America before Welfare

America before Welfare

Franklin Folsom

NEW YORK UNIVERSITY PRESS
New York and London

NEW YORK UNIVERSITY PRESS
New York and London
Copyright © 1991 by Franklin Folsom
All rights reserved
Formerly published as: Impatient Armies of the Poor: The Story of Collective
Action of the Unemployed, 1808–1942

Library of Congress Cataloging-in-Publication Data

Folsom, Franklin, 1907–1995
America before welfare / Franklin Folsom. —
p. cm.
Includes bibliographical references (p.) and index.
ISBN 0-8147-2667-4 pbk.
1. Unemployed—United States—Political activity—History. I. Title.
HD8076.F65 1990
016.322′2—dc20
90-11315
CIP

New York University Press books are printed on acid-free paper,
and their binding materials are chosen for strength and durability.

*This book is dedicated to the unemployed
and the homeless of the 1990s.*

From street and square, from hill and glen,
  Of this vast world beyond my door,
I hear the tread of marching men,
  The patient armies of the poor.

> — Thomas Wentworth Higginson
> "Heirs of Time," 1889

The right to work is the right to life.

> — American Federation of Labor
> Convention, Chicago, December 1893

Other nonfiction books by Franklin Folsom

For adults:

Give Me Liberty: America's Colonial Heritage

America's Ancient Treasures: A Guide to Archaeological Sites and Museums in the United States and Canada (with Mary Elting Folsom)

Exploring American Caves

The Great Peace March: An American Odyssey (with Connie Fledderjohann)

For young readers:

Red Power on the Rio Grande: The Native American Revolution of 1680

The Life and Legend of George McJunkin: Black Cowboy

Science and the Secret of Man's Past

The Language Book

Contents

Abbreviations

ACLU	American Civil Liberties Union
AFL	American Federation of Labor
AICP	Association for Improving the Condition of the Poor
AU	Artists Union
AWP	American Workers Party
AWU	Auto Workers Union
BEF	Bonus Expeditionary Force
CCC	Civilian Conservation Corps
CI	Communist International
CIO	Congress of Industrial Organizations
CP	Communist Party
CPLA	Conference for Progressive Labor Action
CWA	Civil Works Administration
EPIC	End Poverty In California
FAP	Federal Art Project
FERA	Federal Emergency Relief Administration
FWS	Federal Workers Section
HUAC	House Committee on Un-American Activities
ILD	International Labor Defense
IWA	International Workingmen's Association
IWW	Industrial Workers of the World
LID	League for Industrial Democracy
MWIU	Marine Workers Industrial Union
NEB	National Executive Board (of WAA)
NRA	National Recovery Administration
NUL	National Unemployed League

OARP	Old Age Revolving Pension Plan
PWAP	Public Works Art Project
RFC	Reconstruction Finance Corporation
RILU	Red International of Labor Unions
SLP	Socialist Labor Party
TUEL	Trade Union Educational League
TUUL	Trade Union Unity League
UC	Unemployed Council
UCL	Unemployed Citizens League
UL	Unemployed League
UPL	United Producer's League
WAA	Workers Alliance of America
WESL	Workers Ex-Servicemen's League
WIR	Workers International Relief
WPA	Works Progress Administration; Work Projects Administration
WPC	Workingmen's Party of California
WPUS	Workingmen's Party of the United States
YCL	Young Communist League

America before Welfare

Introduction

We are right willing and able to work; and on the Planet Earth
is plenty of work and wages for a million times as many. We
ask if you mean to lead us towards work; to try to lead us, —
by ways new, never yet heard of till this new unheard of Time?
Or if you declare that you cannot lead us? And expect that we
are to remain quietly unled, and in a composed manner perish
of starvation? "What is it you expect of us?" This question I
say has been put in the hearing of all . . . ; and will be again
put, and over again, till some answer be given it.

— Thomas Carlyle
Past and Present, 1844

This is a book about organization among unemployed workers who have not remained "quietly unled." It is a book about
achievements in the face of great obstacles, a history of creative
response to hardship by human beings who have suddenly
been cut loose from society. It is a book about penniless people
who have made history.

With more frequency than we in the United States sometimes recall, the poor have achieved the front page. Static
poverty, quaint indigence, or tight-lipped starvation are usually
good only for feature stories or for filler. Headlines require
action, and the unemployed have often furnished plenty of that,
adding both variety and vigor. More important, industrially
irrelevant people have changed the course of events. And this
book is an effort to record and evaluate the contribution they
have made.

Charity, bounty, alms, doles, relief, welfare: Beginning long
ago, assistance in one or another of these forms has flowed
from the haves to the have-nots — but seldom until the latter
have extended a begging hand or have made more peremptory

gestures. Not only need, but *expressed* need has been a prerequisite of aid. As one of the jobless pointed out during the 1930s, "Insistence is not born in a vacuum; it is the direct result of resistance." The unemploying, in other words, enter into the stories in this book to give necessary background to the actions of the unemployed. I have had to show how the neighborly impulse of decent mutual assistance, how charity, has become less a means of preserving the aided than a means of benefiting the aider. A vast welfare structure has grown up as a kind of buffer state, protecting the possessors from the dispossessed. It is one purpose of my survey to look at the origins of this structure in relation to the recurring chant, "We Demand!"

This chorus has been sung out in spite of the fact that unemployment is centrifugal. Leaving a job means leaving a center and moving toward a periphery. It means leaving a collective pattern and entering formless isolation. Uniting under a boss or against a boss is a clear, understandable concept, but uniting against bosslessness is a very different matter.

In the first place, there must be general agreement among the jobless on whence and how a solution can be forthcoming. Should a self-respecting worker accept relief at all? If so, is it better to turn to the church, or to the rich (via private charity), to the portions of the globe uninhabited by Europeans (recalling that in the nineteenth century a flood of the unemployed poured from Europe into North America), to crime, to scabbing on organized labor, or to the least imaginative solutions of all — tightening the belt or opening the gas jets on the kitchen stove?

These doubts and hesitations are attended by other, dispersive, forces. Differences of race, nationality, religion, sex, and age have been very divisive factors; so, too, have patterns of separations by craft and rank nurtured at the workplace. And there are other inhibiting influences, prominent among them the apathy that attends undernourishment. Against these odds, the miracle is that the unemployed have organized at all. Nevertheless, in hard times, some people have moved toward real solutions of the unemployment problem that other people had created.

During the nineteenth century, which many Americans tend to think back on as a period of vigor and expansion, there were painful episodes that are frequently overlooked. Without enumerating all of these negative realities in our past, this book will concentrate on one series of them, which paradoxically seems to be full of promise for the future. These bleak stretches of the past which have marred — and made — life in the United States, include about a quarter of the years in the century before our own. Such hard times have continued at recurring periods right up to the present.

I hope critics will note that I have studied a part of the American past, that has been too much ignored. I also hope this beginning will suggest to others that many additional studies of the history of the unemployed should be made.

1

Jobless Jack Tars
(1808)

We are for the most part hale, robust, hearty men, and would choose some kind of employment rather than the poorhouse for a livelihood.

> — Unemployed sailors' petition
> January 9, 1808

See the bold Sailor from the Ocean torn,
His element, sink friendless and forlorn!
His suffering spouse the tear of anguish shed,
His starving children cry in vain for bread!

> — William Cullen Bryant (age 13)
> "The Embargo," 1808

Over two hundred sailors gathered, shivering but defiant, in New York's City Hall Park one bitter Saturday morning in January 1808. This gray group made an impressive knot among the trunks of the barren young elms, sycamores, catalpas, and poplars that stood in decorous rows in the four acres surrounding the unfinished City Hall. All of the republican traditions of Greece and Rome were revived in the architecture of this new seat for the city government, and the sailors had gathered before it to put America's still new republicanism to a test — one of the first tests of its kind.

Up Broadway, the cobblestoned show street of New York, the sailors had streamed, their trousers flapping in the wind. Against the doors of dwellings stood curious doctors, lawyers, merchants, traders. They watched until the cold, nipping at thinly stockinged shins exposed beneath knee breeches, drove them indoors. Attentive, almost incredulous faces looked out of the windows over some of the shops that stood on one side of the park. Artisans' eyes glanced up from card games or from the pious books on self-advancement in which the few small librar- ies abounded. Their seafaring brothers were likewise bent on self-advancement, but they were using a novel means toward that end. The sailors moved toward the mayor's office to peti- tion for redress of their grievances — and grievances they had. They and their families, through no fault of their own, had suddenly come face to face with literal starvation.

A governmental embargo, stopping all ships from leaving the United States, had been declared December 22, 1807, in response to war between France and England, a war that threatened to involve the United States. American shipping was being molested on the high seas, and as a means both of defense and of retaliation, a one-country effort at a kind of sanction had been secretly decided on by Congress and Presi- dent Jefferson. Messengers on horseback galloped from Wash- ington to all ports up and down the coast. At 5:00 on the morning of December 25, one of the riders roused the Collector of the Port of New York. By 7:00, he had handbills printed and distributed along the wharves. The immediate effect was to throw many thousands of Yankee seamen out of jobs overnight.

Industry at that time was still in its infancy, but by a freak of history, widespread unemployment, which often accompa- nies our present form of machine production, had appeared at the end of 1807 to torment those who lived in that day of small-scale hand manufacture and commerce.

New Yorkers had already seen terrifying evidence of the approaching mechanized world. On August 7, 1807, every man in the harbor, from bargee to pilot, had looked over the bul- warks of his sailing vessel and had seen — and heard — and smelled — a sail-less vessel moving against the tide. Roaring, clattering, spouting smoke and fire, the new boat had ploughed on. "The devil going to Albany in a sawmill," some said, but it was only Robert Fulton experimenting with his steamship, the *Clermont.* All along the two miles of North River waterfront, old sea dogs had fallen to their knees and prayed, ducked into cabins, or made a dash for shore.

Now, only a few months after the advent of America's first steam-driven vessel, sailors faced a new and even more terrifying forewarning of the future: unemployment.

Savings banks were unknown to sailors in 1808, and little enough of a seafaring man's ten-dollar monthly wage could have been left in a bank anyway. Moreover, he spent his slim earnings quickly, confident that he could find a berth when he needed one in these boom times of American shipping.

Within a few days after the embargo began, the sailors had no money left. No money meant no food. Fortunately, most landlords were lenient and let them stay on for a while, knowing that solvent roomers were not likely to replace the penniless occupants, and shelter was mightily welcome in this unusually severe winter. But whenever a sailor stepped restlessly outdoors to see if by any chance there was a change along the wharves, he was likely to hear the tantalizing cry, "Here's milk, ho!" from a carrier with two heavy milk cans on a yoke across his shoulders. Men began crowding the Battery, from the time the morning gun sounded on Governor's Island until it was too dark to see. There, in the icy winds, bare hands held fish lines over the water.

Some of the sailors' former shipmates had taken up a new trade, the despised calling of ragman. With bags over their shoulders, able seamen nosed around for pieces of canvas or rope. They thronged the dead waterfront mournfully crying, "Tumble Up! Tumble Up! Old Rope!" And many a big climber of masts and rigging envied the pinched and sooty chimney sweeps whose piercing soprano cry was a constant reminder that there was employment for some:

> Sweep, O — O — O — O
> From the bottom to the top,
> Without a ladder or a rope,
> Sweep, O — O — O — O

Mayor Marinus Willett knew very well what was happening in his city of less than 100,000 inhabitants. The astute Revolutionary War veteran was listening everywhere with his unforgettably large ears. Plans had already begun to shape in his lean, significantly coiffured head. In a republican gesture, he refused to wear the powdered wigs still popular with aristocrats, and, although he was bald in front, his straight hair dangled to his shoulders.

Willett and his Common Council had looked at the harbor where the gear hung loose on nearly 700 brigs, schooners, sloops — ships of all kinds. Sailmakers were idle. Shipwrights fingered their tools and their very slender wallets. The richest merchants were buying up all bacon, salt fish, and flour and hiding it away in sturdy warehouses until prices went up — and until their competitors went out of business. The city fathers had an uneasy suspicion that trouble lay ahead.

Some distress had existed before the full effect of the embargo was manifest. At Christmas, the churches in Wall Street and farther uptown had taken up collections for the many paupers. Aware now of the increased hardship, Marinus Willett sensed that there might be problems unless the hungry were fed. Accordingly, he agreed on January 4 with the report of a committee of the Common Council "that . . . it is incumbent on the Corporation at this inclement season to alleviate the evils which must result from a suspension of the ordinary vocations of the laborious part of the community: That the opening of the Broadway road, while it would tend to public convenience and improvement, would also afford employment for a number of industrious persons, who may be suffering for the want of work, and thereby relieve themselves and families from distress."

A few days later, the sailors decided to present to the mayor a petition emphasizing their plight. Some of them remembered the strikes of New York sailors in 1800, and they knew how greatly employers feared united action. At that time, certain citizens had felt it desirable to organize vigilantes to move against the strikers.

Sailors, who made up the largest category of wage earners, were accustomed to working together, and it was natural for them to think of uniting to get relief. Accordingly, they selected a committee, planned a public meeting, and even got a notice of it published in the *Daily Advertiser*.

The mayor, as soon as he read the *Advertiser*, summoned the Common Council on January 8 to see what could be done to prevent any "unpleasant consequences." It would have been unwise to use force because of the numbers and known courage and desperation of the sailors, so the council started an anti-meeting campaign. Adverse notices immediately appeared in the press, and suave leaflets signed by the mayor called on the sailors not to meet. That these efforts had some success is suggested in a report by the *Evening Post* that "all excepting about two hundred omitted to assemble" on Saturday, January 9. These 200 gathered to support their committee as it presented the petition that took note of the mayor's leaflet and asked for "some kind of employment rather than the poorhouse for a livelihood." And not only jobless jack tars demonstrated. The *Evening Post*, no friend of the embargo, reported, "All classes of citizens, led by sailors surged through the streets displaying placards demanding bread or work."

In the stately council chamber with its wood and stone carvings, Mayor Willett awaited the seamen. He sat under a canopy in the same chair on which George Washington had sat during the first Congress of the new republic.

The mayor accepted the petition brought by the demonstrators (see Appendix A) and tried oratory to defuse the crowd: "My lads, I am sensible how hard this embargo bears on you, but it is the *Captain's orders* and you know your duty well enough not to refuse obedience. I can assure you that the Corporation will do everything possible for your relief; but your present measure is an improper one and I hope you will disperse without doing anything further."

The sailors quietly left, and after them, the leather-hatted, club-carrying city watchmen. Outside the hungry seamen encountered boys trotting through the streets with huge baskets on their heads, singing out "Hot Muffins!" "Tea Rusks!" It was

3:00 in the afternoon, and the wives and daughters of ship owners and merchants were receiving their customary tea cakes rushed to them from the bakers' ovens.

Meanwhile, in response to the sailors' "improper measure," the mayor called a special session of the Common Council, which on Monday set aside $1,000 to start relief machinery moving. (The Republican pro-Jefferson newspapers praised this measure, but the Federalist journals, pointing out that it resulted from fear, sought to discredit it.) By Thursday a soup kitchen had been built, and by Friday the Alms House was supplying food to over 1,000 unemployed, five times more than it had served the week before. Saturday, one week after the demonstration, an office was opened at Broadway and Chambers Street to take applications for aid.

Another act of the Common Council, "alarmed at the temper" of the unemployed, established the first work relief project in the United States, and soon sailors and other embargo sufferers were swarming over what is now Murray Hill, instructed to level that frozen eminence — with spades. Other unemployed men began to fill in a pond called the Collect and the marshes surrounding it. This project, like the scratchings on Murray Hill, was badly conceived. Quantities of lightweight garbage had been thrown into the Collect and the marshes. Much of this garbage was forced to the surface by the heavy earth shoveled into the water. The result was a very offensive mass of refuse. Later, the several acres it covered would be the site of a jail called the Tombs, in which future generations of jobless protestors would be locked up.

The project of filling in the Collect was discontinued February 15 by the Common Council, "as this labour is not very profitable, and as means of employment will be afforded at Governor's Island" (more of a hope than a promise).

Still another project had been set up in the meantime in the Brooklyn Navy Yard — "so that no ill consequences can result from their tumultuous associations," according to the city fathers. The sailors, who were urged into the Navy Yard to work under military supervision, were offered not money but "victuals, drink, fuel, candles, and accommodations for lodging.

Soap for washing to be an extra charge." The merchant seamen had no love for the navy. Officers of warships, they knew, had a way of trepanning — kidnapping — husky fellows. To allay fears on this score, official promises were made to a committee of the unemployed: "As some may have apprehensions of being trepanned the Hon. Council pledge that nothing of this sort will take place." For this effort at reassurance, the council got space in the *Evening Post*. Provisions had been made for several hundred workers, but out of the thousands on the beach in New York, only fifty-three had accepted work in the Yard by the end of March, and of these, thirty-nine quit soon after they reported to their unpaid jobs.

By early February, nearly 5,500 unemployed were calling for rations at the Alms House. A month later, over 6,000 were standing in line on the cold mornings when food was distributed. One-sixteenth of the population was on relief. In addition, over 1,000 packed the cells of the debtors prison.

The increasing call for aid was not interpreted by the council as an increased obligation on their part. In fact, they complained that they were being imposed upon. Although a new mayor was to be chosen in the month of February, candidates and political groups had little fear of retaliation from the unemployed, who could not vote because they did not qualify as property owners. Moreover, popular resentment was slow to be registered against mayors because they were chosen indirectly by a council of appointment. Even so, Marinus Willett was defeated for reelection by DeWitt Clinton, the man from whom he had won the office a year before.

Rations, consisting of a quart of soup, a pound of bread, and three-quarters of a pound of "ordinary" beef, were at first issued on Monday, Wednesday, and Friday. In one busy period, the butchers who supplied the Alms House ran out of "ordinary" beef and had to substitute good cuts, but they were recompensed at the going rate for the good cuts. On Saturday the menu was a half-pound of pork instead of soup and a pint of beans instead of beef. After February 8, the council proposed "to issue rations only twice a week, in future, and to examine into claims and necessities of the applicants so far as may be possible to prevent further abuse of the public bounty." At the same time a Mr. McPherson was active on behalf of the Common Council "assisting those families who are reported to be in distress and administering such supplies as their respective cases may require." Mr. McPherson seems to have been the first home relief investigator employed by a governmental agency in the United States.

On April 4, 1808, the unemployed faced a termination of rations, although the embargo was not to be lifted for another eleven months. "As the season has arrived [a local newspaper reported] when the late objects of the public bounty may be able to procure support for themselves and their families by their own industry they [the Common Council] have discontinued issuing any more rations from the Alms House." The unemployed got no city help until the next fall. The countryside — and beyond that, the frontier — was the direction in which the jobless were asked to look. Two days later (April 6), John Jacob Astor's American Fur Company was chartered. This development, which gave promise of some employment in the wilderness, was arranged largely through the influence of Mayor Clinton.

The famous mayor, later governor of New York and even considered for the presidency, was soon busy preparing for the strange series of elections that characterized New York's early governmental system. At the same time, Tammany Hall (very much the same political machine then as later) decided that the logical way to bolster its political prestige was to hold a patriotic parade. Someone remembered that a large number of American soldiers had died on board British prison ships in New York harbor during the Revolutionary War. The bones of these men were reputed to lie in Wallabout Bay, and Tammany petitioned for the right to bury them and set up a monument. Mayor Clinton, although no Tammany man, saw the political possibilities in the scheme and immediately jumped on the bandwagon. At his suggestion the state legislature provided funds for the burial project.

The Tammany Society marched in impressive rank to Wallabout, where it laid the cornerstone of a vault in which were to be placed the remains of 11,500 patriots who had died on board the floating dungeons. On April 26, twenty hogsheads of bones were laid in the unfinished vault. In addition to Tammany, members of Congress, naval officers, and less noted notables took part in the ceremony, with much oratory and rolling of drums. Months later the vault remained unfinished. When asked what had happened to the $1,000 appropriated for it, Tammany replied by petitioning for — and getting — an additional $1,000. Still the vault remained as it was, and the curious were not able to find out what had been done with the funds.

This Wallabout circus may have had some small effect in keeping New York's embargo sufferers from asking for bread, but the approach of summer, with its inevitable return of hope, was more likely the determining factor. Many city dwellers believed that the jobless were less likely to go hungry during the warm months. Farmers, who knew more about food because they grew it, were more pessimistic, although they did offer seasonal work to some laborers.

Elsewhere up and down the coast, sailors and others had been affected as severely as those in New York. Often they, too, paraded, demonstrated, and petitioned, and were told that such actions were "improper." Like the New York unemployed, they faced the obstacles of official evasion, an antagonistic press, and leaders in their own ranks whose motives were dubious. Seamen were reported drowned in Salem — apparent suicides because of unemployment.

In Portland an anti-embargo demonstration was organized. "A long-boat of a ship was loaded onto a car stern foremost and rigged like a ship but made to represent the present state of shipping," said an account of the action. "All the rigging was hanging loose. On the stern was painted "O-GRAB-ME" ['embargo' spelled backwards]. Then all the truckmen of the town hitched their horses to the car, and mounted them, each one holding his whip by the small end . . . then followed a band playing doleful music and the unemployed people followed — masters, mates, and men and all the mechanics connected with commerce." Soup kitchens were soon opened in Portland.

In Boston the unemployed were even quicker to seek relief than in New York. On Thursday, January 7, according to the *Independent Chronicle*, "A procession of from 80 to 100 sailors, carrying a flag, marched with martial music to the Governor's house, and demanded *employment* or *bread.* The governor, as soon as he could be heard, addressed them with a presence of mind which became his exalted character, suggesting the impropriety of their manner of seeking relief and declaring that he could do nothing for them in his official capacity. They finally dispersed without further disturbance."

The next day a petition appealing for relief, signed by 110 men, was handed to the selectmen of Boston. The signers had wanted to appear in a body, but were told that only twenty-five would be received; in the end only six appeared. These men, when quizzed, said that some of the petitioners, being illiterate, had let their names be put down by the man who drew up the petition. On the pretense that this action made the whole thing invalid, the selectmen decided the appeal should be ignored.

In Philadelphia the unemployed were likewise on the move. On Saturday, January 16, the *American Citizen* reported: "A large number of seamen paraded with the flag of the United States to the City Hall, in order to claim the protection of the Corporation, in consequence of being destitute of support. A Committee chosen out of their number entered the Mayor's office, and stated their hardships and the difficulties to which they were subjected, and to use their own expression 'wished to know what was to be done. . . .' "

The mayor took their flag from them, declared them an unlawful assembly, and then said, "My lads, I pity you from the bottom of my heart — I know that yours is a hard case, but the government have deemed this measure to be a proper one, and it is your duty to obey the law. I respect your services to the country. I well know how necessary you are to our commercial and naval prosperity, but to collect in this manner is not proper. You must be sensible of it. The Chamber of Commerce [unofficial then as now] have taken your situation into notice, and a committee appointed to afford you relief. To them in respectful measure I advise you to appeal, and may God bless you all." The honest tars gave three cheers and departed. Three days later the Chamber of Commerce did make some contribution to the sailors and put some of them to work making canvas, rope, coarse mats, oakum, and gaskets. But the city continued to refuse to accept responsibility for the lives of its citizens. In the end, the demonstrating sailors were won over by the anti-embargo Federalists who used them (at one time 1,000 of them) as strong-arm men to protect their meetings from attacks by the pro-embargo Republicans. In return, the unemployed got backslapping and grog in the coffeehouse — but not relief.

Artisans, sailors, farmers, and their families faced a second winter of distress. In New York the relief apparatus summoned into being by the activities of the unemployed renewed its partial aid. Protesting the inadequacy of this handout, a meeting of sailors and others on January 18, 1809, set up a committee to study the situation. The result of the study was an appeal for centralization of all relief agencies under city control. These proposals were discussed but rejected by the Common Council, which left to private charities the job of giving aid. The council members hoped that the charities would be able to turn noisy sufferers into silent ones. An assistance society had already been formed in December 1808 to help certain groups of the unemployed, notably, it declared, those "who from motives of delicacy would not seek it for themselves." The society was also vastly concerned with bestowing "on the sons and daughters of affliction, counsels of prudence and religion, which, if followed, under the influence of grace, would not fail to produce their welfare in future life and their eternal and immeasurable felicity."

On April 14, 1809, Congress lifted the embargo, and ships could sail again. The immediate cause of mass unemployment was gone, but echoes of some related events continued.

In the summer of 1809, certain activities of William Mooney, head of the Alms House and the founder of Tammany Hall, had come under inspection. For the supervision of the Alms House, the rules of which defined it as "a detached part of the regular system of Police, which comprehend the relief of the necessitous, the encouragement of industry, and the prevention of crimes," he was to receive $1,000 a year, plus $500 expense money for his family. These sums he very punctually collected from the Common Council treasury. His Alms House accounts showed a series of curious entries, "Trifles for Mrs. Mooney" totalling $4,000. In addition, Mr. Mooney had appropriated Alms House property to the value of $1,000. He was removed from office in due course, but the Alms House and the unemployed never received restitution for the money he had taken. Tammany, and Mooney himself, easily survived the scandal.

After the first meeting of the unemployed in 1808, group agitation fell off until it disappeared during the second winter of hard times. Many of the seamen gave up hope of work at home and smuggled themselves abroad to man foreign ships. "The British Packet sailed this afternoon," read a typical item in the *Post,* "with her decks literally crowded with sailors going to another country to seek employment." Other jobless joined the great trek to the Mississippi Valley in search of a living on the land. The recent Lewis and Clark expedition had hinted that a hunter might at least find subsistence in the West.

For the most part, only the old, the defeated, and the sick unemployed remained in the cities, and there the factories, which had grown up as a result of the embargo, began to offer a few jobs. Although distress was great, many pinned their hopes on the promise of more employment soon — and they were right.

Some of those who managed to keep their jobs during the embargo were militant in defense of their living standards. A strike of shoemakers that broke out in New York in 1809 possibly owed some of its inspiration to the example of the demonstrating seamen the preceding winter. In the next year, the members of the Philadelphia Typographical Society went on strike.

No permanent organization grew out of the early banding together of unemployed sailors. They did, however, write a prologue to the long drama of struggle for relief. And they won from some officials the tacit admission, albeit temporary, that the community should assume responsibility for relief. The seamen had turned to a governmental agency for help, partly because it was a governmental agency that had made them unemployed and partly because there was a general republican expectancy that *their* government should help them. Whatever their motives, they caused the New York Common Council to set up the first work relief projects, to administer home relief, and to appoint what was apparently the first home relief investigator in the United States. In the dawn of industrial America, workers in adversity acted in groups to bring about governmental action for the common good.

While the New York unemployed played their significant parts, a great man lay dying in a little house in Bleecker Street in Greenwich Village, a short way outside the city. Tom Paine, the professional agitator of the American and French revolutions, had given immeasurable aid to the businessmen, artisans, and farmers of two countries in throwing off restraints. Now, while he was passing from the scene, a new revolution, the Industrial Revolution, was beginning to produce a new class that would repeatedly need to throw off restraints imposed on it by mass unemployment.

The first of the unending cycles of industrial-age joblessness would begin in 1819, after a period of postwar prosperity resulting from the War of 1812 and, farther afield, the Napoleonic Wars in Europe. Very early in the industrial era, war appeared as a solution to unemployment, but there was also on the horizon the economic maladjustment that always seems to follow the end of wars.

2

The First Industrial Unemployed
(1819–1829)

It does not . . . depend upon the will of the man who has no
property, whether he shall have any portion of the product of
labour; but upon the will of the man who has property.

— Daniel Raymond
Thoughts on Political Economy, 1814

Let it not be forgotten, that while on the one hand, labor-saving machinery is advancing in its march to perfection, with
rapid strides, and diminishing demand for labor; so on the
other, are the numbers of the poor, among whom this demand
is to be shared, augmenting in a fearful ratio.

— Thomas Skidmore
The Rights of Man to Property! 1820

"Most of our manufactures have stopped," reported an
alarmed Baltimore newspaper in July 1819. "The prospect before us is that we shall have . . . at least 2,000 men, 2,000
women and 2,000 children idle for the ensuing six months, who
have hitherto been accustomed to labor, and are still willing to
work if they could get it to do. The men might earn one dollar,
the women 40 cents, and the children 20 cents per day, each, if
proper employment were furnished to them."

Some among Baltimore's 2,000 idle males may have been
the "obscure men of humble origin" who, seeking at least fraternal support in this year of great insecurity, organized the
Independent Order of Odd Fellows. In any case, Baltimore
workers were having a most distressing time, and the situation
was the same in other cities.

In Philadelphia, a survey of only half its sixty factories revealed that the number of workers in the shops examined had dropped from 9,700 in 1816 to 2,000 in 1819. In the city as a whole, about 20,000 people were daily seeking work. The distress was greater than anyone in the city could remember.

In New York, estimates of the number of workers turned out into the streets ranged from 15,000 to 20,000. And what the jobless faced there, besides hunger, was described by an English visitor: "The streets are miserably dirty, as to them is consigned the filth of most houses, and suffered to remain all seasons, July and August excepted, and you are continually annoyed by innumerable hungry pigs of all sizes and complexions, great and small beasts prowling in grunting ferocity." The streets on which the poor of Philadelphia lived were no better.

While the pigs fed on the leftovers from the homes of employers or the still employed, the half-million American jobless had to rely on charity often dispensed in soup lines. Some moved into "houses of industry" where they exchanged labor for food and shelter. When they did manage to stay in other quarters, they crowded together at the rate of a dozen families in a one-family home that had been vacated by some merchant, or they existed in what one historian of architecture described as "packing boxes lacking in light and ventilation . . . little more than crowded pens, as crowded as a cattle market."

With the crisis of 1819, the United States (total population not quite 10 million, including slaves) had its first experience of a full-scale, national, modern depression, although the country was still for the most part rural. This economic collapse came close on the heels of technological advance. In 1816 the first modern textile mill went into production, and power-driven machinery began to creep into other kinds of manufacture. The introduction of power did not throw masses of people out of work overnight as the embargo had done ten years earlier. Instead, the growth of unemployment was gradual, but it was already significant two years after the War of 1812. Joblessness increased as businesses faltered and failed because of the corruption and instability of the Second Bank of the United States and the currency it issued. There was no standard national currency. Businessmen would borrow money that had one value, then find they had to repay it with money of a very different value. Chaos resulted, and the situation worsened when the Napoleonic Wars in Europe ended, bringing the reality, or at least the threat, of competing products from that part of the world.

From April 1814 to March 1815 public agencies in New York provided some assistance to 19,078 persons. More than one-fifth of the city's population received relief at some time during this twelve-month period. By February 1817 at least 15,000 persons in the city were completely dependent on public and private charity. The annual expenditure for poor relief was the largest item in the city budget.

In 1817 a number of substantial New Yorkers decided it was time to take additional steps. If they were to remain in the city — and remain alive — they believed it would be prudent to protect themselves from the hordes of poor who might feel driven to choose between begging, stealing, and rioting. Accordingly, a group of solvent citizens created the Society for the Prevention of Pauperism in the City of New York. The society placed the blame for unemployment on those who were out of work and maintained that the cure for idleness lay in improved morals and in working harder for less pay (hence the "houses of industry"). The low level of subsistence provided in these and similar institutions had its uses: Employers in Philadelphia soon brought wages down to the relief level. The New York Society for the Prevention of Pauperism also encouraged frugality by founding a savings bank, the first in the city and the third in the United States.

These actions were taken ostensibly *for* the unemployed, not *by* them, and as far as is known not at their suggestion. During these years, there were no demonstrations as there had been at the time of the embargo. Such group-pressure tactics would not occur again until the industrial working class had grown in size and experience. It was too early for the polyglot unemployed to speak out with one voice. The jobless came from diverse countries in western Europe, spoke many different languages, worshipped in rival churches, and sought companionship or escape in different tippling houses (as bars were called). They had sharply differing attitudes toward authority and the responsibilities of government. Many arrived in American ports already demoralized, having been shipped out of their homelands after long spells of unemployment, when charity organizations, wearied of giving relief, paid for their trans-Atlantic passage to get rid of them.

None of these first-generation immigrants were welcome. Native-born factory workers looked on them as rivals for such jobs as remained. At the same time, the native-born were themselves, as E. J. Hobsbawm put it, "first generation immigrants from pre-industrial societies, even if they never actually moved from the place in which they had been born."

Minor, riotous disturbances did take place in New York, but the time had not come when these various newcomers to a new kind of world could see the need for planned common action to cure a baffling evil. To survive, many of the more vigorous males moved toward the frontier. This was early in the period of the mountain men, who endured lives of hardship and violence pilfering furs on western lands that belonged to Native Americans — who in turn were resentful but relatively helpless in the face of advancing well-armed, capitalist society.

Because of this westward migration, the jobless who remained in the cities included a disproportionate number of women, many of whom chose to become prostitutes rather than starve. Both women and men faced the massive propaganda of preachers who told them that they were out of work because their morals were bad. Reformers campaigned, not for jobs at good wages on socially useful public works, but against tippling houses.

From a desire to reform and to buy a measure of security, as well as from motives of neighborliness, citizens in Philadelphia produced a bewildering variety of charities with names such as the North Soup Society, the Southern Soup Society, the Western Charitable Organization, and the Indigent Widows and Single Women's Society. The soup lines administered by these organizations grew longer and longer. So great was the pressure on the private agencies dispensing relief that they themselves sought relief from public sources. They asked for and got money from the municipal government.

A few individuals spoke out for jobs on public works for the jobless. As early as February 19, 1819, someone signing himself "H. B." proposed in the *New York Columbian* a way of providing "constant employment." He suggested the establishment of a state-owned woolen and cotton factory to teach the youth of New York the "useful art of spinning and weaving, the state to furnish the new material and receive the proceeds as it is finished for the consumer." H. B. also suggested state-owned cotton and woolen warehouses to sell finished cloth both at wholesale and at retail. Apparently nothing came of this idea, which had the misfortune to appear in the same year that the Supreme Court, in the Dartmouth College case, determined that the course of development of the United States economy should be in the channels of privately controlled, rather than state controlled, capital.

Other proposals for public works to support the unemployed also surfaced. For example, a representative from Philadelphia in the Pennsylvania legislature offered a bill early in 1820 for state financing of thirty road projects throughout the state. At the same time, the New Jersey legislature adopted a bill that would have given jobs to many of that state's unemployed. Apparently the financing of this publicly approved project was to have been private, but the funds were not forthcoming and nothing came of it.

The story was generally the same for most proposals for public works that came from middle-class reformers and politicians. In addition, none of the leaders of the new trade unions seems to have regarded the unemployed as a practical base from which to attack the system that they opposed to one degree or another. The ideas of some of these leaders and writers, however, survived into later depressions, when they had their effect on the thinking and the actions of the unemployed as they sought for a way out of the ever-recurring cycle of economic distress.

By 1823, after the distress caused in part by the speculations of the Second Bank of the United States had been greatly reduced, and after relatively stable business practices had resumed, there were still ups and downs in the economy. The various, mutually suspicious, elements of the new and traditionless working class of the United States still faced many problems. Despite the resumption of a good deal of production and trade, workers who had jobs were poorly paid for very long hours of work.

Even before a new depression arrived in 1829, workers manifested several types of response to their problems. One was to form unions. The Mechanics Union of Trade Associations, the first central labor body in the country, took shape in Philadelphia in 1827. Though animated by broad ideas of reform, it grew up primarily to serve those who had jobs and seemingly did not adjust to serving those who had lost employment.

Equally irrelevant to the needs of the jobless was a second phenomenon: a scattering of communitarian settlements that began to appear about the time when factories first made use of power-driven machinery. Although some of these utopian experiments lasted many years, they did not in any important way provide jobs for those displaced from the economy by labor-saving inventions. A radical of the time, Thomas Skidmore, who had a keen sense of identity with working people, had this to say of New Harmony, one of the utopian settlements: "No actual experiment [was] made of the community system at New Harmony — everything being in the proprietorship and under the dictation of a few Aristocratic speculating theorists."

A third response to unemployment and other inequities was political. In Philadelphia in 1828, William Heighton, a shoemaker who was a leader in establishing the Mechanics Union of Trade Associations, went on to form the Working Men's Party. By its very existence, the new party was a statement that a union movement, even one with long-range goals such as those of the Mechanics Union, was not equal to dealing with all of labor's problems. Laws had to be changed, and for that, political action was required. Workers, including most of those who had lost their jobs, suffered from laws that dictated imprisonment for nonpayment of debts. Under these laws, 10,000 New Yorkers were imprisoned annually. How workers felt about going to jail because they were poor was summed up by a workingmen's newspaper: "A law that makes poverty a crime, and a poor man a felon, after those very laws have made poverty inevitable, is not only cruel and oppressive, but absurd and revolting."

On the other side of the books, workers needed a law giving them liens, or claims, against the property of employers who failed to pay the wages they owed. There was also need for a law that would provide public education. All in all, workers had reason to want representatives in legislative bodies who would be responsive to their interests.

To protest against unemployment and to fight against the efforts of employers to lengthen the working day from ten to eleven hours, Thomas Skidmore, a teacher and inventor turned machinist, initiated a Working Men's Party in New York. Skidmore, although abrasive in manner, was an effective speaker and leader. To the amazement of the old parties, his new one soon received about 6,000 votes. Other Working Men's parties followed in most of the states where industry was developing. For two or three years these "Dirty Shirt Parties," as some of their opponents called them, were active. They received support from about fifty newspapers and on occasion elected representatives to local or state office. They played important roles in ending imprisonment for debt, in obtaining mechanics liens, and in winning free public education.

Despite, or perhaps because of, these achievements, the New York Working Men's Party was split, partly by infiltrators from Tammany Hall, into three competing factions. The leader of one of these factions was Robert Dale Owen, son of the English utopian Socialist Robert Owen. A close collaborator with him was an Englishwoman, the anticlerical reformer Frances ("Fanny") Wright. These two, in fervid but genteel tones, inveighed against the rich and urged education for the poor. They faced opposition from the dominant political parties (the Whigs or National Republicans on the one hand and the Tammanyites or Democrats on the other), although Owen was considered sufficiently respectable to be allowed to address the United States Congress. Support from Skidmore would have been unwelcome, for he was deemed altogether too uncompromising in his assault on property holders. In addition, the Owenites, sometimes called the Wright Reasoners in scornful allusion to Frances Wright, were opposed by a farm-based faction of the Working Men's Party that objected to compulsory tax-supported education. The farmers wanted their children at home so they could work, not off in the boarding schools that Owen campaigned for.

Soon enough, factionalism rendered the new party ineffective. Skidmore was isolated. He had roused opposition among old-line politicians by getting wide circulation for resolutions such as this one, which he no doubt wrote: "*Resolved,* The distress of hundreds of the working classes, in the eastern cities of these United States, during the winter of 1828–29, is a specimen of the evil resulting from artificial inequality, which distress was partially relieved by the charity of the wealthy, *Resolved,* That if the working classes were not unjustly deprived of their rights, they would need no charity."

In his campaign for the right of working people to own the wealth they produced, Skidmore attracted not only followers but also skillful enemies. The enemies, mainly Tammany men who claimed to be friends, outmaneuvered him. At the same time, his grand idea of redistributing wealth did not attract the undivided loyalty of men who never knew where their next meal was coming from. What the unemployed wanted before everything else was food; wealth could wait. Skidmore, though cogent in some of his analyses, did not seem to give that fact full weight. The result was that he did not lead the unemployed anywhere politically, not even toward demanding public works. It remained for the Common Council on its own initiative to increase markedly the money it spent on public building when labor was cheap during a depression that began in 1829 — the second depression of the Industrial Revolution.

Buoyed up somewhat by the rising tide of revolution in France, of national liberation in Greece, and of sweeping reforms in England, the American Working Men's movement did not immediately lose hope, in spite of all the dissensions. Too much was happening, too much was at stake, and the whole spirit of the Working Men's Party was too youthful to admit pessimism. Frances Wright, in reviewing the first six months of 1830, said they "have not been sterile in events. They have exhibited a change in the public measures. They have witnessed . . . the breaking up of parties, alarm of politicians, the anathemas of bigots, the noise of demagogues, and the awakening, and gathering, and the uniting of people. . . . The ridden people of the earth . . . are struggling to throw from their backs the 'booted and spurred' riders . . . it is labor rising against idleness."

Less ecstatic, and less urgent in his vision of change, Owen wrote at the same time, "But if the productive powers must increase, then the world must, sooner or later, adopt some system of distribution, that, like the federative system, can bear an abundance and prosperity."

Such noble sentiments flourished in the second and third decades of the nineteenth century. Economic and social theories burgeoned while the soup lines lengthened. The impassioned debaters dwelt more on their pet panaceas than on the immediate problem of getting work and food for the jobless. But in the general ferment, a body of writing appeared that would have its effect on the thinking of leaders of future generations of unemployed. These writings were the most important product of the crises and unemployment in the initial period of industrialization.

The first of these germinal essays has been called the first socialist book published in the United States: *Some Causes of Popular Poverty*, written by a physician, Dr. Cornelius Blatchly, in 1817. Blatchly followed it ten years later with another treatise in a similar vein, *An Essay on Commonwealths*. In these studies he objected to great inequality in the distribution of wealth, which he believed should be distributed in accordance with work performed and not in accordance with property owned.

In 1820 a Baltimore lawyer, Daniel Raymond, added to this idea a noteworthy concept about unemployment. Looking at the new factory system, Raymond contended in his *Thoughts on Political Economy* that unemployment resulted from the separation of workers from the ownership of property. He wrote, "It does not . . . depend upon the will of the man who has no property, whether he will have any portion of the product of labour; but upon the man who has property. If those to whom the whole surface of the earth belongs, choose to say that those . . . who have no property, shall not labour; or, in other words if they do not choose to employ them, they will, by the established laws of property, have no legal right to any portion of the product of labour; and must starve, unless supported by the bounty of others — they must become paupers." Raymond also argued for public works, both as a way of maintaining full employment and as a means of stimulating the economy by providing workers with the means of becoming consumers.

Close on the heels of Raymond came Langdon Byllesby, printer and inventor. In 1826 he published *Observations on the Sources and Effect of Unequal Wealth.* Like Raymond, Byllesby found ample reason to believe that unemployment resulted from the introduction of labor-saving machinery. "Every increase of the *power* [that is, mechanical] of production, under the present systems, actually lessens the *quantity* produced in proportion to the amount of population; and instead of decreasing the number of the needy and their privations, greatly adds to both." Byllesby not only looked for causes, he also prophesied that movement for social change would be a result of unemployment. About the social reforms that were needed, however, he was vague. The best he could recommend was the establishment of communal societies separate from the general economy.

The shoemaker William Heighton was more specific. He was not only an organizer of Philadelphia's central labor union and its Working Men's Party, he was also a frequent speaker, and some of his speeches appeared in print. In his *Address to the Members of Trade Societies* (April 1827), Heighton proposed actions quite different from retreat into communitarian groups. He emphasized the need for organization of workers in order to get their immediate needs satisfied.

Of equal interest were the writings of Thomas Skidmore, who repeated in New York the political inventiveness that Heighton had shown in Philadelphia. In 1829, the year in which Skidmore launched the New York Working Men's Party, his book *The Rights of Man to Property!* was published by Alexander Ming, Sr. An admirer of Thomas Paine and a convinced revolutionary, Skidmore maintained that property gave those who owned it the power to dictate the terms of existence of those who worked, including the power to determine that many should not work.

What Skidmore saw as the evil of private ownership was compounded by the effect of advancing technology. For example, the first gaslights on the streets of New York were installed in the year of crisis, 1829. New inventions were flourishing. At the time of the embargo, the Patent Office was registering new inventions at the rate of about seventy-seven a year. By the time of the 1829–1830 depression, the annual number of new inventions recorded was 544. Both the pace of technological innovations and the rate of unemployment had sped up immensely, and Skidmore, with other radical writers on poverty, was quick to make a connection between the two phenomena. Labor-saving devices, they said, created unemployment. Labor-saving devices, however, did not reduce profits. Here is the way Skidmore put it in *The Rights of Man to Property!*: "If it is seen that the steam engine, for example, is likely to greatly impoverish, or destroy the poor, what have they to do, but to lay hold of it, and make it their own?"

> If a man were to ask me [Skidmore concluded in his final pages], to what I would compare the unequal distribution of property which prevails in the world . . . I would say that it reminds me of a large party of gentlemen, who should have a common right to dine at one and the same public table, a part of whom should arrive first, sit down, and eat what they chose; and then, because the remaining part came later to dinner, would undertake to monopolize the whole; and deprive them of opportunity of satisfying their hunger, but upon terms such as those who had feasted, should be pleased to prescribe.
>
> Such, now, is the actual condition of the whole human race.

Skidmore, while he lived, which was only until 1832, contributed momentum to the democratic movement in the United States. Although his rhetoric stirred many, his efforts at organizing never concentrated on the men who stood in soup lines in 1829. And under Andrew Jackson, who was president from 1829 to 1837, the general movement toward increased democracy, mainly for small producers, drained off most of the reform energy of the country. The Working Men's parties merged into the general democratic upsurge.

The unemployed would have to make a fresh start when the next depression occurred only a few years later.

3

"Go to the Flour Stores!"
(1837)

Cold April; hard times; men breaking who ought not to break;
banks bullied into the bolstering of desperate speculators; all
the newspapers a chorus of owls.

> — Ralph Waldo Emerson
> *Journal*, April 22, 1837

These capitalists generally act harmoniously and in concert,
to fleece the people.

> — Abraham Lincoln
> Speech to the Illinois legislature, January 1837

[In France and England, 1730–1848] . . . the general pattern
of the crowd's behavior . . . [was] direct action and the imposi-
tion of some form of elementary natural justice.

> — George Rudé
> *The Crowd in History*, 1964

The mayors of New York usually held open house about New
Year's time, and as 1837 approached, Mayor Cornelius V.P.
Lawrence took special pains to plan lavish hospitality. He could
not afford to have Tammany Hall bankers and merchants whis-
pering about their stingy representative in the chief office of
this growing city of 200,000, which by now was second only to
London among the commercial cities of the world. It would not
do to have Tammany's rivals, the land owning Whigs, laughing
behind his back.

Tables were heaped high on the morning of January 3.
Bottles of champagne, catawba wine, brandy, and bourbon

stood in groves on the sideboards. Elaborately starched servants fluttered about, more than a little harassed by the rush of giving a special polish to the floors and burnishing the silver as bright as the day it first came from England. When the hour of ten chimed on the grandfather clock, they opened the doors and stood ready to take greatcoats and beaver hats from the friends of their master.

Instead, men with no overcoats pushed by, and many of them left their flat felt caps on their heads. Dozens of these ill-clad unemployed or underemployed or underpaid invaders headed straight for the hillocks of dainties. In this spontaneous, unorganized raid was evidence that a depression was continuing and growing worse.

Before the mayor or anyone else could decide what to do, the marble tops of the tables shone white and bare. The liquor, in most cases reaching empty stomachs, took immediate effect. Finally, police appeared, cleared the chaotic reception rooms, and sent the ragged, jobless men back to the cellars of Five Points, the slum area around the site of the old Collect Pond that had been filled by the unemployed in 1808. Newfangled multiple dwelling tenements had begun to spring up near Five Points in answer to greatly increased real estate values, but these men could not afford to live in them.

The constables, known simply as "leatherheads" to the foragers they evicted, restored order but could not restore the lost drink and victuals. Still, they waited close at hand to thwart any future putsches on the punch bowl. At length the expected guests arrived, sympathized heartily with their host, and joined in the general excited discussion of what the world was coming to. Gang fights and riots, they recalled, had made 1834 memorable. After the great fire of 1835 (the light from it had shone so bright that firemen in New Haven and Philadelphia manned their pumps thinking their own cities ablaze), disorder, riots, and violence had increasingly disturbed the quiet streams of bourgeois lives.

Only the preceding summer, in order to stop the alarming tendency of employees to strike, the Supreme Court of the state had found twenty tailors guilty of "conspiracy to injure trade and commerce." The tailors had struck for higher wages and a ten-hour day; they got the choice of paying a heavy fine or going to jail.

Almost any day brought parades of protest or of pride. Mechanics who had sleek coats and glossy hats dressed up in them, and some union members even sported doeskin gloves on hands that carried placards demanding a ten-hour day. On special occasions all the trade unions of the city paraded together, marching and countermarching, their tightly trousered legs keeping time to the music of drums and fifes and trumpets.

Erupting into staid Massachusetts, the New England Association of Farmers, Mechanics, and Other Workingmen had appeared, importuning loudly for the ten-hour day. Unions mushroomed among the poor whites in the southern states. In New York, workingmen had grown so strong that they organized a revolt in the ranks of Tammany Hall. The paraders and strikers called themselves the Equal Rights Party, and their loudest clamor, reflecting their inferior position as debtors, was for bank reforms, for an end to speculation, and for an end to paper money that was accepted by creditors only at a discount. The Equal Rights faction had even forced Tammany candidates in the last election to take a pledge against monopolies and had elected Ely Moore, a Tammany "labor" man, to Congress.

Complaints about such signs of a new cocky attitude among the lower classes thrust themselves into the mayor's glum celebration. As talk came back to the omnivorous and thirsty invaders earlier in the day, one or two of those present uneasily mulled over what a visiting member of the British parliament had recently said: "I have seen scores of destitute homeless wretches lying on bulks, or under the sheds about the markets of New York and Philadelphia, and I have been eyewitness to great misery, from cold and hunger, in the severe winter of 1835–36. . . . Coroners' inquests were being held time after time on the extenuated bodies of sufferers from privation; and subscriptions repeatedly talked of, but very little entered into."

Only last summer a book, the *Workingmen's Manual*, had

offered an explanation that men quoted, requoted, praised, or attacked: "Pauperism is another of the concomitants of the age of capital, extortion and usury."

Throughout the country, 300,000 workers belonged to trade unions, and many read in the radical paper, the Plain Dealer, that "the employer filches from a poor man a part of his hard earned wages and is guilty of a miserable fraud. . . . The only effective mode of doing away with the evil is by attacking it with the great instrument of the rights of the poor — *associated effort.*"

Dangerous nonsense, the mayor's guests agreed as the party broke up. Cold dug through greatcoats too quickly for lingering under the gaslight in front of the door. One by one the guests hurried to their waiting carriages and, tucked into bear and buffalo robes, rolled off toward their homes. It was an unusually cold winter, although little snow lay on the ground. Ice covered the Hudson from shore to shore. Wolves, so the newspapers said, scavenged in the streets of Danbury and other Connecticut towns.

Bad as the weather was, economic conditions were worse. In 1836, aggressive speculation and hoarding by banks and businesses (both popularly called "monopolies") led to general economic collapse and consequent mass unemployment. Very soon plans emerged that were meant to cope with some of the effects of this, the third depression of the industrial era.

On December 3, 1836, the *National Laborer*, printed in Philadelphia but read in many nearby cities, presented a plea and a purpose on behalf of the jobless and the still-working poor: "Let not the people be deceived, but let all who have no wish to pay ten or twelve dollars for coal, memorialize Congress on this subject. New York and Boston have already presented petitions, while Philadelphia has remained silent. . . . Let us act at once, and tell our representatives plainly that we are opposed to the coal monopolies."

Two weeks later the *National Laborer* featured an editorial that said, "Charity societies are . . . degrading to a free people. . . . The producers of all wealth, and they are mostly 'the poor,' have doubtless learned by this time, that what individual effort cannot do, co-operation can, and it is by this method they can shield themselves from the wretched consequences of poverty." Cooperative buying was thereupon recommended, so that the poor could be "fortified against the extorting schemes," one of which was to give work to unemployed seamstresses. Those who gave money to start this boon to both producers and consumers repeatedly asked Elias Fountain, one of the committee of "gentlemen" in charge of the fund, for an accounting. If one was finally made, it was not forced into the public eye. Such awkward clamor did not discourage Elias Fountain; he again raised money for unemployed seamstresses in 1855.

In mid-January the *National Laborer* granted space to prominent citizens for a communication calling on clergymen to urge private charity for the poor and unemployed. The paper's editor was incensed at this suggestion for solving the problem, but he expressed satisfaction that the distress of the poor was being noted, at least.

Charity did bring a trickle of help. In Philadelphia one philanthropic enterprise, the Southwark Soup Society, supplied 1,100 persons a day with soup. A general ward committee of twenty citizens looked for the causes of the high price of foods and fuel and reported back to an open meeting in the Court House. After hearing theories about "the just cause of complaint" of the unemployed, the meeting approved a plan aimed at getting food for the poor at very low cost. The plan included a recommendation that everyone abstain from all use of alcohol so that grains needed for food would not be diverted to the manufacture of drink.

How well Pennsylvanians practiced total abstinence is not recorded, but the committees that the meeting set up to provide relief did function for some time. Meetings of other groups and general agitation continued, for suffering caused by economic conditions was acute. Gatherings of the unemployed even took the unconventional step of asking for state ownership of granaries and coal yards to break the food and fuel monopolies.

Antimonopolist sentiment was widely held, and it pre-dated this year of increasing distress. In July 1832, President Andrew Jackson had vetoed a bill to recharter the United States Bank,

claiming the institution tended toward monopoly. The electorate upheld his act in the same year by returning him to office
for a second term. Unforeseen troubles, however, followed soon
upon the new freedom and power allowed the eighty-eight state
banks. They issued paper money at will in response to the great
demand for currency to pay for western lands. By 1835, inflation had led to abnormal business expansion as well as a
complex and congested jumble of credits and debits. First gold
and then silver went out of circulation as a result of laws
governing coinage that placed a premium on possession first of
one and then of the other metal. Paper money alone remained,
and workers had to accept it as wages at a discount. Factory
and farm hands were in straits long before any real depression
appeared. But appear it did.

Government land in the West, recently acquired from Indians by dubious and violent means, sold at $1.25 an acre, and
paper money could pay for it; in consequence, a speculation
mania swept the country. The sale of public land increased
fivefold in two years. Ownership tended to center in the hands
of those who had the most paper money: the bankers, or
"monopolists." Seeing that the government realized practically
nothing from these sales, Jackson issued the Specie Circular
on July 11, 1836, which ordered land agents to accept only
hard money after August 15, 1837. This order sent coin scurry-
ing toward the frontier, and the East, where the new industrial
growth centered, depended more than ever on paper. A crash
was on the way.

Paralleling American developments, panic swept the London exchange. Cotton dealers in the southern states found
English markets closed to them. They failed and took with them
into ruin the banks supplying their capital. Nicholas Biddle, the
country's leading financier, established new banks in Missouri,
Arkansas, Alabama, Georgia, and Louisiana. He put in very
little capital and observed no rules in issuing paper money. As
a consequence, the notes quickly fell 30 percent in value and
the planters would not take them.

Banks as a whole, having only $38 million in currency to
back $525 million in loans, began to fail. They took with them

those individuals and banks from whom they had borrowed. Many of the latter had overinvested in factories that closed because of their supporters' failure and because of the diminishing market resulting from the decreasing value of the money that wage earners received. Workers in the factories were immediately thrown out of the ranks of consumers, and they, with the farmer-producers of goods that were no longer consumed, went down in the general heap.

In addition, many of the states had turned their bonds over to agents, who failed without giving the states any return on the bonds. The states, thus saddled with debts, repudiated the bonds in many cases, adding to the turmoil. Finally, after most of the economic row of dominoes had felled each other, all of them rested their full weight on the workers, who either lost their jobs entirely or had to accept greatly reduced wages as a condition of continued employment. This process was particularly apparent in New York, where much of the country's economic life was centered.

New York workingmen, both the jobless and the still-working poor, had begun to suffer long before President Jackson issued the Specie Circular. Their problems were worse, indeed, than those of their Philadelphia confreres, and their resentment took on a more developed character under the leadership of the splinter of Tammany Hall known as the Equal Rights or "Loco Foco" Party. This group, the reincarnation of a section of the Working Men's Party that had formed in New York in 1829, was one small element in a worldwide upsurge of which the struggle for the Reform Bill and Chartism in England, the 1830 July revolt in France, and growing rebellion in Germany were manifestations. As large-scale enterprise wrenched men from their own small farms and businesses, security diminished; resentment and retaliation sprang up everywhere as a natural result.

The rise of the labor movement, which accompanied the growth of industry and commerce, allowed the left-wing Tammany group to become more and more active until it actually threatened the power of the probusiness or "monopolist" faction. At a meeting in Tammany Hall one night, the monopolists discovered they faced a left-wing majority. The outnumbered supporters of privilege fell back on a simple mechanical aid to their cause: They turned off the gas, leaving the assembly in darkness. Some of the radicals, ahead of their time in more ways than one, took out newfangled matches, lit candles, and went on with the meeting. The matches, known commercially as "Loco Focos," supplied a name for the insurgents, at first derisive but later popular. These Loco Focos were to become to some extent the champions of the unemployed.

Soon after the mayor's disastrous January 3 open house, the Loco Focos watched the thermometer going down and the price of wheat going up — it had risen from $8.50 a barrel to $12.50 since September — and they decided to act. At a county convention of the party in the Military and Civic Hotel, on January 17, 1837, they appointed a committee to arrange for a big demonstration against paper money that dramatically decreased in value and against the price of bread, which steadily rose.

Soon handbills were plastered on walls and fences all over the city:

Bread, Meat, Rent, Fuel
Their prices must come down!
The voice of the people shall be heard, and must prevail! The people will meet in the Park *rain or shine*, at four o'clock on Monday afternoon, to inquire into the cause of the present distress and devise a suitable remedy. All friends of humanity, determined to resist monopolists and extortioners, are invited to attend.

On the bitter cold morning of February 13, the *Morning Courier* and *New York Enquirer* noted: "We trust . . . that no respectable citizen will attend the meeting in the Park. No good can come of it." Businessmen warmly toasting their feet in front of their open fireplaces listened to the gale blowing outside and had no fears. No citizens, respectable or otherwise, would appear outdoors on a day like this.

But there were 50,000 unemployed in the city. By 4:00, hundreds of them huddled in front of City Hall. By 4:30, 5,000 chilly men crowded around a huge banner that read, "As the currency expands, the loaf contracts." The chairman, 60-year-old physician Moses Jaques, stood hatless, his hair streaming out in the wind, and shouted, "The banks are oppressors of the poor, for they foster the speculators in real estate, which raise rents, and they raise the prices of the necessaries of life." He exhorted his fellow citizens to seek peaceful remedies for public grievances and "to do no act which might bring into disrepute the fair name of a New Yorker, the honor of a citizen of this Republic, or the character of man."

Alexander Ming, Jr., a liberal and ambitious government customs inspector, then stepped to the platform and read the document of the day, which began, "When in the course of human events it becomes necessary for the many to declare hostility against the rapacity of the few. . . ." The document went on to declare that "the monstrous banking system is the prime, original cause" of the current economic chaos, which included fantastically high prices. The assembled throng agreed that the banks were more "dangerous to the liberties of the people than . . . a standing army." It followed from this analysis that the solution to the crisis was for workingmen to refuse paper money and demand specie instead.

After the shivering assembly unanimously adopted this antibank program, it agreed to memorialize the state legislature to the effect that distressed workingmen were boycotting paper money. This measure may have had more meaning for those who still had jobs and a little income, but the thousands who were jobless could not refuse to use paper money — which they didn't have anyway.

Just then a tumultuous stream of men and boys flowed from Chatham Street toward the peaceful gathering in the park. A man jumped boldly to the platform where Ming was still standing and stole the audience for a moment, long enough to shout, "Go to the flour stores and offer a fair price, and if refused, take the flour." He got no farther. The elderly chairman, Dr. Moses Jaques, aided by the officers of the meeting, pulled the uninvited advocate of direct appropriation off the stand and pushed the meeting toward a headlong adjournment.

Confusion followed, but Alexander Ming, Jr., the orator of the day, was not forgotten. His hat soon appeared high above the crowd, casting a grotesque shadow from the gaslights that lit the rooms in City Hall where uneasy officials had gathered to watch the proceedings. Ming was carried on the shoulders of his admirers across the park to Tammany Hall, half as a joyous rebel returning victorious and half as a wistful exile paying persuasive homage to what later proved to be his true home.

Clattering and roaring away from the park in the direction of Broadway went another section of the meeting, at least 1,000 strong. Tables at home would still be breadless for a long time, even if Mr. Ming's boycott of paper money was successful. It was cold tonight, and wives and children were hungry. Many followed the unknown speaker who had said, "Go to the flour stores!"

Blacks and whites in the crowd hurried shoulder to shoulder down Broadway. A few hackney cabs, coaches, phaetons, and large-wheeled tilburies rumbled over the polished pavement stones between the rows of low, red-brick houses, some of which boasted the plate-glass window fronts just recently introduced in America. Omnibuses swished by, like boats, bearing such names as "George Washington" and "Benjamin Franklin."

Advertisements carved in the sidewalks stared up provocatively at the penniless crowd, and merchants who hovered near their shops sighed with relief when the throng swung off Broadway and headed west to Washington Street near Dey. There stood the storehouse of Eli Hart, with, some said, 53,000 barrels of flour inside. From basement to roof, the precious stuff was crammed, and only a few frightened clerks stood between it and a roaring torrent of hungry, angry humanity.

Soon barrels were rolling out the front door into the street. A gleeful boy dropped one bulging container after another from an upper window shouting, "Here goes flour at $8!" As the barrels struck the pavement, the staves burst apart and the flour for the most part was lost. Five hundred barrels in all rolled out and exploded or had their heads knocked in. The raiders also dragged out a thousand bushels of wheat, and old Swiss women who lived nearby scurried back and forth to their dwellings with boxes, baskets, and aprons full of wheat and flour. Every man in the neighborhood rolled full flour barrels away and hurriedly lugged off sacks of the whole grain. If obeying the law meant starving, the law be damned!

Representatives of the law soon appeared. Justice Blood-good and a small posse of constables swung their clubs, but the angry crowd stripped the officers of their weapons and their clothes, broke the clubs over the constables' leather helmets, and freed the two men whom they had arrested. Mayor Law-rence came from City Hall and tried to speak, but a shower of barrel staves, headings, sticks, stones, balls of flour, and icicles forced him to retreat for his life.

The pillaging went on for hours and ended only after the arrival of more police and hastily summoned soldiers. Instead of beating a disorderly retreat, part of the crowd streamed across the city to the East River and made off with fifty barrels of flour from the Herrick and Co. storehouse at Water Street and Coenties Slip. Here, according to the *Times*, "A gentleman made his appearance and announced to them that the propri-etor of the store had authorized him to pledge to them that if they would desist from destroying his flour, he would the next day give the whole of it for the benefit of the poor." The crowd dispersed, and as it dwindled the police made the first success-ful arrests of the evening. (The next day, as an afterthought, Herrick and Co. concluded it was wiser to sell their flour than to give it away.)

By this time, the constables and soldiers had thrown a cordon around the knee-deep flour in front of Hart's. A few women still dashed away, with containers full of it, but for the most part the crowd that continued to hang around was unwill-ing to risk further conflict. The weather came more and more to the aid of the law, and long before midnight, the street was filled only with the flour shining white in the moonlight and the glint of burnished guns and swords.

The morning after the great riot, hundreds of ragged slum dwellers from Five Points crowded the police station. Fifty-four of their fellows lay in jail. All day the crowd hooted and booed every time a constable passed through the door. It was easy to distinguish the constables, though they dressed like other men: They carried sturdy, fat-bellied clubs.

Sympathizers made several futile attempts to rescue the prisoners who formed a representative lot: young, old, several African-Americans (who were placed in the lowest, least ventilated cells), many native whites, some Irish, and at least one Englishman. The last may have recalled a rhyme from his homeland a few years before, when two millers, Bone and Skin by name, achieved a local monopoly of flour:

> Bone and Skin,
> Two millers thin,
> Would starve us all, or near it:
> Be it known
> To Skin and Bone
> That flesh and blood won't bear it.

The labor press took up the jingle, and it was soon on many American tongues.

The group in the cells represented the New York working class, with one exception. Not a single member of the Loco Foco Party had been arrested at the scene of the disorder. Indeed, the party boasted that it frowned on acts of violence. A leader of the Loco Focos, however, printer John Windt, was taken into custody later (on charges that have been forgotten) and held for $1,000 bail. He was not accused of having been in the riot, nor did the law ever bring him to trial in this connection during his subsequent long career as a labor agitator. After the riot, many of the newspapers lambasted the Loco Focos. Alexander Ming lost his position in the Customs House and got it back much later only after taking his case to Washington.

Two days after the riot, bills of indictment against many of those arrested had already been brought in by a grand jury, which workingmen complained was headed by the former mayor, Philip Hone. "The city was disgraced by a mob," Hone wrote in his diary. A few days later, however, he added,

"What is to become of the laboring classes? The mechanic who has a family does not do so well with his 18 shillings a day [a shilling was not much more than a 1990 nickel — F.F.] as he did when his wages were only 12 shillings. . . . Never have I known so dear a market as the Fulton was this morning. It had the appearance of famine. . . . I record for future observation the cost of my marketing this morning:

A bass, 14 lb.	$2.50
2 small turkeys	3.50
1 pair partridges (forbidden)	1.00
21 veal	3.94
Neck and breast mutton	1.50
6 sweetbreads	1.50
TOTAL	$17.31

"I could not do with less."

On this same day the city fathers took steps to increase the police force "for the suppressing of riots," and a fierce argument about monopoly began in the press. Eli Hart, owner of the plundered warehouse, indignantly protested, "The price is as always, the effect of supply and demand."

An answer came from the *National Laborer:* "Some of the New York sixpennies [that is, newspapers — F.F.] say that the flour hoarded in that city belongs to the millers in the interior, and not to the merchants of the city, who are mere agents. . . . But we do not believe . . . the disclaimer; for we believe that millers and merchants are engaged in the combination, and boards of bank directors."

Leaders of the new Native American Party reasoned that if the Loco Focos "had held no Park meeting there would have been no flour riot." Whigs and many Tammany Democrats agreed. But Loco Focos met immediately in protest and resolved: "That if there had been no Park for the people to meet in, or if there had been no people to assemble there, no public meeting would have taken place. That the people should be shot down, and the Park laid off in building lots and sold at auction to prevent all Park meetings in the future, and consequently, all flour riots."

Five thousand of New York's nearly 50,000 unemployed had gathered in the park that February day. In the weeks that followed, distress from inflation increased. So did resentment among the jobless, and the Loco Focos determined to have something done.

4

Poor in Purse but Rich in Principle
(1837–1840)

Law rules the poor and money rules the law.
> — E. J. Webb
> speech, June 24, 1837

The most dreaded of all wars, the war of the poor against the rich, a war which, however long it may be delayed, will come, and come with all its horrors.
> — Orestes A. Brownson
> "The Laboring Classes," 1840

It is perhaps not unreasonable to see these earlier, immature, and often crude, trials of strength, even when doomed to failure, as fore-runners of later movements whose results and successes have been both significant and enduring.
> — George Rudé
> *The Crowd in History*, 1964

Between 30,000 and 40,000 people jammed New York's City Hall Park on March 6, 1837. Tension was greater this day than it had been on the eve of the flour riot because of a report in the sympathetic *New Era* that said, "There will be a large military force called out today as we are informed from authentic source, IN ANTICIPATION of the Great Meeting of the people in the Park on the subject of all the necessaries of life."

The report proved correct. A brigade of artillery paraded ostentatiously by the meeting (which had been called by the Loco Focos) of which, alleged the *Journal of Commerce*, "nine-tenths . . . were English Radicals, a few were Irishmen, and the rest were New York loafers. . . . Others, as we happen to know, attended with the view of assisting the civil authorities in case this meeting like the other one, should end in a riot." Such measures were being taken against the victims of the depression, which had not abated.

A carpenter's bench, with a table on top, stood in front of City Hall, and from there speaker after speaker sought to send his voice to the limits of the largest mass meeting New York had ever seen. Flags, banners, streamers were scattered through the crowd. "No rag money, give us gold or silver!" they read. "Down with chartered monopolies!" "We are now to see if we can make an effective stand against the spirit of monopoly." "We go for principle. No monopoly." "Equal rights must and shall be preserved." "We enjoy our liberties to the last ditch."

The rattle of cannon on paving stones echoed every rhetorical attack on the banks. Statements in defiance of monopolists were punctuated by the restless clash of staves on the stone walls of City Hall, against which the newly enlarged constabulary leaned. After the meeting ended without incident, the Loco Focos of the Sixteenth Ward gathered again and voted a resolution:

> Whereas the Mayor of the city of New York did in his wisdom and clemency, transmit a solemn request to our military chiefs to order out their regiments on the 6th of March; and whereas, the commanders of their martial invincibility, like the valorous king of France,
> "Did with all their men
> March up the streets and then march down again."
> And whereas, the august Mayor, Watchmen and Constables, were snugly ensconced in the purlieus of the City Hall, where they did the state great service.
> Therefore, be it Resolved, That the Mayor and the Martial Commanders on the memorable day of the 6th of March, cover themselves with all the splendid halo of immortal glory.

Another meeting held on the day of the demonstration condemned the authorities for "anticipating a riot and disgracing our citizen soldiers by placing them in the situation of policemen and keeping them under arms to intimidate their fellow citizens assembled in the Park for redress of grievances."

Ten days later news reached New York of the collapse of New Orleans' greatest flour dealer. Apprehensive Loco Focos called meetings of unemployed in the city and in Greenwich Village to demand work. An aristocratic witness described one of these gatherings of men "standing in ominous darkness, save for the lurid light shed upon their cadaverous looking faces from twenty or thirty flambeaux. . . . Over their heads, floating the dark and poisoned breeze, were a variety of banners . . . underneath these stood the managers and orators, who were straining their lungs to swell the sounds of their cracked voices. We might and should probably have laughed, but for the recollection of the lamp-posts, the . . . Jacobins, and the Guillotine."

On April 3, another large Loco Foco meeting took place in the park, where people supported a resounding pledge read by Revolutionary War veteran Levi D. Slamm, a grocer. The pledge, couched in rhetoric reminiscent of the War of Independence, emphasized the rights of man. It also made a clear appeal on the basis of class: "The world has always abounded with men, who, rather than toil to produce the wealth necessary to their subsistence, have contrived to strip others of the fruits of their labor, either by violence and bloodshed, or by swaggering pretentions to exclusive privileges." The document expressed opposition to rioting and violence and resolved that "we will cause the producing interest to be represented in our legislative halls hereafter by actual producers."

The pledge was clearly an election manifesto, and someone nominated Revolutionary War veteran Dr. Moses Jaques for mayor. Suddenly a banner appeared announcing the nomination in large letters. The audience cheered, and the sun for the first time that day burst from the clouded sky and shone full on the assembly. The coincidence excited renewed cheering.

In the election, which spread over three days (April 11, 12, and 13), Jaques got 4,000 votes out of a total of 34,000, although many workers could not vote because they could not meet property qualifications. The Loco Foco strength came at the expense of Tammany and brought about the defeat of the

Democratic-Republican candidate. The Whig candidate won with 17,000 votes, and his victory forced Tammany to take stock of itself. From this election dates the Tammany policy of befriending the masses by making or appearing to make concessions to their demands.

Nearly every laborer in the city was unemployed by the middle of April 1837. The unemployed in Greenwich Village issued a call for a public meeting, the purpose of which was to petition the city for work. On April 22, the observant former Mayor Philip Hone wrote in his diary, "The poor and laboring classes of the community, who constitute a large proportion of the depositors in those institutions [banks], urged by their necessities, or by want of confidence in all money institutions, are withdrawing their funds in a most alarming manner."

Banks were indeed unsound, as Loco Foco analysts had been contending. Paper money grew more and more worthless. Jobs withered away to mere memories of employment. In spite of the coming of good weather, the whole body politic became increasingly irritable, and only the Loco Focos were there to direct the discontent. On May 3, they held another meeting in the park that dealt more specifically with unemployment than any that preceded it. The day was warm, but very few of the 5,000 present could muster a penny for a drink of water when the spring water wagon lumbered past. Instead, the crowd put unusual fervor into its unanimous vote recommending that the city employ as many laborers as possible "in the construction of the works for running water to the city, and other public works in progress." Speakers also called for reduction of officials' salaries and suggested appointment of unofficial ward committees "to attend to the condition of the destitute immigrants and others who may desire to remove to the country."

Another petition, presented at this time to the Board of Aldermen, asked that the street commissioner be "authorized to employ such persons on any of the public avenues or streets, as he may deem expedient." The aldermen took no action on the petition, but the 5,000 determined men outside City Hall — and the memory of the flour riot — had their effect. Plans for the

Croton Reservoir had lain around for years, but not until May 5, immediately following the demonstration, did anyone shake the dust off them. On that day the mayor signed a resolution "that a reservoir be constructed," and $10,000 was appropriated for the project.

Travelers still came from abroad in spite of hard times, and they found New York a sad city filled with sallow-faced men and women. On May 4, Captain Marryat, the famous sea story writer, landed. "The militia are under arms, as riots are expected," he observed. "Not a smile on one countenance among the crowd who pass and repass. . . . Mechanics thrown out of employment, are pacing up and down with the air of famished wolves. . . . The Irish emigrant leans against his shanty, with his spade idle in his hand, and starves."

"The port indeed was full of shipping," noted another British traveler, "but their hatches were fastened down, and scarcely a sailor was to be found on board. Not a box, bale, cask, barrel, or package was to be seen upon the wharves. Many of the counting houses were shut up, or advertised to be let. . . . The coffee houses were almost empty, the streets near the water side were almost deserted; the grass had begun to grow upon the wharves."

Inland activities as well as those along the coast slowed. "The factory girls are leaving the factories," said the *New Haven Register*, "and going back to help their mothers, and aunts and uncles make cheese and raise poultry, watch bees, pick the geese feathers, and sort the wool." The *Norwalk Chronicle* noted, "Ten or twelve double horse wagons passed through this place on Friday loaded with men, women, guns, rifles, boys, girls, babies, and other knick-knacks, all bound to the far West."

The economic breakdown affected the entire country. On May 7, it reached a dramatic climax in New York in a run on the banks. On May 9, bank officials sitting in their two-story buildings in Wall Street suspended specie payment, thus paralyzing the whole nation, and by the end of the month, Philip Hone wrote, "A deadly calm pervades this lately flourishing city. No goods are selling, no business stirring, no boxes encumber the sidewalks of Pearl Street. Very few houses are being built. . . . [But theaters kept open. — F.F.] Nine of the money drains [that is, theaters] are in operation."

Captain Marryat described how these and other "money drains" carried on business: "Go to the theaters and places of public amusement, and, instead of change, you receive an I.O.U. from the treasury. At the hotels and oyster cellars it is the same thing. Call for a glass of brandy and water and the change is fifteen tickets, each 'good for one glass of brandy and water.' At an oyster-shop [where low-priced food was of great importance to workingmen — F.F.] eat a plate of oysters, and you have in return seven tickets good for one plate of oysters, each. It is the same everywhere."

In the midst of this panic the new anti-Catholic, anti-Irish mayor, Aaron Clark, a Whig, took the oath of office. Disgruntled workers rioted in the Common Council chambers at his inauguration.

Protests of a more organized nature also reached City Hall. On May 29, a petition "in behalf of the unemployed operatives, for relief" was referred to a committee of the Common Council, which later reported that it was in general against work relief but did favor a few projects, both to provide some relief and to obtain material and labor at lower prices. The recommended projects called for the expenditure of $250,000.

The Select Committee, reporting on June 8 on the work projects demanded by the unemployed, showed they had been impressed not only by the constant pressure but also by the type of people asking for relief. They "beg that it be borne in mind by the Common Council, that the persons who now call on you for assistance are not paupers; they merely ask for employment to enable them to procure food for their wives and little ones, until an opportunity offers for them to do something better. Many . . . have supported their families through the rigors of the past winter, on the savings of the previous year, believing that the return of spring would bring with it the accustomed demand for labor; but circumstances have destroyed that hope."

Under pressure of the unemployed, contract work on streets, avenues, and sewers was developed by June, and at a meeting on June 12 the Common Council sped up this work, offering advances to contractors who promised to hire only family men who had been in New York six months or more. Although there was money enough for the expensive methods of relieving unemployment by allowing contractors to relay funds to the jobless, direct payment by the city to the unemployed through work relief was persistently avoided, the aldermen pleading a depleted exchequer.

Just as persistently, the Loco Focos called the anguished citizenry together in City Park. On June 24, a great meeting — some said the largest yet held in the city — resolved "That the banking system was at war with the interests of society and the constitution." The main speaker, E. J. Webb, followed a familiar pattern and used the aspirations of the American Revolution as a point of reference: "However unpalatable the truth may be to our national vanity, it is not the less true that America is not yet a republic. Here as elsewhere 'Law rules the poor and Money rules the Law.' We cannot afford to waste our time in empty formalities while our families are famishing around us."

At the same time, the members of the Board of Aldermen were considering a wage-cutting, spread-the-work plan. On the Fourth of July they all made patriotic speeches beside liberty poles throughout the city. The next day they asked a committee "to report on the propriety of reducing wages of the men employed on sweeping streets to six shillings per day, and that of the carts employed on the same to thirteen shillings per day, and that the street inspectors be required to employ more men, not exceeding the amount of the sum per week at the present wages." There is no record showing whether or not this plan went into effect, but at any rate the city fathers hoped it might be possible to have the employed share the burden of caring for the unemployed by taking a wage cut.

More and more, the Loco Foco resistance to such tactics was replaced with suggestions that the unemployed help themselves by going west — by becoming small landowners. At the same time, the Loco Foco Party became obsessed with the idea of working within the old Democratic Party. On October 27, 1837, Alexander Ming, Jr., one of the nonlabor members in the party, urged reunion with Tammany, on the theory that Tammany had reformed and was now antimonopolist. The *Plaindealer*, a Loco Foco paper, suspended publication at this time, and before long, in the very depth of the depression, the party disappeared. It had compromised itself out of existence, and although its cause was the cause of the unemployed, the party leaders gave it up. They ceased fighting for city relief, and their influence was felt in private charity in only a few New York wards, notably the Sixth, where Horace Greeley led in relief activities.

In his autobiography, *Recollections of a Busy Life*, Greeley described the situation in New York in the fall of 1837:

> In addition to all who may be said to belong here, legions of laborers, servants, etc., are annually dismissed in autumn from the farms, country seats, and watering places of the suburban districts, and drift down to the city, whence they were mainly hired; vaguely hoping to find work here, which a small part of them do; the rest live on the good nature of relatives, if such they have here, or on credit from boarding houses, landlords or grocers, as long as they can; and then make their choice between roguery and beggary. . . . To say that ten thousand young persons here annually take their first lessons in debauchery and crime would be to keep quite within the truth; and . . . I judge that destitution flowing from involuntary idleness sends more men and women to perdition, in this city, than any other cause, intemperance possibly excepted.
>
> I lived that winter [1837–1838] in the 6th Ward. A public meeting of its citizens was duly held early in December and an organization formed by which Committees were appointed to canvass the ward from house to house, collect funds from those who could and would spare anything, ascertain the nature and extent of the destitution and devise ways and means for its systematic relief. Very poor myself, I could give no money, or but a mite; so I gave my time instead, and served through several days, on one of the visiting committees. . . . I saw two families, including six or eight children burrowing in

one cellar under a stable, a prey to famine on the one hand, and to vermin and maladies on the other. . . . I saw men who each, somehow, supported his family on an income of $5 per week or less, yet who cheerfully gave something to mitigate the suffering of those who were really poor. I saw three widows, with as many children, living in an attic on the profits of an apple stand which yielded less than $3 per week, and the landlord came in for a full third of that. But worse to bear of all was the pitiful plea of stout, resolute, single young men and young women, "We do not want Alms; we are not beggars; we hate to sit here day by day idle and useless; help us to work, we want no other help; why is it we can have nothing to do?"

In New York City, the Central Committee for the Relief of the Suffering Poor sponsored lectures and concerts as a means of raising money, while the still prosperous generally complained that hordes of beggars thronged the streets and knocked at doors. The committee made an effort to see that none froze or starved, but once winter was over, the poor were expected to "subsist on the milder state of the atmosphere." Greeley wanted more; he pleaded for the continuance of public works, which alone could help keep wages from falling lower.

Before the end of 1837, nine-tenths of the factories in the eastern states were closed. One hot day in August, 500 men in New York applied for work in response to an advertisement for twenty men to wield a spade in the country at four dollars a month plus board. Men posted notices in City Hall that they would do any kind of work for three dollars a week. And immigrants kept coming. Eighty thousand arrived in New York in 1837, holding the population of the city constant in spite of great western migration.

Rents for tenements in New York were higher than in any city in the world, and as cold weather approached renters made plans for action. The *New Era* boosted the campaign with an editorial titled "The Poor! The Poor! The Poor!" which proposed that the tenants pay no rent and the landlords give receipts up to February 1. "There are at the present moment fifty thousand persons suffering for the common wants of life. Is nothing to be done until it be *too late?* Must a civil volcano, which is gathering in hidden strength and is not the less terrible for the stillness which precedes its eruption, burst over the heads of the people, before they will wake to their true condition?"

The agitation in New York City came to little, but a rent strike centering around Albany came to a great deal. By January 1839, $400,000 in back rent was owed by farmers, who had felt the pinch of depression, to the heirs of Stephen Van Rensselaer. When the estate made efforts to collect, the renters, over 3,000 of them, organized and resisted. A secret underground association called the "Indians" flourished among the farmers for many years. In 1846, with the aid of the labor vote in New York City, they elected a sympathetic governor of the state. By 1847, all of the "Indians" who had been imprisoned for their antirent activities were freed, and in a short time nearly all the demands of the rent strikers were granted.

The year 1838 in the cities saw no easing of conditions for the unemployed. Toward the end of January Horace Greeley called for $50,000 additional relief money, adding, "It ought to be twice that sum." At least 10,000 of those in direst poverty were getting no relief from the overburdened almshouses and charity agencies. Many hundreds more got not relief, but jail. Debtors still had to go to prison, and the single meal served there each day consisted of half-baked bread and boiled beef gristle and bone.

Still the Whig officials took no steps toward giving relief, but Tammany leaders, partly pressed by the newly returned Loco Focos in their ranks and partly acting from shrewd demagogic motives, made a display of distributing clothing, fuel, and even money. One of the leaders, John M. Bloodgood, the chief constable who had directed the attack on the flour rioters, went among the poor with a basket filled with cakes, pies, and meat, and he gave them out to those who asked for them. "It was discovered shortly afterward," said M. R. Werner in his history of Tammany Hall, "that Mr. Bloodgood gained his money by extorting it from counterfeiters, thieves, and prostitutes who were brought into his court." Bloodgood had failed in business in the prosperous year 1823 and had then turned to politics.

The new Tammany friendship for the underdog provoked by the Loco Focos had an expected result: Tammany-supported candidates won the spring election in 1838. Before the election, however, public works (on a contract basis) were revived by the Whig Board of Aldermen, which acted with the already familiar motives of getting necessary improvements at the bargain rates made possible by the helplessness of labor. Labor had, indeed, become helpless. The Loco Foco Party was no more, and its mass tactics were merely bad dreams to the monopolists. Unions, under the double pressures of employers and of unemployment, which ended their treasuries and their basis of organization, had largely ceased to exist. The National Trades Union had dissolved in May 1837. The rest of the labor movement turned away from conflict and toward cooperatives, toward seeking utopian oases in the economic desert. In the next decade more than forty "communist" communities were launched — "duodecimo editions of the New Jerusalem," Karl Marx called them. They all failed, but they were all symptomatic of the aspirations of the times.

A few old Loco Focos maintained their rebellious zeal inside the still corrupt Democratic machine. "Poor in purse, but rich in principle" remained the motto and the mien of the Eleventh Ward Democratic Workingmen, for instance, and a few of the old leaders continued to be militant. Levi D. Slamm said in November 1838, "We are opposed to the modern doctrine that 'the *possession* of property is the proof of merit,' we assert that the *creation or production* of wealth is the evidence of merit, and not the mere possession of it." Such inconspicuous men as Slamm gave a progressive character to a section of the Democratic Party for a decade or more to come. In fact, the whole Democratic Party was called the Loco Foco Party for several years.

Workers in 1839, 1840, and 1841 were discouraged. They had met in great numbers to hear radical talk, but where had it got them? There was no home relief, and no real work relief. They had won a system of public works but it was inadequate and underpaid. They had won an increase of private charity, likewise insufficient. Now that life was harder than ever, some of the leaders no longer struggled against poverty and its causes. They merely tried to evade them. For one thing, they agitated for prohibition (New York averaged three temperance meetings a week). Dr. Sylvester Graham, a dyspeptic temperance reformer who campaigned against white bread and preached in favor of a brown kind he called dyspepsia bread. It became known simply as graham bread, and today we still have graham crackers.

Leaders and reformers of all kinds turned attention away from economic distresses close at hand, but whipped up excitement for prison reform, for free education, for free western land, and for the abolition of slavery in the distant South. To the achievement of all these goals the early American labor movement made a substantial contribution, but it fell far short of solving the problem of unemployment. Meanwhile, the labor movement of the 1830s melted imperceptibly into the general capitalist scene. The reformers who remained active from 1838 on openly encouraged private charity or gave it tacit approval. This fact, together with the efforts of the capitalists and the newspapers, thwarted moves on behalf of the unemployed. The papers, in fact, were merely polite agents-provocateurs. They did their effective best to head off all efforts of the jobless to make society responsible for their survival. Despair crept over those workers who could not migrate or squeeze into one of the still existing jobs. Some writers came to refer to the period as "the age of suicide and mysterious disappearance."

Many a hungry man passed along Chatham Square watching the seventy or so African-American girls there who sold the cheapest of all foods, corn. At 7:00 in the evening it was impossibly expensive at three cents an ear, but by waiting until 10:00 they heard the more pleasant chant, "Hot corn! Two cents!" and those who had two cents then rushed to buy the leftover ears on which they did not even get salt. Many a worker who had once jauntily entered an oyster cellar and called for humble "shilling stew" now stood begging outside the door of the cellar under the bright globe of red muslin over a rattan frame — the oyster "balloon" that hung above the door.

Others, when a few pennies miraculously came their way, stepped into a certain noisy grog shop near the waterfront, where homemade liquor sold for three cents a glass. During the two dark years of 1837 and 1838, the enterprising owner of the dive, young Fernando Wood, managed to buy three sailing vessels out of his profits. (In 1854 and 1857, when hard times returned, Wood again faced the unemployed, not from behind a bar but from behind the mayor's desk, and he fed the hungry cheap rhetoric instead of cheap rum.)

Small hopes still existed here and there. One young mother played a long shot on a December morning in 1838, nearly two years after Mayor Lawrence's reception had been invaded by hungry men. She hurried through the streets before anyone was about and left a large basket containing a tiny baby on the doorstep of 719 Broadway, the home of Philip Hone. The former mayor was still well-off, although he had three grown sons who could find no work. Servants discovered the abandoned child and ran with it to their master. For a moment the handsome, curly-headed Whig toyed with the idea of keeping it. "But," he wrote in his diary, "in that case I would have twenty more such outlets to my benevolence. I reflected, moreover, that if the little urchin should turn out bad, he would prove a troublesome inmate; and if intelligent and good, by the time he became an object of affection the rightful owners might come and take him away. I sent off the little wanderer to the Almshouse."

Next day Hone called at that grim place to reassure his conscience that the child was well cared for, and he was unmoved by a note which had been found among the child's clothing: "Have compassion upon my poor orphan child, its father lost. . . . I am a poor friendless widow in a strange city. Had I kept it, it would have lingered and died with starvation. O, it will drive me frantic to think I must part with my first and only pledge of my departed husband, but God will forgive me."

A few days later, the pious American Tract Society distributed a curious leaflet. "The New Year has commenced, and all around men are active. Commerce has revived," was its cheery but totally untrue message. "The merchant rejoices in the improvement of trade. The mechanic again obtains employment, and all expect still better times." Unemployment continued, and, low wages notwithstanding, the price of wheat kept going up. It reached a higher point in 1839 than at any time since 1819, and a few intellectuals cried out that a revolution was coming. "A crisis as to the relation of wealth and labor is approaching," said the influential and widely read writer, Orestes A. Brownson. "We or our children will have to meet this crisis."

Brownson overlooked the capacity of the great West to absorb population and goods and to supply capitalists with motives for investment. He did not foresee that westward expansion and other factors would supply momentum for more than one more turn of the eccentric wheel of capitalist production. On the other hand, he did observe that the number of small factories increased even during the depression, and that the number of industrial workingmen (he called them "proletaries") had steadily expanded until it had reached 17 percent of the population. He did not see capitalism's untapped sources of strength or the enormous influence it held over the minds of even the most distressed workers and farmers. His attention focused merely on a wish and on the few remaining signs of militancy in the labor world. One of these sources of hope for a change came from workingmen near him in Charlestown, Massachusetts, who considered their plight on the eve of the presidential election in 1840 and wrote in a manifesto:

> Brethren: — The time seems to have arrived, when we, the real workingmen of the country, should pause and survey our condition: . . . We are poor. Our wages barely suffice to give us the necessities of life. We rarely have either leisure or opportunity to cultivate our minds. . . . Not our *rights*, but our *mights* fail us. . . . The privileged classes have always prevailed against us, though we are the many and they are the few, because they have combined their numbers and acted together. . . . We would, therefore, recommend to our brethren to organize themselves into associations, which . . . may bring about a concert of action between the workingmen of the country. . . . Let us become a band of brothers sworn to stand

by one another. . . . With our interests are identified those of the race.

While Americans drew up this call for class struggle and class unity in the face of low wages and unemployment, two young students in Europe — Karl Marx and Friedrich Engels — were reading philosophy and writing poems, only remotely aware of the distressed but potentially dynamic world of working people. But it would not be many years before the two Germans learned much about economic reality in the United States, and, having learned, began to make contributions to it.

Meanwhile, relative prosperity gradually returned. The crisis of mass unemployment had passed and would not recur until 1854.

5

Our Daily Bread
(1854)

The middle class is always a firm champion of equality when it concerns a class above it; but it is its inveterate foe when it concerns elevating a class below it.

— Orestes A. Brownson
The Laboring Classes, 1840

As New York nights grew longer and colder in 1854, the barrels and packing boxes that had once sheltered little Jimmy no longer sufficed. The African-American boy could keep alive on the eels he earned dancing for the delight of fishermen and sailors along the wharves, but he shivered at night. A hope remained, however, and one evening he went to Fulton Street, humming one of the recent song hits:

> When de night walks in as black as a sheep,
> And de hen and her eggs am fast asleep,
> Den into her nest with a sarpent's creep,
> "Pop goes de Weasel!"

In Fulton Street, Jimmy trudged up two flights of stairs at number 192, pushed open the door labeled "Newsboys' Home," and said to the man at a table on one side of the room full of white boys, "I got no place to sleep."

The question, according to the story in the *New York Times,* was whether to trust Jimmy. It cost six cents for the use of a bed in the home, and he hadn't even one cent. After some delay, Mick, one of the older boys, spoke up. "Hey Mr. Tracy, here's three cents to Jimmy's lodging!" Tracy thanked him, and the evening passed quietly, but when bed hour came, Mick had changed his mind. He announced belligerently, "I ain't going to pay that nigger's lodging."

"Very well," said Tracy. "You can do as you choose with your money, but this colored boy is as respectable and well behaved as you are — and you have no right to speak about him in that way. Some of you were ragged and dirty and hungry, and you hadn't anyone to care for you when you came here."

Mick looked ashamed but stubborn. One tall boy, recently a "tough" and proud of it, gave a penny. Other boys followed suit. The six cents were soon made out. "Ye'll have bad luck," some of the boys warned Mick as they went in to bed. "Ye will because ye didn't give nothin' to Jimmy's lodgin'."

In their narrow bunks, the waifs went on talking. One who hadn't given was asked, "Didn't y' ever hear the Golden Rule?" "No." "Well it's in the Bible. 'Do unto others as you would have others do unto you.' What do you think of that?"

The sermonized youth considered a moment. "S'pose you're short and couldn't?"

The number of poor who were short and couldn't was unusually large, both inside and outside the recently established Newsboys' Home, although work had been fairly steady in the last year or two. More than 20,000 paupers — men, women, and children — were living in cellars in Manhattan alone, according to the police. Many of them existed in three-tiered underground apartments, others in the boarding and lodging cellars. First-class guests in these lodging cellars paid even less than the newsboys in their loft: thirty-seven and a half cents a week. They received straw to throw on the floor as a mattress and cover. Second-class guests paid eighteen and three-quarters cents a week for the privilege of sleeping on the bare floor. Third-class tenants paid nine cents a week in a kind of gamble. If a place on the floor remained vacant, they could squeeze into it after the first- and second-class guests had settled down.

The only furniture in the cellars was generally a long table and one or two benches. Once a day, food was served from the table — whatever food the beggar women in the employ of the proprietor had been able to cadge from generous housewives and storekeepers and from refuse heaps. First-class guests took their choice from the indiscriminate pile. After they had finished, the second class ate, and the remnants, if there were any, went to the nine-cent-a-weekers.

Even during the good times of 1853, the cellars had been crowded, but as 1854 drew toward its close, they overflowed. Jobs vanished as fast as the steam from the locomotives that had recently carried so many hundreds of thousands of poor men toward the West in search of gold or land or justice. An amalgam of the latter two motives sent, among other hundreds, three typical farmer brothers from Ohio to Kansas in October of this year. Owen, Frederick, and Salmon Brown went west to grow grain and to choke slavery. John Brown, their father, joined them soon after, and on May 24, 1855, at Ossawatomie, these men struck their first physical blow against slavery.

Abolition and antiabolition news had come to fill the papers more and more in recent years, but in New York the sudden business slump temporarily pushed the slavery question into second place. Newspapers noticed the drastic economic change at once. When the *Times* sketched the story of little Jimmy on October 19, 1854, the paper also wailed,

> The first step on the wharves and the first walk through one of the riverstreets, show the same sad unnatural sights, which haunt one in London and Glasgow alleys. The worn, thin face of the Irish laborer hunting for work; the tawdry and bold women clustered upon house steps; the ragged and shoeless girls, picking a living from heaps of refuse, or begging at the doors of rich warehouses; the motley tattered boys creeping and prowling, and idling about the docks; the foreigner, poor and vagrant at home, yet poorer and more desperate here. The same story written about everywhere on their brutal faces; — of inequality, want, ignorance — all begetting thriftlessness and vile habits.

Throughout the previous four years, wages of some skilled workers (in the building trades, for example) had gone up. But real wages decreased for workers in other trades: shoemakers, clothing workers, printers, cabinetmakers, hatters, iron workers, and handloom weavers. At the same time, profits increased.

All of this cumulative poverty, rubbing frayed elbows with accumulating wealth, naturally had its reflection in politics. A movement for civic reform struggled in opposition to a Tammany that had grown a little richer, a little more corrupt than ever. Tammany men, still called Loco Focos, responded to the pressure for reform in a mild and oblique way. They divided into "Hardshell" and "Softshell," two nearly identical cliques that differed mainly in the Softshells' alliance with the progressive capitalist forces antagonistic to the extension of slavery.

As industry — and poverty — increased, unions grew vigorously. They led 400 strikes in 1853 and 1854, and they gave weight to some incipient reform movements. Boastful of their enmity to the "money power" and swearing allegiance to American-born workers, a new party, the Know-Nothings, swaggered onto the scene. These secretive chauvinists revived the traditions of the Native American Party, rooted as they were in similar conditions twenty years before.

Outside New York the Know-Nothing movement was strong, but the Softshell "reform" party, headed by wealthy Fernando Wood, easily won against it in the city. Wood, who had prospered from his saloon during the depression of 1837, had his own ideas of reform, and he had the full support of the Liquor Dealers Protective Association. He was a powerful man physically, and he dressed in style, with modish lapelled vest, high collar, very broad bow tie, and tall plug hat. He was congenial, but was generally known as "The Fox." One acquaintance called him "the handsomest man I ever saw and the most corrupt man that ever sat in the Mayor's chair." As if trying to prove it, Wood boasted of his machine before the election, "The people will elect me Mayor even though I should commit a murder in my family."

A real, but small, reform group, the Practical Democrats, urged many radical changes in city and national affairs, reviving the revolutionary phrases and fervor of their progenitors, the Loco Foco Party of the 1830s. Ira B. Davis, a leader of this faction, denounced monopoly as roundly as had Alexander

Ming nearly twenty years before. By some miracle Davis had resisted much of the corrosive influence of tempting and possible wealth that had worn away the spirit of revolt in some of the early radicals. Alexander Ming, Jr., for instance, whose father, with Skidmore, led the most uncompromising faction of the Working Men's Party in 1829, and who himself led unemployed demonstrations called by the Loco Focos in 1837, was now a well-to-do and conservative man, possibly even a corrupt one. The day after Wood's election, Ming, who by this time bore the title "Colonel," burst into print with resolutions and great rejoicing. Duly grateful, Wood nominated Ming to be "First Clerk" of the city.

However steadfast Ira B. Davis was to the radical traditions of early America, he was not too radical for the lower middle class. His "practical" democracy combined the agrarianism (the free land movement) fostered by George Henry Evans with the utopian socialism advocated by Charles Fourier. Agrarian thinking was no outworn dogma in the 1850s. The land of half a continent, void of people of European origin, fired the acquisitive imagination of many a white-skinned person for two more generations. Fourier's socialism, however, had been tried and found wanting. Thousands of Americans, seeking an uncontentious mode of escape from their economic limitations, had joined "communist" communities, called phalanxes, built on blueprints drawn from the writings of Fourier and his disciple Albert Brisbane. This phase of the poor man's long search for security was over by 1854; its last remnants went up in smoke that year with the flames that consumed the $12,000 grist mill of the North American Phalanx.

As the economic crisis developed in 1854, many native-born workers resurrected the doctrine formerly held by many members of the Working Men's Party of 1829 and the Loco Foco Party of 1837: The state should be responsible for its unemployed. In addition, the great number of English-born workers remembered the public works that had been wrung from the British government in 1846 as well as the mass methods of Chartism, the first great British proletarian movement. The eastern cities of the United States, New York in particular, were home to still other men who had seen masses of poor people in motion. Many hundreds of Frenchmen, who in 1848 had revolted against the tyranny of the "bourgeois king," Louis Philippe, eked out an exile existence. Germans, too, had fled their country when their struggle for democracy failed in 1848. The *New York Tribune*, wishing to appeal to the sudden influx of Germans, signed on a new correspondent, Karl Marx, to review German and west European affairs. While Marx was learning enough English to fulfill his assignment, his friend Friedrich Engels wrote dispatches for him.

One German exile, quiet, tenacious Joseph Weydemeyer, had been attempting to introduce Marxian socialism to American workers. In April 1853, he established in New York City a workingmen's alliance. Then, together with Sam Briggs, an English agitator in Washington, D.C., he set out to radicalize the rapidly growing labor movement. In 1854, however, the unions fell victim to economic depression. They had no treasuries, and when dues stopped because of unemployment, the unions stopped too.

Signs of the depression had already appeared in 1853, when prosperity had led to overexpansion in production of many commodities. The expansion was encouraged by an industrial exposition in the sprawling Crystal Palace at Forty-second Street and Fifth Avenue. "A Yankee manufacturer passes rapidly through the machinery room," noted Horace Greeley, "until his eye rests on a novel combination for weaving certain fabrics, when, after watching it intently for a few minutes, he claps his hands and exclaims . . . That will pay my expenses for the trip!" Many entrepreneurs made the trip. Their ambitions rose as swiftly and as high as the elevator at the Crystal Palace lifted passengers. (It was the first passenger elevator any of them had ever seen, and it hoisted people quickly up an amazing seven stories.)

Speculation had followed the discovery of gold in California. Banks, paper money, credits, land grabs, railroads — all sprang up along the trail toward gold and were far greater in extent than the immediate or future need demanded. This precarious business structure might have maintained its equilibrium longer than it did if two destabilizing events had not occurred at the same time. The first was an enormous fraud. The president of the New Haven railroad forged $2 million worth of stock in his own company. Second, the Crimean War interrupted the constant transfusion of European capital into American economic ventures.

Moreover, gold was being demanded abroad in payment for the excess of American imports over American exports. The consequent export of bullion reduced the already slight gold backing for the paper money flooding the country. The sudden and simultaneous withdrawal of capital and confidence closed down banks, factories, and railroads. Once again, enormous numbers of workmen walked the streets.

By December 1853, no newspaper in New York could ignore either the "revulsion," as the business collapse was called, or its consequences. One comment was typical:

> People are brushing up and patching up old clothes that were intended for the ragman, so that if the poor tailors have been compelled to throw by the needle it has only been to increase the labors of the thrifty housewife. . . . The streets are thronged by able-bodied mechanics and laborers seeking work in vain. . . . North of the Mason Dixon line we shall come off better than we can now anticipate, if before the expiration of the winter there are less than five hundred thousand working people, including their families, deprived of their employment, and their means of subsistence.

The editors, who reflected the worldview of employers, began looking for the hidden benefits of hard times. "They will prove a blessing if they lead the young to abandon their drinking and smoking and treating, and 'going on a bust,'" said the *Times*. "You can have no idea, if unaccustomed to self-denial, how easily it can be done. . . . The stomach is a most accommodating organ."

A little later, signs of popular disbelief in the contractibility of the digestive tract made the *Times* apprehensive. "Hungry people are by no means the best political economists," it argued and, on December 12, offered an example of what it considered acceptable political theory: "We do not believe the City Government should, even if they could, do anything. . . . It corrupts a people even in starvation, to be fed by a Government." And later, "We have great faith in the whole-hearted liberality of our rich men."

The Association for Improving the Condition of the Poor (AICP) shared this faith and put its full corps of "visitors" in the field to do their double duty of providing charity and spiritual uplift. The well-oiled machine, however, did not run smoothly. Shaggy, pouch-eyed Robert M. Hartley, the pious general director of the organization, was distressed. Fresh from a summer vacation in Europe where he had seen quiet, refined charity offices, he worried over the hectic aspects of his own. The whole trouble, he decided on reflection, lay in the local ward relief committees, which had no connection with the AICP but pestered it no end for funds and services. These ward committees sprang up as they had in 1837. Simple human neighborliness created some of them. Politicians, merchants, and the unemployed themselves created others. All of them made it their business to solicit funds, seek out needy cases, and either provide for them or refer them to the AICP.

The sometimes obstreperous committees were in close touch with the unemployed and made an enormous difference in the living standards of the poor. But Mr. Hartley condemned both them and the labor movement that had originally urged their formation. He insisted, "In no other community have mechanics and laborers had less reason to complain of the rich, than in this city."

Hartley was convinced that private charity was equal to any emergency. Nevertheless, he accepted for his organization $10,000 voted for it by the Common Council out of public funds. The donation, made December 20, was a direct result of the council's fear that the workingmen would begin to use mass tactics. A meeting of the unemployed had been announced for the following day, December 21, and City Hall hastened to inspire hope in private charity rather than accept responsibility for municipal relief. Paradoxically, the ward committees, which had been backed in some cases by the very politicians who wanted to avoid direct city relief, caused an immediate strain to be put on the $10,000.

When the unemployed meeting began, a thousand laborers and mechanics in blue overalls, low-crowned hats, and short jackets clustered around City Hall steps, where, for lack of a platform, the speakers stood. Since the purpose of the meeting was to suggest a plan for relief, a committee to draft resolutions was appointed and left to perform their duty. In their absence, well-known figures in the labor world spoke. A Mr. Wallford, president of the Plasterers Association, whose full name the *Times* did not bother to report, acted as spokesman for Agrarianism, one of the great social movements of the time. He urged that the unemployed be given free land in the West, and warned his audience not to have faith in the Common Council. Their only hope, he contended, was in councils of workingmen, which would remove competition and increase production.

Vociferous approval of his remarks came from an important-looking medical gentleman who waggled his very long beard and stole the crowd, although he spoke from its fringe and not from the steps. "There is nothing dishonourable in begging," the doctor roared. "We must canvass the city and provide for the poor." This doctrine, that the poor should provide for themselves by organized begging, actually prevailed at the meeting, although the original call for the gathering was "to petition the Common Council to commence the construction of the new City Hall and other public work, immediately, in order to give employment to those who are now idle." The idle lacked faith in politicians and in their own power to make politicians provide relief. So they ignored the fact that $10,000 had just been elicited by mere announcement that demands would be made for relief, and they were led instead into turning to private charity.

The meeting adjourned until the following Tuesday, but the next afternoon, Friday, December 22, another thousand people gathered in City Hall Park, exhibiting "many indications of the prevalent distress," according to the *Times*.

"This state cannot continue much longer," those at the meeting agreed, "before there will be a general outbreak, and the scenes of 1837 be re-enacted with double force and loss of property. . . . The question is, are we to have bread? The next question is, how are we to get it?" The meeting then proposed relief offices in every ward and agreed on a campaign to solicit funds and jobs. No one present mentioned the earlier plan to press the city government for relief.

Enthusiasm for self-solicited charity was by no means universal. At noon on Christmas, three days later, an angry, clumsily organized group of 300 men met in the park and complained. The weather was mild, although the ground was wet underfoot, and the speaker, John Paul, easily held the crowds. When he began interlarding resentment with religion, a rich Irish brogue cut across the rapid flow of his American-ese: "Oh, tell us about the price of flour and niver mind yer religion."

> Well [Paul answered], I will tell you what they are doing in the Eleventh Ward. They have organized what they call a Relief Association there, and at the head of it is a master builder, a man who made his money from the labor of the poor; and now in gratitude for what they have done for him, he is willing to treat them to some soup. The prophet of old put meal into his pot, and if you want the soup to be at all tolerable, add a little meal, it will do it good. [The crowd laughed. They had tasted this soup during the last few days.] There are members of the new Common Council who are in the soup movement. . . . These rich men do not live on soup — they have nice roast turkey and cranberry sauce and spring chicken and oyster sauce. . . . But the Lord is in our midst and he will see to it that justice is done his people.

Just then, a sizable military parade swung into the midst of the crowd. Street shows and parades traditionally took place on Christmas. Willy-nilly the unemployed reviewed a crack battalion, the Rynder Grenadiers and their band, which played alternately "Hail Columbia" and "Paddy Will Ye Now" as they strode through the warm mud to Tammany Hall where they were to be guests. A banquet for 400 lay waiting on elegantly appointed tables.

After the military retired, orator Paul continued: "The Creator has given me a desire for those things, and I must gratify that desire. . . ." This was too much for a police officer who had edged through the crowd. He ordered Paul to stop, claiming his remarks might lead to a riot. The crowd buzzed for a moment, then roared for the speaker to go on. But it was no use. The hungry soapboxer and man of God was led away to jail.

A few less forthright speakers tried to hold the crowd's attention, but soon the meeting dwindled away. The unemployed joined other New Yorkers as they lined the curbs of the city watching soldiers strut and mummers pretend an air of well-being.

The mummers got much bigger notices in the press than the meeting of the unemployed, although the *Times* did recognize that a Christmas parade was not enough to take a jobless man's mind off roast turkey. "It is only a crisis; it must be soon over; — do not let it leave you a ruined man where it found you a worthy," the editors advised. "No American working man has ever fairly tried what he can live upon, if driven to a stress. . . . Boggle at nothing which will save a few pennies. Leave off sugar, or potatoes, or even bread, if something nutritious which costs less can be found."

The *Times* then aimed both barrels at "False Friends of the Poor." Referring to the recent meetings of the jobless, it said, "The speakers were without exception, *political* mechanics, — men whose principal trade has been political agitation, and who are far more anxious to secure offices for themselves than to benefit their class for whom they came to speak. . . . We see no occasion whatever for mass meetings in the Park, or elsewhere to devise means for the Poor."

The unemployed did see occasion. Next day, Tuesday, December 26, the meeting the *Times* had hoped to discourage took place. A committee of workingmen appointed on the previous Friday had been active, and upon adoption of its report the Mechanics' and Workingmen's Aid Association emerged. The program proposed by the committee included only the most modest demands. A determined air of geniality at all costs stood in place of any show of partisanship for the unemployed. In-

stead of asking for more city appropriations, the association
urged only private contributions to augment the city's $10,000
gift to the AICP.

One old man at the meeting took mild exception to this
policy. On calling for payment by the city of half the rent of the
unemployed, he got roundly applauded. He did not mind city
aid, but private charity was odious: "For six months in 1817, I
lived on a pound of bread a day. I begged from nobody." His rent
proposal disappeared almost as soon as he offered it, buried
under the oratory of Isaac Relyea, who talked himself into the
presidency of the organization. Relyea opposed public works as
a means of relief on the grounds that they led to graft. Private
charity was his solution.

Relyea's ideas, and the ideas of the mute and hesitant mass
for whom he wanted to be spokesman, took form in part from
the textbooks and religious tracts of the times — the inescap-
able folklore propaganda of the 1850s. Workers who had
learned to read, and who had helped their children puzzle out
their first lessons, were defying social values that had been
educated into them when they demanded relief from society.
"The Poor Old Man," an exercise in the most popular of all texts,
McGuffey's Eclectic First Reader, was typical. A picture at the
head of the story showed a very bent and ragged old man in
too-short trousers and too-long coat. He leaned on a stick and
tipped his hat to two little children on the other side of a
waist-high board fence. The dialogue ran:

Jane, there is a poor old man at the door.
He asks for some-thing to eat.
We will give him some bread and cheese.
He is cold. Will you give him some clothes too?
I will give him a suit of old clothes, which will be new to him.
Poor man! I wish he had a warm house to live in, and kind
    friends to live with him; then he would not have to beg
    from door to door.
We should be kind to the poor. We may be as poor as this old
    man, and need as much as he.
Shall I give him some cents to buy a pair of shoes?
No; you may give him a pair of shoes.

It is hard for the poor to have to beg from house to house.
Poor boys and girls some-times have to sleep out of doors all
    night.
When it snows, they are ver-y cold, and when it rains, they get
    quite wet.
Who is it that gives us food to eat, and clothes to make us
    warm?
It is God, my child; he makes the sun to shine, and sends the
    rain up-on the earth, that we may have food.
God makes the wool grow up-on the lit-tle lambs, that we may
    have clothes to keep us warm.

McGuffey's Second Reader continued this kind of indoctrination in a lesson entitled, "The Good Boy Whose Parents Are
Poor," which included this: "It is God who makes some poor and
others rich. . . . The rich have many troubles which we know
nothing of, and . . . the poor if they are but good, may be very
happy." (The notion that God would provide silenced many. But
as the depression dragged on, the empty pantry came to argue
with McGuffey on more equal terms.)

The mechanics' meetings continued. Reporting them, the
Herald said, "Many of the worst red republicans of Paris —
fellows who would burn, rob, and murder — are hiding their
faces in this city; nor are these wanting a still more detestable
class of incendiaries, in the shape of English Socialists and
German Communists. There are grounds for believing that the
fellows are at the bottom of some of the movements of the
workingmen; and that if trouble were to ensue, they would try
hard to make opportunities for plunder." (The acumen of the
Herald can be judged by an editorial in the adjoining column,
which rejoiced that the abolition movement "had greatly declined and its entire dissolution will transpire at a period not far
distant.")

Another new organization of the unemployed, the Associated Workingmen, offered a more militant program than the
Mechanics' and Workingmen's Aid Association and grew to a
much greater size and influence. Inner as well as outer enemies, however, opposed its forthrightness. A struggle for su-

premacy in the organization soon began. One faction wanted relief in a hurry and did not bother with involved ideas about reforming all of society first. The other faction favored land reform and a housing project, and their greater political skill prevailed. The defeated faction resigned, marched out of the meeting in a huff, and shut off all the gaslights into the bargain. But the lights soon burned again and the meeting proceeded with plans for a delegation to the Common Council.

On January 5, this delegation met with a special committee appointed by the council. They did not seek charity, the delegation said; they wanted jobs. But insistence from only one part of a split organization was not persuasive enough. The matter died without reaching the council itself.

To confuse and divide the unemployed still further, an organization called the Sons of the Republic began at this time to raise private charity funds for the native-born and no others. The long, 100-percent-American arm of the new Know-Nothing Party seemed to be guiding this effort.

Although joblessness was driving some people to consider group action, centrifugal forces were also at work sending the inexperienced unemployed into ever smaller groups rivaling each other, even sending many individuals into isolated obscurity — and destruction. One of the latter was a shy, immigrant bookbinder, John Murphy. He died by his own hand in a situation about which Horace Greeley's *Tribune* reported floridly and pointedly:

> The old year was running out its last sands; the matrons were preparing their sumptuous and elegant tables . . . the viol had uttered its initial squeak premonitory of the ball wherewith the gay and reckless were eager to "dance the Old Year out and the New Year in," when a wail of woe issued from a poor tenement where upon a wretched pallet . . . lay the body of a man . . . John Murphy, born an Englishman, bred a bookbinder, who brought hither his wife and children last August, expecting to support them by diligent labor in his calling. So he did after the best fashion he could, until the 1st of November, when the increasing severity of the pressure

compelled his employers to discharge him. . . . So John Murphy went home to his poor family, and tried, from day to day, from place to place, to find work elsewhere — anywhere — but in vain.

Leaving her pride and her protesting husband at home, Mrs. Murphy finally on the last afternoon of the old year went to the home of one of the Committee for the Relief of the Poor of the Seventh Ward. He was not in.

"She returned to her home," reads the *Times*'s version of the story, "where she heard a noise in the bed room, and inquiring of her children where their father was, they said he was lying down in the bed room. She went to go in and . . . discovered him on his knees, with his hands together as if praying, and his throat cut in a horrible manner. He could just manage to speak . . . 'Oh Sarah! Oh Sarah!'. . . . The youngest child was starving upon the bed, having had nothing to eat for two days. During the inquest upon the father, the mother received news of the child's death."

A week later (January 8), American workingmen and a group of German unemployed met together "forsaking all their old party prejudices . . . to unite and combine their forces for the attainment of a common object, namely, the deliverance of land, labor, and the currency from the grasp of the monopolist and speculator." To achieve this end they proposed a nation-wide association of workingmen.

One German at the gathering said: "In our country we have fought for liberty. . . . If you don't know your rights yet, hunger will teach them to you. You don't get bread nor wood and there is plenty of them. At our Revolution in June [1848] we obtained three months credit, and when we had no bread, we soon obtained it, because we were 200,000 strong. Let us therefore remember that union is strength."

Another German spoke: "It is said that the stomach does not ask if its food is paid for, but I shall not drink the soup given by the rich as if it were given to dogs. I repeat it — I want work, not charity!"

German speakers drew huge applause, but American speakers kept control, although they expressed only bland, vague aspirations and even half-apologics for the lethargic city government. A man named Charles Smith mysteriously became a leader of the group and at the same time an apologist for Mayor Wood.

Two days later, Smith assumed control over part of a spontaneous meeting of 2,000, which the *Herald* described as being made up of a "more intelligent class of men than those present on former occasions." Smith urged patience and peace in the midst of banners reading, "We Want Work and Must Have It!"; "Live and Let Live!"; "This is our Last Resource"; and "Hunger is a Sharp Thorn." An ally of Smith's organized a march — away from City Hall. The crowd, however, soon weary of its unimpressive trudging, returned to the seat of government and sent a committee in to see Mayor Wood. The Fox answered their complaints and demands by saying, "The charter of this city does not allow the Mayor or any head of departments to give more than $250 without a contract, and that sum would go but a small way among so many. . . . No doubt something will be devised for the effectual relief of the poor."

When the committee reported this evasion, the crowd grew angry, and frantic speakers could not persuade it to disperse. Mayor Wood's man Smith shouted: "This is poor conduct for starving men. If the City Charter is defective, let us go to Albany and have it mended. . . . Now boys, we have been here long enough — let us go home and have dinner."

"Where are we going to get it?" came from a chorus of voices. A worried Smith pleaded once more for law observance, but a rough-looking fellow interrupted, "We'll have to break into the stores for food. We won't starve!" A thousand throats cheered. Flour stores might have been looted again as in 1837 had not Smith's oratory finally swayed the crowd. The men went home, many to no supper.

Some response, some concession to the persistent thousands outside City Hall was imperative, and the mayor let it be known that he was pushing a plan to give work on a new reservoir on the site of the projected Central Park. As usual, something checked him, this time the Croton Aqueduct Board, who decided his plan was impossible for legal and practical reasons.

At this point the *Times* very unwillingly reversed its policy. Instead of continuing to call for private charity, it came out on January 12 urging public works immediately. The change apparently was influenced by a veteran's petition and a memorial by the Associated Workingmen. At a January 8 convention in Washington of the veterans of the War of 1812, nearly 2,000 had petitioned Congress for relief. The Associated Workingmen, less formless, and for that reason more formidable than some of the spontaneous gatherings, was a united movement of Germans, French, and Americans led by Ira B. Davis. The group, as in its early meetings, continued to seek free land and unemployment relief. Referring to the "precursors of a hurricane of death over this city," the association hinted that it could not be responsible for acts of the unemployed if their pleas for aid were not granted. Their memorial to the Common Council stated:

1. That there are now in this city 60,000 able bodied men out of employment.
2. That 50,000 women, accustomed to earn their own livelihood, and in many instances to support families by their unaided efforts, are out of employment.
3. That 10,000 children, accustomed to earn their own livelihood, and in many cases to aid materially, if not altogether support dependent relatives, are out of employment.
4. That 75,000 persons are now chiefly, if not altogether dependent upon the 120,000 unemployed . . . thus forming an aggregate of the 195,000 members of our common humanity, all of whom are thus for the most part deprived of their daily bread.
5. That these 195,000 persons have now, in the purchase of food chiefly if not entirely, at a ruinous sacrifice, disposed of what available means they had accumulated in more prosperous times, and we regret to say that the savings

bank robbers have not passed by the "poor man's lamb."

6. That to supply the 195,000 persons with essential food, at the present prices, at least ten cents per day to each individual is required: The aggregate of this is $19,500 per day, or $136,000 per week.

7. That the public duty and private benevolence have, up to this time, been totally inadequate to supply the vital wants of the suffering working classes of this city, and now deep murmurings are heard all around the cheerless hearthstones of proud, stern-hearted men, who would prefer death to the crouching supplications of repulsed beggary.

This memorial provoked not only concessions from the *Times* but also rebuttals from a rival paper. "The whole action of the unemployed workmen is based on the grand fallacy that it is the business of the state to care for them, to give them work when they want it, and generally to relieve them of the responsibility of looking after themselves," said the *Herald*.

The *Times* paradoxically covered its retreat to advocacy of public works thus: "For our part, we sometimes think it is better for an able bodied man to run close risk of starvation than to be fed on public alms." Robert Hartley of the AICP, in a report made about this time on the "Rights of Labor," indicated by alien-baiting what he thought of government aid: "The doctrine so pertinaciously urged, that a man has a right to work and wages from the government . . . whether his services are needed or not . . . is urged mainly by our foreign born citizens."

Unimpressed, the Associated Workingmen kept up their clamor for public aid instead of private charity. On January 15 they managed to bring together most of the tag-ends of unemployed organizations into a meeting of 5,000 — the largest yet held — where Ira B. Davis voiced the changing temper of the unemployed: "We know our distress is too deeply seated to be healed by any temporary charity that may be extended."

The program of this united movement was simpler and clearer than anything so far: charter revision under authority of the state legislature, stoppage of evictions and indemnification of landlords for losses incurred by nonpayment of rent distribution of free public lands, and memorialization of Congress by the city authorities for a homestead bill.

The Common Council was in session during the meeting and watched the crowd surge away under a dull sky, smoke-laden even though the fires in most of the factory furnaces had died. The men walked together up Broadway, past the straggling handful of their fellows who had got jobs as sandwich men and were sharing with lampposts the burden of propping up the city's advertisements. Eighty marshals led the column along Broadway, disorganizing the helter-skelter flow of carts and carriages and buses, then west to Fifth Avenue, where the march ended under the eyes of the well-to-do — the "codfish aristocracy," many called them, with unmistakable allusion to odor. Here lived many of the bankers who thought relief was demoralizing to the unemployed but who recently in one day had paid out $4 million in hard cash in order to save railroad properties.

Within a few days another large gathering of unemployed filled the park, and Charles Smith bustled around. This time he was challenged, according to the *Times:*

> Some individual that looked like a man that thought more of his dinner than poverty, hinted that Mr. Smith was lazy and liked better to talk than to work. Mr. Smith replied indignantly. The sleek individual refused to retract, and offered to put the orator to work instantly at the rate of $1 per day. His employer took him to the ruins of the New City Hall [the present City Hall; it had been slightly damaged by fire — F.F.] and desired him to remove thence a pile of old brick and lay them up neatly and expeditiously in another place. Mr. Smith took off his cloak (he wears a cloak) and "rolled up his sleeves," and . . . worked hard and well for about an hour and a half when his employer expressed himself satisfied and rewarded his employee with the sum of fifty cents. Mr. Smith gained the day . . . and soon after he delivered another speech.

The next day twenty men were put to work cleaning up the debris around City Hall. The mayor explained that more could not be done because of the limitation in the charter.

The weather suddenly changed to bitter cold on Friday, January 19. The cold, together with rumors of impending military discipline for the unemployed, kept the park free of meetings. Moreover, 8,000, many of whom had customarily met, had found their way into shelters under the control of the governors of the Almshouse.

Other thousands were still neglected, and persistent newspaper stories countered every move to organize them. "It has an Alien Look!" ran the head over an editorial in the *Times*, which made red-scare allusions to "revolutionary flags of 'we want bread and *will* have it,' " and to "Demagogues of very small calibre . . . [who] harangue and resolve in the Park for the amusement of the miscellaneous crowd of alien chartists, communists, and agrarians. . . . One of the speakers on Monday demanded *in German* immediate employment."

The notion of adequate relief from private charity was not allowed to collapse undefended before the onslaught of radical ideas. P. T. Barnum, with suitable publicity, gave a full day's receipts from his American Museum to the AICP. Private relief for "females out of employment" was organized. Funds for the "Home of Protection and Instruction for the Benefit of Female Servants" were actively solicited until an awkward scandal crippled that venture. Earnest notices of benefits for the poor began to appear in newspapers. "The Fourth Annual Meeting of the Minerva Mutual Improvement Society will be held this evening," ran one item. "The proceeds are to be given to the poor of the city." The American Widows Relief Association sprang up, aiding carefully selected cases. Society women arranged a calico ball for the poor. Old dresses and calico frocks took the place of finery on the occasion. After the party, the costumes were given to the poor. "There were about 400 persons present," said the *Tribune*, "from the fashionable circles of society in the City. . . . The dresses of the ladies were only remarkable for their plainness and neatness, while jewelry was almost entirely discarded. . . . As these dresses are to be distributed to the poor . . . we may hope that their future wearers will endeavor to preserve not only the neatness of their attire, but a comeliness of person and manner corresponding therewith."

At the same time, *Graham's Magazine* noted:

> Dress is this season most costly, perhaps never was more so,
> for, in addition to the richness of the material employed, the
> quantity and expense of the trimmings, without which a dress
> cannot now be made, render winter prospects very appalling
> for the papa's and husband's purses. To ordinary silk dresses
> — those destined for the house — flounces are indispensable.
> Some have as many as eighteen, so small they look like frills.
> Each of these is edged with a narrow worsted lace. The color
> of the silk . . . is *poussière de Sebastopol.*

Emphasis on gaiety tended to replace serious consideration
of unemployment in the papers. "Broadway was in a din yesterday," began one notice on January 26, when an unemployed
meeting had to be called off because of the cold. "The sleighing,
good for the City, was taken advantage of. All sorts and conditions of sleighs, and manner of horse-flesh, were in active
commotion. The fancy pung and the gigantic omnibus on run-
ners ran along together, their occupants vociferating, and the
street lads pelting them all. . . . Whole regiments of men and
boys and even women shovelled tons of snow. The charges they
made were not in all cases so modest as starving people would
generally be supposed to have asked."

While some unemployed suddenly got temporary work
shovelling snow, most got no work at all. Robert Hartley reported to the AICP that the number of persons aided in January
was 49,986 — three times as many as had been aided the
preceding January. Hartley filled in details: "Even the office of
the board, where relief is never given, was crowded by clamor-
ous beggars who had been sent there by the Ward Committees.
. . . The city was overrun by unmanageable crowds of men,
women, and children, not only clamoring for aid and seemingly
in great wretchedness, but who often manifested much asperity
and bitterness if they did not get all they asked."

Twelve of the twenty-two wards had relief committees, and
a glance at Hartley's own figures gives a key to the source of his
irritation. In the ten wards that had no committees, the average
increase in the AICP case load this winter over the preceding

was 225 percent. The average increase in expenditure was the same. (Funds paid for Indian meal, hominy, beans, peas, salt pork, and dried fish.) In the twelve wards that did have committees to help the unemployed get relief, the average increase in the case load was 337 percent and in expenditure was 674 percent. In these wards, the unemployed were likely to get a little bread, tea, sugar, and fresh meat now and then, in addition to the foods mentioned above. The AICP outlay, of course, did not constitute the sum total of relief. The ward committees aided many not reached by the AICP, and individual donors supported soup lines.

The origins of the relief committees were as various, and often as venal, as the socioeconomic pattern of which they were a small but characteristic part. For instance, William Bloodgood, who as a magistrate in 1838 had shared some of his graft with the unemployed, was now chairman of the relief committee in the Fourteenth Ward. In the Seventeenth, butchers organized the relief setup. At first they donated the beef for soup, but as soon as a dependable soup-line demand had been created, they sold it. Of the charity fare in this ward, the *Herald* said, on Christmas, "It is unnecessary that it should be so good for the purpose to which it is put."

In February, kitchen doors were still besieged from morning to night by men, women, and children seeking handouts. Lest these demands become too importunate or too highly organized, a new campaign was started. "The winter is almost over," said the *Times* on February 4. A few days later, however, the same paper had to report that "bitter pinching cold congealed the breath upon neck comforters, so that they became as solid as cakes of ice." To make matters worse, an influenza epidemic raged through the city, and another huge snow fell. Hundreds, however, were neither ill nor penniless. They rejoiced, drank more than enough of warming liquor, and sleighed wildly up and down Broadway tooting fish horns. Prostitutes, seeing a chance to combine an outing with business, hired six-in-hand sleighs and drove ostentatiously about. Many a girl who was recently a seamstress or maid or factory hand was now riding in one of these sleighs. Dr. William W. Sanger, in his *History of*

Prostitution, written two years later, noted that the number of young girls who turned to that calling increased during the hard times, even though money was harder to come by. Over 4,000 prostitutes existed, after their fashion, in New York in 1855, and venereal disease in the city increased rapidly during the next two years.

With the snow deep enough for sleighing, many African-Americans wrapped themselves up in whatever warm things they could find and went out to serenade whoever looked rich enough or drunk enough to toss them a few pennies.

During 1854–1855, while some who may have been former slaves resorted to such measures to stay alive, agitation steadily increased in the North against slavery in the South. More and more newspaper space was given to the abolition movement. To some it seemed clear how slaves could be freed, but how could people be freed from bread lines?

As the Civil War approached, the energies of many liberal reformers and radical agitators turned to the slavery question. Both groups eventually got what they wanted: the Emancipation Proclamation in 1863, and the Homestead Bill which became law in 1862. In the same period, another group of agitators opposed the further influx of foreign labor, and the national government stepped in, early in 1855, to prevent immigration of convicts and paupers — that is, the unemployed from abroad. Meanwhile, the resident unemployed did not get relief.

The drive of the unemployed to become owners of land was a drive to become capitalists. The Homestead Bill tended to weaken the power of the land monopolists but it also, paradoxically, turned both the unemployed and the labor movements to daydreams of confronting capitalists not as worker-antagonists, but as owner-antagonists. Here was a plausible avenue of escape, less troublesome than the alternative of struggle to make society shoulder responsibility for those deprived of work through no fault of their own.

Restricted immigration became a fetish with a large part of the working class during this depression. The latest arrivals from abroad were regarded as scabs, underbidders in the labor market, a threatening increment to the reservoirs of the job-hungry — hence, enemies. Seeing no further than this, much of the labor movement opposed, and opposed effectively, the immediate continuance of large immigration. At the same time, employers called for protection, not from foreign workers but from foreign goods.

Throughout the depression a small but by no means negligible section of workers persisted in emphasizing the need for public relief and public works. They suggested municipal shoe factories, housing projects, the creation of Central Park, and an entirely new City Hall. In answer, they received mainly private charity, albeit much increased.

The unemployed movement had been hampered by the conflicting social philosophies that had appeared within its leadership. The group efforts of the unemployed never grew much larger than some other contemporary mass phenomena. For example, at the outset of the depression, as many as 4,000 people traveled to Grass Valley outside New York City to see a prize fight. An underworld gang leader, Bill Poole, was shot and killed by a rival in a saloon brawl, and his funeral drew 5,000 mourners. Ornate humbuggery also had its charms. During the time of greatest suffering, spiritualists drew crowds nearly as large as did the unemployed leaders.

In spite of such distractions and the hesitation of leaders, the basic tendency and impulse of the unemployed had its specific effect on relief. The benefits of the ward committee system, disorganized and inadequate though it was, were felt throughout the winter of 1855–1856. Workers continued to insist bluntly, stubbornly, on the importance of food and shelter — of tangible things. Against this tendency, employers and the press, such as the *Times* and the *Herald,* posed the values of self-denial and patience — intangible spiritual qualities.

Bridging these two groups of opposed attitudes and actions were a few members of one group or the other. Horace Greeley was one who admitted to being uncertain of his road. On the one hand he joined the rich in making mildly helpful suggestions for household economies. On the other he differed with them sharply in the matter of mass pressure. Of the unemployed meetings, which all the other editors attacked, Horace Greeley said, "The workmen showed the spirit of independence which underlies freedom and the conquest of man over difficulties."

This spirit of independence, this rudimentary consciousness of class, was kept alive in spite of the shortcomings of the unemployed in seeking what they most desired, security and equality. However much they flirted with problems other than unemployment, some of their leaders still kept up their quest for unity.

At a dinner on February 24 commemorating the anniversary of the French Revolution of 1848, leaders of various workingmen's organizations made resounding speeches against tyranny. All of them, however, saw tyranny only in a muffled press, in a prison, or in a workshop; the tyranny of the soup line was never mentioned, even by Ira Davis, who spoke on behalf of the Practical Democrats. After several months of organizing the unemployed he might have been expected to call their plight to mind. But no. Vague politics and vaguer aspirations were on the bill of fare for this banquet.

Someone from nearly every group spoke — except from the *Arbeiter Bund,* whose leader was Joseph Weydemeyer, a friend of Karl Marx. This German exile was always deliberate and slow to speak or act. But perhaps just now his silence hid a mingling of practical hope and hardheaded skepticism at the words of the leader of the Free Democrats, William J. Rose, who declared to the cheers of the earnest gathering: "In the last 12 months the revolution has made 1,200 years of progress. The revolution has begun in America."

Very soon, not even Rose was talking about nascent revolution. A kind of prosperity that might grow and last a long time returned in 1856, and with it came increased employment, including a job for 16-year-old John D. Rockefeller, who had been unable to find work for many weeks in 1855.

6

Panic-Stricken
(1857)

It is not pleasant to grope among the muck and the slime. Cover it up! Do you say that pestilence will arise? Never mind — cover it up — never look "down below."

> — Walt Whitman
> *The Brooklyn Times*, July 12, 1858

I, John Brown, am now quite certain that the crimes of this guilty land will never be purged away but with blood.

> — John Brown
> last statement, December 2, 1859

We will now discuss in a little more detail the struggle for existence.

> — Charles Darwin
> *The Origin of Species*, 1859

"This time the crash will beat anything known before," said Friedrich Engels, forecasting the end of the boom of 1856 in a letter to Karl Marx on April 14 of that year. Replying a few days later, the exiled economist agreed with his collaborator. "The thing is on a European scale," Marx said.

Within eighteen months both Europe and the United States were involved in the first great worldwide depression. A contemporary jingle described events this way:

> Monday, I started my bank operations;
> Tuesday, owned millions by all calculations;
> Wednesday, my Fifth Avenue Palace began;

Thursday, I drove out a spanking bay span;
Friday, I gave a magnificent ball;
And Saturday, smashed with just nothing at all.

A hectic boom had followed the depression of 1854–1855. In the United States it had consisted of a vast expansion of railroads, new industries, and new cities. But there were soon more transportation and more production than the country could absorb. One writer summed up what was going on: "Premature railroads at the West had fostered premature cities, teeming with premature traffic for a premature population; and while canals and railroads had conspired to reduce the mileage rate of transportation, the dispersion of American farmers over a vastly wider area counterbalanced that advantage."

The disturbances in finance were dramatic, beginning in August 1857 when the Ohio Life Insurance and Trust Company failed and triggered a series of other failures. The resulting confusion was suggested in a contemporary anecdote. In the story, a drunk clung to a lamppost one night in the fall of 1857. When a watchman protested the noise he was making, the drunk replied, "It tain't me that's a making of the noise. They are a breakin' a crushin' and a smashin' of all things to an incredible amount."

"You are as tight as a brick in a new wall," the officer countered.

"It's not me that's tight," the drunk insisted. "Money is tight."

"Then you are drunk."

"The world is drunk," the man replied. "The whole country is a staggerin' round, buttin' their head agin stone walls and a skinnin' of their noses on the curbstone of adversity. Sir, everybody's drunk but me. I'm afflicted. I've got the panic. I've tried to drink it off, but it's no use."

Neither the drunk nor anybody else could drink off, or shake off, or sleep off the panic.

Bread lines had lengthened steadily during the late summer months, and as they grew, the pay envelopes of those still employed began to dwindle. When the labor supply reached flood proportions, a strike wave, previously set in motion by a newly revived labor movement, receded. Soon the new unions, in spite of their militancy, sank out of sight for the most part, and the unemployed formed what labor movement there was.

In the biggest industrial centers, agitation, provoked by unemployment, was first encouraged by German immigrants. Many of them were exiles from the terror following the unsuccessful revolt in their homeland in 1848, and most of them had heard one or another of various radical theories, which held one proposition in common: that the state should serve the needs of the people.

Philadelphia Germans, at a mass meeting in Spring Garden on October 25, decided to boycott all articles of food for which speculators were asking exorbitant prices. The boycotters then established a kind of cooperative for buying food at wholesale rates and selling it at cost to the poor. In addition, they appointed a committee to make plans for the future. Their program as finally formulated called for instant employment of the unemployed by the city, state, or federal government; reduced tariff; sound currency; no small bank bills; and reduced food prices. The proposals, for the most part hermetically sealed in the German language, did not become part of the thinking of the great body of Philadelphia's unemployed.

Meetings were called, however, to back this program, and the Germans played some part in bringing about change by setting in motion the native-born workers, whose social philosophy was less consistent but whose presence in Independence Square bore more weight with the mayor and the two branches of the City Council. Due largely to the mobilization of the unemployed in unaccustomed numbers, the city government finally set up construction projects on culverts and reservoirs, but not before the New York unemployed (unwittingly aided by a provocative press) had put the fear of mobs into the hearts of Philadelphia politicians. Some relief out of public funds likewise was given in Boston and Chicago.

Unemployed gatherings took place in other cities, in Harrisburg and Louisville, for example, and in nearly every case they were first suggested by Germans. And almost always the Germans were isolated as soon as the movement got under way.

Differences between them and the American unemployed developed, particularly on the question of inflation, which the Germans opposed. But on one thing all groups agreed. They wanted work, not charity. Typical of this spirit was a banner carried in a Trenton, New Jersey, parade: "We ask not alms but work, that our wives and children may not starve. Peace and good will is our motto."

In Newark, a call was sent out on Saturday, November 7, for a meeting the following Monday. At 7 A.M. on November 9, a few laborers collected in front of the Market House. Shortly afterward another knot appeared on the opposite side of Broad Street. Then another group collected in the open area under the Liberty Pole, forming altogether an assembly of over 1,000 people. At about 8:00, the unidentified managers of the meeting procured a large dry-goods box for a stage and carried it into the common. The various scattered groups gathered around it. Once begun, this meeting repeated the old refrain, "We do not wish alms, but the opportunity to earn our living by peaceful industry."

Within thirty days after the beginning of the bank crash on August 24, estimates of New York's unemployed wage earners ran as high as 40,000 out of a total population of 700,000. Some of this number had already been unable to find jobs when the first financial flurry in April dramatized the coming of a great depression. "There was a more appalling picture of social wretchedness than was probably ever witnessed this side of the Atlantic," said the Association for Improving the Condition of the Poor. Nevertheless, the association aided only one-fourth of those applying to it for aid — an efficiency record of which its secretary Robert Hartley did some boasting.

Two years before, the association had given aid more fully, but the ward committees, which then served the unemployed by forcing the AICP to increase its outlays, did not reemerge, in part at least because of AICP strategy. In 1857, the association did not set up branch offices in the working-class neighborhoods as it had done in 1854–1855. Many of the unemployed were now forced to go some distance to the central office. In addition, it became more difficult for the unemployed to bring pressure on field representatives of the AICP. New, rigorous tests of need were imposed by trained personnel. In addition, a careful watch was kept, and any sign of the formation of the troublesome ward committees was countered with propaganda showing the competency of the AICP to deal with the situation.

These maneuvers served to cut down expenses and to achieve a veritable miracle of philanthropy. During October, more than 8,000 families received aid from the AICP — a *decrease* of 25 percent in this depression year over the same period in the preceding normal year.

Faced with the AICP's virtual monopoly of private charity — and its resistance to giving real aid, the unemployed quickly turned to demanding employment on public works. The "impulsive local movements" of 1854–1855, as Hartley called the Ward Relief Association, gave way to a citywide movement. This movement, as viewed by some, was even more disturbing than the earlier activities on a ward level. The disturbed ones felt that social responsibility for the unemployed should be avoided at all costs, and it was for this reason that the well-to-do supported private charity. But, like the unemployed in Philadelphia and a dozen other cities, New Yorkers in distress now turned to City Hall.

Officials there were silent at first when they saw banners reading "Political knaves and speculators have robbed us of our bread. They offer us soup. Behold your work! This you have done in the name of God and Liberty. We have borne the stripes of men, we now claim the stars."

The noise made by the unemployed at least called attention to poverty.

> The wheezy sharp-eyed old women who deal in apples and pears are sadly puzzled how to dispose of their stock [observed William Cullen Bryant's Evening Post]. There is a marked falling off in the business of those urchins who insist upon "blacking your boots, sir!" at every corner in the Park and in the vicinity of the downtown hotels. People either black their own boots or leave them to the influence of time

and nature. . . . The Chinamen who peddle cigars by the wayside now have their patience tried more severely than ever. . . . The receipts of the organ grinders have very materially diminished . . . the monkeys perform to much less appreciating spectators.

The unemployed also thrust themselves on the attention of editor Walt Whitman of the *Brooklyn Times.* On October 21, he wrote:

Vainly the Laborer cries out in the market places and at the corners of the streets —

> No parish money or loaf.
> No pauper badges for me,
> A son of the soil, by the right of toil
> Entitled to my fee.
> No alms I ask, give me my task:
> Here are the arms, the leg,
> The strength, the sinews of a man,
> To work and not to beg.

We believe that the estimate of the probable number of unemployed [25,000] who will have to be provided for in some form, by us, is under the mark. But concede that it is greatly exaggerated — was it ever yet known that the treasuries of our public charities were burthened with a surplus or that the means and ministrations of private benevolence were too profuse and assiduous?

The day after Whitman implored his readers to think of "what was to be done," Mayor Fernando Wood offered an answer to him and to the scattered but growing number of demonstrators beneath his office windows. Fernando the Fox, with an eye on the coming local elections, decided to startle the world. On October 22, he read a radical-sounding message that rumor insisted was written by the city clerk, Alexander Ming, who had addressed the poor of New York twenty years before, on the eve of the flour riot. Whether Ming wrote it or not, the prolabor phraseology derived from Loco Foco days.

"In New York," the message ran, "it may be said that those who produce everything, get nothing, and those who produce nothing, get everything. They labor without income while surrounded by thousands living in affluence and splendor and who have income without labor." The mayor proposed that $250,000 be spent at once to create Central Park. Plans to establish the park already existed. Land had been acquired and commissioners had been appointed, but little other action had been taken. "I recommend that the Corporation be authorized to advertise for estimates for furnishing the Corporation with fifty thousand barrels of flour and a corresponding quantity of cornmeal and potatoes . . . these provisions to be disposed of to laborers to be employed upon the public works referred to, in lieu of money."

Uproar followed this proposal. "Such words would excite the harassed unemployed rather than allay their fears and lead to humble forbearance," complained the AICP. Similar objections came from other quarters, but there were some who approved. The net result of the mayor's bombshell was that attention more than ever focused on that ineradicable embarrassment, the unemployed.

Now it was imperative for the least sympathetic papers to recognize the changed contours of the workingmen's world. The press correctly prophesied,

> Many a worthy home this winter will be half-stripped of the cherished things on which the good wife had prided herself. The indication already is that mechanics throng the pawn brokers' offices with their tools. . . . The Newsboys' Lodging House is crowded nightly. Every bed is full, and in many cases *two* boys have been only too glad to sleep spoon fashion in one bed two feet wide. . . . The poorest people are pawning their children's clothes. . . . The penitentiary shows a large increase in the number of convicts sent up for small crimes. . . . The women in prison are uncommonly numerous. Nearly all of them are prostitutes.

The *Times* went so far as to say that some action was called for and, along with others, recommended migration. The AICP actively tried to interest the unemployed in moving to the West.

In the East, money for salt cod was hard to get, but in the West fresh buffalo and venison could be had for the shooting. And in California, in addition to food, there was gold.

A vigorous publicity campaign supporting migration had immediate effect, relying as it did on that folk belief, the American Dream: Every man could be a small independent property owner if he worked hard and obeyed the Ten Commandments. New railroads, the fingers of a profit economy, clawed with increasing certainty at the West — and they beckoned the unemployed. So great indeed was the migration at this time that a despairing Sioux chief addressing President Buchanan said, "If we look to the East, we see the track of the first white man on the grave of the last red man."

Another exodus led eastward. Boatload after boatload of Irish sought repatriation when their means of support in the New World vanished. The population of New York fell many thousands by the first of the year (1858) because of the flushing out of unwanted human beings into the sea on the one hand and into the prairie on the other.

Draining off surplus labor and avoiding government relief might have seemed adequate to the *Times*, but many workingmen thought differently. One sign of this restiveness was the establishment of the Communist Club, a German group under the leadership of an obscure music teacher, F. A. Sorge, who later rose to be secretary of the First International and has come to be called the father of modern socialism in America. Members of the Communist Club aspired, according to their constitution, to "abolish the so-called *bourgeois* property, both inherited and acquired, in order to replace it by a reasonable participation in earthly enjoyment, accessible to all, and satisfying the needs of all."

With one eye on the state election to be held November 2 and the city election December 1 and the other eye on the unemployed, the anti-Wood commissioners for Central Park voted October 30 that they would "sanction the employment of a suitable force for advantageous work whenever the necessary funds are furnished by the city authorities."

German Communists approved of the general features of the mayor's plan for work and of the Park Commission's avowed willingness to provide it. On November 2, more than a thousand German workmen met in Tompkins Square. Led by a drummer and waving a banner reading "*Arbeit!*" ("Work!"), they marched to City Hall, where they presented petitions for work. If the petitions should not be granted, speakers said, in both English and German, pointing to the occupants of the municipal offices, "We shall force them to help the people." They also threatened the various political parties with their combined opposition and pledged not to let one child die of starvation.

This was election day (for state offices only), and a clever soapboxer popped up in the midst of the disgruntled throng, attacking all political parties but proceeding by his own short-cut methods to the conclusion: "Go the whole Democratic ticket." His speech probably changed few votes, but scores like it — and the drinks and bribes that had been flooding the city for weeks — would assure Tammany of victory at the polls.

Some of the word-wary unemployed who had attended the meeting were not satisfied. That night a procession of ragged men and women dragging a cannon marched through the streets of the fashionable quarter.

Two days later the police commissioner asked leave to arm ten "prudent and discreet patrolmen with revolvers that a suffi-cient force may in any contingency be called upon to suppress any riots or unlawful assemblages, without the necessity for invoking the aid of the military." That same day the German workmen, now accompanied by a contingent of Irish, held another "hunger meeting" in Tompkins Square. It was cold, and some of the unemployed tore down the fence surrounding the square and used the boards for fuel.

Another and larger crowd gathered in Tompkins Square the next day, November 5. Some said there were 4,000 in the column that filed toward City Hall carrying banners reading: "Work, Flour, Bread" and "Every workman has a right to a living." Before the march, speakers standing on the dried-up fountain basin that served them for a platform noted that

"Ladies throng Broadway every day buying silk robes, while the wives and children of honest laborers are starving. . . . What man, with a soul in him would see his wife and offspring famish when bread was to be had for the taking of it?"

At City Hall, a committee of the paraders presented to the mayor a "Mass Petition for the Unemployed," asking him "to convene without delay the Aldermen and Commonalty of the City for the purpose of ordaining the immediate employment of workmen at the Central Park, Grand Reservoir, New Post Office, levelling or sewering streets, or any other public works so indispensable for the sanitary condition of the people and the comfort and safety of the wealthy themselves." The mayor promised he would do all he could, counselled against any excitement, and promised to send the petition the following week to the Board of Aldermen. He and the aldermen happened to be at odds, and Wood had no desire to be speedily rebuffed just then.

"Mr. Wood, you propose only to communicate our memorial to the Common Council next week, not before," said a man named Bieler, a spokesman for the committee. "We cannot wait so long in our misery. . . . The people cannot wait any longer, . . . and we cannot warrant that, their patience being exhausted, they will not help themselves by employing physical power with its accompanying brutalities. We, of the Committee, have done all we can to keep the peace, but the alternative is now before us, and we ask for work or death." The mayor, apparently frightened, replied that he would bring the petition before the Board of Aldermen that same evening.

Before the crowd outside City Hall dispersed, a figure who had been familiar at demonstrations two years before put in his appearance. Charles Smith had helped to pacify the unemployed in 1854–1855 and he still did pinch-hitting for Mayor Wood. He called on the City Council to save the city from "revolution, ransack and riot" by setting up public works and paying the unemployed in flour as the mayor had proposed.

Still the crowd in front of City Hall lingered, and another Wood henchman, ex-Councilman Hart, jumped to the platform:

"You should be the slaves of the rich no longer, for this is what you are now. You should be your own master, and what you toil for you should keep, and it should not be taken from you." Cheers interrupted him, but he got in his final word: "Mayor Wood is the man for the poor."

That night the mayor was as good as his word. He presented the "Mass Petition" to the Board of Aldermen, and that group made a discreet gesture toward providing jobs. They decided to advertise for bids on the levelling of Hamilton Square.

Next morning the *Times* insisted, "The leaders in these demonstrations are foreigners. . . . Their actions will be very likely to arouse the native American element. . . . It is very evident that our city stands on the brink of great dangers."

The *Herald* went further. "Rioters, like other people, have heads to be broken, and bodies to be perforated with ball and steel. As our militia would make no scruples to shoot down any quantity of Irish or Germans, or other people who proposed to rob or riot, we take it that the peace will be preserved."

Whatever the anxious merchants and bankers thought of this ominous blustering, the unemployed were not frightened out of meeting again. By 10:00 Friday morning (this was November 6), 5,000 were in Tompkins Square — the largest crowd since the daily demonstrations began on the preceding Monday. Wood's faithful lieutenant, Charles Smith, made a speech opposing further demonstrations until Monday. Part of the audience disagreed and instead decided to march to the Stock Exchange. A huge sign reading "We Want Work" headed the procession as it wormed through the streets of the slum district and finally entered Wall Street. The area in front of the Stock Exchange was completely jammed, and a new leader, a blacksmith named Bowles, spoke: "You owe us a living and we mean to have it!" he shouted. "What we want is work, is it not? It is all on that banner. Is it not?" Amid cries of "Yes!" the police made a show of taking the banner down. The crowd resisted, and the police retired, their long coat tails flapping a little more quickly than usual.

Abandoning Wall Street, the demonstrators then moved up

Broadway to City Hall, where Smith again tried to discourage further action. Instead of disbanding, the crowd shouted approval of a petition to landlords to be lenient. Bowles, who had led the descent on Wall Street, went in with a small committee to see the mayor, who said that he thought on Tuesday next something would be done for them. After giving Wood's answer, Bowles announced adjournment. But he, appearing now as another of Wood's agents, succeeded no better than Smith. An hour later many workers still shuffled about in front of City Hall.

The chaos and formlessness of the unemployed movement became more apparent, even as its size continued to increase. That same Friday afternoon, another meeting was going on in Tompkins Square. A mechanic, Philip Wilton, spoke: "I have not tasted anything to eat for eighteen hours, and unless I get work shortly I must resort to stealing something. A little while ago I went into a bakery on Avenue D and asked them if they would give me a loaf of bread, which they refused, and were going to have me arrested because I took a bun from the counter. The temptation was too great to resist."

All of the efforts of Smith and the other agents of Mayor Wood did not prevent another demonstration early the next morning (Saturday, November 7), and the police were stationed around City Hall. These were the first police that had been allowed near the seat of municipal government since the previous summer, when the mayor expelled them after a political squabble. It was becoming clear that the promayor leaders of the unemployed had either been tampered with or had been planted in the beginning. Voices shouted frequently at the meetings that these men had sold out for a bribe of three dollars a day. F. A. Sorge, leader of the Communist Club, also pointed out the betrayal.

In the absence of other leaders and speakers, the crowd in Tompkins Square gradually became quiet and waited around in little groups talking among themselves. Old John H. Paul, who had defied the police while addressing the unemployed on Christmas Day in 1854, tried to speak for a while. Now, however, in addition to his religious doctrines, he had a profound faith that prohibition could end all difficulties, including unemployment. He was jeered off the platform.

Aimlessness seemed about to claim the demonstrators again when a small group of workmen entered the square carrying a banner, "Work We Want or Bread." This new group, a kind of rank-and-file committee, was apparently free of all political connection, either radical or conservative. Their leader was an Irish bricklayer and sailor named Gordon who had been in the country sixteen years. He was a small, tough man, of red face and somewhat rummy breath, who described himself as "only a bundle of bones and a shadow."

Gordon began to speak, advising another march on City Hall, but someone interrupted him with the cry of the hungry in 1837 — "Let's break into the flour stores!" An uproar followed, but Gordon and his little group of new leaders quieted it with plans for the morning's march. "We don't want temperance! We don't want politics! We want bread." Gordon ended his harangue and was vastly cheered. His order to fall into line, however, met only apathy. Had they not been marching for days, and what had it got them? Another speaker tried to fill up the forming column. He too failed. Finally a German, speaking briefly in his native tongue, turned the trick. A fair part of the crowd joined the ranks of what turned out to be not the largest, but certainly the most spirited, in the whole series of parades. It was clear that the Germans, believing in the class struggle as many of them did, were the most militant and the most disciplined section of the unemployed. Their ideas apparently served as some kind of armor against Smith, Bowles, and the other pro-Wood orators.

At City Hall Gordon and over fifty of the marchers pushed into the mayor's office, but they found it empty. These men were not leaders The Fox cared to encourage. Furthermore, he was thoroughly frightened, knowing words would no longer suffice. To another committee that mysteriously presented itself at this time, however, he repeated the same old story for lack of any other. He expected there would be work on Tuesday or

Wednesday, and he added a word of caution against being led astray by bad leaders. This committee reported favorably to the men still waiting in Tompkins Square.

The crowd at City Hall was bigger than ever on Monday, November 9. Many of the men threatened to enter the chambers where the aldermen and councilmen were meeting to make their all-important decisions about public works. Police were in evidence, with the complete approval of the jittery Wood. In Wall Street at the Sub-Treasury Building, the U.S. assistant treasurer, recalling previous visits of the unemployed to the district, telegraphed Washington for military protection. So great was apprehension in the capital that the cabinet was specially convened and a high-ranking military officer was assigned to keep an eye on the bullion stored in New York.

One of the police commissioners, General Nye, was not to be outfrenzied. He prepared a resolution for his fellow commissioners to sign: "Whereas this department is not blind to the fact that under the cry for bread by persons not hungered, cities have been sacked and governments overthrown, and fully aware how easy it is to excite the prejudice of the poor against the rich, and knowing when so excited they forget the almost unbounded hospitality and the heavy and constant drafts that are made upon the wealth of the rich for the support of the indigent poor; . . . Resolved . . . that the citizens . . . desist from further attempts to excite or keep alive the present excitement in our City with regard to labor or the supplies of food." Police officials discussed this document and approved it, and Mayor Wood sitting with them, supported a motion that they reconvene the following day at 2 P.M., saying, "It may be necessary."

The mayor's fears were understandable in view of his inaction. The crowd outside in City Hall Park persisted, and about noon it grew more than usually excited. Many of those present shouted that Mayor Wood had been humbugging them, that he could give more work immediately and pay them from the treasury, if he was so inclined. Several men who had signed the mass petition spoke, attempting to quiet the unrest. They urged patience, and although loudly booed, helped to disintegrate the meeting. Also aiding in this process was the deus-ex-machina appearance of a Brooklyn hose company that at the moment of greatest tension began playing a stream of water on and near City Hall.

The men left, but they had learned a number of things, not the least of which was that there were now two committees claiming to represent them — the original signatories of the Mass Petition, who merely tried to keep them quiet, and the rank-and-file group headed by Gordon, which insisted loudly that jobs be supplied at once. It was the emergence of this new, uncompromising group that had caused all the excitement. Their insistence, novel as it was in the circumstances, did not fail to get results. The Board of Aldermen officially offered the plan for a $250,000 Central Park bond issue for the mayor's signature. Presumably 1,500 to 2,000 men were to be employed forthwith. The city fathers also discussed speeding up work on Croton Reservoir, and they approved a paving project for Second Avenue.

At the time the city administration was providing some of the jobs that the unemployed had publicly demanded, a *Times* editorial writer was composing "a word of advice to intelligent workingmen": "As far as the mere supply of work or food is concerned, there cannot be a worse way to come at either one or the other than to demand them as a right, when every kind of intelligence in the whole community knows there is no such right." The *Herald*, ordinarily Mayor Wood's paper, spoke out more bluntly. It called for "volleys of musketry" to "repress" the unemployed. And, indeed, musketry awaited them.

On Tuesday fifty-seven soldiers and fifty-seven sailors hid among the granite arches in the basement of the Custom House and the Sub-Treasury Building. Three hundred police drew up outside the fence around City Hall Park, where the unemployed gathered once more. A brigade of militia paraded in front of City Hall.

As had been the custom, the unemployed gathered simultaneously in both the park and Tompkins Square, although notices in the newspapers this morning had sought to divert all of them to Tompkins Square. There, Charles Smith brought news of the concessions granted by the Common Council. Great cheers and a vote of thanks followed this announcement, but a note of stern skeptical qualification went with it. On a lamppost near the fountain hung a banner showing a hand holding a hammer, the old labor symbol dating back to the Working Men's Party of 1829. Under the symbol was the legend "The working-men will meet this evening."

Other evidence of the spirit in which the unemployed took their victory appeared at a table in the corner of the square. There, under the direction of Gordon and his rank-and-file committee, hundreds were giving their names and addresses, hoping by so doing to speed up the hour when they would receive work. Before noon the man at the table had over 600 names.

All day the crowd lingered around the fountain. By 4:00, five hours after the meeting had started, the 5,000 in the square were getting impatient. When was work to begin? The growing restlessness appeared likely to breed action. Eventually one of Wood's men — this time it was Bowles — put in an appearance. He could give no news about when work would begin, "But since you want only work, you must keep the peace and you must not accuse the rich of being your enemies." "Yes they are," cried many.

After Bowles, middle-aged Ira B. Davis took his place on the fountain platform. Davis, who had been a Loco Foco during the hard times of 1837 and had led the unemployed in 1854 and 1855, had more recently mingled with the revolutionary exiles from abroad, appealing for unity. He also called for action at the polls against bad politicians and for continuance of the organization they had started. "Keep your organization even if you get work," he said, "in order to crush out of existence the cormorants that swindle society." Then, sowing confusion, Davis ended by appealing for votes for Mayor Wood.

Had the old veteran been "reached" by Wood along with most of the other leaders of the movement? Or were his energetic words and his weary conclusions merely the behavior of a tired radical whose love of rebellion outdistanced his faith in his fellow workers? Either way, he was on the bandwagon of the most corrupt mayor the city had ever seen, and he discouraged the use of mass tactics he himself had advocated so long ago.

The peace at Tompkins Square contrasted markedly with the tense scene in City Hall Park that day. There, hemmed in by police and militia, provocative speakers held forth. One said, "If any 'big man' were to say he intended to visit New York, the Common Council and the mayor could call special meetings and spend $20,000 . . . to receive him, but when hungry men wanted to work, the necessary proceeding to give it them must be put off and put off, although there was plenty of work to be done." A ragged-looking man asked whether any in the crowd were ready to do anything like men. Soon he left, with the remark that some had no spirit even when pushed. They would only yelp when kicked.

A speaker who said the unemployed could use muskets as well as the soldiers was thrown off the stand. In the disorder that followed, two men tried to speak at once from the steps of City Hall, and the city marshal, against the wishes of the crowd, discouraged both of them. One who was particularly loud in protests was threatened with arrest, but later he turned up near Tammany Hall arm in arm with the marshal himself. Was all this hubbub and rumor of violence merely one phase of the mayor's preelection publicity? At this late date it is impossible to tell, but half of the moves and countermoves were certainly manipulated by those who held and wanted to keep the key to the city's coffers.

The whole action of the unemployed on this day of expected riot was formless, partly spontaneous, partly phoney, partly carefully planned by honest workingmen. In the ensuing days, activities in City Hall Park and Tompkins Square went on as usual, with one exception. The militant labor element shifted its activities elsewhere.

The day after the great sword rattling, there was still much general excitement, although there had been no arrests. Many curious onlookers appeared in Tompkins Square on November 11. Even two or three ladies, heavily escorted by side-whiskered gentlemen, looked at the gathering from a distance. Their voluminous skirts and gay silks contrasted inescapably with the grays, blacks, and faded blues of the workingmen's costumes.

The crowd on November 11 was smaller than on previous days, for division among the unemployed was having its effect. The Germans discussed in little groups the formation of a separate organization. Even among them there was dissension. When a man named Noll spoke recommending the quality of patience so dear to Mayor Wood, he was insulted and beaten. Funds for Central Park had not yet been released, and the men were disillusioned and restless. Moreover, the assemblage had acted as a magnet for gangs of ruffians who seized every opportunity to raid butchers' wagons. Men obviously in need of bread emptied the basket of one baker's boy as he passed the square. A few minutes later, another delivery man passed with twenty loaves, but this time the "Dead Rabbits" gang, the most powerful in the city and notoriously pro-Wood, got the bread and to the expressed horror of the workingmen used the loaves for footballs. Turning from this sport, they captured a passing troupe of musicians and forced them to play.

In the midst of all this, voices still called to the unemployed for unity and for action. "Let us set aside all political considerations. Where we are united we may defy the police and the army of Goliath," cried John H. Paul, veteran evangelist, prohibitionist, and agitator.

While he spoke at Tompkins Square, another veteran, a tall, neatly dressed old man, climbed the steps of City Hall trying to get publicity for a scheme of his. He wanted a mass meeting in Tompkins Square Thursday noon of all the unemployed of Brooklyn, New York, Jersey City, Newark, and Trenton. Sixty thousand, he estimated, would be there. Then he wanted a march past City Hall into Wall Street.

"But of what service would that be? How could that relieve the hungry?" a reporter asked.

"Good heavens, Sir! Will Wall Street, will the City Government . . . see that army of sufferers and devise no relief? . . . Hundreds of your streets need repairing, scores of them need grading. There is work enough for an army to do, and the city has money enough at its command."

The old man, who did not give his name, offered as a kind of credential for himself that he was in the flour riots in 1837 and had been put under bond for keeping the peace. Only one man was released on bail after that affair, the printer John A. Windt, who later became a labor editor. Whoever the old man was, he and the weary Davis, who had urged votes for Mayor Wood, together embodied the divergent traditions of unsophisticated militancy on one hand and radical talk and conservative action on the other.

After ten more days of uninterrupted demonstrations, the crowds in Tompkins Square gradually disappeared, and there was less clamor at City Hall. Police retired from sight. Soldiers and sailors left their hiding places in the government vaults. Either the fears of violence had been proved groundless or the supposed basis for them had ceased to exist. The militia were withdrawn but possibly for an entirely different reason. They were not dependable in this situation, as many of the demonstrators knew. One of the unemployed said at a meeting that "some of them are as bad off as any of us. I know half a dozen of them who have got no breakfast yet."

A few hundred working women and men had already been transported by private charity to the West, and the minds of many more were fastened on migration as the only hope. Many Irish were already leaving or planning to leave for Ireland. Divisions in the ranks of the leaders and obvious political chicanery on the part of most of them made many workers skeptical about the virtues of organized action. Moreover, starvation, beyond its initial stages, did not make men into adequate public pleaders, even on their own behalf.

Finally, a period of mild, continuously pleasant weather set in. Families sat with windows open. Fires were out. Barefoot children played in the streets and the few laborers who had work did not have to worry at the moment if they lacked warm clothes. Indian summer played its part in taking the minds of many who still had a little food off the prospect of a penniless winter.

A few thousand laborers and mechanics continued to agitate, however. Under the leadership of the rank-and-file committee headed by Gordon, they turned from City Hall where, on paper at least, the first battle for jobs had been won and went to the place where the jobs were supposed to be— the proposed site of Central Park. The committee collected more and more names of the destitute and made daily reports on the prospects for relief jobs. These reports, full of emphasis on existing distress, appeared even in papers that were bitterly opposed to group action by the unemployed.

This continued activity had been responsible for the signing, on November 1, of warrants for $30,000 to provide work in Central Park. By the fifteenth, however, no jobs had come through, and crowds of men were waiting all over the unpromising area that was destined to become the world's first great people's park. A year before, the city had taken title to the large area, which was covered with squatters, shacks, slaughterhouses, stinking bone-boiling works, and pigpens. Frederick Law Olmsted, the man whose plan and supervision were to turn all this squalor into a place of beauty, soon received a list of 10,000 men who were in desperate need of work on the wasteland in order to support their families.

Clerks stationed at the site to receive applications for work in the park worried as they looked at milling demonstrators, some of whom had fashioned signs that read "Bread or Blood." Hoping to defuse the demonstrations, the clerks offered jobs to Gordon and his most active assistants, but these men were not to be bought off. Gordon and his followers continued what they had been doing; they established local ward organizations. Out of these committees had come 2,500 would-be workers who lined up at one time, in spite of a large showing of police, in front of the clerks stationed at the site.

The next day a notice appeared on a fence at the edge of the site and on a tree near which the crowd had been gathering to hear speeches. It read, "No more applications for work will be received (here) at present. The laborers who have been engaged will be notified at their residence."

The park commissioners wanted to be free of pressure as they gave out jobs to nondemonstrating applicants, who would producc good results at the polls in the fast-approaching election. To intimidate demonstrators who might suspect the import of the posted notices, thirty-five policemen were stationed nearby, and in case they and their clubs did not prove equal to the situation, guns in the arsenal were loaded.

The commissioners' precise plan was this: Each alderman was to have the appointment of fifteen men to be put to work the following day, and no radicals and no friends of Mayor Wood were to be given jobs. Obviously not only Wood but his enemies had their eyes on the mayoralty election, which was only a few days away. Counselled by Gordon, the unemployed met the next day in Tompkins Square and marched once more to City Hall, announcing they would all refuse to vote for anybody — until they received work.

The next morning demonstrators once more milled around in front of City Hall. The recently discredited Charles Smith regained sympathetic attention by playing on the great resentment against the Central Park Commissioners.

Four days later there were still no jobs in the park. Then, desperately and as if for the last time, men met in Tompkins Square and appointed a committee of two to make a final call on the commissioners. The commissioners protected themselves from this committee and said they would reply only upon receipt of a written complaint. Meanwhile, there were no jobs, and the police commissioners busied themselves with approval of a new club or nightstick for policemen. It had a trigger in the handle, which, if pulled, sent out sharp points all along the sides of the weapon. These were described as "calculated to wound the hands of the assailant, and not only cause them to let go, but will mark them so as to identify the rascal for future arrest."

Indian summer ended. November 24 was very cold, and few of the men had overcoats. This day, there were no good words for either Mayor Wood or for his rivals, the park commissioners. Even Charles Smith did not dare to praise Wood. Rather, he distracted attention by proposing tar and feathers for the commissioners. He also disagreed with the proposed boycott of the

ballot, pretending he did not care how the unemployed cast
their ballots as long as they voted.

Thanksgiving Day was the occasion for the *Times* to say:

> During the past fortnight there has been a very perceptible
> and painful increase in the number of our street mendicants.
> . . . They give us no rest. They intrude themselves. . . . Little
> barefooted children, with their pale faces, look up from the
> crowded sidewalks, and in their piping voices ask for money to
> buy food for their sick mothers. . . . Gay promenaders who
> come out to enjoy the pleasure of shopping in Broadway are
> annoyed at every step by pertinacious little creatures who
> follow them with outstretched hands beseeching for two cents
> towards buying a loaf of bread — for our street mendicants are
> seldom so humble as to ask for one cent. . . . The police should
> have strict orders given them to arrest and send to the station
> houses every person, man, woman, or child, who may be
> found begging in the streets.

Undismayed by recent events, Dr. Henry Ward Beecher
expressed gratitude, in his Thanksgiving Day sermon, that
trouble "which falls upon individuals is but temporary and is
compensated by collateral benefits." As pocketbooks shrank,
evangelism prospered. If Earth was dreary, there was always
Heaven and, for variety's sake, Hell. One of the great revivals of
modern times came not long after the depression of 1857.
Hymn singing and street-corner meetings filled Wall Street. In
the raw western city of Chicago, Dwight Moody was starting on
his career of fishing for souls. Talk of spiritualism, already
widespread, increased.

But before men gave up parading and began praying for
their daily bread, the cumulative effect of the ceaseless demand
for work had made itself finally, although not fully, felt. Nine
hundred men had been put to work on Central Park before
election day. Everything pointed toward the election. Mayor
Wood's men, Charles Smith and Ira B. Davis, worked hard
trying to win the unemployed by emphasizing the mayor's
radical talk. Unpleasant facts, however, outweighed talk of any

kind: On November 30, 1,200 men applied to the city for shelter for the night. There were accommodations for only a third of that number. The following day at the local election, Mayor Wood was defeated.

The new mayor, Daniel F. Tiemann, a "regular" Tammany man, was inaugurated January 5. Wood had been expelled from Tammany Hall. Tiemann's chief recommendation was that he had a less bad record than Wood. Remembering the hornet's nest that Wood had stirred up by his professed sympathy for the unemployed, Tiemann avoided the unemployment question altogether, and his evasion was never successfully challenged. The vigorous unemployed who might have opposed him had either left the city (as they did in 1808, 1837, and 1854) or had found relief work among about 1,000 men employed in Central Park or among a much smaller number engaged in the demolition of buildings or in one of the paving projects that were at last begun. Walt Whitman visited one such project in the sister city of Brooklyn, where men worked "hip-deep in the water, eleven hours per day for a dollar." Many unemployed, of course, sank into what Marx called "the dangerous class," the "passively rotting mass" that politicians might well use for "reactionary intrigue."

The degradation to which some of the population had been driven was noted under the caption "A Starving Woman" in the *Times*, January 27, 1858:

> A lady passing down Broadway, near Fourteenth Street, a few days since, when opposite a butcher's stand, was startled by the excited appearance of an intelligent-looking woman rushing toward her, with clasped hands and a look of despair, exclaiming, "I am hungry, I am hungry." Stepping inside the store, the lady procured for her some potatoes and a piece of meat. The hungry woman put the meat to her lips and *ate it to the bone!* then saying, "I must take this home to Eddie," rushed wildly from the store, leaving the salesman and the lady astounded. Incredible as this seems, we have every reason to believe it true.

Six thousand women tried to keep alive on their earnings as prostitutes — one woman, that is, for every sixty-four adult males in New York. In 1857 seventy-five acres were set aside on Ward's Island as a pauper's cemetery, and it rapidly filled.

It was in the depression year of 1857 that Louis Pasteur discovered that spontaneous generation did not exist in the organic world. In that same year there was evidence that spontaneous generation does not exist in the social world. Conditions may be ripe for the growth of the "bacteria" of social change, but if they are isolated from a culture in which they can grow, or if they grow in the same culture as disease germs, they shrivel and die.

The depression of that year had forced the unemployed to act before they had the necessary consciousness of their cause or the necessary unity to achieve adequate government relief for all. Nevertheless, in the cautious words of Dr. Leah Feder in *Unemployment Relief in Periods of Depression,* "In New York and Philadelphia labor demonstrations helped indirectly in securing appropriations for public works or relief of the unemployed."

By the first months of 1859, the hard times had come to an end. The one million wage workers in the United States again had their jobs, and they quickly put out of mind the trials and struggles of their unemployed years. They turned instead to changing the South from semi-feudalism and slavery to wage-work capitalism. During the depression, John Brown had been gathering arms for the defense of Kansas against those who wanted it for slaveholding territory. And during the depression, J. P. Morgan went into business.

It was not long before new developments began among workers. In January 1861, a union, the American Miners Association, formed and adopted this unusual introduction to its constitution:

> Step by step the longest march
> Can be won, can be won;
> Single stones will form an arch
> One by one, one by one.

> And by union, what we will,
>> Can be all accomplished still,
> Drops of water turn a mill,
>> Singly none, singly none.

As miners began to try to create a union, the union of the United States was on the verge of breaking up. During the Civil War that followed this crisis, mass unemployment was not a major feature of the social chaos. A new, sharp downturn in the economy began toward the end of 1873.

7

Red Flag in Tompkins Square
(1874)

Where there is more than enough for all, all should have at least enough.
— banner in Tompkins Square, 1874

Ulysses S. Grant, president of the United States, had breakfast with his trusted friend, the financier Jay Cooke, on the morning of September 17, 1873. These two bearded men, the political and economic leaders of a continent, ate heartily, chatting over the previous day's accomplishment, which had been to put Grant's son in the school Cooke recommended. Pudgy Grant had great respect for wealth wherever he saw it, and fragile Cooke did eager obeisance before tractable power.

Their friendship, which Cooke had made a point of starting, prospered against a background of scandals that were epidemic in this age when the government had the giving of great favors. These favors included grants of public lands to encourage the building of the 30,000 miles of railroads that were constructed between 1872 and 1877. One of the scandals had surfaced in 1872 when it was discovered that a government-subsidized company, the Credit Mobilier, had bribed Vice-President Schuyler Colfax by giving him stock in the company. More recently, a speculation mania had swept the stock exchanges. Such events had built up a kind of pyramid of public doubt, with Cooke seated at its apex. Grant, however, stood unshaken in his fidelity. Had not he and Cooke won the Civil War? He had grown famous generalling the army that the banker had grown rich financing.

The harmony between the state and big business was probably not in Grant's mind as he breakfasted amid the splendor of Ogontz, Cooke's estate outside Philadelphia (the ownership of which the president envied his host). Cooke, however, may well have had occasion this morning to think of the relationship. More than once during the meal, a servant sitting at the financier's private telegraph hurried to his employer with messages from New York. Each time, after glancing intently at the news, Cooke turned quickly back to his guest without revealing what the messages were about.

The meal over, the two men rode in Cooke's elegant carriage to the railroad station where they parted. Grant took a westbound train, and Cooke went to Philadelphia to his bank in Third Street. Not many minutes after the heavy doors of that institution swung open to let him in, they closed to keep clamoring depositors out.

The financial panic of 1873 had started, and the great depression of which it was a symptom had begun its six-year course. The unemployed faced the greatest suffering so far known in American history, and struggling against it they tried to develop organizations equal to obtaining public works and public relief.

Possibly three million people were thrown out of work by the depression, and at the same time refugees from Europe continued to arrive, although in smaller than usual numbers. Some had fled France after the failure of their effort to establish a people's government in Paris in 1871. Anti-Socialist pressures affected Germans under Bismarck, and the tide of German immigration was higher than at any time since the failure of the Revolution of 1848. In New York, a dramatic high point in the efforts of these unemployed was a mass rally for jobs on public works, which the police turned into a four-hour riot.

President Grant did not foresee any of this or grasp its meaning. Those around him seldom brought troublesome concepts to his attention, and he persisted in trusting his advisors, who frequently misled him. Throughout the hard times of the 1870s, he remained as unaware of the facts of the depression as he had been in Cooke's home at the moment of its inception.

With Cooke, he symbolized the combined blindness and ruthlessness of the forces that first deprived workers of jobs and then refused to feed them.

The Gilded Age, Mark Twain called this period. For the conspicuous minority it meant sudden opulence and steady corruption. Cities as well as the central government were affected. For years the Tweed Ring had been writing in enormous figures on the blank checks it forced the citizens of New York to sign. Researchers have said that possibly as much as $30 million were looted from the New York City treasury in thirty months. Ballyhoo for the great American System (a phrase used for the local manifestation of the worldwide capitalist economy) mesmerized a great many people.

Another feature of the Gilded Age was the great activity of the Ku Klux Klan in the South. Vigilantes were busy on the frontier. Chinese were being brutally attacked in California and Washington state. Protestants rioted against Catholics in the East. Strikes were frequent, sometimes violent. In New York alone in 1872 nearly 100,000 workers in the mechanical and building trades struck for an eight-hour day.

At about this time Friedrich Engels, a refugee from the German Revolution of 1848 living in Manchester, England, summarized doctrines that had dug deep into the minds and movement of European workers:

> The whole industrial and commercial world, production and exchange among all civilized peoples and their more or less barbaric hangers-on are thrown out of joint about once every ten years. . . . Little by little the pace quickens. It becomes a trot. The industrial trot breaks into a canter, the canter in turn grows into the headlong gallop of a perfect steeplechase of industry, commercial credit, and speculation, which finally, after breakneck leaps, ends where it began — in the ditch of a crisis. And so over and over again. . . . And the character of these crises is so clearly defined that Fourier hit all of them off, when he described the first as "*crise plethorique*," a crisis from plethora. . . . *The mode of production is in rebellion against the mode of exchange.*

Saying this, Engels was paralleling ideas about depressions expressed earlier in the United States by Byllesby, Raymond, and Skidmore, among others.

Engels did more than diagnose economic ills. For several years he and Karl Marx had helped European workers organize the International Workingmen's Association, now often called the First International. This loose grouping included Anarchists, liberal reformers, and Communists. Followers of the Anarchist Mikhail Bakunin opposed political action. Followers of Ferdinand Lassalle urged the working class to rely only on electoral action as a way of bettering their lot. Backers of Marx and Engels urged workers to use both unions and political action in its broadest sense. The latter group transferred the headquarters of the organization to New York in 1873 as an anti-Bakunin measure.

At that time there were 5,000 American members of the International, organized into thirty sections. In 1872 one of the members, Victoria Woodhull, became the first woman candidate for the presidency, running as a member of the Equal Rights Party. That same year, with her co-editor Tennessee Claflin, she published in *Woodhull and Claflin's Weekly* the first English translation of the *Communist Manifesto* to appear in the United States.

Meanwhile the secretary of the International, F. A. Sorge, went about the melancholy work of winding up its affairs. Another International must come, Sorge believed, one with less inner conflict. Still, the American sections of the strife-ridden organization did have active members when the depression arrived. They soon petitioned the mayor of New York and the Congress for public works; they even asked President Grant to summon a special session of Congress to initiate a large program of civic improvements. For the most part, however, the International spent its energy reenacting the conflicts that had come with it from Europe. In addition, it had developed new conflicts that derived from the surrounding United States culture. Some native-born, middle-class members tied their radicalism to fads such as spiritualism and free love or to panaceas such as currency reform. They were the ones who dominated

Section 12 of the North American Central Committee of the International. In 1872 this section had been expelled, but it maintained a skeleton organization known popularly as the Spring Street Council, which was later to make itself heard.

Members of a larger group were mostly foreign born and from the working class. On December 17, 1871, many in this group had forced the New York police to revoke a ban against a parade they wanted to hold on Fifth Avenue to commemorate the Paris Commune. This successful thrust for the right of public assembly has been called the "first First Amendment case."

In March 1872, well before the onset of the most severe crisis, sections of the International in New York had led a demonstration of unemployed workers. One of the banners expressed the central policy of the International: "The unemployed demand work of the government."

The International did little to animate the general American labor scene, and there was even less vigor in the indigenous National Labor Union, which had been headed by the energetic William J. Sylvis until his death in 1869. Lacking his directing genius, the National Labor Union was considering notions about transforming unions into producers' cooperatives. In good government, its leaders thought, lay the hope of workers, and panaceas such as paper money, not economic action, were favored. Indeed, electoral activity, to the exclusion of mass pressure or trade union organizing, became the obsession of many American workingmen during the depression. These doctrines of Lassalle had their inning but were not the only ones to come up to bat in 1873.

Most of 1873 was a time of weariness and wordiness, a time of closing out old things in the labor movement. But before the year's end, much that was new and vigorous began to appear. The quasi-industrial union known as the Knights of Labor was secretly forming. The Molly Maguires, a grossly slandered organization of Pennsylvania coal miners, fiercely defended their wage scales. Elsewhere large numbers struck for the eight-hour day and for better wages. As the depression developed, a strike movement against wage cuts began. It continued until it reached a dramatic climax in vast and turbulent railroad strikes in 1877.

When unemployment became epidemic, the jobless in many cities met and petitioned for public works. A mason in Newark at one of the meetings suggested the general mood of desperate determination: "Hunger will go through a stone wall," he said. In New York the Spring Street Council, perhaps because some of its members were fluent journalists, took the lead in drafting a "declaration" against unemployment and for public works. The non-Socialist central labor body and twenty unions joined in support of a demand for public works, and 800 trade unionists attended a rally in mid-November.

Soon the German-speaking Tenth Ward Workingmen's Association formed and began methodically to organize the unemployed. A 22-year-old carpenter who was active in the Tenth Ward group and apparently also in the Spring Street Council and in union affairs, was of Irish origin. Although he was born and raised in New York, Peter J. McGuire, who was to become an influential labor leader, had associated so much with German and French immigrants that he had become fluent in their languages.

The ward was divided into four parts, and a census of the unemployed was undertaken. After the jobless had been located, they met and agreed on three demands:

1. Work to be provided for all those willing and able to work, at the usual wages and on the eight-hours plan.
2. An advance of either money or produce sufficient for one week's sustenance to be made to laborers and their families in actual distress.
3. No ejectment from lodgings to be made for non-payment of rent from December 1st, 1873 to May 1st, 1874.

Believing that effective organization could grow up around this program, the International proposed in a manifesto that a plan modeled on that of the Tenth Ward Association be applied by the unemployed everywhere (see Appendix B). The manifesto was vehement in denunciation of capitalism and its effect on workers. Acting on suggestions in the document, some of the unemployed in New York undertook activities citywide.

The German Socialist members of the International persuaded the non-Socialist Workingmen's Central Council to encourage the ward form of organization, and the Spring Street Council also agreed. Together the three organizations endorsed a call to a meeting of the unemployed on December 11, 1873, at Cooper Institute.

"Is there any less real wealth in the country now," ran the call, "than when the monte-tables of Wall Street turned against those who were so recklessly gambling in the *People's Highways* — our common railroads? . . . Is it employment and pay that the working people should demand or the grudgingly given and debasing bread of charity?" The call continued, "N.B. *Politicians and Demagogues please take notice*, HANDS OFF! This is a people's gathering, and they are entirely competent to conduct its interests in behalf of the whole people. . . . For the first time hear truths spoken that shall *fire the Nation's heart.*"

Out of the December 11 meeting grew a citywide committee of fifty members. It chose a name likely to appeal to both patriotic native Americans and radical foreign-born workers: the Committee of Safety. The words recalled to Americans an active antiestablishment people's organization in the Colonies before the Declaration of Independence. To foreign-born workers they recalled an organ of the French Revolution.

This New York Committee of Safety undertook to organize the unemployed in a mass demonstration and march to City Hall on January 13, 1874, to demand work. (See Appendix C and Appendix D for examples of handbills.) The Committee of Safety worked with others in preparing for the march. The coalition reflected the divisions that had paralyzed the working-class movement both in the United States and abroad. Within each were factions, and the police, the newspapers, and the remnants of the Tweed Ring rejoiced to find confusion among the jobless.

Placards at the Cooper Institute meeting of December 11 had told the story of the times, as some of the unemployed saw it: "When Workingmen Begin to Think, Monopoly Begins to Tremble"; "10,000 Homeless Men and Women in our Streets"; "7,500 Lodged in Overcrowded Charnel Station Houses per week" (in bad weather, homeless men and women were allowed to sleep in police stations); "20,250 Idle Men from 11 Trade Unions — 5,950 Employed"; "182,000 skilled Union Workmen Idle in New York State"; "110,000 Idle of All Classes in New York City." These figures, as well as the widely circulated national estimate of 3 million jobless, are hard to prove or disprove. A national bureau of labor statistics, which the International took the lead in proposing, had not yet been established. In any case, no one could deny that unemployment was vast in extent.

With unemployment came evictions, for the great majority of the jobless could not possibly have had any savings, as a survey conducted by the *New York World* showed. Cheese-paring economies were necessary even in prosperous times. Unskilled laborers averaged fourteen dollars a week, skilled women workers seven dollars. No cozy place existed on the street in which to weather the economic storm. Even in the dullest times a welter of wagons, carriages, and ragpickers and their dog carts kept the dirty asphalt and cobblestones too hectic to accommodate the homeless. Free public bathing houses were incessantly crowded and were only a temporary haven at best. Confusion, turmoil, despair, and aimless anger consumed the unemployed until leaders appeared.

New York, always important in unemployed activity because of its size and its relatively high percentage of radical workers, was not the only city in which the jobless became active as winter advanced. Need, seldom an entirely mute teacher, had suggested mass action elsewhere. Moreover, the manifesto and the International's plan for organizing had been widely circulated. In Louisville, Kentucky, the unemployed met and called on the city for public works. Boston laborers also petitioned for public works. There the mayor went so far in his efforts to discourage their pleas as to make this prophecy: "There will soon be work for all who desire it." Chicago had a very militant movement (described in Chapter 8).

Meanwhile, attempting to take advantage of the rising interest in organization that was stimulated by preparations for the January 13 march in New York, an independent group of non-Communist Irishmen called a meeting in Union Square January 5. But instead of being opened by Patrick E. Dunn, the chief sponsor, the meeting found itself with Theodore Banks, a Committee of Safety man, as chairman. A few minutes later bespectacled old Patrick Dunn pushed his way to the platform and spoke from the side of younger, larger Banks: "We don't want anything to do with Communists, and the Committee of Safety is a humbug. What we want is work and pay for it, and if we ain't given what we want we'll take it." The city's assistant aldermen, it seemed to Dunn, were particularly to blame for not providing work. "The miserable, dirty blackguards, if they don't do it, we'll throw the wretches out of the windows of their Chamber."

Peter J. McGuire, also of the Committee of Safety, spoke next. Until December 5 when he lost his job, McGuire had been a wood joiner by trade in the daytime and a high school student at night. He was also a member of the International Working-men's Association and about this time became an organizer for the Social Democratic Party, later renamed the Socialist Labor Party. A few years later he was to be the originator of the first Labor Day and organizer of the Brotherhood of Carpenters and Joiners, which he headed for a quarter-century.

The problem for McGuire and Banks, on the rainy morning of January 5, was how to keep this non-Communist gathering from resulting in violence or inanity, which would tend to hamper the success of the great meeting planned for the thir-teenth. The solution they found was simply to take over leader-ship as the jobless marched to City Hall and to make sure that Dunn and his friends were given positions on the committee to see the mayor.

Four abreast down the sidewalks along Broadway the few hundred men marched, frightening the merchants who had not seen such a parade since 1857. At City Hall the ragged little army found the iron gates closed against them. Only the com-mittee chosen to see the assistant aldermen was admitted; it spoke its mind through Banks and received a legalistically

phrased runaround. When the arrogance of the assistant aldermen was reported back to the crowd, one of the organizers of
the meeting proposed that the group "throw those whelps out of
the windows." But Banks and McGuire argued that the best
measure was to organize many more of the unemployed, and
their counsel prevailed.

Dunn tried, a few days later, to hold another meeting, but
for the second time the Committee of Safety leaders spoke
words more to the liking of the unemployed. The battle of
factions was on. Countermoves, denunciations, and resolutions
began to flood the papers, which willingly published anything
that might discredit the obviously formidable organizing power
of the Committee of Safety, which was loudly — and wrongly —
accused of being completely communist.

Handbills indicating the strength of the unemployed movement were given out all over the city. Police spying increased as
the activity of the unemployed increased. The printer of a leaflet
that appeared in both German and English had to face a long
police interrogation.

Street meetings increased in number. A newspaper reported
that "to recognize the principal leaders a number of private
detectives were present." On one occasion, an army captain
somehow became chairman of a street corner meeting, only to
have the meeting resolve, "We consider it the duty of the working classes all over the United States to commence the struggle
for the emancipation of labor and the abolition of class rule,
and we most solemnly pledge ourselves to aid the glorious
work."

The Committee of Safety invited Mayor Havemeyer to address the meeting of the unemployed in Tompkins Square
planned for January 13, and apparently the mayor accepted the
invitation. Permits to exercise freedom of speech and assembly
were required in 1874, and the Committee of Safety sent Mc-
Guire and a delegation to get two permits, one for the meeting
in Tompkins Square and another for the march to City Hall. The
park commissioners were elaborately cordial at first. Finally,
however, the interview came down to the following, as one
newspaper reported:

Police Commissioner Gardner (firmly). You can go to Canal Street and not below it. You can send your delegates to City Hall and your processionists can await an answer.

Mr. McGuire. And if the masses wish to accompany them and break through at Centre Street, what then?

Mr. Gardner. Then there will be trouble for which we will hold you to answer. Now, mind what I say.

Mr. McGuire (angrily). Is that the law?

Mr. Gardner. Law or no law we will not permit it.

The interview occurred on Saturday, January 10, three days before the demonstration, on the success of which hung the hopes of so many. On Sunday the Committee of Safety sent an unavailing telegram to the governor of the state, hoping he would intervene to guarantee them the use of the streets. The committee also made a general appeal to the public for a hearing. Ward organizations set up by the committees took elaborate precautions to keep police provocateurs out of the ranks on the day of the march. Among other things, they arranged special credentials to make it difficult for police agents to pose as workingmen.

The Workingmen's Central Council chose Sunday to announce a program that was clearly distinguished from the simpler demands that the Committee of Safety made. Whether or not this program was intentionally diversionary, it had that effect. It included no direct demands for the unemployed but called instead for complete unionization of working people, more leisure, more benefits, a federal bureau of labor statistics, cooperatives, public lands for the people and not for the railroads, an end to laws giving capital special privileges, a beginning of health and safety laws, arbitration instead of strikes wherever possible, prohibition of the importation of "all servile races," better apprentice laws, abolishment of the contract system of prisons, the eight-hour day, and a "flexible national circulating medium" (that is, inflation). This list was the program of the Industrial Party, one of three short-lived radical parties that appeared in New York during the depression.

On Monday, harassed young McGuire rushed down to City Hall again to make another appeal for the right of the unemployed to complete the march as planned. Police Commissioner Gardner received him and revealed that his agents had been busy. They had somehow got to McGuire's father, a poorly paid porter working for the Lord and Taylor store for women's clothing. The elder McGuire had actually stood on the steps of a Catholic church and denounced his son, calling him a Communist. When young McGuire heard this he wept.

The same day, another committee of the unemployed — or so they described themselves — appeared before the police commissioners and urged that the police prevent the meeting in Tompkins Square. Led by Dunn, who had been notoriously unsuccessful in earlier efforts to organize the unemployed, and backed up now by a majority of the Workingmen's Central Council, they received an immediate hearing, and their request was promptly granted. Less than twenty-four hours before the announced meeting, permission to hold it was revoked. None of the members of the Committee of Safety, however, received notice of the revocation.

Editorials in the press said that the meeting was being advocated in "bread-or-blood speeches of bar-room orators." But news columns gave no evidence that any speaker called for or threatened bloodshed. There is some evidence that the reports of threats came from police agents. The fact was that the Committee of Safety diligently tried to avoid violence. Declarations of policy were sent to newspaper offices, and such declarations as were published called only for discipline among the unemployed and pointed to the likelihood and danger of police-instigated disruption.

The Committee of Safety was not alone in its fear of police violence. The *Times*, as eager as any paper or politician to have the meeting called off, grew a little squeamish at the last minute: "Our confidence in the preservation of order is not strengthened by the information that Matsell is to be in active command of the police." Matsell, it seems, had commanded only once before, and on that occasion a riot had ensued. Even so, the *Times* concluded, "The disposition made of the police force is of such a nature as to insure a quiet day, but if a collision between the processionists and the police should occur, the conflict will be short and decisive. The whole force will be ordered on duty at six a.m."

The night of January 12, police officers called at the homes of all the leaders of the announced demonstration, ostensibly to give them official notice, and for the first time, that the permit for the meeting had been revoked. Possibly fearing that the police might arrest them on the eve of the meeting, the leaders of the Committee of Safety were all away from home, so none of them received notice of the cancellation. While policemen hunted for the leaders through one tenement dwelling after another, a well-known labor official, Ferdinand Laurrell, scurried from one workers' meeting to another, pleading with every group not to gather the next day. He was not cordially received.

Others too, were busy trying to head off the mass meeting. "There are apprehensions in some quarters," the *Times* said, "that serious disturbance will occur tomorrow, but we do not share in them. We do not credit these agitators with much sense, but they certainly must have enough to avoid an open and flagrant violation of the law."

Ignoring — or unaware of — all efforts that had been made to discourage them, men, women, and children began to walk through the gates of Tompkins Square at about 10:00 the morning of January 13. Gathered in small knots behind the iron fence around the square, they waited to hear what the mayor had to say about relief for the unemployed. No police officers were stationed at the gates to keep them out or even to notify them that the permit for the meeting had been withdrawn.

Before long, at the north end of the square, a young German Socialist, Christian Meyer, raised a banner reading "TENTH WARD WORKINGMEN'S ASSOCIATION." Around it stood the largest knot of demonstrators. One tawny-bearded, magnificent-looking man, who reminded some people of a hero in Wagnerian opera, carried a red flag. Such a flag had long been a symbol of defiance in Europe; it had been used in revolts against tyranny in France in 1790 and in 1791. The flag carrier was Justus Schwab, a former mason, well known among German refugees. Now he operated a saloon that was a kind of headquarters for newly arrived immigrants and for radicals already in residence. Samuel Gompers, who knew the saloon well, described it as "the post office and information center for the underground of revolution." It served as hospital and hostelry as well.

Throughout the crowd in the square volunteers distributed leaflets announcing the program the meeting had been called to support. It had been prepared for the Committee of Safety by Peter McGuire and Lucien Saniel, veteran of the Paris Commune, who would remain an ardent Socialist until his death in 1927. Around the edges of the crowd, Mrs. Tom-Ri John, carrying a walking staff for protection and wearing trousers out of unconventional preference, offered for sale copies of *The Volcano*, an eccentric periodical printed in red ink on bright yellow paper by her husband, editor Tom-Ri John. Wherever demonstrators gathered, the John's three daughters, Eruptor, Vesuvia, and Emancipator, were present.

By 10:30 (the *Post* estimated), at least 6,000 men, women, and children were in the square, and the number continued to grow until it reached possibly as high as 15,000. Even so, all was peace and quiet. Major Havemeyer had not appeared, but Police Commissioner Duryea was on hand. Suddenly, about 100 policemen, with clubs drawn, stepped out of the nearby 17th Precinct Station House and marched in formation through the crowd to the center of the square. There they lined up before Commissioner Duryea.

"Now you all go home," Commissioner Duryea shouted. "Right away!"

Immediately the police began to swing their clubs. At about the same moment thirty mounted police appeared and began to strike indiscriminately at women and children as well as men. The surprised and terrified crowd fled through the gates with the police in pursuit. Only the men around the banner of the Tenth Ward Workingmen's Association remained. Christian Meyer held the banner high and would not move. To defend himself, the press reported, he had in his hand a hammer, a tool of the trade in which he could not find work.

"By dint of sharp clubbing" the police dispersed the crowd, but not before someone — the police said it was the German Meyer with his hammer — had cut a gash in the scalp of a police sergeant. Meyer was severely clubbed and arrested, along with forty-six other demonstrators. Hundreds were injured. Besides the sergeant, there was one other police casualty. An officer was struck, so a reporter said, by an old man who claimed to be a Communist and who carried a club. Against one hammer and one club the police brought up reinforcements — the *Times* said a total of 1,500 officers, but this figure cannot be confirmed. (Official records of the riot have been destroyed.)

The police attacks continued. One eyewitness said they went on all day, "wherever the police saw a group of poorly dressed persons standing or moving together." The eyewitness was Samuel Gompers, who would one day become president of the American Federation of Labor. He saved his own head from being cracked by jumping down a cellarway. Peter McGuire wasn't so lucky. In his diary he later made this wry entry: "McGuire, looking for someone to help him nurse his bleeding head, was officially initiated into the class struggle."

About noon, five leaders of the Committee of Safety went to City Hall, still hoping to persuade the mayor to fulfill his speaking engagement in Tompkins Square.

"I do not choose to address crazy or excited people who may be anxious to send brickbats flying," the mayor told them. As he spoke, Police Commissioner Duryea stood at his side. Quietly but firmly the delegation pressed their invitation. One of them said that all had been peaceful at the meeting until the police attacked "mercilessly." Commissioner Duryea insisted that his men had attacked only after a man with a hammer had struck a police officer on the head — a story that did not coincide even with accounts printed by antidemonstration newspapers.

Before the conference between the mayor and the Committee of Safety broke up, the mayor, a Republican and the owner of a sugar factory, explained what he regarded as the main difficulty in the way of granting the demands of the unemployed. "The market is glutted with labor, and men will not work unless they get the price they ask. I believe that there is work enough for everybody but not at the wages demanded." In reply, the committee insisted that workingmen had to get fair wages in order to survive. They also pointed out that they could not demand employment from private business, so they must demand it from the government.

That was the crux of the dispute between the unemployed and the city administration, and it was not resolved in the mayor's office. After the committee left, the mayor said, within hearing of the press, that he favored raising private (that is, not public) funds to aid the unemployed.

That night protest meetings were held in many parts of the city. The next day the New York State Assembly in Albany appointed a committee to look into unemployment.

Of the forty-six men arrested on the day of the Tompkins Square riot, twenty-four were Germans, ten were native Americans, and the remainder were Poles, Italians, Swedes, Irish, and French. Justus Schwab, carrier of the red flag, was charged with inciting to riot. In response, he defiantly insisted, according to a confused account in the *Times*, that he was a member of "the Commune" (some French demonstrators had been supporters of the Paris Commune, and a number of German demonstrators were members of the International, which included Communists). Schwab told the court he went to Tompkins Square to parade, but not to break the peace. He recognized the red flag as the emblem all over the world of unity among workingmen. He was remanded to jail.

The court gave the harshest sentence to Christian Meyer, standard-bearer of the unemployed from the Tenth Ward. He was sent to work six months in the Charity Hospital and Penitentiary. At the same time, "Boss" Tweed, head of the Tweed Ring, was also in jail for stealing millions of dollars from the city. But there was a difference between the two sentences. Tweed's jailers took him daily in a carriage to Central Park (which had been built following unemployed demonstrations in 1857), where he had a pleasant walk. Then he went to his nearby home for dinner before returning to jail for the night. Christian Meyer, except when he was working or eating, did not leave his bug-infested cell.

After six months and while he was still in jail, Meyer insisted, "I am here not for any wrong, but because I was in the right." Those who shared Meyer's view vehemently protested his imprisonment, and the governor pardoned him at about the time he was due to be released anyway.

John Swinton, a veteran member of the staff of the *Times*, had been a scheduled speaker at the Tompkins Square meeting. What he saw there propelled him, already a labor sympathizer, into a lifetime of agitation for labor. He felt so strongly following the riot that he carried his protest to the New York State Assembly, where he said, "The authorities were not quelling a riot, for there was no riot, and not a man had raised a finger when the police unexpectedly sprang to the assault. . . . The editorial funks and intellectual policemen have roused prejudices against their victims by saying they were Communists, in league with the impending earthquake. Gentlemen, be not alarmed by mysterious words, and let not the epithet "Communist" stir up the same sort of hydrophobia that the epithet "Abolitionist" once did. Suppose the ideas of these people were the sort which editors and policemen call "Communistic": does anyone suppose the thing can be scribbled out of their hearts or clubbed out of their heads?

Not surprisingly, immigrants from Britain's Irish colony joined the protest. A newspaper serving their community asked, "Suppose it was a Know-Nothing meeting? Suppose it was a meeting of monopolists or of stock gamblers? . . . Would such a meeting be prohibited? Would not the police and military be called out in force to protect them?"

A Democratic voice that had spoken differently in the depression of 1857 also joined in protesting the action of the Republican city administration in New York. Fernando Wood, once a mayor and now a congressman from New York, said, "The police authorities have no right to break up a public meeting called for any purpose by the people."

From the point of view of the unemployed, the results of their organizational efforts were mixed. They did not get the public works they sought, but they did get greatly increased relief — from private sources. During the period of most intense agitation, the New York Commissioners of Charity gave out more relief than they had in the entire twelve months prior to November 1873.

Another result of the efforts of the Committee of Safety and its allies was the appearance in the *World* in late January of a series of articles making clear that the plight of the unemployed was every bit as bad as their leaders had claimed.

Although the depression dragged on for years, the unemployed did not succeed in keeping their organization alive. Samuel Gompers has recorded their problems: "The Tompkins Square outrage was followed by a period of extreme repression. The New York police borrowed continental methods of espionage. Private indoor meetings were invaded and summarily ended by the ejection of those present. The police frustrated several meetings held to protest against brutality and in defense of the right of free assemblage for a lawful purpose." Police repression also drove Gompers into a decision that dictated the course of his whole life. "I saw how professions of radicalism concentrated all the forces of organized society against a labor movement and nullified in advance normal, necessary activity."

While Gompers resolved to keep a safe distance between himself and radicals, Swinton moved in the opposite direction. He went on to run for mayor later in 1874 on a Socialist ticket. The split typified by Gompers and Swinton, along with other differences, hindered the effort of the unemployed to get public works. The most resolute section of the protesting workers was German. They stubbornly continued to speak German and to stand aloof from native American workers. Politicians from the Republican and Democratic parties made use of divisions and antagonisms of every sort, infiltrating the organizations of the unemployed, and leading them away from effective action. With surprising suddenness, the New York jobless could not agree on anything. At the same time, they faced representatives of economic and political power more arrogant and more hostile than any who had hitherto ruled in the United States. Without the weapon of unity, they were paralyzed.

8

From Arsenic to Arson
(1873–1874)

When a tramp asks you for bread, put strychnine or arsenic in it, and he will not trouble you any more, and others will keep out of the neighborhood.

— *Chicago Tribune*, 1884

An unlikely couple, newcomers from Texas, watched and wondered at a series of parades of Chicago's unemployed during the Christmas season in 1873. The man was a white Confederate veteran; the young woman, his wife, was of African-American and Native American descent. Neither was used to seeing masses of workers, let alone masses of unemployed workers. They had never heard speeches of the kind that orators offered day after day to the jobless gathered on the Lake Front. The young man, Albert R. Parsons, a printer and a member of the Typographical Union, was aware that no effective national organization of trade unions existed, yet literature was distributed at these gatherings by organizers who obviously had some kind of national structure. They called themselves Socialists or Anarchists and belonged to the International Workingmen's Association.

Parsons, when a teenager, had risked his life on the slaveowners' side of the Civil War, but soon after hostilities ended, he came full circle. In Waco, Texas, he edited a paper that advocated full rights for former slaves. Now, in Chicago, he was seeing evidence that others besides slaves suffered intensely under the economic system in the United States. Parsons was not yet ready to believe all the unfamiliar theories he heard from the orators, and he certainly could not guess that in a few years he would accept some of their ideas and become a leader of Chicago's organized labor or that in less than fifteen years he would be world famous, martyred in the Haymarket affair by the same social forces against which the jobless were parading in 1873.

Albert's wife, Lucy, had probably been born a slave, but the Ku Klux Klan was active around Waco where she lived, and she had not said that she had African ancestors when she and a white man became known as a married couple. Instead, she claimed Indian and Spanish forebears, which she also may have had. Like her husband, she was moved by the distress of 1873. Her sympathy led to a lifetime of organizing workers — beginning with seamstresses, women in her own trade — in every depression up to and including the 1930s.

Among the unemployed in December 1873, neither Lucy nor Albert Parsons was a leader, but both were learners. What they saw and learned in Chicago had a special quality because of special conditions in that city.

A large, unused relief fund ($700,000) existed in Chicago in 1873, and the unemployed wanted it released. The fund remained from gifts that had been sent to the Chicago Relief and Aid Society from all over the world following the great fire that had destroyed much of the city in 1871. This fund made history in the field of social work by initiating the practice of giving cash grants, but the recipients of the grants were generally those who had been deprived of property or its use by a physical disaster, not those who had been deprived of work by the decision of employers. The businessmen who supervised the fund had not distributed all the money that had been collected, and there were accusations (denied, of course) that they borrowed from the unspent surplus at bargain rates to finance their own enterprises.

The response of the unemployed was: If the money exists, it should be spent. We are Chicagoans, and we need relief. On December 21, 5,000 workers brought together by the International and trade unions demanded employment at a living wage and an eight-hour day for all who were willing to work. They also demanded food and money for their immediate needs and proposed that this relief be distributed by a committee appointed by the unemployed themselves. The next day, 20,000 workers marched to City Hall and asked that the money be distributed immediately. At a meeting the day after Christmas that included representatives of the unemployed, Mayor Joseph Medill, a committee of the Common Council, and representatives of the Relief and Aid Society, the society refused to turn over its surplus to the city.

The next step in the campaign was a demonstration at the headquarters of the society. The officers refused to meet with representatives of the unemployed, but when a thousand of them tried to crowd into the small rooms, the officers changed their minds. They promised to give relief, but only after the applicants had been vaccinated. A thousand jobless then tried to storm into the office of the society's doctor. At this point the society gave up, hired a corps of social workers to screen applications, and began to distribute some of its large surplus. Many applicants were refused, but about 10,000 families did get some help. The city of Chicago itself gave no relief.

All the demonstrations of the unemployed were closely watched and sometimes interfered with by the police — coppers or cops, Chicagoans called them. This title had been popular ever since 1858 when John C. Haines took office as mayor. He was known as "Copper Stock" Haines because of his speculation in the stocks of copper mining companies. The nickname applied to him quickly spread to his police and the name "Copper," shortened to "cop," stuck, possibly because policemen had copper buttons on their uniforms.

After the tense days at Christmastime, 1873, unemployed demonstrations continued. Before long, employers formed private military organizations and began to call for violence against "tramps" and strikers. Sentiments such as the following appeared in the press: "Hand grenades should be thrown among these union sailors, who are striving to obtain higher wages and less hours. By such treatment they would be taught a valuable lesson and other strikers would take warning from their fate." Tom Scott, president of the Pennsylvania Railroad, said, "Give them the rifle diet!"

In response, workers formed military organizations of their own. Germans enlisted in the *Lehr und Wehr Verein.* Bohemians had an organization they called the Sharp Shooters, and there were also the Irish Guards. An angry Lucy Parsons began using impassioned rhetoric. "When the ruling class advocated arsenic," said her biographer, "Lucy advocated arson. When the ruling class said destroy the human being, Lucy said destroy their property."

Violence was much in the air in the 1870s. The Ku Klux Klan prospered in the South. The army and frontiersmen were busy driving Indians off their land so that white settlers might enjoy it, and to many it seemed quite natural to recommend violence against the jobless who were insisting that they had rights. One solution to their problem, the jobless said, was the reduction of the working hours of the employed from twelve or ten hours a day to eight hours, without any reduction in wages. The eight-hour day would benefit both those who had jobs and those who needed them. If production levels were to be maintained with the same technology, employers would have to hire additional workers, thus reducing unemployment.

The campaign for the eight-hour day at no less pay had already gained some momentum by the time the crisis of 1873 set in. In spite of hard times, the labor organizations led by the International continued the campaign. Nevertheless, employers began to cut wages. The clear threat was "If you don't accept the wage cut, you will be replaced by an unemployed man who will be glad to get any pay at all."

Miners and railroad workers struck against both the wage cuts and efforts to destroy their unions. The late 1870s became one of the bloodiest periods in the long, bloody history of American employer-employee relationships. Many strikers were killed in encounters with private strike-breaking armies maintained by employers, some of which were organized by the Pinkerton Detective Agency. The Pinkertons, as the strike breakers were called, joined the police, the militia, and the regular army in using violence against strikers. These confrontations, although they were only indirectly related to unemployment, brought a new development to the labor movement during the great railroad strike of 1877. At that time, many of the unemployed joined the strikers and gave support by refusing to scab.

Before the depression ended, someone gave Albert Parsons a handbill announcing that Peter J. McGuire would speak at Turner Hall on the economic crisis. McGuire, a leader of the New York unemployed at the time of the Tompkins Square riot, was in Chicago representing the Social Democratic Party. "We have come together," he said, "without bands of music or waving banners. We have no money. . . . The workingman labors with all his strength not for himself and those rightly dependent upon him, but for every mean despot who has money in his pocket, and no principle in his head." At the end of the meeting, Parsons applied for membership in the party.

9

Dictator for a Season
(1877)

Resolved, All so-called tramp laws punishing unemployed working men as tramps are unconstitutional and inhuman as poverty is thereby made a crime. Therefore we demand their repeal.
— Socialist Labor Party National Convention, 1879

Eighteen seventy-seven was a year of great unemployment and of great violence in the relations between capital and labor. In California, a 32-year-old teamster tried to parlay turbulence into power, and in the process, Dennis Kearney, a native of Ireland, almost became an American Ceasar — or an American Hitler.

Kearney had already had a taste of bossing men. From 1868 to 1872 he had served as first officer on steamers in and out of San Francisco. Later, after the newly completed transcontinental railroad increased the overland flow of traffic, he saw a chance to invest his savings. First he bought a modest draying business consisting of three heavy wagons and the horses to pull them. Soon he also acquired political ambitions. When he became a United States citizen in 1876, he decided to prepare for political life by getting some education (his schooling had ended when he left Ireland at age 11 and went to sea).

In San Francisco, the place for adult education was the Lyceum of Self Culture. Debates went on there endlessly, and Kearney took part in them to develop the speaking skill he would need as he became a public figure. Time after time the nervous, but nervy, young man jumped up to hold forth in hesitant Irish English, and often what he said was not well received by the workingmen present. Those among them who had no jobs resented Kearney's insistence that they wouldn't be in distress if they had worked hard, saved their money, and abstained from alcohol and tobacco, as he did.

Fifteen thousand San Franciscans were idle in the spring of 1877 — and that number did not include the impoverished former speculators who now lived in Pauper Alley. Moreover, there had been other hard times in the recent past. In 1870, 3,000 men had tried to get work when 125 jobs opened up at Yerba Buena Park. A few days later those who were disappointed had gathered on the Sand Lot, a vacant space in front of the new City Hall, formed the San Francisco Workingmen's Society, and gone to the nearby mayor's office to demand jobs.

Failing to get work, they had hit upon what seemed an obvious cause for their troubles: the Chinese laborers, laundrymen, domestic servants, and gardeners who were still employed, albeit at very low wages. Although mass unemployment was general throughout the country and not just an affliction of the West Coast, many of San Francisco's jobless had leaped to the conclusion that these alien underbidders for work were to blame for unemployment. Committees had gone to employers demanding that the Chinese be fired and that white workers be hired to take their places. Few, if any, such appeals had been heeded in 1870.

The same kind of anti-Chinese agitation continued into 1877 and would go on for years to come. Still, Dennis Kearney maintained that the solution to the problems of the unemployed lay in diligence. The Chinese had a reputation for working hard, and he approved of that.

Even while Kearney argued, he saw crowds gathering on the Sand Lot to hear a very different point of view. At the Sand Lot (San Francisco's equivalent of London's Hyde Park), advocates of spiritualism and phrenology and every kind of religious and political belief vied for attention. Among them were speakers who agitated for the Workingmen's Party of the United States (WPUS). This party had been formed only the year before in

Philadelphia after the International Workingmen's Association (IWA) had dissolved, immobilized by three-way disputes between its Marxian, Lassallean, and Anarchist members.

Some of the IWA's members, nationally and in San Francisco, had joined the WPUS. Kearney saw vigor in their activities, even if their theories were strange to him, so he applied for membership. Some WPUS members, however, knew of his anti-working-class remarks at the Lyceum, where he was supposed to have referred to his audience as "them chaws," apparently scornfully stereotyping all workers as tobacco chewers. His application to the WPUS was rejected.

At about this time, the WPUS in San Francisco took steps to support a vast railroad strike that had broken out in the East and spread to the Midwest. The railroads, after imposing a 10-percent wage cut, announced a second cut. The railroad workers rebelled, and a ferocious struggle followed between the largest industry in the country and the men whose labor was essential to it. In what has been called the most violent year in American labor history, upheavals shook the country, and San Francisco felt the tremors.

The police were fearful on July 23, a day chosen by the WPUS for a rally in support of the railroad strikers. As a precautionary measure, officers arrested several men carrying banners through the streets to advertise the meeting. Before the police would allow the rally to go on, they demanded — and got — guarantees from the WPUS that its speakers would make no incendiary remarks. When 8,000 people gathered, they heard no calls for violence. Had the meeting been held anywhere else, and without prior police censorship, the tone of the speeches would, no doubt, have been the same. The WPUS was not a haven for terrorists.[1]

But violence was in the minds of some in San Francisco on July 23. Before the WPUS rally adjourned, an anti-Chinese organization marched up to the margin of the crowd with drums beating and flags flying. These "hoodlums" (a name that may have originated in San Francisco in the 1870s) wanted action. With their ranks enlarged by people whom they drew away from the WPUS rally, the hoodlums proceeded to demolish more than twenty Chinese laundries, and in an excess of zeal they also destroyed a plumbing shop that was not at all Chinese.

Rumors quickly spread that the hoodlums and the jobless planned to attack the dock of the Pacific Mail Steamship Company. This firm was widely regarded as the real cause of the Chinese "problem," for Pacific Mail ships had brought, and were still bringing, thousands of immigrants from China to California.

Businessmen were aghast. Some of them had profited by employing Chinese labor at very low wages. Others feared that if violence started, their property would be destroyed even though they did not hire Chinese. To prevent any assault on their very comfortable way of life, they followed an old San Francisco tradition: They organized vigilantes. In no time about 4,000 men were enrolled in the Committee of Safety and armed with hickory pick handles. Each handle was equipped with a thong that could be secured to its wielder's wrist. The vigilantes, among them Dennis Kearney, did not intend to be separated from their weapons in the heat of battle.

In addition to the Committee of Safety, soon known as the "pick handle brigade," all of the city police were mobilized. Units of the state militia also stood by, as did elements of the United States Army, Navy, and Marine Corps. Together, these forces prevented destruction of the Pacific Mail dock, but they did not save other parts of the city from massive arson. Many businesses went up in flames during three days of rioting. San Francisco, in all its turbulent years, had never seen such violence, and the rich of the city were afraid. As San Franciscan Henry George put it, they felt "the timidity which attaches to great wealth gained by questionable means." George also speculated about the state of mind of "the man who from the windows of a two million dollar mansion looks down on his fellow citizens begging for the chance to work for a dollar a day."

Dennis Kearney had joined the "pick handle brigade" on the side of businesses that employed Chinese, but when he saw the furious outpouring of hatred against the rich, he had second thoughts. The hoodlums and jobless together seemed to be a force that could propel him far and fast on a political career. Within a month of the WPUS rally and the riot that followed, Kearney had become anti-Chinese. He appeared only in workingmen's clothes and tried to set up an organization to compete with the WPUS. This first effort, called the Workingmen's Trade and Labor Union of San Francisco, failed. But Kearney persisted, and soon formed the Workingmen's Party of California (WPC), which quickly attracted followers. Almost overnight, he became a flamboyant soapboxer. His language, albeit inelegant, was picturesque and forceful.

In the name of the WPC, Kearney began to hold meetings, sometimes in halls or on street corners and every Sunday afternoon on the Sand Lot. Repeatedly he led hundreds, even thousands, of unemployed men to City Hall in fruitless searches for relief or jobs. Relief was given to some of the jobless by private charities, and some jobs were created by private sources, but the city assumed no responsibility.

Division had sharpened rapidly between the haves and have-nots of San Francisco. The unemployed were bitter toward the banks and large landowners and in particular the Central Pacific Railroad, which had a monopoly of railroad transportation in California.

On several occasions Kearney was arrested for inciting the wrath of the unemployed with statements such as "A little judicious hanging would be the best course to pursue with the Capitalists" and "Judge Lynch is the judge wanted by the workingmen of California. I advise you all to own a musket and a hundred rounds of ammunition." Arrests, plus a stay in jail awaiting trial, were all that he suffered for his utterances. He was convicted of "incendiary speech and terrorism," but the California Supreme Court reversed the conviction. Apparently the fire-eater did not lack powerful friends.

Kearney also had a goon squad that accompanied him to meetings, including rallies called by the WPUS, which he raided with considerable success. At all of his own gatherings,

Kearney's hoodlums took care of hecklers. They made credible the boast he seems to have shouted more than once: "I am the dictator!"

There is a familiar ring in Kearney's explosion onto the political scene and in the way he either opened or ended his speeches with the cry, "The Chinese must go!" Like a German would-be dictator fifty years later, Kearney soon had groups of unemployed men armed and drilled as military units, with San Francisco's businessmen-vigilantes as models. He also developed ward organizations throughout the city, apparently taking over at least a few Democratic Party clubs.

By the new year, Kearney's Workingmen's Party was ready to run candidates and to offer a platform calling for equal taxation, life imprisonment for malfeasance in office, restriction of the size of landholdings, abolition of Chinese labor, an end to prison contract labor, and an eight-hour day. The points on Chinese labor, prison labor, and the eight-hour day were particularly attractive to the unemployed because they aimed directly at making more work available to the jobless.

In a special election in January 1878 to fill a vacancy in the state senate, the winner was J. W. Bones, candidate of the Workingmen's Party. In elections held in February and March, Workingmen's candidates gained office in Oakland and Sacramento.

When Kearney's crusade first began to attract followers, one of those who attached themselves to the "dictator" was Carl Browne, a young man with eclectic offbeat sympathies and a talent for publicity. Browne soon found himself one of three members of the executive committee of the Workingmen's Party of California. He also established a weekly paper, the *Open Letter,* as organ of the party, and he cannily kept for himself a large block of stock in the corporation that controlled it. Kearney was the corporation's president. Browne did most of the writing for the *Open Letter* and drew cartoons and other illustrations for it. Before long he became private secretary to Kearney.

Meanwhile, the *San Francisco Chronicle* was glad to tempt readers away from its rival, the *Call,* by giving ample coverage to the doings and the sayings of the suddenly popular Sand Lot orator. While the *Chronicle* and the *Open Letter* whipped up excitement, Kearney was in and out of jail, as were several of his lieutenants. When he was free to do so, he led unemployed rallies and marches.

On January 3, 1878, 1,500 men gathered at City Hall to demand "work, bread or a place in the county jail." Civil servants inside the City Hall building were visibly shaken. Three men representing the crowd told the mayor they could no longer control their angry brothers. They proposed that capitalists contribute enough money to establish an industrial colony that could provide jobs for the jobless. The mayor himself had nothing to offer but promises, and the city, in fact, did nothing. It did not even support a move made in the legislature that was aimed at enabling San Francisco to employ 2,000 men for three months.

All in all, Kearney's movement prospered, although the unemployed did not, and Kearney, encouraged by Browne, began to have national ambitions. In July 1878, the two men went to Boston, ostensibly to see Kearney's aged mother but really to sound out sentiment in the East. Their discoveries did not lead to the formation of a national organization, but on the West Coast the Workingmen's Party of California continued to be an important force on the general political scene.

While Kearney was away from home, other leaders not connected with the Workingmen's Party of California had begun to lead unemployed marches. Clearly the "dictator's" presence was not required to prompt the jobless to seek means of solving their desperate problems. So militant were the new demonstrations that businessmen once more formed themselves into a vigilante Committee of Safety. They assembled an arsenal and paid the state militia to guard it.

No rioting broke out, but the continued agitation, particularly by the Workingmen's Party of California, did much to provoke the drafting in 1879 of a new state constitution. At the constitutional convention a third of the delegates were WPC members. Their point of view did not often prevail in the deliberations, but the document produced with their help, considerably amended over the years, is still in effect. In addition, one national consequence resulted from the WPC program. Congress passed legislation in 1882 that put a stop to Chinese immigration. Of course, the law did not stop unemployment. In fact, a new wave of joblessness began about the time Congress approved its racist-inspired exclusion of Chinese.

What produced the anti-Chinese movement that began in California and finally affected the whole country, including organized labor? Some historians have looked for its roots in the Know-Nothing movement in pre–Civil War days. This nativist effort probably did influence some among those who suddenly found themselves out of jobs in 1877, but American political life did not lack for racists before (or after) the Know-Nothings. Those who employed labor or wielded power had often found it useful to have division in the ranks of workers. They had also found it to their advantage when employees fought an enemy other than employers. Kearney, like other demagogues, was quick to learn the use of what historian Alexander Saxton called "the indispensable enemy."

American workers had plenty of reason to hate the "monopolies," Kearney's term for all big business. Profits were immense, and at the same time the distress of workers, both employed and unemployed, was equally formidable. By an easy displacement, many workers identified the Chinese with the businesses that employed Chinese. Both, many of the jobless demonstrators came to feel, had to be opposed. Neither the unemployed nor the employed workers considered organizing the Chinese into unions with the aim of protecting the American wage standard by bringing the wages of the Chinese up to that level.

Writing on the anti-Chinese agitation, John Philip Young said in his *San Francisco: A History of the Pacific Coast Metropolis* that it was "not a workingmen's movement. It is a false impression that it was due to the labor unions or to the prejudice of the working classes of the city." Young said the movement was "popular," apparently meaning it embraced people from a variety of walks of life. Kearney, however, called the movement a "workingmen's party," although it was as attractive to declassed hoodlums on the one hand and to certain businessmen and professionals on the other as it was to workers. He hoped to rise in the political world by directing the wrath of this amorphous lot of whites, including workers, against the Chinese. How conscious he was that his role would divide labor may never be known, but some of his enemies within the working-class movement accused him of accepting bribes from railroad interests. His speeches, they said, were written for him by Chester Hull, a reporter on the *Chronicle*, which was no working-class organ. The merit of such charges is now hard to gauge.

Dennis Kearney subsided almost as quickly as he erupted on the political scene. His WPC was soon absorbed into the Democratic Party. After he served briefly on the national executive committee of the short-lived Greenback Labor Party, he lapsed into mysterious silence. By 1884 he was entirely out of politics. Later he ran an employment agency and became a broker dealing in real estate and stocks.

Earlier, while Kearney was trying to turn the anger of the unemployed to his own advantage, others were prompted by the popular turbulence to move in their own ways. Henry George, a civil servant in the city, observed the juxtaposition of rich and poor, and on September 18, 1877, began to write *Progress and Poverty*, an unsettling book that was to have an immense audience.

With the collapse of the Workingmen's Party of California, and with increased employment, a curious and disturbing episode in unemployed history had come to a close.

10

Black Flag in America
(1883–1885)

At no time since the panic of 1873 have such large sums been expended in the erection of first-class business blocks and elegant and substantial private dwellings as at present.
— *New York Times*, July 14, 1880

The public be damned.
— William Henry Vanderbilt

All history has been a history of class struggles, of struggles between dominated and dominating classes at various stages of social development.
— Friedrich Engels

Peter McGuire, of the Tompkins Square demonstration, recruited not only Albert Parsons but also many others into the Social Democratic Party in the late 1870s. In 1881, as a founding member of the Brotherhood of Carpenters and Joiners, McGuire drafted the call for the convention that led to the formation of the American Federation of Labor. In the spring of 1882 he proposed to the Central Labor Union in New York that the first Monday in each September be set aside as a labor holiday. Thus Labor Day began, started by a carpenter and erstwhile leader of the unemployed.

For the first celebration of the new holiday, September 5, 1882, workers in New York assembled near City Hall without the difficulty they had experienced in 1874. They paraded up Broadway to what is now Bryant Park behind the Public Library

on Forty-second Street. There, they and their families pic-
nicked, danced, and listened to speeches.

McGuire and some other initiators of the festivities were
Socialists, but it was a sign of the times that their parade took
them past the Union Square Theater where a play, *The Black
Flag*, was currently showing. The black flag was a symbol of
Anarchism, and interest in this trend within the radical movement was considerable in 1882, the year Johann Most, a leading Anarchist, arrived from Europe.

Another man who remained in Europe but who influenced
the radical unemployed in the United States did not think
highly of Most, whom he knew well. Karl Marx called the
Anarchist a person "of most childish vanity. Every change of the
wind blows him first in one direction and then in another like a
weathercock." Marx would not have long to oppose the Anarchist's influence in the New World. Marx died in 1883, and Peter
McGuire was one of those who spoke at a New York memorial
service for him. Johann Most lived on until 1906.

An audience for agitators such as Most definitely existed in
1882. That year in Manhattan alone more than $5 million was
dispensed in charity, and in Brooklyn (still not connected to
Manhattan by a bridge) charity totalled another $1.5 million.
After a brief period of prosperity, a new depression was creeping
up, and the word *creeping* must be emphasized. It did not come
with a sudden shock, propelling workers into sudden reaction
as some previous depressions had done. Technological advances had led to overproduction; that is, consumption did not
keep pace with production. Prices fell, and factory owners then
curtailed production and laid off workers. This depression,
unlike some that had gone before, did not begin with a collapse
of banks, but its effect on workers was the same as in all the
others: They could not find jobs.

To measure unemployment there was now a new federal
agency, the Bureau of Labor Statistics, which the International
Workingmen's Association had been the first to propose. In
1882, the bureau sent fifteen investigators into the field to take
a census of the jobless. They came up with a figure of 1 million,
which was 7.5 percent of the work force.

Terence V. Powderly, master workman of the Knights of Labor, put the figure for the unemployed at 2 million. Powderly was fearful of any action by either this large number of jobless or by the employed. He said in an inner organization circular:

> The number of the unemployed is very great and constantly increasing. Reduction of wages, suspension of men, stoppage of factories and furnaces are a daily occurrence. With such a state of affairs staring us in the face, a word of warning cannot be amiss. Indulge in no hasty or ill-advised action, no matter how great the provocation to strike against an injustice or a grievance of any kind. Count well the costs before taking the action. Remember that the winter is upon us, the dull season of the year is at hand, the number of unemployed so great that the chances of filling the places of strikers are very numerous.

In spite of such advice, workers, seeking aid from some kind of organization, turned to the Knights of Labor in increasing numbers. In 1883 the organization had 52,000 members, the next year the number grew to 71,000, and in 1885 it was 111,000. By 1886, estimates ranged from 300,000 to 500,000. Some even said there were 1 million in the organization, which admitted unskilled workers, employers, women, and African-Americans, as well as the skilled male white workers sought after by craft unions.

Not all members of this semifraternal, educational organization were as timid as Powderly. Some local branches conducted strikes. One strike led by Joseph Buchanan against a group of railroads (the Wabash, Missouri Pacific, and Union Pacific) owned by Jay Gould was vast in scope and successful.

The rebellious mood of many in the organization was reflected in songs like the following, which were popular among the Knights:

> Up with the banner, boys,
>   Blow the trumpet's call;
> Fall in and march, be brave, boys—
>   Monopoly must fall.

While the continuing depression stirred antimonopoly sentiments among both the employed and the jobless, new immigrants kept arriving. In 1883, Emma Lazarus, a banker's daughter who had sympathy for the unemployed (but no direct experience of unemployment), wrote a verse for the pedestal of the Statue of Liberty:

> Give me your tired, your poor,
> Your huddled masses yearning to breathe free,
> The wretched refuse of your teeming shore.
> Send these, the homeless, tempest-tossed to me,
> I lift my lamp beside the golden door!

At the end of the year in which these words were unveiled, New York politicians in a public relations gesture announced that there would be one-time distribution of free food — "Bread for the Hungry" — on December 29. So many women and children appeared that day on the steps of City Hall that there was almost a riot.

America's Gilded Age was an epoch, to use the words of Charles and Mary Beard, "when physical force was a normal part of business procedure." Brickyard workers in New Jersey worked under brutal conditions, and J. P. McDonnell, a left-wing editor of the Paterson, New Jersey *Labor Standard*, was jailed for publishing a letter that exposed those working conditions. In Chicago, seamstresses, many of whom were immigrants, often worked in crowded, unsanitary rooms for twelve, sometimes even sixteen, hours a day, and they barely earned enough to exist on. More visible in Chicago were the thousands of men who gravitated to the city hoping to find work. There, large numbers of them could not even find shelter. On the coldest nights many tried to keep warm by constantly moving around outdoor fires. When they quit trying, their bodies were found in Lake Michigan.

Earlier, at the time of the 1877 railroad strike, Lucy Parsons had seen local police, state militia, and finally federal troops used against striking workers. She read in the *Socialist* accounts of widows of workers who died because they could not afford medical care. She knew of children who had starved to death. She who had come from a slave background had seen that only the violence of the Civil War had ended the violence that was the institution of slavery. More and more it seemed to her that the callousness of Chicago's wealthy could only be ended by their forcible overthrow. The Anarchist theories of Johann Most were at hand to reinforce her own deeply emotional responses to the suffering she saw around her.

In 1884 when Albert Parsons, who had risen to a position of influence in the Chicago labor movement, started a new radical paper, the *Alarm*, Lucy contributed to the first issue an open letter to "tramps":

> A word to the 30,000 now tramping the streets of this great city, with hands in pockets, gazing listlessly about you at the evidences of wealth and pleasure of which you own no part, not sufficient even to purchase your self a bit of food with which to appease the pangs of hunger gnawing at your vitals.
>
> Have you not worked hard all your life, since you were old enough for your labor to be of use in the production of wealth? . . . Yet your employer told you that it was overproduction that made him close up.

She then addressed those among the unemployed who, she had good reason to believe, were contemplating suicide. She proposed that they leap into the lake in front of the "voluptuous" homes of the rich after availing themselves of "those little methods of warfare which Science has placed in the hands of the poor man. . . . *Learn the use of explosives!*" There is no record that individual acts of terror increased following this advice, which was general in tone and did not suggest specific targets.

Other voices at the same time gave more hope, urging acts less likely to provoke violent retaliation. The *Alarm* itself, in a column adjoining the one in which Lucy Parsons made her emotional appeal, ran a satiric fable by the English Socialist William Morris. In the form of a debate of chickens before a feast, the topic discussed was "With what sauce shall we be eaten?" At a certain point one of the chickens rudely interrupted the argument by announcing, "I don't want to be eaten at all!" In spite of Anarchist calls for flamboyant deeds by individuals and for individual acts of violence, many workers gravitated toward collective actions that fell far short of using dynamite.

At weekly meetings on a desolate strip of land on the Lake Front, speakers made platforms out of salt barrels. Depending on the weather, sometimes as many as 1,000 employed and unemployed workers gathered to hear attacks on the private ownership of the means of production. There were few, if any, demands for public works. The speakers of all shades of socialist opinion seemed to have lost any hope they once might have had that Chicago's officials would give them work.

The focus of pressure was not on government, but on the "rich." A demonstration called for Thanksgiving Day, 1884, is an example of the texture and tendency of the movement. The International Working People's Association, which was the current title of the Anarchist-tinged break away from the International Workingmen's Association, distributed 25,000 leaflets before Thanksgiving. These fliers, announcing the demonstrations, were addressed "TO WAGE-WORKERS, THE UNEMPLOYED AND 'TRAMPS!', *Women and Men, Sisters and Brothers.*"

In spite of rain mixed with snow that lasted all day, several thousand appeared and stayed in attendance. Albert Parsons chaired the meeting and made heavy use of biblical quotations to attack the rich. He introduced a lengthy resolution vaguely insisting that the wealth and the work of the world should be shared by all. After more long speeches, the shivering crowd marched through the Chicago streets where many bankers, railroad owners, and merchants had their homes. At the head of the procession were the black flag of anarchism and the red flag of communism.

Here was high drama — the angry poor marching to the doorsteps of the rich. There was no lack of courage among the marchers, but out of the affair came no practical plan to feed the hungry tomorrow, next week, or next year. Labor organizer Mother Jones saw some of the demonstrations in Chicago and said, "The workers asked only for bread and the shortening of

the long hours of toil. The agitators gave them visions. The
police gave them clubs."

Unemployment continued to rise. Applications for help from
the Chicago Relief and Aid Society were up 61 percent in 1885
compared with 1884. But the staff of the society was skillful at
its task of protecting dwindling resources. In 1874, only 50
percent of those who applied for relief received it from the
society, and there is no reason to believe that the percentage
was greater ten years later. The response of the unemployed,
led by the International Working People's Association, was to
stage another huge demonstration and parade on Thanksgiving
Day, 1885.

What else could they do? One dramatic suggestion of a
national plan to try to solve the problem of unemployment
originated in San Francisco. There, in 1886, Joseph R. Buchanan, who had led the great Knights of Labor strike against
the Gould railroads, had been asked to try to bring about some
unity within the sharply divided radical labor movement. In the
course of a speech to a labor group, Buchanan urged workers
to elect workingmen to Congress. A carpenter in the audience
interrupted.

> Your advice as to voting for the right kind of men for Congress
> may be all right, and I am willing to act upon it when the time
> comes; but it will be a long time before that course, even if
> successful, can bring us the relief we so sorely need. The
> question is what can we do now? I am one of the million who
> are hunting for work; begging for the opportunity to earn the
> food my wife and children must have if they are not to starve.
> I agree with you that Congress should do something for us in
> this awful emergency, but it is blind to our sufferings and deaf
> to our appeals. How will you arouse it? What will we do now —
> tonight — this very hour?

The hall was silent. Buchanan rose and spoke. "Stand up
comrade," he said to the carpenter.

> I am going to answer your question to the best of my ability.
> You did not ask it to corner me or to cause annoyance; I know

that cry; it came from your bursting heart. First let me say that I never give advice that I am not willing to act upon myself; but it is for you to lead in this matter; I promise to follow you and to aid in your support.

You are a carpenter. Go out from here and build a banner or transparency. I will give the little money required to purchase the sticks, nails, and muslin. Find a painter who, like yourself, is asking, "What shall we do now?" and have him paint upon the sides of your banner the words, "ON TO WASHINGTON!" At sunrise to-morrow morning, with your painter comrade meet me on the Sand-Lots and bring the banner with you. We will open a recruiting office on the Lots, and when we have a score of marchers in line we will start down Market Street, gathering the unemployed, the hungry, the wretched as we go. We'll cross the bay and in Oakland will confiscate a train, if that is thought desirable, or tramp along on foot, but with our faces ever turned toward the East. . . . We will gather the disinherited as we march and the millions of betrayed and plundered will cry with us, "ON TO WASHINGTON!" We will take the food we require for our actual needs, leaving vouchers to be cashed at Washington when the people once more regain their government.

When we have massed our great host of Industrial Crusaders about the Capitol, and packed Pennsylvania Avenue from Capitol to White House, we will demand of our servant, Congress, that it give us at once the justice that has been so long delayed. If it heeds not our commands, if it still defies us, we will hurl the whole treacherous swarm into the Potomac!

Buchanan's proposal astonished everyone, including the carpenter who had asked the question. "But my dear sir," he said, "what you propose might come to revolution."

Buchanan gulped. He was an advocate of peaceful transition to socialism. "I hadn't thought of that," he said lamely.

The meeting approved Buchanan's proposal of a march on Washington, although nothing practical was done that night or in the following days to implement it. But when the next depression came, in the inexorable way of depressions, the workers of San Francisco remembered the slogan, "ON TO WASHINGTON!" It was from that city that the biggest of many armies of unemployed workers started for the nation's capital in 1894.

11

Anarchists and Agitators
(1883–1893)

If you dam up the river of progress —
    At your peril and cost let it be;
That river must seawards despite you —
    'Twill break down your dams and be free;
And we heed not the pitiful barriers
    That you in its way have down cast;
For your efforts but add to the torrent,
    Whose flood must overwhelm you at last.

CHORUS:
For our banner is raised and unfurled;
At your head our defiance is hurled;
Our cry is the cry of the ages —
Our hope is the hope of the world.
              — "The Hope of the Ages," words by E. Nesbit
        in *I.W.W. Songs to Fan the Flames of Discontent*, n.d.

In February 1893, a big business, the National Cordage Company, paid its stockholders a 100-percent dividend. Five months later the company closed its doors because it could not pay its debts. Creditors began to demand payment from other companies, and many of them could not meet their obligations. Soon 16,000 firms were bankrupt, and hundreds of banks had collapsed. Economists disagree about what caused the ensuing depression, but all agree that the decline of business activity was catastrophic. According to some estimates, almost three-fourths of the work force in the United States was unemployed by the end of the year. In August, when it became clear that unemployment was increasing, Emma Goldman, a 24-year-old Jewish refugee from Tsarist Russia, was in Rochester, New York. She had gone there to rest, because her doctor had told her she had incipient tuberculosis. Before that, she had been working long hours as a seamstress and longer hours organizing the defense of her Anarchist lover, Alexander Berkman, who was on trial for attempted murder. (Berkman, as a grand gesture against oppression, had tried to assassinate Henry C. Frick, harsh enemy of labor, who was chairman of the Carnegie Steel Company.) But when the economic crisis of 1893 sent thousands of workers into the streets, Goldman forgot about her health, went back to New York City, and rushed into strenuous activity among the jobless.

Goldman was not quite five feet tall, but she made up in energy what she lacked in height. Early and late she collected food, ran errands, and helped to conduct meetings in Union Square. With a permit duly obtained from the police, a rally in the square was called August 23 "to promote local, state and public works for the unemployed." The state legislature had just refused to do anything for the jobless, and the 3,000 to 4,000 workers who assembled to hear Goldman speak listened eagerly to the furious words that poured from the diminutive Anarchist, who was eloquent in several languages. She had never moved an audience more than on that evening, especially in a portion of her speech that was delivered in German, urging workers to demand what was rightfully theirs — beginning with the bread they so sorely needed. The audience cheered and waved, and Goldman said afterward their hands looked like "the wings of white birds fluttering."

The next day Goldman went to Philadelphia for further agitation among the unemployed. As she entered the meeting hall where she was to speak, she was arrested for her part in the Union Square gathering. A New York police officer, Detective Charles Jacobs, conducted her back to Manhattan. On the train he offered her inducements, including money, to become a spy in the radical movement. Goldman replied by throwing a glass of water in his face.

New York's Superintendent of Police, Thomas F. Byrnes, angered by Goldman's refusal to cooperate, threatened her with a long stay in jail. (He also threatened physical violence, but then thought better of it.) Goldman was sentenced to a year on Blackwell's Island after she was found guilty of inciting to riot. At the trial, Detective Jacobs testified against her. Although he admitted he was no stenographer, Jacobs claimed he had taken down verbatim what she said in her Union Square speech. He insisted she had urged workers to go out and seize bread by force. Emma Goldman denied saying this, and Jacob's testimony was not decisive in her conviction. In truth, she was found guilty because of her anticapitalist ideas and radical beliefs.

Goldman's beliefs were those of the rather formless group of New York Anarchists. They opposed what they called the exploitation of man by man, and they looked forward to a cooperative society infused with the spirit of equality and love. Many of them felt that it was pointless for workers to try to remedy their situation at the ballot box, as bourgeois politics was corrupt and rigged to benefit the employing class. Trade unions, too, were largely traps, tying workers to the capitalist system. Some Anarchists preached what they called "propaganda of the word." Others preached "propaganda of the deed," which meant direct action, including violence, to bring about a world in which love and justice could prevail. It did not matter whether Anarchists spread their gospel by word or by deed; all were assumed by the authorities to favor violence, and the reaction was vigorous — in Goldman's case a year in jail, which effectively separated her from the unemployed she was trying to influence. (This lopping-off of leaders such as Goldman was to be a continuing tactic of authorities throughout the depression.)

When she was released from jail, enthusiastic friends held a public meeting in her honor. There was also a welcome for her at the saloon on First Street that was the unofficial headquarters of radicals in 1894, as it had been in 1874. The cordial proprietor was still Justus Schwab, one of those arrested at the riot in Tompkins Square.

While still in jail, Emma Goldman had become interested in nursing. After her release she took training, and later she had a job caring for a madam who was a drug addict. One of the woman's former clients, Goldman discovered, had been Detective Jacobs. In the meantime, Police Superintendent Byrnes had been forced to resign because an investigating committee had revealed that he and many of his officers had been taking kickbacks from brothel keepers, streetwalkers, criminal gangs, and pickpockets. Men such as Detective Jacobs and Superintendent Byrnes did nothing to change Goldman's ideas about politics.

While Emma Goldman was preparing her Union Square rally, Lucy Parsons was arranging a similar meeting in Chicago. Now the widow of Albert Parsons, who had been executed for his anarchist ideas, she received a tremendous welcome August 21, 1893, from thousands of unemployed workers in Metropolitan Hall.

"Now is my harvest time," she said. "I attempt no concealment of the fact that I, with other true-hearted Anarchists will take advantage of your present condition to teach you the principles of the true faith. . . . You are the sole producers; why should you not consume? . . . Your salvation lies in stirring you to desperate action. . . . Let our streets run with gore but let us have justice. . . . You must no longer die and rot in tenement houses. . . . Shoulder to shoulder with one accord you should rise and take what is yours."

Both Goldman, a Jewish refugee, and Parsons, an African-American woman from the South, had voiced the angers and hostilities of the jobless. But anarchist "principles of faith" had little effect in the world outside the meeting hall.

In the summer of 1893, the American Federation of Labor responded to the new depression with measures to defend its members. The national leaders, one of whom was Peter J. McGuire, began to urge that the jobless hold mass demonstrations. McGuire continued to have an interest in the unemployed, just as he had in 1874, when he played a role in the Tompkins Square demonstration. The AFL now began to organize the unemployed into federal labor unions, and the national office sent George Edwin McNeill on a tour to speak at meetings of the jobless in Albany, Buffalo, Toledo, Detroit, Owosso, Indianapolis, Cincinnati, Columbus, and Chicago.

In Chicago, trade unions held a meeting on the Lake Front in August. Speakers urged that the hours of the employed be reduced so that there could be work for all, that the government establish public works and build roads, and that the jobless be given fiat money (specially printed paper bills that were not backed by specie). After the meeting the workers marched through the city streets to make known their demands and the nature of the organizations supporting them: trade unions and the Socialist Labor Party.

Out of this activity grew a union-controlled Labor and Temporary Relief Committee, which forced the city council to appropriate funds for public works and relief to be administered by the committee. It was the first time anywhere in the United States that workers obtained control over relief funds. They succeeded in getting jobs for 1,400 men on public works, specifically on a drainage canal. Two thousand more were employed at substandard wages on street repairs. The jobs lasted only a month.

The depression continued to deepen as the thirteenth annual convention of the American Federation of Labor assembled in Chicago December 11–19. A vice-president of the organization, Thomas J. Morgan, a Chicagoan and a member of the Machinists International Union, proposed that the assembled delegates go on record in support of two resolutions he introduced. The first read: "*Resolved,* That while this convention applauds the humane efforts of private individuals to relieve the terrible distress of the unemployed, at the same time we must respectfully, but emphatically insist that it is the province, duty and in the power of our city, state and national governments to give immediate and adequate relief."

The second resolution read: "*Resolved,* That a system of society which denies to the willing man the opportunity to work, then treats him as an outcast, arrests him as a vagrant and punishes him as a felon, is by this convention condemned as inhuman and destructive of the liberties of the human race, and *Resolved,* That the right to work is the right to life, that to deny the one is to destroy the other. That when the private employer cannot or will not give work the municipality, state or nation must."

Both resolutions were adopted by the convention with Samuel Gompers presiding. Perhaps Gompers, as he heard these proposals, recalled the events in Tompkins Square that he had witnessed two decades before. Certainly it is known that he was moved by the new wave of joblessness. At a meeting of the unemployed in Madison Square Garden in New York on January 30, 1894, he protested the starvation that affected large masses of citizens, and then recited the following inflammatory lines (a performance that he, an essentially conservative person, later regretted):

> Let conflagration illumine the outraged skies!
> Let red Nemesis burn the hellish clan
> And Chaos end the slavery of man!

The AFL agitated actively among the jobless in eastern cities and may have had some influence on events in Danbury, Connecticut, where hat workers were unemployed because of a lockout. The workers availed themselves of the New England institution called a town meeting, at which all citizens can take part in making decisions for the community. The jobless hatters attended the Danbury town meeting in such numbers that they were able to vote themselves $50,000 for relief. The town selectmen, however, had veto power over such decisions, and they barred payment of this relief money.

In Chicago in the winter of 1893–1894, at least 65,000 men were out of work, according to a survey conducted by *Bradstreets,* a business publication. A University of Chicago professor estimated 100,000 Chicagoans were unemployed. Cash relief, in addition to the public works, averaged only ten dollars per person and was given out to a total of only 30,000 persons. In New York City, which had 80,000 to 85,000 unemployed, according to the same surveys, relief was given to only 50,000 and averaged fifty dollars per person for the entire winter.

Local relief measures were clearly inadequate in relation to a problem that was vast and national. Estimates of the jobless in the whole country ranged from 1 million to 4.5 million, and there was no national program for dealing with all of these people, who until recently had been employed and self-supporting.

Perhaps some unemployed workers wished they still had the frontier as a possible route of escape from some of their difficulties. Earlier the jobless had been among those who followed Horace Greeley's advice: "Go West, young man." When the final depression of the nineteenth century paralyzed the economy, however, that route had virtually disappeared, and the unemployed had to seek another.

In their search they sometimes had the aid of labor organizers in places besides Chicago and Danbury. In Denver, unemployed miners who came in from the mountains were aided by the Trade and Labor Assembly, which set up a tent colony called Camp Relief. This settlement was entirely administered by its jobless residents. The Trade and Labor Assembly also fed 550 jobless workers a day at the Maverick Restaurant.

In many parts of the West, the jobless started to move around in search of work. In California, at first, they simply went up and down the coast looking for job openings. On harvesting and railroad construction crews, on ships, and in mining and lumber camps, they had worked in groups. Now it followed, almost as a matter of routine, that they tried to solve their common problem of joblessness in groups. This time they tried to make the railroads, the nation's largest industry, help them. The West Coast unemployed rode trains without paying fares as they looked for work in private industry. In 1894, they began using the railroads, which many of them had helped build, as instruments in a vast effort to persuade the federal government to employ them on public works. From all over the country, at least forty-two armies of unemployed men (and some women) headed for Washington, D.C., in order to petition Congress.

12

Armies Form
(1894)

Starving in a land of plenty
Hunger-lines on haggard faces
Thousands tramping on and on —
In search of work in far off places.

— P. J. Maas
The *American Federationist*, May 1895

As far as I am aware no attempt has yet been made in any country to deal comprehensively with the question of the unemployed.

— Geoffrey Drage
The Unemployed, 1894

"On to Washington!" had been a slogan proposed by trade union leader Joseph Buchanan in San Francisco in 1886. By the spring of 1894, after nearly a year of mass unemployment, the slogan was transformed into action. Certainly the idea of petitioning Congress for public works was in the wind, in part as a result of one man's flair for getting publicity. Carl Browne, who had been an imaginative assistant to Dennis Kearney when he agitated among the jobless in San Francisco in 1877, was now in the Midwest. There he put his talent to work for Jacob S. Coxey, who had developed a grand scheme for ending unemployment. Thanks in large part to Browne's public relations activity, the small army that Coxey assembled and led to Washington has received attention out of proportion to its real role in other migrations of the jobless in 1894. Coxey's Army is covered in Chapter 14, but to put the record straight about masses of the unemployed who were in motion on the West Coast, their story leads off.

On April 2, 1894, a great crowd of unemployed men in San Francisco petitioned Mayor Ellert for enough money to buy ferry tickets so they could cross the bay to Oakland on the first leg of a projected journey to the nation's capital. At first the mayor refused, but demonstrations continued, and on April 4 he agreed to pay twenty-five dollars for passage on the ferry for 600 of the jobless. Another 900, who wanted to go by ferry but did not get tickets, set out by whatever means they could. Many bypassed Oakland and headed straight for Sacramento, where they planned to rendezvous with the 600 ferry riders.

Most of these men were already familiar with the only means of transportation that made possible direct contact between the people and their representatives in the national capital. In the course of job hunting, they had learned how to avoid railroad guards and to ride in, on top of, or underneath boxcars. On passenger trains they could cling to the end of a baggage car that had no opening into the next car. Here, on the "blind," they had a fair chance of being unnoticed once the train had picked up speed.

The delegation from San Francisco planned to cross the entire continent in this fashion, although they had no money for shelter or clothes or food along the way. However, as Jack London, who joined the migration, said later, "The very poor constitute the last resource of the hungry tramp. The very poor can always be depended on. They never turn away the hungry. Time and again all over the United States have I been refused food at the big house on the hill; and always have I received food from the little shack on the creek or marsh, with its broken windows stuffed with rags and its tired-faced mother, broken with labor."

As matters turned out, the unemployed on their way to Washington often had help from people who weren't very poor. Gifts came from canny citizens who simply wanted to get the hungry army out of town. There were also gifts from the Knights of Labor, from Populists, and from labor unions made up of those who still had jobs.

Meanwhile, the mayor of Oakland was less than cordial when the 600 unemployed from San Francisco arrived suddenly on his doorstep. Although his own supply of jobless was large, he was prevailed on to provide temporary shelter in the Mills Tabernacle, a building big enough to hold the visitors. Oakland citizens collected $200 to help defray their expenses.

Before these San Franciscans crossed the bay, a man known as "Colonel" William Baker had given them a semblance of form. They were divided into companies, and each company had officers. Here was an army, calling itself an Industrial Army (possibly after a term used in Edward Bellamy's recent, widely read utopian novel *Looking Backward*). In Oakland, Baker suddenly announced that he had to go home. Overnight a short, slender, 32-year-old printer and member of the Socialist Labor Party, Charles T. Kelly, took command. Kelly had held no post at all when the army left San Francisco, but as an active union man, he had learned something about organizing, and he had also served an apprenticeship in the Salvation Army. Now he was leaving home, he said, because, "In a matter like this, a man must be either a man or a serf. He must do his duty, and his family must be a second consideration."

Although he was usually soft-spoken, seeming to observers rather like a divinity student, Kelly soon showed that he could be decisive. The men began to call him "General" and considered him above all the officers they already had, including the absent Colonel Baker. Probably the leap from private to general happened on the morning of April 5. The mayor of Oakland had said that the marchers must leave town that day, and the Southern Pacific Railroad had agreed to transport them to Sacramento if they would part with the $200 that had been collected from Oakland citizens. For this sum the army expected to ride in coaches, but the railroad supplied only six boxcars.

Kelly looked at the men. There were between 1,500 and 2,000 of them now, and they were all supposed to ride in six boxcars. "We do not propose to be pushed into such cars like hogs!" he shouted. At once he had the men with him, and he led them back to the Tabernacle where they had spent the previous night. They had been ordered not to reenter it, but reenter they did.

The mayor fancied he knew a crisis when he saw one. He mobilized the entire police force, had the sheriff swear in a great many deputies, and demanded militia from the governor. All of these forces of law and order planned to surround the Tabernacle at 2:00 on the morning of April 6, drive the jobless out, and herd them into freight cars — of which the Southern Pacific had now agreed to supply seven.

When the men in the Tabernacle heard the order to leave, suddenly issued in the middle of the night, they refused to obey. The police entered, arrested Kelly, and took him away. The men refused to budge without him. He was returned to them and led them to the waiting train — the same six cars. Again they refused to enter. A seventh car appeared before dawn, and only then did the army leave. To avoid what had happened in Oakland, officials in Sacramento hastened to arrange transportation and sped the train on its way eastward.

The governor of Utah, warned of the approach of this horde of the dispossessed, refused to cooperate. He ordered the railroad not to bring the army into his state, but the loaded train arrived anyway. The Utah courts then ordered the Southern Pacific to take the men back to California. Both the railroad officials and the men on their train refused to obey.

At this point Governor Waite of Colorado stepped into the controversy. He was a Populist, a vehement reformer, and he thoroughly approved of the demands of the unemployed for public works. Waite invited the army to pass through Colorado, but both the Union Pacific and the Denver & Rio Grande railroads, giving different reasons, declined to carry the jobless through the state free of charge. The members of the army not only could not pay, they would not pay passenger fares. They shared a Populist hatred of the railroad corporations that had been given huge quantities of public land and subsidies out of the public treasury, and then charged what they pleased for transporting freight and passengers and paid what they pleased to their employees. Some in Kelly's army had been involved in the bloody railroad strikes of 1877, and another big strike was approaching. They all wanted something now from the railroads to which the public had contributed so much. Some Socialists in the army ("Colonel" George Speed, the leader from Sacramento, for one) helped keep these sentiments alive.

During the court controversy between Utah's governor and the railroads, Kelly's army remained stalled at Ogden, where 10,000 people, many with guns, lined the streets when the train arrived. At this point Kelly was absent for several days, but the structure of the army remained intact. Order prevailed in the camp the men made near the tracks, and the citizens of Ogden, who had been frightened at first, turned friendly.

Meanwhile, Kelly had gone to Salt Lake City to confer with the governor. Colonel Baker was also on hand again. They had both just rejoined the army when the mayor of Ogden came to their camp and ordered them to leave. Kelly quietly agreed to obey, apparently because he had worked out a plan for transportation.

The men left Ogden on foot, preceded and followed by cavalry, but they did not walk very far. They soon came to a twenty-six-car Union Pacific freight train. When the 1,200 members of the army proceeded to "capture" the train, its crew put up no resistance.

The cars rolled eastward, with only a few stops. Fortunately the army's commissary had three days' rations that had been collected in Ogden, and at some towns along the way more food was donated. In Cheyenne, for example, the army received 3,000 loaves of bread and six beeves to be slaughtered for meat. All was well, or at least as comfortable as boxcars could be in weather that went below freezing at night.

Jack London recorded the depth of the cold in a diary he kept while he tried to catch up with the main body of the army. He had missed connections in Oakland because of its hasty forced departure. One night along the way, the young tramp woke up "half frozen to death"; it took him thirty minutes of vigorous walking to restore sensation to his feet.

London was not alone in trying to overtake the train. There were hundreds, most of whom seemed to have fought a losing battle with railroad guards. One who had managed to join the army for a short while as it crossed western Nevada was William

D. ("Big Bill") Haywood, a tall, husky, one-eyed, 25-year-old who at times had been a cowboy and at other times a miner. Right now he couldn't find work at either trade and was deeply depressed. "I could not understand the problem of unemployment," he wrote in his autobiography years later. "Nor could I find the reason for thousands of men crossing the continent and going to Washington. . . . These panics in which workers were the chief sufferers were the outgrowth of the capitalist system. But the cure or preventive did not then occur to me. I struggled along in mental darkness."

In April 1894, Haywood was so discouraged that he soon dropped out of Kelly's army at Winnemucca, Nevada, and turned back westward to the slight comfort his family could give him. Eleven years later, he opened the founding convention of the Industrial Workers of the World (the IWW) a revolutionary syndicalist organization that was to lead some of the unemployed in another depression. Among those over whom Haywood presided at this founding convention was Colonel George Speed of Kelly's army. By the time Haywood wrote his autobiography in 1920, he had come to regard Kelly's and other Industrial Armies as "one of the greatest unemployed demonstrations that ever took place in the United States."

Jack London also had failed to understand the mass movement of "tramps" or "hoboes" in which he had taken part briefly. His diary has almost nothing to say about the political objectives of Kelly's army, which had first excited him in Oakland, his hometown. At that time, young London was doing the work of two men in order to get one man's pay, shoveling coal for thirteen hours a day, twenty-nine days a month. When he heard about the hundreds of men headed for far places, he suddenly chucked his job and set out, just a few hours too late, to join them. It took him days to overtake Kelly, and at one place he encountered eighty-four other jobless men who, like himself, were trying to catch up with the army.

"I found . . . a big refrigerator car with the leeward door open to give ventilation, and I climbed in," London wrote. "I stepped on a man's leg, next on some other man's arm. The light was

dim, and all I could make out was arms and legs and bodies...
. They were all lying in the straw, and over, and under and
around one another."

The men cheerfully tossed London above them until he
landed in a small bit of unoccupied space. "I was initiated," he
said,

> and into a jolly crowd. All the rest of the day we rode through
> [a] blizzard, and to while time away it was decided that each
> man was to tell a story. It . . . must be a good one, and
> furthermore it must be a story no one had ever heard before.
> The penalty for failure was the thrashing machine [that is, the
> process of being tossed around — F.F.]. Nobody failed. And I
> want to say right here, never again have I sat at so marvelous
> a story telling debauch. Here were eighty-four from all over the
> world — I made eighty-five, and each man told a masterpiece.

The yarn-spinning, roughhousing tramps eluded the railroad bulls, as they called the guards, and some of them, London included, reached Omaha. There they joined the main body
of Kelly's army, which had arrived three days after leaving
Ogden.

Thousands of Nebraskans on the west bank of the Missouri
River cheered the train. In Omaha, trade unions held rallies,
passed resolutions in favor of petitioning Congress for public
works, and raised food and funds for the "Industrials," as
Kelly's followers had begun to call themselves. The Knights of
Labor and the Woodmen of the World also busied themselves on
behalf of the boxcar riders. Populists on both sides of the river
gave enthusiastic support.

The Industrials passed through Omaha, then across the
river, through Council Bluffs, and on east of the city to the
Chautauqua grounds, where they camped and waited for new
transportation to be arranged. Although there was a large
empty auditorium nearby, the men, exhausted from their long
journey in freight cars, were not allowed to take shelter in it.
They had to sleep in mud and spent the following day outdoors
in the rain. Newspapers estimated that about 30,000 sightseers

came from Omaha and Council Bluffs to marvel at the army that had "stolen" a train and also to protest the conditions under which the men were forced to camp.

It turned out that new transportation was not forthcoming. One and all, the railroads east of the Missouri refused to allow the men to ride except at full passenger rates. The attorney for one of the railroads, however, offered to provide free transportation to the Iowa militia. Several hundred militiamen were soon on hand — using the big auditorium.

After four days of misery on the Chautauqua grounds, Kelly gave up hope of getting a train and prepared his army to leave on foot. Now it truly would be a "petition in boots," as many were already calling it. Meanwhile, the unions in Omaha had decided to march to Council Bluffs and demand that the railroads provide a train for the men so they could present their petition in Washington.

Union representatives asked the operators of the bridge across the river to waive the usual toll, and the operators readily agreed to do so if the union members would break step as they crossed. There was a very real danger that the bridge might collapse if too many marched on it striding in unison. A count was kept of the tolls *not* collected. The number was 3,500. Another 1,000 sympathizers crossed over by train. The demonstration that these 4,500 union members held in Council Bluffs was spirited but fruitless. The railroad companies were not moved. There would be no train provided for Kelly's army.

After hearing this, 200 Council Bluffs women, headed by Mrs. Fred Harmon, tried to see Iowa's Governor Jackson, who was in the city. They wanted him to order the railroads to provide a train. The governor was not available, but the attorney for one of the railroads was. He admitted that the governor had the legal power to demand a train to move the men across the state. The women then asked the lawyer a pointed question. "Will we be punished if we seize a train?" The lawyer, startled, replied, "I guess not; that is, not severely punished."

At about this time frustrated union men in Omaha tried to steal a train for the use of the Industrials. The attempt failed, and the railroads quickly took preventive steps: They ordered all engines and trains removed from the area. But somehow one switch engine in Omaha was overlooked in the scramble. Several supporters of Kelly's army converged on it and clambered into the cab. Among them were two women, Edna Harper of Omaha and her friend Annie Hooton of Council Bluffs. Edna Harper was a newspaper reporter in a day when the press hired very few women. Annie Hooton was a hairdresser.

The engineer in the cab, no doubt with his job security in mind, said it was against regulations for him to start the engine under existing circumstances. But he pointed to the throttle and said the engine would start if the throttle was pulled. Either Edna Harper or Annie Hooton got the point and pulled. The little engine started and chugged off, coupled to two freight cars. After this small train got under way, the rule-conscious engineer protected railroad property by driving the engine himself. It didn't go far, however: The railroad company had ordered a rail removed from the track. (Apparently it was better to damage an engine and kill people than to risk transporting the unemployed free of charge.) From somewhere there appeared sympathizers who had done railroad work, and before long the missing rail was back in position. The train proceeded with its small cargo of well-wishers from Omaha, including Edna Harper and Annie Hooton.

At midnight the engine pulled up near the spot where the Industrials were encamped. General Kelly considered the militiamen, who were bivouacked only a few hundred yards away, and the puny switch engine with two cars. This train couldn't solve his huge transportation problem, so he sent it back to Omaha, loaded with men who had sickened after sleeping outdoors in the rain.

As for Edna Harper and Annie Hooton, the Union Pacific had sworn out warrants for their arrest. To keep them from the clutches of the law, Kelly suggested that the two women go east with his army, which would now be traveling on foot. The women accepted, but they did not have to walk. A supporter contributed a horse and buggy for what the press began to call Kelly's two "angels." Someone also donated a tent for their exclusive use. Edna Harper obtained a typewriter and busied herself writing. If her news stories appeared in the Omaha *Bee* for which she said she was a reporter, they were not dignified with her byline.

The story of "Kelly's Angels" appeared widely in the press, and, perhaps inspired by their example, several women from the town of Oakland, east of Council Bluffs, signed a petition they hoped would get them railroad transportation to the nation's capital. Some distance away, in the town of Washington in northern Iowa, 150 unemployed people, including 50 women, commandeered a train.

For nearly a month Edna Harper and Annie Hooton accompanied the army that stubbornly marched eastward across Iowa. Their part in the venture came to an end before they reached the Mississippi, however. Edna Harper decided that General Kelly was a self-seeking opportunist. She accused him of pocketing for his personal use money that had been contributed for the whole army. (Colonel Speed had made the same accusation.) She also noted that although he would not let women enlist in the army and would not let privates have female companions, he spent more time with Annie Hooton than became a married man. He was, she thought, losing sight of his political objective in the nation's capital.

There seems to be no record of what happened to Mrs. Harmon and the 200 women she organized in support of Kelly's army in Council Bluffs. Nor do we know any more about the women of Oakland who wanted to join Kelly, or about the fifty women of Washington, Iowa, who joined unemployed men in stealing a train. Perhaps because so many historians have been men, silence has also settled over the lives of Edna Harper and Annie Hooton.

The march across Iowa persisted in spite of some dissension in the ranks. Kelly rode about on a magnificent black horse that a local sympathizer had given him and encouraged the men to get up entertainment — a fife and drum corps, bands, and parades. But such morale building did not set trains in motion. The army still had to walk. Very soon shoes, already old, wore out, and there were almost no new ones in the commissary wagons. Like many, Jack London was soon so crippled with blisters that he had to be carried for a while on one of the wagons generously provided by local farmers. Along the roads and streets people usually poured out to cheer and to offer food.

A full kind of community life evolved in this organized migration. Squads went out ahead of the main army soliciting contributions. Cooks prepared and served meals. An unemployed dentist pulled teeth when he thought such treatment necessary. Extraction was done without anesthetic but with the help of husky members of the army who held the patient immobile until the tooth was out. Some of the marchers formed glee clubs and sang at night. Song and dance teams performed, and impromptu orators gave political speeches. At many stops local ministers appeared and delivered sermons. There was even a baseball team that played local nines along the line of march.

Altogether, Kelly's army was a spirited group, with the marchers finding out that there was much to live for, even though they did not have jobs. They enjoyed each other's company, and they had a shared goal. In a way they were creating a new society within the one from which they had been cast loose.

Meanwhile, progress eastward was painfully slow, and it would be months at this rate before the marchers could reach Congress, which they believed had the power to solve their problems. To speed up and to ease the journey, someone thought of building boats on which the army could float down the Des Moines River 300 miles to Keokuk. From there, the boats could continue on the Mississippi to the Ohio and then could be towed up the Ohio to the Allegheny Mountains. The final stage of the journey would be on foot.

Carpenters in the army set to work on donated material and built a fleet of flat boats. Although the Des Moines River was narrow and shallow, the boats finally reached the Mississippi. On this leg of the journey, living was good for a short while, but feeding the army soon went beyond the resources of the sparse population along the Des Moines and later along the Mississippi. Jack London told what happened:

On one stretch the Army went forty-eight hours without grub; and then it arrived at a small village of some three hundred inhabitants, the name of which I do not remember, though I think it was Red Rock. This town, following the practice of all towns through which the Army passed, had appointed a committee of safety. Counting five to a family, Red Rock consisted of sixty households. Her committee of safety was scared stiff by the eruption of two thousand hungry hoboes who lined their boats two and three deep along the river bank. General Kelly was a fair man. He had no intention of working a hardship on the village. He did not expect sixty households to furnish two thousand meals. Besides, the Army had its treasure-chest.

But the committee of safety lost its head. "No encouragement to the invader" was its programme, and when General Kelly wanted to buy food, the committee turned him down. It had nothing to sell; General Kelly's money was "no good" in their burg. And then General Kelly went into action. The bugles blew. The Army left the boats and on top of the bank formed in battle array. The committee was there to see. General Kelly's speech was brief.

"Boys," he said, "when did you eat last?"

"Day before yesterday," they shouted.

"Are you hungry?"

A mighty affirmation from two thousand throats shook the atmosphere. Then General Kelly turned to the committee of safety: —

"You see, gentlemen, the situation. My men have eaten nothing in forty-eight hours. If I turn them loose upon your town, I'll not be responsible for what happens. They are desperate. I offered to buy food for them, but you refused to sell. I now withdraw my offer. Instead, I shall demand. I give you five minutes to decide. Either kill me six steers and give me four thousand rations, or I turn the men loose. Five minutes, gentlemen."

The terrified committee of safety looked at the two thousand hungry hoboes and collapsed. It didn't wait the five minutes. It wasn't going to take any chances. The killing of the steers and the collecting of the requisition began forthwith, and the Army dined.

Two thousand hungry mouths were a lot of mouths to feed. Jack London noted that 42,000 meals a week had to come from somewhere, and too often the meals did not appear. Members of the army, in increasing numbers, chose to forage on their own rather than go hungry as members of a large group. One of the deserters was Jack London. "I can't stand starvation," he wrote in his diary. At Hannibal, Missouri, the birthplace of Mark Twain, the young writer-to-be turned north toward Chicago.

London continued to travel as a tramp, but it would be many weeks before he began to draw conclusions about capitalist society. He was arrested early one morning for the crime of being unemployed and on the streets of Niagara Falls, New York. After a mockery of a trial, he was sent to prison. There he found work — at forced labor. The experience helped lead him rapidly to Socialism.

General Kelly continued to lead his army, which was increasingly resisted by law enforcement officers in towns along the way. Nevertheless, recruits kept appearing. Those who were admitted to the army (not all were thought sufficiently serious minded) took the place of deserters. In spite of some strong differences between General Kelly and some of his colonels, his troops held together.

All the way up the Ohio River police officers, sheriffs' deputies, and vigilante groups calling themselves committees of safety made life difficult for the waterborne army. Before it reached Wheeling, West Virginia, Kelly went ahead to make arrangements in Washington. He arrived there July 12, almost two and a half months after the original target date of May 1.

In Wheeling, the police arrested many of the army's members and sent them to the workhouse for fifteen days. Word went out to the rest of the men that anyone headed for Washington would get the same treatment. Under this pressure, the destitute, and now leaderless, army disintegrated, and only a small number finally managed to reach the capital. The few who filtered through all the sieves prepared against them did so in spite of federal, state, and local authorities, vigilante groups, and the manipulations of the country's greatest industry, the railroads. Congress had no problem ignoring them, although most of the small delegation of Populist senators and representatives were in sympathy with the idea of public works.

Populists, members of or supporters of the People's Party formed in 1892, had sent to Congress three senators and ten representatives, all from western states. They were clear evidence of a strong movement among farmers to fight against the high costs of transporting their products to market, the low prices at which they had to sell their products, and the high costs of the goods they had to buy. The core of the Populist movement was agrarian in the West and in the South, where it was also strong, but the People's Party was also generally sympathetic to labor. It was not, however, sufficiently revolutionary to please the very much smaller Socialist Labor Party, and it was too political to please the American Federation of Labor.

The platform adopted by the People's Party in 1892 had called for government ownership of railroads, steamship lines, and telephone and telegraph services; the election of senators by direct ballot instead of by state legislatures; the abolition of national banks; and the free coinage of silver. In the presidential campaign of 1892, General James B. Weaver of Iowa had received a million votes as the nominee of the People's Party. When Kelly's army came through Iowa, General Weaver warmly greeted the Industrials in person, something the leading Democratic and Republican politicians certainly did not do, in Iowa or in Washington.

Kelly continued to favor public works to relieve the sufferings of the jobless, but in 1924 he vehemently attacked the radical ideas that had moved him in 1894 and again in 1914, when he tried to lead another army of unemployed men to Washington. On this second attempt he got only as far as Sacramento, where the police saw to it that he served a term in jail. Behind bars, he came to the conclusion that radicalism did not pay.

13

More Armies
(1894)

It may be all right to "put your shoulder to the wheel," but
what are you to do when you lack the wheel?
> — Chesterfield W. Myers
> poet laureate of Coxey's Army, 1894

What cometh here from the west to east a-wending?
And who are these, the marchers stern and slow?
We bear the message that the rich are sending
Aback to those who bade them wake and know.
Not one, not one, nor thousands must they slay,
But one and all if they would dusk the day.
> — William Morris
> "The Death Song," 1887

More than three weeks after General Kelly's departure from
the Bay Area, a contingent of 1,100 left Oakland. At the head of
500 of this group was Mrs. Anna F. Smith, "a woman of great
decision and of commanding presence," according to the *New
York Times.* Mrs. Smith had been unanimously chosen "after
several leaders of the other sex had failed to start them on the
way to Washington." Unfortunately for Mrs. Smith and her
followers, the resistance of the railroads had greatly increased.
She and her army did not get far — just how far is not known.

Among other Industrial Armies were two from Los Angeles.
One, led by Arthur Vinette, a general organizer of the American
Federation of Labor, started out with more than 200 men but
had only 10 left when it reached Washington. The second was

headed by Lewis C. Fry, like Vinette a general organizer of the AFL and a member of the Socialist Labor Party (SLP). This group, a lineal descendent of earlier Marxist organizations, sought in 1894 to achieve a socialist society by winning workers to a program that combined the use of the ballot with the organization of radical unions competing with the American Federation of Labor. Socialist Labor Party members opposed anarchism, and it was order, not anarchy, that fascinated Lewis Fry.

At one time Fry had been a soldier, and he gave quasi-military shape and direction to the Los Angeles jobless who joined him. His well-drilled companies paraded the streets and on occasion strode in formation into meeting halls to hear discussions of social questions. Of one such episode a professional lecturer, Henry Frank, said:

> In Los Angeles, Cal., I delivered a lecture in a large hall on Sunday morning. Among the multitude of people who came to listen to a discussion of social and religious problems, I observed to my amazement several companies of the recently organized "Industrial Army." They marched through the streets of the city, in front of many of the churches, with emblematic ensigns flying, five hundred strong, and as they filed into the hall and quietly took their seats they were greeted with thunderous applause. I noticed that my most attentive and appreciative listeners were these same sallow-faced and sad-hearted unemployed.
>
> I very earnestly interviewed "General" Lewis Fry, who has since marched seven hundred men from California, and at this writing has successfully carried them as far as Missouri, with the desertion of scarcely a man. I publicly asserted my opposition to his scheme on prudential grounds. Therefore I keenly catechized him. But I soon learned that the purpose of the "army" was wholly peaceful, and no thought of insurrection or depredation was entertained.
>
> The following question was sternly put to him: "If you succeed in assembling an army as you hope to, what action will you take provided the government interposes and prevents your progress?"

> Quick as a flash came the . . . response, "Lay down as prisoners of war and demand that the government provide for us."

After careful screening of all who wanted to join his army, Fry enrolled 850. He then tried to get free transportation for them on the Southern Pacific Railroad. He failed, and on March 26 he and 600 men set out on foot for Washington, provisioned by many supporters. At Ontario, California, the army seized a train, which took it on to Colton. At Colton sympathizers made more donations: 3,000 pounds of hardtack, 250 pounds of bacon, and 200 pounds of beans. The men then moved, by stolen train, east across the desert.

Alarming rumors raced ahead of them. The mayor of El Paso, Texas, mobilized the city. He called a public meeting (which citizens attended, Texas fashion, wearing guns), and then asked Governor J. S. Hogg to bring in federal troops to protect El Paso and presumably all of Texas. But Hogg, like Governor Waite of Colorado, was a Populist and not inclined to use force. He saw no evidence that the army was a threat, although some newspaper stories suggested it was made up of dangerous Communists.

When the train reached El Paso, Fry was arrested for vagrancy. He was soon released and busied himself explaining the aims of the army and its need for food. The trouble the mayor had expected did not materialize. Instead, the Industrials marched peacefully through town, then proceeded to take possession of another Southern Pacific train. The railroad officials allowed the train to go on but had it sidetracked at Sierra Blanca, a whistlestop in a desert region where there was neither food nor water. The 800 men who now made up the army were stranded and in real peril. The Southern Pacific's strategy may have been to provoke the men to escape from the desert by stealing another train that was carrying mail. Such action would have allowed the railroad to get around Governor Hogg: Federal troops could be called in to protect the mails.

While the Industrials' freight train was stalled, Texas Rangers appeared, ostensibly to protect railroad property but actually to hold the army prisoner. Governor Hogg wrathfully

ordered the Rangers to stop harassing the "petition in boots."
Then, in the rhetoric of Populism, he sent a telegram to the
Dallas *Times Herald* showing that he was evenhandedly against
both big business and communism:

> You can truthfully say that neither the cormorant nor the
> commune can disgrace Texas while I am Governor. When a
> railroad company hauls tramps or unemployed penniless men
> into this State it cannot dump them into a barren desert and
> murder them by torture and starvation without atoning for it,
> if there is any virtue in the machinery of justice. Nor will I
> permit them to be shot down on Texas soil by any armed force
> whatever, no matter how much the Southern Pacific and the
> other enemies of the State may howl about the commune.

Organized labor supported Hogg and Fry's army. The Central Industrial Council of Texas made this position clear in a
resolution, but such resolutions did not dissuade the Southern
Pacific. The railroad continued to hold the army helpless in the
desert. The impasse was broken only when citizens in El Paso
sent out $200 worth of provisions and paid for a special train
with five coaches and two baggage cars to move the men farther
away from El Paso and on to San Antonio.

Meanwhile Fry eluded the Rangers, boarded a passing
freight train, and went ahead to organize support in the state
capital. Although he was discovered in the ice box of a refrigerator car and put off the train, he soon turned up in Austin,
where he hoped to march his army to the mansion of Governor
Hogg and thank him for his help. The local police prevented the
march, and the men had to move on, this time packed so tightly
in boxcars that everyone had to stand all the way across Texas.
Still riding freight trains, and still 600 strong, the army reached
St. Louis on April 3.

Railroads east of the Mississippi refused transportation,
and the men continued on foot. With new recruits bringing its
size up to 800, the army hiked eastward, although food and
good shoes were scarce. By-products of hunger and sore feet
were exhaustion, dissension, and desertion. The strategy of the
railroads and local police began to pay off. What had started out

as one large unified army in California became two small rival groups in Indiana. Finally, only a handful of men with Fry reached Washington.

While Fry and Kelly were on the march, many of the more radical unemployed miners in Butte, Montana, gathered at a bar called the Sump. There they fretted and fumed until the night of April 7, when they joined a crowd of several thousand gathered on the courthouse steps to hear about the widely publicized Industrial Army led by Jacob Coxey that was on its way to Washington. Chairman of the meeting was William Hogan, an unemployed teamster given to lecturing on Shakespeare who, he thought, was more on the side of the ruling class than he should have been. The meeting ended with a proposal to form a branch of a workingmen's organization called the Industrial Legion.

Stimulated by the Populists who belonged to the Montana Peoples Party, the Industrial Legion became the nucleus of an army led by Hogan that would soon leave to petition Congress for public works. In growing numbers the men made camp near the Northern Pacific Railroad yards, while Hogan, dubbed a general by the press, negotiated with the railroad for transportation eastward. The signals he received encouraged him. All courtesy and politeness, he and his men boarded a train. Then began a confusing struggle. Some railroad officials, many local police officials, and even a federal marshal seemed disposed to help the army. The federal courts and the federal government, up to and including President Grover Cleveland, were against it. The railroad had filed for bankruptcy and was in the hands of federal receivers, which meant that the state authorities, many of whom were sympathetic to Hogan's army, had no jurisdiction.

When an injunction was issued forbidding interference with the trains, the particular federal marshal responsible was pointedly slow in delivering the order to Hogan. When experienced railroad men in the army found a suitable engine, it seemed clear to them that, so far as the Northern Pacific was concerned, they could borrow a train. For two hours, as they readied the engine and cars, not a soul appeared to protest their very obvious activities. William McDermott, the dilatory

marshal, was again evasive when ordered to protect a scheduled run of another train that might be commandeered. He said
he could not carry out the orders "on account of its being St.
George's Day," a day of parades and festivities celebrating
spring. At last Hogan and his army got under way, and Mc-
Dermott chased them — very slowly — in another train that
started seventeen hours behind its quarry.

Hogan's army rushed east and grew as it traveled. Sympathizers at stops along the way donated food. Telegrams from
Butte went out ordering law enforcement officers to stop the
train, but the sheriff in Billings replied: "County attorney and
sheriff out in Bull Mountains laying out additions to Billings.
All able bodied men are now busy selling real estate. Stop
[Hogan's] army at Livingston." Livingston residents, however,
turned out to welcome the train, and Hogan even got a fresh
engine there.

East of Livingston, somebody, using dynamite, created a
landslide across the tracks. With tools from a tool car that was
now part of the train, the army quickly removed the barrier and
then, as one report put it, "thoughtfully replaced the obstruc-
tion" behind them.

A different law officer, Deputy Sheriff M. J. Haley, was now
in charge of the pursuit. His posse was a scruffy lot of barflies,
but even some of them could not live with the idea of chasing
unemployed men on their way to petition Congress for work.
Twenty-three of the original 100 in the posse failed to show up
for the pursuit, which did not go ahead with much vigor.
Although he was now only three or four miles behind Hogan,
Deputy Haley — who, like Hogan's supporters, was in favor of
resumption of government purchase of silver — ordered the
posse off his train. First, he slowly called the roll, then spent
more time pinning insignia on each man. Finally he read the
entire court order aloud, and explained in detail the duties of
the posse. In spite of such stalling tactics, Haley's train kept
overtaking Hogan's all the way to Billings, where a large crowd
had turned out to show support for the army. Haley, with only
twelve of his men, only eight of whom were armed, approached
Hogan's train and at last ordered the Industrials to surrender.

Billings supporters stepped in at this point to protect the Industrials. Someone, apparently a deputy, opened fire and killed a Billings resident. In no time, the crowd disarmed the deputies, and the stolen train raced on out of town.

Meanwhile, President Cleveland had ordered out federal troops. They placed a barricade across the tracks near Glendive, Montana, and had Gatling guns set up by the time the train was brought to a stop. The United States regulars captured the Industrial Army, and the surrender took place in the following fashion, according to a reporter who interviewed General Hogan nearly thirty years later, after he had become a fruit farmer in California:

A pompous, booted and spurred army officer hustled about among the group, asking for "General" Hogan. Though Hogan was standing several times within a few feet of him, idly whittling a stick with a pen knife, the [man] addressed always peered around and remarked:

"Well, he was here a few minutes ago, but I don't see him now."

For over an hour the colonel went raging about fuming threats, until finally one of the soldiers, pointing out Hogan, told him he thought that was the man.

The army officer came to a halt in front of Hogan, who continued whittling the stick.

"Are you in command of this damn rabble?" he roared.

"I was until an hour ago," Hogan grinned.

"Do you surrender?"

Hogan sighed. "It is the fortune of war," he said sadly. Then reversing his pen knife, with the blade in his hand, he handed it to the colonel, with a low bow and the remark, "Please accept my sword."

For his part as commander of the train-stealing army, Hogan was sentenced to six months in the county jail. Some others got lesser sentences.

Hogan's imprisonment did not stop the army. With support from the citizens of Helena, it moved on to Fort Benton, 140 miles to the east. There, following the plan General Kelly had used in Iowa, the men built flat boats and floated down the

Missouri River to St. Joseph. At least 400 Industrials arrived there July 9. Traces of the army disappear at that point, but apparently a small part of it persisted and reached Washington.

Earlier, in the spring, a group from Portland, Oregon, and another from California had combined and called themselves the "Fifth Regiment United States Industrial Army," under the leadership of a stonemason, S. L. Scheffler. The Union Pacific Railroad refused to provide transportation out of Portland, even though Governor Pennoyer of Oregon interceded on the regiment's behalf. The men then walked fifteen miles to Troutdale, where experienced railroaders among them quietly took possession of the local depot. While they tried to find out when to expect a train they could commandeer, they carried out all the necessary work at the station, including the receiving and sending of telegraph messages. Nobody along the line suspected the takeover, but before an eastbound train reached Troutdale, one regular employee at the depot escaped and sounded the alarm.

Soon United States Marshal Grady appeared with deputies. When he could not find out who was in charge of the strange, efficient men in the depot, he satisfied himself by reading an injunction forbidding them to interfere with railroad property. The men quietly dispersed, and Grady, thinking his work done, returned to Portland. As soon as he was out of town, the Industrials went back to the depot and resumed its operation.

Marshal Grady next asked Governor Pennoyer for militia. The governor, more friendly to the unemployed than to the railroad, replied: "This is a civil and not a military government, and it is your duty to exercise the civil power to quell any disturbance when it occurs, and not to call upon the militia before it occurs."

At that point, Grady wired U.S. Attorney General Richard Olney for help from the regular army. While he waited, Grady and the local sheriff, with forty-six men, went to evict Scheffler and his army from their camp near the railroad. They found the men lined up in good order, all packed as if ready to move. Hospitably the well-provisioned Industrials offered to give the law men a meal. The deputies, who had been very coolly received by the citizens of Troutdale, declined and returned to Portland.

Grady and the Union Pacific officials then thought of a gimmick. They sent to Troutdale a train of empty boxcars in each of which was a copy of an injunction forbidding the Industrials to take railroad property. The trap worked. The men boarded the cars, found and ignored the injunction, and took over the train, thus making themselves guilty of contempt of court.

Now a chase began in earnest. Grady pursued them from the west, and the United States Army came at them from the east. They had to surrender. When Grady, who had told the attorney general that the men were dangerous, had them searched, he found to his embarrassment that there were only three guns among the 507 prisoners. Supported by public demonstrations, the Industrials went into court back in Portland. The judge let them go with a warning not to repeat their offense.

Three hundred and fifty of the men immediately announced their decision to start out again for Washington, and on April 31, 3,000 workers in Portland paraded in their support. The next day, May 1, was devoted by labor to another big parade and to campaigning for the eight-hour day.

Shortly afterward, the Portland Industrials heard that the famous Coxey (see Chapter 14) had been arrested and had not been allowed to petition Congress. Though they were not cheered by the news, they continued in small groups toward the capital. At one point, Scheffler and 228 men stole an Oregon Short Line train and were arrested in Idaho. Several of Scheffler's aides received five-month jail terms. Another section of the Portland army stole a different train, with similar results. Scheffler himself got six months in jail, and the rank and file received sentences up to sixty days.

The men had to build their own prison camp, and later, Idaho's Governor McConnell complained to the attorney general that the jailers had not complied with the "demands of civilization." The prisoners were released only a few at a time, so it was virtually impossible for them to reassemble. At the expense of tens of thousands of dollars, the law-enforcing agencies had defeated the Portland army.

A similar movement started in Tacoma, Washington, where women tried to join but were rejected. The leadership of this army fell to Frank T. "Jumbo" Cantwell, a prosperous prize-fighter and saloon bouncer. The program his followers adopted was unique in several ways. It called for government financing of liberal education for all, construction of a canal in Nicaragua (to aid West Coast shipping), restrictions on immigration, and work on irrigation projects in dry land areas. These detailed demands provided strong motivation for Jumbo's army, although at first he had no better luck with the railroads than other leaders had. He even offered $10,000 of his own money to buy transportation, but the railroads refused to haul the men as freight. Jumbo's wife then offered to pay for boxcars in which to ship cattle, planning to put one cow in each car with thirty or forty men to tend the animal. No, said the railroads, they weren't going to be tricked. Later, Jumbo's maneuvering was more successful, and a good part of his better-financed army, unlike most of the others, managed to reach Washington. Their petition, like all the others, went unheeded.

Other armies had different experiences, none of them good. On May 4 in Yakima, Washington, a whole group of Industrials was arrested, and on May 9 deputies jailed many more after a bloody battle. Men who tried to free the prisoners the following day were also arrested. Some men, attempting to avoid the deputies who were guarding trains, decided to travel by boat on the Yakima River; thirteen of them drowned. In Pasco, Washington, 200 men were arrested as they tried to hop trains.

A Spokane contingent tried to get transportation to the Mississippi River by offering to repair Great Northern tracks along the way. The railroad's president, James J. Hill, rejected their offer, calling them "the worst class of men." Early on, this Spokane section found itself under the leadership of J. W. Kelly, a brother of General Charles Kelly whose army had started from San Francisco. J. W. Kelly and his men stole a train in Montana but were stopped before getting far. Kelly was kept in jail.

Train stealing was epidemic all over the Northwest, but few of the thousands of men who started for Washington managed to solve the transportation problem. Fewer still managed to slip through the obstacles placed in their way by some local and state officials and by the hostility of Attorney General Olney and President Cleveland. Both of these powerful figures opposed what the unemployed sought — public works.

The members of the Industrial Army that passed through Denver tried to ease their journey by launching a flotilla of flatboats on the South Platte. The boats were wrecked, and there may have been fatalities.

The Northeast, too, had an Industrial Army. It was led by Morrison I. Swift, a Ph.D. from Johns Hopkins University, who devoted most of a long life to trying to help the jobless and other disadvantaged groups. The New Englanders fared a little better than the western armies, who had so much farther to travel. Part of Swift's army did reach the capital and did leave its petition (see Appendix E).

14

Coxey's Army
(1894)

We would show our real condition —
Take a living, true petition
Unto Congress now in session,
Upward, then, and onward!

— Chesterfield W. Myers
Coxey's Warning: A Vindication of Coxeyism, 1894

None of the Industrial Armies, in which many thousands took part at one time or another, was as well publicized as the contingent called Coxey's Army. Although it was one of the smallest units in the whole movement, by the time it got on the road to Washington the entire country had heard about it. Often other contingents were called "Coxey's Army," no matter what their origin or leadership, and their members were dubbed "Coxeyites."

Coxey's army started its journey in Massillon, Ohio, on March 25 (its leader's birthday), It had had its genesis months earlier on Chicago's Lake Front at a union-organized meeting (see Chapter 11). Like Union Square in New York, the Lake Front was a place where every kind of agitator, political or religious, held forth, along with vendors of patent medicine. Among the soapboxers who spoke there, one of the most colorful was Carl Browne, who had taken part with Dennis Kearney in the San Francisco demonstrations of 1877. Browne was now a paid organizer for the People's Party and also an organizer for the AFL. It was his job to build industrial legions, which at first were a general working-class arm of the Populist movement not exclusively concerned with unemployment. As the depression developed, however, Browne spoke out more and more for the jobless and for public works. In his Lake Front talks, he repeated the call, "On to Washington!" which he may have heard Joseph Buchanan utter in San Francisco in 1886.

Jacob S. Coxey, who was in the city attending a Populist convention on fiscal reform, heard the call and was impressed. Coxey, besides being an earnest reformer, was the very prosperous owner of a sand quarry, a farm in Ohio, and a racehorse breeding establishment in Kentucky. Some estimates place his wealth at $200,000 in 1893 dollars; today he would be called a millionaire.

At the time Coxey heard Browne propose a march to petition Congress for public works, he had already launched a program designed to help both farmers and the unemployed. He had drafted a Good Roads Bill and arranged to have it introduced in Congress. The bill called for hiring all unemployed men who applied for work at the then fairly decent wage of $1.50 for an eight-hour day — a goal much sought by labor. The estimated $500 million needed to repair existing roads and build new ones would be obtained by simply printing paper (fiat) money, thus increasing the money supply, which Coxey thought desirable anyway. (See Appendix F for the text of the bill.)

After his Good Roads Bill had been introduced, Coxey came to realize that the roads he projected would mainly serve the interests of the rural population. To serve urban dwellers, he drafted another bill entitled the Non–Interest-Bearing Bond Bill. This one called for repairing streets and constructing schools and public buildings. It, too, was to be financed by fiat money backed by municipal bonds, which in turn would be secured by half the assessed valuation of all property in each issuing community. The bonds would be retired over a twenty-five-year period by funds from taxes, and at the same time the fiat money would be withdrawn on a regular schedule. In addition, the bonds were to be non–interest-bearing, a feature that provided the name for the bill. (Appendix F contains the text of the bill.)

Dipping into his personal resources, Coxey hired Browne to

whip up support for his bills. With the energy that seemed to mark everything he did, Browne drew big cartoons and set them up on a wagon where they could be seen even from the outer fringes of large crowds. The drawings, which Browne called a "financial panorama," expressed his — and Coxey's — distrust of the country's banking and financial system. After the panorama had attracted the curious, Browne proceeded to hold them with his speaking talent. His lectures urged support of the Good Roads Bill as a way out of the depression and unemployment. He also plugged his dream of a march to Washington, which Coxey liked so much that he began to believe it was his own invention.

Browne's Lake Front performances attracted such large numbers of jobless that the mayor of Chicago grew alarmed and warned him to leave town. Browne went to consult Coxey in Massillon, then reappeared, incognito, in Chicago and joined a man who sold a patent medicine called "Kickapoo Indian Blood Remedy." Spieling gave him a chance to go on promoting the Good Roads Bill while praising the medicine man's nostrum.

Chicago, with its thousands of jobless, seemed to Browne a good place from which to launch the march to Washington. But Coxey, now president of the J. S. Coxey Good Roads Association, wanted to have it start from his hometown. So Browne returned to Massillon and moved into Coxey's house.

In January 1894, while his employer was launching his Non–Interest-Bearing Bond Bill, Browne busied himself writing and illustrating circulars announcing the march that he and Coxey had begun to call a "petition in boots." It also had a more official name — the Commonweal of Christ — and Browne developed a semi-military plan for organizing it. Possibly he modeled it on some armed military organizations that had been established by radical workers in Chicago in the 1880s, but his proposal for the Commonweal differed in one major respect from the workers' militia. There were to be no arms of any kind in this army. For his peaceful cohorts, he designed badges replete with symbols and slogans that distinguished officers of different rank, and he painted banners that proclaimed the heavily religious character of the assemblage.

Browne's circulars reached a wide audience. He had the ear of national officers of the American Federation of Labor, and he was well known to the Knights of Labor. Either directly or indirectly, he also reached the Socialist Labor Party, which had groups in many cities.

Contingents of the Commonweal of Christ were organized in many places. As one of them began to form in Chicago, Lucy Parsons and her friend Lizzie Swank came and talked to the men who had enlisted. Although the two Anarchist women approved of the march, they made speeches against a society based on profit and tried to persuade the recruits that much more change was needed in the world than merely the construction of good roads financed by non–interest-bearing bonds.

Just before the Chicago group was to leave, led by "Commander" Randall, Parsons and some other women provided a dinner to cheer the men on. After the meal, according to Henry Vincent, official historian of Coxey's Army, several of the women made encouraging speeches to those gathered in the courtyard of the barracks where they had been assembling.

With these short talks (wrote Vincent) Commander Randall expected to close the proceedings. Not so, however. Some of the men recognized Lucy Parsons. They yelled for her and she promptly came to the front. The commander was taken by surprise, and he did not have time to think before the voluble Lucy was at it. He removed his hat and fingered it nervously, meanwhile noting the effect of her words upon the men. Mrs. Parsons told them, among other things, that they were belched up from the hearts of the people and indicated a condition. They were incorruptible, she said, and they were going to Washington to present in person their petition. They knew, she added, that when Wall Street railway-wreckers and billionaires wanted anything from the National Government, they got it. She told them they weren't going down there for a miserable dollar and a half a day, but they should demand sufficient money to educate their children. Inasmuch as they had built America, they deserved the good things of the earth. She recalled that they must be tired sweeping Chicago streets for bad soup. She had much more to say on the same lines and Commander Randall was much relieved when she retired to a position adjacent to the fence. He lost no time in stepping forward and telling the men that the speeches were at an end and that he would permit no more. "I will lead nothing but a peace movement," he said, "and we will stick to our text. I have not organized you to pursue any policy indicative of force, and the man who does not want to march under the Coxey banner cannot remain a part of this cause." "Rally 'Round the Flag, Boys" followed.

Ministers had visited the army as it was getting started. Detectives also had come, disguised as unemployed workers, and remained even in the section headed by General Coxey himself.

The central core of the Commonweal assembled near Coxey's home in Massillon, where Browne (who had married Coxey's daughter) was stirring up vast newspaper publicity, not only for good roads and non–interest-bearing bonds, but also for theosophy, in which he had developed great interest. All the Commonwealers, it seems, were reincarnations of Christ. Browne was the cerebellum of Christ and Coxey the cerebrum. (These novel ideas may have helped to attract to the army Douglas McCullum, author of *The Dogs and the Fleas by One of the Dogs*. There was also an astrologer, and a mysterious figure generally referred to as "the Great Unknown.") In general, theosophy roused little enthusiasm among most of the 100 men who finally assembled in Massillon. It was jobs that had meaning for them, and they hoped to get them constructing roads and buildings.

On Easter morning the procession started in a chill rain. No train stealing or boat building for the Commonwealers; they walked. They did have wagons for their commissary and a huge circus tent for shelter and meetings. Coxey himself rode in a carriage with a new wife and their new baby, Legal Tender Coxey. Sometimes Browne, in buckskins and sombrero, rode a fine horse, and often he and Coxey stayed in hotels while the common Commonwealers slept on the ground.

On schedule, the army arrived in Washington in time to parade up Pennsylvania Avenue on May 1. At the Capitol, between 15,000 and 20,000 people awaited the marchers who now numbered about 500. Then came the anticlimax: Browne, Coxey, and another colorful leader, Christopher Columbus Jones, were arrested for walking on the grass of the Capitol lawn and were soon sentenced to twenty days in jail. They did not succeed in presenting their petition to Congress. (See Appendix G for the text of the petition.)

Official Washington had been scared witless by the approach of Coxey's harmless army. Fifteen hundred soldiers were stationed in the city in case of "trouble," and several thousand more were ready in Baltimore, Annapolis, and Philadelphia. Tens of thousands of dollars were spent mustering federal troops here and in other parts of the country.

Why did the Industrial Armies provoke such resistance? Why did Congress, although the need was nationwide, make no concessions in response to the petitions of the unemployed? Local administrations in earlier depressions, and to some extent in this one, had sometimes yielded in one degree or another to the demands of demonstrators. But in 1894, although the effort of the unemployed was great, it won no national public works whatsoever. As one account put it, "Coxey's Army wrote only its name in history, not its program."

The various programs of the Industrials achieved somewhat more local than federal response because local government officials were closer to their jobless constituents than were those in Washington, and some of the former were influenced by grass-roots support for the armies. Those who had great political and economic power had removed themselves from those who did the country's work. Their power, which was centralized, prevailed over the decentralized efforts of the unemployed. Police often jailed the armies' leaders, with the most militant and the most radical receiving the harshest sentences. Police action was also taken against such middle-of-the-road reformist leaders as Coxey, but their treatment was less severe. Often it was not only police but also vigilantes and federal troops who moved against both leaders and the rank and file, and their effect was crippling. In the final analysis, what the unemployed needed was something that neither employers nor the federal government that spoke for them felt obliged to give.

Although the unemployed in 1894 moved in large numbers, and courageously, in what they conceived to be their own interest, they had not learned how to move effectively, given the forces they had to overcome. They did not know how to keep themselves from being divided by squabbles or from being diverted into pursuit of irrelevancies. Still, the Industrial Armies had borrowed from the past and projected into the future one fundamental idea: Public works were essential in times of mass unemployment.

When, after three years of depression, large banking firms found it to their advantage to help the government stabilize the currency on the basis of gold, the economy revived. Mass unemployment gradually subsided. But anticapitalist groups, such as the Socialist Labor Party and its offshoots — first the Socialist Party and later the Industrial Workers of the World — remembered that depressions and unemployment were recurrent phenomena. These radicals, the dwindling numbers of Anarchists, and reformers, including Jacob S. Coxey, were ready to move among the jobless when new crises came, telling them that society was to blame for their troubles and society should be required to remedy them.

15

Hallelujah, I'm a Bum
(1907)

Conservatism, being an upper-class characteristic, is decorous; and conversely, innovation, being a lower-class phenomenon, is vulgar.

— Thorstein Veblen
The Theory of the Leisure Class, 1899

The working class and the employing class have nothing in common. There can be no peace so long as hunger and want are found among millions of working people, and the few, who make up the employing class, have all the good things of life.

— Preamble to the Constitution
of the Industrial Workers of the World, 1905

The greatest of our evils and the worst of our crimes is poverty.

— George Bernard Shaw
preface, *Major Barbara,* 1907

In October 1907, following a period of wild speculation, the stock market crashed. Many banks failed, damaging businesses, and many employers discharged workers. Hundreds of thousands, perhaps millions, of ordinarily employed workers were out on the street. Their unemployment lasted through 1908.

Among the jobless, those who had any savings to fall back on were few, and their savings were small and soon gone. Single men and women were evicted from rooming houses. Married men and their families were evicted from their homes, usually rented. People went hungry as they walked from one shop gate to another, all with signs that said, "No help needed" or "Not hiring." Discouragement and despair overcame many, and the suicide rate rose (it was 50 percent higher in 1908 than in 1907).

Such phenomena did not interest President Theodore Roosevelt, whose attention was more often on the foreign scene. Beginning with the Spanish-American War, the United States had become an imperialist power that had displaced Spain from Cuba, Puerto Rico, and the Philippines. Violence abroad became part of United States policy, just as it had long been part of the domestic scene where the use of force on occasion was considered an acceptable way to assure a docile reservoir of unemployed workers. Any sign of militance among the jobless was likely to be handled brusquely, even brutally. To make clear where he stood, President Roosevelt said, "When compared with the suppression of anarchy, every other question sinks into insignificance."

Anarchists were actually few in number, and they held a wide range of views, most of which did not include advocacy of violence. Americans, however, were aware that a man who called himself an Anarchist had assassinated President McKinley in 1901. Most Americans also believed, although supporting evidence was lacking, that Anarchists had been responsible for the sensational Haymarket Massacre in 1886.[1] There was indeed a receptive audience for any attack on anarchism — and such an attack could divert attention from more fundamental problems.

Anarchists had not, of course, caused the economic collapse of 1907, and there were not many of them on the scene when the unemployed began to look toward radicals and reformers, hoping to find some force that could help them out of their difficulties. Some Anarchist activity did continue in spite of government repression and in spite of the barren aspects of Anarchist thinking, which offered workers no hope of immediate improvement in their lot. There was even a little Anarchist influence in a new working-class organization, the Industrial Workers of the World (IWW), which had already appeared on the scene in January 1905 at a meeting in Chicago, just two blocks from where Albert Parsons and other Haymarket martyrs had been executed in 1887. Presiding over the opening session, attended by men and women who would come to be known as Wobblies, was Big Bill Haywood. Haywood had been part of Kelly's unemployed army for a while in 1894. (George Speed, a cantankerous colonel in that same army, was also present.) Among the speakers was Lucy Parsons, who proposed a tactic that would be used to great effect by the unemployed in the 1930s. She suggested the sit-in as a device for the new revolutionary organization to use during strikes.

The IWW had its origin in a belief, held by many workers, that they needed industrial unions rather than the unions based on craft that the American Federation of Labor favored. There seemed to be little hope that the AFL would serve workers in any militant way, and indeed it was not even the aim of the AFL to serve the entire working class.

Active in launching the IWW were Eugene V. Debs, who had built an industrial union among railroad workers, and leaders of the Western Federation of Miners, together with some labor men affiliated with the Socialist Party and the Socialist Labor Party. Mary Harris "Mother" Jones, acting as an individual, though she was an organizer for the United Mine Workers, and socialist-minded Thomas J. Hagerty, a Roman Catholic priest, were also involved in starting the IWW. Two other early leaders were Elizabeth Gurley Flynn and William Z. Foster, both of whom later became leaders of the not-yet-formed Communist Party.

To announce the creation of the new organization, Father Hagerty drafted a manifesto that, among other things, continued a long tradition of economic thought in the United States on the subject of unemployment:

> New machines, ever replacing less productive ones, wipe out whole trades and plunge new bodies of workers into the ever-growing army of tradeless, hopeless unemployed. As human beings and human skill are displaced by mechanical progress, the capitalists need use the workers only during that brief period when muscles and nerves respond most

intensely. The moment the laborer no longer yields the maximum of profits, he is thrown upon the scrap pile to starve alongside the discarded machine.

The manifesto also spoke of "the irrepressible conflict between the capitalist class and the working class" and emphasized the importance of working-class unity. Nevertheless, the IWW was soon torn by disputes. Some of its Socialist Party members had reformist ideals. Socialist Labor Party members among the IWW founders were ardent trade unionists or anarchosyndicalists who belittled political activity. By the time the depression began in 1907, two years after the IWW was formed, ideological differences among these factions had weakened the organization. Its treasury was shrinking because its unemployed members could not pay dues. Nevertheless, the Wobblies turned stubbornly to organizing the jobless, a task not undertaken in this depression by the craft unions of the American Federation of Labor.

Skilled craftsmen could get higher wages than the unskilled and could offer good pay to union officials. If employers found they had to deal with unions, they preferred to handle them craft by craft, rather than tackle all who worked in a given industry. With craft unions it was possible for employers to play one off against the other. In addition, craft unions did not subscribe to large, troublesome objectives such as replacing capitalism with socialism; they merely wanted a little larger slice of the existing economic pie.

To strengthen their position, craft unions always tried to limit the number of those qualified to do skilled jobs. One aspect of this limiting process was to close doors to African-Americans, the foreign-born, women, and the unskilled. This policy left a great many workers outside any union, and the IWW set itself the task of bringing them all into one organization, set up so that all workers in any industry could act as a unit in dealing with the owners of that industry. And to make sure that the unemployed would not take jobs away from union workers, the IWW organized the jobless, depleted though their treasury was.

In a few places, notably Los Angeles and Youngstown, Ohio, the IWW had a good deal of success leading local demonstrations to demand work or food and shelter. But there was no nationwide effort for a march on Washington to bring pressure on the federal government, as Coxey had done in 1894. Most Wobblies were too cynical about the federal government and about capitalism to expend energy in an effort they were sure would bring no results. "We do not share the view that the unemployed can be entirely eliminated under the capitalist system," said an editorial in the *Industrial Union Bulletin.* "But that unemployment can be greatly reduced in volume by action of an economic organization in shortening the work day and dividing up the work at hand, goes without much argument." The unemployed Wobblies believed in the shorter workweek, but they spent most of their time demonstrating for "ham and eggs" or "porkchops."

On street corners and in meeting halls they assailed the ruling class which, they always loudly recalled, they, the workers, had helped to make rich. They derided charity organizations that gave meager alms to the meek, and they encouraged unemployed workers not to scab on union labor even though they disapproved of the old-line craft unions.

The Wobblies were not alone at the time in pointing out that employers would try to use the unemployed as underbidders in the labor market. In a book he published in 1909, E. T. Devine, a professor of social work, stated the point of view of conservatives, who, he said, considered the unemployed

an incident, and an inevitable, normal, and desirable incident, of the labor market. If there were no unemployed, no new enterprises could be undertaken, labor organizations would become too powerful, wages would soar upwards, and the demands of workingmen for all kinds of reasonable and un-reasonable conditions would have to be granted. A large surplus body of workers keeps those who are employed in a proper state of discipline, leaves the capitalist free to encourage any new undertaking which requires labor, confident that he can make his own terms with no nonsense about recogniz-ing a union or agreeing on terms of a collective bargain.

The IWW did what it could to keep jobless workers from being used to lower the living standards of their employed "fellow workers" (a term introduced by Big Bill Haywood at the first convention).

Perhaps remembering the Industrial Armies of 1894 that had gone down to defeat singing hymns, the Wobblies of the Northwest sought local victories, animated by songs whose words mocked religion and other proprieties and whose tunes were sardonically borrowed from church music. A 1908 song from Spokane used the Salvation Army tune "Revive Us Again" for such verses as these:

> O, why don't you work
> Like other men do?
> How in hell can I work
> When there's no work to do?
> Hallelujah, I'm a bum!
> Hallelujah, bum again!
> Hallelujah, give us a handout
> To revive us again.

At its convention in 1901, the Socialist Party, which had formed in part as an offshoot of the Socialist Labor Party, had proposed "state or national insurance of working people in case of accidents, lack of employment, sickness and want in old age; the funds for this purpose to be furnished by the government and to be administered under the control of the working class." By 1908, the party had aroused little support for unemployment insurance, but it did have a presidential candidate, Eugene V. Debs, on the ballot. Debs got 400,000 votes even though many unemployed supporters were disfranchised because they were homeless — "on the road" — looking for work. The strong electoral campaign of the Socialists, however, did not bring food to the hungry, nor did it force the government to provide employment on public works.

Many agitators proposed various actions to help the jobless get short-term relief. One of these was General Coxey, this time without an army. As an individual he called on President Roosevelt and was received. As he had in 1894, Coxey argued for public works, together with his ingenious scheme for financing them. Roosevelt was heartily cordial — and in full disagreement.

Another activist was J. Eads How, often called the "millionaire hobo" because he came from a prominent family of considerable wealth. On January 14, 1890, How led 800 unemployed men to City Hall in St. Louis to ask the city for help in getting work. He also had dreams of leading a Coxey-like army to Washington, but nothing came of this project.

A more colorful agitator was Ben Reitman, a long-haired medical doctor employed by the city of Chicago to treat venereal disease among prostitutes and homeless men. Reitman was soon to become the lover of Anarchist Emma Goldman while he acted as her business manager, booking her lecture engagements and arranging for her meeting halls. Of himself he said, "I am an American by birth, a Jew by parentage, a Baptist by adoption, single by good fortune, a physician and teacher by profession, cosmopolitan by choice, a Socialist by inclination, a radical by nature, a celebrity by accident, a tramp by twenty years experience, and a tramp reformer by inspiration."

Like How, Reitman failed to pull together a march on Washington as he talked of doing. Both he and How were better at getting publicity for the underdog than they were at the hard practical work of organizing. Reitman inveighed against inhumane charities and inadequate soup lines, and he called himself the president of the Chicago Chapter of the Brotherhood Welfare Association. One of his big schemes, in Chicago and later in New York, was a public dinner to be attended by 100 unemployed men. The "toasts" for the dinner, well publicized in advance, included "Why I haven't worked in twenty years," "How much I make on a good day," and "How my face got hard."

It is not clear whether Reitman actually pulled off all his flamboyant dinners, but while he talked, some Socialists in New York tried a different way of helping the jobless. Pointing out that it would be a physical impossibility to overcome intense local resistance and evict large numbers of tenants concentrated in one area, a Socialist Committee of Ten urged everyone in that area to refuse to pay rent unless it was reduced. On January 8, 1908, the *New York Times* reported some success for this venture. "Many Landlords Yield in Rent War," ran a headline.

The unemployed needed more than lower rent. Thousands had no housing at all. Men were applying for shelter in greatly increased numbers at the Municipal Lodging House. (At the same time, the general secretary of the Industrial Christian Alliance investigated the Lodging House and claimed that less than 1 percent of the applicants for shelter were really unemployed.) Frank Bohn, who had been among the founders of the IWW and was secretary of New York's Central Federated Union, reported that 70,000 union men and 100,000 unorganized workers were looking for jobs in the city. Army and navy recruiting offices were overwhelmed with applicants trying to escape from unemployment by way of the armed services. Hundreds applied without success for work at Pocantico Hills, the estate of John D. Rockefeller near Tarrytown, New York.

In Boston, Morrison I. Swift, who had led an Industrial Army to Washington in 1894, led a new army into the richest Episcopal church in the city. The demonstrators quite simply wanted food and shelter, and wasn't a church supposed to be charitable? The rector seemed disposed to help and took up a collection for their benefit. According to the *New York Times*, the collection amounted to exactly one-sixth of what the rector had received the previous week when he solicited money for foreign missions.

Considering the unemployment problem in New York early in February 1908, the *Times* summed up the opinion of many industrialists, economists, politicians, and social workers: Labor was to blame. Unions, the paper said, had raised wages by "extortionate methods of combinations in restraint of trade." If employers could not afford to hire workers, it was the workers' fault. The solution to unemployment was lower wages. A week after offering this remedy, the *Times* endorsed another plan worked out by the United Charities Organization. This one called for a rural agricultural colony, reminiscent of the failed utopian colonies of the previous century, which would support itself and also produce food for state institutions.

On February 19, the New York police announced that they were looking for the Anarchist authors and distributors of a leaflet, said to have been printed by "unemployed printers in Chicago," that urged the jobless to take arms and seize whatever they needed. Those responsible for the leaflet were never identified, and the police search led only to more hysteria against radicals, not to relief for the jobless.

The day after the New York police began their hunt for Anarchists, a meeting of the unemployed was held in Philadelphia. This gathering was clearly called by Anarchists. The 2,000 men and women who attended were largely of Italian and Russian Jewish origin, and speakers addressed them in Italian and Yiddish. The chairperson and one other, Voltairine de Cleyre, spoke in English. Although the purpose of the meeting seems to have been purely educational, some of those present wanted action, perhaps for sinister reasons. In spite of protests by the speakers, who thought they were too few for a successful demonstration, unknown persons led the audience out of the meeting rooms and toward City Hall. Carrying a red flag with a black border, they were ostensibly bent on seeking relief and public works from the municipal government. All was peaceful until some teamsters attempted to drive their horses and wagons through the crowd and the marchers resisted. The police intervened, and soon officers on "motor bicycles" raced around the city calling out all the mounted police. After a considerable force of officers on horseback arrived with batons flying, somebody started shooting, creating more confusion but apparently doing little damage.

When the melée was over, four policemen and one bystander had been slightly injured, a driver of one of the wagons had lost most of his clothing, and fourteen Italian demonstrators had been so severely beaten that they had to be hospitalized. All of the last group were arrested.

The next day, the speakers who at the indoor meeting had tried to head off the outdoor demonstration were also arrested. Their case eventually was dismissed for lack of evidence, but four of the badly beaten Italian workers did not fare so well. Months later, three of them who belonged to an Anarchist group known as Social Revolutionaries were still in custody. The fourth, known simply as an Anarchist, was sentenced to five years in jail.

Winter was a time of great distress for the jobless everywhere. In Chicago the Socialist Party called for a demonstration at City Hall to present a petition demanding work. The police refused to grant permission for a parade, but the Socialists decided to march anyway. They changed their minds, however, when a large force of police gathered at the announced assembly point. Instead of marching, they held a meeting at their headquarters where they passed resolutions denouncing the police.

Ben Reitman, who was present, was not so easily discouraged. Somehow he managed to get marchers together and led them toward City Hall. At State and Quincy streets, mounted police dispersed the men after ten minutes of fighting. The marchers then reassembled and were attacked again. "Vigorous action by the police prevented a socialistic demonstration, but not until many heads were broken," said a newspaper report. Dr. Reitman was arrested, "and this practically [ended] the demonstration."

Newspapers editorialized, and politicians talked, but unemployment did not go away. In New York, a Conference of the Unemployed supported by both the Socialist and Socialist Labor parties resolved to hold a mass meeting in Union Square in an effort to get something done for the jobless. The police at first granted, then denied, a permit. When about 1,000 people assembled anyway, the police managed to prevent any speech making. Up to this point, the affair was only one of routine harassment and interference with free speech. Matters suddenly changed when a homemade bomb went off. A sickly young loner, Selig Silverstein, had managed to enter the square concealing a device made from the top of a brass bedpost, into which he had poured a quarter of a pound of nails, each broken in half. On top of the nails he had put some nitroglycerine, and on top of that some gunpowder. The bomb lacked only a fuse.

Later, Silverstein said he became excited when he saw in the square a policeman who had once beaten him. He inserted a fuse into his contraption and started to light it with a burning cigarette. But in his agitation he missed the fuse and applied the cigarette to the wrong part of the bomb. The resulting explosion killed a tailor who happened to be standing nearby. It blinded Silverstein and blew off one of his hands. He survived only a few days.

After the bomb exploded, the police launched an attack on the 7,000 people outside and the 1,000 inside the square. Detectives hurried through the stunned crowd "arresting every man who looked suspicious," according to the *New York Times*.

The night was filled with terror for all radicals. The police watched every known leftist hangout. They crowded into a memorial meeting held for a little-known European revolutionary. Magistrates set high bail for some of those arrested and refused any bail at all for one man who apparently knew absolutely nothing about the bombing.

Robert Hunter, a leading Socialist who had been scheduled to speak at Union Square, issued a denunciation of the police, saying: "The gathering in the square would have been peaceable had the police not intervened." Of the bomb thrower, he said, "If the poor creature was interested in the rights of the unemployed or in the rights of free speech he could hardly have chosen a more effective method of injuring these causes."

The next morning, the *New York Times* reported that a bill would be introduced in the state senate to provide for a commission to study unemployment and recommend remedial legislation. The same day, worried prominent citizens meeting in the rooms of the Manufacturers Association passed a resolution calling on state and city authorities to institute public improvements as a means of alleviating distress among the jobless. A few days later, a large conference of social workers also called for public works.

The police soon admitted that they had no evidence of any "red" plot behind the explosion of the bomb in Union Square. On the contrary, Sol Fieldman, who was to have been chairman of the Union Square gathering, insisted "the explosion was a prearranged plot on the part of the police to destroy our meeting."

A week later, delegates from a hundred labor and Socialist organizations sent a committee to the mayor of New York to seek relief measures. That same day, the press reported that three unemployed workers had shot themselves, a fourth had died after turning on the gas, and a fifth had hanged himself. Also that day, President Roosevelt sent a message to Congress calling for the construction of four first-class battleships instead of the two fighting craft recommended by the House Naval Committee. He defended his project in imperial terms, not as a relief measure to provide work for the unemployed.

As spring and warm weather approached in 1908, the Bowery Mission closed its bread line, which the *Times* reported had fed 238,500 men in the preceding winter. The *Times* added that "as a closing manifestation of good will, each man [present] received two hard-boiled eggs and two rolls in addition to the regular bread supply." Neither the mission nor the *Times* explained what the unemployed were to eat until the depression was over.

There was still mass unemployment in late August. The *Philadelphia Press* reported, "There were more unemployed at the City Hall Plaza to hear speakers representing the Industrial Workers of the World than have ever attended a demonstration in this city in recent years." One of the speakers was 18-year-old Elizabeth Gurley Flynn, known as the "Rebel Girl," who would be heard at many unemployed demonstrations in depressions still to come.

Congress legislated some banking and monetary reforms in 1908 that brought a degree of order into banking procedures. What many called the "banker panic" came to an end, and businesses resumed normal activity. Unemployment decreased, but it did not end. It continued for years, at an average level of about 10 percent. Even after the end of the depression the unemployed continued to protest. Morrison I. Swift, for example, led a demonstration in Boston in 1909. But there still was no answer to the question in the Wobbly song:

> How in hell can I work
> When there's no work to do?

16

Pie in the Sky
(1914)

Everyone has an absolute, and inalienable right to work. . . .
If he is deprived of this he is robbed of the means of life and
therefore of life itself . . . he must therefore take food, clothing
and shelter where he can.
— Resolution adopted by the Boston Unemployed
on Boston Common, March 14, 1914

It is precisely in the century which has seen the greatest
increase in productivity since the fall of the Roman Empire
that economic discontent has been most acute.
— R. H. Tawney
The Acquisitive Society, 1920

Following a period of expansion of American business at
home and abroad, a depression began in 1913. It was the old
story of production being curtailed because it exceeded consumption. First, manufacturing in some basic industries declined, then other businesses began to fail, and before the end
of 1913 mass unemployment had arrived. It grew when World
War I disrupted ordinary economic life first in Europe, and then
throughout the world.

As in past depressions, the unemployed had to rely to a
great extent on themselves — and on radicals — to get relief,
and the activities of the jobless under radical leadership did
much to bring into existence local private charities and relief
organizations.

The left-wing resources that were available to the unemployed had never been better, in spite of the fact that the

Socialist Labor Party had almost withered away and took no interest in the day-to-day problems of the jobless. In fact, the SLP at this time actually disapproved of such activities. In contrast, the Socialist Party was thriving. More than 900,000 citizens had voted the Socialist ticket in the presidential election of 1912. Two hundred newspapers throughout the country called themselves Socialist, as did hundreds of elected local officials. The party had about 150,000 dues-paying members.

The number of Socialist Party members contrasted sharply with the 11,000 people who paid dues to the IWW in 1914. Membership had been reduced by unemployment from 18,000 before the depression. The number of workers who had been Wobblies at one time or another since 1905, however, was at least 100,000, and many of these were still moved by the rebellious spirit of the loose-knit, aggressive, democratic organization that sought to build "One Big Union." Indeed, the IWW in 1913 was intensely active and very militant. It led a bitter strike in Paterson, New Jersey, and the workers, employed and unemployed, of New York City were swept into support of the strike by an immense pageant about it that was staged in Madison Square Garden. The moving spirit behind the production was the young writer John Reed (about whom, in 1982, the movie *Reds* was created).

In spite of their smaller numbers, it was the IWW and a few remaining Anarchists, much more than the Socialists, who did the arduous and often dangerous work of trying to get food and shelter and employment for the jobless.

The IWW responded to the depression by forming what were often called Unemployed Leagues, auxiliaries attached to their regular locals. Each jobless worker who joined an Unemployed League paid five cents (or sometimes nothing) a month in dues. Within the leagues, the IWW followed a policy that was different in one important respect from the policy it supported in 1907–1908. At their convention in October 1914, Wobbly delegates voted that unemployed "parades to City Halls, Capitols, etc., should be discouraged as nothing more substantial than hot air is to be found in these political centers."

Instead of petitioning government agencies, Wobblies now taught workers that they might have to help themselves to the food they needed. Not too clearly, the IWW at this point proposed actions that seemed to range from simply exerting pressure to actual looting. The IWW publication *Solidarity* included the following in its report of the 1914 Wobbly convention: "The delegates agreed with [Bill] Haywood that the places for the unemployed to demonstrate were the places where there was plenty of food and clothing so that they could help themselves."

This policy, when put into practice, involved pressure, usually by weight of massed numbers, on those who had food. The IWW did not actually organize looting, but its advocacy of a policy that the jobless help themselves won no friends among such groups as the Socialists, who were sensitive to what large sections of society would tolerate. Practically, the Wobblies did more than use militant language to encourage the jobless to appropriate the necessities of life. They led demonstrations and also urged the employed to take action of a sort designed to help create more jobs. They advocated and practiced sabotage, by which they meant slowing down production or damaging machinery. Wobblies maintained that bosses broke the bodies of workers in the process of getting as much profit from them as possible, so it was appropriate for workers to respond by breaking machinery, thus forcing bosses to hire more workers in order to maintain production.

Like many other IWW leaders, Wobbly poet Joe Hill disagreed with the few Anarchists who advocated the use of armed violence by the unemployed. Workers, he said in an article in the *International Socialist Review*, could not possibly finance the weapons they would need to fight off the private armies paid for and equipped by the employers. He told the following story in his article:

> Some time ago the writer was working in a big lumber yard on the west coast. On the coast nearly all the work around the water fronts and lumber yards is temporary.
>
> When a boat comes in a large number of men are hired and when the boat is unloaded these men are "laid off." Conse-

quently it is to the interest of the workers "to make the job last" as long as possible.

The writer and three others got orders to load up five box cars with shingles. When we commenced the work we found, to our surprise, that every shingle bundle had been cut open. That is, the little strip of sheet iron that holds the shingles tightly together in a bundle, had been cut with a knife or a pair of shears, on every bundle in the pile — about three thousand bundles in all.

When the boss came around we notified him about the accident and, after exhausting his supply of profanity, he ordered us to get the shingle press and re-bundle the whole batch. It took the four of us ten whole days to put that shingle pile into shape again. And our wages for that time at the rate of 32 cents per hour, amounted to $134.00. By adding the loss on account of delay in shipment, the "holding money" for the five box cars, etc., we found that the company's profit for that day had been reduced about $300. . . .

This same method of fighting can be used in a thousand different ways by the skilled mechanic or machine hand as well as by the common laborer. This weapon is always at the finger tips of the worker, employed or unemployed.

The first IWW action (the first action by any group) against unemployment in the prewar depression was a parade and open-air meeting in Los Angeles the day after Christmas, 1913. Wobbly speakers, addressing a large gathering that included Mexicans, denounced "starvation amid plenty," and the police response was to attack with clubs and revolvers. They arrested seventy-five of the demonstrators and killed one. The *Los Angeles Times* reported that "the meeting was peaceful until the police arrived."

By the first of the year, 10,000 people in San Francisco were standing in soup lines each day, and 65,000 altogether were estimated to be out of work in the city. At this time Lucy Parsons cooperated with the IWW in San Francisco, where she was making her living by lecturing and selling books about her husband, Albert Parsons. On January 20, she rented Jefferson Hall for a lecture about unemployment. When she appeared, the proprietor of the hall refused to let the meeting be held, claiming he had not been paid. Not to be frustrated, Parsons, with many who had come to hear her, moved across the street. She began to talk and was immediately arrested. The police also arrested, among others, the Wobbly who was head of the San Francisco Unemployment Committee.

About 1,000 people who had gathered to hear Lucy Parsons or had been attracted by the disturbance now tried to hold their own meeting, which the police blocked. Members of the crowd responded by smashing nearby plate-glass windows. The charge against Parsons became inciting to riot. The police magistrate dismissed this charge for lack of evidence, but the police immediately rearrested Parsons and charged her with actual rioting.

In court, Parsons produced receipts for the rent of the hall, and the magistrate recognized that she could not have been rioting, for she was in custody when the riot occurred. It also developed in court that the proprietor of Jefferson Hall had been urged by the police to prevent the meeting and that the police were conveniently on hand — with an ambulance — when the audience could not get into the hall. As was to happen many times in 1914, a meeting of the unemployed had developed into a fight for free speech.

Unemployment was acute earlier in San Francisco than in some other cities because a world fair was to be held there. Men had come from all over seeking work, only to find there were not nearly enough jobs to go around. The Wobblies, who loved to sing, had a collection of bitter songs about the fair. One, sung to the tune of "Tipperary," was written by Joe Hill, soon to be executed in Utah for a murder to which no evidence linked him.

> Bill Brown came a thousand miles to work
>   on Frisco Fair
> All the papers said a million men were
>   wanted there
> Bill Brown hung around and asked for work
>   three times a day,
> Til finally he went busted flat, then
>   he did sadly say,

CHORUS:
It's a long way down to the soupline.
    It's a long way to go.
It's a long way down to the soupline
    And the soup is weak I know.
Good-bye, good old pork chops.
    Farewell beefsteak rare,
It's a long, long way down to the soupline,
    But my soup is there.

In Detroit, the Unemployed League ran its own soup kitchen in a former church building provided by Unitarians. Along with mulligan stew, the Wobblies gave lectures and held street meetings. So active was the Detroit Unemployed League in arguing for reduced hours and increased pay that the Wobblies believed they played a major role in persuading Henry Ford to raise wages to five dollars a day — a move that outraged other automobile manufacturers.

Not all churches were as hospitable as the Unitarians in Detroit, and there was a deep antireligious, or anticlerical, mood among some of the jobless. Out of this mood came a famous Joe Hill song:

Long-haired preachers come out every night,
Try to tell you what's wrong and what's right;
But when asked how 'bout something to eat
They will answer with voices so sweet:

You will eat, bye and bye,
In that glorious land above the sky;
Work and pray, live on hay,
You'll get pie in the sky when you die.

Wobblies could certainly be irreverent, but it was as much from need as from a desire to needle that the IWW began to lead jobless men, and an occasional woman, to churches in New York City. The idea originated with Frank Tannenbaum, a 21-year-old immigrant who was an unemployed member of the Waiters International Union. Tannenbaum was not only an IWW member but also a friend of the Anarchist Emma Goldman, and he spent a good deal of time reading and helping out in the office of Goldman's magazine, *Mother Earth*. Tannenbaum first suggested his idea of going to churches at a meeting of all the IWW locals in New York City in January 1914. The plan was approved, and Tannenbaum and others were assigned to carry it out.

The night of February 27, Tannenbaum led 1,000 jobless men to the Baptist Tabernacle. The next night, he led 600 to the Labor Temple, and on March 2 he and his followers went to the Fifth Avenue First Presbyterian Church. On each of these nights, the churches let the unemployed in and gave them food and shelter. After each visit the jobless army tidied up.

On the evening of March 4, Frank Tannenbaum addressed the jobless as usual in Rutgers Square before going to a church. He was explaining why there was unemployment in capitalist society when (according to Max Eastman, who reported the speech for his magazine the *Masses*) a woman interrupted, saying that in France the people had had to use force to win their independence. "In Paris the streets ran with blood," she said.

"Yes," said Tannenbaum, "and it will take force to overthrow capitalism here, too. And the I.W.W. is organizing the force that will do it when the time comes."

Asked why he led the jobless to churches instead of the Fifth Avenue clubs of the wealthy, Tannenbaum replied, "Because the church seemed a natural place for a hungry and homeless man to go to ask for food and shelter."

New York's police commissioner had noted complaints coming from influential quarters about the activities of the IWW. He had also been asked by fearful church members to keep an eye on the nocturnal marches of the jobless, peaceful though they had been. Accordingly, he had officers on hand when Tannenbaum and 500 men and 1 woman arrived at St. Alphonsus Catholic Church on West Broadway. Tannenbaum, accompanied by detectives, went to the rectory to ask Father John G. Schneider for permission to enter the church. Father Schneider refused, and Tannenbaum returned to the front of the building to lead his men elsewhere. While he was absent, someone had opened the church door and the men had filed in. Tannenbaum asked them to leave, and about 300 of them did so before the police closed the doors, preventing further departures.

Tannenbaum found that he and the remaining 200 were trapped inside, along with some newspaper reporters. He asked the reporters to note that if any violence occurred it would be the police who caused it. There was no disorder in the church, as a photograph taken by one of the reporters showed. There was no violence when the police arrived, but Tannenbaum, 190 men, and 1 woman were arrested.

The results of such episodes were to be felt a generation later. One witness, a young fellow who became known as Mike Gold, was so angered by the police action that he was moved to join the IWW. During the Great Depression of the 1930s, Gold, now a Communist, became a frequent and eloquent writer on behalf of the jobless.

Each of the penniless unemployed who was arrested with Tannenbaum was held for $100 bail; Tannenbaum's bail was $5,000. When he was tried, he was sentenced to a year on Blackwell's Island plus a $500 fine to be paid off at the rate of a day in jail for each dollar. The fine was later paid by sympathizers. (Frank Tannenbaum was so outraged by conditions in the Blackwell's Island jail that he began a campaign against them after his release. His efforts forced some reforms.)

Impressed by the militant young immigrant, Upton Sinclair wrote an angry, despairing poem, "To Frank Tannenbaum in Prison," which ended:

> A world enslaved, I cannot set it free!
> So I excuse myself, and do my task,
> And let thee rot, poor sad-eyed foreign boy —
> One hero-soul in this our coward State!

One of those arrested with Tannenbaum was Arthur Caron, an unemployed textile worker. Later he was arrested again on his way home after another unemployed meeting. This time he was thrown into a car by two detectives and beaten so badly that he had to be hospitalized. Still later, while awaiting trial, Caron turned up as a picket outside the Rockefeller estate at

Tarrytown, where workers were protesting the massacre of miners, women, and children during a strike against Rockefeller-owned mines at Ludlow, Colorado. This time stones were thrown at him. Back in the house he shared with several others, he was killed by a bomb on July 4, the day before his trial. Who was responsible for the bomb has been disputed. At a large Union Square memorial meeting for Caron, Elizabeth Gurley Flynn asked: "If this young man did turn to violence as a last resort, *who is responsible? Who taught it to him?*"

Support for Tannenbaum's activities had been far from unanimous among leftist and liberal people, some of whom also disapproved of the activities in connection with his legal defense. Although as an individual he received financial aid from a few well-to-do persons, many leftists were unwilling to support any IWW cause.[1] Employers now found the time favorable for a campaign against the IWW, Anarchism, and Socialism, which were all loosely lumped together. For some time newspapers had been concerned about the growing influence of Wobblies among the unemployed. American Federation of Labor officials joined in attacking the IWW, and Socialist reformers, often from the middle class, were uneasy about the sometimes rowdy and indiscreet Wobbly tactics. An important organizer of propaganda against radicals was the National Civic Federation, which included not only big capitalists but also Samuel Gompers, head of the AFL. Because of the growing hostility, the IWW set up a Labor Defense Committee.

Meanwhile, the IWW, the Socialists, and the Anarchists could not find ways of working together for the unemployed. It did not help that a few of the Anarchists who believed in "propaganda of the deed" were still active. On October 13, anniversary of the death of Spanish Anarchist Francisco Ferrer, two bombs exploded in New York, one of them at St. Alphonsus Catholic Church.

Against such a background, there was a scramble — while Tannenbaum was in jail — to provide for the unemployed a leadership that was safely antiradical. A man named Jefferson Davis appeared on the scene. Calling himself "King of the Hoboes," he had founded an organization, the Hoboes of America. In 1908 in Seattle, he had started a housing scheme for homeless men that he called "Hotel de Gink." Now, in New York City, he set up another Hotel de Gink, for which he solicited support on the grounds that it would keep homeless men from following the IWW.

Still the IWW persisted. Its Labor Defense Committee had helped at the trial of Tannenbaum and his companions, and in the spring of 1914, Wobblies in New York created an Unemployed Union. One of those who formed this organization was Elizabeth Gurley Flynn, the "Rebel Girl" speaker at meetings of the Philadelphia jobless in 1908. In her autobiography, she quoted the program that was printed on a red card:

> The Mayor's Committee has been investigating us for weeks and has done nothing. The CITY says it can do nothing. The STATE can do but little. The BOSSES say they have no work for us. LET'S GET TOGETHER AND SEE IF WE CAN DO SOMETHING FOR OURSELVES!
>
> In order to force immediate and serious consideration of the Unemployed Problem, the I.W.W. Unemployed Union of New York advocates the following measures:
>
> 1. Organization of the Unemployed. (In Union there is Strength.)
> 2. A Rent Strike. (No wages, no rent.)
> 3. A Workers' Moratorium. (Don't pay your debts till the jobs come around.)
> 4. Refusal to work at Scab Wages. (Don't let the boss use your misery to pull down the workers' standard of life.)
> 5. A demand for Work or Bread. (If the bosses won't let you earn a decent livelihood then they must foot the bill for your keep.) The workers make the wealth of the world. It's up to us to get our share!

On the reverse side of the card were several quotations, mostly from religious sources:

> Cardinal Manning said: "Necessity knows no law and a starving man has a natural right to a share of his neighbor's bread."

Father Vaughn said: "The Catholic Church teaches that a man who is in extreme need of the means of subsistence may take from whatsoever sources, what is necessary for him to keep from actual starvation. . . ."

Jesus said (*Matthew*, Chapter X, Verse 2): "And into whatsoever city or town you shall enter inquire who in it is worthy and there abide till you go hence. And into whatsoever house you enter, remain — eating, drinking such things as they have. For the laborer is worthy of his hire."

The Unemployed Union tried a variety of picaresque publicity stunts to attract attention to the problems of the jobless. For one thing, they printed tickets that read: "Good for One Meal. Charge to the Mayor's Committee on Unemployment." Armed with these tickets, Wobblies went into fancy restaurants and demanded — and got — meals. This scheme continued until newspapers carried stories about the hoax. Individual Wobblies also volunteered to help the Mayor's Committee on Unemployment sort clothes donated during a clothing drive. The volunteers appropriated the best of the garments, put them on, wore them back to Wobbly headquarters, and distributed them among their needy fellows.

Out of the bitter events in the spring of 1914 came many different responses. One was a satire in the form of newspaper dispatches purporting to come from Jerusalem at the time of Jesus. "JESUS ARRESTED, ARRAIGNED BEFORE FEDERAL AUTHORITIES" read one headline. (Later, during the Great Depression of the 1930s, the author of the satire, Henry G. Alsberg, was in charge of the Federal Writers Project, a public works program for unemployed writers.) The Alsberg pieces appeared in the *Masses*, as did many angry cartoons about unemployment by John Sloan, Art Young, and other well-known artists.

The *Masses* tried to be practical, too. It published an article by Meyer London, the lone Socialist congressman, calling for unemployment insurance. A few unions had by now set up modest out-of-work benefit plans for their own members, but the idea of government unemployment insurance had not yet appeared in any significant way on the national scene.

In San Francisco, the needs of the jobless continued. Charles Kelly, leader of an Industrial Army across the country in 1894, decided on another mass lobbying trip to petition the federal government to set up public works. George Speed, now a Wobbly, had travelled with Kelly twenty years before, but he opposed this new project and called Kelly a faker. The army took shape anyway, and finally IWW members joined it, forming a separate company within the larger movement.

Kelly led the whole army out of San Francisco, but they got no farther than Sacramento. The Southern Pacific Railroad would do no more than allow the men to camp on railroad property after they refused an offer of transportation back to San Francisco. Soon Kelly and the head of the IWW segment of the army were arrested. While they were in jail, the city of Sacramento supplied food for a few days and hoped that something would happen to get the men out of town.

Nothing did happen. The city asked Governor Hiram Johnson, of the new Progressive Party, for militia, which he refused to supply. Local officials then sent armed police, sheriffs, and deputies to evict the army. Wielding pick handles and aided by firemen using a fire hose with water under high pressure, they attacked the camp. A number of men, including an African-American IWW member, were so badly beaten that they had to be hospitalized, and others claimed they had proof that one of their number was killed.

It so happened that Helen Keller was billed to lecture in Sacramento at this time. This amazing woman had become famous for her work on behalf of the deaf and the blind, and she had, in the words of the *International Socialist Review*, "come to the conclusion that the unemployment of the blind is only part of a greater social question. 'It is not physical blindness, but social blindness, that cheats our hands of their right to work,' " she declared.

Keller, a Socialist, announced that at her Sacramento lecture she would speak in defense of the brutalized unemployed. Word soon reached her that if she did so, she would be hauled from the platform and driven out of town. Nevertheless, she gave her speech. She talked about unemployment, its causes, and its only possible cure, which she said was socialism. Nobody dared to carry out the threat.

To the chagrin of Sacramento officials, much of the unemployed army they had evicted was able to stay close by, but out of legal reach. A sympathizer had invited them to use an acre and a half of choice land he owned in an area just beyond the city limits where the very wealthy had homes. Hundreds of men camped on this wooded plot, and they had the legal papers they needed to keep evictors away.

Charles Kelly served a six-month sentence in jail. He came out convinced that radicalism was the wrong route for workers to follow.

The IWW continued to go where the jobless were. They formed an Unemployed League and began to conduct street-corner meetings in Sioux City, Iowa, where hundreds of men were stranded in October 1914 after summer work on railroad construction and in the wheat fields had shut down. With a kitchen set up in the local Socialist Hall, the Wobblies fed the jobless. They also began to organize a union among those who could get jobs working ten hours at fifty cents a day. In protest, the local merchants stopped contributing food for the IWW soup kitchen. The Wobbly response was to lead 150 followers into a luncheon meeting of the businessmen's organization known as the Commercial Club. The jobless ate the meal prepared for the club members, and also made it clear they wanted action in response to their demand for food and shelter.

The businessmen now put pressure on Sioux City officials to get the unemployed out of town, and police officers began to arrest IWW speakers at street-corner meetings. The charges were vagrancy, and soon most of the local unemployed were locked up. The IWW then sent out a call for help. Wobblies began to drift into town in great numbers. The new arrivals held street meetings and demanded the release of their fellows. Soon all were out of jail, but the street meetings continued, and they always demanded relief for the jobless. Crowds of at least 600, sometimes 1,000, gathered, and the police arrested anyone who got up to speak.

To prepare for the large numbers who would soon be in jail,

the city had built a stockade and ordered a great quantity of big rocks hauled in. The prisoners were supposed to break up the rocks, apparently for use in road or other construction. But when they were ordered to the rock pile, the prisoners merely sat on it. Nothing could persuade them to work without decent pay. Sent back to the jail, the men went on a hunger strike, burned their vermin-infested blankets, and vowed not to eat until all were released and their right to free speech returned.

The authorities agreed to release them if they would promise to leave town. The men refused to do so. The Wobblies maintained that each man should be free to leave town or stay, as he wished. Finally the authorities gave up completely. Eighty-six half-starved hunger strikers walked out of jail, free to speak and to hold a victory celebration on top of the rock pile, where they cooked mulligan stew in cans labelled "Standard Oil." Their victory did not end there. Soon the Sioux City authorities set up a fund to provide relief for the unemployed.

Activities of all kinds occurred all over the country. J. Eads How, the "millionaire hobo" who had led an unemployed march in St. Louis in 1908, hired the San Francisco Civic Auditorium for an Unemployed Convention February 18–23, 1915. The IWW, which did not have the money to hire such a hall, did have the energy to take over the meeting once it got under way.

They acted in the spirit of the concluding stanza of the poem "Us, The Hoboes" which Covington Hall had published in the *International Socialist Review* only a few months before:

> We shall laugh to scorn your power that
> now holds the world in awe.
> We shall trample on your customs and
> shall spit upon your law;
> We shall outrage all your temples, — we
> shall blaspheme all your gods,
> We shall turn the old world over as a
> plowman turns the clods.

Rebellious though they were, the Wobblies offered no general program that could help the jobless. Their main achievement was to mobilize support for jailed workers, whom they regarded as political prisoners.

In Chicago, "hunger demonstrations" were frequent. Anarchists planned a big one for Sunday, January 17, 1915. It would begin with an indoor meeting at Hull House, the settlement house run by Jane Addams. Over the speaker's stand hung a black banner with the word HUNGER on it in white letters, and other signs around the hall said, "We Want WORK Not Charity," "Why Starve in the Midst of Plenty?" and "Hunger Knows No Law." Among the speakers was Lucy Parsons, who told her audience, "As long as you accept charity, capitalists will not give you work."

The police waited outside, but they did not succeed in preventing the march from the meeting hall to the area of rich men's clubs and hotels in the heart of the financial district. Along the route police kept up a steady attack on the marchers. At one point, an Episcopal priest, Irwin St. John Tucker (known among the poor as Friar Tuck) picked up and walked with a banner the police had thrown to the ground. Appropriately, its message was "Give Us This Day Our Daily Bread." The priest, Lucy Parsons, five other women, and fifteen men were arrested.

Encouraged by some reformers and intellectuals in Chicago, the courts ruled that the chief of police did not have the right to license street parades. The prisoners were freed. Meanwhile, however, the Corporation Counsel had ruled that the police *did* have the right to issue parade permits. The hunger demonstrators felt that this ruling called for another march. This time they paraded with very little harassment from the police, and they passed resolutions saying, "We, the unemployed of Chicago . . . shall continue to use the public streets . . . and fight for bread and work."

No solution to the problem of unemployment came from these hunger demonstrations, but a favorite union song did — "Solidarity Forever." Ralph Chaplin, the IWW leader who wrote the song, finished it the morning of January 17 and sang it to the tune of "John Brown's Body" as he walked toward Hull House:

> When the Union's inspiration through the
> workers' blood shall run.
> There can be no power greater anywhere
> beneath the sun.
> Yet what force on earth is weaker than
> the feeble strength of one?
> But the Union makes us strong.
> SOLIDARITY FOREVER!
> SOLIDARITY FOREVER!
> SOLIDARITY FOREVER!
> FOR THE UNION MAKES US STRONG.

With this song and in other ways the Wobblies left their mark. The Anarchists, though many fewer in number, also made a lasting impression. For instance, a teenaged boy named Benjamin Grefenson never forgot a hunger demonstration he witnessed. When he grew up and became known as Herbert Benjamin, he led two National Hunger Marches in the 1930s.[2]

Coming from surprising quarters were expressions of bitterness. Here is part of a poem by Britain's Rudyard Kipling that reached many American workers in 1914 when it was published in the *International Socialist Review*:

> We have fed you all for a thousand years, but that
> was our doom, you know;
> From the time you chained us in the fields, to the
> strike of a week ago.
> You have eaten our lives, our babies and wives,
> but that was your legal share;
> But if blood be the price of your legal wealth,
> good God, we have bought it fair.

Meanwhile, millionaire Jacob Coxey continued to advocate public works and his unique proposal for financing them. His files still in Massillon, Ohio, show earnest correspondence on the subject with public figures in 1914. That year he also organized, without great success, another march on Washington. He did succeed this time, however, in making a speech from the Capitol steps.

Carl Browne, also in Washington, renewed efforts he had begun in 1894 to speak from the Capitol steps about the need for public works. While he lived in a twenty-five-cent-a day room, he pleaded his case before the presiding officers of both houses of Congress. Finally he got permission from Champ Clark, Speaker of the House. On Christmas Day, 1913, Browne mounted the Capitol steps and started to speak. As in 1894, however, the police were on hand, and they stopped him because he had not got the permission of Vice-President Marshall, presiding officer of the Senate. This time Browne outwitted the police. Later in the day, surrounded by what he called a "band of brave fellows," he returned and gave his long delayed speech. Afterward he appeared as usual on the street corners of Washington dressed in an outfit that looked like a suit of armor, selling his own mimeographed publication, the *Labor Knight.*

Browne died on January 10, 1914. In reporting his final efforts for the unemployed, the *Masses* concluded, "He took Washington too seriously." There was reason for this cynical remark. During the eighteen months of the 1913–1915 depression, the federal government in Washington took no action to help the unemployed. No branch of the federal government even tried to measure the extent of unemployment, and President Woodrow Wilson ignored all of the proposals that came to him from many quarters urging that public works be established. (For an indication of the mood of some of the unemployed at this time, see Appendix H.)

No state provided public works during this depression, and among the major cities only Philadelphia appropriated public funds for relief. It is hard to gauge to what extent this pattern reflected the absence of a campaign for public works by Anarchist- and IWW-led unemployed. But the IWW, with here and there a little help from AFL locals, did induce a number of communities to provide relief.

Without the efforts of the Wobblies in 1914, the suffering of American working people would have been much greater than it was. Without the agitation of Socialists, Anarchists, and particularly the IWW, there would have been no advance among workers in their perennial effort to figure out what to do about unemployment or how to get rid of it altogether. In a very small way, they realized the dream expressed in the conclusion of Reginald Wright Kauffman's 1914 poem, "The March of the Hungry Men":

> Through the depths of the devil's darkness, with
>   the distant stars for light,
> They are coming the while you slumber, and they
>   come with the might of Right.
> On a morrow — perhaps tomorrow — you will waken
>   and see, and then
> You will hand the keys of the cities to the ranks
>   of the Hungry Men.

What some regarded as a solution to the problem appeared when war industries began to expand, thus helping to bring an end to the depression. But the war that would soon include the United States was totally unacceptable to the Wobblies as a way of dealing with the unemployment problem. The IWW believed that the chief sufferers on the battlefield would be workers, and it opposed the war in every way it could, both before and after U.S. involvement. As a result, the IWW felt the full force of government repression and was virtually immobilized when a new depression arrived following the end of World War I.

17

"Fight and Live!"
(1921–1929)

The business of America is business.
— Calvin Coolidge, president of the United States
1925–1929

My experience is that the greatest aid to efficiency of labor is a long line of men waiting at the gate.
— Samuel Insull, public utilities executive

The man who fights for his fellow-man is a better man than the one who fights for himself.
— Clarence S. Darrow
address to jury, Chicago, 1920

During and immediately after World War I, private enterprise and sections of the public in the United States fell into a kind of paranoia. The stimulus to hysteria in some quarters was the socialist revolution in Russia, which seemed likely to succeed. Many workers and radicals in the United States were exhilarated by it, and their opponents lost no chance to head off any kind of American socialist revolution. As a result, democratic attitudes and institutions were subverted as they had never been before except in the slave-holding South. The federal government, headed by President Woodrow Wilson, and many state and local governments and vigilante groups engaged in assaults on radical labor organizations, radical political leaders, and radical publications.

On January 15, 1917, Congress passed the Espionage Act. Under this law, 877 persons were arrested, although not one was ever brought to trial on a charge of actual spying. Nor was anyone tried or convicted of espionage under a companion law, the Sedition Act of 1918. The Post Office suspended mailing privileges for many unorthodox publications. In New York State, several Communists were found guilty of criminal anarchy and received sentences of from five to ten years in prison.

The Wobblies, who had been active in organizing unions, strikes, and the unemployed and in resisting curtailment of freedom of speech, were a particular object of attack. In July 1917, during a strike in Bisbee, Arizona, vigilantes rounded up and kidnapped 1,200 striking miners and townspeople who were suspected of being Wobblies or Wobbly sympathizers, took them all to a remote spot in the New Mexico desert, and held them there for thirty-six hours without food or water. After beating the prisoners, the vigilantes drove them into a federally operated detention camp from which they were not released for three months, although no charges were brought against them.

In Seattle, where the IWW had been very influential, immigration authorities arrested large numbers of aliens, looking for Wobblies they could deport. So many were taken in that the jail could not hold them all, and prisoners had to be farmed out to jails in other Washington towns and cities. In Butte, Montana, vigilantes lynched Frank Little, a crippled Native American who was a popular IWW organizer. In Tulsa, Oklahoma, vigilantes tarred and feathered seventeen Wobblies.

Nevertheless, in 1919, in response to the agitation of radicals, the Democratic administration endorsed the principle of appropriating funds to provide jobs on public works. At the same time, the government continued its repression. In August, President Woodrow Wilson, in a private letter, called the Wobblies "a menace to organized society and to the right conduct of industry." Soon after, every IWW hall in the country was raided and 160 Wobblies were arrested, including Bill Haywood and Elizabeth Gurley Flynn. Emma Goldman, not a Wobbly but an Anarchist, was tried for obstructing the draft and was deported along with nearly 250 other aliens.

In the general frenzy, Socialists who opposed the war were harassed. As early as June 1917, vigilantes had destroyed many Socialist headquarters, and even after the war, the New York State Assembly refused to seat five elected Socialist legislators.

Trials of IWW members were held in Omaha, Spokane, Wichita, and Sacramento. More than 100 Wobblies were tried in Chicago; they were accused of committing among them over 10,000 crimes. The sentences imposed on some of them were long. Haywood, who was not in good health, received a twenty-year sentence. He appealed, and when his appeal was denied he jumped bail and took refuge in the Soviet Union.

As a result of the repression, the IWW was nearly crushed. It was in no position to concern itself with the unemployed in the postwar depression that was coming on. On January 2, 1920, Department of Justice agents under A. Mitchell Palmer and J. Edgar Hoover rounded up 10,000 radicals throughout the nation. In New York State, a special investigating group known as the Lusk Committee added to the general terror by confiscating tons of radical literature, arresting thousands of people, and helping district attorneys obtain indictments and immigration officials carry out deportations. (Palmer, who hoped he would one day be president, saw "reds" as a menace in the event of a new economic depression. The "disease of evil thinking," he said, "would prove grave indeed" during a time of want.) Early in 1920, Police Commissioner Enright of New York City got the city aldermen to approve plans for a special police regiment to combat revolutionary agitators.

Partly because its members had held differing views about the war, the Socialist Party in the United States was in crisis. Many of its members had opposed the war as imperialist while others had supported the government. Many Socialists supported the Soviet revolution while others did not. From the debate on these and related subjects emerged two Communist parties and a weakened Socialist Party. One Communist group was made up largely of foreign-born workers who had been organized into federations according to the languages they spoke. The other revolutionary group included more native-born Americans.

These two new parties, both very small, took shape in the

midst of the terror against the Left, and they began operations as underground organizations. They were also consumed with sectarian quarrels. People who are combative enough to take on the whole capitalist system are often quite capable of doing battle with each other. In addition, the two parties were infiltrated by government spies who encouraged the quarrels. (Some historians have estimated that one-fourth of the members of these tiny underground groups were government agents or provocateurs.) There was a spy present when the two parties finally settled their differences in 1922 and became one openly functioning party, which was called for a while the Workers (Communist) Party.[1]

All things considered, the organizations of the Left were in a remarkably poor position to help the multitudes of unemployed who were, by the late summer of 1920, looking for work. War industries had closed down and huge numbers of ex-servicemen had entered the job market. Just how many were unemployed is not known with certainty. One expert estimated the number of jobless at 4 million; another estimated there were twice as many jobless in 1920 as in 1908 or 1914. Though these figures were vague, clearly millions were out of work.

It was also clear that the United States had grown rich in the 100 years since the first industrial depression. The number of workers in industry was four times as great as it had been in 1819. Their output had increased thirteenfold in the same period, according to some estimates, and the wealth held by the employing class was twenty-three times what it had been a century before.

Now, following World War I, great repression and great unemployment accompanied great wealth. Among the jobless, the radicals continued a tradition begun a century before: doing what they could to aid and to educate those in distress. In New York, the largest city and the one where misery was greatest — and where one-third of the population was foreign-born — the underground Communist movement began organizing. A husband-and-wife team, Israel Amter and Sadie Van Veen, was assigned to concentrate on the problems of the jobless. They could not be deported because they were native-born.

Israel Amter was born in Denver, Colorado, in 1881. Unable to go to college because of the depression of the 1890s, he worked at various jobs while trying to get a musical education. He wanted to be a composer, and in time he did write an opera about American Indians who had been familiar sights to his parents when they settled on a Colorado farm in the 1860s.

In his teens Amter managed to become an accomplished pianist. At a concert he gave in the Denver synagogue, he met Sadie Van Veen, an artist who had come to Denver from New York when she was a child. Her family read *Appeal To Reason*, a Socialist paper published in Girard, Kansas, and she introduced Amter to Socialist ideas. Together they met Bill Haywood and Eugene V. Debs, and in 1901 they joined the Socialist Party. After their marriage two years later, they went to Vienna to study, and there they both took part in Austrian Socialist activities. When they returned to the United States they settled in New York, where Amter worked as a musician and a translator from the German. Along with many other Socialists, they opposed World War I and the entry of the United States into it. They were supporters of Debs, who had been sentenced to prison in 1919 for his earlier antiwar activities, and who in prison received nearly a million votes as the Socialist candidate for president. In 1922 Amter and Van Veen helped form what became the Communist Party.

The plight of the unemployed moved Amter deeply. He said in his memoir, "Do you know what it means to be unemployed — to be denied the right to work? The unemployed worker has no income. He may be kicked out of his home at any time. His furniture may be put out on the street. If he is a home-owner, he may lose his home. His family may be broken up, and he will have to farm out his children or place them in institutions." The reason for periodic depressions was, he felt sure, "because the capitalist system cannot operate without an army of unemployed."

As the postwar depression grew, Communist leader Nikolai Lenin advised Communists in the United States to operate openly and to form alliances with existing working-class organizations. American Communists took this advice to heart, and soon Amter and his wife were assigned to discuss unemployment with various unions, a few of which had developed modest unemployment insurance plans for their members.

By March 1921, thirty-five local AFL, IWW, and independent unions had arranged to send delegates to the Unemployment Conference of Greater New York. The conference set up a continuing organization, the Unemployment (also called the Unemployed) Council of New York, and Israel Amter became its secretary. Adopting the slogan "Fight and Live: Work or Compensation," the council began to hold meetings at which speakers advocated unemployment relief, public works, and low-cost housing.

Soon after the formation of the Unemployed Council (UC), Amter was arrested and charged with criminal anarchy. When he was released on bail, he continued to work for the organization, editing a small paper he called *Jobless* and speaking at street-corner meetings. The meetings drew crowds of unemployed men as well as police agents.

One meeting, held in a hall, was arranged especially for ex-servicemen. After Amter finished his talk, he gave the floor to speakers from among the crowd. One man, still in military uniform, asked, "Why should we be sitting here, when there are places on Riverside Drive where we can lay our heads at night?"

"Yes," shouted another, "and why should we let off so much steam in this hall, when there are plenty of stores and restaurants where we could go and fill our bellies?"

Many in the audience agreed. Amter knew they were hungry, and to keep them from rushing away on a foraging expedition, he had come prepared to serve coffee and sandwiches, which he now did. He was also prepared to believe that the proposals for immediate seizure of food and shelter came from police provocateurs, which had happened before. (At a similar meeting in Philadelphia in 1908, unknown persons in the audience had persuaded the unemployed, against the speaker's pleas, to leave the hall bent on looting. They were attacked by waiting police.) Amter did not intend to play into hostile hands or to adopt some of the colorful activities of the IWW's Unemployed Leagues, whose members had on occasion helped themselves to meals.

In another respect, the program of Communists in 1921–1922 differed from the activities of the Wobblies in 1914. The New York Unemployed Council began a propaganda campaign for unemployment insurance, which the Socialist Congressman Meyer London had called for in the *Masses* in 1915, and which the Socialist Party advocated in its 1920 program. Instead of approaching churches or rich men's clubs for relief, as Anarchists and Wobblies had done, the council went to the municipal government. On one occasion it planned two simultaneous marches to converge from opposite directions on City Hall, where the acting mayor would be given a petition for relief. (The mayor himself was vacationing in Florida.)

The police moved to head off the demonstration. So many officers were stationed along the proposed routes that the marchers thought better of parading. Instead they faded away — but not because they had lost interest in reaching City Hall; they knew that there was more than one way to get there. Only a token handful followed Amter on his part of the announced parade route, but 10,000 slipped quietly into Foley Square behind City Hall. Taken by surprise, the police gave up their efforts to prevent the meeting. They even opened a corridor through the crowd so that Amter and a delegation from among the demonstrators could enter City Hall and see the acting mayor.

"Police will not solve the unemployment problem," Amter told that startled gentleman. "It is ridiculous for you to line up police against us when we demand relief, lodging and unemployment insurance."

The problem of economic crisis and resulting unemployment did not exist just in the minds of radicals. In 1921, at the suggestion of Secretary of Commerce Herbert Hoover, President Warren G. Harding called together representatives of business, industry, government, and social work to act as the President's Conference on Unemployment. This group, noting the absence of solid statistics, estimated the number of unemployed, exclusive of farm labor, to be 3.5 million early in September 1921. The figure was soon revised upward, and some estimates ran as high as 10 million jobless.

A related agency, the Economic Advisory Committee, made recommendations to the full conference, and these recommendations became more or less the conference's official findings. The central concept was that local governments must solve the emergency relief problem. In addition, industry should improve its efficiency so that unemployment would not recur, and government at all levels should plan public works to provide jobs, now and in the future.

Although in 1921 African-American workers were moving from the South into urban centers in great numbers and suffered most acutely from unemployment, the president's conference was made up entirely of white members. An African-American editor protested, and an African-American church leader was appointed. President Harding then noted that a newly enfranchised half of all voters was underrepresented and added women. Neither Hoover nor Harding proposed adding a representative from among the unemployed themselves. The closest the conference came was to include Samuel Gompers, head of the American Federation of Labor, who opposed unemployment insurance. The AFL did offer a theory about the cause of unemployment. At the AFL convention in June 1919, delegates had agreed it is "due to under-consumption. Underconsumption is caused by low or insufficient wages. Just wages will prevent industrial stagnation and lessen periodical unemployment."

President Harding may have known of this resolution. At any rate, when he appointed Gompers to the conference, he told him, "The whole trouble with the labor movement, Mr. Gompers, is that you and a lot of other labor men are not advising workmen to accept necessary reductions in wages and give an opportunity for a revival of industry."

The main objective of the conference was to get voluntary action against unemployment at the local level. By December 1921, 209 cities had set up mayor's committees to deal with the problem. The voluntary actions they encouraged, however, were piecemeal and inadequate. Portland, Oregon, for instance, did little more than set up emergency housing for homeless men. Detroit, where tens of thousands were out of work, encouraged citizens to hire men for odd jobs. Fewer than 1,000 got some work as a result of that campaign. Los Angeles set aside $2 million for public works. Kansas City reported an increase in the money contributed to private charity. Waterloo, Iowa, used the unemployment crisis to shift the burden of relief measures away from employers and the city government onto those who were still employed. Workers there were pressured into contributing 1 percent of their wages (that is, taking a 1 percent wage cut) to provide funds for the jobless. In Philadelphia, Holy Trinity Church set up an employment bureau, but to be eligible for help a jobless person had to be a member of the church's Bible class. The director of the president's conference, Colonel Arthur Wood, said of the Trinity Church program, "If a job isn't worth praying for, it isn't worth having." Wood, former head of the New York City police force, was now assistant secretary of war.

Other police- and military-minded men were also active in carrying out conference activities. An Army officer and an officer from the Navy were members of the conference staff. So, too, were agents of the Justice Department, who went out over the country and dealt directly with mayors. According to historian Carolyn Grin, "They also attended several radical meetings in New York, where Communists were allegedly attempting to capitalize on the unemployment situation, and their reports on these sometimes were used . . . to impress mayors with the need for local action."

In general the recommendations of the President's Conference on Unemployment centered on steps designed to improve the economy rather than to provide relief for the jobless. Congress accepted only a small part of such modest suggestions as were made. One of these was a proposal to increase road building — just what Jacob Coxey had advocated in 1894, 1908, 1914, and April 1922, when he met with President Harding and tried to talk him into endorsing the perennial Coxey public works scheme.

The conference also suggested that plans for public works be drawn up in readiness for the next period of mass unemployment. Congress did not agree. Following the return of relative prosperity as the 1920s advanced, Herbert Hoover continued — unsuccessfully — his attempts to get support from Congress for the idea of a public works program prepared in advance.

In summarizing the results of the conference, historian Carolyn Grin said, "At best it had inaugurated minor relief, a few jobs, and some studies, but studies used by academicians rather than politicians able to translate them into practical reform." Nevertheless, Herbert Hoover, who had dreamed up the conference, thought it was a great success, "a milestone in the progress of social thought." Later, Hoover was president when increased unemployment again plagued the country, and he opposed relief for the unemployed.

One individual who tried to do something effective for the jobless was Urbain Ledoux, former Harvard lecturer, United States Consul in Prague, and successful businessman, who was now a convert to Buddhism. Known in Boston as "Mr. Zero," Ledoux got various institutions there to supply homeless men with sleeping quarters that came to be called "Hotels de Jobless" or "Hotels de Gink." In New York, Mr. Zero, on behalf of a hundred unemployed men, asked for invitations to President Harding's inaugural ball. He even arranged for transportation for his party, but the invitations never arrived. Determined to call public attention to the suffering of those who could not find work, Ledoux held what he called "slave auctions." On Boston Common he put men, stripped to the waist as if they were slaves, on the auction block before crowds and asked for bids by employers. Only two "slaves" were bid for, although many were available. Those two went to "buyers" who offered only board and room and very small pay for a week's work.

When Mr. Zero tried to hold a similar auction in New York, he had even less luck, although he got a good response from thousands of homeless men who were sleeping on newspapers in public parks. To publicize his plan, he rode around in a bakery wagon, giving out free rolls and announcing that the auction would be held on the steps of the Public Library at Fifth

Avenue and Forty-second Street. The police soon put a stop to this unauthorized distribution of free food, and Mr. Zero continued on foot. Wherever he went, police officers went with him. They even followed him into a church where he stopped for a half-hour of rest and meditation. More were on hand behind the library in Bryant Park when at least 4,000 jobless men began to gather. Before Ledoux could start his auction, a formation of mounted police rode their horses into the crowd. From another direction a squadron of police rode in on motorcycles while officers on foot wielded clubs. Ledoux, motivated by religion rather than radicalism, was aghast, but the police assault had its effect. Mr. Zero gave up trying to call large numbers of unemployed together. He confined himself instead to persuading churches in New York and Boston to offer food and sleeping space to destitute men (for which he did not receive the same harsh treatment that Frank Tannenbaum had in 1914).

By the end of 1922, the depression was nearly over. Prices of commodities, which had been greatly inflated during the war, dropped substantially, making increased consumption possible. Business began to produce again and to hire workers. Even so, unemployment did not disappear. A reservoir of jobless men and women remained, even in times that were good from the employers' point of view.

The unemployment that Mr. Zero, Jacob Coxey, and Israel Amter protested simply did not go away. Neither did the radicals. The Communist Party in 1924 adopted a program that called for, among other things, a united front of all working-class organizations in a fight against continuing unemployment. Next year the CP made clear it was no longer underground, but it was still underfinanced. When it sent Israel Amter that year to be its district organizer in Cleveland, Ohio, he and his wife and two children had to hitchhike from New York.

In Cleveland, large numbers of men went daily to shop gates, looking for but not finding work. At factories and in working-class neighborhoods, the Amters passed out leaflets discussing unemployment and the Unemployed Council, which they believed should be ready to organize when the really big crash that they expected finally arrived. (The Amters knew that unemployment was spreading worldwide. In Germany, the National Congress of Unemployed Workers representing several hundred thousand jobless called for a shorter workday and shorter workweek for the employed and a consequent increase in jobs for those out of work. It also called for special efforts by trade unions on behalf of the jobless and urged united action against unemployment by all working-class organizations.)

The Unemployed Council in Cleveland set up a huge kettle in the Public Square and served free soup to the jobless. The organization also led groups of men and women into the offices of the Community Chest, where they demanded and got relief. Time and again Amter was arrested, as he had been earlier in New York. The criminal anarchy charge against him there had finally been dropped, but new nuisance charges were made in Cleveland, where obviously he was a nuisance and an embarrassment to authorities.

As Christmas 1928 approached, the Unemployed Council called attention to the plight of the jobless by setting up a ghastly Christmas tree in the Public Square. In lieu of the usual decorations, chicken heads hung from the branches, along with old pants, rags, and worn-out shoes. The Unemployed Council also borrowed from Mr. Zero the idea of holding a "slave auction" in the Public Square. The police dispersed the crowd and arrested Sadie Van Veen, who was tried and convicted under an 1865 law that forbade the selling of slaves.

When Cleveland officials did nothing in response to the continuing pleas for relief, members of the Unemployed Council appeared at one of the City Council meetings. Amter rose and asked for action on petitions the unemployed had presented. Other speakers, both unemployed and employed, supported his request. In reply to demands that they leave, the delegation said they had no intention of leaving until they got what they had come for. The City Council then walked out. Amter and his group took over the vacant seats and ran an orderly meeting on the subject of unemployment and relief, which was reported in detail, though not sympathetically, by the press.

Altogether, the activities of the Unemployed Council in Cleveland produced only some small help from the Community Chest and the city government by October 29, 1929, when the stock market crashed and verified what the jobless already knew: that there was a deep crisis in American economic life. In the years since the postwar depression of 1921–1922, the weak radical movement had not grown very much stronger or more capable of influencing national policy. In spite of the radicals' constant demands for public works, neither the government nor private industry provided for large-scale work relief projects.

Still, the leaders of the unemployed had learned a good deal that would be useful when the next, very different, stage in unemployed history opened with the onset of the Great Depression of the 1930s. The numbers of those out of work would be much greater than ever before, and their unemployment would last much longer.

Beginning in 1930, the organizations of the jobless would spread nationwide, become more stable than in the past, and expand in response to activities by both non-Communist radicals and Communists. Finally, the various trends among the organized jobless would merge into one national organization, and through it they would have power and reach goals they had always sought but had never before been able to attain. The dramatic achievements of the 1930s — federal assumption of responsibility for the jobless, vast work relief projects, and unemployment insurance — were outgrowths of the constant efforts that had gone on from 1808 to 1929.

18

The Beginning of the Great Depression (1929)

When more and more people are thrown out of work, unemployment results.
> — Calvin Coolidge, president of the United States
> 1925–1929

He who kills a job begins to kill a person.
> — author unknown

One of the most responsible tasks of the historian is to distinguish between the tinder and the spark.
> — Owen Lattimore
> *Nomads and Commissars*

Over half a century after the Great Depression, many people recall the desolation caused by the worst economic collapse in United States history, but few remain who remember the creativity with which citizens pressed the federal government to rid the country of the plague of unemployment. Because there have been more than fifty years of unrelenting indoctrination by the media, the educational system, many religious institutions, and most politicians, there are even fewer who recall with any clarity the role that radicals of several kinds played in furthering the interests of the millions who were out of work.

One who witnessed the radicals in action was Len De Caux, a trade union editor and publicity director of the energetic Congress of Industrial Organizations (CIO), established in the 1930s. De Caux said:

The most fully employed persons I met during the depression were the Communists. They worked 10 or 12 hours a day — maybe 16, if you counted yakking time. Most got no pay. A few full-timers had theoretical salaries, more theory than salary. The money was contingent — if some came in, you might get some. Most worked for love, or spite, if you prefer.

Work they did. They were in on every protest I saw or heard of. If they didn't start things themselves, they were Johnnies-on-the-spot. The anti-eviction fights were their babies, or adopted babies. They brought demanding crowds to the relief offices. They organized block committees, mass meetings, demonstrations. The Communist-led Unemployed Councils later took over this work. . . .

The Communists brought misery out of hiding in the workers' neighborhoods. They paraded it with angry demands through the main streets to the Public Square, and on to City Hall. They raised particular hell. . . .

If the Communists were as nasty, cantankerous, conspiratorial, and subversive as charged, that scared the ruling class of people all the more and forced more concessions. Somehow the Communists didn't scare the unemployed. In hundreds of jobless meetings, I heard no objections to the points the Communists made, and much applause for them. Sometimes I'd hear a Communist speaker say something so bitter and extreme I'd feel embarrassed. Then I'd look around at the unemployed audience — shabby clothes, expressions worried and sour. Faces would start to glow, heads to nod, hands to clap. They liked that stuff best of all.

De Caux then described a Communist-led demonstration in Cleveland protesting police brutality at an earlier action. The police stayed out of sight while the crowd "surged through the streets. I wondered if some incident mightn't turn them into an unruly mob. Then I noticed men with red armbands — stewards from the Unemployed Councils — moving quietly among the people, preventing congestion, directing circulation."

Communists and other organized radicals, along with individuals who were somehow not in the mainstream, stepped forward amid the economic distress and helped give direction to large numbers of workers who had been set adrift. For example, on March 17, 1928, well before the Wall Street crash of October 29, 1929, (usually regarded as the beginning of the depression), the maverick millionaire, J. Eads How from St. Louis, organized a National Unemployment Conference in New York. It was well attended by homeless, wandering men — hoboes.

Jacob S. Coxey, who had campaigned for public works in 1894 and in every succeeding depression, arrived a day late for the gathering, but his pronouncements made headlines. Among other things, he proposed a new march on Washington like the one he had led in 1894. There were, he said, 5 million unemployed, compared to the 3 million who had been jobless when he led the Army of the Commonweal to the nation's capital thirty-four years before. Coxey's estimate of 5 million may have been high, but there were undeniably a great many people out of work.

Mr. Zero, who had fed the jobless in New York and Boston in the depression of 1921, was also on hand. He offered coffee to the delegates.

Among the speakers was John DiSanto, a radical and a representative of another conference that had been called for that same day by the Unemployed Council, an organization initiated by the Communist Party (CP).

Perhaps there were also Wobblies among the hoboes, but the IWW had been greatly weakened during World War I and after by the savage government raids and related vigilante actions. The organization accurately predicted the approach of the depression and urged the jobless to organize, but it was not able to provide much leadership during the late 1920s and the 1930s.

The same was true of the Socialist Labor Party (SLP), witness of several depressions. In 1929 it was, as it has remained, only a very small sect. It issued leaflets to the jobless asserting that capitalism was the cause of unemployment, but it offered no immediate help to those who desperately wanted to know where their next meal was coming from. Reforms cannot solve unemployment, said the SLP; socialism was the only answer. The SLP did not attempt to lead in fighting for relief and against evictions or participate in campaigns for unemployment insurance.

The Socialist Party, by contrast, did believe in reforms. It concentrated on education and lobbying and did some direct distribution of charitable relief to the jobless. Although the Socialists were aware of the rising level of unemployment, they were apparently not much involved in the March 17 conference that attracted hoboes or in the other conference that had been called by the Unemployed Council. The second conference was supported by the Communist-backed Trade Union Educational League (TUEL). The same day (March 17, 1928), still another conference began in Moscow, this one held by the Red International of Labor Unions (RILU), with which the TUEL was associated. Delegates from many countries brought reports of increasing unemployment. The problem was worldwide. It was agreed that all left-wing activists in the capitalist world should devote increased energy to organizing the jobless.

The RILU and the related New York Conference of the Unemployed Council both called for government unemployment insurance and for equal rights for unemployed women.

The two New York conferences on March 17 stirred the New York Central Trades and Labor Council to announce a third conference on unemployment a few days later, March 24 and 25. This trade union gathering had as one of its speakers Matthew Woll, vice-president of the American Federation of Labor. Woll's participation did not mean that the AFL had suddenly become supportive of direct unemployment relief, work relief, or unemployment insurance. On the contrary, Woll seems to have put in an appearance in order to blunt the campaign launched by Communists. Woll's presence, however, was evidence that mass unemployment did exist and the Communists were active among the jobless.

Even before these various conferences were planned, the Communists had already turned their attention to the jobless. In February 1928, Herbert Benjamin, a member of the CP, had spoken at an open-air meeting in Philadelphia on the causes of unemployment and the need for the jobless to organize. The ultimate cure for unemployment was socialism, he said. At that point the police moved in and broke up the meeting before Benjamin finished talking. His response was to go to the Communist Party headquarters two blocks away, leading as many listeners as he could. From the open window of the office he continued his talk until the police broke into the building and arrested him and some of his companions.

The Central Executive Committee of the CP adopted a program later in 1928 that called for organization of the jobless and proposed methods of agitation and propaganda. Actually, these efforts did not amount to much more than plans to persuade the unemployed to join the party, but the CP was acutely aware of economic problems. The Sixth World Congress of the Communist International (CI), held in July and August 1928, had come to the conclusion that the capitalist economy was moving into a depression and that Communists everywhere should step up their organizational work among the jobless.

Even before the depression, joblessness was of major proportions. Paul U. Kellogg, a prominent social worker, estimated that in the most prosperous years of the 1920s "We had a body of one million unemployed." In April 1929, two social workers from the University Settlement said in the *Survey* magazine, "We like to feel that no neighbor knocks in vain at the settlement door, but these days . . . these knockings reach a crescendo. In years of apparent prosperity, they have become insistent." Lilian Brandt, another social worker, said that in New York City nurses and social workers "with few exceptions . . . saw much more distress last winter [1929–1930] . . . than they have ever seen before." In spite of such evidence, which began to accumulate long before Lilian Brandt's report, President-elect Herbert Hoover continued to voice the response to unemployment that had been traditional ever since the Elizabethan Poor Law of 1601: Joblessness should be dealt with by private and local agencies, not by the central government. Furthermore, Hoover did not agree with the Marxists' prediction of disaster. On August 11, 1928, he said, "We in America today are nearer to final triumph over poverty than ever before in the history of any land. The poorhouse is vanishing from among us. . . . We shall soon with the help of God be in sight of the day when poverty shall be banished from this nation."

On December 4, 1928, outgoing President Calvin Coolidge

said, "No Congress of the United States ever assembled, on surveying the state of the Union, has met with a more pleasing prospect than that which appears at the present time." The cheery attitude of Coolidge and Hoover was widely shared. On October 15, 1929, the well-known economist Irving Fisher said, "Stock prices have reached what look like a permanently high plateau." William Green, president of the AFL, advised workers to invest in stocks.

Hungarian Marxist economist Eugene Varga, working in Moscow, made it clear that he did not think capitalists should feel so pleased about the prospects of their system. He foresaw an immediate shift from boom to bust. So, too, did Leon Trotsky, who wrote in the *Militant* on June 1, 1929: "A social crisis in the United States may arrive a good deal sooner than many think, and have a feverish development from the beginning. Hence the conclusion: It is necessary to prepare."

Roger Babson, a capitalist economist, who may or may not have known of the analyses of Marxists, said, "Sooner or later a crash is coming and it may be terrific . . . factories will be shut down . . . men will be thrown out of work . . . the vicious cycle will get in full swing and the result will be a serious business depression."

What happened on the stock market closely paralleled Babson's prediction. In 1925 the Dow Jones Industrial Average had stood at 99.18. By September 3, 1929, it had risen to 381.17. At the end of October, speculators lost faith in the economy and began to sell stocks. Everybody sold. By noon of October 24, 1929, the four most powerful bankers in the country met in the office of J. P. Morgan and put up a vast sum of money to buy stocks in an effort to stop the downward plunge. The effort failed, and stock values continued disastrously downward. By November 13 the Dow Jones average had fallen to 198.67. The ability of capitalists to raise money for their enterprises was only a fraction of what it had been. Business activity dwindled, throwing millions out of work, and consumer goods, already in oversupply, had few buyers. The unemployed certainly could not consume. Manufacturers cut production still farther, creating still more unemployment. The entire economy collapsed.

Exactly how many were out of work in the United States? Nobody really knew. Mary Van Kleek, who chaired a committee on governmental labor statistics of the American Statistical Association, recommended in December 1928 that the Census Bureau count the unemployed, which it had never done. On January 8, 1929, Senator Robert Wagner responded to this urging — and to the mounting evidence of mass unemployment — by introducing a bill, which soon became law, requiring the Census Bureau to count the jobless. There were 2.286 million unemployed in the United States in the spring of 1929, according to the estimate of Robert R. Nathan that was published several years later by the International Labor Office in Geneva. Finally, on the last day of April 1930, the Census Bureau revealed the count of the unemployed required by the new law: 3,187,947. Some experts said the figure should have been larger, about 4.4 million. President Hoover complained that the Census Bureau figure was much too high. He asserted that the real figure was more like 1.9 million and continued to deny that there was a depression. In June 1930, when the head of the National Catholic Welfare Council urged Hoover to expand federally subsidized public works immediately, he replied, "Gentlemen you have come 60 days too late. The Depression is over."

Six months later, Hoover called a conference of governors and appointed a national committee to deal with unemployment. The governors in turn appointed state committees. Another six months passed. Although unemployment was still rising, Hoover asked for only $150 million for six months to provide work on projects already undertaken by federal departments. In his annual message to Congress he made only one mention of relief: He recommended an appropriation for the Department of Agriculture to lend money to protesting farmers, who had suffered from drought, so they could buy seed and feed for animals.

Meanwhile, Hoover's emergency Committee for Employment had undertaken to end the problem with slogans such as "Give a job" and "Spread the work." The committee, whose members were a virtual "who's who" of the business world, encouraged private charity and also urged people to conserve food and grow subsistence gardens. It did recommend public works, but Hoover resisted spending money on such projects. In addition, the Federal Farm Board had 600,000 bushels of wheat in the fall of 1930, but Hoover waited until 1932 before authorizing the use of any of it to feed the hungry. He did approve giving some of it to feed farm animals, prompting Senator George Norris to say, "Blessed be they who starve while asses and mules are fed, for they shall be buried at public expense."

As they had always done in past depressions, newspapers supported the notion that private charities, not the federal government, should aid the jobless. In New York City alone in 1930, 1,200 private charities reported that they were giving relief. By October 1930 one agency, the Emergency Employment Council (known as the Prosser Committee) had raised over $8 million for relief of the unemployed. The fund was to provide five dollars a day to workers who would spend three days a week building fences, water fountains, roads, and playgrounds; repairing public buildings; and, if they were women, making clothes for others who were out of work.

In another move, New York's mayor, James Walker, dealt with the unemployment problem by appointing a committee made up of the heads of the various departments of city government. The committee recommended that city employees contribute 1 percent of their wages to a fund for the jobless to be distributed by the police department. New York teachers contributed to buy free lunches for hungry schoolchildren.

Roger W. Babson, the economist who had looked at the evidence and forecast the depression, now said, without offering supporting evidence, that religious revivals would solve the problem created by the slump. Fortunately for the jobless, some churches did more than try to revive faith. In Harlem, the ghetto where New York's African-Americans lived and where unemployment afflicted workers at three times the rate it did in white neighborhoods, churches were particularly active. They served several thousand free meals a week in the winter of 1930–1931.

Even in the "prosperous" years from 1922 to 1929, 40 percent of the population did not earn enough to afford an optimum diet (that is, a diet that could keep people in good health), according to left-wing researchers who called themselves "Pen and Hammer." The government's Children's Bureau reported that one child in five was not getting enough of the right things to eat and that shocking undernourishment, even starvation, appeared in coal mining communities in several states. In *Nation in Torment,* Edward Robb Ellis tells the story of a teacher in a coal mining town who asked a little girl in her class if she was ill. The child replied, "No, I'm all right. I'm just hungry." The teacher urged her to go home and eat something. "I can't," the child said. "This is my sister's day to eat." In the absence of governmental relief, the Children's Bureau asked the American Friends Service Committee to feed the children of unemployed miners.

In many cities children rang doorbells and asked for food. A priest in San Antonio, Texas, told Heywood Broun, "Last month we buried thirty-nine persons, most children, from this little church alone." As early as December 1930, milk consumption in New York City was running a million quarts a week below normal.

Thousands of boys and girls left home and moved restlessly around the country hoping somehow to find work or food. Usually they travelled in, on top of, or under cars in freight trains. Adults took to riding freight trains in greater numbers than ever before. Just one railroad, the Southern Pacific, ejected 683,457 people from its trains in 1932.

An official of another railroad gave the following testimony to a Senate subcommittee:

> We took official notice, in 1928, of 13,745 transients, trespassers that we found on our trains and property.
> In 1929 that figure was 13,875.
> In 1930 we took a record of 23,982.
> In 1931 that volume jumped to 186,028.

In 1932 it receded a little bit to 149,773, or a total, for the five years, of 387,313 persons that we found trespassing upon our trains and property [among these, the official listed hundreds as killed or injured — F.F.]. . . . At the beginning of this large increase in travel by trespassers, the railroad officers would threaten these men with arrest and in most instances, they would laugh at the officers and say, "That is what we want. That will give us a place to sleep and eat."

About this time Thomas Minehan, a graduate student of sociology, became so much interested in the migrating swarms of homeless children that he spent two years living in their jungles and riding freight trains as they did. The result was a fascinating book, *Boy and Girl Tramps of America*. Many other writers in the 1930s gave glimpses — or extended pictures — of how unemployment affected the quality of life for workers. One of these books was Jack Conroy's *The Disinherited*. Another, Tom Kramer's *Waiting for Nothing*, is less well known, but was republished in 1988. In his novel *Land of Plenty*, Robert Cantwell spoke for many in a conversation between two workers, Winters and Hagen, employed in a sawmill where Hagen's son also had a job. Hagen said, speaking of his son:

"A year ago I figured I'd have him in school. Now I got a daughter and two kids living with me. Now we got word my oldest daughter's husband's out of work."
Winters said, "It's hell, ain't it?"
Hagen jerked his hand toward the boy. "It's hell for him."

It was hell for older workers, too. Many of them had been laid off since before the onset of the depression. And women, of course, had acute problems. They were not as large a part of the work force as they are today, but wives and daughters suffered when husbands and fathers lost jobs. Women workers, because they were lower paid than men, found themselves less directly affected by unemployment than their male competitors.

In response to distress, spontaneous acts of appropriation became common. According to Carl Winter, who later became a leader of the jobless, "Mass street demonstrations and other

gatherings of the unemployed were followed by their participants swarming into nearby restaurants, eating their fill, and
then departing with advice to the cashier to 'charge it to the
mayor.' " Theft was widespread, and there were food riots just
as there had been in New York in 1837.

In the town of Henrietta, Oklahoma, unemployed workers
appeared in front of stores and threatened storekeepers into
handing out food. In New York City, 1,100 men waiting in the
Salvation Army bread line saw bakery goods being delivered to
a nearby hotel. The men raided the trucks and helped themselves. One group of unemployed workers raided a packing-
house in St. Paul, Minnesota, and made off with hundreds of
hams and sides of bacon. The young man who led the raid was
strongly criticized by the Communist Party, which issued a
statement against direct appropriation of food. It was wrong,
said the statement, to sacrifice long-term objectives for limited
gains by a few individuals. (The young raider was Gus Hall, who
many years later became head of the CP.)

As the realities of the depression grew clearer, various political groups responded by organizing the unemployed. The Socialist Party became active and supported organizations of the
jobless that later merged into the Workers Alliance. Followers of
the Reverend A. J. Muste established very vigorous organizing
centers in Pennsylvania, Ohio, West Virginia, and the Pacific
Northwest. In California, a massive self-help movement sprang
up and spread to other states. By the mid-1930s right-wing
politicians saw the potential in the restless millions of unemployed. Huey Long, governor of Louisiana, built a movement so
powerful that it thoroughly frightened the Democratic Party. So
did the vast radio audience assembled by Father Charles E.
Coughlin. Dr. Francis E. Townsend gathered a huge following of
older citizens to lobby for old age pensions, and Socialist writer
Upton Sinclair, no right-winger, led a revolt in the Democratic
Party called "End Poverty in California" (EPIC) that almost put
him in the governor's mansion.

Efforts initiated by the Communists were the first of the
mass social movements to be of consequence. They served as a
model for much of the agitation that marked the end of the

presidency of Herbert Hoover, who continued to deny the reality of what was happening in the job market.

In late 1929, the Central Committee of the CP had adopted and published demands for the jobless: unemployment insurance administered by workers; abolition of private employment agencies and the establishment of free agencies administered by workers; a seven-hour day and five-day week with even shorter hours in mining; no underground work for women; no child labor; public funds for emergency relief; no evictions; union scale of pay on public works; and recognition of the USSR (a gesture of international working-class solidarity as well as a move that presumably would lead to increased trade and more jobs).

In a pamphlet, *Out of a Job*, written at about the same time, Communist leader Earl Browder had proposed a detailed "Program of Work Among the Unemployed" that included the recommendation that the Left-led Trade Union Unity League (TUUL), formerly the Trade Union Educational League, take the initiative in what he called "Councils of the Unemployed."

The secretary of the TUUL was William Z. Foster, a former Wobbly. Foster had worked at many jobs on railroads and as a seaman, and he had experienced unemployment. As a labor organizer he had led in unionizing the meat packing industry, and in 1919 he had led a great strike in the steel industry. There was no labor leader with greater talent as an organizer, said labor journalist Mary Heaton Vorse, who had witnessed the performance of all of the important trade union officials of her time. In early 1930, Foster attended a meeting in Moscow with Communist leaders from all over the world. As part of the Communist International (CI), the group helped plan a worldwide response to the worldwide phenomenon of unemployment.

Back in the United States, Foster enlisted the help of Israel Amter, Robert Minor, and Herbert Benjamin. Gaunt, Lincolnesque Amter was now district organizer of the CP in New York. Minor, after becoming well known as a cartoonist for the St. Louis *Post Dispatch*, had turned to the Left and was associated with various radical groups before he joined the CP and became editor of the *Daily Worker*. Benjamin, an ex-Wobbly, had observed Anarchist-led unemployed demonstrations in Chicago when he was a boy, and he had absorbed some anticapitalist views from an older sister who was an active Anarchist. He had had experience as a member of the International Association of Machinists and had been involved with the unemployed in Philadelphia.

These four — Amter, Foster, Minor, and Benjamin — and many others did what they could on the American scene to make an important event out of International Unemployment Day, which the CI had proposed as a response to economic disaster in all major capitalist countries.

The call for the worldwide demonstration, to be held on February 24, was issued in late January 1930. Organizers rushed plans to get a large turnout. Guided by Foster, the TUUL members, CP members, and Young Communist League (YCL) members used a variety of organizing techniques. For example, members of the TUUL set up a picket line on January 16 at a market in the Bronx when several food workers were discharged and forced into the ranks of the unemployed. Police attacked the picketers. In the ensuing melée an officer drew his gun and fired, striking a young Communist, Steve Katovis, and shattering his spine.

In the hospital, although Katovis was completely helpless and near death, the police kept him under constant guard, took his fingerprints, and allowed him no visitors. On January 24 Steve Katovis died, and the CP urged workers to appear at City Hall to express their anger.

The CP, YCL, and TUUL had at their disposal in preparing for this and other events newspapers with a total national circulation of about 250,000: the English-language *Daily Worker* (circulation about 10,000), two Finnish-language dailies, one Russian-language daily, one Yiddish daily, and a dozen other foreign-language papers that appeared less frequently. Communists also had influence in various foreign-language fraternal orders and in sports clubs and cultural clubs.

In addition to distributing the *Daily Worker*, party members and sympathizers passed out 100,000 mimeographed leaflets about the young man who had been killed while trying to get back jobs for workers who had been fired. In response to this agitation, 3,000 people appeared at City Hall. There, police attacked them and broke up the gathering.

On January 27, the *Daily Worker* issued the call for International Unemployment Day, February 24. On January 28, the day of Katovis's funeral, the Communist paper estimated that 10,000 people filed past the body as it lay in state at the Workers Center, 20,000 followed the cortege at the funeral, and 50,000 gathered to pay tribute in Union Square. Altogether, 100,000 people were said to have watched one phase or another of the proceedings.

Most of the demands to be made by the demonstration were full of meaning for the jobless. "Immediate relief!" was uppermost in the minds of all who had lost their source of income. Money fo food and shelter was absolutely essential. "A shorter work day!" — this slogan meant to the unemployed that if those who had jobs worked fewer hours at the same pay, there could be work and wages for those out of work. "Work or Wages!" said countless leaflets. *Work* was clear enough, but what about *or wages*? The slogan was meant to propose that those out of work should be paid unemployment insurance at the rate of the full wages they had received when on the job. The cost of this insurance, to be paid from the day work stopped until employment resumed, was to be covered by the employers who had profited from the labor of the workers they had discarded.

The Communists kept spreading the news that the demonstration would take place in many cities in the United States and indeed would be worldwide. Unemployment, in other words, was a general malady not caused by workers. It was not a reflection of the shortcomings of individuals. In addition, the demonstration would help the jobless feel hope and self-respect in the presence of humiliating, desperate adversity.

19

The Great Response
(March 6, 1930)

The final solution of unemployment is work.
— Calvin Coolidge, president of the United States
1925–1929

There is plenty of law at the end of a nightstick.
— Grover A. Whalen, police commissioner of New York
1930

To the working class there is no foreigner but the capitalist.
— Big Bill Haywood

In response to complaints that there had not been time enough to organize, the Communist International (Comintern, or CI) changed to March 6, 1930, the date for the worldwide demonstration. (By chance, this was the anniversary of a great meeting of the unemployed that had been held in New York in 1837.) The *Party Organizer*, a small house organ for CP leaders, gave detailed instructions on how to prepare for the event. Each party member had very specific assignments to carry out in order to get as much publicity as possible in his or her union or sports club or foreign-language fraternal order. Some were to organize street-corner meetings in neighborhoods. Others arranged to rent halls for lectures or to hold benefits to raise money.

In addition to the 7,500 CP members, most of whom were preparing for demonstrations in various cities in the United States, a smaller number of YCL members publicized the demonstrations. Members of the TUUL, many of whom were not Communists, also participated.

Organizers made special efforts among the African-Americans who suffered more than whites from the spreading unemployment. For example, the Upper Harlem Unemployed Council came into existence in February. Its first objective was to mobilize black and white Harlemites for the March 6 demonstration.

Demonstrations in advance of the big day began to take place. One YCL member, Al Richmond, a 16-year-old high school student at the time, recalled what he termed "skirmishes" that preceded March 6:

> In the first skirmish 3,000 demonstrators and 200 cops battled in New York's City Hall Park on January 25.
>
> A month later (February 27) police attacked thousands of unemployed massed at City Hall to demand immediate relief. In the final skirmish, Saturday, March 1, several hundred women and children demonstrated at City Hall. Or as near City Hall as they could get. They were met by 100 uniformed policemen and detectives with orders to prevent the demonstration.

Many demonstrators were arrested, among them Sadie Van Veen, wife of Israel Amter. The five-foot-tall, 100-pound woman was charged with kicking a police officer in the stomach while she was protesting that she had a right to speak.

Demonstrations were also taking place in other big cities. In Cleveland on February 11, when the City Council met, 3,000 unemployed workers marched to City Hall to demand food and clothing. Police attacked them in an effort to hold them back.

In Chicago, the CP printed 50,000 stickers, 50,000 papers for distribution in shops, and 200,000 leaflets announcing the March 6 demonstration. Steve Nelson, a Communist, has given his recollection of what happened at a meeting in Chicago's Mechanics Hall that had been called to prepare for March 6:

> The meeting was very successful, with over six hundred neighbors, [Unemployed] Council leaders, union activists, and Party people responding to the call. As the session was about

to break up, a dozen paddy wagons pulled up to the entrance, and the hall was surrounded by uniformed police. All doors were shut, and we were all questioned and searched as we walked out, in single file, between a double row of cops. One hundred thirteen of us were separated from the rest and jammed into the wagons. This group was questioned by members of the Red Squad, who identified the "real agitators" on sight, and all but fourteen were released.

These "masterminds" of the Red Conspiracy were a rather motley group and included Nels Kjar, the old carpenter and leader of the Party Trade Union Committee; Andy Newhoff, who worked with the ILD [International Labor Defense]; Gene Rodman, an unemployed painter; Joe Dallet, who led the Steel and Metal Workers Industrial Union; two Black Party activists from out of town; B. D. Amos and Harold Williams; Fred Fine, a fourteen-year-old boy whom we called "the Kid"; myself; and a few others. Dora Lifshitz, the only woman arrested, was separated from the rest.

We sat for five hours, wondering what would happen to us, while Nels tried to prepare us for the inevitable. "This is a setup for a beating. Just don't give in. If they divide us, it will be tougher for each one."

Eight detectives came in, all big guys, and sat on a platform facing our bench. "Jesus," someone said, "they don't look alike, but you couldn't tell them apart." The biggest of the bunch, Sergeant Barker, motioned for two other dicks to join him as he walked over to the bench. Without a word they grabbed two of our men, shoved them out into the corridor, and closed the door. Soon we heard screams, and the twelve remaining men stiffened. Barker and the two detectives came back smiling crookedly and elaborately wiping their hands with handkerchiefs. "You," Barker yelled, pointing a finger at the Kid, "you little monkey."

"Who, me?" The Kid stood up.

"Yeah, you — you little bastard — come up here."

The Kid, ninety pounds and five feet four, walked up to meet Detective Barker. Barker stood towering over the boy, and his face was redder than usual. After a pause the detective put one big hand on the youngster's thin shoulder and slapped him hard across the face. The Kid stood hunched silently with the spotlight glaring in his eyes, staring the detective square in the face. The second slap, fast and chopping from the other side, was harder.

"Now you talk, you little bastard! Look me in the eyes, you little punk — come on, look me in the eyes! You'll go home to mama and stay there, won't you? You'll have enough of these Reds before I'm through with you." Another slap. As if blinded momentarily, the Kid started to sway. Then another hard slap turned him half around, and his knees began to fold. The men on the bench shifted nervously.

"Comrades, keep your heads," Nels whispered, not forgetting the seven other detectives, who sat fingering their revolvers. "You see their game. They'll shoot the first one of us that takes a step. They'll say we started a fight, and they'll have an excuse to attack and arrest more of our people." Joe Dallet was losing his temper. "How the hell can we sit here and do nothing?" he demanded. "He'll kill the Kid."

"Sit down, Joe. Don't be a fool," the old man said. "You see how happy they are. They think their game is working." Gradually Joe calmed down.

Detective Barker turned back to the Kid, dramatically throwing open his coat to reveal the holstered revolver on his hip. The Kid's eyes were riveted on the gun.

"What are you looking at that gun for?" Barker asked slowly.

The Kid stood motionless, not saying anything.

"What are you looking at that gun for!" shouted the dick. The Kid remained silent.

"What would you do with it, you dirty little Jew bastard, if you did have it? You'd shoot me with it! You'd kill me, that's what you'd do! Wouldn't you? Wouldn't you!"

The Kid's eyes were steady, and blood dripped down his chin. Hesitating, he suddenly shouted, "Yes, I would!"

The men on the bench broke into loud laughs. Joe pounded me on the back, saying, "What a Kid, what a Kid!"

But the ordeal was far from over. I was sitting next to the last man when two detectives pushed me through a door into another room. They forced me into something that looked like a dentist's chair and strapped me in it. Detective Miller, whose five brothers ran the gangs on the West Side, came into the room. He turned, slowly removing his glasses and wristwatch, and unbuckled his holster, laying it on a small table near the door, which he locked. Then he put on a pair of canvas gloves and pulled out a blackjack with a mother-of-pearl handle. "So you're a big shot agitator. So you won't leave town, eh? You'll get out all right, even if I have to send you in a nice wooden box!"

The blackjack clipped me across the head, and then he carefully worked me over. After some fifteen blows, I gave a twisting jerk with all my strength, tore the chair loose, and fell flat on the floor, pretending to be unconscious. I heard Miller's assistant say, "Maybe you'd better lay off the son-of-a-bitch. He'll leave town now. He's had enough."

Miller unstrapped me, pulled me clear of the chair, and kicked me in the ribs as hard as he could. I went out like a light. When I regained consciousness, I cleaned my bloody face in the washroom and wandered over to an open window for some air. Still dazed, I stared out of the window at the city. Consciousness came suddenly when I saw Detective Miller standing at my side. "What are you looking out the window for? Were you going to jump? I'll open it for you, go ahead. You got no reason to live." He shoved me. "Go on, jump. What are you waiting for?" Realizing that the bastard meant business, I braced myself against another shove and edged away from the window.

An hour later I found my friends sitting on a cement floor in front of the elevator. Harold Williams was stretched out, his torn pants revealing an enormous rupture, and B. D. Amos had had his front teeth knocked out. Joe Dallet was bleeding from the mouth and had a gash on his cheek. Andy had a big lump on his cheek, and Rodman's thick black hair was caked with blood. The Kid stood there, his eyes all bloodshot. Only two men in the group, Kjar and Paul Cline, had not been beaten. This, we figured, was done deliberately so as to throw suspicion onto their integrity. . . .

We were brought to trial on charges of sedition and organizing for an armed revolution. The prosecution presented a very flamboyant case designed to show how dangerous we were. Fortunately for us, we had a jury trial and we had the International Labor Defense in our corner. . . .

The trial lasted about a week. The jury, comprised mostly of workers, a number of whom were unemployed, voted for acquittal. The case made the government look bad, and it slowed the repression down a little.

In New York, on the eve of the March 6 demonstration, Police Commissioner Grover Whalen gave the press the text of an unsigned letter he had been sent by the Department of Justice. The letter alleged that Reds in New York had received orders from Moscow to destroy, beginning March 6, City Hall, the Woolworth Building (at that time the world's tallest building), police headquarters, the New York Stock Exchange, and various other buildings. Moscow, this document alleged, also ordered the assassination of various prominent figures, including President Hoover; Alfred E. Smith, former governor of New York State; John D. Rockefeller; and Mayor James J. Walker.

What some Reds were really doing when this provocative forgery appeared in the news is told in Al Richmond's autobiography:

> My YCL team of five is in the Bronx, where all dynamite stores are under police guard. It is midnight and our behavior is furtive. But we do not have dynamite. We are armed with posters, a jar filled with paste, and a brush. . . .
>
> On this night in early March we are bent on putting up posters where they will be seen by workers and others who come to seek work at the [Dubilier condenser factory]. . . . Five of us in this empty street; I with the posters under my arm, someone else with a jar of paste in a brown paper bag, and a third comrade with the brush wrapped in rags. . . . The three of us with the paraphernalia are to put up the posters. The other two are to serve as lookouts. One lookout is Brooklyn-born and bred, the purity of his Brooklynese accent unblemished by the efforts of New York's schools. . . . "If someone is coming," I ask [him], "what will be your signal?" He replies, "I'll whistle da sextet from Lucia de Lammermoor." That cuts the tension. But there is enough of it left so that between our nervousness and a strong breeze we have trouble with the flutter of the first poster. The rest, about a dozen, go up smoothly and quickly on walls and fences. Donizetti's sextet is not whistled that night.

Although Richmond was not among them, some other students from the Bronx were arrested on March 5. The crime: posting and distributing literature about International Unemployment Day.

As YCLers worked hard to publicize the upcoming demonstration, others were busy trying to mobilize against it. Matthew Woll, vice-president of the AFL, sent a letter to 500 business organizations and to members of Congress. Woll alleged that the Soviet Union was behind the agitation among the American unemployed, and he repeated charges made by the Department of Justice that William Z. Foster had brought from Russia $1.25 million to finance social disruption. The *New York Times* gave Woll's letter front page coverage.

The night before the demonstration, organizers held meetings in small groups all over the city to give out final instructions. On the morning of March 6, a massive headline on the front page of the *Times* read:

ALL POLICE ON DUTY
TO AVERT VIOLENCE AT RED RALLY TODAY

FIRE DEPARTMENT
ALSO HELD IN READINESS TO QUELL RIOTING
ANYWHERE IN THE CITY

PUBLIC BUILDINGS GUARDED

WHALEN TO COMMAND BIG FORCE
EQUIPPED WITH TEAR AND GAS BOMBS
AT UNION SQUARE

The story that followed began: "The most extensive preparations ever made by the police here to meet a possible emergency were worked out yesterday for the unemployment demonstration to be staged by the Communists in Union Square at noon today."

The next day the *Times* gave a good deal of space to William Z. Foster's speech at the demonstration. According to the re porter, Foster told the audience about a meeting he had had with the police commissioner:

"We asked Whalen if we could go to City Hall and present our petition. The answer was, 'No.' Any celebrities coming to town are allowed to use Broadway. When the workers want it they can't have it. Are we going to take 'No' for an answer?"

"No," roared the Communists [by which the *Times* meant the crowd, which it estimated at 35,000 and which the Communists put at 100,000, only a small fraction of whom could have been members of the small CP and smaller YCL — F.F.].

Foster later gave his own version of his encounter with Whalen: "Our committee demanded a parade permit. We pointed out that the Queen of Rumania, sundry military butchers and many capitalist organizations had been allowed to parade freely, but now the class that built Broadway was being denied the right to walk along it."

Soon after Foster's speech at the demonstration, the police attacked. The *New York World* reporter gave the following account:

[Demonstrators and bystanders] were slugged and kicked, blackjacked and knocked down by mounted police in the frantic fifteen minutes that followed the policemen's charge on the straggling parade of placard carriers. That attack altered the scene with incredible swiftness from one of good-natured mass apathy and order to the most panic-stricken confusion. . . . Mounted police were setting their horses at the trot into mobs so tightly packed that there was no escape.

[There were] women struck in the face with blackjacks, boys beaten by gangs of seven and eight policemen, and an old man backed into a doorway and knocked down time after time, only to be dragged to his feet and struck with fists and clubs.

Many of the women were kicked as they lay on the ground or [were] hoisted to their feet and . . . slapped by the policemen. . . . One of them fought savagely howling curses and a bluecoat seized her around the shoulders with one arm and punched her with his free hand. A detective ran up and while the policemen held her crashed his blackjack into her face three times before a man dragged her away.

Their faces contorted and raving and cursing, [the police] plunged into the crowd . . . which did its terror-stricken best to flee. One . . . in tan mackinaw, shield #2836 . . . charging without any plan into any group and breaking it apart with a club . . . wrapped with adhesive tape . . . he used his left fist and both legs.

[There were] men with blood streaming down their faces dragged into the temporary police headquarters and flung down to await the patrol wagons to cart them away.

Members of the staff of *Outlook Magazine* looking down on Union Square witnessed a scene in which two men were singled out by police and plainclothesmen who "beat them, knocked them down . . . kicked them about the face, chased them around Irving Place separately where they were met by another crowd of police and plainclothesmen who backed them up against the fence of Washington Irving High School, smashed their heads back against the fence, kicked them and slugged them. . . . At no time were the two men endeavoring to fight back."

As violence began in Union Square, Herbert Benjamin, in a room just off the square, tried without much success to direct defense squads to protect the demonstrators.

The committee that had been unable to get permission for a parade to City Hall pushed toward Broadway to lead the march. The confusion was too great, however, and they could not make their way through the crowd. Advance planning had taken into account this possibility, and the committee had agreed on a meeting place two blocks from City Hall. Four of the five members managed to reassemble there. Foster, at least, came by taxi. Together the four went up the steps of the seat of municipal government and demanded permission to present to the mayor the program they proposed for the unemployed. Immediately they were arrested and charged with unlawful assembly. Later they were rearrested on charges of felonious assault.

News of the demonstration, as interpreted by newspapers mostly hostile to the unemployed, reached a very large audience. Coverage of the event was curiously lacking in the recently developed newsreel "talkies." Cameras with sound recording equipment were operating at the time of the speech making and the ensuing police attack. But viewers of newsreels (at least those prepared by the two largest companies in the business) were not to hear what the speakers actually said or see what the police actually did. Before any films could be distributed, Will Hays, head of the Motion Picture Producers and Distributors of America, got on the phone and persuaded the heads of the companies not to release their sound films. The Hays office subsequently denied that any political pressure had been used to suppress the March 6 sound recordings. As it turned out, at least a half-dozen people, all organizers of the demonstration, did see the suppressed newsreel.[1] Benjamin told how this came about:

> At about nine that evening I was called to the phone to speak to some one who said he had something very important to tell me. The caller told me he was owner or manager of a movie house; that he had received film from one of the newsreel companies of the demonstration but before he could show them a police officer had appeared to tell him that the Police Commissioner does not want this film exhibited. He intended to obey, but would put on a private showing that night for me, if I wanted to see it before it went back to the distributor. Six or seven of us went. The film ran about seven minutes. It showed the overflowing square, the speaker's stand, the police headquarters with Grover Whalen and the charge of the mounted police that started the battles. Watching some of the scenes as men and women were being mercilessly beaten with long clubs, thrown under galloping horses and chased by plain clothesmen, press badges in their hat bands, it was understandable why Grover Whalen wanted the film sup-pressed. It would have explained also why New York workers felt such a deep hatred for those who wore the uniform or badge of the New York City Police Department.

After being arrested, Foster, Amter, Minor, and two young seamen named Liston and Harry Raymond were held without bail on the order of Chief Magistrate William McAdoo. Later, in court, they were denied a trial by jury and were convicted of unlawful assembly and sentenced to three years in various city prisons. Liston served one month. Foster, Amter, and Minor served six months and were then released on parole. Raymond was released a few months later.

These jail sentences, plus many scores of bloody heads, were the price paid for the right to parade from Union Square. Apparently never since March 6, 1930, have the New York Police denied a permit for such a parade.

The New York demonstration was only a part of the nation-wide mobilization of the jobless that same day. New York and Detroit crowds were the largest — 100,000 or more in each city. About 50,000 gathered in Boston and in Chicago, 30,000 in Philadelphia, 25,000 in Cleveland, and 20,000 in Youngstown and in Pittsburgh. In addition, at least 125,000 demonstrated in a total of two dozen other cities across the country.

A half-million or more people came to the demonstrations March 6 in response to the call for International Unemployment Day by the Comintern. The magnitude of this response not only shocked the authorities in New York but also surprised the organizers.

At this point it is fair to ask, was the CP's organizing of the jobless on March 6 and throughout the depression solely a response to the desperate need of American people, or was it primarily a response to external manipulation? The answer seems to be that the intense activity of the CP was the product of both stimuli, and the so-called external manipulation was the Comintern's response to the plight of the jobless every-where. When the Comintern called for international demonstra-tions, it had no interest that was hostile to the American unemployed. Moreover, the mass movement of the unemployed was very much a creation of non-Communist workers.

To be sure, the Communists did provide skilled leadership and careful, well-publicized preparation, which made the dem-onstrations big and effective. The results, both good and bad, were soon to appear.

No doubt aware of the announced plans for demonstrations on March 6, the Commerce Committee of the United States Senate scheduled hearings for that day on three bills submitted by Senator Robert Wagner of New York. The historic bills would for the first time put the federal government in the business of alleviating unemployment.

On March 17, Norman Thomas, Socialist leader, made public a petition signed by ninety-two prominent non-Communist men and women asking Mayor Walker to remove Grover Whalen from his post as police commissioner. The signers included Charles and Mary Beard, John Dewey, Rexford Guy Tugwell, the Reverend John Haynes Holmes, and Art Young. The American Civil Liberties Union joined in the campaign against Whalen. Under the auspices of the ACLU, a group of lawyers met to consider action to be taken against him. (Eventually such pressure did produce the commissioner's dismissal.) On March 19 in New York, labor leaders, many of whom were Socialists, held a conference on unemployment that added the voices of 300 local unions to the increasing clamor for relief for the jobless.

On the day of the demonstrations, the Socialist Party had sent a wire to Franklin D. Roosevelt, governor of New York, urging him to do something about unemployment. At the end of the month, Governor Roosevelt appointed the State Committee on Stabilization of Industry to develop long-range plans for dealing with unemployment. He also announced that he was in favor of unemployment insurance, and he told the mayors of cities in New York State that they could use the state armories for sheltering homeless people.

The demonstrations were not simply a case of militant action followed by results that were beneficial to the jobless. There were many casualties among the participants. Two days after the demonstrations, the *Daily Worker* offered a tally of the numbers arrested and injured in a few of the cities:

New York	37 arrested	130 injured
Detroit	45 arrested	25 injured
Los Angeles	60 arrested	20 injured
Seattle	12 arrested	10 injured
Washington	11 arrested	6 injured

The authorities in many cities had been frightened and, having no plan for solving the unemployment problem, had used force. March Pierce, police commissioner of Los Angeles, told the Reverend Clinton Taft, who was protesting illegal arrests, "I won't listen to any arguments on behalf of Communists. The more the police beat them up and wreck their headquarters, the better. Communists have no constitutional rights, and I won't listen to anybody who defends them." Lieutenant William F. Hynes, head of the Red Squad in Los Angeles, claimed that his men "have never beaten up anybody, unless they are justified."

The March 6 demonstrations produced other counteractions. Some authorities made concessions that they hoped would defuse an explosive situation; others resorted to repression in the hope of crushing the militants among the jobless. In at least part of the working class, the result was a new sense of hope and of self-confidence.

Among the concessions won following the March 6 and other demonstrations was a move to establish some kind of government public relief apparatus where none had existed before. In New York, Governor Roosevelt and the legislators responded to the mood and the strength of the jobless when a group of unemployed came to Albany on a hunger march and tried to enter the legislative chambers. The state police drove the marchers away after a forty-five-minute battle, but shortly thereafter the legislature passed the Wicks Law under which relief activities began in November 1931.

Elsewhere, there were moves to increase relief already granted by cities. Cries of alarm came from mayors. In mid-February 1931, Mayor Mackey of Philadelphia, while appealing for charitable contributions from a wealthy audience, recommended that his listeners give to the poor "for their own safety." An observer said the city's "critical emergency shocked its most tradition-oriented citizens and aroused them to advocate direct federal relief." In Chicago, the *Progressive* wrote, only fear of a rebellion forced the legislature to pass a $90-million relief measure. Helen Seymour, a graduate student of economics at the University of Chicago at this time, commented in a thesis that the activities of the relief-seeking unemployed "often with a philosophy of class struggle, in most large cities, [have] led directly or indirectly, to the setting up of machinery for systematic clearing of client complaints. Its influence on administrative thinking along the line of client participation has been considerable."

Hopes of the unemployed were high following March 6. Certainly the small CP had reason to feel exhilarated; its membership nearly doubled between March 6 and May 1. By September, however, some of the euphoria had dissipated. Marxist economists said the depression would get worse. This forecast, which proved to be true, required sober analysis of what could be done to organize the growing numbers of jobless into Unemployed Councils. The scene of action from now on was increasingly in neighborhoods, where people lived and needed relief. Pressure on city administrations continued as well.

The March 6 demonstrations had made very clear that municipal treasuries and tax bases were not equal to the demands for relief. Accordingly, mayors of big cities began to appeal for federal help. The Conference of Mayors was formed in this period, called into existence by the organized unemployed. In Chicago mass pressure had its effect, according to writers Frances Fox Piven and Richard A. Cloward: "Where half the working force was unemployed and Socialists and Communists were organizing mass demonstrations, the mayor pleaded for the federal government to send $150,000,000 for relief immediately rather than federal troops later."

Not surprisingly, many city governments responded to the March 6 protests with force. In Detroit, a massive mobilization of police, including thirty-six mounted officers, launched an attack just when speakers began to address a crowd variously estimated at 50,000 to 100,000. A fight between the police and the jobless went on for two hours. In a similar battle in Milwaukee, forty-seven workers were arrested, among them the young Finnish-American, Gus Hall, who would one day become general secretary of the Communist Party. In Flint, Michigan, the police arrested all of the speakers before the demonstration began.

Four months after the March 6 demonstration, John Dos Passos, writing in the *New Republic*, offered a summary of the continued violent responses by authorities to the dynamism of the Left-led unemployed: "Since April [1930], there have been about four thousand arrests in the United States of members of the Communist Party, alleged Communists, or working people attempting to go to meetings on subjects considered 'radical' or 'dangerous' by the police. Many of the arrests were for distributing leaflets or speaking in connection with the March 6 or May 1 demonstrations."

Dos Passos tabulated the violence against people that was initiated by the police. There was also violence initiated by the jobless against rules and regulations and against poverty, but the unemployed rarely initiated violence against people. Often, a result of disruptive antiregulation acts by the unemployed was that the jobless got what they wanted and needed. The opposite result, however, was that acts of disruption often stimulated severe responses. The results of the militant mobilization of March 6 showed both tendencies.

Although the demonstrators in New York did not plan to use force except in self-defense, they did plan to disobey orders given by the police commissioner (they planned to go to City Hall when they were ordered not to). One response by authorities in New York was to grant immediate relief and to establish a committee to study the unemployment problem. The other response was the violent attack by the police. In effect, the city of New York said, "You have called a real problem to our attention, but you shouldn't have done so in the way in which you did it."

The dual nature of the reaction to the March 6 demonstration appeared also on the state and national scenes. On the one hand, Governor Roosevelt established the first statewide emergency relief apparatus. On the other hand, U.S. Representative Hamilton Fish, on the very day of the demonstration, proposed an investigating committee that later became the House Committee on Un-American Activities, a committee that was costly to the unemployed and to radicals and liberals for decades.

In spite of massive repression, the unemployed movement grew amid worsening economic conditions, and cheery pronouncements continued to pour from Washington. The *New York Times* front page headline on May 2 read, "Worst of Depression is Over . . . Recovery Near [Hoover] States." Just after the March 6 demonstrations, one of which took place in Washington within view of the White House, President Hoover had insisted, "All the evidences indicate that the worst effects of the crash on unemployment will have passed during the next sixty days." (Actually, mass unemployment lasted until the United States prepared to enter World War II.)

Hoover also insisted that helping the jobless should not be a federal responsibility. Late in 1930 he threatened to veto a bill that would have provided American Indians with a $15-million loan for food.

Secretary of Commerce Thomas W. Lamont, a partner of J. P. Morgan, did his share of morale raising. The *Times* of September 23, 1930, ran a front page headline reading, "Lamont declares decline has ceased." By December, however, when President Hoover delivered his annual address to Congress, he grudgingly admitted that something had to be done about unemployment. He proposed an appropriation of $100 million to $150 million for public works in order to provide jobs. This amount would have meant somewhere between ten and fifteen dollars for each jobless person, if all of the appropriation went to the unemployed, which of course it wouldn't. Much of the money would have to go for materials and equipment and administrative costs. Congress appropriated $116 million, which left most of the unemployed exactly where they were before the bill became law — destitute.

Six months later, June 16, 1931, the *Times* headline read: "Hoover decries depression panaceas . . . pictures glowing future for nation."

20

Unemployed Councils
(1930–1936)

This is a good time for social workers: the only people who seem to be employed — alas.
— Lillian Wald in a letter dated January 12, 1932

"A red is any son of a bitch who wants thirty cents when we're paying twenty-five."
— Mr. Hines, a peach grower, in John Steinbeck's
The Grapes of Wrath, 1939

When radical leaders talked about hungry workers in 1930 they were not just using rhetoric. That year, the hospitals in New York City reported ninety-five deaths from starvation, and that figure may not have been complete. Moreover, for every person who starved, a great many others went hungry, and undernourishment contributed to deaths from other causes.

The Preliminary National Conference on Unemployment was held March 29 and 30, 1930, in New York City. John Schmies, an auto worker and Communist Party district organizer from Detroit, chaired the conference, which was designed to prepare for the establishment of a national organization of the unemployed. Two hundred fifteen delegates came from forty-nine cities in eighteen states. Some were sent by Left-led trade unions and others by neighborhood organizations of the unemployed. Twelve delegates were women. (Low-paid women workers were not laid off jobs as quickly as higher-paid men, and women constituted less than a quarter of the nation's employed work force.) Thirty-two delegates were young workers. Forty-seven (more than 20 percent) were African-Americans. This high number reflected both the particularly severe impact of the depression on African-Americans and the absence of discrimination against them in this Communist-led movement. Among the speakers were William Z. Foster, Israel Amter, and Robert Minor, all out on bail and awaiting trial on charges connected with the March 6 demonstration.

Local organizations called Unemployed Councils[1] already existed in some places. The councils represented at the National Conference on Unemployment had been drawn together in a variety of ways. Some had formed when radicals called neighbors together to prevent the eviction of one of them. Others formed as neighbors joined in efforts to get relief for a family that was on the brink of starvation. Hosea Hudson, an African-American, talking to Nell Irwin Painter, described council activities in Birmingham, Alabama:

> We [in the Unemployed Council] was always busybodies. We didn't wait for people to come to get us when they didn't get they grocery order or they coal order from the welfare. We would go around to see what the conditions was.
>
> If someone get out of food and been down to the welfare two or three times and still ain't got no grocery order, quite naturally the people talk about it. We wouldn't go around and just say, "That's too bad." We make it our business to go see this person, find out what the conditions was. And if the person was willing for the unemployed block committee person or the Party person to work with them and help them get something, we'd work with them. . . .
>
> We'd go to the house of the person that's involved, the victim, let her tell her story. Then we'd ask all the people, "What do you all think could be done about it?" We wouldn't just jump up and say what to do. We let the neighbors talk about it for a while, and then it would be some of us in the crowd, we going say, "If the lady wants to go back down to the welfare, if she wants, I suggest we have a little committee to go with her and find out what the conditions is."
>
> After the committee go down to the welfare office, we come back to the neighborhood, pass the word around that this

committee done gone downtown. Everybody wants to know what happen. But we won't going walk around tell everybody what's happened. We call a meeting. Sometimes we'd had 25–30 people in a room — won't no hall, we didn't have meetings in a hall, we had meetings in a room. We'd sort of have to raise the meeting kind of careful, because we didn't want the police to run in and break it up. Irregardless of what you was, they'd call you Red. . . .

We would conduct the meetings in a businesslike way. We would have one in the committee to make a report on what happened at the welfare office. . . . Then we'd throw the meeting open for discussion, let them say what they think. The purpose of it was to let them say they thought it was a good thing, that we ought to keep this up, all of us come together to be a regular organization. If there wasn't already a neighborhood unemployed committee on that block, the floor would be open for membership. All they had to do was sign up, sign a card, and didn't pay no dues.

Unemployed Council leaders made it clear that they were unalterably opposed to racism. In almost every city in which there was a large African-American community — Atlanta, Birmingham, and Richmond, for example — African-American and white Communist organizers went to the African-American unemployed, organized them into Unemployed Councils, and fought to get them relief.

Delegates from the varied lot of organizations represented at the Preliminary Conference adopted a program which was, with small modifications, to be that of a national organization of Unemployed Councils for several years. This program, like those in earlier depressions, called for federal relief and federal unemployment insurance. It opposed discrimination in the re-hiring of unemployed workers because of race, radical views, religion, or sex. It urged that the jobless be exempt from taxes and mortgage payments, and it proposed a shorter working day for employed workers with no reduction in wages.

The delegates to the conference also had other questions on their minds, and not all of these were easily answered. Should the councils themselves organize and distribute direct relief?

Should there be Unemployed Council soup kitchens? Opinions varied as delegates sought the right formulas for organizing. Advice that came from the CI to American Communists was that they should be flexible.

No matter what organization a delegate represented at the Preliminary Conference, he or she brought some experience of protest and resistance. There was a long American tradition of militant actions in earlier depressions, but there was no American pattern to follow in establishing a stable national organization of the jobless. Precedents were few in other countries, as well. In Germany, which was tormented by the same depression that afflicted the United States, workers led by Communists had formed councils. Members not only used mass marches and demonstrations, but also followed a practice of conferring with authorities in efforts to get relief. In Tsarist St. Petersburg, organizations of the jobless called Unemployed Councils had been established as far back as 1906. These councils (like the groups led by Israel Amter in the United States in the 1920s) had suggested to Americans a name and an organizational form and pointed toward various actions and policies.

In the end, the Preliminary Conference delegates agreed to hold a full-scale formal conference in Chicago early in July 1930. (The Unemployed Council did not achieve a formal constitution until it held its third national convention in Washington, D.C., in February 1934. For the text of this constitution, see Appendix I.) In the meantime, Unemployed Councils had been springing up in Chicago — twelve of them with 1,000 members. A council in Minneapolis enrolled 375 members, and Milwaukee, Duluth, and Indianapolis had growing organizations. By and large, these councils differed from some existing councils sponsored by the TUUL, which was mainly preoccupied with organizing workers who still had jobs. Some workers who were associated with militant unions (such as fur workers) got active union help when they became jobless, and they organized Unemployed Councils on an industrial basis. The unemployed who were on relief or were in need of relief could most easily be organized in relation to the relief-dispensing agencies. Frequently the activities of these agencies coincided with residential areas, so the Unemployed Councils grew up in neighborhoods and had subdivisions called "block committees."

The Milwaukee councils had an organizational chart that went this way:

1. Block committees are elected by workers in one or two blocks where the workers gather in meetings.
2. This block committee sends delegates to the Neighborhood Council. Neighborhood Council should be composed of 1 or 2 Wards with delegates for all block committees, fraternal organizations, Trade Unions, etc., in that territory. This is the Neighborhood Unemployed Council.
3. The Neighborhood Unemployed Councils elect delegates (3, 5, 10) according to the size, and these delegates are sent to the County Unemployed Council (in Chicago we have City Unemployed Council). Here in Milwaukee, because we are more closely connected (West Allis, etc.) we form the County Unemployed Council.

The block-committee form of organization was good for dealing with the problem of evictions. Members of the council were close at hand when marshals suddenly appeared to move a family out of a home for which it could not pay rent. Very often the committees prevented evictions. These block committees and the larger neighborhood organizations of which they were a part served another function: They provided fellowship for those whose workplace relationships had been totally disrupted when they were dismissed.

Not all problems of the jobless could be solved close to where they lived, of course. Except for dwindling private charity funds, the money for relief would have to come first from cities, then from states, and finally from the federal government. So the unemployed organizations had to find a way to bring pressure on mayors and city councils, on governors and state legislatures, and on the executive and legislative branches of the government in Washington. The neighborhood councils solved the problem by sending delegates to citywide councils, which, on occasion, then joined together for lobbying in state capitals and in Washington. To aid in lobbying for federal relief and work projects and unemployment insurance, a national federation of state and local councils had to come into being, and it did so at the conference in Chicago in July 1930.

The 1,320 delegates who attended this gathering set up the Unemployed Council of the USA, which began to take nation-wide initiatives on behalf of the jobless. Dependence on the TUUL was now largely a thing of the past, but the Communist Party continued to give active support, and Communists among the unemployed became leaders of the new organization.

The upsurge that had led to the conference in Chicago was national in scope. In the South, in Atlanta, dramatic events had taken place only a few weeks earlier. At a rally against unemployment and racism in May, four speakers had been arrested because the meeting had ignored segregated seating laws. They were charged with attempting to incite insurrection, as defined in a pre–Civil War law. The four were Anne Burlak, a 19-year-white textile worker who had recently become a Communist and was now a full-time organizer for the National Textile Workers Union; Mary Dalton, another white textile organizer; Henry Storey, an African-American printer from Atlanta; and Herbert Newton, an African-American schoolteacher from New York. Soon their case was joined with that of two others who had been organizing the unemployed on an integrated basis: M. H. Powers, a Communist, and Joe Carr, a YCL member. The Atlanta Six, as they became known, challenged the Georgia insurrection statute, which had had its origins in the days of slavery.

Burlak's activity among the jobless continued as she toured the country mobilizing support for the Atlanta Six. The United States Supreme Court finally heard the Burlak case, which had been joined to that of Angelo Herndon, a young African-American man who had been arrested under the same law. The court declared the Georgia statute unconstitutional.[2]

In August, immediately following the founding conference of the national Unemployed Council, the Communist Party established a newspaper in the South. The *Southern Worker* put great emphasis on organizing the jobless. In the extremely hostile states of the former Confederacy, the CP managed to maintain this paper, which had a mailing address in Alabama, was edited in Tennessee, and was printed in Georgia. One of the two owners of the print shop was the Kleagle (leader) of the Ku Klux Klan in Georgia. At first the Klansman didn't know what his presses were turning out, but when he discovered it he kept quiet. He, like the unemployed, felt the pinch of the depression and was glad to get the cash — which editor James Allen somehow always scraped together to pay the bill.

Distributing the paper to the jobless was a problem. To avoid the hazards of the mails, copies were spread throughout the South largely from hand to hand. Couriers left bundles in prearranged places, often hidden in trees. A great many of the jobless African-Americans were illiterate, and organizers read the newspapers aloud to them. In such ways word began to spread about the Unemployed Councils and the actions they conducted on behalf of the jobless.

In time the fight for jobs and relief in the South merged with the fight for the Scottsboro Boys, nine African-American youths who were framed on charges of raping two white women. The ferment among African-Americans was general and led to a demonstration of 7,000 unemployed African-Americans and whites in Birmingham in November 1932.

Indicating its flexible approach to organizational problems, which differed among regions and cities, the new Unemployed Council of the USA did not adopt a constitution. Such a step was not to come for four years, but the form of organization that evolved provided opportunities for exchanging experience and pooling energies.

In northern cities militant actions against evictions continued. In *Black Metropolis*, St. Clair Drake and Horace Cayton suggested the mood of the time: " 'Run quick and find the Reds!' More than one Harlem mother shouted this to her children when she was faced with eviction."

Not all eviction crises were so simple. In Chicago, early in August 1931, the police shot and killed three African-American men during an eviction fight. The following day 5,000 people protested in Washington Park, and the next day another demonstration of equal size took place. Then came news of the death of a fourth man who had been shot in the same eviction struggle. Sixty thousand people, of whom 40,000 were African-Americans, attended the funeral of the four.

Carl Winter, a Communist leader in the Unemployed Councils, recalled what happened when there was a wave of evictions in New York for nonpayment of rent:

> Squads of neighbors were organized to bar the way to the dispossessing officers. Whole neighborhoods were frequently mobilized to take part in this mutual assistance. Where superior police force prevailed, it became common practice for the Unemployed Councils to lead volunteer squads in carrying the displaced furniture and belongings back into the home after the police had departed. Council organizers became adept in fashioning meter-jumps to restore disconnected electric service and gas.

Using a variety of resistance techniques, the councils had practically stopped evictions in Detroit by March 1931, according to Edmund Wilson writing for the *New Republic* (March 26, 1931). Helen Seymour in "The Organized Unemployed" noted, "Of an eviction one unemployed worker said, 'We chased the constable twelve blocks. And we would have beat the hell out of him. The Unemployed Council is built on action, not promises. The eviction was stopped. For three weeks, we would wait for recognition from a relief office. Our committee got it for us in fifteen minutes.' "

One eviction in Brooklyn resulted in a demonstration by several thousand people at which a Democratic Party politician spoke in support of the community protest, although it had been organized by the Communist Party and an Unemployed Council. On another occasion, several hundred workers gathered outside an apartment in Harlem where a landlord was making a second attempt to evict some tenants. When the marshals arrived, they saw banners reading, "No Work, No Rent!" This time the marshals prevailed. They arrested two African-Americans and two whites from among the protesters, and the four had to serve ten days in jail. In other cases Unemployed Council members were more successful. They went to courts to warn judges there would be resistance if marshals tried to carry through evictions. More than once they persuaded judges who had heavy caseloads to let tenants remain in their apartments. During the first half of 1930 in New York City, 72,798 warrants for evictions were served. Unemployed Councils successfully resisted a great many attempts to carry them out. During eight months of 1932, 185,794 families in New York City received such notices. According to Richard O. Boyer and Herbert M. Morais in *Labor's Untold Story*, the Unemployed Council managed to move 77,000 of these families back into their homes. Whether or not this figure is accurate, there was an astonishing amount of successful resistance.

Evictions were epidemic on a national scale. In five industrial cities in Ohio between January 1930 and July 1932, for example, nearly 100,000 dispossess notices were issued.

In *Strike!* labor historian Jeremy Brecher quoted the following from a Chicago newspaper:

> A woman living in a certain block in Chicago has five children; her husband is a stockyards workman who has been out of a job a year and a half. But on ten dollars a month sent by her brother-in-law, and borrowing now and then from the neighbors' pantries, she has fed her family. There is no money left for rent. So after two warnings from the landlord — a crisis. She is to be evicted next Tuesday at five.
>
> In the same block lives a member of the local branch of the Unemployed Council, who has been through it all before. He talks to the men and women and together they call a meeting of all the families on the block. Most of them have known Mrs. MacNamara for years and know that the baby has tonsilitis. At 4:30 on Tuesday you find them in an organized body outside the MacNamara flat. The sheriff arrives and in the face of protest does his work. Mrs. MacNamara's bed, bureau, stove and children are translated to the street. Then the Council acts. With great gusto the bed, bureau, stove, and children are put back in the house. Then the neighbors proceed to the local relief bureau, where a Council spokesman displays the children, presents the facts, and demands that

the Relief Commission pay the rent or find another flat for the MacNamaras. The local relief worker expresses dismay but says the rent fund is exhausted. The spokesman goes through the MacNamara story again with a new emphasis, and repeats his demands. If the Commission is adamant, he leaves and reappears at general headquarters with a hundred Council members instead of fifty. Usually the Commission digs up the $6 a month rent or the landlord throws up his hands, and Mrs. MacNamara's children have a roof over their heads.

Often no one knew when or where a new eviction notice would be posted. Teams of furniture removers would appear suddenly without a day or even an hour of warning. But the unemployed turned this handicap into an advantage. Men who were out of work often hung around the local headquarters of the Unemployed Council, where they found companionship. When a breathless messenger came with news that an eviction was starting, these jobless men were ready, willing, and able to dash off and lend a hand to a neighbor. The very unpredictability of the eviction process offered another advantage to the jobless: It meant that police agents in their midst had very little time to alert the police.

In these eviction fights, the will to survive came into direct, raw conflict with the will to make a profit from property. Flesh resisted force — and flesh and spirit, aided by a spontaneously developing sense of comradeship, often prevailed. Arrests were frequent, and there were many casualties when neighbors moved furniture back into apartments from which marshals had just taken it. An American Civil Liberties Union survey published early in 1935 counted at least fourteen deaths at the hands of the police, many of which occurred as angry people fought for shelter.

The eviction fights were part of the general upsurge that had led to the conference of the Unemployed Councils in Chicago in July 1930. The ferment continued after the conference. In New York City, the Unemployed Council organized a demonstration on October 17, 1930, at City Hall to demand relief. The leaders of this meeting were arrested and severely beaten, but the Board of Estimate of the city met the next day and appropriated

$1 million for relief. It was the first such appropriation made by the city in the Great Depression.

The New York Unemployed Council also pioneered in a form of pressure that was later to be adopted by auto workers in Detroit: the sit-in, which had originally been proposed by Lucy Parsons at the founding convention of the IWW. Often council members filled a relief station and then refused to leave until they got their grievances settled to their satisfaction.

In February 1931, Unemployed Councils and the TUUL organized a delegation of 140 persons from all over the country to petition Congress for relief and for unemployment insurance. In every major city demonstrations took place while, on National Unemployment Insurance Day, the delegation was in Washington.

Early in 1931, some leaders of Unemployed Councils had recommended setting up food kitchens, and Communists helped organize food collections. These were humane acts of assistance to people who needed something to eat immediately. In a few months, however, both the Communists and the Unemployed Councils abandoned the idea, saying it had nothing to do with solving the basic problems of the unemployed. Similarly, Communist and council policy on the subject of looting varied depending on time and place. In the early days of mass unemployment some Communists encouraged the direct appropriation of food. Later the practice was frowned on because it solved no long-term problem and could provoke very costly counteraction.

The Communist Party was usually against spontaneous acts of appropriation, but coal bootlegging became so widespread that the CP thought it wise not to oppose it. Unemployed Pennsylvania coal miners began to go back to the closed-down mines to dig coal for themselves rather than for the profit of others. They also dug in poor seams close to the surface. This spontaneous and illegal activity grew to astonishing size. In 1931 the jobless miners bootlegged about a half-million tons of anthracite, some of which they used and some of which they sold. In 1932 the bootlegged coal amounted to a million and a half tons. By then about 1,000 jobless miners had gone into business. They sold their coal on the market in big eastern cities in competition with the coal being offered by owners of mines that were still operating. So strong was this illegal movement, and so widespread its support in the mining districts of Pennsylvania, that the police and the courts looked the other way.

The Unemployed Council did not initiate the bootlegging, but it did build a strong organization among the jobless miners taking part in it. Steve Nelson, then a Communist leader of the council, summed up the situation:

> Naturally the political significance of the bootlegging was discussed at Party meetings, and we took it as a positive sign. Instead of lying down next to the coal piles and freezing, the bootleggers sold it to buy them food. Their acts affirmed the concept that human life comes first and private property second. To this extent the experience represented a political advance by thousands of miners, but we didn't overestimate the meaning of bootlegging. We saw it primarily as an immediate response to a problem and not as a major step on the road to socialism.

While some members of the Unemployed Council in Pennsylvania were bootlegging coal, councils elsewhere were using very legitimate techniques. In the iron mining town of Crosby, Minnesota, for example, Emil Nygard, a Communist and a leader of the local Unemployed Council, ran for mayor as part of a campaign for relief and jobs on public works. He also promised, if elected, to set up a Workers Advisory Committee to check up on the City Council. Nygard won the election and immediately hired jobless miners to do work improving the town, including planting trees. The City Council tried to thwart Nygard at every step but the mayor carried his fight to the state capital. He led a Workers and Farmers Hunger March to petition the governor and the legislature. Nygard might have been reelected, but the mine owners said they would close down the mines completely (and cause increased unemployment) if he remained in office.

Electoral methods were also used in Illinois in 1935. In the village of Forest View in Cook County, four members of the Unemployed Council were elected village trustees. One of these was John Wright, a Communist who had been very active in the work of the Unemployed Council in various Chicago suburbs.

The Communists were busy everywhere. They were diligent and eager to have the unemployed adopt a whole range of communist policies — many of which appeared to the jobless to have little or nothing to do with getting relief or preventing evictions. The contentious quality that prompted the Communist David to do battle with the capitalist Goliath spilled over into quarrels with others on the Left. Back in the 1920s, intense squabbles had occurred between factions within the party. After two of the factions, the Trotskyists and the Lovestoneites, were expelled, they operated outside the CP, and the antagonisms continued. In addition, Socialists were objects of strong CP attack. Indeed, they were often called "Social Fascists" and were opposed with the same kind of vituperative language used against German, Italian, and American fascists.

At times it seemed that Communists were contentious simply for the sake of being ornery, and certainly this chip-on-the-shoulder aspect of the movement won few converts either to immediate reform or to ultimate revolution. Irrelevant contentiousness did, however, give impetus to and put its stamp on some of the actions of the Unemployed Councils. Witness this report in 1933 in the first issue of the *Catholic Worker:*

> It is the policy of the Unemployed Council which is recruiting members through its block committees by canvassing and by circular appeals, to keep religion out of their discussions . . . and the Council grows. . . .
>
> [However] a group of Italian families had gathered together under the auspices of the Unemployed Councils to witness a little entertainment provided by the young people of another section. The Block Committee did not know what the entertainment was to consist of. They were as horrified as the Italian visitors when they found that the organization of children had elected to put on a little drama called, "Mr. God is

Not at Home," which treated of religion scornfully and scoffingly. . . . So the little affair on East Fifteenth Street turned out to be one of those occasions when the young Communists played into the hands of the priests, and we must thank them for their zeal.

There were other problems. Clarence Hathaway, a CP leader, made a tour of industrial cities, after which he urged that more attention be paid to the immediate needs of the jobless, with less talk about far-off colonial wars and less agitation for the defense of the Soviet Union. In addition, the CP's Central Committee urged its members to use fewer slogans that seemed to the jobless to be alien to their needs. Even in Moscow, a leader of the Comintern strongly criticized many of the abstract slogans that the U.S. Communists were using in propaganda addressed to the jobless.

Nevertheless, the Unemployed Council of the USA grew. By 1933 it had 150,000 members, according to its secretary, Herbert Benjamin. Much of the activity conducted by the jobless was aided by Communist Party members, and testimony to the quality of their work sometimes came from unlikely quarters. Norman Thomas, a Socialist leader who had been sharply attacked by the CP, said, "The Communists — the best of them — were devoted people, able in organizing labor and the unemployed."

One such devoted Communist organizer in the Unemployed Council (and later in the Workers Alliance) was Helen Lynch, a poet and a graduate of the University of Michigan. Her home town was Muncie, Indiana. At first, when she came to New York, she had a job teaching in a private school. Next, she shared the life of the unemployed, and although she was a quiet, self-effacing person, she soon became a leader in many demonstrations, sit-ins, and eviction fights. She was in charge of all the trucks on a hunger march to Albany in 1934. Mike Davidow, who was the New York City organizer of the Unemployed Council and later of the Workers Alliance, recalled Helen Lynch as both courageous and selfless. In the early days of the depression, said Davidow, before there was any cash relief, she often gave her food tickets to people who seemed to need food more than she did. And she always wore the same navy blue blouse, skirt, and tam. The council leaders wanted her to have another outfit, and they assigned council member Frieda Jackson to see that Helen got it. Frieda bought Helen a new dress and made sure she put it on. The next day it was gone; Helen had given it away to a woman who, she said, "needed it more than I."

Such lack of attention to her own welfare undermined her health. She was not well on February 17, 1938, when the relief authorities refused to grant relief to Mrs. Mamie Abrahamson, an African-American mother of a four-year-old child. Mrs. Abrahamson had refused to accept a job at substandard pay that would have required her to be separated from her child not only during the day but also at night. Helen Lynch would not accept the decision of the relief officials and continued the fight, directing the activities of Workers Alliance members from her bed, to which pneumonia had driven her. On February 24, word came that the fight was successful; Mrs. Abrahamson got her relief. On February 27, Helen Lynch died.

On the morning of her funeral, 2,000 mourners jammed into the Church of All Nations, and 5,000 Workers Alliance members and friends made a funeral procession from the church to Tompkins Square, scene of many of the struggles that Helen Lynch had led, and back to the church, all in a driving rain.

In the West, Carl Yoneda, a man of Japanese ancestry, worked for years as selflessly as had Helen Lynch. He led many demonstrations of the Japanese Local of the Unemployed Council in Los Angeles. He was active in many citywide and statewide actions and hunger marches, and he was often arrested and beaten by members of a special unit of the Los Angeles police force that came to be known as the Red Squad. In his autobiography, *Ganbatte*, Yoneda described one of the worst of these beatings: On February 15, 1933, a Committee of Fifty, representing the ACLU, TUUL unions, Japanese workers, the International Labor Defense (ILD), and others, went to City Hall to ask the City Council to censure William F. Hynes, the head of the Red Squad, for violating their right to freedom of assembly. Leo Gallagher, an attorney, started to address the

City Council on behalf of the committee. Hynes immediately tried to arrest Gallagher. When members of the Committee of Fifty, including Yoneda, came to Gallagher's aid, Hynes signalled to members of his squad to seize Yoneda. They took him into an elevator that was manually operated, stopped it between floors, and, using brass knuckles, began to hit him in the abdomen. There were to be no signs of blows to his face. Finally, they took the elevator to the basement and dumped him on the floor, where a City Hall worker found him and managed to get him to a doctor. It was many weeks before Yoneda could return to full-time work for the Unemployed Council and other organizations.

From the point of view of the unemployed, what did people like Helen Lynch and Carl Yoneda and others in the Unemployed Councils accomplish? C. R. Walker, after a tour of several regions in the country, gave his conclusion in the *Forum* magazine of September 1932: "In the cities I visited the economic status of the unemployed workers, the amount of relief, etc., was directly proportional to the strength of the Unemployed Councils." Josephine Chapin Brown, a historian of relief in the 1930s, echoed this opinion: "Unquestionably pressures exerted by organized client groups not only succeeded in correcting numerous local deficiencies in the administration of emergency relief but were potent in securing larger appropriations of funds from local, state and federal governments."

21

The Nonconfrontational Alternative: Self-Help (1931 and later)

I'm learnin' one thing good. Learnin' it all a time, ever' day. If you're in trouble, or hurt or need — go to the poor people. They're the only ones that'll help — the only ones.
— Casey in John Steinbeck's *The Grapes of Wrath*, 1939

While Communists were developing a confrontational movement that demanded federal aid for the jobless, other movements were springing up based on the belief that the unemployed should and could help themselves. Of course, many had to help themselves if they were to survive. In cities everywhere, clusters of homeless men and some homeless families gradually built up shanty towns that came to be called Hoovervilles. As these Hoovervilles grew on patches of unoccupied land, they began to resemble organized communities. The shacks, made from all kinds of discarded materials, tended to be arranged in rows. Paths between the rows were called streets and given names. With a determination to survive, the citizens of Hoovervilles tried, with no resources, to reconstruct at least a shadow of the life from which they had been driven by mysterious economic forces.

For the most part they were not derelicts who had been broken by society (and drink) in years of prosperity. They were stable citizens who not so long ago had been hardworking, contributing members of society. They were people who did not insist on starving if the government lagged in establishing public works. They and other hundreds of thousands of the jobless engaged in a wide variety of self-help projects.

Many of the unemployed recapitulated in a very short time the economic history of the human race. When they were separated from the prevailing economy, the jobless found food where they could, often in garbage cans. They became hunters and gatherers. At a slightly higher level, they tried to stay alive by exchanging labor for meals. Direct barter came next. People exchanged haircuts for bread, wood chopping for groceries, garden vegetables for clothes, and so on. Some of the jobless reinvented money. They printed unofficial paper money called "scrip" that served as pay in return for labor. With scrip, they bought goods that were often in oversupply in the general economy. Soon enough, inflation decreased the value of scrip. People outside the mainline economy found themselves working more and getting less in return for their labor. When surplus goods were no longer available, the jobless attempted to become producers, growing and making the necessities of life. In order to do this they needed capital, which they got in a modest way from county, state, and federal sources.

One widely publicized activity was apple selling. In cities everywhere, men stood on street corners offering apples at a nickel apiece. This was not self-help activity generated by the jobless, however. It was a strictly commercial enterprise initiated by apple growers who saw a chance to use the desperate unemployed as salespersons who could help unload a bumper apple crop.

California's large self-help movement has been described in detail by Clark Kerr in his Ph.D. dissertation for the University of California, "Productive Enterprises of the Unemployed 1931–1938." At one time or another, 500,000 families were affiliated with this movement, which had about 75,000 active members. By the end of 1932, it had spread to thirty-seven states, although the largest concentration of self-help organizations, often called "productive enterprises," remained in California. Kerr summarized the social impact of the movement: "The effect of participation in self-help production on the social attitude of the members was to concentrate their interest on productive activities rather than on protest or higher relief payments."

Communists called the self-help movement a "self-starvation" movement. In California, in the season when carrots were plentiful, radicals made up a song that became popular:

> But carrots, carrots, carrots,
> Are nine tenths of all you eat.
> Your innards get to hankering
> for a good old chunk of meat,
> so I can't refrain from lifting
> this prayer to god on high,
> "Grant me one more leg of chicken
> on my plate before I die."

A second large center of self-help activity developed in Seattle, which had long had a strong union movement. Two different radical traditions met there. One, stemming from the Industrial Workers of the World (IWW), had been very vigorous in Seattle in the 1920s, and some of the unemployed in the 1930s were former or long-time Wobblies. The other source of radical energy was the Seattle Labor College and its parent organization, the Conference for Progressive Labor Action (CPLA). Both institutions were led by A. J. Muste.

The indigenous IWW tradition held that society should be reorganized along industrial lines, with workers in control. The Musteite tradition at that point (it soon changed) favored a kind of benevolent, nonconfrontational approach to solving labor's problems. Both traditions meshed during the 1931 summer months in support of a worker-administered communal self-help program. The result was a remarkable outburst of activity through an organization called the Unemployed Citizens League (UCL). Its founder in Seattle was Carl Brannin, editor of the *Vanguard*, a paper he used in his organizing efforts.

By the end of 1931, the UCL claimed 12,000 members. In the next twelve months it spread through the state of Washington, and its membership rose to 80,000 in 1933. During those two years its emphasis changed considerably, but in the beginning its activities centered around mutual aid.

Each local of the UCL sent five delegates to the central body, which met weekly. The first chairman of the federated locals was an elderly out-of-work building contractor, J. F. Cronin. Although not a worker, Cronin pointed with pride to his membership many years earlier in the Knights of Labor, which had been sympathetic to the Industrial Armies of 1894.

During the growing and harvesting season in 1931, the self-help program appealed to UCL members who came from a variety of trades (listed in descending order according to their numbers in the membership): carpenters, loggers and lumber workers, truck drivers, lumber laborers, steel and other metal workers, common laborers, salesmen, office workers, deep sea fishermen, painters, ship carpenters and shipwrights, auto and aviation mechanics, electricians, machinists and helpers, building laborers, cooks, bakers and candy makers, engineers, plumbers, artists, sign writers and lithographers, concrete workers, fishing laborers, plasterers and lathers, railroad workers, steam firemen, boilermakers, miners, musicians, waitresses, bricklayers and tile-setters, cabinet workers, draftsmen, and a few other trades represented by only one to three persons.

The UCL locals got the fishermen's union to lend boats so they could fish. Members persuaded farmers to let them harvest the fruit and potatoes for which there was no market, and they borrowed trucks to transport this produce. Women exchanged sewing for food. Barbers cut hair for canned berries. The practice of barter spread and was highly organized.

The harvesting of surplus farm crops in 1931 produced eight freight-car loads of potatoes, pears, and apples. The borrowed fishing boats brought in 120,000 pounds of fish in the fall and winter of 1931. Some men collected firewood from cutover forested areas; in all, they cut, split, and hauled 11,000 cords. The products of these labors were shared by UCL members. Some members repaired houses or worked in shoe repair shops, while others did gardening. There were also child welfare and legal aid projects in which lawyers contributed their services. The extent of UCL activity was carefully recorded by members who had been clerical workers. Between January 1 and July 21, 1932, an average of 5,000 persons worked sixteen hours each week.

The UCL self-help program, carried out by skilled workers from the various trades, generated a considerable amount of economic activity outside the general economy. For a few months it helped stave off starvation or at least severe deprivation for thousands of workers in Seattle.

To many it seemed that a formula had been found for using the manifold talents of the jobless in their own behalf. The Seattle unemployed were mainly skilled workers in their middle years, and they were eager to support themselves as they always had. They would go to great lengths to avoid taking charity, which was what they considered relief to be. But neighborliness and admirable impulses toward cooperation were not enough. By the winter of 1931, it was already apparent that the needs of the jobless greatly exceeded the ability of a mutual aid program to meet them.

Some UCL members looked for a while with hope toward the Technocrats. This movement took the position that highly technical, intelligent, rational planning in society could eliminate unnecessary work and at the same time make work opportunities for the unemployed. But the Technocrats faded from political view as quickly as they appeared. Technocracy could not convince enough people that clever schemes could bring order into the capitalist system.

Unwillingly, the UCL turned more and more to the city for relief. With the aid of a sympathetic administrator, members were able to take over for a time the distribution of much of the city relief. At about this time, the Unemployed Council began to organize in Seattle, and some of its members became active in UCL locals.

The Unemployed Council had never approved of self-help programs. In the opinion of Herbert Benjamin: "This form of relief is comparable to the relief that a starving dog might get by eating his own tail." For the ruling class, he said, "a good relief plan is any plan whereby the working class would feed on itself and relieve those who own the wealth from obligation and responsibility."

When the UCL in Seattle organized a hunger march that occupied the County City Building, for some reason the Communists in the Unemployed Council opposed this popular sit-in move. In effect, the clumsy action of the Communists aided the police in bringing an early end to the sit-in. The national CP, however, was extremely critical of the local members and of a slogan of the Seattle Unemployed Council, "Smash the UCL."

Old IWW members in the UCL were among those who began objecting to self-help, which they came to regard as little more than a way for the jobless to share poverty with one another. The militant tradition of the IWW fitted well with the confrontational methods that were being recommended by the Unemployed Council.

The UCL policy of voluntarism was now facing challenges from all sides, including the city relief apparatus, which did not like to see unpaid amateurs doing its work. Professional politicians wanted to have control over a large relief fund that, as a result of pressure, had been growing. Under such stresses, one after another of the UCL leaders resigned. At the same time (early in 1932), UCL members became intensely interested in an upcoming municipal election and in the activities of politicians who were running for office. Candidates saw in the large and well-organized UCL a chance to win the support of a sizable bloc of voters (about one-third of the Seattle electorate belonged to the UCL). One of the candidates for mayor, John F. Dore, made speeches that were proworker and antirich, thus pleasing many of the jobless. As a result, Dore received UCL endorsement in his campaign, and he won the election that took place in the spring of 1932.

Once he was in office, Dore's militancy went into reverse. The new mayor bore no resemblance to the man who was recently so friendly to the jobless. He even threatened to use machine guns against their demonstrations. To the unemployed he became known as "Revolving Dore." The UCL quickly repudiated him, but UCL members did not despair of political action. They decided to shift support from candidates who belonged to the old parties and nominate candidates from their own ranks. By now the UCL had established locals throughout the state. On May 30, 1932, delegates from nearly ninety locals met in Tacoma and established the United Producers League (UPL), which aimed to include farmers. The UCL and UPL nominated seven of their members to run for the state legislature, and in November 1932 all of these candidates were elected.

But state legislatures, even when they included representatives of the unemployed, and even when they were lobbied for three days by 1,000 hunger marchers — as they were in Olympia in January 1933 — could not solve the unemployment problem. By February 1933, the UCL had become for the most part an organization, as one observer noted, "not unlike the Unemployed Councils in philosophy and tactics." This rapid transformation from a self-help to an electoral organization and then to a radical protest group paralleled to some extent the evolution that was taking place nationally in the UCL's parent organization headed by A. J. Muste.

22

The First National Hunger March
(December 1931)

Just grin, keep on working, stop worrying about the future
and go ahead as best you can. We always have a way of living
through hard times.
                    — Charles W. Schwab, chairman of the board
                           Bethlehem Steel Corporation, 1931

Power concedes nothing without a demand. It never did, and
it never will. Find out just what people will submit to, and you
have found out the exact amount of injustice and wrong which
will be imposed upon them; and these will continue till they
have resisted with either words or blows, or both. The limits of
tyrants are prescribed by the endurance of those whom they
suppress.
                                         — Frederick Douglass, 1849

Which side are you on?

                                              — Florence Reese
                                           song written in 1931

In the spring and summer of 1931, the jobless were on the
march. On April 1, a throng in Maryland forced its way into the
state legislature and demanded relief. Later that month, five
columns of unemployed marchers started out from different
points in Ohio. They met in Columbus, the state capital, where
in spite of a heavy rain 3,000 people turned out to greet them.
During the last week of May, four columns of marchers started
out for Lansing, Michigan's capital. Along the way large gatherings of workers greeted one column or another in Kalamazoo,

Battle Creek, Pontiac, Wayland, and Detroit. Fifteen thousand people were on hand when the columns met in Lansing. Later hunger marches stirred people up in at least forty cities, and there were statewide hunger marches in California, Minnesota, New York, Maryland, New Jersey, Pennsylvania, Indiana, Illinois, and Missouri.

All of the marches were part of a plan drawn up by the TUUL to dramatize the demands of the jobless for relief and unemployment insurance. All were in preparation for a national action reminiscent of the Industrial Armies of 1894: a National Hunger March, scheduled to arrive in the nation's capital on December 7, the day Congress would begin a new session. The Central Committee of the Communist Party urged its members to give the fullest possible support to this effort.

In overall charge of the Hunger March was Herbert Benjamin, a small, frail man who had worked at many trades, including umbrella mending. Len De Caux had encountered him in Cleveland when Benjamin was district organizer there for the Communist Party. De Caux, a graduate of Cambridge University in England, said of Benjamin, whose education ended with the sixth grade, "He had wit and sophistication. He was reasonable and readily grasped situations — a good organizer."

"I came into the unemployed movement by reason of undernourishment," Benjamin said. He was, in fact, ill when CP leader Earl Browder asked him to take charge of all party work among the unemployed. Benjamin had already played an important part, offstage, in the demonstration of March 6, 1930. In preparation for this new assignment, he hurried to Europe to attend a conference, "Unemployment in the Capitalist World," in Prague, where people from various countries pooled information about how they were organizing the jobless. He arrived too late for the conference, but he did study unemployed organizations in Germany and then went on to Moscow. He returned to the United States in October 1931.

The Hunger March that Benjamin led differed sharply from the marches of the Industrial Armies that had moved toward Washington in 1894. In the first place, it was not a mass migration of the jobless. It was strictly limited in size and made up only of elected delegates from labor and unemployed organizations. Unlike the 1894 armies, the Hunger March was highly organized and had a much more class-conscious program to present. It represented a disciplined organizational effort by Communists in the United States, about half of whom were out of work.

The planners of the Hunger March put forward the following demands:

1. Immediate unemployment insurance at full wages administered by workers for all workers without discrimination of any kind.
2. Social insurance payments for illness, accident, old age and maternity.
3. Winter relief of $50 for each unemployed worker plus $10 for each dependent, the money to come from funds hitherto allocated for military purposes.
4. Transformation of huge stocks of wheat and cotton held by the Farm Board into bread and clothing for the jobless.
5. No eviction of unemployed workers. Free rent, gas and light to all unemployed.
6. A seven hour day with no reduction in wages for most workers, and a six hour day for miners, railroad workers and young workers.
7. Prohibition of all forced labor in connection with relief or insurance, and no discrimination.
8. Full and immediate payment of the balance of the veterans bonus to ex-servicemen.

The Unemployed Councils publicized this program in neighborhoods, and local demonstrations and warm-up actions made it known. One warm-up action took place in front of the Briggs Manufacturing Company in Detroit, which made car bodies for Ford. This demonstration, organized by the YCL, made demands on behalf of the families of seventy-five men who had been thrown out of work at the closely related Briggs and Ford plants. It also called for support of the upcoming National Hunger March. The day before the demonstration, children appeared near the plant carrying signs, one of which read, "Walter P. Brigg's children have their own ponies. Briggs workers' children starve. All out to the Briggs Hunger March!"

About 600 people started the march on November 22 (the day before Thanksgiving) at the Unemployed Council headquarters. By the time they reached the Briggs plant, the number had grown to about 5,000. At the gate, inside which the still-employed workers were locked, speakers urged the men to strike and pledged that the jobless would not scab. Then the hungry crowd voted to go to the nearby Ford company store, which had supplies of things the unemployed desperately needed. The store locked its doors, and the police attacked the marchers. Two were arrested.

In spite of the police, the demonstrators then and there held a protest meeting and approved a plan to march on the big Ford plant at a future date. Organizers also signed up two new members for the auto union.

More typical of the preparations for the National Hunger March were neighborhood conferences, often called united front conferences. These brought together representatives of unions, fraternal organizations, and other groups, and each gathering elected delegates to take part in the national march. The issue of the *Party Organizer* that circulated at this time was vehement in its insistence that members of the CP help build their conferences and help the march in every way, including getting organizations to elect delegates. The number of delegates elected depended on the size of the community. Fund-raising went on to finance them, and support was solicited and often obtained from unions and community organizations. The entire march was to be made by car or truck, so jalopies had to be borrowed and trucks borrowed or rented. Along the lines of march, the Unemployed Councils, working with local branches of a left-wing organization called Workers International Relief (WIR), obtained donations of food and offers of shelter, sometimes in public buildings and sometimes in private homes.

All of this activity attracted attention. The *New York Times* reported that the New York City Bureau of the Secret Service had notified the head of that organization in Washington that the marchers "all will be furnished with rifles." After airing this provocative fabrication, the Secret Service said it believed that the *Times* report was farfetched, and indeed it was. Arms were absolutely forbidden to all who took part in the march.

Plans called for the formation of four separate columns, all of which would meet in Washington on December 6 to be on hand for the opening of Congress the next day. On December 1, Column 1 was to leave Boston and Column 2 would leave Buffalo. On November 30, Column 3 would leave Chicago and Column 4 would leave St. Louis. Delegates from the West Coast would leave cities there on November 23 and would join columns in either Chicago or St. Louis. Of the delegates, 46 percent were CP members and 5 percent YCLers. Thirteen percent were African-Americans and 11 percent were women. Forty of the marchers belonged to the AFL; seventy-five were TUUL members. Heading the group of delegates that went from Kansas City to join the St. Louis column was a young African-American man, Henry Winston, who would one day become national chairman of the Communist Party.

It was no simple matter to get 1,670 delegates transported, fed, clothed, and sheltered — all on a strict schedule. Each delegate wore an armband reading, "National Hunger March, December 7, 1931." Each truck, which typically carried ten delegates, elected a captain, and each column of trucks elected a guiding committee and a leader. In every truck there was a map telling exactly the route to be followed, and with each column went a scout car, sometimes pushing ahead to look for difficulties and sometimes following behind to watch for breakdowns. Each column also had a medical aid squad and a mechanic. Under Herbert Benjamin, who was in command nationally and was also responsible for all arrangements in Washington, A. W. Mills acted as chief organizer. Benjamin shuttled back and forth between Washington and different points along the lines of march, checking on details. Everything was handled with military precision; nothing was left to chance.

Police along the line of march were often unfriendly. In Hammond, Indiana, they seemed determined to stop a rally called to support the march. But the crowd was so large and so militant that the police gave up trying to disperse it.

An account by Sadie Van Veen of events in Cumberland, Maryland, will suggest what happened repeatedly along the way to Washington. Van Veen had been asked to arrange food and shelter in Cumberland for one column of marchers on the night before they reached Washington. The mayor of nearby Fredericksburg had told the Washington Post that he was sure Cumberland would meet the marchers with hostility. What happened was somewhat different, according to Van Veen's account:

> I was told that I would have to rely chiefly on my own resourcefulness. I was given a small sum of money — I think it was the munificent sum of $40 for all expenses including food for the marchers. Those were hard times. . . .
>
> Arriving in Cumberland, . . . I phoned one of the three people to whom I had been directed.
>
> When we met, we took up the first and most important matter on our agenda, and that was shelter for the marchers, for the weather was freezing cold. . . .
>
> I was advised to see the mayor of the town, who was a physician, not running for re-election and evidently indifferent as to his political reputation with Cumberland politicians.
>
> But the only place he could get for us, with space enough for so many marchers was, of all places, an old skating rink on the outskirts of the city. . . .
>
> The mayor went out of his way to have two great pot-bellied stoves installed and ordered coal and wood to keep the fires going. It was the best that could be done.
>
> The food problem was a weighty one. I visited the wholesale butchers and grocers. I told them that we had to have quantities of food; meat, cheese, bread, coffee, canned milk and sugar. . . . They came across handsomely. . . .
>
> From the wholesale bakers we got all the bread we needed, at cost. It was mid-winter and we decided on Mulligan stew. The butchers gave us 25 pounds of good beef. We got a bushel of onions and carrots for very little money. We did as well with the canned milk, cheese and sugar. I believe we paid for half.
>
> The skating rink was cold. Fires had to be built and the food

had to be cooked. We needed workers — willing, trusted men who would go out of their way to help their unemployed brothers and sisters.

Cumberland, like all the cities of the South, was a jim-crow town. There were hundreds of Negroes in the hunger march. Whom could we trust?

I decided to go to the Negro (and segregated) section of the town. I took a bus and got off where I believed I might find people willing to help. I walked into a bar and poolroom in the Negro community. There were possibly a dozen men, drinking [beer], playing pool, talking. When they saw me, a dead silence fell over the place and amazement was on every face. What did a white woman want here?

"Brothers," I began, without losing a moment of time, "there is something very important I have to tell you—it won't take me five minutes to explain. I'm not selling anything. I am not a preacher. I don't want any money.

"In two days there will be 600 unemployed workers here. They are marching this way from all over the country. They are on their way to Washington, D.C., to demand Government relief for the unemployed and unemployment insurance.

"Now I'll tell you why I came to you. About a third of these people are Negro men and women. I came to ask you to help us cook and care for them for a day and a night. They will be weary, cold and hungry. They are delegates from the Unemployed Councils all over this country. I come to you because I don't know anyone else in this town that I can trust to help poor Negro and white folks. We need a committee of about a dozen people who will prepare the food and build the fires at the old skating rink.

"If you come, you will meet some wonderful people. You'll see a crowd where there is real brotherhood between Negro and white. What do you say?"

There was silence for a moment; then they began to talk.... They asked questions and wanted details. They said they would come, sure thing! And they did come. At the appointed time, hours before the marchers entered the city, we met in the huge, cold barn of a place, and started to work. Fires were built in the two big stoves. It was impossible to get the place warm, even though the stoves were kept red hot. The best we could do was to get the chill out.

Our new friends built fires outside for cooking the chow. They brought with them two or three great stew pots, such as are used in the army; one for coffee. (They probably borrowed them from a friendly restaurant.) They attacked the sides of beef and vegetables, sliced the bread and cheese. What a stew they made! I can still remember the aroma! Boards were laid across the barrels and boxes in the hall. Paper plates, containers and spoons were laid out. Cheese sandwiches were piled high. . . .

It was already dusk and time for the great arrival. We had sent out scouts to lead the way. Everything was ready.

Suddenly we saw the lights of the cavalcade at the foot of the winding road leading to our camping place. On they came, straggling up the hill. Then one car after another began to pull up. . . . The crowd piled out and streamed into the barn-like hall. On and on they came. It took more than an hour for the travelers to park their tin lizzies and shabby jalopies and encamp. They brought gunny sacks and blankets with them.

Cold and hungry, they were glad to stand and stretch their limbs after their long tour cramped into vehicles not big enough for half their number. Then they lined up for chow. . . . Everyone got a plate of the hot stew, a sandwich and coffee. Cigarettes and pipes came out. They threw down their blankets and camped about the two stoves at either end of the hall.

A little later the March Committee asked for silence and held a brief meeting to make plans for the next day. . . .

Within an hour after the short meeting the marchers were asleep on the floor on their blankets and bundles. Committees had been appointed to stay and watch in shifts.

The men who had come to help us stayed with us all night. They did not rest. They went from group to group, meeting people from all over the country. It was a revelation to them. Indeed, there were many revelations in those years of organizing the unemployed!

Early the next morning, the marchers pulled out, after hot coffee, bread and cheese. We had no other food.

They climbed into their cars and tin lizzies. Slowly and carefully they moved on down the winding road. The next stop was Washington, D.C.

The columns all reached Washington December 6, on schedule. Police Commissioner Pelham Glassford, who had been on the job less than a month, said of the approaching Hunger Marchers, "The city was very apprehensive about them, and the preparations I made for police control were as much to allay public alarm as to handle the actual situation." As his preparations began, Glassford sent for Benjamin, who was well aware that enemies of the march were predicting violence.

Benjamin told in his memoirs how this invitation originated. He was staying in the home of Joe Rinis, a Jewish carpenter and CP member who had spent several years working as a volunteer technician in the Soviet Union.

> One evening in November, Joe, speaking with studied casualness as we were having tea before going to bed, said, "I know a young woman who is dating the new Chief of Police. If you could get a message to him through her, what would you say?" The idea of Joe Rinis knowing someone who would date a chief of police seemed too implausible and ridiculous to credit. However, Joe seemed to be seriously trying to tell me something and he was someone worthy of respect, and it was an intriguing thought. So after a few minutes I replied, speaking aloud as much to myself as to him, "I would tell him that he has a chance to become the most celebrated police chief in the U.S. by having a demonstration of unemployed take place in the capital at a time like this, without violence." Two days later I answered my phone.

It was Glassford, pleasantly asking if Benjamin could come to see him that afternoon. In Glassford's office Benjamin made a novel proposal. "All right," he said, "you people always claim that we are the ones who want bloody heads so we can shout police brutality. We'll give you a chance. You contain your people, and I will guarantee that there won't be any violence."

Glassford was eager to start off his career as a police official with a peaceful operation, and he worked closely with Benjamin to this end. He arranged for shelter for the marchers and saw to it that soup, stew, bread, and coffee awaited them. Still, he took no chances. He had as many police as marchers lining the streets when the determined mass of petitioners entered the city. After all, Washington had not seen anything remotely like this since the days of the militant suffragists.

Federal officials did not leave matters in the hands of Glassford. Secretary of War Patrick J. Hurley had ordered all soldiers at nearby Fort Meyer to be ready for active service. Two companies of Marines had been called by the time the marchers reached Washington, and nearly 1,000 additional Marines were brought from Quantico to the Marine barracks in Washington. According to one newspaper, 400 police were imported from eastern cities to augment the District of Columbia force. Guards were posted at the home of Representative Hamilton Fish, author of legislation that would lead to the establishment of the House Committee on Un-American Activities. (The previous evening Fish had attacked the Hunger March over radio station WJSV. The marchers, he said, did not represent American workers, and Benjamin, leader of the march, took his orders from Moscow.) Guards also were posted at the home of Senator Tasker L. Oddie of Nevada, another vocal anti-Communist.

The night of December 6, the marchers met in the Washington Auditorium to hear speeches by Herbert Benjamin, William Z. Foster, and others. They could also hear music from the floor below the auditorium, where a marathon dance had been going on for days. The marathoners were dancing for prize money as a solution to their unemployment problems.

The Hunger Marchers had their own music, provided by the Unemployed Workers Club Martini Horn Band. This ensemble consisted of a drum major, a snare drum, a bass drum, a cornet, five martini horns, and an instrument made up of sixteen pan pipes. At times the band burst forth with what the *Evening Graphic* called "revolutionary tunes."

The delegates, to show where their sympathies lay, elected an honorary presiding committee consisting of Tom Mooney; Warren K. Billings; the Scottsboro Boys; Harlan (Kentucky) coal strikers who were in prison, plus other jailed coal strikers in Ohio, West Virginia, and Pennsylvania; seventeen workers who had been arrested for marching around the White House a few days before; farm workers from Imperial Valley, California, who were on strike; and IWW members from Centralia, Washington, imprisoned as a result of their fight for free speech.

The next morning the marchers met at John Marshall Place. Some of the placards they carried read: "We demand unemployment insurance equal to full wages"; "Down with charity slop, We demand cash relief"; "Down with the Hoover Hunger Government"; "AF of L leaders are against unemployment insurance"; "Equal political and social rights for Negroes"; "Milk for our children"; "We American workers refuse to starve"; "Not a cent for war — All funds for the unemployed."

The line of march to be followed in Washington had been planned by Commissioner Glassford. The *New York Times* noted that he had "deliberately laid out the longest routes for them to traverse," in order to tire the marchers as much as possible. At John Marshall Place, Glassford, out of uniform, cruised about on a motorcycle smoking a long-stemmed pipe.

The press as a whole was hostile. The *Daily Mirror* reported, "The marchers were of several races, mostly whites and negroes but among them were several scores of yellow men from various climes. Many women appeared in the column."

Along the line of march stood two rows of policemen, according to one estimate 1,000 in all, and at the Capitol were 400 to 500 more. There, an elaborate plan had been worked out so that the marchers had to move into a roped-off area where they were widely separated from the thousands who had come to watch them. Machine guns were trained on the marchers. Police officers were armed with sawed-off shotguns and tear-gas guns. One reporter claimed there were also hand grenade launchers. An emergency ambulance stood nearby. Everything was calculated to produce maximum intimidation.

Vice-President Charles Curtis had sent word that the marchers could not enter the Capitol grounds carrying any placards with slogans that criticized the president or the two houses of Congress or that were in any way objectionable. But no one had thought of forbidding music. On the steps of the Capitol the band that accompanied the marchers blared out the "International":

Arise, ye prisoners of starvation!
    Arise, ye wretched of the earth,
For justice thunders condemnation,
    A better world's in birth.
No more tradition's chains shall bind us,
    Arise, ye slaves; no more in thrall!
The earth shall rise on new foundations,
    We have been naught, we shall be all.

Organizers of the march hoped to send committees onto the floor of the House of Representatives and the Senate to present their demands. Benjamin had earlier met with Senator William E. Borah, a Republican from Idaho, in an effort to arrange for unemployed leaders to address the Senate, but the committees were not admitted to either the Republican-controlled Senate or the Democratic House. On the Senate side, they had to present their demands to the Sergeant at Arms while they were standing at a basement door. After being refused admission to the Capitol, William F. Dunne, leader of the Hunger Marchers Committee, said to his followers, "The Congress has refused to hear proposals of the Unemployed Councils through the Hunger Marchers. The entire negotiation so far as your committee is concerned was conducted through police. We were not permitted to address any of the civilian members of the Congress."

Inside the Capitol, Vice-President Curtis called the Senate to order in the first session of the Seventy-second Congress, and the chaplain, the Reverend ZeBarney T. Phillips, D.D., offered a prayer that concluded, "Fill us with a Christ-like tenderness for all who are heavy laden or overborne with care. Give us grace fearlessly to contend against evil; and that we may reverently use our freedom, help us to employ it on the maintenance of justice among men and nations, to the glory of Thy Holy name. Through Jesus Christ our Lord. Amen."

From the Capitol the marchers went to the White House and tried to present their demands directly to President Hoover. Inside the White House grounds, "the police fairly fell over each other," according to an International News Service story, and there were ambulances and patrol wagons nearby.

At the White House gate, Herbert Benjamin, with a committee, insisted that they wanted to see the president himself. All the committee members, he said, were unarmed and willing to be searched. But the Secret Service agent at the gate was emphatic. The president, although he was in the building, would not see the committee. According to one newspaper account, dictaphones were operating outside the White House to record what the committee said. Meanwhile, thirteen (some reports said eighteen) men and women from among the marchers were arrested and charged with parading without a license. They were held for $500 bail each. According to the Washington *Herald*, one of those arrested was beaten by the police.

The main body of the marchers now moved on from the White House to the headquarters of the American Federation of Labor, only a few blocks away. They wanted to protest the refusal of the AFL to support unemployment insurance and other demands of the organized unemployed. William Green, AFL president, met with the committee and berated them. This confrontation did not produce an immediate change in AFL policy. That would come later.

Among a number of prominent figures drawn to Washington at the time of the Hunger March was the philosopher John Dewey. He was there as head of an organization called the People's Lobby.[1] On November 20 and December 1, Dewey and 300 intellectuals had held a conference to discuss "The Unemployment Program for Congress." Those attending the discussions, many of whom were Socialists, heard reports on joblessness from ten different cities. Following their discussions, they met with a dozen senators and representatives and proposed that Congress appropriate $240 million for relief, $250 million for aid to state unemployment insurance plans, and $3 billion for roads, public works, and cheap housing. The funds were to be raised by increased taxes on the rich. Relief was to be given without applying any "pauper test." In other words, applicants for relief were not to be forced to divest themselves of all their belongings before they qualified for government aid.

The Hunger Marchers, who had not succeeded in meeting members of Congress during their two-day stay, started back to their various points of origin. At each overnight stop, mass meetings heard marchers' reports on what had happened when they tried to speak to Congress and to the president. Some of the newspapers covering the march referred to the "retreat" of the marchers. Their return was in fact no retreat; they proceeded exactly according to a plan worked out well in advance.

After the march, William Z. Foster, writing in *Labor Unity*, the organ of the TUUL, called it an example of the power workers could exert. He noted that at the time the march was being prepared, the government had used great force against unemployed picketers at the White House. Militants had received heavy jail sentences.

While Foster saw the disciplined march as a successful display of working-class strength against the force mobilized by the Hoover administration, another Communist leader, Earl Browder, drew a different conclusion. Unknown to the press, Browder was in the capital at the time of the march. He said later that violence was averted because of negotiations he initiated through Congressman Vito Marcantonio. Quite possibly Browder's intervention reinforced the efforts Benjamin was making with Police Commissioner Glassford.

The contrasting views of Foster and Browder reflected the differing tactics pursued in the unemployed movement. The two approaches — one emphasizing confrontation and mass pressure, the other emphasizing negotiation and cooperation — continued in unstable equilibrium through the depression years. As for the Hunger March of 1931, its impressive organization, together with behind-the-scenes negotiation, elicited response from some members of Congress. Within two months, Senators LaFollette and Costigan introduced a bill proposing to grant the states $375 million to be used for relief. The Hoover administration defeated it.

The Hunger March contributed greatly to making the jobless of the country aware that a militant organization was on their side. And it established (or reestablished) for all Americans a right they have since used many times: the right of citizens *en masse* to petition the government.

Although in official government circles the Hunger Marchers had been rebuffed, they had succeeded handsomely with sympathetic crowds in the city and had called the nation's attention to the need for both the short-term and the long-term goals of the Unemployed Council: immediate winter relief and unemployment insurance.

Among the thousands of observers in Washington was 77-year-old Jacob S. Coxey, now mayor-elect of Massillon, Ohio. "As I expected," he wrote for the United Press, "it was an orderly as well as an impressive demonstration." He viewed the whole Hunger March with "keen interest and delight," according to another story. Coxey pointed out that the roads he campaigned for in 1894 had been built, and it took the trucks of the Hunger Marchers only three days to travel the distance his army had needed thirty-five days to cover. "I'm still working for the same financial plan as on May Day, 1894, to furnish money without interest to states and subdivisions thereof to put the idle to work on public improvements as needed when there is no demand for labor in factory production," Coxey said.

The leaders of the Hunger March were well aware of Coxey and his army and of his comments on their activities in 1931. Clippings about him were carefully saved in the scrapbook kept in the national office of the Unemployed Council. Just as the roads for which Coxey demonstrated finally came into being, so did, in a few years, a form of the unemployment insurance and social security that the Unemployed Council sought.

Although the Hunger March did not immediately persuade most members of Congress to support adequate emergency relief, long-term unemployment insurance, old-age pensions, a shorter workday with no decrease in wages, or immediate payment of a bonus to veterans, the march, along with events preceding and surrounding it, did contribute to ferment among those who still had jobs. A hunger march in Pennsylvania that preceded the national march was believed by many to have stimulated 40,000 miners in the state to go on strike. Similarly, local hunger marches in Ohio seem to have sped up the process of organizing steel workers into a union.

Just as the effect of the march was considerable, so, too, were efforts to minimize its impact. One such effort was made by Father James R. Cox, a Roman Catholic priest in Pittsburgh, who was sufficiently active among the jobless there to be known as Mayor of Shantytown. The Hunger Marchers had scarcely left Washington when he led his own march on the capital. On January 6, 1932, 12,000 went with Father Cox to Washington. In explaining his march, Cox told a reporter:

> Some weeks ago I read of the invasion of Washington by a Communistic group of marchers waving the red flag singing the International and demanding all sorts of fantastic things. This is repugnant to me, and I so stated casually over the radio. I remarked that while I condemned these demonstrations, I believed a body of real American citizens should go to Washington and protest against unemployment conditions which exist in the United States today.

The Unemployed Council Hunger Marchers had indeed sung revolutionary songs, including the "International." Father Cox's followers arrived in the District of Columbia singing "America" and "Keep the Home Fires Burning." They traveled in cars that the *People's Lobby Bulletin* noted were much better than those available to the Communist-led Hunger March. The socialist *New Leader*, commenting on the kind of backing Father Cox had, asserted that his march was financed by the small store owners who belonged to the Allegheny County Merchants Association.

Commissioner Glassford's police handled Father Cox gently and President Hoover met with him. Hoover personally heard Cox's proposals for a $5 billion bond issue for public construction, for funds for relief, and for loans to farmers and taxation of the rich. Hoover's reply was, "In the present and what I believe is the final campaign against the Depression, I have laid a program before Congress and I trust we will secure its early adoption. The real victory is to restore men to employment through their regular jobs. That is our object. We are giving this question our undivided attention."

Ultimately, the conventional behavior of Father Cox and his supporters was no more successful than the radical demeanor of the Hunger Marchers had been. Neither gained immediate concessions from the government.

Soon after his march to Washington, Father Cox began to have dreams of becoming president. *Father Cox's Blue Shirt News* announced that a convention would be held later in St. Louis to found the Jobless-Blue-Shirt Party. Nothing came of it, and soon Father Cox faded from the depression scene. If his movement proved anything, it was that large numbers of unemployed workers were ready to move, and felt they could properly turn to the federal government for the help they needed.

23

The Ford Hunger March
(March 7, 1932)

History is more or less bunk.

— Henry Ford, 1919

Posterity has picked practically all its heroes from the agitators. They are the saints and holy men of our religion.
— Heywood Broun in the *Nation*, December 30, 1939

In 1929 American auto factories produced over 5 million
cars. In 1932 the figure dropped to less than 1.5 million. As a
result, unemployment in the Detroit area was much higher
than the high national average. By the end of 1931, over 75
percent of the unemployed workers in Detroit were already
destitute and deeply in debt. At that time, of course, there was
no unemployment insurance or social security. Workers owed
stores for food and clothing. Many had lost their homes and
were doubling up with friends or relatives. And now the banks
were going broke.

Maurice Sugar, a young Detroit labor lawyer who was convinced of the need for basic social change, frequently accepted
invitations to explain his views to groups of workers. One such
invitation came from homeless men who were living in a large
barracks-like shelter. The room in which Sugar was to talk had
no chairs, but it did have a table, which he used for a platform
while his audience stood. What the young man said that night
is not remembered, but what happened to him as he looked into
the gray faces of the men in front of him had an unexpected
result. Sugar went home and put together the words of the

"Soup Song," sung to the tune of "My Bonnie Lies Over the Ocean":

> I'm spending my nights at the flophouse
> I'm spending my days on the street
> I'm looking for work and I find none
> I wish I had something to eat.
>
> CHORUS:
> Sooo-oup, sooo-oup, they give me a bowl of sooo-oup
> Sooo-oup, sooo-oup, they give me a bowl of soup.
>
> I spent twenty years in the factory
> I did everything I was told
> They said I was loyal and faithful
> Now, even before I get old.
>
> CHORUS
>
> I saved fifteen bucks with my banker
> To buy me a car and a yacht
> I went down to draw out my fortune
> And this is the answer I got.
>
> CHORUS
>
> I fought in the war for my country
> I went out to bleed and to die
> I thought that my country would help me
> But this was my country's reply.
>
> CHORUS
>
> I went on my knees to my Maker
> I prayed every night to the Lord
> I vowed I'd be meek and submissive
> And now I've received my reward.
>
> CHORUS

Soon the "Soup Song" was heard on unemployed picket lines and marches and at demonstrations all over the country. It was very popular in Detroit, where tens of thousands of Ford employees were out of work. Forty percent of the jobless in Detroit had once worked in the Ford plant, but Henry Ford was getting publicity with his claim that only those who were lazy couldn't find jobs. Contrary to general belief, Ford now paid wages below the average in the automobile industry. To make sure that his workers did not join a union, he had in his plants a private police force that included toughs of several kinds, professional wrestlers and ex-convicts among them. Ford was a virulent anti-Semite, had strong antiblack prejudices, and discriminated against African-American workers. He ran the city of Dearborn, which adjoined Detroit, like a dictator. A cousin of his was the mayor, and the chief of police had been a detective on his payroll. Henry Ford had accumulated a vast fortune. It was natural that ex-Ford workers who were facing literal starvation should regard him as more than slightly responsible for their plight.

Following the November 1931, hunger march on the Ford-related Briggs plant, the Detroit Unemployed Council began to plan a demonstration at the Ford plant itself. Usually an Unemployed Council carried its demands to the general public or to public relief agencies or to one level or another of government. It was in those areas that solutions might be found for the problems of the jobless. But there were exceptions. Sometimes picketers carried protests to the offices of private charities or to former workplaces where they had spent much of their lives. Now that unemployed Ford workers were in great distress after having served the company long and well, they thought that it could — and morally should — help them.

In planning the demonstration at one Ford plant, the Detroit Council had the cooperation of the Auto Workers Union (AWU). The AWU, which was affiliated with the TUUL, had been trying against intense company resistance to unionize the Ford plants.

Former Ford workers mobilized to go to the Ford employment office in Dearborn on March 7, 1932, and to make the following demands:

1. Jobs for all laid-off Ford workers.
2. Immediate payment of 50 percent of full wages.
3. Seven-hour day without reduction in pay.
4. Slowing down of the deadly speed-up.
5. Two 15-minute rest periods.
6. No discrimination against Negroes as to jobs, relief, or medical service.
7. Free medical aid in the Ford Hospital for all employed and unemployed Ford workers and their families.
8. Five tons of coke or coal for the winter.
9. Abolition of service men [spies, private police].
10. No foreclosure on homes of former Ford workers — Ford to assume the responsibility for all mortgages, land contracts, and back taxes on homes until six months after regular full-time employment.
11. Immediate payment of a lump sum of fifty dollars for winter relief.
12. Full wages for part-time workers.
13. Abolition of the graft system in hiring workers.
14. The right to organize.

This list, which much more accurately reflected what workers needed than what they could expect to get, helped attract 4,000 to a rally in a big dance hall the day before the demonstration. One speaker was the head of the TUUL, William Z. Foster, who had been jailed at the New York demonstration March 6, 1930, and was now out on bail. To no one's surprise, Foster contrasted the life of workers once employed by the capitalist Ford with the life of workers in the socialist Soviet Union, where there was a shortage of labor as that country was becoming industrialized.

The next afternoon, with a parade permit that had been granted by Detroit Mayor Frank Murphy, and with no interference by the Detroit police, the marchers assembled in weather that turned out to be bitterly cold. When about 3,000 were on hand, Albert Goetz, leader of the march, addressed the crowd.

The *Detroit News* reported that Goetz exhorted the crowd to be orderly. "No trouble, no fighting," he said, even though the police might try to stop them.

As the marchers started to walk the short distance toward the invisible line that separated Detroit from Dearborn, they sang and carried placards that read: "We want bread not crumbs!"; "Give us work"; "Tax the rich and feed the poor"; "Fight dumping of milk while babies starve"; "Open rooms at the 'Y' for homeless youth"; and "All war funds for the unemployed."

At the Dearborn city boundary, about fifty Dearborn police and private police from the Ford plant blocked the road.

"Who are your leaders?" an officer called out.

"We are all leaders!" someone shouted back.

"Stop, or we'll shoot!" came an order from the police, and at the same time they fired tear gas. The marchers, coughing and weeping from the gas, were confused and ran in all directions. Some remained on the street and felt the full effect of police night sticks. One officer fired a gun. At this point, the unemployed counterattacked. From a nearby field they picked up stones and pelted the police. Soon the supply of tear gas ran out, and, followed by a hail of stones and frozen mud, the police fled. The marchers continued toward the Ford plant.

Firemen now joined the police and tried to hook up hoses so they could shoot water on the marchers. Their first efforts failed, and they withdrew to the plant. At Gate Three, near the employment office, they succeeded in attaching their hoses. From a bridge over the street they poured icy water on the already chilled marchers. The police now regrouped, their numbers increased by additional personnel from Ford's private army and by officers from the Detroit and state police forces.

As the battle continued, the police drew their pistols and started to fire. Before this round of shooting stopped, they had killed four men and wounded about seventy-five. The figure for the wounded is not precise because many of them apparently took refuge in their own homes instead of going to hospitals.

At this point the Unemployed Council leaders proposed to call off the demonstration to prevent further bloodshed. In the chaos they asked those who could hear them to vote on whether or not to end the demonstration. Then, declaring it ended, the men began to withdraw.

Suddenly Harry Bennett, the hated head of the Ford private police force, drove out of the plant in a car and started to shoot. The marchers responded with stones and hit him. Bennett stepped out of his car bleeding and fell to the ground. From there he was taken to the hospital.

The police and the Ford servicemen opened fire with machine guns, killing one more man and wounding many. One of the wounded was a photographer taking pictures for the *Detroit Free Press* and the *New York Times*. He later said the marchers were quiet and orderly until the tear gas attack began. He did not see a single armed worker. Another photographer who was stationed with the police said that he had not seen any marcher use firearms, but he had seen the police fire what he estimated to be hundreds of shots. Certainly not one police officer received a bullet wound.

Many of the wounded were under arrest in the hospital and chained to their beds "to prevent possible escape," according to Police Commissioner James Watkins. Others were arrested on the streets, and raids extended to private homes, where more were taken into custody. The Detroit police arrested some demonstrators in Detroit and turned them over to the officers in Dearborn.

In his account of the Ford Hunger March, labor historian Alex Baskin, who is no apologist for the Communists, emphasized that the demonstrators were unarmed and that the leaders did not plan any violence. Maurice Sugar investigated the affair thoroughly after he became attorney for the victims. He wrote,

> In all our experiences with so-called riots in the United States we know of none started by the people assembled. We know of plenty where they have defended themselves against attack by the police or by self-constituted guardians of law and order. There is no case on record of a conviction for an act of violence or advocacy of violence by communists or any other workers in all the unemployment demonstrations which have taken

place in the last two years, except for admitted self-defense after attack.

During the violent battle between the armed private and public police on the one hand and the unarmed unemployed demonstrators on the other, some of the windows of the Ford plant near Gate Three were filled with observers about whose reaction one can only speculate. They were engineers and technicians studying the Ford production methods. They came from the Soviet Union.

In Detroit, where the Ford family had immense power, the following headlines appeared in the newspapers the next day:

REVOLVERS AND CLUBS USED BY BOTH SIDES
Harry Bennett, Head of the Ford Police Was Shot in the Head
Two Civilians and Four Policemen Were Reported Shot

COMMUNISTS INFLAMED BY FOSTER HURL STONES AND CLUBS
IN PREARRANGED OUTBREAK
Harry Bennett and Others in Hospital Following Battle
Started When Agitator Fires Six Shots

HARRY BENNETT'S COURAGE
Ford Service Chief Leaves Safety to Hurl Himself Into Thick
of Fighting

Hoping to forestall any efforts to misrepresent the cause of the four deaths, Maurice Sugar, acting for the families of the deceased, tried to arrange for a physician of his choice to be present at the autopsies. Although this practice was common, Sugar did not succeed in having the bodies examined by a doctor.

One of the dead was 16-year-old Joe Bussell, a high school student and son of militant worker parents. He had left school in the middle of the day to take part in the demonstration. The others were Joe York, age 22, the district organizer of the YCL; Joseph deBlasio, age 32, a Communist Party member; and Coleman J. Leiny, 27, a member of the Unemployed Council. The funeral of these four turned into one of the largest demonstrations ever held in Detroit. Estimates of the number of mourners ranged from 8,000 to 70,000. The *New York Times* reported that 30,000 were seen by Mayor Frank Murphy, who watched the funeral. At the head of the procession was a banner proclaiming, "Smash the Ford-Murphy Terror!"

At once a search began for William Z. Foster, whom the press accused of stirring up the Detroit jobless to use violence against the police. Foster, after speaking at the rally in Detroit, had taken a train to Milwaukee for a speaking engagement there. From Milwaukee he returned to New York for a scheduled meeting with his parole officer. In New York a room full of police awaited him, and it looked as if serious new charges might be lodged against him.

In the meantime, the Detroit Employers Association, which had great influence on police policy, had held a secret meeting, news of which finally leaked out. One faction among the employers urged that the strongest possible assault be made on the leaders of the unemployed, all of whom were called Communists. The other faction recommended a milder course, which would be less likely to radicalize people. A show of sympathy might win them away from communism. The latter policy was adopted by the businessmen's organization and by the Detroit police, and charges were not pressed against Foster. He merely had his freedom of movement restricted to Greater New York.

After the funeral, the four who had been killed were buried in the cemetery close to the scene of the massacre. (There, in 1982, labor leaders and political figures in Detroit met with veterans of the Hunger March and others to honor the dead fifty years after the event.) Not only had the violence of March 7, 1932, strengthened the unemployed movement, the unemployed movement had also helped unionize the Ford plant.

According to some accounts, a fifth man died as a result of the police action March 7. He was Curtis Williams, an African-American who was said to have been gassed so severely that he died in August. A funeral committee formed and tried to have his body buried in the plot with the four white victims. Permission was denied by the cemetery and the mayor of Detroit. The funeral committee answered with a threat to scatter Williams' ashes from a plane flying over the Ford plant. Ford sent up a plane to avert this danger, but when it returned to the ground to refuel another plane hired by the committee took to the air. Ashes of the Jim-Crowed man were then scattered where he had once worked.

Public outrage at the killings brought protests from Socialists, the American Civil Liberties Union, and liberal publications, and in the end there was not a single indictment brought against any of the marchers. The Detroit police and law enforcement officers had complied with the decision of the Detroit Employers Association to play down the violence and to appear sympathetic to the jobless. The conciliatory behavior of officialdom did not dampen the militancy of the Detroit unemployed, however. Soon many of those among them who were veterans of World War I joined in the next major event that would stir the jobless and the nation.

24

The Bonus March
(Summer 1932)

The men of profession stoop to trade,
The tradesmen are resigned to labor.
The laborers also drop a grade
And idly live with Death for neighbor.

> — Seymour G. Link
> *The Rebel Poet*, March 1931

They'll red-cross all the sick and maimed,
They'll wooden-cross all those who fall,
They'll iron-cross the hero guys,
And double-cross us all.

> — sung by World War I Veterans

All you there, all you there —
Pay the bonus, pay the bonus —
For the Yanks are starving,
The Yanks are starving everywhere.

> — Variant of "The Yanks Are Coming"
> sung by Bonus Marchers, 1932

After Black Thursday, the day of the stock market crash in October 1929, people turned to every possible financial resource to stay alive. Those of the unemployed who were veterans of World War I turned to IOUs they had received, documents saying that the government would pay them an average of about $1,000 each as adjusted compensation for their military service. The pay of a private had been only one dollar a day — much less than civilians working in the war industry had received — and veterans' organizations had lobbied for an upward adjustment. Congress had approved this extra pay which came to be called a bonus, but first President Harding and then President Coolidge had vetoed the congressional action. Finally, however, the Bonus Bill became law over Coolidge's veto and the veterans could look forward to receiving their bonus — in 1945. The promise of money in 1945 did not put food in the mouths of jobless vets in the time of great distress that had begun in 1929. To many of them it seemed reasonable to ask for immediate payment.

In 1929, responding to their pleas, Representative Wright Patman of Texas, a former machine gunner who was in some ways a latter-day Populist, introduced a bill providing for immediate payment in full. Although it was defeated, Patman kept the bill before Congress. It began to act as a magnet, attracting unemployed ex-servicemen, to Washington where they lobbied for its passage.

Among political parties, only the Communists supported immediate payment, and representatives of a small Communist-led organization of veterans, the Workers Ex-Servicemen's League (WESL) testified in favor of it before a congressional committee in April 1932. The WESL spokesmen (James W. Ford, an African-American and the Communist candidate for vice-president, and Samuel J. Stember, a white) also told the committee that veterans should come to Washington to lobby for the bonus, which the establishment-minded American Legion officials opposed. They suggested the date of June 8, 1932.

The WESL Committee and the Congressmen were surely aware that wandering over the country was by now a way of life for a great many unemployed. At least a million and perhaps as many as 2 million migrants, including 200,000 boys and girls, were shifting from place to place, looking for work, begging, hoping. The notion of a veterans' march grew naturally from this background of uneasy, restless search, but the Bonus March, when it developed, stood out from hobo migrations because it had a clear political and geographic goal.

The Communist proposal for a national march of veterans

drew little attention, and the party made no dramatic effort to equal the remarkable organizing achievement of the 1931 Hunger March. Indeed, the events that followed the announcement were largely spontaneous, whereas the Hunger March had been carefully planned, and the efforts to organize the veterans' march were mostly non-Communist, even anti-Communist. Agitation among veterans, in fact, had fascist overtones. It was a period when news came daily from Germany that Hitler's Nazis were gaining power, and gaining it in part by successful manipulation of many of the unemployed.

On May 10, a few days after the Communist leaders of the WESL (of course it was called "weasel") met with the congressional committee, about 300 former soldiers and sailors started for Washington from Portland, Oregon. No researchers have found any indication that these veterans were responding to the WESL proposal for a march. It seems more likely that they had heard the news that the House Ways and Means Committee had shelved the bill that proposed immediate payment of the bonus. They set out for Washington to lobby, and a charismatic but unstable unemployed car salesman, Walter W. Waters, emerged as their leader. Waters's followers rode boxcars, hobo fashion, as had members of the Industrial Armies about forty years before, and somehow word of their migration spread, despite minimal press coverage.

From one city after another groups of vets began to move toward Washington. Some men brought their wives and children. There were stories about a woman who led a group of Texas veterans. The press called her "a Joan of Arc in overalls," and noted that she traveled with a burro named Patman, after the congressman who had introduced the Bonus Bill, and a goat named Hoover.

In Camden, New Jersey, veterans used a bizarre stunt to raise funds for the march. They buried a hungry vet alive, making sure that he would stay alive, and then charged people to look through a funnel at the man in his grave. Later in Washington, D.C., vets used the same sensational stunt.

Soon a considerable movement was getting under way.

News stories about it increased, and they had the effect of increasing the size of the migrating army.

On the journey from the West Coast to the Mississippi River, contingents of the Bonus Army traveled mostly in freight cars. The western railroads were accustomed to having migratory workers ride without paying as they moved about looking for jobs, so only a few obstacles were placed in the way of the advancing and growing army of jobless veterans. A former locomotive engineer, well acquainted with the railroad world, went ahead of the Portland, Oregon, contingent and made advance arrangements for food and shelter.

The marchers were a varied lot. "The vast majority . . . were middle-aged and middle-class — small businessmen, skilled tradesmen, white collar workers, with a sprinkling of professionals such as teachers, lawyers and dentists," said one historian. Other observers saw very few middle-class veterans and many more workers, unskilled as well as skilled. Whatever their social origin, a great many of the Bonus Marchers wore overalls. Others had on parts of army uniforms. Each man carried his own bedroll and a duffel bag. One contingent, traveling by freight car from Minnesota, put on their car a bill of lading that read, "Pennsylvania Railroad #36865 — Destination Washington, contents, livestock, 55 veterans." When one contingent reached Ohio, the governor of the state put thirty-five highway trucks at its disposal to hurry it through the area over which he had jurisdiction. In general, authorities had decided on a policy of getting rid of the vets rather than resisting them.

No effort was made by any central organizing body to synchronize the movements of different sections of the Bonus Army. For instance, on the day when 400 men left a small town in Indiana, another 400 left California, 400 more were crossing Illinois, and 500 were preparing to leave Boston.

The veterans came from every direction, and among them was a very small minority of Communists organized by the Workers Ex-Servicemen's League. One of them was Peter V. Cacchione, an Italian-American who had been raised a Catholic. At his home in Sayre, Pennsylvania, Cacchione had been a railroad worker. He had voted sometimes Republican, sometimes Democratic. In 1928 the Democrat Alfred Smith got Cacchione's vote in the presidential election, possibly because Smith was against prohibition, possibly because he was a Catholic. Thoughts about unemployment had not been much on Cacchione's mind until 1932, when, at the age of 35 he joined the growing army of unemployed. Cacchione went west to work on the huge Hoover Dam in Nevada, but he was soon out of work there, too, and flat broke. Hoping to find something to do in the country's biggest city, he hoboed back east. When he got to the ferry that plied between New Jersey and New York, he had to borrow the nickel fare. Once in New York, he had no place to sleep, so he went to the Municipal Lodging House, which had beds for homeless single men and a few single women. There he spent the night and, together with all the other men in the place, he was hustled out onto the street in the morning before even having a chance to wash.

Some of the men who objected to this treatment formed a committee to protest to the management of the shelter. Cacchione asked to go along. The officials at the municipal "flophouse," listened to the complaints politely, and in the middle of the following night drove all the members of the committee out onto the street. The evicted men, among others, were clustered around the flophouse door the next day when somebody from the Unemployed Council appeared with a speaker's stand. A meeting started, and Peter Cacchione, thoroughly angered by what he called "conditions" in the shelter, got up on the stand and spoke.

Members of the Unemployed Council talked to him after the meeting, and he joined the organization. Not long after that, he joined the Communist Party, members of which were working to build the council. Cacchione went on to join the WESL and soon afterward led a contingent of unemployed veterans from New York to Washington to take part in the nationwide Bonus March.[1]

Washington's Police Commissioner Pelham D. Glassford had experienced the National Hunger March just a few months before, and when word reached him that large numbers of veterans were moving toward the capital, he began to use, he later explained, "every method to check its development. I wired and wrote the governors of the various states in which contingents were being organized, asking them to discourage the movement." He also urged Congress to act quickly on the Patman Bill. Glassford reasoned that if Congress rejected the bill (as he hoped it would) and then adjourned, the veterans, lacking congressmen to see, would have no target against which to direct their anger, and so would lose their incentive for continuing their march. But Congress was slow to act, and the veterans came.

When they began to arrive in Washington, they faced various forms of petty harassment. For example, the water sprinklers on the Capitol grounds were kept running around the clock so that marchers could not sleep on the grass. (Those who remembered their history would have recalled that Jacob Coxey, who led unemployed marchers in 1894, was arrested at the Capitol for walking on the grass.)

When it became clear that large numbers of veterans were actually going to stay in Washington, Glassford, in the interest of controlling them, asked the secretary of war to provide the Bonus Marchers with food and shelter at places judiciously scattered around the city at some distance from each other. These measures were intended to keep the men fed and divided and thus less likely to cause trouble.

President Hoover asked for and got from Congress funds with which to buy the marchers transportation home. He announced that 6,000 men accepted this offer, but many more than 6,000 remained in Washington. Governor Roosevelt of New York sent a representative to Washington to make a similar offer of free transportation for New York veterans. It is not clear how many accepted, but no one claimed it was a large number.

Obviously many veterans intended to remain close to the seat of the power that could solve their problem. Commissioner Glassford shrewdly made plans to take over leadership of the movement. On May 26 in Judiciary Square, at the first big meeting of the Bonus Marchers in Washington, an unknown man in the audience called on Glassford to speak. Glassford readily agreed, and in his speech he proposed a name for the veterans to use — the Bonus Expeditionary Force (BEF). He was somehow elected secretary-treasurer of the new organization, and very soon he "appointed" Walter W. Waters to be commander-in-chief. Waters accepted, according to a press release issued by Glassford, "upon a strict disciplinary agreement, including the elimination of radicals." Here was the key element of Glassford's strategy: to try to set the Bonus Marchers against each other by raising a red scare. Glassford has described how he did this: "The BEF military police worked intimately with the Metropolitan Police under my command. [I] used BEF to combat the influence of the Communists, even to the point of intimidating and threatening those who came to the BEF Camps. Often Communists were 'beaten-up.'"

When the small minority of Communists among the veterans planned a demonstration June 8, Glassford said, "To avoid any pretext for trouble I granted a permit for the parade and then set about blocking any chance for its success. . . . We induced the BEF to stage a parade on Pennsylvania Avenue on the evening of June 7, which so overshadowed anything the Communists were able to do that they called off their demonstration." In addition to using the BEF against the Communists, Glassford continued to discourage the main body of veterans. He did not succeed.

Many veterans were occupying unused government buildings in various parts of the city. Others had settled in an area called Anacostia Flats, southeast of the Capitol across the Anacostia River. There the vets had put together a whole town of makeshift shacks, complete with streets and street signs. Some of the shacks housed not only homeless men but their families as well.

How many vets were in Washington? Glassford put the number at 22,000; President Hoover said there were only half that many. Figures issuing from the veterans' groups were much higher than Glassford's. Whatever the number, thousands began to assemble at the Capitol on June 17 for a "Death Watch." Congress was due to adjourn the following day. The House had acted favorably on the Patman Bill, but the Senate had not yet taken action, although it was considering the bill.

Glassford, realizing that the veterans were moving toward the Capitol, took extraordinary defense measures.

In his *Veterans on the March*, Jack Douglas told what happened:

> The Anacostia Bridge was raised after a few Marchers had passed, and held open for over two hours while the Senate was killing the Bill. Some twelve thousand veterans found themselves cut off from the city. Two police boats took positions under the bridge. A war plane sailed like a buzzard, back and forth, over the camp [at Anacostia] for an hour and a half. A few of the veterans jumped into the river and tried to swim across.

Passage over two other bridges was blocked. Meanwhile, the Capitol was fortified with extra police, and 200 Marines were ready nearby. Four to five thousand veterans who had not been stranded in Anacostia arrived at the Capitol, and they waited for hours, growing angrier with each placating speech made by Waters or by a senator. Thousands of sympathetic citizens joined them in their vigil. The Anacostia Bridge finally was opened after angry citizens, trying to get home, demanded it. The thousands of veterans who had been trapped across the river arrived at the Capitol just as the Senate was voting to reject the bill. "Police and Senators wondered what would happen when it was announced that the Bill had failed," Douglas's account continued. Senators were "wondering whether it would be safe for them to leave the building."

> To get out of the dilemma, they did just what Glassford had been doing all along — got Waters to help. Waters was called in. Matters were explained to him. He came out, blew his whistle, and told the men (while the police inside stood ready in case he failed): "Men, I have just had word that we've received a temporary set-back. The Bonus Bill has been defeated in the Senate. But that's all it is — a set-back. We're here to stay. We'll show those guys in there that we can take it on the chin. . . . But now I suggest that you form yourselves into an orderly group and march back to your camps singing America . . ."

An Army band, which had appeared mysteriously just before the announcement, nervously began to play "America."

The BEF had been rebuffed by both the Senate and the president. According to Arthur M. Schlesinger, Jr., "The President had ample time in these weeks [while the veterans were in Washington — F.F.] to receive Jim Londos, the heavyweight wrestling champion, delegations from Eta Upsilon Gamma Sorority and from Baraca Philathea Union, adolescent winners of essay contests, and other dignitaries, but audiences were denied to the leaders of the BEF." Hoover defended his attitude toward the veterans by saying, twenty years later, that the BEF "was in considerable part organized and promoted by Communists and included a large number of hoodlums and ex-convicts determined to raise a public disturbance."

The anti-Communist cry also came from other quarters. The fascistic Roman Catholic priest Father Coughlin of Royal Oak, Michigan, sent $5,000 to the BEF with the stipulation that it was to be used only by non-Communists. Father Cox, a Catholic priest from Pittsburgh who had led a march on Washington earlier in the year, made efforts to take over the BEF. He qualified as a veteran, having served as an army chaplain. Waters, the commander-in-chief of the BEF, talked about organizing something comparable to the Nazi storm troopers and the Italian Black Shirts. The name of his organization would be the Khaki Shirts of America. Instead of the standard military salute, Waters began to salute with the stiff arm gesture of the fascists.

The press was unrelenting in its attack on alleged Communist influence among the veterans. Although newspaper editors were careful in their selection of reporters to cover the Bonus March, the Hearst papers made what they came to regard as a big mistake. They sent Louise Bryant, widow of Communist John Reed, to Washington. Reed had covered the storming by the Bolsheviks of the Winter Palace in St. Petersburg. Perhaps the Hearst editors thought that they would have some kind of scoop if they had Reed's widow cover what they thought might be the storming of the Capitol in Washington. The story Louise Bryant turned in, however, so displeased the Hearst editors that they would not print it. Nevertheless, her report did reach the readers of the Communist *Daily Worker*, which ran it.

After the defeat of the Bonus Bill, many veterans did not leave Washington. Where would they go? They had no homes or jobs to return to, so they stayed. At this point the Treasury Department stepped in. Some of the veterans were housed in an old building that department officials said had to be demolished so that a new one could go up, thus providing work for the unemployed. Officials ordered the veterans out. Word of the impending expulsion spread quickly, and men from other camps, as the scattered clusters of veterans were called, came running to help prevent the eviction.

When the Treasury Police (not under Glassford's command) attempted to use force to remove the occupants of the old building, a full-scale riot developed, in the course of which the Treasury Police shot and killed two men. Commissioner Glassford described the situation this way: "The Administration created an episode to serve as an excuse to call out troops which had for several weeks been given special training in street fighting and coping with a mob." Glassford also described as "absolutely untrue" the statement by President Hoover that the BEF contained an "extraordinary proportion of criminal, communist and non-veteran elements." Glassford said, "In making this statement President Hoover sought to deceive the people as to his motive" in ordering the use of force against the veterans. Glassford did not say what he thought Hoover's motive was, but it is reasonable to think that the president might have had the coming election in mind. (For his part, Hoover had been critical of Glassford's strategy in dealing with the Bonus Marchers, saying of the incident that Glassford had "failed to organize his men, thus causing the injury of several police officers." Not a word was said about the dead veterans.)

After this violence, the District Commissioners asked for military assistance to restore order. "At my direction to Secretary of War Hurley," said Hoover in his memoirs, "General Douglas MacArthur was directed to take charge. General Eisenhower (then Major) was second in command."

On July 28, regular army troops assembled on Pennsylvania Avenue. General MacArthur and Major Eisenhower put in their appearance at about four in the afternoon. Their main objective was the veterans' settlement in Anacostia Flats, but first some veterans who had barricaded themselves in a village of shacks at Third Street had to be removed. The *New York Times* ran the following account:

> Down Pennsylvania Avenue . . . the regulars came, the cavalry leading the way, and after them the tanks, the machine-gunners and the infantry. . . . There was a wait of maybe half an hour while the Army officers talked it over with the Police and the bonus marchers shouted defiance. . . .
>
> Twenty steel-helmeted soldiers led the way with revolvers in their hands until 200 were in position in front of the "bonus fort." Then the mounted men charged. They rode downstreet clearing the path with their sabres, striking those within reach with the flat of their blades.
>
> The action was precise, well-executed from a military stand-point, but not pretty to the thoughtful in the crowd. There were those who resisted the troops, fought back, cursed, kicked at the horses. . . .
>
> Amidst scenes reminiscent of the mopping up of a town in the World War, Federal troops . . . drove the army of bonus seekers from the shanty village near Pennsylvania Avenue.

Late in the day troops attacked Anacostia Flats with tear gas, giving the residents no time to remove whatever small possessions they had. The soldiers simply drove out the veterans and their wives and children and then set fire to the shanties. Across the river in the distance, the dome of the Capitol showed clearly in the night, and thousands of spectators gathered to watch the destruction of the flimsy shelters of men and families who now had absolutely no place to go.

General MacArthur later said of those whom his soldiers had attacked, "That mob . . . was a bad looking mob. It was animated by the essence of revolution. . . . They were about to take over in some arbitrary way either direct control of the government or else to control it by indirect methods."

MacArthur claimed that the "insurrectionists" themselves set their shacks afire, and Hoover claimed that MacArthur had exceeded his orders. The public revulsion against the attack on Anacostia Flats was so great that everybody concerned wanted to place the blame on somebody else. Newspaper columnist Heywood Broun voiced an attitude shared by many: "The administration which began with the promise of two cars in each garage, is ending with the accomplishment of a bomb for every shack." Referring to the massive aid given to banks and businesses by Hoover's Reconstruction Finance Corporation and to the use of tear gas against veterans, Broun said, "For the banks of America Mr. Hoover has prescribed oxygen. For the unemployed, chlorine."

Many years later, Congressman C. Wright Patman, speaking with Studs Terkel, described the Bonus Marchers who had come to demand passage of his bill.

> There was twenty thousand here at one time. I addressed them out there on the Capitol steps.
>
> Who were the so-called bonus marchers? They were lobbyists for a cause. Just like the ones in the Mayflower Hotel. They didn't try to evict *them*. Why the poor come to town, they're trouble makers. Why, certainly. They step on the grass and they're put in jail for stepping on the grass. The Mayflower crowd, they don't have any problem at all. They're on every floor of every building of Capitol Hill all the time.
>
> The marchers were good, law-abiding citizens. They built these lodgings down here from waste paper and boxes and things. They had lots of streets and everything. . . . Those buildings were burned down by the army, the military, under the direction of Mr. MacArthur and Mr. Eisenhower. Mr. MacArthur was strutting down the street just like it was a big parade.
>
> The next morning, after driving them out, using tear gas, you'd see little babies and mothers on the side of the road.

What Patman said was perfectly true, of course, but neither Patman nor any other politician admitted the real reason why the jobless veterans were so mistreated. Politicians could not bring themselves to admit that they could but would not give what the jobless sought: a minimum of security. And, as before and since, anti-Communism was the slogan used by those who wanted to deny relief to the jobless.

As the night sky of Washington turned red from the fire at Anacostia Flats, left-wing veterans held a previously announced meeting at Eighth Street and Pennsylvania Avenue. The police had passed along to the committee in charge "rumors" that the meeting would be stoned by BEF members but it went forward anyway. According to one estimate, 2,000 men were present. A speaker reported to the crowd the threat that the police had made and said, "If the police keep their hands off, there will be no rioting." And there was none.

The attack on Anacostia Flats had begun on Thursday, July 28 — Bloody Thursday, the veterans called it. All day Friday and all Friday night attacks continued as veterans were evicted from one encampment after another.

The Bonus March was over, but even hostile critics admitted that it had been partially successful. John Dos Passos, soon after the event, put it this way:

> The Bonus March in the summer of 1932 was one of the most instructive things that ever happened in this country. As time goes on I think it will assume more and more importance in the history of the present phase of American capitalism. Both its failures and its successes cast light on the realities of popular democracy under the great monopolies. The March was a spontaneous movement of protest, arising in virtually every one of the forty-eight states. Times were hard. . . . One thing they did accomplish. They gave the Powers That Be the scare of their lives, and set rolling the huge snowball of popular discontent that the next fall substituted the jackass for the elephant on Capitol Hill.

Unemployment continued, and so did agitation for the bonus. Veterans, as many as 3,000, continued to haunt Washington. Finally, in 1936, over the veto of President Roosevelt, Congress passed the Patman Bill. The vets had lost the battle of Bloody Thursday, but they won the war for the bonus.

25

Action Everywhere
(1932)

There is nothing to worry about. Better times are ahead for all.
— John D. Rockefeller, Sr., president of Standard Oil
January 21, 1932

Some of the weaker, according to the law of nature, will naturally die under the stress of the times. The strong and hardy will survive and reproduce, and thus the human race will be strengthened.
— Professor E. G. Conklin, Princeton University
January 1932

At the time of the National Hunger March of 1931, private charities and local and state governments were already running out of relief funds. Although the need was increasing, the Home Relief Bureaus in New York, for example, refused to accept any more applications for aid beginning January 8, 1932. The next day, crowds at the relief offices began to demand food, and on January 17 the bureaus thought it wise to reverse their policy.

The disparity between the need and the available relief was nationwide. In January, the Unemployed Council led a march of 5,000 that demanded — and won — better conditions for the 20,000 inhabitants of flophouses in Chicago. On February 4 (National Unemployment Day), large demonstrations called the demands of the jobless to the attention of officials in New York, Boston, Cleveland, Knoxville, Youngstown, New Haven, Lawrence, New Castle, McKeesport, Decatur, and Philadelphia. In April there was a big demonstration in Massachusetts, and police attacked 3,000 hunger marchers in New York. Other demonstrations followed in Connecticut, Wisconsin, South Dakota, Pennsylvania, and California. Early in 1932, following mass demonstrations in Chicago, the Illinois legislature, fearful of rebellion, appropriated $90 million for relief.

Social workers, accustomed to dispensing relief from private and local sources, had always assumed that this was the proper way to handle unemployment. But by May 1932, the magnitude of the problem had won them over to the policy that reality — and the Unemployed Councils — demanded. The National Conference of Social Work meeting in Philadelphia strongly supported federal relief. President Hoover, meanwhile, continued to insist that the way to aid the jobless was to aid business, which would in turn provide jobs. If business had all the capital it wanted, some of the money would trickle down to the poor. The agency for making capital available was the Reconstruction Finance Corporation (RFC). The RFC meant massive intervention in the economy by the government, which Hoover had earlier objected to. He also responded to pressure by supporting a public works program that had been set in motion, including the building of war vessels. The total amount of money to be spent on these projects was $1 billion, of which a good deal was to go for materials and not directly for wages.

As for federal relief, Congress, with Hoover's approval, at last responded to the growing clamor and set up a fund to provide loans to the states for relief purposes — but only on condition that state and local agencies could show that they were doing their best to solve problems themselves. This plan would keep the federal government out of the business of giving direct relief, and the funds would be administered under the supervision of "leading citizens," not representatives of the unemployed.

The amount allocated for the fund in July 1932 was $3 million. The subsequent amounts allocated during Hoover's last months in office were:

August 1932	$13,931,669
September 1932	$18,523,502
October 1932	$22,594,762
November 1932	$18,484,923

December 1932	$35,958,117
January 1933	$49,435,416
February 1933	$48,187,271

At their highest level, these amounts were less than three dollars per month for each of the unemployed workers, who may have numbered 17 million, with nothing for their dependents.

Ignoring such economic realities, Secretary of the Interior, Dr. Ray Lyman Wilbur, made a tour of the country and concluded, "There is no poverty in the United States despite the fact that 10,000,000 people are unemployed. The 10,000,000 are being cared for 'one way or another.' "

Hoover himself continued to repeat his assertion that "no one has starved." The editors of *Fortune* magazine later in the year used this slogan as the title for a detailed study of the depression. They made clear, however, that the slogan was not valid, and went on to predict that 25 million might be unemployed before the winter of 1932 was over. Money did not trickle down in any effective way from the institutions that received loans from the RFC. Instead, the depression continued to deepen.

During the months of the 1932 presidential campaign, the organized unemployed, particularly the Unemployed Councils, kept up demands for immediate relief, public works, and unemployment insurance. Certainly the councils could not put enough weight into the electoral scale to tip it against Hoover and for Roosevelt. In fact, the councils did not urge voters to support Roosevelt. Instead, in some places (Chicago, for example) the councils endorsed the Communist ticket. At this time, the councils published newspapers only in New York, Chicago, and Salt Lake City, and by August the part of the unemployed movement that was led by Communists did not exceed 50,000 members. Nevertheless, according to Mauritz Hallgren, a writer for the *Nation*, "Social workers everywhere told me that without street demonstrations and hunger marches of the Unemployed Councils no relief whatever would have been provided in some communities, while in others even less help than that which had been extended, would have been forthcoming."

Some council activity took on dramatic form. In Indianapolis in the summer of 1932, council members built a shack on the courthouse lawn, and a homeless unemployed family moved in. When winter came, the council put up another shack for another homeless family on the State House grounds. These actions, which dramatized the housing problem, drew such strong support that the governor of Indiana set up a housing commission that was instrumental in bringing evictions in the state to a virtual halt. In Ohio, the Unemployed Council set up an organization of workers who were homeowners to protect themselves from eviction. As autumn advanced, protest activity involved others beyond the membership of the Unemployed Council. In Washington a Farmers National Relief Conference was held, and in Cincinnati a Left-led group within the AFL formed the Committee for Unemployment Insurance and Social Security (discussed in Chapter 33).

After the presidential election but before Roosevelt took office, the Children's Misery March approached the White House on Thanksgiving Day, November 24. (The government's own Children's Bureau had already reported that one-fifth of the children in the country were showing the effects of poor nutrition, inadequate housing, lack of medical care, anxiety, and insecurity.) Riding in taxicabs, the marchers numbering more than 100, were accompanied by a physician, Dr. Emile Conason, Mrs. Pauline Gitneck, and Miss Gertrude Haessler. Whether the children sang as they came near the White House is not remembered, but the *Hunger Fighter* in New Haven, Connecticut, published a song that had been written for the occasion:

> Empty is the cupboard,
> No pillow for the head,
> We are the hunger children
> Who cry for milk and bread.
> We are the hunger children
> Who cry for milk and bread,
> We are the workers' children
> Who must, who must be fed.

> We want
> Shelter and clothes,
> Shoes for our toes,
> Bread for the body,
> A roof for the head.

When the children asked to present a petition to President Hoover, a force of 150 police stopped them and also prevented some other children from joining the main group. Then, invoking laws concerning child delinquency, the police arrested the two women, one elderly and white-haired, the other a social worker formerly employed at the Department of Labor. When ordered to leave the scene, the social worker lay down on the sidewalk, and the police had to carry her away. The African-American driver who had brought Dr. Conason in a taxi was also arrested.

As the police pushed some of the children into a patrol wagon, a girl in the group was heard to protest, "Why are we arrested? Because we are hungry and came to tell Mr. Hoover so?" The police changed their tactics, and sent the children away on streetcars.

Activities of the Unemployed Councils spread in the South as well as in the cities of the North. One important development involved a young African-American, Angelo Herndon.

When he was 17 years old and fresh from his home in the North, Herndon had somehow found work in Birmingham, Alabama, in 1930. Even so, he remained keenly aware of joblessness. Later he said:

> I wish I could remember the exact date when I first attended a meeting of the Unemployed Council, and met up with a couple of members of the Communist Party. That date means a lot more to me than my birthday or any other day in my life. . . .
> I came across some handbills put out by the Unemployed Council. . . . They said, "Would you rather fight or starve?" They called on workers to come out to a mass meeting at 3 o'clock. . . . I got to the meeting while a white fellow was speaking. I didn't get everything he said, but this much hit me and stuck with me: that the workers could only get things by fighting for them, and the Negro and white workers had to

stick together to get results. . . . Then a Negro worker spoke from the same platform, and somehow I knew this was what I had been looking for all my life.

Herndon joined the council, then the Communist Party, and in the summer of 1932 he was working among the jobless in Atlanta. In mid-June the state of Georgia had closed down all of its relief stations in spite of the high rate of unemployment. Herndon was convinced that this was a move to force the urban jobless to go into the countryside and accept work on farms at what was almost literally a slave wage.

Led by Herndon, council members passed out leaflets calling for a demonstration at the courthouse to demand that relief be continued (see Appendix J). Four hundred African-Americans and 600 whites took part together in this protest in the segregated South. The city officials claimed they could not continue relief, saying they had no money. Speakers for the council pointed out that $800,000 had just been collected in the Community Chest drive. The next day the city appropriated $6,000 for relief.

The matter might have ended there with a minor victory for the council, but officials in Atlanta were alarmed. Whites were cooperating with African-Americans, which wasn't supposed to happen in the South, and together they were making demands that could be costly.

Angelo Herndon was arrested at the Post Office where he had gone to pick up his mail. He was charged (as Anne Burlak had been earlier) under a pre–Civil War statute with attempting to incite insurrection. The arrest began an ordeal for the young man that would go on for more than four years. During much of that time he had to endure brutal prison conditions, and he faced the prospect of having to spend twenty years in confinement for distributing a leaflet.

The Unemployed Councils, the International Labor Defense, and millions of people joined in the effort to free Herndon. Among those taking part was Anne Burlak, out on bail after a campaign on her own behalf. She, with others who made up the Atlanta Six, urged the release of Herndon from Fulton Tower, where they had all been imprisoned. Herndon finally won his case after two appeals to the United States Supreme Court, and the state of Georgia then dropped the case against the Atlanta Six. The militant unemployed leaders had killed a repressive Georgia statute that had survived from the days of slavery.[1]

By the fall of 1932, the Unemployed Council had grown so strong in Birmingham that it could hold a demonstration — vehemently opposed by the powerful Ku Klux Klan — that brought together African-Americans and whites to demand and obtain promises of relief from city authorities. Hosea Hudson, an African-American leader of the Unemployed Council in Birmingham, tells of another demonstration a little later on the courthouse steps, where about 7,000 people gathered to demand more relief:

> We had a committee of nine to go up to talk to Jimmie Jones the mayor of Birmingham. Mary Stevens was the spokesman for that committee. She was the onliest woman, and Jimmie Hooper Sr. was the onliest Negro on that committee of nine. The rest of them was white, because we didn't expose too many Negroes. . . . Jimmie Jones asked Mary in the course of his remarks to her after she had opened up their case to him, he asked her, "Do you believe in social equality for niggers?"
>
> She told Jimmie Jones, "Yes, why not? They are just as good as you and I are. Why not?"
>
> Jimmie Jones stopped her and told Mary Stevens that he didn't want to hear any more from her. "That's enough from you," and he told his police and plain-clothesmen to go up there and get all of these people from the courthouse steps.
>
> These big strong-arm men rushed up there ahead of Mary and the committee and made the announcement to the crowd that there would not be any meeting here this afternoon. When they said that, the police who was standing among the people in the crowd began to shove and push the whites who was a little stubborn about moving, because this was the first time that many of them had ever been pushed around like that by the police. They had always been made to believe that they were better than the niggers was, because they were white people. That was a great eye-opening for a many of them that afternoon.

The Unemployed Council was the main organizing force among the jobless in many places. Meanwhile, the IWW was still trying to play a role, although it was only a shadow of its former rambunctious self. In the final year of the Hoover administration, it was still alive and still able to have a last word. Its newspaper, the *Industrial Worker*, ran a fable entitled "Depression Hits Robinson Crusoe's Island":

"Friday," said Robinson Crusoe, "I'm sorry, I fear I must lay you off."

"What do you mean, Master?"

"Why, you know there's a big surplus of last year's crop. I don't need you to plant another this year. I've got enough goatskin coats to last me a lifetime. My house needs no repairs. I can gather turtle eggs myself. There's an overproduction. When I need you I will send for you. You needn't wait around here."

"That's all right, Master, I'll plant my own crop, build up my own hut and gather all the eggs and nuts I want myself. I'll get along fine."

"Where will you do all this, Friday?"

"Here on this island."

"This island belongs to me, you know. I can't allow you to do that. When you can't pay me anything I need I might as well not own it."

"Then I'll build a canoe and fish in the ocean. You don't own that."

"That's all right, provided you don't use any of my trees for your canoe, or build it on my land, or use my beach for a landing place, and do your fishing far enough away so you don't interfere with my riparian rights."

"I never thought of that, Master. I can do without a boat, though. I can swim over to that rock and fish there and gather sea-gull eggs."

"No you won't, Friday. The rock is mine. I own riparian rights."

"What shall I do, Master?"

"That's your problem, Friday. You're a free man, and you know about rugged individualism being maintained here."

"I guess I'll starve. Master. May I stay here until I do? Or shall I swim beyond your riparian rights and drown or starve there?"

"I've thought of something, Friday. I don't like to carry my garbage down to the shore each day. You may stay and do that. Then whatever is left of it, after my dog and cat have fed, you may eat. You're in luck."

"Thank you, Master. That is true charity."

"One more thing, Friday. This island is overpopulated. Fifty percent of the people are unemployed. We are undergoing a severe depression, and there is no way that I can see to end it. No one but a charlatan would say that he could. So keep a lookout and let no one land here to settle. And if any ship comes don't let them land any goods of any kind. You must be protected against foreign labor. Conditions are fundamentally sound, though. And prosperity is just around the corner."

26

The Second National Hunger March
(December 4–6, 1932)

In reality the Great Depression was not depressing. The lean
years of the New Deal became a period of lively ferment.
— Mathew Josephson
Infidel in the Temple

We march on starvation, we march against death,
We're ragged, we've nothing but body and breath;
From North and from South, from East and from West
The army of hunger is marching.
— Hunger Marchers' song, 1932

In the election of November 4, 1932, many unemployed
voters who saw no hope of getting relief from the Republican
administration also withheld their support from Roosevelt. But
rebellious and sceptical though they were, they did not take the
step of casting their votes for William Z. Foster and James W.
Ford, the Communist candidates. About a quarter of a million,
however, did actively support the second National Hunger
March.

In September 1932, the Unemployed Councils in Chicago
had begun to make plans for this second march. Among those
invited to attend a preliminary conference was Socialist Karl
Borders, leader of many of the unemployed in the city. Borders
declined to participate, but some other non-Communist groups

did take part, among them some organizations called Unemployed Citizens Leagues.

The planners decided that this time there should be nearly twice as many delegates as in the 1931 march, and the numbers to be chosen by various organizations were precisely allocated:

1. By neighborhood groups, from bread lines, flop houses, etc. for every 100 workers or major fraction thereof
   1 delegate each

2. From shop groups and shop locals   1 delegate each

3. From Unemployed Citizens Leagues and branches
   1 delegate each

4. From Lodges and Local fraternal Organizations
   1 delegate each

5. From AFL and other Union Locals   2 delegates each

6. From each City Unemployed Council   2 delegates each

The number of people represented by the delegates was about 250,000.

From the surviving registration blanks of nine men who were part of the delegation from Oregon, we can get some idea of who the marchers were:

- Walter E. Hekala, 21, was a plumber who had been out of work for three years. He was organizer of a YCL unit and represented 500 young people.
- Carl R. Syranen, 20, was a YCL member who did not give his occupation. He had been out of work for two years and objected to what he called the "forced labor" he was required to do for twenty-five cents an hour, "once in a while," in order to get relief.

- Oscar Ruutul, a 26-year-old Communist Party member, had been out of work for eight months and got relief of four dollars a month in scrip from the Salvation Army.
- Max Farrar, 28, a CP member, listed his occupation as "organizer, Unemployed Council, Salem, Oregon." He got no relief at all.
- Clair H. Fessler, 42, had not worked at his trade in electrical construction for eighteen months. The relief he got consisted of government flour, which he received from the Red Cross. He had eight children, and specified that he had no political or trade union affiliation.
- M. J. Somers, a 24-year-old laborer, did not give any union or political affiliation. He was receiving $2.50 a month from County Welfare.
- William Cominski, 26, a candy worker who had been unemployed for two years, was a delegate from the Unemployed Citizens League, although he was a CP member.
- F. J. Varnese, 20, a laborer and Communist Party member, had been out of work for nine months. He said he did not get "very much relief" and what he got came from the "commissary," which may have been a mutual aid project.
- James B. King, 26, a mechanic and a CP member, had been out of work for three years and said he got no relief.

All of these delegates were male, but there were many women among the 3,000 marchers. All but one of the nine Oregonians were young, as were one-third of the marchers. Those from Oregon included a much higher proportion of Communist Party and YCL members (seven out of eight) than the march as a whole, in which those who belonged to Communist organizations were a little less than one-third of the total. There were 250 members of AFL unions in the march, and the entire body included a high percentage of African-American men and women, especially from the South.

The outcome of the presidential election on November 4, 1932, had little effect on plans for the march. Although Roosevelt had won a sweeping victory, opinion in the councils was that pressure on the incoming administration should be increased.

Starting in late November, delegates from forty-six of the forty-eight states traveled in old trucks and battered jalopies, which carried banners and signs that told why the marchers were going to the capital. The main objectives of the march were money from the federal government to supplement local relief by giving every unemployed worker fifty dollars cash winter relief, plus ten dollars for each dependent; immediate unemployment insurance to be paid for by the government and employers; a halt to tax rebates for the wealthy and for corporations, a halt to military expenditures; and a tax levy on the capital of large corporation owners.

Coming from different parts of the country, eight columns of marchers had been fused into three by the time they reached Washington. Along the way, each contingent had tried to tell the thousands of observers what the aims of the march were, and their reception was often enthusiastic. Many workers in Trenton, New Jersey, staged a one-hour strike in their support as the marchers passed through the city. But in Charlotte, Birmingham, and Chattanooga, police attacked the marchers.

Hostile press coverage of the march was routine, and the *New York Daily News* was particularly vicious. On December 4 it ran a story under the headline "Reds Threaten Bloodshed on Capitol March." The story alleged that Herbert Benjamin threatened to break into the Capitol by force and prophesied a massacre if President Hoover called out troops. "Pennsylvania Avenue Will Run with Blood," Benjamin was supposed to have said. He sued the *News* for $1 million, pointing out that he had not even been where the paper said the speech had been made. Moreover, the *News* was for sale on the street before the time of a speech he did make, in which there was no reference to violence. Four months after the event, the *News* printed a retraction, but the story had contributed to an anti–Hunger March hysteria in Washington.

Edward Dahlberg, who covered the March for the *Nation*, a liberal publication, reported that in Wilmington, Delaware,

> . . . men and women were indiscriminately clubbed and beaten because they had attempted to assemble and speak; they were,

besides, tear-gassed inside the church which they had rented. Moreover, all along the line repeated attempts were made to discourage and dispirit the marchers. Difficulties were made so that they could not obtain sleeping quarters, hold demonstrations, or even communicate with hundreds of thousands of other hungry Americans. . . .

On Sunday, December 4, the hunger marchers were met in Washington [at the edge of the city — F. F.] by a large police escort and shunted into an isolated street, which was immediately sealed by heavy cordons of police at both ends. [Police Commissioner Brown had replaced Commissioner Glassford, with whom Benjamin had had a working relationship. — F. F.] Twelve hundred policemen, seven hundred deputized firemen equipped with tear gas, sawed-off rifles, and sub-machine-guns, in addition to the militia which was held in readiness in the barracks, were prepared to meet three thousand unarmed, weary, worn, and undernourished men and women.

The street in which the marchers were imprisoned for nearly three days lies between a railroad yard and a treeless hill on the outskirts of town. . . . On top of the hill were machine-guns, which at first, and to an unprepared observer, looked like a battery of cameras. The tear-gas squad was stationed on the bluff. . . . One of the officers of the tear-gas squad said to a reporter . . . that $10,000 had been spent on gas for the present "hunger marchers' job." Four trucks were filled with it. In each policeman's kit there were two lots of tear gas to one of sickening or D.N. gas.

On Sunday the marchers were held virtually incommunicado. Besides, there was no water, no hydrant on the street. Not until evening was a truck permitted to leave to bring back cans of water. Many of the men and women went to bed without it. . . . There were no sanitary arrangements either, and the men and women were harassed and chased from one place to another by jeering policemen. The second day the marchers were given permission to build a toilet. Four different times the men had gone ahead with this, in each instance having received the approval of the police inspector, and each time the police doctor had informed them that they would have to construct it elsewhere in order to comply with sanitary regulations! In the face of this, and notwithstanding the fact that the police had violated the most fundamental health rules provided by law and medicine, the marchers maintained unbroken discipline and order. They carefully refrained from offering the police the slightest provocation.

There were no cots or beds in the camp. Although "sympathizers," among whom were Quakers, radicals, working-men, and humanitarian citizens of Washington, had offered accommodations sufficient to house a thousand hunger delegates, the police would not release them for the night. Some slept in the trucks. Others . . . lay down on the cold asphalt. . . .

Sick men and women could not get hospital attention without the approval of the police doctor. . . . As one was being carried out to the ambulance, a policeman said: "Let him die here. We don't want him to die in Washington." It would not do to allow a hungry American to die of starvation on the streets of the capital. The hunger marchers were political prisoners and were accorded the treatment meted out to criminals, with the difference that even in the most backward jails convicts are at least provided with food and water.

The next day . . . the police, having failed to incite the hunger marchers to riot, started a campaign of more pernicious provocations and red-baiting. The tear-gas squad on the hill began to "test" the bombs by throwing them into a bonfire. As the bombs exploded, the wind, which was blowing in the direction of the delegates below, carried the sickening fumes into the trucks where men and women were sitting and standing, causing them much discomfort. . . .

Doubtless the press played a large role in all this. In order to give their stories a sexy and gamy flavor some papers stated that men and women were sleeping standing up locked in each other's arms. The newspapers had previously run column articles declaring that each hunger marcher was receiving five dollars a day from Moscow. . . . A headline ran: "Rumor, Dynamite in Communists' Trucks." Below, in small letters, was "Rumor Unfounded." This must have helped to inflame the police force. . . . And even when articles, representing the opinions of individual reporters who had actually witnessed the scene, were sympathetic to the hunger marchers, the headlines, expressing the editorial policies of the paper, were more often than not at complete variance with the stories. . . .

Later, Senator Costigan came out and was indignant at what he saw. LaGuardia was there and equally aroused. Congressmen Swing and Amlie visited the camp, among others. . . . That night about four hundred men and women were allowed to leave the camp and sleep in lodgings in Washington. The police, many of whom were drunk, broke loose and slashed the tires of seventeen trucks.

The permit to parade the next day was granted, but the guard surrounding the marchers was so thick that some of the unsuspecting spectators in the throngs must have thought it was a police and firemen's parade. . . . The crowds neither booed nor cheered. There was in Washington that morning all the semblance and surcharged atmosphere of martial law.

At the Capitol two committees of twenty-five each sought audiences with the presiding officers of the House and Senate. Vice-President Curtis was angry as committee leaders tried to state the demands in their petition. "Don't cast any reflections on me!" he snapped. "Just hand me your petition. You needn't make any speech. I have only a few minutes time." The committee to see the Speaker of the House, John Nance Garner, included Anne Burlak, co-chairperson, and David Levinson, a left-wing lawyer. Democrat Garner was as hostile as Republican Curtis, and he referred to Mr. Levinson as Mr. Levinsky. The lawyer corrected him, saying his name was Levinson. "What's the difference?" Garner replied.

Their message delivered, the Hunger Marchers returned to the street where they had been forced to camp for three days, held a brief meeting, and began to depart. Their progress homeward was not smooth. In many places the police harassed them, and there were mutterings among the delegates that the high standards of organization that had marked their approach to Washington had not been maintained on the way back. Apparently the defense squads that had helped to protect the marchers from police as they approached the capital had fallen apart. Still, the delegates did reach home and make their reports to the organizations that had sent them.

Clearly the marchers had not won on the spot what they sought. Nor had John Dewey's Socialist-influenced conference in Washington on December 23, nor Father Cox's anti-Communist demonstrations. But the incoming administration could see strong evidence that anger was widespread and organized.

A significant section of the jobless was in motion, and it had allies and impact. One indication that the movement was growing can be found in the response of Dorothy Day, a Catholic who witnessed the second Hunger March. She was shocked that the Catholic Church had not officially backed this action by the jobless, and five months later she launched the *Catholic Worker*, a radical journal that has had a vigorous life ever since.

The Democratic Party had already shown awareness of the importance of the unemployed. One plank in its 1932 election platform had called for unemployment insurance, but the Democrats did not favor the method of financing that the Unemployed Council advocated. The council wanted insurance entirely financed by the government and by the employers, who profited by the labor of their employees and then cast them adrift when it suited them. The Democrats approved proposals for insurance for which workers themselves would bear part of the cost.

Following the march, proposals for the solution to unemployment came from many quarters. Former Washington Police Commissioner Glassford suggested that camps under the control of the military be established for young workers. Considering the rise of Fascism in Italy and Germany and the attempts there to militarize unemployed youths, it was not surprising that the Unemployed Council leaders and the Socialists were suspicious of this proposal. Only later, as the camps became reality and lost some of their military coloration, did the councils relax their opposition.

President-elect Roosevelt had already felt pressure from the organized unemployed, who had been pushing him in the direction of what Hoover had called squandering and what the dispossessed called social security or the right to live. Almost as soon as Roosevelt took office, he began to respond.

27

Mergers, Mergers:
Socialists and the Workers Alliance
(1932–1936)

Morgan Paid No Income Tax for the Years 1931 and 1932;
Neither Did His Partners
— *New York Times* headline, May 24, 1932

Depending on which statistics you believe, by 1933 there were between 13 million and 17 million jobless (and their families) and a like number of part-time workers (and their families). At the same time, the number of radicals who concerned themselves with the unemployed had also increased. These left-wingers fell into three main groups: the Communists, the Socialists, and adherents to the Conference for Progressive Labor Action (CPLA), generally known as Musteites after the name of their leader, A. J. Muste. Both of the non-Communist groups built organizations among the unemployed and achieved local and regional strength after appearing on the scene later than the Communist-initiated Unemployed Council.

Even before the Wall Street crash in 1929, the National Executive Committee of the Socialist Party had recommended the establishment of "unemployed councils," using a phrase already in currency. The Socialist councils were intended simply to educate and agitate on behalf of the jobless and for public works programs and better relief measures. Socialists nationally did not, at the outset, undertake to organize the jobless to act for themselves. The situation soon changed in Chicago, however, where SP members were in revolt against the national leadership of their party.

It was not until January 1933 — that is, not until after the second National Hunger March — that the Socialist Party in New York gave up its "study and educate" position and began active organization among the jobless. At that point, some New York SP members clearly showed the influence of their colleagues in Chicago. In fact, they said that they had studied the organizing methods used there. Later, the national Socialist leader, Norman Thomas, gave his support to the Chicago group.

The Socialist leader in Chicago was Karl Borders, who had been executive secretary of the Chicago branch of the League for Industrial Democracy (LID). The LID was directly descended from the Intercollegiate Socialist Society (for which Jack London had been a popular speaker after his brief participation in the Industrial Army of 1894). The organization Borders founded became known as the Chicago Workers Committee on Unemployment. Although no workers belonged to the committee at the outset, its goals were similar to those of the Unemployed Councils, but its methods were different. According to Helen Seymour, who studied both groups:

> Unlike the Council, which attempted to stop evictions and increase relief by mass physical protest, the Workers Committee inclined toward conference methods; it also made an appeal to the community, sponsoring a series of hearings in various parts of the city at which workers, grocers, landlords, and professional persons testified on effects of the depression. Like all unemployed organizations, however, it held its rank and file through grievance work on individual complaints against relief regulations and administration.

Karl Borders was a social worker who had close relations with prominent persons and with settlement houses in Chicago. He was well informed about existing relief facilities, and he sought harmonious ways to get from these facilities such benefits as he could for the jobless. He began by doing things for the unemployed rather than with them, but in time he developed some awareness of the need to involve the jobless themselves in solving their problems.

Borders formed his committee after the dramatic eviction

fight of August 1931 in which the police killed three Unemployed Council members. He had two purposes in mind. One was to persuade the governor of Illinois to call a special session of the legislature to enact legislation to meet the unemployment crisis. His second purpose was to provide the unemployed with an organization other than the Unemployed Council to which they could turn. Borders was hostile to the council and to Communists who supported it. It is not clear whether he was anti-Communist before he went to the Soviet Union, where he spent two years before the depression, or whether his hostility developed while he was in the USSR or after he returned to the United States. In any case, by 1931 he had harmonious relations with Chicago officials who were anti-Communist.[1] Before long he was on good terms with officials in Washington and moved on to a job in the New Deal.

By the summer of 1932, the Chicago Workers Committee had three active locals, and it continued to grow. Reflecting Borders's aversion to joint action with the Unemployed Council, the committee refused to participate in the conference called to prepare for the second National Hunger March. On December 3 and 4, 1932, while the Hunger Marchers were the center of great excitement, penned up day and night outdoors on a chilly Washington street, Borders was in the Capitol testifying before a congressional committee.

Borders's organization grew under his energetic leadership until it had sixty-seven locals in Chicago and a few locals elsewhere in Illinois and in other parts of the Midwest. In March 1933, the Workers Committee on Unemployment began to publish a biweekly, the *New Frontier*, which reprinted in its first issue this satiric poem from *Hobo News:*

The Ignorant Masses

The social uplifters, those eminent sifters
Of merit and poor people's needs,
Went down to the slums to regenerate bums,
And do meritorious deeds.

We washed them, we dressed them, with libraries blessed
    them.
We prayed with those ignorant mobs —
And the wretches were hateful, and vilely ungrateful,
And said what they wanted was jobs!!!

Our noble committee then searched thru' the city
To find all the fallen and lost;
We learned how they came to be living in shame —
This, mind you, at no little cost.

We swamped them with tracts and statistical facts,
But the creatures were terribly rude;
They acknowledged 'twas nice to be free from all vice
But they said what they wanted was food!!!

They're just as God made them — it's useless to aid them,
The brutes do not ask for reform;
Intellectual feasts are all wasted on beasts
Who want to be fed and kept warm.

Let them keep their allotted positions, besotted
And blind! When you bid them advance —
The ignorant asses, the underworld classes
Will say all they want is a chance.

In its second issue (March 4, 1933), the *New Frontier* noted
that the AFL convention in September 1932 had announced
approval of two measures that the Borders committee had long
recommended. One was a shorter workday and workweek; the
other (reflecting a reversal of the AFL stand) was endorsement
of the general idea of unemployment insurance. There was no
mention in the article of a committee of AFL members headed
by Louis Weinstock, which had mobilized sufficient union support to bring about this reversal. Weinstock was a Communist.
(There will be more about this internal AFL conflict in Chapter
33.)

Earlier, on February 8, 1932, at a citywide meeting of
representatives of its various locals, the Workers Committee

"practically unanimously passed a resolution instructing all locals not to enter into any united front activities with the Unemployed Councils." The councils for their part seem to have been very eager for a united front: They announced that some locals of the Workers Committee were cooperating with the councils. Borders insisted there was no such cooperation. In many ways the quarrels between the two organizations in Chicago were bitter and continuous, with no visible benefit to the unemployed.

Nevertheless, there were some similarities between the two groups — for example, the *New Frontier's* choice of songs recommended to the unemployed. In addition to the old IWW song "Solidarity Forever," the paper reprinted the anthem that the Communists considered their own: "The International." The paper also recommended the old socialist song "Red Flag," which had been adopted by the Communists. The *New Frontier* also offered the words of the new favorite, "The Soup Song," which had been written within the year by Maurice Sugar, who was very close to the Communists.

Even as the Workers Committee quarreled with the Unemployed Council, it kept in close touch with problems faced by the jobless. One of the committee's locals investigated garbage eating among the unemployed. Among other things, it reported:

> Miss F—— was an unemployed housemaid. She had applied for relief, but because she was a single person, they would only put her in a shelter. She had a little furniture and felt that she would lose her home and also her chance of getting a job if she went into a shelter, where she understood that she would be shut up and only let out at certain times. At present she was just working for her room, but did not get anything to eat and therefore went to Ohlsen's dump. When asked what kind of food she got there she replied, "Sometimes good, sometimes not fit to eat. Those greedy men sometimes get into the trucks before they are dumped and get the things away from us women without us getting a fair chance." People are not supposed to stay around all day, but only at certain times so as to make room for others. When asked if this was a regulation made by Mr. Ohlsen, she replied, "No, just an understanding among ourselves."

The activity of the Chicago Workers Committee stimulated Socialists in other midwestern cities, and in November 1933, the locals of the Workers Committee, led by Karl Borders, held a convention to found a national organization called the Unemployed Workers League of America (see Appendix K). Forty-four delegates from more than thirty groups in Illinois, Ohio, Missouri, Michigan, Iowa, and Texas attended. The gathering adopted resolutions opposing child labor, the sales tax, and the "stagger system" of employment (a scheme for shifting some of the burden of unemployment to those who had jobs) and demanding a government form of social relief to be financed by taxing the rich. This new Socialist-led organization struggled along in the Midwest and did not quickly achieve influence nationally. Later it linked up with other Socialist-led organizations that became important to the national scene.

A leader of these organizations in the East was David Lasser, a young MIT graduate and author of *The Conquest of Space* (the first book in English on space exploration). Lasser had joined the Socialist Party and the LID in 1932. He started an unemployed organization in his Greenwich Village neighborhood and then moved on to become organizer of one of the four New York locals of the Workers Committee on Unemployment. Soon he helped to arrange the merger of the Workers Committee with the small, independent organization, the Workers Unemployed League. Then came another merger with the Association of the Unemployed, which was led by followers of Jay Lovestone who had been expelled from the Communist Party because the party regarded them as too right wing. The result of this coalition was a new organization, the Workers Unemployed Union, which had twenty-eight locals in New York City. From this base, Lasser went on to become head of an organization in a wider area, the Eastern Federation of the Unemployed and Emergency Workers.

At one point, as the series of mergers developed, Lasser and Mary Fox invited Carl Winter, then head of the Unemployed Council (UC) in New York, to merge his older, larger organization into the Socialist-led group. Winter expressed interest in joint actions with Lasser's organization, but joint action was not what Lasser sought; he wanted the UC to give up its identity. Winter saw no advantage to the jobless in such a step.

Much to the consternation of some of those who were called Old-Guard Socialists, militant activity developed from David Lasser's growing Socialist-led movement. One of the Old Guard, Louis Waldman, used the columns of the *New York Times* to attack Lasser for leading a demonstration at City Hall on the first day in office of Mayor Fiorello LaGuardia. A later demonstration led by Lasser attracted 8,000 to Union Square. On March 4, 1933, and again on November 14, 1934, Socialist-led groups organized demonstrations throughout the country.

Yet another group of Socialists developed militant activity in Maryland. Dianne Feeley described the movement in her privately circulated history of unemployed organizations, *In Unity There is Strength:*

> Perhaps the most impressive of all the Socialist Party led groups was the People's Unemployment League of Baltimore. Within a year they built an active movement of 7,000–12,000 members in twenty different locals. Combining direct action with self-help activity, the Baltimore group became a powerful force for the unemployed. They led sit-ins and demonstrations, and favored the device of sending unemployed delegations to the mayor or head of the relief agency. Their self-help activities included the distribution of free food and the repair of abandoned houses for their members.
>
> They were well-organized within Baltimore's Black community. The committee organizers opened and closed their street corner talks — mounted on the back of a food distribution truck — with the slogan: "Black and White, Unite and Fight." The Baltimore committee had 2,000 to 3,000 Black members.

Socialist-led organizations continued to merge, and the idea of strengthening the jobless by cooperating with the Unemployed Council gained more and more support among the rank and file in Lasser's organization.

28

"Don't Tread On Me!"
(The Unemployed Leagues)
(1932–1936)

I dig your ditches. I'm Labor.
I man your switches. I'm Labor.
I teach your kids and make your shoes,
I sew your pants and write your news,
With brain and brawn, with nerve and thews,
I'm Labor.

I'm on relief. I'm Labor.
Life's full of grief. I'm Labor.
I eat salt pork and navy beans
With now and then some turnip greens.
I'm finding out what hunger means,
I'm Labor.

At last I'm waking. I'm Labor.
My chains are breaking. I'm Labor.
No more to wealth and might I'll cower
But rise, unite and use my power.
I'm Labor.

— from *Ohio Unemployed League Songs*

In 1932 in Ohio and parts of Pennsylvania and West Virginia, members of the Conference for Progressive Labor Action (CPLA) began to draw groups of workers together into Unemployed Leagues (UL), as they had done in Seattle.[1] Most of these CPLA organizers were graduates of Brookwood Labor College, a school attended by trade union activists and radical young intellectuals. The college had been established by A. J. Muste, who had attained distinction as leader of a 1919 strike of textile workers in Lawrence, Massachusetts. Because of their close association with Muste, the organizers who went out from Brookwood were often referred to as Musteites.

As they moved among the jobless in Ohio, they started Leagues in small communities where they found relatively stable populations. From small beginnings, they often spread out by getting recruits to approach their nearby relatives. These new recruits would in turn talk to their relatives in adjoining townships. Organizing in large industrial centers came later, after the leagues were well established in the smaller places. By January 1933, the various leagues in Ohio had come together in a state organization, and by July 4, the Leagues claimed 100,000 members in Ohio, 40,000 in Pennsylvania, and a total of 10,000 in West Virginia, New Jersey, and North Carolina. On Independence Day 1933, these league members sent delegates to a convention in Columbus, Ohio, that founded the National Unemployed League (NUL).

The organization was not really national, but it had grown vigorously, and as the depression became more brutal, many of the Musteites who organized the league became more radical. Reflecting their mood, they adopted at their convention a Declaration of Workers and Farmers Rights, which was modeled after the Declaration of Independence. (The text of this document appears in Appendix L.) In addition, they adopted as the league logo the Rattlesnake Flag of the American Revolution with its slogan "Don't Tread on Me!" Finally, the convention overcame some heated squabbling between left-wing and right-wing delegates.

A month after this founding convention, the NUL organized a march of 7,000 jobless workers to the state capital in Ohio. In the months that followed, the Musteite organizers of the NUL moved quickly to the left. By December 1933, the Conference for Progressive Labor Action, to which almost all of them belonged, had dissolved and its members had formed the American Workers Party (AWP). By the time of the second national convention of the NUL in the summer of 1934, the delegates in attendance voted for the abolition of the capitalist system.

Six months later, the Trotskyists, who had been expelled from the Communist Party in 1928, joined the AWP, bringing with them their anti-Stalinist views and also their factional squabbles. They were divided into at least four groups that quarreled heatedly among themselves.

As the political churning went on, so, too, did active organizing work among the jobless. In Pittsburgh, a leading UL organizer was Ernest McKinney, an African-American who later became an organizer for the CIO. McKinney said that the UL was:

> trying to inculcate in these unemployed workers (many of whom had been in the organized labor movement, many thousands had not) that they must become part of the regular labor movement. It was part of our theoretical concept, in connection with the organization, that we did not want a continuing of unemployed organizations. We wanted the day to come when unemployed organizations would be done away with and there would only be organizations of employed workers.

Other goals of the Unemployed League were described by Louis Budenz in a pamphlet, *Organizing the Jobless.* He emphasized the importance of convincing those among the jobless who had no experience with organizations to learn orderly procedures and to learn that a continuing organization was important. It was not enough just to get people together for a particular demonstration or one-shot action of some other kind. He also argued for the need to be inclusive, to take in all kinds of workers without ignoring those who were "backward" politically. He insisted that the UL must oppose self-help (which it had not done in the beginning) and should object to private relief. The demand, he said, would be for government relief, and one reason he gave was that the mounting costs of relief would weaken the government and thus "hasten a show down" — meaning, apparently, hasten the day when a revolution could take place.[2]

As the UL mobilized workers to try to put the financial burden of unemployment on the state, it also tried to get specific immediate benefits for the membership. For example, in the fall of 1935, the UL in Pittsburgh drew up a list of 4,400 children who could not go to school because they did not have shoes. The UL then campaigned to get city officials to provide shoes. They succeeded in persuading the City Council to hold a hearing and to appropriate $40,000 for this purpose, but Pittsburgh's Mayor McNair refused to release the money. The UL then set up two picket lines of women, one at the mayor's home, the other at his office. They picketed for six weeks, and the children finally got their shoes and could go to school.

The UL also engaged in sit-ins in relief offices. One sit-in in Pittsburgh lasted for fifty-nine days. Occasionally the UL organized direct appropriation of food. For example, upon discovering that seventy-nine sacks of flour were lying in a government warehouse in Pittsburgh, a small group of UL members simply walked in and in an organized manner took possession of the flour and put it to good use. There was no mob looting as there had been in the New York flour riot of 1837. League members were simply acting on a slogan that Arnold Johnson had used as the title to a pamphlet: "Give Us Relief, Or We'll Take It."

> In another incident in Ohio, a group of men who had been miners in the marginal mines of Athens County, marched into Glouster, Ohio, which was the trade center for the surrounding area. Each man was armed with a gunny sack; each man was uttering demands for food — food for his family, food for himself. These desperate men waved their gunny sacks in the air and threatened to return in a week if they received no relief in the transpiring period. And if they did return, they vowed to leave only when their sacks were filled with food even if they had to take it from the shelves of stores. These men got their relief.

John R. Stockham, who told this story in his M.A. thesis for Ohio State University, stated that the march with gunnysacks was spontaneous. Others claimed it was organized by the UL. It seems likely, at the very least, that ideas coming from the UL stimulated the marchers.

A UL paper, *Voice of the Worker,* told of a community action in Pennsylvania:

> An infuriated crowd of Unemployed League members twice this afternoon, within the period of an hour, smashed attempted evictions. . . . A messenger came running into the UL headquarters: "A widow is being evicted." In 10 seconds scores of husky Leaguers were tearing down Hamilton St. . . . In two minutes they ran into and around the home where the eviction was taking place — Mrs. K—— was cowering in a corner, almost fainting with fright, tears streaming down her wrinkled old face, as the brutal thugs tossed her last few possessions out and started to move them off in a truck. . . . League members pressed the thugs to the wall. . . . Fists were raised. . . . Willing hands took the furniture from the truck and carried it back to the house. . . . Half an hour later, while the office staff had scarcely time to catch its breath, another messenger burst in: "Come quick, the thugs are back and have smashed the old lady's door!" Once more the League men sped to the scene. "Eviction on Chestnut Street," they cried to curious spectators as they ran down the streets and alleys. . . . In spite of numerous police on the scene, League members ran into the house and drove the sniveling thugs into the street. The crowd booed lustily. As they saw the splintered door their anger rose. "Where are the rats that did this?" they shouted. The thugs were pointed out, cowering behind the coat-tails of the cops. More police cars drew up as the crowd strained to get at the eviction gang. . . . The truck-drivers climbed into the van and prepared to move away. But they had a hard time getting started as water had accidently gotten into the gas tank.

Along with such actions, the UL constantly educated members about the need for basic changes in society. In Ohio, membership soared at one point to 150,000, organized into more than 250 local leagues. The CPLA (later the AWP) did not have enough members to build leagues everywhere, but the Musteites did start locals as far away as Seattle, where they had a vigorous history (see Chapter 21). In general, the Unemployed League represented a considerable movement wherever it existed.

In Ohio in 1934, the militancy and prolabor policy of the UL led to its dramatic participation, along with the locally smaller Unemployed Council, in a strike at the Auto-Lite plant in Toledo. Although the Musteites, who had now become the American Workers Party, and the Communists mistrusted each other, they worked together in support of the strike. Both the AWP and the CP strongly emphasized the importance of solidarity between the employed and the unemployed workers, and a picket line of UL and UC members played an important role in turning a failing strike into a partial victory for employed auto workers.

The cooperative action of the two organizations of the jobless in support of employed Auto-Lite workers was in open defiance of an injunction that forbade picketing by persons who were not union members. On May 15 and 16, more than 150 members of the UL and UC were arrested by 150 deputies whose wages were being paid by the Auto-Lite Company. Then came demonstrations at the jail and courthouse. At the same time, the picket line not only continued, it grew to 1,000, then 4,000, and then 6,000.

The deputies kept up their attacks, but the picketers began a round-the-clock siege of the plant, inside which were many deputies, scabs, and police officers. Hand-to-hand fighting went on all through the night of May 23. Governor George W. White now called out the National Guard, which attacked the picketers, killing a striker and an unemployed worker and tear-gassing many. The guardsmen, numbering 1,350, fought the strikers and the unemployed for an entire day. At this point, the AFL unions in Toledo threatened a general strike, and Department of Labor mediators appeared. Finally, the strikers and the company agreed on a settlement that included gains for the Auto-Lite workers.

Of this event, an astonished Roy W. Howard of the Scripps-Howard newspapers said that the unemployed "appeared on the picketlines to help striking employees win a strike, though you would expect their interest would lie the other way — that is, in going in and getting the jobs the other men had laid down."

Another significant aspect of this joint UL and UC action was that the unemployed had attained a degree of unity among themselves as well as demonstrating unity with those who had jobs — unity against the common problems of low wages and unemployment. The jobless had also helped employed workers carry through a strike that was opposed by the cautious top AFL leadership. In the process, the striking workers became more militant, thanks to the education they got from their jobless supporters.

At the time of the Auto-Lite strike, a major strike was shaping up in San Francisco. Longshoremen and seamen were entering a struggle with ship owners that would develop into a general strike of almost all workers in the Bay Area. And there, as in Toledo, the organized unemployed supported the strikers. They were successful in persuading migratory farm workers in the Sacramento area not to go to San Francisco to take jobs as strikebreakers. For her part in this action, an Unemployed Council leader in Sacramento, Nora Conklin, was arrested with others and after a year-long trial found guilty of conspiring to overthrow the United States government by force and violence. Many unemployed members of the Workers Ex-Servicemen's League also were jailed when they took part in a peaceful meeting aimed at dissuading jobless workers on the waterfront from scabbing.

In Baltimore, in 1934, the Marine Workers Industrial Union (MWIU) led seamen who were "on the beach" in a campaign against the "fakers" in the Seamen's YMCA, who were administering relief for the federal government. The seamen rebelled against these "hypocritical tyrants" and "grafters," and they sent a delegation to Washington to protest and to make an unconventional proposal. The committee met with Elizabeth Wickenden of the Federal Emergency Relief Administration (FERA), who found that their "terminology and temper was obviously radical" and that they were "extremely intelligent men."

What the men wanted was to administer relief through "an

elected committee of their own." They won this right, and soon unemployed seamen were handing out more money than before because bureaucrats were no longer being paid to do so. The quality of relief greatly improved. Not only were the jobless seamen better off, but employed seamen also benefited. The committee in charge of relief several times gave relief to seamen who went on strike in Baltimore against miserable conditions on ships.

In the contentious year of 1934, labor made many advances. The Auto-Lite strike was a high point not only for the union but also for the organized jobless. Thereafter, however, the Unemployed League began to weaken. Roy Rosenzweig, in a study of the UL published in *Labor History*, blamed the decline in part on the Musteite shift in primary emphasis: less on helping the jobless satisfy their immediate needs and more on remote revolutionary objectives. Certainly the Musteites went through some obvious policy changes between 1932 and 1936. After initially condoning self-help, as they had in Seattle, they adopted a Marxist ideology when they became the American Workers Party. They then merged with the Trotskyists. By this time they had moved away from their original focus on the American scene. Instead, they were much distracted by disputes about Trotskyist theories on an international level. But the American scene had changed as well. The number of unemployed had somewhat decreased, and the jobless had won their fight for federal work relief. They now had to deal with the national relief apparatus, but the UL was still essentially only a regional organization without the resources necessary to mount national campaigns.

As the UL weakened, the other unemployed organizations were gaining experience in the new circumstances. More and more they saw advantages to cooperating with each other. Anthony Ramuglia, president of the National Unemployed Leagues, was more hopeful than accurate when he summed up developments in the UL, saying, "It is a straggling army, but it is moving forward all the time." By 1936 it had ceased to move forward, and in a weakened state it joined the Workers Alliance of America.

29

The Army of the Aged
(1933–1942)

The Townsend Plan is "the most Christ-like plan that has been conceived since the crucifixion."
— "Big Bill" Thompson, mayor of Chicago

The Townsend Plan is marching —
It will never know defeat —
It will vanish want and sorrow
And will make our years more sweet;
Heal the dread of our tomorrows —
It will make our lives complete —
God's Plan is marching on!
— sung to the tune of "Battle Hymn of the Republic"

When most older Americans felt the full force of the depression, they had no pensions to soften the blow. A few states and some business enterprises had meager pension plans, the latter often only for employees with records of long service. Top executives in industry often received pensions when they retired, as did civil service workers and members of the military. But with a few other minor exceptions, the 10 million citizens over the age of 60 had no pensions to look forward to, and about half of them were dependent on their families or on private or community charity for financial support. As the crisis deepened, the ability of sons and daughters and charitable institutions to help dwindled rapidly.

Although a number of industrialized capitalist countries (Sweden, Denmark, Great Britain, New Zealand, and Argentina) had made some provision for workers who reached the age at which their labor was no longer profitable to employers, the United States with its prosperous economy had no national pension plan in operation in 1929. In most countries where plans existed, they were the result of pressure by labor and Socialist movements. In the United States, however, neither education by committees of intellectual reformers nor government attempts to head off agitation by radicals had produced any such federal legislation for the aged.

By 1929 only one older person in five in the United States had enough savings to be independent after retirement, and on average these old folks had more than ten years of living still to do. In 1928, a respected American advocate of old age pensions, Abraham Epstein, had calculated that 30 percent of people over 65 were dependent on others for support. Government sources put the figure at 20 percent. Whatever estimate one chooses, there was clearly a large and growing number of the elderly who had no way of supporting themselves.

During the 1920s, scores of bills proposing plans to take care of the aged had been introduced in state legislatures and in Congress. The National Archives hold a flood of letters to the Department of Labor from individuals and a wide variety of organizations pleading for old age pensions. Among the organizations, the Socialist and Communist parties at various times urged pensions for the elderly, but the millions who were still regarded as employable attracted more of the attention of radicals than did the smaller number of those who would never work again because of their age.

Commissions to study the pension problem littered the political landscape. In New York, when Franklin D. Roosevelt was governor, one of these commissions led to legislation that established a very modest retirement pension of $22.16 per month for state citizens. Nationally the situation, which was bad before 1929, rapidly became desperate for many after the stock market crash in the autumn of that year.

It fell to the elderly to lobby on their own behalf, and one of those who knew the insecurity that comes with advancing years was a physician named Charles F. Townsend. Dr. Townsend

had never prospered in youth or in middle age, and his prospects now were bleak indeed. After working as a rancher, a
farmer, a miner, and stove salesman, he had led a very modest
life as a general practitioner in the Midwest and later turned to
selling real estate in California in a not very successful effort to
increase his income. Then, as the depression strangled the
economy, he lost the small job he had as an assistant county
health officer in Long Beach, California. There, during his
unemployment, he somehow had a remarkable idea for solving
his financial problems and those of all others in his age group.
He won support for his scheme from a real estate promoter who
had an obvious talent for getting publicity and for organizing. In
a very short time these two men developed a movement among
older Americans that had a powerful impact in the nation's
capital. The physician and the real estate promoter, Robert E.
Clements, were jointly responsible for developing one of the
most important mass movements of the depression years.

Townsend, in his youth, had been influenced by Socialist
notions of reform. Late in life he learned something about
promotion and organizing. In 1933, when he was 66 years old
and completely out of a job, he had time to think about unem
ployment and the plight of old people. He gathered his thoughts
together and sent them off to the *Long Beach Times Telegram* in
a letter that appeared September 30, less than seven months
after Roosevelt had become president. What Townsend proposed aroused a great deal of interest among the large elderly
population of southern California.

In its simplest form Dr. Townsend's idea was this: The
government should pay every person over 60 a monthly pension
of $200 — a lot of money in 1933. Each recipient of this amount
would be obliged to spend it all within thirty days. With about
10 million people spending $200 a month, there would be a vast
increase in consumption of goods and services. Production
would increase to meet this demand, the unemployed would go
back to work, and the depression would come to an end.

Where would the government get the many billions of dollars needed to finance this plan? The money would come from a

2-percent sales tax, levied each time a transaction took place, beginning with payment for raw material and continuing through every stage of manufacturing and distribution, ending with the final sale to a consumer. It became known as a transaction tax, and it would have added about 10 percent, not 2 percent, to the cost of every item consumed.

All economists agreed that the plan was impractical, absurd, even mad. The amount of money needed to finance it each year was not known. Estimates ran as high as $24 billion. The amount that could be raised by the transaction tax was also unknown, but the burden of the tax would fall most heavily on those least able to pay it. Because people would be obliged to spend all their pension within thirty days, merchants, seeing this captive market, would raise their prices. Inflation would result, increasing costs for everybody and particularly hurting the poor. Plans for making sure that every old person spent all of his or her $200 within the month were nebulous. Right, left, and middle, the experts said the Townsend Plan would create more problems than it would solve. Their opinions made little impression on Dr. Townsend or on millions of desperate old people who became his followers. They were largely churchgoing folk, and they listened to ministers who became prominent speakers for the Townsend movement. God, they were convinced, would somehow take care of the problems that economists found in the plan.

Duly incorporated under California law as the Old Age Revolving Pension Plan (OARP), Townsend's organization began to function and to give out charters for clubs nationwide. Soon there were 7,000 of them. Each club meeting ended with members joining in the Townsend Pledge: "The Townsend Plan WILL succeed. I therefore pledge my allegiance to its principles, to its founder, Dr. Francis E. Townsend, to its leaders, and to all loyal members."

All power in the OARP remained in the hands of Townsend and Clements. They not only collected dues but also started a newspaper, the *Townsend Weekly*, which was their private property and was very profitable, carrying as it did many ads for patent medicines. The owners also sold pamphlets, insignia, bumper stickers, buttons, banners, and vitamins. Nickels and dimes and quarters poured into OARP headquarters. People poured into the organization — 4 million of them, if you believe the figures that Townsend and Clements put out, many fewer if you believe critics of the organization. Whatever the actual size of the membership, it was large and represented a tightly organized force for lobbying by letter. It was "the most colossal campaign," said one observer, "ever waged by pen and ink."

Increasingly, elected officials listened to the demands of the organized elderly whose hopes had been raised by the vision of $200 a month, which was roughly ten times as much as any of the few existing state pension systems offered them. Representative John S. McGroarty from California introduced a bill in Congress in April 1935 that spelled out the Townsend Plan in some detail and began to attract support of other congressmen who were being heavily lobbied. Townsend claimed he had petitions supporting the McGroarty bill that were signed by 20 million citizens.

At least partly in response to the growing strength of the Townsend movement, President Roosevelt saw to it that an old age pension plan was written into the Social Security Act that became law on August 14, 1935. The act provided far less than the Townsend Plan called for — $30 per month for each person over 70. It was far less, also, than the Communists, Socialists, and Musteites demanded, and it was less than the aged needed in order to live in some kind of dignity. Nevertheless, it did avoid the catastrophic expense that Townsend's plan entailed, and it served to reduce agitation for $200 a month.

It is worth repeating that the agitation for old age pensions, which had gone on before the Townsend movement, had obtained no legislative results nationally. Only when the movement set people in motion — "when despair among the aged assumed a threatening political form," according to one observer — did elected officials decide that it was necessary to provide some form of federal plan.

The contrasts between the Townsend organization of the

unemployed elderly and the militant organizations of the general unemployed population were numerous and sharp. The general organizations had broader objectives and served a wider variety of interests. Beginning with the Unemployed Councils, they focused much attention on ethnic minorities, particularly on African-Americans. They had strong central leadership, but, unlike the Townsend movement, they had provisions for input by the rank and file.

The working-class component in the unemployed organizations was large, and the attitude toward governmental authority ranged from skeptical to confrontational. To one degree or another, the initiators of the unemployed organizations held visions of a Socialist society as a way out of the problems of unemployment, although the movement as a whole did not hold such views. And the unemployed movement was in large part secular and not religious in tone, although A. J. Muste, one of the important leaders, was a minister, as was Norman Thomas, the Socialist leader.

In contrast to the unemployed organizations, the Townsend movement was a one-issue organization made up largely of small-town and rural people who tended to share a common ethnic background. There were few African-Americans or industrial workers in the movement. Townsend had no large revolutionary goals. His followers supported capitalism and were determined to make the system work for them. They accepted highly centralized control of the OARP, which had a strong Christian religious tone and did not tolerate deviation from the policies that came down from the all-powerful leaders.

Before passage of the 1935 Social Security Act, President Roosevelt refused to meet with Townsend. The snub, along with the president's successful maneuvering of the pension issue, angered Townsend, and he continued agitating for his own plan. For a while members of the OARP continued to follow their leader. At the same time, opposition to the Townsend Plan increased, and in February 1936 its enemies in Congress managed to have an investigating committee established. The committee soon made it widely known that Clements was becoming wealthy from funds that old people sent to OARP headquarters. In his testimony before the committee, Dr. Townsend was exceedingly vague about the practical details of the plan that bore his name. He stalked out of a committee hearing and was cited for contempt of Congress.

The congressional investigation hurt the Townsend movement, but the need of the elderly was so great that large numbers of older citizens clung to the Townsend clubs. Many seemed genuinely to believe that God would step in and straighten out any problems about financing the plan. The only alternative they saw was poverty and lack of medical care, but when Social Security legislation was passed, the zeal of the Townsendites faded.

The decline in the movement, together with its leaders' opposition to Roosevelt, moved Townsend to seek allies from the right end of the political spectrum. At the OARP convention in Cleveland in 1936, Father Charles Coughlin came to speak. Coughlin had built up an audience of perhaps 10 million for his weekly nationwide radio talks. In his broadcasts, he gave voice to the economic frustrations of a vast number of Americans, and he directed their anger against big banks, Roosevelt, and Jews. Coughlin admired Hitler, and in a few years the Department of Justice would consider prosecuting him as a German agent. Another cleric who spoke at the OARP convention was the Reverend Gerald L.K. Smith, who had tried to keep the Share Our Wealth Clubs (see Chapter 31) alive after their founder, Senator Huey Long, was assassinated.

Very soon Townsend, Coughlin, and Smith formed an alliance with Representative William Lemke, a right-wing Republican. Together these four launched the Union Party, which entered the 1936 presidential campaign with Lemke as its candidate. This third party sought to defeat Roosevelt, but the millions of supporters of Townsend and his new allies faded away when they entered the voting booth. The incumbent president, who had made some concessions to the unemployed, was reelected. The whiff of fascism that accompanied the Union Party did not attract voters. As they cast their ballots, they seemed to be saying that their serious problems, which remained, would have to be solved in some other way.

Neither Townsend nor Long, Coughlin, nor Smith led unemployed workers to home relief bureaus to get relief. They did not encourage their followers to prevent evictions, or mobilize them to support unemployment insurance. Nevertheless, all these movements did facilitate change, and the one led by Dr. Townsend clearly contributed to obtaining some aid in the form of pensions for the elderly portion of the jobless community.

30

End Poverty in California (EPIC)
(1934)

Good times are surely coming,
Soon business will be humming,
And we'll give old poverty the air.
If EPIC is phony,
Then the rest is all baloney,
So vote for Downey and Upton Sinclair.
— EPIC election campaign song, 1934

Hard on the heels of Dr. Townsend's utopian blueprint for ending poverty among old people came another California scheme to end poverty for everyone. Backed by thousands of people who were out of work, the plan almost changed the government of the populous western state, and it had more than a little influence in shaping federal legislation that would soon be enacted by the Roosevelt administration in Washington. This immensely popular movement went by the name of "End Poverty in California" (EPIC, for short), and it was the creation of one man, Upton Sinclair. Although Sinclair borrowed momentum and some ideas from the self-help movement, from Dr. Townsend, and perhaps from Huey Long and Father Coughlin, many of his ideas came from his lifelong adherence to reformist socialism.

Sinclair was not a late arrival on the political scene. In 1905 he and Jack London had founded the Intercollegiate Socialist Society (later called the League for Industrial Democracy). In 1906 he had been very influential in Washington, D.C., when he shocked the country by revealing in a widely read novel, *The Jungle*, the horrible working and sanitary conditions in the meat-packing industry. This book was the single most powerful factor that led to the passage in 1906 of the Pure Food and Drug Act. In addition to *The Jungle*, Sinclair wrote many other novels exposing corruption and attacking injustice, and he was widely known as a muckraking journalist — so well known that he was listed in a poll conducted by the *Literary Digest* as one of the four most outstanding men in the world. The other three were Franklin D. Roosevelt, Adolf Hitler, and Benito Mussolini.

Although Sinclair was passionately interested in politics, he spent most of his time writing and lecturing rather than running for office. One day in 1933, a prominent Democrat suggested to him that he run for governor of California on the Democratic Party ticket. Almost immediately Sinclair changed his registration from Socialist to Democrat and began to outline a platform and do the practical work of organizing a political campaign. He had given up hope of interesting Americans in Socialism, if that word was used. Instead he proposed to lead the country toward a Socialist society in a way that would avoid the deep prejudice of voters against radical ideologies. He did not focus attention on the working class, which he thought was disappearing, at least in a psychological sense.

Soon after changing his registration, Sinclair announced his End Poverty in California (EPIC) campaign. He said:

> The backbone of the plan is a state system of production for use, to be applied for the benefit of those now unemployed. As matters stand the unemployed are fed at public expense, and this is leading the state into bankruptcy and inflation. The only solution is to give the unemployed access to land and factories and let them produce what they are going to consume, thus taking them off the taxpayers' backs.

Sinclair believed that his plan offered "the only way to save our democratic nation from a tumble into civil war, Fascism, and ultimately Bolshevism."

To spread the word about his program, Sinclair wrote a pamphlet, "I, Governor of California and How I Ended Poverty:

A True Story of the Future," which soon reached a very large audience. To get out voters, Sinclair established the End Poverty League and set up 2,000 local organizations of the league in communities all over the state. In a primary contest against seven other candidates, Sinclair won the Democratic nomination for governor. He received more votes than the seven other candidates combined (one of whom was George Creel, an important figure in the national Democratic Party and an official in the Roosevelt administration).

Sinclair's plan called for the state to buy bankrupt farms and factories at a nominal price and then set them to producing for the unemployed. The idea attracted tens of thousands of people who were already making efforts under great difficulties to survive through self-help organizations. The production-for-use movement, which had started in California, had made people familiar with the outline of Sinclair's scheme. The jobless saw in it a way to improve their lot. The employed thought it was a way to reduce the cost of relief by getting the needy to produce for themselves. In addition, it would reduce the tax burden on those who were employed. From many quarters came support for the EPIC plan to provide for the jobless an economy of their own outside the general economy.

So powerful was Sinclair's appeal that conventional politicians used all kinds of measures to bring about his defeat. They encouraged Raymond Haight to run for governor as a Progressive Party candidate. A number of well-known Democrats came out in support of Frank Merriam, the Republican candidate, and the leading Democrat in the country, President Roosevelt, did not support Sinclair. Merriam got help from one quarter that definitely cut into Sinclair's vote. Dr. Townsend, embittered by the refusal of President Roosevelt to support his Old Age Revolving Pension Plan, came out for the Republican candidate. The Socialists, who felt betrayed by Sinclair, ran a candidate against him, as did the Communists, who regarded the EPIC plan as demagogic. By their opposition to Sinclair, both the Socialists and the Communists isolated themselves from many of their allies to whom the EPIC plan seemed a ray of hope in a dismal world.

Although Sinclair was obviously the leader of EPIC, he made ample opportunity for thousands of workers and lower-middle-class voters to participate in the EPIC campaign to improve their lot. A number of prominent individuals ran with Sinclair on the EPIC ticket, and some of them went on to high office in later elections. For example, Sheridan Downey, the EPIC candidate for lieutenant governor, became a United States senator, and Jerry Voorhis, an EPIC candidate for the State Assembly, became a representative in Washington and remained one until he was defeated by the red-baiting tactics of Richard Nixon. Thousands of less-prominent, unpaid volunteers did election work for EPIC. They rang doorbells, distributed leaflets and pamphlets, and ran offices with the zeal of crusaders. They circulated copies of *EPIC News*, the movement paper that had the considerable task of dealing with the virulent attacks that the entire press of California made on Sinclair.

At the same time, Merriam supporters used techniques that are now all too familiar in election campaigns. They hired public relations experts to smear Sinclair. He was called an agent of Moscow — a Communist — even while the Communist Party called him an ally of the capitalists. Forged newsreels were widely circulated, purporting to show hordes of hoboes heading for California in boxcars so they could live on the handouts Sinclair promised the poor. Earl Warren, then a district attorney who would later become chief justice of the U.S. Supreme Court, joined in the hysteria. He said, "We must fortify ourselves against a resolute purpose to overwhelm California with Communism." Red-scare billboards appeared along the highways. Disreputable derelicts were hired to carry signs urging people to vote for Upton Sinclair. The red-baiting of Sinclair, who was anti-Communist, the hostility of Townsend and the Socialists and Communists, and the third-party candidacy of Haight paid off. Merriam won the election with 1,138,620 votes. Sinclair's vote was 879,567. Haight was third with 302,519, and the Socialists and Communists together got less than 9,000 votes. Merriam soon rewarded Townsend for his support by coming out in favor of the Old Age Revolving Pension Plan.

Before long, Sinclair was back at his typewriter producing novels, and California's unemployed had to stop short of the State House in their search for the power they needed to end their poverty.

Those who were determined to prevent the jobless from controlling their own lives prevailed in the California election of 1934, but from then on the Democrats in that state were much stronger than they had been for decades. Nationally, pressure for federal aid to the unemployed was greater than it would have been if Sinclair had not helped to set hundreds of thousands of jobless and poor people in motion. Within a year, President Roosevelt proposed that Congress support increased inheritance taxes, adopt a gift tax, and impose graduated corporate and personal income taxes — all measures that Upton Sinclair had advocated in his EPIC campaign.

End Poverty in California had definitely left its mark on the social scene. The section of the population in direst need of basic economic reforms, however, had not learned to wield the tool it most needed in order to solve its problem. The jobless had not achieved unity in a mass movement that could produce really decent emergency relief jobs and, for the long term, really adequate unemployment insurance.

31

Huey Long's Share Our Wealth Movement (1934–1935)

> Huey Long is the greatest headline writer I have ever seen.... He is the greatest political strategist alive. Huey Long is a superman.
>
> — The Reverend Gerald L.K. Smith

Although the capitalist economy was international, and although its spasms of mass unemployment affected many countries, some of the schemes proposed for dealing with joblessness and poverty in the United States were purely national in nature. None of these offered any fundamental threat to the worldwide system that had produced the distresses of the 1930s, nor were they any real threat to the U.S. sector of capitalism. Sinclair, Townsend, and Father Coughlin and their supporters advocated only some changes in capitalism, and their recommended reforms did not focus attention primarily on the unemployed. They cast a wider net.

Huey Long, originator of the Share Our Wealth movement, operated a similarly capitalist-oriented program. Long was a Louisiana lawyer who called himself "the Kingfish." He had built a powerful political machine based on the poor whites in his home state, and in 1928 he became governor at the age of 35. Long was not an impressive man physically. He was small, chubby, and homely. His manners were atrocious by upper-class standards. He could be outrageously offensive, but he never was dull and often was very funny. His uncouth behavior seemed to endear him to millions who resented the gentility of those who lived well at the expense of the poor.

By shrewd and devious political maneuvers in the Louisiana legislature, Long outwitted the small handful of very wealthy individuals and corporations that were accustomed to ruling the state, and he forced them to accept higher taxes. Then he saw to it that the tax money paid for much-needed roads, added new buildings to the university campus, built a lavish new state Capitol, and provided free textbooks to schoolchildren. At the same time he managed to push through legislation that abolished the poll tax; reduced auto license fees; aided farmers; and lowered gas, electric, and telephone rates. Some of these reforms he achieved by methods that only his most loyal followers called legal.

Long, who came from a rural background, had a strong attraction for small farmers and small-town people. His following was largely made up of whites, but he did not exclude African-Americans from the organization he established. He did insist on their right to an education, which other politicians in Louisiana had long denied them, but at the same time he persisted in referring to them as "niggers."

Using the impoverished state of Louisiana as a base, Long soon moved out onto the national scene as a U.S. senator. In Washington, on February 23, 1934 — just before the fourth anniversary of the enormous March 6 Communist-led demonstration against unemployment — Long announced on national radio a scheme to help the poor and save capitalism from the Socialists and Communists.

Following his dramatic radio speech, he introduced in Congress legislation that embodied his plan, which he later described in his autobiography, *Every Man a King*:

1. A capital levy on the property owned by any one person of 1% of all over $1,000,000; 2% of all over $100,000,000, the government takes all above that figure; which means a limit on the size of any one man's fortune to something like $50,000,000 — the balance to go to the government to spread out in its work among all the people.
2. An inheritance tax which does not allow any one person to receive more than $5,000,000 in a lifetime without work-

ing for it, all over that amount to go to the government to be spread among the people for its work.

3. An income tax which does not allow any one man to make more than $1,000,000 in one year, exclusive of taxes, the balance to go to the United States for general work among the people.

The foregoing program means all taxes paid by the fortune holders at the top and none by the people at the bottom; the spreading of wealth among all the people and the breaking up of a system of Lords and Slaves in our economic life.

Coupled with this legislative proposal for soaking the rich, Long initiated an organization he called the "Share Our Wealth Society." Its slogan was "Every Man a King." Soon there were thousands of Share Our Wealth clubs nationwide. Anyone could join, and there were no dues. Simply by signing a card that supposedly went on file in the Kingfish's office, club members would be in on the ground floor when the great wealth-sharing day came.

By the end of 1934, Long claimed the clubs had 3 million members. His staff said that another 1.6 million joined during the next nine months. Few of Long's many critics believed these figures, but no one doubted that he had a very large following.

Like Dr. Townsend, whose movement was also attracting millions of followers, Long appealed strongly to many of the unemployed who had become dissatisfied with what they believed to be the meager accomplishments of the New Deal, President Roosevelt's plan of reform and recovery. Neither Long nor Townsend organized the jobless to take action on their own behalf, as did the Unemployed Council, the Unemployed League, and the Workers Alliance. Long's method was to promise to do things *for,* not with, the jobless and the farmers and small-town people. He won his following by resounding attacks on the rich and repeated promises to the poor, promises he made credible by pointing to the very real improvements he had engineered in Louisiana. Besides, he could put on a show unsurpassed by any other politician.

Unlike the Left, Long operated as a conventional politician, using parliamentary tricks to gain power. Then he used his power to increase his mastery of the machinery of government. Often, as he expanded his control, he did so by means that had little or no legal basis. Voters were accustomed to seeing a corrupt politician use dirty tricks to their disadvantage — but here was an adroit performer of such tricks who talked as if he were on the side of the poor and could demonstrate reforms he had already made in his own state. In Louisiana he had had a well-organized corps of lieutenants who ran errands for him, making deals and silencing opponents. While he was governor, he had begun to develop such a corps on a national scale, and at the national Democratic convention in 1932, he had used his wheeling and dealing skills in support of the candidacy of Franklin D. Roosevelt.

After his election to the Senate, Long tried to manipulate Roosevelt. In this he failed, and he changed from a strong supporter of the president to a powerful rival with presidential aspirations of his own. James A. Farley, a leading professional Democratic politician, feared that Long might actually succeed in ousting Roosevelt at the 1936 Democratic convention and might actually win the election.

In speech after speech, Long excoriated the rich and exploited the suspicion of socialism and communism that was endemic and widespread in the country. "Huey Long," he boasted, "is the greatest enemy that the Socialists and Communists have to deal with." Scarcely a month after he launched his Share Our Wealth movement, he debated Socialist leader Norman Thomas before a large audience in New York's Madison Square Garden. Thomas attempted to use logic and reason to show that Long's economic theories were impractical. In reply, Long turned his back on logic and legality, which he, as an able lawyer, knew very well. Instead he reverted to the guise of southern rustic, which also fitted him well. He pretended not to understand the economic theories that Thomas had been propounding, but he promised that when he had figured them out he would write Thomas a letter. Then, with great bluster, he insisted that all debts should be "ipso facto" remitted. "Maybe you don't know what I mean by ipso facto," he added. "Well, I don't either." The audience, which had been friendly to Thomas, now laughed and applauded the Kingfish.

Long's very American-sounding Share Our Wealth plan came at a time when Fascism had taken over the governments of Italy and Germany. He said, "If Fascism comes to America, it will come on a program of 'Americanism.' " In every possible way he made a folksy "American" appeal, but he was careful not to use the label *Fascist* to describe the movement he headed. Some of his critics, however, did see a Fascist future for this charismatic politician who had moved with great speed to center stage. In his assault on socialism and communism, Long paralleled the demagogy of Hitler, who sought to attract workers away from Socialism by incorporating the word *socialist* in the name of his party. Its full title was National Socialist German Workers Party — Nazi, for short. With this model before him on the world scene, Long attacked the Left on the American scene.

In his rush toward power, Long gave voice to the very real grievances of the poor and the unemployed and sought to use this suffering section of the population to further his aims. But they would never find out where the Kingfish might have led them: He died on September 10, 1935, the victim of an assassin's bullet.

We will never know what, if anything, Huey Long would have done for those out of work. The pattern of action in his rise to national prominence does not suggest any major assault on the causes of mass unemployment. Nor does his record suggest that he would have carried through any major remedial legislation for those in need of jobs. There is no indication in his behavior that the unemployed themselves would have played any real role in helping to shape legislation that would have provided work. The pattern was that Huey Long himself made all the decisions and all the deals. He did everything, and he did only what would enhance the power of Huey Long.

Sounding like a Populist who was one of the common people, Long had won not only a following but also ambitious lieutenants. One of them was the talented orator, the Reverend Gerald L.K. Smith, pastor of a church in Louisiana. Smith was an energetic organizer as well as a dynamic speaker, and he gave Long a great deal of help in spreading the Share Our Wealth movement.

After Long's death, Smith tried to carry on the movement, but rivals in the Long political machine soon found ways of excluding him from the organization he had helped to build. Without Long or Smith, the Share Our Wealth clubs died almost as quickly as they had come into existence. Smith had to look elsewhere for people to lead. He found them in the Townsend movement and in a vast radio audience assembled by Father Coughlin.

32

Federal Work Relief at Last
(1934–1936)

The volume of unemployment is merely a statement of how hard it is to remain employed.

— Harry Hopkins
Spending to Save

I had felt [at the relief station] the possibility of creating a new understanding of life in the minds of people rejected by the society in which they lived.

— Richard Wright
American Hunger, 1944, 1977

And holler, "Hey man,
Great God, let me go yo' way,
I just want a job workin'
For the CWA."

— a Depression song

As long as the Republicans, led by Hoover, ran the federal government, their response to the depression had been to deny economic reality and to make almost no concessions to the demands of the jobless. By the end of Hoover's term, only one unemployed person out of four was getting any relief from any source, and the amount of relief received by each family was minuscule. In New York, for example, it averaged only $2.39 per week. When the Democrats, led by Roosevelt, took over power on March 4, 1933, their response was to make some concessions, but economic reality continued to be a very painful mess. In a great flurry of activity, the New Deal gave some of the unemployed some of the things they had been seeking, but many got nothing. According to sociologists Frances Fox Piven and Richard A. Cloward, "For a brief time, there were twenty million people on the relief rolls, but millions more badly needed relief and never got it."

The concessions granted by the New Deal did, however, represent victories for the unemployed, whose pressures on the government had been centrally planned and highly organized. To this pressure, the first response of the Roosevelt administration was to acknowledge what the radicals had long been saying: The economic disaster that faced the working class was national in scope. No private charities or city or state governments could by themselves keep alive the spirits and the skills and the bodies of the 12 or 15 or 17 million jobless and their dependents. Only the federal government could muster the necessary resources.

A month after he took office (three months after the second National Hunger March), Roosevelt launched the Civilian Conservation Corps (CCC), a plan that would employ 250,000 jobless young men. Radicals concerned with unemployment were deeply suspicious of this move, which was under the control of the army. John Dewey's Committee on Unemployment denounced the idea. The Unemployed Council, thinking of the youth movement of Hitler, who had just won control of the German Reichstag, feared the CCC was a step toward militarizing the youth of the United States. The council and the Communists also noted that only a small minority of the young men who were out of work would get jobs on the CCC and that their wages would be very low. Perhaps the fears and protests of the radicals had some effect. The CCC did not create a body of militarized youth, and the public lands benefited greatly.

Two months after taking office, Roosevelt set up the Federal Emergency Relief Administration (FERA) to dispense direct relief. This agency was modeled on the Temporary Emergency Relief Administration that Roosevelt had established in New York, where the jobless had been very active while he was governor. The same man, Harry Hopkins, who had headed the state organization headed the FERA. Now, for the first time in

United States history, the federal government was taking responsibility for relief.

In an effort to create jobs in private industry by bringing some order into the chaotic practices of businesses, Roosevelt launched a program of voluntary cooperation among businessmen, the National Recovery Administration (NRA). At the head of this agency he put a colorful, conservative military man, General Hugh Johnson. Under the NRA, whose symbol was a blue eagle, employers ostensibly agreed to sign codes that set minimum wages and maximum hours for workers. Employees were to be free to join unions of their own choice. Manufacturers were to agree on stabilizing the prices of their products. Child labor was to end. Such were the stated goals, but in reality the NRA was a vast public relations operation. Nels Anderson, a New Deal official, frankly admitted, "The experiment was a colossal failure. Industry could not be persuaded to impose rules on itself, nor to keep them when they were imposed. . . . The jobless remained jobless."

The direct relief provided by the FERA did not satisfy anyone. The jobless wanted work. In November 1933, Roosevelt established the Civil Works Administration (CWA) to provide temporary jobs to a few million of the unemployed. The jobs would be on projects requiring little capital. Men would do such things as tidy up run-down neighborhoods, clear waste land, dig drainage ditches, and prevent soil erosion. The pay was low — far below prevailing wages — but it was a beginning. Here was work relief instead of cash relief.

In 1934, I interviewed and registered some of those who applied for CWA jobs. I was unemployed after months of job hunting in New York, and someone in the New York Employment Service had thought that because I was a college graduate, I might qualify to take down the names and occupations of others who were out of work. I was told to report to an armory in Brooklyn.

When I appeared for this first day of interviewing the unemployed, I found a long line of men waiting outdoors. Many had been standing in line for hours. The November morning was bitter cold, and the men shuffled and stamped their feet, trying to keep warm as they hunkered inside ragged overcoats — if they had overcoats.

It was warm in the armory, but those waiting were let in only one or two at a time. The building was large enough to hold all of them, and they could have been reasonably comfortable while they waited. I pointed this out to my supervisor, a civil servant on loan from a state office. The supervisor ignored the suggestion and told me to get back to doing what I had been hired to do.

Sitting in comfort, I listed skills, work records, race, nationality, age, and religion, and I heard, but had no place to list, stories of tragedy. A subway worker had been laid off after twenty-one years when an accident on the job incapacitated him. His medical expenses shot up at the very time his income stopped. A Parks Department worker noted with heavy emphasis that he had been laid off the day after election day. African-Americans with marginal skills had been out of work longer than most of the whites. One of them explained that he had left Alabama "on account of Scottsboro and lynchings." A scenery decorator for the Ziegfeld Follies couldn't leave town to look for work because of a court order that required him to stay in the city and pay alimony to his former common-law wife. A man by the name of O'Brien, who somehow thought it relevant in the circumstances, burst out, "I don't believe in God, but I can swear in Jewish." Time and again, someone reported that he had been fired because of Roosevelt's NRA. Sometimes these men had been fired from shops before their bosses signed the NRA code, a maneuver that allowed the employer to be classified as a small business and thus avoid having to change his pay rate or establish the working conditions that the NRA code called for.

A 64-year-old man who had been a tile-layer's helper for twenty-five years had managed to buy a home, but he had lost it because he could not get work and could not keep up the mortgage payments. A 66-year-old Jewish cabinetmaker, illiterate and hungry, showed, by pointing to the notches he had taken up in his belt, that he had lost weight. Many men reported how much they had lost — 20 pounds, 30 pounds.

Two had lost 40 pounds since being laid off, and their clothes hung loose on them. A deaf-mute wrote down answers to written questions. He knew how to be a baker's helper, but he couldn't find work and had to live on whatever food he could get from friends. Pipefitters, roofers, tinsmiths, lathers, pocketbook makers, tailors, bank clerks, draftsmen, warehouse managers, cable splicers — none could find work, and many literally did not know where their next meal would come from.

On the way home on the subway that night, I wept. The next day I appeared at the armory with back issues of a newspaper for the men to read as they shuffled in line outside the armory. The paper was the only one I knew of in the city that took an interest in the jobless and that had proposals about how they could better their lot by uniting. The paper was the *Daily Worker*, with which I had just become acquainted.

When I reached the armory, however, there was no line outside. Apparently my protest the day before had not been wasted; the supervisor had let the men into the warm room. I passed out the papers before I took my place at the desk. At the end of the workday I was handed a pink slip, which meant I was fired for handing out the newspaper. As I left the building, someone told me quietly that there would be a meeting of relief workers that night and gave me an address.

The dingy meeting room was crammed with men eager to tell about problems in the first days of CWA. Many had been victims of administrative bungling. They had reported to addresses where there had been no preparation and there was no work to do. Many had been forced to stand outdoors in the cold when they could have been in warm buildings.

A slender, small man at the back of the room seemed to know a good deal about how to bring organization out of such a formless collection of people who were strangers to each other. He spoke briefly a few times. Before the meeting was over, the men had elected temporary officers, including me, after I had told my story. Thus the Relief Workers League came into existence. The small man at the back of the room who had given shape to the meeting was Herbert Benjamin, leader of two national hunger marches. (Appendix M contains the text of the preamble to the league's constitution.)

The Relief Workers League attracted mainly blue-collar workers. Some of the white-collar unemployed joined groups that clamored for work of the kind that required their skills. These groups in turn managed to get in touch with each other, aided by members of the already existing Unemployed Council and by members of the Communist Party. As the workers gathered, they began to devise suitable organizational forms and policies.

Inequalities in CWA operations were widespread throughout the country. In Colorado, for example, Spanish-speaking workers, unlike workers who spoke English, had to prove their citizenship to get on CWA rolls. This task was often impossible, if only because many Chicano babies were born at home and their births were not registered. At best, only one-third of the jobless could get work on the CWA, and few of the successful applicants in Colorado were Spanish speaking. Some of them got jobs in the town of Lafayette, where they worked on a swimming pool. When they discovered that Chicanos would not be allowed to swim in it, they went on strike, and in the uproar that followed, nobody won. The project was abandoned, and the excavation for the pool was simply filled in.

In New York, at one point, discontent focused on a different kind of discrimination. On December 12, four representatives of white-collar workers who had joined organizations went to Washington to protest work relief wages that were lower for white-collar workers than for laborers. The delegates returned, believing they had been told by officials in Washington that the wage discrimination would end. But back in New York, relief administrators denied they had received such orders from Washington. Besides, they said, relief workers had no right to organize. In protest against this ruling and against the continuance of higher pay for laborers, the white-collar workers held a march to CWA headquarters December 29.

The CWA had come into existence suddenly and would go out of existence suddenly in the spring of 1934, although the problem with which it was supposed to deal was far from temporary. Discontent increased sharply in New York as announcements appeared that CWA was to be terminated because funds appropriated for it had run out. Several organizations sent a joint delegation to the office of the newly installed mayor, Fiorello H. LaGuardia. I was a member of this delegation. Our spokesman was a professional man, an engineer. He had been one of the builders of the Hell Gate Bridge and was now earning twenty-three dollars a week on CWA.

As we met with LaGuardia in his office, the engineer expressed hope that the mayor of the richest city in the world would give help to the helpless in the crisis that lay immediately ahead when CWA employment would end. LaGuardia sat at his desk and listened for a while and then suddenly exploded in what could best be described as a tantrum. He jumped up, jutted out his big jaw more than usual, brought two clenched fists down on the desk top, and accused the unemployed engineer of "living off the nickels and dimes of the unemployed." Was this the same man who as a liberal in Congress had lent a helping hand to the Hunger March in 1931?

The next day, the mayor spoke about the city's problems to a group of bankers at a luncheon. There he did not throw a tantrum. He did, however, soon take a leading part in forming the Conference of Mayors, which became an instrument that the cities would use in trying to get more federal funds for unemployment relief. The conference still existed a half-century later and still performed a similar function.

It would take more than a newly formed organization of mayors to help LaGuardia resolve the dilemma of limited relief funds on one hand and seemingly limitless demands for relief on the other. When spring came in 1934, the New York Welfare Department thought it could safely save money by ceasing to pay rent for many of those who were on relief. Presumably the jobless who would have to live on the streets and sleep outdoors would suffer less now that the nights were warming up.

The Unemployed Council and the Relief Workers League formed the United Action Committee and called for a protest demonstration. On the rainy morning of May 26, 1934, 500 unemployed gathered before the office of Commissioner of Public Welfare William Hodson at 50 Lafayette Street to picket and demand the money for rent that was being withheld.

Picket lines had been regular institutions at the Welfare Department ever since the termination of the CWA, and committees from the picket lines had always got hearings. This morning, however, closed doors greeted the delegation, although it had taken the customary and previously successful steps, including sending a telegram, to get in. This morning the delegation very much wanted a hearing, because the picketers needed money for rent. What they got was a charge into their midst by mounted police. At a signal, officers on horseback came at the demonstrators from every direction, cutting off all means of escape.

The police beat an unknown number of picketers and arrested thirteen. Of the latter, mild-mannered Core D'Amicis suffered particularly. He had to have medical treatment twice on the day of his arrest, once after the riot and a second time after his "examination," in the course of which a detective, whose foot he was forced to kiss, kicked him in the mouth.

Immediately following these arrests, the committee that had been denied a meeting with Welfare Commissioner Hodson went to LaGuardia's home. Many people had a picture of LaGuardia as a great liberal, but the unemployed saw a very different man. When he was confronted with unemployment, he threw up his hands and evaded. He refused to meet the committee on the ground that he carried on official business only in his office. When the committee asked to meet him in his office, LaGuardia said that he only made appointments when he was in his office.

While the committee was being rebuffed by the mayor, most of the arrested protestors were being beaten in jail. The author of this book was among them and was an eyewitness to the beatings. On Monday the mayor was caught by the delegation as he tried to leave unobserved by the back door of City Hall (a practice that the unemployed had already learned about and anticipated), but this confrontation brought no immediate results. The beatings in jail continued. D'Amicis was clubbed every day for a week until he was so feeble that he could not stand in the courtroom. His cell mate, Joseph Schindler, bore witness to the beatings and was clubbed himself. He noted bitterly that the beatings went on behind steel doors that he, as an iron worker, had set up years before. The blows he received loosened all his teeth on one side so that he could not chew, and during the three weeks he waited for bail, he lost a pound a day. Bail for these two was $1,500 each. Where were they to get the money? Schindler, a relief worker, had only two dollars when taken into custody. One went for a pitcher of ice water prescribed for him by the prison doctor. The other was used to bribe a guard who would not furnish deloused bedclothes free of charge. For Schindler and D'Amicis, the story was excessive bail, daily beatings, and finally a verdict of "not guilty." A homeless man arrested at the same time told almost the same story.

Conviction on the charges against the picketers was apparently not the main concern of the police and prosecution. Two months was the heaviest sentence imposed, although individual bail ran as high as $3,500. Police Sergeant Duffy made a revealing admission outside of court to one of the prisoners, a man named Jenkins. Bail for Jenkins had originally been $1,500. After several days, his fellow picketers raised that amount, whereupon the police rearrested Jenkins on a new charge and demanded additional bail. Friends managed to raise this amount, only to see Jenkins arrested a third time. At this point Sergeant Duffy said, "We'll break you bastards yet." He was referring to the Unemployed Council and Relief Workers League, which had supported the picket line.

Duffy and his cronies nearly succeeded. The impoverished unemployed organizations paid over $1,000 as purchase price for the $18,000 total bail set for those arrested on May 26. Abuse of bail was widespread at the time. Civil liberties organizations reported that about 3,000 people were in jail at any moment in 1934 because of activities on behalf of strikers, the unemployed, or minority political groups. Many of these militants were in effect bailed into jail rather than bailed out of it.

What instructions Mayor LaGuardia may have given the police on May 26 and 27 is not known, but he could not have remained ignorant of what happened on those days. The Sunday papers carried stories and photographs that clearly showed the violence used by the police in front of 50 Lafayette Street. On Sunday morning, many unemployed went to the Tombs Court, where those arrested the previous day were to be arraigned. When Magistrate McGee set bail at $1,500 each for some of them, a spontaneous cry of outrage went up in the courtroom. The judge's response was quick. "Clear the court!" he ordered, and policemen rushed in through every door, making an orderly departure impossible. Many people were clubbed in the courtroom. Others were beaten on the street, where there was no traffic because it was Sunday. Some officers followed unemployed men and women for as much as two blocks, striking them with their nightsticks the whole way. Two of the unemployed, an artist and his wife, were beaten so badly on the street that some reporters from the big newspapers protested (*New York News*, May 28, 1934). The reporters themselves were then beaten (*Hunger Fighter*, June 2, 1934).

The LaGuardia administration had seemed determined to carry through its cut in rent relief, but as a result of these actions by the unemployed, the city soon withdrew the cut. It appeared after all that there was money enough in the city treasury.

Nationwide, efforts to reduce all kinds of relief payment did not end. Businesses — and representatives in Congress who were sympathetic to them — did not relish having to pay taxes to support the workers they had discharged. Moreover, work relief, which required materials and equipment, was more costly than cash relief. Many businessmen protested against all make-work programs, and only a little less loudly against cash relief.

In the face of this opposition, the Roosevelt administration did not attempt at first to extend the CWA, which had been conceived of only as a temporary, emergency measure. But the pressure of the former relief workers and the other unemployed grew as Roosevelt retreated. Harry Hopkins, who headed the cash-relief-giving FERA as well as the CWA, found ways to transfer some FERA funds from direct relief to work relief projects.

Confusion was great as CWA closed down and new construction and repair projects administered by states with federal money opened up. The jobless flocked to the new projects, which paid more than people were getting on direct relief. But as soon as they began work, they protested that the pay was lower than the pay for similar work in private industry. This unsatisfactory wage scale, known as a "security wage," brought many new organizations into existence. Their objective was first to get the security wage for unemployed workers, then to get that wage raised.

Resistance to relief cutting at the end of the CWA occurred in many parts of the country. In Oklahoma City, protesting unemployed workers assembled in front of City Hall in May 1934. Police attacked them and arrested twenty-one, ten of whom were still in jail nine months later when their trial was finally held. In Ohio, 7,000 unemployed marched on the state capital. In Denver, in October, police fired at striking relief workers and killed one man. When the state legislature in Colorado failed to appropriate money for relief, jobless workers occupied the legislative chambers. Two weeks later the legislature made the sought-after appropriations.

In New York, as the prospect of a bleak winter loomed ahead, the Unemployed Council and relief workers' organizations formed the United Action Conference on Work, Relief and Unemployment. This coordinating organization began a campaign to get adequate appropriations for the jobless, including increased funds from the state treasury. On September 22, in preparation for a state hunger march, a March of Forgotten Men wound through the working-class streets of the East Side en route from Union Square to City Hall. For the time being, police action against the jobless in the city was more restrained than it had been at the time of the attempted relief cut in May. But the police responded quite differently when the state hunger march approached Albany on October 30.

Several hundred delegates had gathered from New York City and other parts of the state to petition for a special session of the legislature to enact laws providing adequate relief. Governor Herbert Lehman had been informed of the date the jobless would be in the state capital and would send representatives to see him. The mayor of Albany also knew when the marchers would appear. Both were away from the city the day the marchers arrived with their petition.

The attitude of Commissioner of Public Safety William V. Cooke was not so evasive. He said, "The police will stop the dumping of the riff-raff and the scum of other cities into Albany. The town is closed to that element . . . half of them are not citizens and most of them can't speak English."

As hunger marchers in trucks started to cross Dunn Memorial Bridge into the city, police stopped the first vehicle and ordered the driver to get out and show his license. Before the driver could comply, according to the *Knickerbocker Press*, an officer dragged him from his seat and began clubbing him. Men in the trucks tried to defend him, and in a flash there was general turmoil. According to the *Albany Evening News*, "Police beat at least 25, sent 11 to hospitals, and arrested 74 others and drove away hundreds." A reporter for the *Times Union* wrote: "At one time, about 20 Hunger Marchers were sprawled over each other on the ground. They had been battered into unconsciousness and partial consciousness. The street was spattered with blood."

Another eyewitness was Robert Moses, Republican candidate for governor in the approaching election, who drove by the scene of the police attack immediately after it had taken place. He told the International News Service, "I saw dozens of the so-called Hunger Marchers who had been headed for the Capitol demanding winter relief lying bleeding by the side of the road. They had been brutally beaten by the Albany police. These men were not given a chance. They did nothing but march on the Capitol to make a protest."

The battered delegates spent the night in an open field, nursing the injured among them as well as they could. People who lived nearby brought food and coffee and some blankets. A nurse appeared and helped. According to a *Knickerbocker Press* reporter, there were calls for a doctor, "But there was no doctor, for the man who had rushed out with a medical bag at the bridge and who, the marchers said, was beaten with police clubs, was one of those who lay unconscious in the field."

Acting Mayor Lester W. Herzog excitedly supported police efforts to keep the marchers out of town and to drive them out if they succeeded in getting in, as many of them did. Those who slipped by the police cordon even managed to hold meetings in Albany, at one of which 300 gathered on the Capitol steps. At the final meeting, held in a rented hall, one of the chief organizers of the hunger march, Richard Sullivan, was arrested and charged with vagrancy. His jailing, and the jailing of others, led to renewed protests by the marchers. Many of them, thanks to alert attorneys, had entered the city in response to court orders to appear as witnesses at the trials of those arrested on Dunn Memorial Bridge.

The absent Governor Lehman was picketed at his home in New York City, and he wired the municipal authorities in Albany, urging that the jobless be allowed to parade in the city. After all, he was a candidate for reelection, and voters would be going to the polls in less than ten days. When he was asked to investigate the violence, however, he declined to do so, saying the affair was a local Albany matter.

The confrontation in Albany did not end with a clear, immediate victory for the jobless, but their insistence was clear and, along with demonstrations in many other cities, doubtless contributed to the continuance of relief during the sixth winter of the depression.

Everywhere in the United States, relief workers' organizations were coming into existence — hundreds of them. Some were spontaneous developments with no known connection to any radical political group. Others were stimulated by obscure groups that had splintered away from the main groups of radicals. Many were initiated by Socialists, Musteites, or Communists. All were feeling their way toward new forms of organization, taking on some of the features of trade unions. In addition, groups of jobless workers began to form along occupational lines and to lobby for special work relief projects that were designed to utilize their special skills. By January 1935, when a National Congress for Social and Unemployment Insurance took place, 101 widely different organizations were strong enough to send delegates to that gathering.

Who belonged to these organizations? In Cleveland, Virginia C. Searls, a graduate student at Western Reserve University, spent three months at the end of 1934 and the beginning of 1935 trying to find out. The group she studied in detail was one local of the Unemployed Council. Council members, she found, tended to be middle-aged, married men, a little older than the average unemployed worker. The great majority were citizens, although more than half were foreign born. The ethnic makeup of this council membership was almost identical with that of the neighborhoods in which they lived. Forty-one percent were skilled workers, 35 percent were unskilled, 14 percent were housewives, 4 percent were white-collar workers, 2.8 percent were businessmen, 1.4 percent were professionals, and 1.4 percent were foremen. Very few had poor work records, and few had ever had contact with relief agencies before the depression. Among the thirty Council members about whom Searls could get information, it appeared that six had never gone to school, four had gone no further than the fourth grade, six had gone to high school, and one was a college graduate.

This council, which seemed typical, was made up of a fair sampling of the country's working population, and it was this group and hundreds of others like it that persistently agitated for improvements in direct relief and work relief.

As this uniting and agitating went on, the Roosevelt administration changed its course. Instead of retreating from work relief in response to pressure from the big business community, the New Deal began to favor work relief over direct relief. Perhaps Roosevelt saw a stronger coalition supporting him if he went in this direction. At any rate, urged on by the unemployed, his administration established work relief projects of many kinds (see Chapter 34).

33

The Campaign
for Unemployment Insurance
(1931–1935)

[T]here can be no peaceful advance as long as the pressing problems of human destitution remain unsolved, and nothing short of a comprehensive national system of social insurance against all the factors of poverty, such as death, or unemployment, offers even a semblance of an immediate solution.

— Isaac M. Rubinow
Social Insurance, 1913

This is the sixth winter,
this is the season of death
when lungs contract and the breath of homeless men
freezes on restaurant window panes — men seeking
the sight of rare food
before the head is lowered into the upturned collar
and the shoulders hunched and the shuffling feet
move away slowly, slowly disappear
into a darkened street.

— Edwin Rolfe
from "Season of Death," 1934

In the 1880s in Prussia, Chancellor Bismarck supported various measures to provide what we today call social security. He was not showing sympathy for the unemployed, the poor, or the aged; he was trying to remove from the radicals of his day, the Socialists, a weapon they could use against him and the class he represented. After the days of Bismarck, unemployment insurance gradually became a normal part of life in

Sweden, Australia, New Zealand, and some other countries. Britain adopted an unemployment insurance plan in 1911. No such national plan, however, had come into existence in the United States by the beginning of the Great Depression. In 1928, only 34,700 trade union members in the United States had unemployment insurance through their unions. A few other voluntary plans had been set up, but they covered less than 1 percent of the work force. For many years, social workers and liberal reformers in this country had been recommending one form or another of governmental insurance for those out of work. In 1914, Meyer London, Socialist congressman from New York, had advocated it, and his party in its 1928 election platform had strongly approved this form of protection for the jobless, as did the Communist Party in its election platform the same year.

Agitation for such protection increased after the Wall Street crash of 1929, and it provoked counteraction from President Hoover, who disapproved of any social security legislation. In 1931 he appointed a group of officials of the Metropolitan Life Insurance Company to study the existing unemployment insurance plans in Europe. Predictably, these private business experts reported that no governmental plan should be introduced in the United States. One observer said that Hoover's action was like appointing the gangster Al Capone and a commission of bootleggers to report on the success of prohibition.

On December 27, 1930, Senator Robert Wagner of New York introduced a proposal for a committee to investigate unemployment insurance. The Senate approved it on February 28, 1931. President Hoover then maneuvered Senator Wagner out of the chairmanship of the committee that, now headed by a loyal Hoover man, reported against any such legislation.

By now, three distinct opinions had become apparent in the growing agitation around insurance for the jobless. The one held by Hoover and many leading capitalists was firmly in opposition to it. At the opposite extreme were the Unemployed Councils, which had been vociferous in support of a plan to be paid for by a tax on business and to be controlled by workers. The third and middle opinion was represented by Senator

Wagner and supported by Governor Franklin D. Roosevelt of New York. They proposed a limited amount of unemployment insurance for a limited period of time, administered by the states and financed by a tax on payrolls. Such insurance would not cover those already out of work — those most in need of help.

Reflecting Roosevelt's policy on this point, his assistant, Colonel Louis M. Howe, told a delegation from the Unemployed Councils, "You cannot go to a fire insurance company and ask them for a policy after your house has burned down. In the same way you cannot get insurance against unemployment after you have become unemployed."

After Senator Wagner introduced his proposal, Roosevelt called a conference of the governors of northeastern states to discuss insurance against unemployment. The governors and their advisors advocated various schemes, not one of which would place control of the insurance in the hands of those most concerned with it — the workers. Most of the schemes would have shifted the cost to the workers who would be insured. At the time of the conference, A. J. Muste put the matter this way: "Unemployment insurance should be regarded primarily as wages. You don't ask a worker to take money out of his wages to pay himself wages." A month after the governors' conference, Communist-led groups held demonstrations for a plan to be financed by employers. William Z. Foster, head of the TUUL, estimated that 400,000 workers took part in these demonstrations.

Agitation for the insurance kept expanding. Before the election campaign of 1932, the Democratic National Convention endorsed state but not federal unemployment insurance. Meanwhile, the Unemployed Councils stepped up their campaign. February 4, 1932, was National Unemployment Insurance Day, and Unemployed Councils conducted activities in many cities. Late in 1932, the second Hunger March clamored loudly for jobless insurance, as did every demonstration and convention of the councils. On March 4, 1933, the day that President Roosevelt took office, Socialists and Communists all over the country nudged Roosevelt by staging demonstrations that emphasized the need for action on unemployment insurance. Roosevelt had not moved beyond expressing approval of the idea.

Frances Perkins, secretary of labor, used a Bismarckian argument in an attempt to build support for some kind of unemployment insurance. According to the *New York Times*, January 27, 1934, she said, "The security felt by the worker protected by social insurance is credited by leading European statesmen with the prevention of major industrial disturbances in the difficult years since the war [World War I]."

A few days later, on February 2, 1934, Representative Ernest Lundeen (Farmer-Labor, Minnesota) introduced in Congress the Workers Unemployment and Social Insurance Bill, which had been drafted for him. The exact authorship of this bill has been differently reported by persons who were involved. (The 1935 version of the bill is reproduced in Appendix N.)

Earl Browder, for many years the leader of the Communist Party, said that he wrote the bill. Herbert Benjamin, the leader of the Unemployed Council and in effect the Communist Party lobbyist in Washington, said that he wrote the final draft of the bill in the office of Representative Lundeen and arranged to have Lundeen introduce it. Louis Weinstock said that Mary Van Kleek, director of Industrial Studies of the Russell Sage Foundation, helped formulate the bill. Van Kleek certainly was an ardent advocate of the bill. She was largely responsible for founding the Interprofessional Association for Social Insurance. Israel Amter, testifying before a congressional committee, said, "The original writer of the . . . bill was the Communist Party." Probably it would be wise to rely on Amter's statement, which was made at a time closest to the event and suggested collective Communist authorship.

Support for the bill came immediately from the Unemployed Councils and from Socialist and Musteite unemployed organizations. On September 16, 1934, the Lundeen measure was endorsed by a conference in Chicago, the participants of which were the National Unemployed Leagues, the Illinois Workers' Alliance, the Eastern Federation of Unemployed and Emergency

Workers Unions, and the Wisconsin Unemployed League — all
Socialist and Musteite organizations with a collective membership of perhaps 750,000.

In spite of agitation for the bill, Congress was not quick to
act. On January 5–7, 1935, almost a year after it was introduced, a National Congress for Social and Unemployment Insurance, held in Washington, expressed the support of a wide
variety of organizations for the Lundeen Bill. Literally millions
of people were represented at this conference by 2,506 elected
delegates from trade unions (including 742 AFL locals) and
scores of unemployed organizations including the Unemployed
Councils, African-American organizations, and social work
groups. Among the delegates were members of the New York
Social Workers Discussion Club, one of whom, Jacob Fisher,
kept notes at the time. In describing one episode, Fisher said:

> [A] delegation . . . met with the FERA: It is a large delegation,
> maybe twenty-five or thirty, headed by Israel Amter of the
> National Unemployed Councils. Amter an old hand at confron-
> tations with public officials; tough, hard-boiled, direct; con-
> veys strong sense of command in any situation in which he
> finds self. Hdq. of FERA is on New York Ave., only a block and
> a half from auditorium. At door guard says will admit only
> small committee. But pressure of delegation behind Amter too
> much. We flood into small lobby, filling it. We want to see
> Hopkins, says Amter. Hopkins is sick, says the guard; get out
> of here. No one moves. Guard phones for a policeman. An
> FERA official appears from nowhere; says Aubrey Williams,
> assistant administrator, will see a small committee. Amter is
> invited into the reception room off the lobby. We all push in;
> occupy chairs, stand against the wall. Williams enters, a tall,
> thin, dark-haired man. Sits on the edge of a desk, says "Go
> ahead and talk, I'm listening." His folksy manner is disarming,
> for some of us, but Amter is not susceptible to its charms. He
> ticks off counts in bill of indictment against government's
> program. Relief payments are inadequate. Wages on work-re-
> lief are too low. Negroes get short end of stick in size of relief
> allowance, number and kinds of jobs on work projects.
> Williams says nothing, takes notes, smiles now and then at
> a vivid turn of phrase. Amter calls on members of the delega-

tion to speak their piece. Personal experiences looking for a job, getting relief, working on a project. They come from Olathe, Kansas; Abbeville, Louisiana; Flint, Michigan; New Bedford, Massachusetts; Klamath Falls, Oregon. A woman from Jacksonville, Florida thrusts at Williams a voucher for a week's wages on work-relief: $1.24. "We want an answer," says Amter at end.

"We'll look into all complaints," says Williams. "We have programs, but we don't always get what we want out of them. Some local administrators are mean and hard. We're trying to weed them out. We're not sure we have all the answers, but the administration is doing its best to protect the unemployed against the forces trying to destroy them—powerful private interests, local officials in league with them, reactionary senators and congressmen." He asks patience and trust. FDR will go down in history as the man who made the first great move to help the unemployed in the Depression. Derisive shouts. Amter demands a timetable, figures on how many dollars will be spent, how many families aided, how many people employed on the new work program. Williams pushes him off, says he is in no position to make promises, wants to finish the discussion, get back to his office. The meeting ends lamely as the exchange between the two becomes repetitive, dwindles, and Williams leaves.

The Lundeen Bill, which Fisher and the other delegates had come together to support, had become the property of a broad coalition that included several different political trends on the Left, and it was important in facilitating joint action by these Left and labor groups. But at this point not all of organized labor supported the bill.

The AFL had long been among the powerful forces that had opposed any unemployment insurance. In response, the Unemployed Councils and the Communists had conducted a campaign among AFL members, urging support for measures that would protect the jobless. Early in 1932, they arranged a conference in New York that was attended by delegates from seventeen local AFL unions. At the conference, the AFL Committee for Unemployment Insurance and Social Security (not officially connected with the AFL) was set up. Soon Louis Weinstock, age

29, an English-speaking immigrant from Hungary and a house painter by trade, became the leader of this committee with the title of secretary-treasurer.

Committee members knew that President William Green of the AFL had not only stubbornly resisted any unemployment insurance plan but had also opposed letting AFL members continue to belong to their unions after they became unemployed and could no longer keep up their dues. Rank-and-file resentment against Green's policy was widespread, and Weinstock was often welcomed as he approached AFL locals.

Weinstock, with great energy, was building fires under the conservative AFL leadership. He toured the country and spoke before 300 trade union locals and central labor bodies. The Socialist-oriented Joint Committee on Unemployment was also active in 1932. It held a conference in Washington attended by many prominent individuals, including a representative of the Musteite Conference for Progressive Labor Action. A nationwide radio audience listened to some of the conference speakers, who demanded action from Congress to alleviate the unemployment crisis.

In a remarkably short time, 5 international unions, 35 central labor bodies, and more than 3,000 local unions had approved of the Lundeen Bill. In addition, rank-and-file committees formed all over the country, and Weinstock's committee, which coordinated their work, published the *Rank and File Federationist.* Not only rank-and-file members but also well-known labor leaders joined in the campaign, among them Harry Bridges of the West Coast longshoremen. Tom Mooney, the most famous political prisoner in the country, supported the bill from prison.

Continuing its pressure, Weinstock's committee called a rank-and-file conference on unemployment insurance in Cincinnati in September 1932, when the AFL National Convention was going on there. Weinstock has told how his committee worked:

> We decided to send a delegation of at least 25 people to the AF of L convention and present insurance and social security.

When we got to the convention hall in the hotel, we found out that the hotel had non-union employees. We were questioning the union sense of leadership of the AF of L to hold a convention in a non-union hotel! So we decided that we were going to put up a show to indicate that the hotel was non-union. We put up a picket of about a hundred people, around the hotel.

Once the picketing was over, we sent in the delegation to the convention to give William Green a request to grant us the floor on unemployment insurance.

Instead, the sergeant-at-arms at the door took the credential, took it to Bill Green, but came back with about sixteen policemen, because they knew what was going on; they knew what we wanted. And they said, "You can't come in."

But the balcony was open for the public, and the majority of our delegates were told in advance, "After the picketing is over, go up to the balcony."

And we went up to the balcony, and there was a huge chandelier somewhere close to the balcony.

I figured, "I'm going to call the attention of the delegates to the fact there is a delegation here, all members of the AF of L." And I climbed on that chandelier, and I started to yell, "Mr. Chairman."

And William Green would knock with the gavel, and say, "No."

So, the delegates were interested in what was going on, and I got to make my five minute speech. And they were listening. I was shouting, "The convention must think of the 12 million unemployed, and you must legislate, and change the position of the AF of L executive council and support unemployment insurance!" This came through clear.

Then they brought in the firemen and got me out, because I couldn't get back to the balcony.

Following this bit of dramatics, the convention voted 300 to 5 to support the principle of unemployment insurance. It had become an important tool in the hands of those who wanted to wake up the AFL so that it could better serve workers.

Two years later, Weinstock appeared before the Senate Labor Committee, speaking for 800 AFL locals and central bodies and reporting the support of a great many other organizations for the Lundeen Bill, which was still before Congress. Weinstock recalled this hearing and Senator Copeland's question, "How much money do you want?"

> I showed them the Lundeen bill — It's $15 (per week) and $3 for each dependent.
> "How many unemployed are there in the United States?"
> So I answered, "Senator, you know as well as I do, it's at least around 10 million unemployed now, and there will be many more as we go along."
> They started to figure it quickly: 10 million unemployed . . . you mean to tell me that each week this government is going to pay out 15 times 10 million dollars? That's a $150 million just on the $15 basis a week! Then you add the dependents, and you multiply this 52 times, it will run into billions! Where are we going to get that money?
> So I looked at him. I says, "Senator, suppose a war breaks out tomorrow. And we have to mobilize the youth of this country. Will the money stop us from fighting for our country? We are going to get the money. But if you are going to leave the youth of today starving, and growing up sick and unhealthy, you'll never have even a defense force in this country to defend the country. So you are making an investment to defend the United States. That's where you are going to get the money. As far as money's concerned, there's plenty of money. You got plenty of millionaires in this country. You can create the taxation where you can get the money from those who are still making millions of profits."

While Weinstock campaigned among workers who were still employed, others talked to the jobless. Steve Nelson, for example, said to unemployed coal miners: "Coming into town, I saw the mules that pull the coal cars. What do the owners do with *them* when unemployment sets in? Well, they put the mules out to pasture. In fact, they feed them well and fatten them until work starts up again. They feel a responsibility to those mules because they represent an investment, but they refuse to accept any responsibility for the miner and his family. What can we do? I say we must fight for unemployment insurance."

President Roosevelt was not inclined to give the Lundeen Bill a sympathetic hearing. The bill proposed social insurance for all of the jobless, the sick, and the elderly, without discrimination, at the expense of employers. This was too much for Roosevelt to swallow, and he appointed a committee to develop social security legislation that he could accept. On January 17, 1935, he sent a special message to Congress calling in general for unemployment insurance and old age insurance. In response, the Wagner-Lewis Bill was introduced and met Roosevelt's approval. It did not, however, meet the approval of the Unemployed Council, which listed the following seven objections:

1. The bill gave no protection to the estimated 16 million then out of work.
2. The bill excluded farm workers, domestic workers, teachers, transport workers, government employees, doctors, nurses, and workers in small shops. In all, more than half of all workers would not be covered.
3. After a waiting period without insurance a worker who lost his job would get only $7 a week for ten weeks (or for 15 weeks if he had been employed for five years). The waiting period was interpreted as a device to keep workers from striking.
4. The bill provided no insurance for sickness, accident, old age, or maternity.
5. The insurance fund would be raised by a 5% payroll tax, which employers would deduct from their tax bill. This deduction would mean a decrease in taxes paid into the Federal Treasury by employers, and other taxes which would fall heavily on workers would be required to get the money needed to cover the government's expenses.
6. The bill would not go into operation until July 1936 at the earliest and would be operative much later than that in many states because it was not mandatory on the states.
7. Provisions by which an employer could put the payroll tax into a separate fund could mean that an employer could go out of business before the fund was large enough to cover the small amount of insurance the discharged workers were entitled to receive.

The Unemployed Council was not alone in opposing the Wagner-Lewis Bill. On February 1, 1935, David Lasser, Socialist leader of the Workers Alliance, condemned the bill in testimony he gave before the House Ways and Means Committee, and the Workers Alliance continued to oppose the Wagner-Lewis Bill and to favor the Lundeen Bill. So, too, did a great many other organizations. They were sufficiently powerful to persuade the House Committee on Labor to report the Lundeen Bill out favorably on May 15 with only one dissenting vote. The supporters of the Lundeen Bill were not able, however, to win over Congress as a whole. The Wagner-Lewis Bill was passed and the president signed it into law on August 14, 1935. With revisions, it has remained the law of the land ever since.

The unemployed leaders were less than jubilant at this partial victory. African-American leaders were very critical of the measure, as were leaders of the Townsend movement. The law provided much less than Townsend had sought for persons over age 60.

But Bismarck would have understood.

The campaign of the unemployed had produced results (although the results were skewed by the unemploying). Their efforts had greatly helped the jobless of future years by obtaining passage of a law that required payment of some income at least for a limited period. Still, they had not won insurance for those already out of work or insurance financed solely by employers.

As unemployment insurance became law, federal work relief also increased. In consequence, the target of the militants among the jobless changed. Their objective now was to secure more and better work relief jobs. In response to both domestic and international developments (primarily the rise of fascism), reform, not revolution, held the attention of unemployed organizations in the next period.

Radicals — at least most of them — as well as their adversaries now made compromises. And the organizations of the jobless moved toward unity, the better to act as a quasi-trade union, vis-à-vis the government.

34

Works Progress Administration (WPA)
(1935–1942)

[The Art Projects are] the closest to the Renaissance of any-
thing that has ever happened before in the States.
— Anton Refregier, muralist
Diary, 1939

"Never before in the history of the human race has a public
works program, whose principal object was the mitigation of
need due to unemployment, reached the magnitude of the Work
Projects Administration. This is true, however you measure it
by persons employed, money expended, or volume of results."
This statement by Joanna C. Colcord, a leading authority on
social work, is true as far as it goes, but a matching generaliza-
tion is needed: Never before have the unemployed forced a
government to establish a public works program of the magnitude of the WPA.[1]

This vast work relief enterprise began in 1935, when Congress made the first appropriation for it. Thereafter Congress
provided funds for the WPA for no more than a year at a time,
and on several occasions that body felt obliged to make supple-
mental appropriations in order to avert some feared consequence such as militant activity by the Workers Alliance.
Depending on what pressures Congress was responding to, the
numbers of WPA workers varied from year to year. In 1936 the
average number employed on WPA in any month was nearly 2
million. The figure for 1937 was 2.2 million; for 1938, 1.8
million; for 1939, 2.9 million; for 1940, 1.9 million; and for

1941, 1.6 million. By February 1943, the WPA was out of existence.

What did the unemployed do when they got jobs on the WPA? They built nearly 600,000 miles of new roads and repaired 32,000 miles of existing roads. They built 75,000 bridges and repaired another 42,000. They installed over 1 million culverts, built 2,800 storage tanks and reservoirs, put in nearly 23,000 miles of storm and sanitary sewers, constructed 880 sewage disposal plants, and repaired nearly 400 more. Two hundred fifty-six new landing fields for airplanes appeared as a result of WPA labor, and nearly 400 old airports were repaired. The WPA workers constructed nearly 6,000 athletic fields and playgrounds and repaired nearly 2,000 more. Because of the WPA, people all over the country could enjoy nearly 6,000 new swimming pools, and nearly 2,000 old pools were repaired. Works Progress Administration labor built nearly 1,700 new parks, fairgrounds, and rodeo grounds; 5,584 new school buildings; and 1,500 new administration buildings in addition to repairing nearly 80 million library books, exterminating unknown numbers of rats, and serving nearly 900 million school lunches.

A related project, the Civilian Conservation Corps (CCC), employed in nine years a total of 2.5 million young men. They left cities to live in 400 remote camps, where they built thousands of miles of hiking trails, planted millions of trees, fought hundreds of forest fires, laid 45,000 miles of telephone lines, and built 42,000 dams.

The list of benefits to society of the unleashed energy of the unemployed, skilled and unskilled, goes on and on. And these workers were not the only ones in the jobless community who improved the quality of life of their compatriots. Pressure from organized white-collar workers brought projects into existence for artists, musicians, and theater people. Richard Wright tells in *American Hunger* how some of the pressure for projects began:

> I sat through several meetings of the [John Reed] club and was impressed by the scope and seriousness of its activities. The club was demanding that the government create jobs for

unemployed artists; it planned and organized art exhibits; it raised funds for the publication of *Left Front;* and it sent scores of speakers to trade-union meetings. The members were fervent, democratic, restless, eager, self-sacrificing.

In New York, an early response to the clamor of unemployed white-collar workers was the formation of the Emergency Work Bureau, which gave meager support for a short time to artists who sought jobs doing what they had been trained for. On September 23, 1933, twenty-five of the jobless artists formed an organization soon to be called the Unemployed Artists Group. They wrote to Harry Hopkins asking for a federal project for unemployed people in their field. In response, Hopkins set up a Public Works Art Project (PWAP) under the Treasury Department. The PWAP, which operated in New York under the director of the Whitney Museum, was not really a work relief project. Because it employed a number of artists who were not taken from the relief rolls, the unemployed artists were not satisfied. Their organization grew and became the militant Artists Union (AU).

The Artists Union held demonstrations in front of the Whitney Museum and demanded an expansion of the program. Soon branches of the AU appeared in many cities, and as a national organization it began in January 1935 to press Congress for a federal arts bill to establish a federal department of fine arts. This campaign did not succeed, but the WPA did make provision for the insistent artists. Soon thousands of them were at work painting murals, making prints, turning out easel paintings, making posters, shaping sculptures, and teaching art classes for children.

The interests of the Artists Union went beyond getting jobs. The organization wanted audiences for art and facilities for art education that would be open to all. As a result of these proposals, more than 100 community art centers grew up in various parts of the country.

Even while such expansion was going on, cuts in appropriations were frequent. The task of agitating for funds to maintain all of these activities kept the Artists Union busy. By December 1937, it had become a full-fledged trade union with 2,500

402 / America before Welfare

members under the umbrella of the United Office and Professional Workers of America, which belonged to the rapidly growing Congress of Industrial Organizations.

In his introduction to *Art for the Millions*, an anthology of eloquent statements by WPA artists, Francis V. O'Connor commented on the "militancy on the part of American artists — a militancy which was peculiar to the 1930's." American art, with its federal financial support, was more vital than it had ever been. Statistics are not usually well suited to art, but figures for the output of the WPA/FAP (Federal Art Project) give some idea of the productivity of those who worked on the projects. According to O'Connor, 2,566 murals were painted in public places as a result of the WPA/FAP (Federal Arts Project) program. These murals were in addition to many that were created by the earlier short-lived PWAP. Artists in the Federal Art Project turned out 108,099 easel paintings and watercolors, 17,744 sculptures, and 11,285 fine prints. In addition, they made 35,000 WPA posters and 22,000 plates for the Index of American Design.

Theater workers among the unemployed had special problems. Because the motion picture industry made it possible for a very few actors to reach a very large audience, actors, directors, and stage designers were rapidly losing jobs even before the beginning of the depression. The fund for jobless actors that was administered by Actors Equity was not equal to supporting the growing number who were out of work. In New York, a group of twenty-five actors realized that the only remedy lay in getting financial help from public sources. They set up an acting company to provide entertainment in schools, and they got support from the city's Recreational Department. This aid, however, was only a tiny drop in a very large bucket. Clearly, only the federal government could handle their problems. Before the end of 1934, actors' organizations proposed that the government employ jobless theater workers on a project that could use their professional skills.

Harry Hopkins, head of the WPA, responded to this proposal by asking Hallie Flanagan to set up a theater project. Hopkins and Flanagan had gone to Grinnell College together, and he knew that she had rare energy and innovative talent. Under her guidance, in an amazingly short time, the Federal Theater was producing plays all over the country before audiences that had never before had a chance to enjoy any legitimate theater. People in Harlem were seeing actors of African descent perform Shakespeare. Children in schools and patients in hospitals were able to enjoy plays. A new kind of dramatic entertainment called the *Living Newspaper* became very popular; it reenacted important current events and introduced audiences to some fundamental aspects of the real world in which they lived. Because the Federal Theater vividly reflected many aspects of contemporary life, it attracted the opposition of reactionaries and was the center of enormous controversy.

Musicians, like actors, suffered from technological unemployment. Mechanical recordings made it possible for commercial theaters to dispense with live orchestras. Just as other artists did, jobless musicians sought for and got WPA jobs that kept their special skills alive. At the same time, they were able to enrich the lives of audiences far from the few big music centers in the country.

The unemployed with other skills found jobs on other projects of a less spectacular kind. Archivists and clerical workers preserved and brought order to countless old documents and public records. Jobless architects made scale drawings of historic buildings, thus preserving for posterity information about the past.

"American literature, no less than American music, art and theater, came of age in the period of the Depression; and the Federal Writers Project, like the other [WPA arts projects] . . . expressed this new maturity." So wrote William MacDonald in *Federal Relief Administration and the Arts*. Many literary critics share this view of the accomplishment of the project, but not many of them have paid attention to how the *American Guide Series*, the greatest achievement of the project, came into being.

In *The Dream and the Deal*, a history of the Writers Project, Jerre Mangione speculated that the *American Guide Series* originated with an FERA administrator in Michigan. Other people, both private citizens and government employees, had also suggested that guidebooks to various states would be good projects. Finally Henry Alsberg, director of the Writers Project, asked two women who had government jobs to write a prospectus for the guidebooks. They provided the format that was followed successfully in producing the best guides ever to appear in the United States. Most of this suggesting and planning took place after the establishment of the Federal Writers Project. Mangione's account of the project's origins overlooks the initiating role played by unemployed workers. Of this episode I have some firsthand knowledge.

Shortly after Roosevelt took office in 1933, a group of unemployed writers in New York followed the example of others who were jobless and formed an organization, the Unemployed Writers Association. Most of the writers were young, and many had been members of the John Reed Club. One was Leon Srabian Herald, a poet of Armenian origin who on occasion wrote for the *New Republic*. The chairman of the Unemployed Writers Association was Robert Whitcomb. At first the association met in his tiny Greenwich Village apartment. Very soon a much larger gathering place was needed — one large enough to hold nearly 1,000 people. Following a meeting of this large membership, the association sent a plan for a writers project to Harry Hopkins.

The WPA still had not acted on the proposal by the time of the National Convention Against Unemployment, in Washington, February 3–5, 1934. The Unemployed Writers Association sent three delegates — Robert Whitcomb, Leon Herald, and me — to the convention with instructions to press the WPA for action on behalf of writers. The committee of three met with Aubrey Williams, assistant to Harry Hopkins, who agreed on a rough plan for a guidebook to New York City as a pilot project. On February 26, 1934, when no action had taken place, writers Robert Whitcomb, Fanya Foss, and Samuel Putnam sent the following telegram to WPA headquarters: "Unemployed Writers Association membership of one thousand must know immediately for mass meeting what is being done about our project.... Please wire answer." Whitcomb reported this campaign in the *Commonweal:*

When money comes through a proportion will be allocated to writers, depending on how many unemployed writers there are; there of course will not be enough to take care of them all. Who asks for money from Congress, who estimates how much there should be? Why, it is Harry L. Hopkins who asks Congress for so-much. All right, then the writers demand that a lump sum be asked of Congress for the writers; we demand that each and every unemployed writer be planned for, in advance.

The Authors' League, many of whose members were out of work, also asked the WPA for funds, and money for the *New York Guide Book* did materialize. The pilot project did work out, and the Unemployed Writers Association, which had become the Writers Union, continued to push for guidebooks in all the states. Through one of its members (me), ten writers were proposed and accepted as state directors of the projects, and the guides began to appear.

In all, fifty-one major volumes in the *American Guide Series* were published, and there were numerous lesser publications. Other books of folklore and oral history came from the previously unemployed writers whom the project supported. At its peak in April 1936, a total of 6,686 writers, researchers, and others were employed on the Writers Project. At one or another time during its eight years of existence, the following men and women were among those on its payroll: Ralph Ellison, John Cheever, Conrad Aiken, Nelson Algren, Richard Wright, Saul Bellow, Edward Dahlberg, Margaret Walker, Jack Conroy, Vardis Fisher, Frank Yerby, Katherine Dunham, Studs Terkel, Maxwell Bodenheim, and Kenneth Rexroth.

Not all was peace and quiet on the project, however. The same political currents that sent turbulence through the rest of the unemployed movement affected the writers. Indeed, they were especially contentious, possibly because they were skilled communicators to whom ideas were very important. But in spite of disruptions, a great deal of work got done and a great deal of published work resulted. A great deal more work was never published because the project was abruptly ended. (Ann

Banks went through some of this abandoned material and produced a fascinating book of oral histories, *First Person America*. Other researchers may find other ways of continuing the contribution of yesterday's unemployed to the readers of today.)

From the beginning, many influential individuals and organizations opposed the WPA. They never gave up the view dating from Elizabethan times in England that it was not the business of the central government to relieve poverty. In addition, they objected to the taxes that were necessary to finance federal relief.

As the economy shifted more and more to producing for war, the objections of many businessmen to the WPA became more strident, and their objections became more influential with members of Congress. One of the representatives who held considerable influence on the Appropriations Committee was Clifton A. Woodrum, a Democrat from Virginia, long an ardent advocate of preparedness. In the first years of the Roosevelt administration, Woodrum had supported relief appropriations, but as war approached his position shifted. He found he could get strong support if he attacked appropriations for relief, and he mounted a campaign against the WPA and the organizations of the unemployed. In this effort his activities followed those of the House Committee on Un-American Activities (HUAC), and like the members of that committee, he made great use of red-baiting.[2] Through committee hearings he got nationwide publicity for allegations that the arts projects in particular were Communist-dominated. The red-baiting had its effect among the general public. President Roosevelt, who had supported the arts projects, now saw no political advantage in continuing to do so. As Jerre Mangione reported from firsthand observation, FDR's interests had shifted by May 1939 to the war in Europe, and he gave no support to the projects, which were under severe pressure. The result was that Congress killed first the Federal Theater, then the other arts projects, and finally the WPA as a whole.

For most of the unemployed blue-collar workers, there were now job openings in the war-vitalized economy. But for artists of all kinds, the great period of creativity had ended. Some of the painters, writers, musicians, and actors could find ways to use their talents in the war effort — if they could prove they were not "reds." But for the most part, those who had produced the cultural renaissance of the depression years had to take jobs outside their chosen professions. If they managed to stay in their professions, they found a whole range of subjects on which they had to be mute. Having to be silent, to engage in self-censorship, was burdensome for people whose business in life it was to communicate.

35

Marching to a Different Drummer: Federal Workers Section (Minneapolis) (1935–1939)

Fascism is nothing but capitalist reaction; from the point of view of the proletariat the difference between the types of reaction is meaningless.

— Leon Trotsky
What Next, 1932

Fascism is the open, terrorist dictatorship of the most reactionary, most chauvinistic and most imperialist elements of finance capital.

— Georgi Dimitroff, general secretary of the CI at its 1935 Congress

Events in Europe sometimes had a strong impact on unemployed organizations in the United States. This happened when the Comintern called for demonstrations on March 6, 1930. It also happened after the anti-Communist Nazis took power in Germany in 1933. Radical organizations everywhere debated how best to respond to the expanding fascist aggression against workers and their organizations and against middle-class democracy. For the unemployed in the United States, the debate was between those who advocated all-out resistance to administrators of relief, who were regarded as agents of capitalism, and those who advocated the seeking of allies, including some among personnel in the relief apparatus.

In the first part of the 1930s, Communists had been on the offensive, but after Hitler took over Germany, the initiative lay with the Fascists. How should Socialists, Communists, and middle-class targets of Fascism deal with the growing threat? Indeed, how should rival capitalists respond to the Fascist capitalists who clearly wanted to replace them? This new political phenomenon had first appeared in Italy, then moved to Germany, and aimed to take over everywhere. "Tomorrow, the world!" was one of Hitler's slogans. If Fascism prevailed, would the plight of the jobless grow worse than it already was? Some radicals said, "Yes"; others said it couldn't get worse.

At the 1935 Congress of the Comintern, Georgi Dimitroff, the Bulgarian who was general secretary of the CI, proposed a strategy for dealing with Fascism. He advocated a coalition or united front of anti-Fascist forces. This coalition of all the groups that had reason to oppose Fascism soon became known as the Popular Front. It was widely adopted and contributed to the defeat of the fascist upsurge.

What Dimitroff proposed in 1935 was a defensive posture. It meant that groups that had been competing with each other for leadership of the working class should cease their sometimes destructive rivalry and work together against a common enemy. For Communists it meant abandoning their sterile dogma that Socialists were "Social Fascists" — that is, hidden allies of the Fascists. For the Socialists, the United Front or Popular Front meant that they would have to give up their long-held suspicions of the Communists. It meant that Socialists and Communists would have to cooperate, which the two parties had not done in Germany, where, as a consequence, Hitler had come to power. In the unemployed organizations, the Popular Front meant that the Communist-led Unemployed Councils and the Socialist-led Workers Alliance would work together.

The Popular Front also meant a shift away from fighting all capitalists and a shift toward collaborating, temporarily, with some of them. This development seemed to certain radicals to be a betrayal of the working class. Followers of Leon Trotsky, whom Stalin had driven out of the Soviet Union, held that view, and wherever Trotskyists had influence, they continued uncompromising opposition to the Popular Front. They would not cooperate with capitalists or any of their institutions.

In Minneapolis, where Trotskyists had influence, they led hostile actions in which relief workers pressed for better pay and better conditions. In these actions, the unemployed had a powerful ally in a local of the International Brotherhood of Teamsters. Trotskyists controlled this local and were able to do what Stalinists and Musteites had always advocated but had not always been able to accomplish. They made a very close linkage between workers who were employed and those who were out of jobs.

In the spring of 1935, General Drivers Local 544 of the Teamsters set up an auxiliary organization called the Federal Workers Section. Its function was to organize the unemployed, particularly those on work relief. One of the leaders of this section was Max Geldman, who left an unpublished memoir of his activities among the jobless. Another leader was Edward Palmquist who, according to Geldman, was a courageous person but impulsive and likely to see everything in terms of black or white. Also prominent among the Minneapolis Teamsters and the unemployed were three brothers, Grant, Ray, and Miles Dunne, all Trotskyists and all brothers of CP member William Dunne, who disagreed completely with them. William Dunne had been a spokesperson in Washington for the 1931 National Hunger March organized by the Unemployed Council.

For Grant, Ray, and Miles Dunne, the Unemployed Council was anathema. They contended that it had betrayed the unemployed, and they and Palmquist and Geldman fought the council with as much vigor as they fought the relief officials. Geldman's contribution to attacking bureaucrats was not only as an organizer. In his memoir (as quoted by Farrell Dobbs), he said:

On the workers education program, a project developed after the Works Progress Administration was set up by Roosevelt, we used to write and enact plays dealing with the plight of the unemployed. I wrote one which didn't have much of a plot. The opening scene told how Mr. Smith, employed on a good job for years and years, comes home and informs his family he has been laid off and there is no possibility of his being rehired or finding a new job. The next scene has the family gathered in their living room. A woman in a fur coat, note pad and pen in hand, is seated before them and conducting an interview along the lines of the customary abusive treatment received by applicants for public relief. This scene had a devastating effect on every audience before which we played. Those present sobbed, lived again through their own bitter experiences and hissed and booed our actress relief investigator.

The mass of unemployed hated the relief setup: resented the indignities they were subjected to; shed tears over their plight; and broke out in angry actions such as protest demonstrations, sit-ins at state capitals, hunger marches, and raids on food warehouses in which food was expropriated and distributed to the needy.

Farrell Dobbs, in *Teamster Politics*, emphasized the objection that the unemployed had to the "made work" that had been concocted by the early work relief programs of the New Deal. The unemployed, he said, felt confused when one relief program was withdrawn and another put in its place, as often happened. Dobbs considered these numerous changes to be deliberate efforts to upset the organizations of the unemployed. After they had set themselves up to deal with one group of problems, the organizations found that those problems had disappeared when the project with which they were associated was terminated. Each new project brought about a different grouping of relief workers who faced new and different problems. In effect, the jobless had to create an entire new organization whenever one project was replaced by another.

Geldman, again quoted by Dobbs, added:

The workers soon found that there was not much satisfaction in working on WPA projects. In the cities they were usually paid $60.50 a month, plus distribution of surplus food products. The wage was less in rural areas, around $40.00 a month in northern states and even lower in the South. Whatever the rate, it was hardly enough to keep body and soul together. Besides, there was little dignity in the assigned work. Here and there something useful was accomplished, like the belt-line road around Minneapolis, or the murals painted by needy artists on post office walls and public buildings, but for the great part it was unproductive, made-up, busywork.

Considering the billions spent that could have been used to creative ends, it was like dumping products to maintain high prices and fat profits. The labor power of millions was wasted, so as not to upset the balance of the capitalist system.

In their fight against capitalist bosses, the Trotskyists in Drivers Local 544 of the Teamsters saw a valuable resource in the unemployed. Through its Federal Workers Section (FWS), the local, with its established structure, was able to mobilize large numbers of the jobless to help in truckers' strikes. In return, the truck drivers gave real, stabilizing help to relief workers as they went about handling their grievances.

With the aid of the FWS, relief workers often obtained increases in relief payments. Following confrontations with relief authorities, they also obtained higher family budgets from the City Council. These confrontations, said Dobbs, had the result of establishing in Minneapolis one of the highest relief budgets in the United States.

John Stockham, who studied the FWS for his master's thesis at Ohio State University, reported on one episode in the effort to prevent a cut in the relief budget: "A number of representatives of the various unions, the Workers' Alliance and the Federal Workers Section appeared before the Welfare Board in protest against this procedure. Max Geldman of the Federal Workers Section acted as chairman of the delegation. As a result, the budget was immediately rescinded."

As the FWS pursued its campaigns for improved relief, it continued to quarrel with the Unemployed Council, with its successor organization, the United Relief Workers Association, and still later with the Workers Alliance of America (WAA). In an official statement of the Socialist Workers Party (the Trotskyist), directors of the FWS criticized the political activity of the WAA:

[It] is a dead certainty that the attempt to tie the Alliance to the kite of one of the capitalist parties, which is pledged to maintain the rotten system that has brought so much misery and pain to the unemployed in particular, is a decidedly reactionary step. It not only does not bring the workers closer to their goal — it pulls them farther away from it. It is a cynical betrayal of the Alliance membership and of the position taken by its convention.

The main job of the American working class today is to break away, most rapidly and most drastically, from their dependence upon the political parties of their enemy, the capitalists. The main job is to find the road to independent working-class political action, with a militant program of struggle directed against the capitalist government and its system.

Commenting on those who criticized the WAA for being merely lobbyists and not being sufficiently militant, Herbert Benjamin told an interviewer, "We didn't go around to beg or to plead with Congressmen or to bribe them to do something for us. We went there to make it hot for them, to put heat on them. And the only kind of heat we could put on them that they would respect was mass action, mass heat."

36

United We Stand — Divided We Fall
(1936–1942)

Bolshevism is knocking at our gates. We can't afford to let it in. We have got to organize ourselves against it, and put our shoulders together and hold fast. We must keep America whole and safe and unspoiled. We must keep the worker away from red literature and red ruses; we must see that his mind remains healthy.

— Al Capone, gangster, in *Liberty Magazine*

The only way to save our empires from the encroachment of the people is to engage in war, and thus substitute national passions for social aspirations.

— Empress Catherine of Russia

The master class has always brought a war and the subject class has always fought the battle. The master class has had all to gain and nothing to lose, and the subject class has had all to lose and nothing to gain.

— Eugene V. Debs, Socialist leader
imprisoned for opposing World War I, 1918

"They parade; they protest; they make demands; they write millions of letters to officials. . . . They are irreconcilable . . . they never stop asking. They state their demands in every conceivable way. They crowd through the doors of every relief station and of every WPA office. They surround social workers on the street. They exhibit the American spirit of determination." So wrote Nels Anderson, director of the Section on Labor Relations of the Works Progress Administration in the *Survey*

Graphic in March 1936. He went on to say, "As far as I know there is no nationwide organization of the unemployed."

One month later, there was such an organization, the Workers Alliance of America. Merged in it were the Workers Alliance, the Unemployed Council, the Unemployed League, and some small independent organizations. The road to unity had not been smooth, although all the major unemployed organizations and most of the scattered minor ones publicly favored unification. Many Socialists remembered the pre-Popular Front days when they had been called "Social Fascists" by the Communists. Moreover, the Communist emphasis on mass pressure was hard for many Socialists to accept, and they continued to be primarily interested in education and in nonconfrontational negotiating techniques and parliamentary procedures.

Over the years, letters from organizers of the Unemployed Leagues to A. J. Muste had revealed their anti-Communist attitude. For example, Elmer Cope wrote on November 11, 1932, of an unemployed conference in Ohio: "[The Unemployed Councils] handled themselves so well that the uninitiated were led to believe that they could be trusted." A little later Cope wrote, "It is pretty much agreed that we will have to keep the Communists entirely out of our organization. At the convention we will adopt a constitution which will make it impossible for them to get in and gain a foothold." Such suspicions continued, and Unemployed Council overtures for unity at that time were rebuffed.

Suspicions also existed between the Musteite-led Unemployed Leagues and the Socialist-led Unemployed Citizens League in Chicago. These were basically turf wars. They were widespread and not easily handled, but by 1935 most Socialist-led organizations and part of the Unemployed Leagues had come together and formed the Workers Alliance of America. Only the Unemployed Council and a few small independent groups remained outside the WAA. The UC at least wanted to be included, and it finally was included early in April 1936, after delicate negotiations. The finally united Workers Alliance of America remained united until the eve of the entry of the United States into World War II.

The unity of the unemployed organizations did not happen in a vacuum. Nels Anderson, in the Survey Graphic article quoted above, made clear that the federal government (the Roosevelt government) had "accepted relief responsibility reluctantly" and had continued the federal program with only "temporary intentions." However, the long-term nature of unemployment — and the insistence of the organized unemployed — was forcing the government to reassess its aims. "We are approaching the point," said Anderson, "where the government will have to decide whether it can quit."

The organizations merging into the WAA said emphatically it could not quit. And the problem of keeping the government in the relief business was a powerful force that held the unemployed together in one national structure.

At the time of the 1936 unity convention, every unemployed organization was weaker than it had been earlier. David Lasser noted the weakness of the Unemployed Council in his report to the convention, but he did not mention a major reason for the lowered membership and activity of the council. Some of the most effective leaders of the UC (and the WAA and UL) had left the unemployed movement for full-time employment as organizers for the Congress of Industrial Organizations, which was suddenly appearing in the center of the labor world. Another reason for the weakness of the UC was that in its desire to promote the unity of all unemployed organizations, the Communist Party had directed some of its unemployed members to drop out of the UC, join the Unemployed Leagues, and put their energies into building one unified organization. This decision was costly to the UC. Its activity and membership dropped, but Lasser and others interpreted the drop only as evidence of sectarian flaws in the practices of the organization.

Weakened the UC was, Herbert Benjamin admitted in a discussion with national CP leaders. "For us unity was absolutely essential. . . . We couldn't afford to go along without it. . . . That is why we made certain concessions [in the unity negotiations]. . . . The Unemployed Council by themselves did not represent any more the majority of the unemployed."

As part of the campaign for unity, the Unemployed Council participated in circulating a pamphlet, *A Handbook for Project Workers*, written by Benjamin, that aimed to build morale among relief workers and to increase rank-and-file support for a single nationwide organization. One morale-building feature of the pamphlet was the following table showing the results of militant actions by relief workers in 1935 (see Table 36.1).

The process of achieving unity at the convention in Washington, April 7–10, 1936, was not easy. Some delegates who were Old Guard Socialists wanted delays. Trotskyist leaders, including now A. J. Muste, gathered in Washington and met with delegates, but to many present it was not clear what policy they were recommending. Many national CP leaders were also in Washington, observing and advising. Norman Thomas, the Socialist leader, was a featured speaker at the convention. Frank Morrison, a leading official in the American Federation of Labor, also spoke. The convention was a major event in the affairs of labor and the Left, and in spite of the dealing that went on as each group maneuvered for position, the unemployed as a whole benefited. What had been three major organizations and a number of minor ones became a single entity able to bring increased pressure on behalf of the jobless. Altogether, 600,000 dues-paying members were incorporated into one national formation. David Lasser was elected president, and Herbert Benjamin organization secretary. (See Appendix O for the text of the WAA constitution.) Among the twenty-seven members elected to the National Executive Board (NEB), there was no political grouping that had a majority. Although the UC, the first organization to propose unity, had only seven members on the NEB, there were eleven CP members on the board. The Socialists on the board were divided into three groups, some Old Guard in their sympathies, some Trotskyist, and some not identified with either of these groups. Among the Socialists were no African-Americans; the three who were on the board were either UC members or were nominated by UC members.

With all the major tendencies in the unemployed movement now committed to working together, many in the WAA saw

Some Successful WPA Strikes and Stoppages (Compiled by Labor Research Association)

Date	Location	No. Involved	Grievances*	Outcome*
Aug. 7–Sept. 24	New York City	1,500 skilled	$93.50 for 120 hours	Won $93.50 for 60 hours**
Aug. 21	New York City	1,000 white-collar workers, 90 projects	Failure to receive back pay for three weeks	Won a $1,000,000 gift hapment — not a wage payment
Aug. 21–22	Chicago, Ill.	600 mostly unskilled	$75 on relief, $55 on WPA	Won reduced hours of work
Sept. 11	Allentown, Pa., and vicinity	1,000 unskilled	$55 for 140 hours	Won 10 percent wage increase and reduction to 120 hours
3 Weeks to Oct. 7	Walker Co., Ala.	2,500 unskilled	Cut from 30¢ to 15½ ¢ an hour — 140 hours	Won rate of 27¢ an hour for 116 hours***
Oct.	Somerset Co., Pa.	2,000 unskilled	31¢ an hour	10 percent wage increase and reduction to 128 hours
Oct. 10	Madison Co., Ala.	500–600	Same as Walker Co., above	Same as Walker Co., above
Oct.	Prince George and Montgomery Counties, Md.	100, mostly construction workers	Wages $32	Won wages of $45
Oct.	Princess Anne, Md.	100 woodcutters	$32 for 140 hours	10 percent increase in wages and reduction to 130 hours
Oct. 28–31	Cumberland, Md.	100, mostly unskilled	28.6¢ an hour for 140 hours	Won prevailing wage of 50¢ an hour for 126 hours
Oct. 30	Reading, Pa.	1,000 skilled and unskilled	Low wages for unskilled and below union wages for skilled	Won $60.50 for 120 hours for unskilled
Nov. 8–12	Allegheny Co., Pa.	500	Failure to receive back pay	Won back pay
Nov. 16–21	New York City		Demanded payment for holidays	Won payment for holidays
Nov. 21	Pittsburgh, Pa.	500	Back pay demanded	Won regular and full payment
Nov. 26–29	Chicago, Ill.	1,500, Reese Park Project	Back pay	Won back pay
Nov.	Newport News, Va.	50	Back pay	Overdue checks paid Nov. 28
Dec. 3–7	Key West, Fla.	1,500 unskilled	Wage increases	a 25 percent increase to $30, with corresponding increase in working hours
Dec. 10–14	Greensboro, N.C.	White and Negro	Back wages and increase in wages	10 percent wage increase and guarantees of regular pay; reduction in hours and other concessions
Dec. 6	Baltimore, Md.	13,000–14,000 skilled and unskilled	$45–$79 for 140 hours	10 percent increase for all; 130 hours for unskilled, 108 hours for skilled
Dec. 30	Detroit, Mich.`	900, A.S.R. Project	Back wages	Secured for 8,000 project workers overdue wages in time for New Year

prospects for a permanent organization with many hundreds of thousands of members — a labor organization allied with the AFL that would give the jobless a position of dignity and importance on the national scene.

The new strength of the WAA was made evident on November 2, when it was able to circulate a copy of an agreement signed by Harry Hopkins assuring the WAA that it had the right to organize relief workers. But the WAA was not yet strong enough to get an appointment with the president: When Lasser and Benjamin appeared at the White House in an effort to see FDR, they were arrested.

The militant mood of the WAA after the unity convention showed itself in various ways. In Kentucky the folk poet Don West collected songs for the Alliance. One of them, by Jim Garland, sung to the tune of "Greenback Dollar," went this way:

Give Me Back My Job Again

I don't want your millions, mister,
I don't want your diamond ring.
All I want is the right to live, mister —
Give me back my job again.
. . . .
Yes you have a land deed, mister,
The money all is in your name,
      But where's the work that you did, mister,
I'm demanding back my job again.

In New Jersey, members of the WAA engaged in a dramatic performance that focused attention on the fact that the legislature was doing nothing to solve a severe crisis in the funding of relief. On April 20, David Lasser managed to address the legislature in the Assembly Chamber. The legislators listened as he told them they were sitting on a volcano, but they took no action. The next day, members of the WAA moved into the Assembly Chamber when the regular session adjourned, and there the jobless remained. Day after day they stayed, mimicking the mannerisms of the legislators, which they had carefully observed, and following all the rules of procedure as they debated and passed ridiculous laws. The jobless occupiers slept in their seats, just as the elected lawmakers often did. They smoked imaginary cigars and made windy speeches — and forced the elected legislators to hold their meetings elsewhere. Amazingly, the legislators made no move to evict the unemployed from the Assembly Chamber.

The histrionics of the WAA did not bring immediate solutions, but the people of New Jersey learned that there was a real relief crisis and that their elected officials were doing nothing about it. The jobless learned that the WAA was very busy trying to serve their interests. The educational effect of the sit-in was extended still further by a widely circulated pamphlet, "The Trenton Siege of the Army of Unoccupation," written by George Breitman, state organizational secretary of the WAA and a Trotskyist.[1]

In Pennsylvania, unemployed workers also responded dramatically to the approaching cut off of relief. The WAA called a statewide convention to be held in Harrisburg, the capital, May 10. To make the gathering as effective as possible, columns of hunger marchers from all over the state converged on Harrisburg. They arrived one day before relief funds were to run out. Fearing that the WAA would occupy the State House as it had in New Jersey, the legislators hastily recessed and had "Closed for Repairs" signs hung on the doors of the Senate and House chambers.

The May 10 hunger march was not immediately successful. More marches followed in the summer of 1936 before the Pennsylvania legislature finally appropriated funds to keep relief going.

In New York, a demonstration was held inside the building where WPA administrator Victor Ridder had offices. Ridder later told a Rotary Club meeting how he prepared for the event. He said he "instructed the guards to see to it that no one who came up for that demonstration would get out of the hospital inside of two weeks, or, if they got out of the hospital inside of two weeks, I would drop all of the guards." Later, in 1938, after the

Workers Alliance had forced his removal, Ridder boasted of this incitement to violence in testimony he gave before the House Committee on Un-American Activities (HUAC).

The militant mood of the WAA continued through its next convention, held in Milwaukee in 1937. At that time, events in Spain drew the attention of the unemployed. Fascists were invading the Spanish Republic, and the WAA voted to send David Lasser to the beleaguered country to carry a message of support.

When the Works Progress Administration announced that 600,000 WPA workers would be dropped July 1, 1937, the WAA sent 2,000 delegates on a job march to Washington. The action prompted one congressman, Clifton A. Woodrum of Virginia, to warn that the WAA would soon be a powerful political organization unless the federal government shifted relief back to the states and municipalities. If this did not happen, said Woodrum, no congressman would be able to win reelection without acceding to WAA demands.

The post-unity vigor in Washington and industrial centers in the East and Midwest also reached areas that had been very little touched by the labor movement. In San Antonio, Texas, a city with a large Hispanic population, the Workers Alliance, led by Emma Tenayuca, made labor history.

Tenayuca was born in 1916 of a mother whose Mexican ancestors had settled in the San Antonio area in 1793. Her father was a Cherokee Indian. When Emma was 6 or 7 years old, her father took her to a local park to hear Anarchists and members of the IWW talk about justice. Labor and civic concerns interested her increasingly from that day on. In Catholic high school she joined a discussion club whose members stayed together after they graduated and published a little newspaper that showed deep concern about social questions.

When Emma Tenayuca was 18, she saw a photograph of the local police chief putting on new boots and boasting that he would use them to kick some women cigar workers who were on strike. Immediately, Tenayuca took a step she had never taken before: She joined the cigar workers' picket line. There she protested when she saw the police mistreating women, and she was arrested. It was her first arrest, but by no means her last.

About this time she was attending political meetings held by Socialists and Trotskyists, but she did not join either group. After its unity convention, Emma Tenayuca heard of the Workers Alliance of America, and in this organization she saw something she liked. "Communists and Socialists got together," she said. Soon she became active in the WAA. On January 29, 1937, she organized a sit-in in the San Antonio WPA offices to protest the announced layoff of thirty WPA workers. She was arrested and tried, but not found guilty of any breach of the law. The police, apparently angered, went a few days later to the headquarters of the Workers Alliance and trashed the place.

At about this time, Tenayuca finally decided to join the Communist Party. Before another year was out, she emerged as leader of what was apparently the largest strike that had ever taken place in Texas. It was not a strike of relief workers, but it showed the close linkage that the Alliance made between jobless workers and those who were employed. Workers in the pecan-shelling sheds had been getting only $2.73 a week, and when they were laid off, as they were periodically, many of them had been joining the Workers Alliance. There, they got to know Emma Tenayuca, who had learned a lot about organizing. In 1937 she pulled together workers first in one pecan-shelling shed, then in another. In a very short time, 10,000 walked off their jobs, and they elected Emma Tenayuca honorary chairperson of the strike, which was ostensibly run by a union[2] to which she did not even belong.

The strike was successful. The pecan shellers got higher wages and the right to organize, and the Workers Alliance in San Antonio grew until it had 10,000 members. But the success of the Alliance and the union had created enemies. The union was attacked as Communist-dominated, and union officials, hoping to evade the charge, brought great pressure on Emma Tenayuca to withdraw from her leadership of the pecan workers. The Communist Party, also hoping to reduce red-baiting of the union, asked her to resign, and she did. But she continued to be active in the Workers Alliance. In 1937 she went to

Milwaukee as a delegate to the national convention of the WAA and was elected to the National Executive Board.

Another person on the board was an African-American woman, Frankie Duty, also a Communist. Frankie Duty, mother of three, was born in Georgia, where she had graduated from college as a music major. Later she sang in many church choirs and choruses in New York. In 1934, she had to go on relief, but in 1935, city officials relied on rumors that she had hidden wealth and cut off her relief. In January 1936 she asked the Unemployed Council for help. The Harlem local of the council came to her rescue, got her back on relief, and got an aggressive new leader in the process. The local, which consisted of only 5 members when Frankie Duty joined it, soon grew to 350 members. They all became members of the Workers Alliance following the unity convention. After she joined the National Executive Board, Frankie Duty continued to be active in her community. On one occasion she directed an all-night sit-in at a Harlem Home Relief Bureau.

Such actions went on in many places. In a pamphlet published in 1937,[3] the WAA summarized events that followed the reelection of Roosevelt. Addressing workers who were on relief or who were on work projects, the pamphlet read:

> Do you remember what happened right after the elections last November? The Works Progress Administration announced that 475,000 W.P.A. workers would be fired. No sooner did we hear this than the Workers Alliance members and branches in all parts of the country went into action. We had expected something like this to happen and we were prepared.
>
> Throughout the country a wave of protest actions began. By means of sit-downs, sit-ins, stoppages, picketing, demonstrations, mass meetings, we showed our enemies that we were prepared to hold our own. Delegations marched to city officials. Resolutions and telegrams came pouring into the offices of Congressmen, as well as the President and Harry Hopkins. Within a few days it was plain that something had to be done, and the U.S. Conference of Mayors called a special meeting in Washington. They sent frantic telegrams to the President, who was then in South America. The result was an announcement that "it was all a mistake." There would be no mass layoffs.

A few weeks later, the newspapers reported that the President would ask for only $500,000,000 as a deficiency appropriation to keep W.P.A. going for the rest of this fiscal year, because there was no money left. Again the Workers Alliance went into action. We pointed out that this was not enough to keep W.P.A. going; that it would mean hundreds of thousands of W.P.A. workers would be fired.

We prepared our own program, which called for an appropriation of $1,040,000,000, so that those already on W.P.A. might keep their jobs. This included enough money to add 300,000 more jobs and increase the wages of all W.P.A. workers by 20 per cent.

But presenting this program to the President and Congress was not enough. To back up these demands the Workers Alliance called demonstrations in every city in the country. We enlisted the cooperation of trade unions and other progressive organizations. Within a period of about two weeks we succeeded in carrying through a march to Washington which brought nearly three thousand elected delegates to the capital from all parts of the country.

Our action was so impressive that President Roosevelt immediately raised his request to Congress from $500,000,000 to $655,000,000.

The WAA engaged not only in mass pressure but in broadly educational activities as well. For example, in Alabama it elected several delegates to represent it at a meeting in Birmingham called by the Southern Conference for Human Welfare. Among those present were Eleanor Roosevelt and Supreme Court Justice Hugo Black. The conference drew close to 16,000. One of the speakers was Hosea Hudson, an African-American Communist and a WAA delegate.

I spoke that evening [he said] on the question of more relief for the unemployed people, more jobs, and an increased wage scale, because we were then only getting $40 and 40 cents a month on the WPA. These was the things we talked about, was hoping the conference would address itself to, that something would come out of this conference on the wage question of the South.

A lot of these delegates was attending that conference, they tried to put that under the rug. It was a ticklish question, cause it would infringe on their relationship with some of the good white industrialists in the South — these schoolteachers, professors, them kind of people at this conference.

The WAA also sought to serve other groups who were victims of the continuing depression. For example, David Lasser appeared before the Ways and Means Committee of the House of Representatives in March 1939 and gave detailed testimony in support of a bill to increase the Social Security pension of workers age 60 and older. The WAA plan, much more modest than the Townsend Plan, was to increase monthly pensions to sixty dollars.

Toward the end of 1938, the House Committee on Un-American Activities (the Dies Committee) had begun to call the WAA "Communist" and "a Communist front." At the same time, a large factional fight had erupted in the WAA in New York City. Several locals accused the WAA of being Communist-dominated. They withdrew and started a separate organization that was called Trotskyist by the locals that remained in the WAA. Communists were indeed active in the various projects of the WAA. In Washington, D.C., Phillip Bonosky, a CP member and president of the D.C. WAA local, arranged for a group of women who were protesting relief cuts to meet with Mrs. Roosevelt in the White House. Bonosky has described this encounter in an article in *Mainstream:*

We brought together about 50 of our women members, who were mostly Negro in that Jim Crow capital, and proceeded to the White House at the appointed hour. Our women had put on their best clothes for the event and were terribly excited. I cannot understand why I was so blasé about it then, except that politically the atmosphere had changed and Mrs. Roosevelt was not my favorite person. In any case we ranged ourselves around the Blue Room where, the story in the newspaper next day noted, Mrs. Roosevelt "has greeted visiting royalty." We were not royalty. In her column *My Day*, Mrs. Roosevelt was to write:

I have just met with as heart-rending a group of
people as it has been my misfortune to see in a long
time; largely a colored group, though some white
women were among them. They came to tell me of
their helpless situation and I can best describe it by
telling you one woman's story. She was laid off WPA
last August [this was April, P.B.] and has a bed-ridden
mother, a sister and a nephew living with her. She
lived until January 4 by begging and borrowing and
then was put back on WPA. The tears stood in her
eyes when she told me she was laid off again and had
an eviction notice and was to appear in court tomorrow morning. Two months' rent is due, and even by
attempting to rent out some rooms she cannot meet
the payments. In the District there is an understanding in the Public Assistance Division that no employable person may be given relief. . . . The cut has come
in WPA and people have to be laid off, and what is
going to happen to them? How would you meet this
situation?

That last question was so typical of her. Coming almost as
an anti-climax, it betrayed her approach to the problem of
poverty and unemployment as a purely sociological one; it was
still an appeal to the conscience of the rich. . . .

The news account that appeared in the newspaper the
following morning described us this way: "Thirty-one neatly
dressed and respectable-looking citizens, about half white
and half Negro, stood in a silent row around the circular walls
of the stately reception room, while President Phillip Bonosky
of the District Workers Alliance read a prepared statement
describing inadequate local relief." We had resounding titles to
cover our poverty — "president" at least!

The statement, long lost by me, is partly resurrected in the
press account, which quoted me as saying:

"The women for whom I am spokesman are all women
who have recently been laid off WPA and find themselves stripped of all resources and completely helpless to support themselves and their families. Not only
do they find it impossible to get private employment,
but they find also that they are not permitted to

receive district relief. There is no industry here into which they can be absorbed. The District Employment Center has informed them that there are already 40,000 people awaiting jobs on its list; and the Public Assistance Division informs them they are ineligible for direct relief because they are able-bodied.

"An average of more than 300 people a month are turned away from District Public Assistance Division because they are 'employable,' although their need has been established and they have no resources whatsoever.

"Such a restriction on eligibility for relief exists in only two other U.S. cities the size of Washington. Also, of 18 leading cities, Washington pays the lowest relief grant, in spite of the fact that rents are highest in the country and living costs among the highest."

In September 1939, a new and unexpected crisis troubled the WAA. Along with many other American organizations, the WAA found it could not ignore events in Europe, where Communist Soviet Union had signed a nonaggression pact with Fascist Germany. The USSR had previously tried and failed to get just such a nonaggression pact between itself and Britain and France. The Soviet Union was now convinced that imperial Britain and France (and the United States) wanted Germany to move eastward against it. The pact with Hitler was an effort to stop that.

This development took the unemployed, and everyone else, by surprise. The WAA had been strongly anti-Fascist and anti-war, but now the United States government and the press made it appear that the USSR had abandoned the anti-Fascist camp and was in alliance with war-making Germany. Some now proposed that the WAA condemn the Soviet Union and side with Britain and France. On the other hand, Communists and many non-Communists in the WAA believed they saw the U.S. government moving toward support of one side in a war in which both sides were imperialist in their objectives. Socialists and many with no Left leanings disagreed. They interpreted American steps toward rearmament as steps toward fighting Fascism. With this as a starting point, antagonisms began to grow on issues much closer to home than foreign policy, and these antagonisms began to threaten the unity of the WAA.

Indicative of the climate in which the WAA was trying to operate was a letter sent on June 28, 1939, to Stephen Early, press secretary to President Roosevelt, by George Creel, a powerful figure in the Democratic Party. Creel enclosed a report written by Kate Richard O'Hare, whom he praised as a careful researcher and whom he identified as a "rabid Socialist." O'Hare's report maintained that the WAA was Communist-controlled. She said, "It [the WAA] is the biggest and sharpest tooth of the wolf that has finally arrived." O'Hare said that she had known Herbert Benjamin for more than thirty years and that he was the "real brains and power behind the throne" in the WAA. She also alleged that there was an agreement whereby the WAA "runs things at the bottom" and in return did not interfere with the grafters at the top of the government's relief apparatus. Such a report to a man close to the president certainly did not smooth the road for the one national organization of the jobless.

David Lasser, as WAA president, often encountered redbaiting. When a reporter for the *San Francisco Chronicle* asked him about allegations that the WAA was under Communist control, Lasser replied that no more than 1 percent of the WAA membership was Communist and that talk of Communist control of his organization was all "plain bosh" (*San Francisco Chronicle*, December 18, 1938).

Nevertheless, many forces, including well-publicized hearings held by the HUAC, had their effect on the WAA and on Lasser. In 1938 he had been expelled from the Socialist Party because of his Popular Front–style activities in the WAA. In September 1939, when the German-Soviet pact caused great turmoil in all Popular Front movements, including the WAA, Lasser sided with the Roosevelt administration on the pact, and he became more isolated in his organization. He wanted to leave his post, and he made this known to Eleanor Roosevelt, with whom he had become friendly. Mrs. Roosevelt reported Lasser's desire to the president. The president sent word back to Lasser, urging him to stay in the organization, to rid it of Communists, and to change its name.[4]

Instead of continuing to insist that talk of Communist domination was "plain bosh," Lasser decided on a different approach. He tried to get rid of the most obvious target of the red-baiters: He asked Benjamin to resign. But Benjamin had the confidence of non-Communist as well as Communist leaders of the organization, and the National Executive Board of the Alliance opposed his resignation.

The red-baiting of the WAA did not let up. In an effort to reduce the attacks, which were, he believed, limiting the usefulness of the WAA, Earl Browder, head of the Communist Party, now made the same proposal that Lasser had made. He asked Benjamin to leave the WAA. Benjamin did resign, and he went on to do other work for the CP. Later, in his unpublished memoirs, he wrote of his regret at leaving the unemployed movement to which he had devoted what he regarded the best years of his life.[5]

Benjamin's sacrifice did not stop the red-baiting attacks on the WAA, but his absence did weaken the organization. In addition to the departure of some of the most effective UC members for full-time employment on the staff of the CIO, several leaders of the Unemployed League and the pre-unity Workers Alliance had become organizers of the new industrial unions. The Socialists who remained in the WAA were not very active. More and more of the work of the organization was being done by people who were either members of or close to the Communist Party.

It was not easy for Lasser to purge the WAA of Communists. They had worked hard to defend the interests of the unemployed and to build the WAA. Not many WAA members felt much enthusiasm for expelling them. These internal factional squabbles caused many WAA members to lose interest and drift away. Meanwhile, attacks by reactionaries were intense. On May 20, 1940, immediately after Roosevelt announced his proposals for military buildup, Lasser met with the president to discuss what he called "the problem of the unemployed in national defense." A month later, on June 18, 1940, Lasser resigned and issued a strong attack on Communists in the Alliance, including Benjamin, who had already resigned. Perhaps Lasser had forgotten a song by Henry George Weiss that had appeared in the first issue of his paper, the *Workers Alliance:*

> If "red" means bread
> For wife and kid,
> A job for you and me,
> Why be afraid of being red,
> Of wanting work, of wanting bread?
> If organizing means we're red,
> Then red's the thing to be!

Lasser expanded his attack on the CP and Benjamin in a series of articles in the *New York Post.* What Benjamin thought of Lasser appears in some handwritten undated notes that were among his papers:

> Relationship with Lasser closer, more amicable than with anyone in all my political career. — The first thing to understand — we each were most useful precisely because of our differences. — We had to set an example — prove to our respective constituencies that we could maintain our differing political views, affiliations, and loyalties even while serving a common org [sic] and immediate program — And we did it —

In the same vein, Benjamin wrote the following in a letter to historian James E. Sargent on August 31, 1981: "Lasser was never a Communist. Never a dedicated Socialist. He believed he was a Socialist for a short time. Mostly he was an able, ambitious liberally-disposed opportunist, I worked well with him. We got along well together. I think FDR had much to do with the unification [of the unemployed organizations]. I know FDR directed the dissolution of our Alliance."

A few weeks after resigning from the WAA, Lasser tried to start a rival organization of unemployed and relief workers. He issued a call for an American Security Conference to be held in Chicago August 19, 1940. Lasser kept Roosevelt informed of the steps he was taking, and he said his aim was to found an organization that was "100 percent American and free of -isms."

His new effort never had much influence among the unemployed.

The WAA grew steadily weaker as it was badgered by investigating committees and as unemployment decreased with the arrival of war orders in the factories of the United States. The dwindling organization could not last much longer. What David Lasser thought about the last days of the Workers Alliance fifty years after it disbanded is not known; he refused to be interviewed for this book.[6]

On the eve of the United States' entry into World War II, the organization that David Lasser, Herbert Benjamin, and countless unemployed workers had built came to an end. It left behind a remarkable record. The WAA and its predecessors had prodded the federal government into assuming responsibility for the unemployed, had persistently fought off governmental efforts to give up that responsibility, and had saved the lives and health of a vast number of Americans. In addition, the Alliance and its predecessors had created a body of thousands of workers who had learned a great deal about how to organize and get results. One of them was Emma Tenayuca, who said more than fifty years later, "We [in the Workers Alliance] were fighting against poverty, starvation, fighting against high infant death rate, disease and misery. Believe me . . . I'd do the same thing again."

Epilogue

Why does this account of organizations of the unemployed end with the beginning of World War II, although mass unemployment was continuous after the end of that war and is present to this day — whatever this day may be?

One reason is that a major phase of history ended with the beginning of the Second World War. Another reason is that I will be 83 years old when this book appears. I don't have enough time left to bring the story up to date. Any exploration of the continuing actions of the discarded portion of the working class will have to be done by a younger person. I hope such a person appears and has the vision to see strong new life taking root among the debris of our society, which, like me, has passed its prime.

I began work on this book shortly before the 1936 unity conference of unemployed organizations. At that time I had spent nearly two years editing newspapers for the Unemployed Council. At intervals after 1936, whenever I was not working for a living — in other words, when I was unemployed — I continued to dig into the history of the jobless.

Since the day when the first page of the book came from my typewriter, a world war has raged and subsided. A cold war has come and is going as I conclude. In that period, the portion of the world economy in which private employers could prevent employees from doing work that needed to be done grew smaller. In the same period, the area expanded in which the state promised economic security to workers. Nevertheless, mass unemployment has continued in the United States, and is now expanding in some countries that were formerly Communist. "By conservative estimates," wrote William Serrin in the *Nation,* January 23, 1989, "some 16.5 million people in the

United States are unemployed and want work, or work part-time but want full-time jobs. That is an unemployment rate of nearly 14 percent, not 5.4 percent as the Bureau of Labor Statistics would have us believe — and still other jobless can be added in."

I like to think that my obsession with the jobless will be of use to the 16.5 million of my compatriots who at this late date still cannot find enough work. It is unlikely that they will discover that patterns borrowed from the past will make perfect blueprints for the future, but these patterns may give some useful hints about how the jobless can rid themselves of a great burden — and how they can help society rid itself of a great shame. It is not possible in the fast-changing world to spell out all the specific steps that the jobless must take, but it is possible to know that masses of people moving in unison can force concessions from those who can give jobs but don't do so. And it is possible to foresee that in fully democratic control of the economy lies a solution to the great waste that is unemployment and that is inseparable from the system we still have with us.

I hope this book tells people there are better times ahead because there are people who will insist on creating them.

Acknowledgments

Before acknowledging my indebtedness to the many people who have given all manner of help as I have worked on *Impatient Armies of the Poor*, I must express my deep overall obligation to my wife Mary Elting Folsom. From the beginning she has given unstinting aid of every possible kind including expert editorial assistance. The book would not have been possible without her support.

Timely completion of the project was greatly helped by a grant from the Margaret S. Mahler Institute of the Gray Panthers. The grant made it possible for Carrie Jenkins to do research and conduct interviews in San Francisco; Los Angeles; Chicago; Washington, D.C.; New York; and Boulder, Colorado. She also provided editorial help on the final version of the text and played a major role in preparing the bibliography.

For patient typing of earlier drafts and for transcribing my longhand scrawls, I am more grateful than they may know to Sarah Van Keuren, Karen Benge Rosson, and Abby Fountain.

I must also thank the following for a great variety of courtesies graciously offered and gratefully received:

Regina Ahram, library technician, Interlibrary Loan, University of Colorado, Boulder

Bruce H. Akers, vice president, Ameritrust Company, Cleveland, Ohio

James S. Allen, former editor of *The Southern Worker*

Myron B. Allerton of the Historical Society of Pottawatomie County, Council Bluffs, Iowa

Peter Allison, Tamiment Library, New York University

Donald Amter, custodian of Amter Papers

Dr. Herbert Aptheker, historian

Gary J. Arnold, assistant archivist, Ohio Historical Society, Columbus

William Asadorian, assistant curator of manuscripts, New York Historical Society, New York City

Betty Bacon, researcher

Bill Bailey, former unemployment activist

Cynthia J. Beeman, historian, State Marker Program Texas Historical Commission, Austin

Ernst Benjamin, custodian of the Herbert Benjamin Papers

Jody Berman, editor, University Press of Colorado

Patricia Bleich, Social Sciences Department, Omaha Public Library, Omaha, Nebraska

Steve Bloom, Fourth International Tendency, Brooklyn

Phillip Bonosky, author and former unemployment activist

Boulder (Colorado) Public Library Reference Desk

Virginia Bouche, department head, Interlibrary Loan, University of Colorado, Boulder

Richard Boyden, National Archives, Washington, D.C.

Beth Brannen, archivist, State Historical Society of Iowa, Des Moines

Dr. Paul Buhle, Oral History of the American Left, Tamiment Library, New York University

Leslie Burger, copy editor

Ann Caiger, manuscripts librarian, Pelham D. Glassford Papers, University of California, Los Angeles

Cedar Rapids Public Library, Cedar Rapids, Iowa

Elvira Chavaria, librarian, Mexican American Library Program, Austin, Texas

Kenneth Cobb, deputy director, Municipal Archives, New York City

J. Robert Constantine, Eugene V. Debs Foundation, Terre Haute, Indiana

Sarah Cooper, Southern California Library for Social Studies and Research, Los Angeles, California

John Corns, researcher

Council Bluffs Public Library, Council Bluffs, Iowa

Nancy Dahlberg, researcher

Mike Davidow, author and former unemployment activist

Albert Deutsch, social worker

George E. DLaid, former unemployment activist

Dianne Feeley, unemployment activist

Eugene Ferrara, photo librarian, *Daily News*, New York City

Peter Filardo, collection assistant, Tamiment Library, New York University

Bob Flood, Omaha Public Library, Omaha, Nebraska

Fred G. Folsom, lawyer

Michael Folsom, historian

Rachel Folsom, former student activist

Sender Garlin, historian

Shevi Geldman, former unemployment activist

Simon W. Gerson, journalist and former unemployment activist

Joyce Giaquinta, Iowa State Department of History and Archives, Iowa City

Erika Gottfried, librarian, Tamiment Library, New York University

W. Douglas Gow, Federal Bureau of Investigation, Washington, D.C.

Ronald J. Grele, director, Oral History Research Center, Butler Library, Columbia University, New York City

Mary Jo Guinan, Douglas County Historical Society, Omaha, Nebraska

Professor emeritus E. R. Hagemann, University of Louisville, Kentucky

Jim Hanselman, teacher

Dorothy Healey, former unemployment activist

Professor Darlene Clark Hine, vice president, Purdue University, and head of Black Women's History Network, West Lafayette, Indiana

Jane E. Hodes, Niebyl Marxist Library, Berkeley, California

Carol Humphrey, design and production manager, University Press of Colorado

Anita C. Hurley, researcher

Eunice and Herbert Huse, researchers

Arnold and Aurelia Johnson, former unemployment activists

Professor Howard Kimelsdorf, Department of Sociology, University of Michigan, Ann Arbor

Kathy Knox, associate reference archivist, Emory University, Atlanta, Georgia

Tab Lewis, National Archives, Washington, D.C.

Elizabeth K. Lockwood, Civil Reference Branch, National Archives, Washington, D.C.

Kathrine Marris, researcher

Ann Matlin, librarian, Reference Center for Marxist Studies, New York City

Dale C. Mayer, archivist, Herbert Hoover Library, West Branch, Iowa

Phyllis E. McLaughlin, Iowa State Department of History and Archives, Iowa City

Harriet McLoone, assistant curator, Americana Manuscripts, The Huntington Library, San Mateo, California

Emil P. Moschella, chief, Freedom of Information Act/Privacy Section, Federal Bureau of Investigation, Washington, D.C.

National Archives and Record Service, Still Pictures Branch, Washington, D.C.

Frances C. Pestalozzi, researcher

Walter M. Pflug, assistant director, Walter P. Reuther Library, Wayne State University, Detroit, Michigan

James B. Potter, state archivist, Nebraska State Historical Society, Lincoln

Dr. Albert Prago, historian

Jay Quadracci, photographer, *Daily Camera*, Boulder, Colorado

Nora Quinlan, head of Special Collections, University of Colorado Libraries, Boulder

Al Richmond, former unemployment activist

Leonard S. Rodberg, Institute for Policy Studies, Washington, D.C.

Joann Ronzio, teacher

Carl Ross, Minnesota Historical Society, St. Paul

Professor James E. Sargent, History Department, Virginia Western Community College, Roanoke, Virginia

Kenneth P. Scheffel, Bentley Historical Library, University of Michigan, Ann Arbor

Jeff Schneider, historian

Leo Seltzer, photographer

Philip C. Settles, word processor

Tom F. Shelton, Institute of Texas Cultures, University of Texas, San Antonio

Beth Shulman, historian

David E. Skaggs, representative, U.S. Congress, 2nd District of Colorado

John Skarstad, assistant department head archivist, Department of Special Collections, The University Library, University of California, Davis

Ann Snuggs, chief operations staff, Information Access Branch, U.S. Department of State, Washington, D.C.

Social Sciences Department, W. Dale Clark Library, Omaha, Nebraska

Walter J. Stack, former unemployment activist

John Stevenson, director, Graduate Program, English Department, University of Colorado, Boulder

Dorothy Swanson, head librarian, Tamiment Library, New York University

Raymond Teichman, supervisory archivist, Franklin D. Roosevelt Library, Hyde Park, New York

Emma Tenayuca, former unemployment activist

Jeff Thomas, reference archivist, Ohio Historical Society, Columbus

Ann Burlak Timpson, former unemployment activist

Margy Vogt, The Massillon Museum, Massillon, Ohio

Professor Alan Wald, Program in American Studies, University of Michigan, Ann Arbor

Dave Walter, reference librarian, Montana Historical Society Library, Helena

Grace Warfield, manager, Mahler Institute of the Gray Panthers

Edward C. Weber, head librarian, Labadie Collection, University of Michigan, Ann Arbor

Reid Williams, researcher

Luther Wilson, director, University Press of Colorado, Niwot

Carl Winter, Midwest Labor Institute for Social Studies, Detroit; former unemployment activist

Alfred J. Young, detective and curator, Police Academy Museum, New York City

Rita Yribar, special collections librarian, Texas Women's University, Denton

Arthur Zipser, historian

Permissions

I thank the following:

Donald Amter, for permission to reprint the excerpt on pages 289–291, from *The Memoirs of Israel Amter and Sadie Van Veen* , unpublished.

Phillip Bonosky, for permission to reprint the excerpt on pages 425–426, from "A Letter to Mrs. Roosevelt," *Mainstream*, January 1963.

Jacques de Spoelberch for the excerpt on page 246 from Alexander Richmond, *A Long View from the Left: Memoirs of an American Revolutionary*, Boston: Houghton Mifflin, 1973. Copyright 1973.

Harvard University Press, for permission to reprint excerpts on pages 262–263, 329, 424–425, from *The Narrative of Hosea Hudson: His Life as a Negro Communist in the South*, by Nell Irwin Painter. Copyright 1980 by the President and Fellows of Harvard College.

Charles Kerr Publishing Company for permission to reprint the Rudyard Kipling poem on page 214, from *International Socialist Review*, February 1914; for the Covington Hall poem on page 212, from *International Socialist Review*, April 1914; for the Reginald Kauffman poem on page 216, from *International Socialist Review*, May 1814; for the Joe Hill excerpt on pages 201–202, from *International Socialist Review*, December 1914.

Industrial Workers of the World, 3435 N. Sheffield #202, Chicago, IL 60657, for permission to reprint on pages 330–331 Mrs. Mary Atterbury's "Depression Hits Robinson Crusoe's Island," *Industrial Worker*, 1932; for permission to reprint on page 214 Ralph Chaplin's "Solidarity Forever," from *Songs of the Workers to Fan the Flames of Discontent*, 34th Edition, 1974; Joe Hill's "The Preacher and the

Slave," page 204; "Hallelujah I'm a Bum!" page 192; and from an undated earlier edition of *Songs of the Workers*, "Bill Brown Came a Thousand Miles," page 203–204.

Meiklejohn Civil Liberties Institute, PO Box 673, Berkeley, CA 94701, for permission to reprint on page 302 Maurice Sugar's "Soup Song," from *The Ford Hunger March*, 1980.

The Nation magazine, for permission to reprint the Edward Dahlberg excerpt from an article entitled "Hunger on the March," December 28, 1932, page 335–338. Copyright 1932 by The Nation Company, Inc.

For excerpts on pages 246–249, reprinted from *Steve Nelson, American Radical*, by Steve Nelson, James R. Barrett, and Rob Ruck, by permission of the University of Pittsburgh Press. Copyright 1981 by University of Pittsburgh Press.

New Outlook Publishing Company, for permission to reprint excerpts on page 317, from Jack Douglas, *Veterans on the March*. Copyright 1934.

For excerpts on pages 410–411, 411–412, from *Teamster Politics*, by Farrell Dobbs. Reprinted by permission of Pathfinder Press. Copyright 1975 by the Anchor Foundation.

For the excerpt on pages 392–393, from Jacob Fisher, *The Response of Social Work to the Depression*. Copyright 1980 and reprinted with the permission of Twayne Publishers, a division of G. K. Hall & Co., Boston.

Eugene Winick, Attorney-at-Law, for permission to reprint on page 206 the Upton Sinclair poem "Frank Tannenbaum in Prison," from *International Socialist Review*, June 1914.

Appendix A

Petition of Unemployed Sailors, 1808

The full text of the 1808 petition of unemployed sailors as published in the *Evening Post* (New York):

To the Hon. Mayor of the City of New York:

Hon. Sir:

Our situation is not only distressing, but truly alarming. The Embargo lately levied on our shipping has not only destroyed all employment by Sea, but rendered it impossible to gain a sustainence by our labor on shore. Our humble petition, to you Sir, is to know how we are to act in this case, and to beg of you to provide some means for our subsistence during the winter, should not the embargo be immediately taken off. What has America to boast of but her Agriculture and Commerce? The destruction of one will mean the ruin of the other.

The greatest part of the wages due us from our last voyages is already expended, and more, we are already indebted for our boarding. By what means shall we discharge these debts? Should we plunder, thieve, or rob, the State prison will be our certain doom.

In a handbill this morning, you tried to dissuade us from our purpose, mentioning that provision was made for objects of pity. We are not objects of pity yet, but soon shall be, if there is not some method taken for our support. We are the most part hale, robust, hearty men, and would choose some kind of employment rather than the poor house for a livelihood. We humbly beg therefore, you will provide some means for our subsistence, or the consequences may not only prove fatal for ourselves, but ominous to the flourishing Commerce of America, as we shall be necessitated to go on board foreign vessels.

Saturday, January 9, 1808

Appendix B

An Unemployment Manifesto, 1873

Manifesto

The Federal Council of the North American Federation
To The Working People Of North America!
Fellow-Workingmen!

The present conditions of society have virtually become a repetition of the brutalities and barbarism of the middle ages.

At those dark times the laborers and industrials were forced by sheer violence to give up the results of their labor to the highwaymen. That was the nobility of the country who despised labor but considered it a good thing and quite honorable to live on the labor of others. All political power, the making and executing of laws, being monopolized by those highwaymen themselves, by the nobility, there was no redress for the producing classes, no law to protect them.

Our actual situation is precisely similar. The present nobility and those highwaymen, called great industrialists, railroads and manufacturing companies and the like, who consider it quite as natural and fair, as the noblemen of the middle ages to live and prosper on the work of others, taking special care for spreading the cloth of legality over their ill-gotten gains and protecting by law not only their treasures, the products of labor appropriated by them, but even the swindling operations of those unholy speculators bent upon realizing hundreds of millions at once.

Now, workingmen, where is your share of these millions? What part of these treasures is allotted to those who create them all?

Your share is the misery resulting from being thrown out of work by the failure of the wild speculation of the ruling class! The part of treasures allotted to you are the shallow phrases of our modern noblemen and reduced wages if you are working.

These evils have grown to such an extent that today there are hundreds of thousands of workingmen, without employment and consequently without means to support themselves and their families, who are suffering for want of the necessities of life. And this state of hopelessness, fellow workingmen, is it not maintained greatly by our own fault?

Have you not listened so long and patiently to the siren voices of the capitalists and their mouthpieces, the press, singing the chant of harmony between capital and labor, identity of interests between those two poles of present society? Alas! You lent your ears too long to those captivating tones of harmony, clouds surrounded your judgement, and you closed your ears to the warring voices of your fellow workers, of those of your co-laborers, who told you always and will tell you ever; There is no harmony between capital and labor, but strife, incessant strife, only to be ended by the complete subjugation of one or the other, and the only way to guard against the subjugation of labor, to advance the interest of workingmen is to organize the forces of labor, to combine and centralize them. Capital, organized and wielding the whole power of the state, can never be conquered or brought to terms by the unorganized disconnected masses of labor. To avoid the fate of slaves all workingmen must organize, combine their forces, increase their numbers and centralize their powers.

The criminal practices of the wealthy classes and the corrupt connivance of the government have brought about the present disasters and disturbances of credit and business, whose consequences are adroitly shifted on the shoulders of the working masses. The workingmen are dismissed and thrown on the street, cold and hunger staring in their faces and inviting them to examine that boasted harmony between capital and labor. Want of solidarity amongst ourselves has given our capitalist rulers the opportunity to act as they like. The absence of fraternal bonds of Union between the manifold divisions of labor has prevented successful resistance to the encroachments of capital til now. Shall this state of degradation continue forever? No, workingmen, no! Workingmen, don't be deluded by the phrases of your oppressors! They will preach free trade for the benefit of the working classes, but enact a protective tariff. They will talk of equality before the law, but make laws against your organization. They will assert the inalienable right to the persuit of happiness but live in luxury, whilst you are deprived of the necessities of life. They will chant Liberty but drill their mercenaries for assaulting and crushing you. They will praise justice, but build prisons and poorhouses for you, and this last is certainly that business wherein they manifest earnestly and without reserve their goodwill and sincere intentions towards you. During the last few days, the whole capitalist press shouted War Against Spain, liberty for Cuba! The cry of distress of the working people must be overhauled and the war — a men-slaughtering en masse — is another blessing of the governing class to the benefit of labor.

Should not the working men be thankful for so much benevolence?

Why, the benevolence itself is an insult to the working class, who have earned by the sweat of their brow the right to demand, not to beg what is due. The working men don't want charity, but work, they scorn alms, but claim the products of their labor for its equivilance, for securing a human existence to themselves and families. Our watchword, therefore, will be: fair work—fair living and woe to the traducers and oppressors of labor.

Organize then, fellow working men, unite and combine to form a living wall such as will be able to withstand the storms from whatever quarter they may come — and the extortion of capital and the misery of labor will belong to the past — and our children and grandchildren will bless the day of our union, the great union of all working men.

We submit and recommend to you the following plan of organization, put into effect already sucessfully by our German fellow workers:

The working men of one, two or more blocks form a district club; the district clubs combine to form Ward Committees, the Ward committees will form a central body by deputizing three (3) delegates from every such Ward committee.

The united working men thus organized will make the following demands to the respective authorities.

1) Work to be provided for all those willing and able to work, at the usual wages and on the 8 hours plan.

2) An advance of either money or produce, sufficent for one week's sustenance, to be made to laborers and their families in actual distress.

3) No ejectment from lodging to be made for non-payment of rent, from December 1st, 1873 to May 1st, 1874.

More than 200,000 working men are residing in New York and the same proportions are existing in almost every city and state of this country. Would it not be an easy thing for this vast majority of the adult citizens to put a stop to the vile practices of capital, to the greediness and the pillaging habits of our modern highwaymen? Could or would any authorities, legislative or executive, be bold enough to resist our demands, if sustained by the undivided front of the laboring masses?

FELLOW WORKINGMEN AROUSE AND UNITE!

By order of the Federal Council, N.A., Federation I.W.A.

F. Bolte, Sec.

From the *Communist*, June 1931.

Appendix C

Announcement of an Unemployed Meeting, 1874

A Monster Mass Meeting of the Unemployed

Will be held at Tompkins Square, Tuesday, Jan. 13, 1874, at 11 AM.

All the unemployed people of this city, irrespective of occupation, are invited to be present on that occasion, likewise all those who are in sympathy with the suffering poor of this city!

Fellow-working men! Your committee of Safety has done its duty; it remains for you to do yours.

We have laid before the City authorities the demand you requested us to make. No Answer. They ignore your committee! Will they ignore you? By the

Committee of Safety

Appendix D

Announcement of an Unemployed Meeting, 1874

Working-men — Attention — Nineteenth Ward!

Winter is upon us and nearly all employment has been suspended. Cold and hunger are staring in our faces. Nobody can tell how long the misery will last; nobody will attempt to help, if we don't do something ourselves.

Now is the time to meet and consider how we are to get work, food, clothing, and shelter.

The Germans are organized; why not the Irish, English, and other nationalities? Come, let us work together. In unity there is strength.

Let every man attend the Ward meeting Saturday, Jan 10th, at 8PM, Concordia Hall, Forty-first St., between Second and Third Avenues, to make necessary arrangements for the monster Mass-meeting, Jan. 13, 1874. By the order of the

Safety Committee

Appendix E

A Petition of the Unemployed of New England, 1894

A PETITION TO THE UNITED STATES
CONGRESS IN BEHALF OF THE
PEOPLE OF THE COUNTRY.

This winter the working people of the United States have suffered as never before, although the country's wealth and supply of food are almost beyond the reach of figures. This shows an economic condition profoundly wrong. But it is only the exaggeration of an evil every year growing more pronounced and dangerous. The rank and file of the working people of the country, both farmers and artisans, are receiving as wages so small a part of what they produce that they are being degraded, and often they are without the necessaries of life. How long do you think the Republic will stand if this injustice continues? The country is already a plutocracy. The wealth power must be curbed and civilized or our days of National happiness and prosperity are numbered.

We therefore request you:

I. To provide farms and factories where the unemployed now and at all times hereafter may be able to apply their labor productively for the supply of their own wants.

II. To take steps to amend the Constitution of the United States so that it shall affirm the right of every one to have work.

III. To abolish interest-bearing bonds.

IV. To furnish immediate employment for the unemployed by beginning the construction of good roads on a large scale throughout the country.

V. To nationalize the Railroads, the Telegraph, and the Mines.

VI. To see that all land not in actual use is thrown open to cultivation by those who are willing to cultivate it.

VII. To establish a commission to investigate the advisability of nationalizing Trusts.

Endorsed by many meetings of working men in New England and brought to Washington by the New England Industrial Delegation.

Adopted by the Delegation in special session, May 29th, 1894, Washington, D.C.

(The signatures of Morrison I. Swift and many others follow. This petition is in the National Archives.)

Appendix F

Coxey's Bills, 1894

1. The Good Roads Bill. — 53rd Congress, 2d Session, H.R. 7438, June 12, 1894.

A BILL to provide for the improvement of public roads, and for other purposes.

Be it enacted by the Senate and the House of Representatives of the United States of America in Congress assembled, That the Secretary of the Treasury of the United States is hereby authorized and instructed to have engraved and have printed, immediately after the passage of this bill, five hundred millions of dollars of Treasury notes, a legal tender for all debts, public and private, said notes to be in denominations of one, two, five, and ten dollars, and to be placed in a fund to be known as the "general county-road fund system of the United States," and to be expended solely for said purpose.

Sec. 2. That it shall be the duty of the Secretary of War to take charge of the construction of the said general county-road system of the United States, and said construction to commence as soon as the Secretary of the Treasury shall inform the Secretary of War that the said fund is available, which shall not be later than sixty days from and after the passage of this bill, when it shall be the duty of the Secretary of War to inaugurate the work and expend the sum of twenty millions of dollars per month pro rata with the number of miles of road in each State and Territory in the United States.

Sec. 3. That all labor other than that of the office of the Secretary of War, "whose compensations are already fixed by law," shall be paid by the day, and that the rate be not less than one dollar and fifty cents per day for common labor and three dollars and fifty cents for team and labor, and that eight hours per day shall constitute a day's labor under the provisions of this bill, and that all citizens of the United States making application to labor shall be employed.

2. The Non–Interest Bearing Bond Bill. — 53rd Congress, 2d Session, H.R. 7463, June 15, 1894.

A BILL to provide for public improvements and employment of the citizens of the United States.

Be it enacted by the Senate and House of Representatives of the United States of America in Congress assembled, That whenever any State, Territory, county, township, municipality, or incorporated town or village deem it necessary to make any public improvements they shall deposit with the Secretary of the Treasury of the United States a non-interest-bearing twenty-five-year bond, not to exceed one-half of the assessed valuation of the property in said State, Territory, county, township, municipality, or incorporated town or village, and said bond to be retired at the rate of four per centum per annum.

Sec. 2. That whenever the foregoing section of this act has been complied with it shall be mandatory upon the Secretary of the Treasury of the United States to have engraved and printed Treasury notes in the denominations of one, two, five and ten dollars each, which shall be a full legal tender for all debts, public and private, to the face value of said bond and deliver to said State, Territory, county, township, municipality, or incorporated town or village ninety-nine per centum of said notes, and retain one per centum for expense of engraving and printing same.

Sec. 3. That after the passage of this act it shall be compulsory upon every incorporated town or village, municipality, township, county, State or Territory to give employment to any idle man applying for work, and that the rate be not less than one dollar and fifty cents per day for common labor and three dollars and fifty cents per day for team and labor, and that eight hours per day shall constitute a day's labor under the provisions of this act.

The texts of these bills are from Coxey's publication, *Cause and Cure*, Vol. 2, No. 2.

Appendix G

A Petition of the Unemployed, 1894

The United States Industrial Army is composed of many thousands of unemployed American citizens, and represents, by general consent, millions of unemployed or partly unemployed and underpaid workingmen. They have naught but their ability to labor to provide for themselves and families, and the average wealth possessed by them would not purchase a decent coffin.

A portion of this army is now encamped near Washington, thousands more are on the way and thousands now languish in jail who from hunger were driven to trespass on railroad property. For years they have peacefully and hopefully awaited for private and public enterprise to give them work, and their condition is now such that their loyalty to the laws of the land is being put to a very severe test, as witness the violent outbreaks that are becoming so alarmingly frequent and are so ominous of catastrophe to the nation. Political liberty is a mockery where economic slavery exists.

This army is organized in the interests of peace and, apart from the borrowing of transportation in an emergency, it has been, and will continue to be, law abiding, half starved and ragged as it is, thus showing to the world an example of patient endurance and determination that is unparalleled in history.

Had we the time and facilities we could have brought a ton's weight of petitions from the poverty-stricken masses.

They ask for immediate employment on public works at fair wages or else national assistance to supply their own wants by cooperative industry.

To have our leading industries nationalized and the product or service to be furnished at cost.

Free coinage of silver and a legal-tender currency issued direct to the people.

To have the immigration of foreign laborers stopped until there is a demand for their labor or until the serfdom of the wage earner is abolished.

Therefore, as the hour of adjournment approaches and our needs are urgent, we the undersigned, at the request of the army and the millions it represents, do respectfully petition your honorable body to pass some measure of immediate and temporary relief.

Petition of the unemployed, Camp Rosslyn, August 1, 1894. The signers were Lewis C. Fry, Los Angeles, Cal.; Arthur Vinette, Los Angeles, Cal.; Thos. Galvin, Los Angeles, Cal.; Frank Cantwell, Seattle, Wash.; Chas. T. Kelly, San Francisco, Cal.; Geo. Howard, San Francisco, Cal.; Sh. Thomas, Cincinnati, Ohio; Chas. Clark, Minneapolis, Minn.; Allen Jennings, Indianapolis, Ind.

From 53rd Congress, 2d Session, *Senate Miscellaneous Document* No. 251.

Appendix H

A Resolution of the Boston Unemployed, 1914

The Right To Steal

Resolutions adopted by the Boston Unemployed on Boston Common, March 14th, 1914.

We, the Unemployed of Greater Boston, having learned that the rich are completely hard hearted toward us in our suffering from want of work, that they prefer to reduce us to the degradation of pauperism or let us starve rather than to open their full pocket-books to give us work;

Having learned from facts that they think more of their dogs and dog shows than they do of us, and that they go on flaunting their criminal wealth-wasting social functions in the face of our desperation while many of us are driven to eat garbage from the restaurant pails to keep life in our bodies, and to sleep on the Common or in alleys;

Having learned that the rich rob us of the wealth which we create, and play commercial poker among themselves to see who shall have the most of it, and call that earning it;

Therefore, Resolved: That here on historic Boston Common we enact a new morality.

We declare that every one has an absolute and inalienable right to work; that if he is deprived of this he is robbed of the means of life and therefore of life itself; that this is not only robbery but the committal of constructive murder against him by society; that in thus casting him out from all social care and protection society excludes him from the operation of its laws and absolves him from all duty of obedience to them; that he is thenceforth authorized and obliged to preserve life by his own efforts; that he must therefore take food, clothing and shelter where he can, regardless of social edicts against his doing so.

We consequently advise the unemployed everywhere to steal food and whatever else they need to maintain their health and welfare, and we affirm that it is stealing only in name and not in fact. Society forces it upon them and society is the primary thief and criminal by doing so, and by robbing them of all fundamental rights of man. A society which does this must either admit the inalienable right to steal, or must expect revolution and dissolution in chaos. The primal rights of man are supreme, above the artificial laws of a greed caste and the servile lawmakers who are commanded by them.

That a statement of this new union and advice to follow it be sent out to the unemployed of the United States.

These Resolutions were passed at a large meeting of the unemployed with but one dissenting vote.

MORRISON I. SWIFT, Roxbury P.O. Sta., Boston, 1914

The Resolutions are now reprinted as historic proof of the birth of a higher morality. Confiscate Rich men's wealth. M. I. S., 1932.

From Morrison I. Swift, *There Must Be Revolution* (Boston, 1932).

Appendix I

Constitution and Regulations of the National Unemployment Council of the U.S.A. (Foreword by Herbert Benjamin), 1934

Foreword

The Constitution of the National Unemployment Council of the United States was adopted at the Third National Convention which was held in Washington, D.C., on February 3, 4, and 5, 1934. The fact that for nearly four years up to that time, the leading national unemployed movement in the United States functioned and conducted brilliant campaigns and struggles without benefit of a formal Constitution is noteworthy.

The Unemployment Councils are organizations that grew up out of the desperate need for defensive action on the part of the millions of workers who found themselves deprived of the opportunity to work and provide a livelihood for themselves and their families. The first consideration of the workers who formed these fighting organizations was, and is, the immediate need for food, clothing, shelter and other necessities of life. How to get these essentials quickly and in sufficient measure is the chief problem of the victims of mass unemployment and consequently of the groups that formed themselves as Unemployment Councils.

The organizers of the Unemployment Councils had no time or inclination to draw blue-prints of imaginary "perfect" organizations. They realized that experience gained in the course of struggle would provide the best pattern for a fighting organization. In the course of the struggle itself, the workers established rules, regulations, and organizational forms that would serve to make their organizations stronger and more effective.

The Constitution of the National Unemployment Council is therefore the concentrated experience of hundreds of thousands of courageous, uncompromising fighters who claim that the right to decent existence, for the great masses who are unemployed through no fault of their own, must stand above the profit interests of those who hold and control the wealth of this country.

Therefore, the first law of the National Unemployment Council is that "Not one worker or his family shall be without decent food, clothing and shelter!" Every provision of the Constitution has for its purpose the enforcement of this law. This must be the guiding principle in the application and interpretation of this Constitution.

For this reason, the Constitution is intended as a guide to action and not as a straitjacket. The National Unemployment Council is a voluntary association of those who desire to further the interests of the workers (employed as well as unemployed) who suffer as a result of mass unemployment. Our success depends upon the initiative which the masses develop in action. This initiative will serve to produce constant suggestions for improvement in the organizational structure and regulations of our movement. As quickly as they are tested in struggle and found effective, such suggestions are made a part of the daily practice and basic rules of our movement.

At the same time we must recognize that mass action is essential just because individual action is helpless and useless. Therefore, any individual or group who may attempt to set themselves, their will and their laws up above and against the collective will and law which is embodied in this Constitution, cannot help our fight. Our movement depends upon the united strength of the masses and not upon the "genius" of some "great" individual or isolated group. Our organization belongs to the whole body of workers that make up the membership and to the greater body of workers whom our movement aims to serve. Anyone who attempts to bend our movement to his personal interests and will has no place in this organization. Any individual who attempts to accomplish individually the tasks of the organization is bound to fail. Collective leadership and mass action are the keystone of our organization.

Mass unemployment is now a permanent feature of present-day capitalist society. An organized movement to defend the economic interests of the workers who are the first victims of unemployment is as necessary and as inevitable as is the trade union movement that has developed out of the needs and struggles of the workers in the industries. The National Unemployment Council is the product of this need. It has faced and will continue to face the sharp, brutal attacks of the ruling class which is responsible for unemployment and which bitterly resists every attempt to compel adequate provision for the maintenance of decent living standards and even the very existence of the masses.

In these attacks, the ruling class makes use of every form of terror and trickery. It will continue to employ its police and military power, its politicians, demagogues, traitors, splitters, and disruptors.

The National Unemployment Council is built upon a full realization of the kind of struggles that must be waged and the forces against whom this struggle must be directed.

We build a movement that is composed of, and open to, every honest worker who agrees with our aims, regardless of political, religious, racial, or national differences. We aim to establish a united front that will embrace all workers' organizations and lead to the necessary complete unification of all existing organizations into one mighty organization.

We build a movement that concerns itself with the most minute needs of the unemployed worker and his family, but which never forgets that our every struggle is directed towards winning greater and more permanent economic security by compelling the establishment of a federal system of unemployment and social insurance.

We build a movement that demands rights and begs no favors; that does not plead but fights; that does not make deals but exerts organized pressure; that does not expect miracles but realizes that gains are made through struggle, effort, and sacrifice.

We build a movement that trusts no promises but depends upon its organized power to win and hold concessions.

We build a movement that scorns the petty bribes with which the ruling class sometimes seeks to buy freedom to continue its program of robbery and exploitation. We fight for the whole working class and therefore for the most oppressed sections, such as the Negro and foreign-born, because this is the only way to gain permanent benefits for all.

We gain inspiration and strength from every struggle of any and every group of workers against the common enemy of all — the oppressors and exploiters of the masses. That is why we support by every possible means every such struggle of the workers, employed and unemployed, in this or any other country.

We recognize as friends and allies the toiling farmers and the professional workers. We regard as enemies all who, in whatever disguise, urge us to be patient in our suffering, meek before our oppressors, modest in our demands, tolerant toward traitors, thankful for scraps of "charity," and dependent upon the kind favors and glib promises of self-seeking political tools of the ruling class.

Ours is the movement and organization of the most useful and therefore most powerful section of the population — the workers who by their labor have produced the great wealth of this country. We claim the right to work and to produce the necessities of life for ourselves and for all other useful members of society.

Whether those who claim ownership of the natural wealth and productive machinery of this country can give us work or not— we claim and fight for the right to live!

Herbert Benjamin

CONSTITUTION
of the National Unemployment Council

Adopted at the National Convention Against Unemployment, February 3, 4 and 5, 1934, Washington, D.C.

PREAMBLE

Mass unemployment has now become a permanent feature of the economic system under which we live. Millions are denied the opportunity to work and earn a livelihood for themselves and their families. The menace of unemployment hangs over the head of every worker in every industry and occupation. Agricultural as well as industrial; professional as well as manual workers, all suffer and all are menaced by the deep, lasting and intense crisis into which present day society has been thrown by the decay of the system in which production is directed in the interest of profits for a few rather than to supply the needs of the many.

Ownership of the wealth and means of production — the mines, mills, factories, railroads and land — is concentrated in the hands of an ever-diminishing number of bankers and industrialists. Control of this great wealth also gives them the power to control the government and thus withhold from the starving masses the right to produce and enjoy the essentials of life.

Only the organized mass pressure and struggle of all victims of mass unemployment and insecurity, Negro and white, can force the owners of wealth and their governmental agents to provide the means of safeguarding the home, the family, and the very existence of the masses who face and suffer poverty in the midst of plenty. Only by forcing the government to establish unemployment and social insurance at rates equal to average wages can even partial economic security and the preservation of living standards be assured for all.

Our task is to see that not one unemployed worker or his family shall be without decent food, housing and clothing.

Our aim is to win security by forcing enactment of the Workers' Unemployment and Social Insurance Bill.

As the means to this end we direct ourselves to the development of a mighty united fighting movement that shall include all workers and poor farmers, regardless of sex, race, nationality, religious or political faith, or other affiliation. This unity, for militant and determined struggle, shall be effected through the National Unemployment Council of the United States of America.

ARTICLE I.

Name and Character

1. The name of the united front movement is the National Unemployment Council of the U.S.A.
2. The National Unemployment Council of the U.S.A. accepts into its ranks workers, toiling farmers, professionals and their organizations, without distinction as to nationality, race, color, sex, religious or political affiliation or belief.

ARTICLE II.

Sub-Divisions

The National Unemployment Council is based upon the following sub-divisions and units: State; County; City and Regional Councils and Locals.

1. The State organization shall be known by the name of the state in which it operates, thus: Illinois Unemployment Council, and indicate affiliation to National Council.
2. The County organization shall be known by the name of the county, thus: Allegheny County Unemployment Council, and indicate affiliation to State and National Council.

3. The city or town councils shall be known by the name of their city or town, thus: Unemployment Council of Indianapolis, and indicate affiliation to County, State, and National Council.
4. The ward or precinct council or local shall be known by the number of the given ward or precinct, thus: Fifteenth Ward Unemployment Council (or local), and indicate affiliation to city and county.
5. Locals (or councils) formed on an industrial or trade basis, or in a given section of a city or town or within any organization or shop, shall be known accordingly, thus: Textile Workers' Unemployment Council (or Local), or Logan Circle; or Brotherhood of Carpenters Local (and number), or Relief Workers' Local; or Unemployed Citizens' Local (or Council).

ARTICLE III.

Emblem

The emblem of the National Unemployment Council shall be an arm grasping at the throat of a skeleton head (representing hunger). Under this shall appear the slogan: "Fight Against Hunger" and around this a circular border in which shall be imprinted "National Unemployment Council — For Workers' Bill."

ARTICLE IV.

National Convention and National Executive Board of the National Unemployment Council

1. The highest body of the Council is the National Convention, representing the rank and file, which shall be held annually.
2. The National Convention shall elect a National Executive Board of not less than 50 members which shall govern our movement between Conventions.
3. Any member of a properly affiliated organization shall be eligible for membership on the National Executive Board. Between the National Conventions, the National Executive Board of the N.U.C. is the governing body. The National Executive Board shall have the authority to speak in the name of the entire organization on all matters of concern to the victims of mass unemployment, launch national campaigns and fix days of national struggle and demonstrations. It sets the date of the National Convention, subject to the approval of the affiliated organizations.
4. The National Convention shall elect the following officers of the National Unemployment Council: the Chairman, two Vice-Chairmen, the Secretary-Treasurer, and the National Organizer.
5. The National Executive Board shall subdivide its work and select its heads of departments as the work requires, and have the right to propose assignments of field organizers subject to the approval of the affiliated organizations in the given territory.
6. The National Executive Board shall issue charters, membership books, and stamps to all affiliates.
7. The National Executive Board elects a National Committee of not more than 13 of its members who live in the vicinity of the National Office. The

Committee shall act for the National Executive Board between meetings of the N.E.B.

8. The National Committee shall be in regular communication with the N.E.B. members; help guide the activities of the affiliated organizations and set up State, County and local organizations where none exists.
9. The National Executive Board shall submit a quarterly report on activities, decisions, organizational work, and finances to the rank and file of all affiliated organizations.
10. The National Executive Board shall give 60 days' advance notice before calling of Conventions and shall provide proposed agenda, draft resolutions, etc., for discussion, emergency situations excepted. Special Conventions can be called upon the request of one-third of all the affiliated organizations.

ARTICLE V.

Referendum and Recall

1. The membership of the N.U.C. shall have the right to demand a general referendum vote on all fundamental questions affecting the vital interests of the unemployed and part-time workers and their organization. The National Executive Board shall make provisions for such referendum when occasion arises.
2. The membership of the National Unemployment Council shall have the right to demand the recall or removal of any National, State, County, city or local officers who, in the opinion of the majority of the membership of the respective area or sub-division, fail to perform their duty in the interests of the organization.
0. Any member or affiliated organization that desires to launch a referendum or recall as provided in this article shall have the right to forward such proposal to the National Committee which shall then publish such request in the first Bulletin of the N.U.C. which appears within ten days after such request is received. When such proposal is approved by affiliated organizations in not less than fifteen cities or counties (or by a majority of such organizations), the referendum or recall shall be formally submitted for a decisive vote.

ARTICLE VI.

Locals

1. The basic organizational unit of the N.U.C. is the local. The local may be based on the block, precinct, or neighborhood; and in smaller towns on the ward or general township. Where necessary and practical, trade, industrial and language locals may be formed. In order to be chartered as a local, a minimum of 25 members and the approval of the next higher sub-division in the area are required.
2. Each local should elect an executive committee of five or more members. This committee shall have power to act for the local between regular meetings and may call special meetings when necessary.
3. The following officers should also be elected and should be included in the Executive Committee: a chairman, organizer, secretary, and treasurer.

4.   Standing committees such as Welfare and Grievances; Eviction and Utilities; Education and Social; Women's; Youth; Negro, etc., shall be elected as needed.
5.   All efforts should be made to involve every possible member in committee work. Committees of one are incompatible with the principles of the N.U.C., which bases its activities on mass action and broad collective committee work.
6.   Elections for all standing committees and officers shall take place in the local every three or six months as desired by the members themselves. Before the elections, committees should submit a report of their activities which should be thoroughly discussed by the local. Vacancies shall be filled at special elections of the local.

ARTICLE VII.

Neighborhood, Ward, Precinct and City Unemployment Councils

1.   As rapidly as possible neighborhood, ward, precinct, sectional or city Unemployment Councils should be set up. The Council is a body composed of delegates from the locals, the local unions, fraternal lodges, shops and relief jobs, and from other unemployed organizations existing in the territory. Locals affiliated to a ward or neighborhood Council are represented in the next higher Council by the delegates from such Council, and therefore are not required to send direct and duplicating delegates.
2.   It is the task of the neighborhood, sectional, ward, precinct or city Councils to set up locals in all parts of their territory, help direct and coordinate their general activities, furnish them with cards, literature and other supplies of N.U.C.
3.   It is a special task of the neighborhood, sectional, ward and city Councils to form groups of workers in the shops and assist the workers in the shops, industries and unions by aiding them in every action and in all strikes conducted in an effort to defend and improve wage, living and working conditions and standards.
4.   The City Unemployment Council shall be a delegated body representing the locals and/or Councils of the N.U.C. within the city, and the corresponding city bodies of the trade unions, fraternal societies, etc. It shall give leadership and guidance in all matters relating to unemployment to all locals and other mass organizations in the respective city. The City Unemployment Council shall meet no less than once a month. It shall elect an executive committee of no less than nine members and no more than fifteen, which shall include the City Organizer, Secretary and Treasurer.

ARTICLE VIII.

County Unemployment Council

1.   In localities where there are a large number of small towns, County Councils shall be established. This should be done on the initiative of the Unemployed (sic) Council in the county seat or largest town or by the State Committee if such exists.
2.   A County Conference of all locals and/or city and town Councils of the N.U.C., working class and toiling farmer organizations should be called

and constitute the County Unemployment Council. The County Unemployment Council shall be the leading and guiding body of the unemployment locals and all organizations in the respective counties.

3. The County Unemployment Council shall meet no less than once a month. It shall be composed of delegates from corresponding bodies (county) of all working class organizations and from city and township Councils and of locals that are not represented in an already affiliated central body.

4. A County Executive Committee of the N.U.C. shall be elected of no less than nine and no more than twenty-five members including the County Chairman, two Vice-Chairmen, Secretary and Treasurer. The County Executive shall be responsible for the current work to carry out the decisions of the County Unemployment Council. The County Executive shall meet no less than once every two weeks.

5. The County Unemployment Council shall receive all materials, supplies, literature for its territory from the State Committee, if such exists, or from the National Unemployment Council, and in turn shall relay such supplies to its affiliated units.

6. The County Unemployment Council shall make regular reports on activities, plans, etc., and at least quarterly financial reports to its rank and file and N.U.C.

ARTICLE IX.

State Council

1. Where sufficient organization has developed, and conditions indicate the need and possibility for the establishment of a State Unemployment Council, it should, upon the approval of the National Executive Board, be organized through the calling of a State Convention of all locals of the National Unemployment Council, trade unions, etc., following the pattern of the County Unemployed Councils.

2. The Convention shall elect a State Executive Committee of fifteen to thirty-five members, including a State Chairman, two Vice-Chairmen, a Secretary, Organizer, and Treasurer. These officers and not more than five additional members shall constitute a Buro. The State Executive Committee is to meet at least once every three months. The State Buro shall meet at least once a month. Where State Unemployment Councils are set up, they shall receive all supplies and material from the National Office to relay to the counties and other subordinate units.

ARTICLE X.

United Front With Unions, Negro, Fraternal, Unemployed, Veterans' Organizations, Clubs, Small Home Owners, etc.

1. It is the task of the local, city, county, State and National Committees to induce all working class organizations in their jurisdiction (such as unions, fraternal, Negro and veterans' organizations, etc.) to set up unemployment committees or locals within their respective organizations and to unite with and affiliate to the Unemployment Council of their community.

2. The task of such unemployment committee is to register the unemployed members of the organization; to organize them into an unemployment local

where this is possible; and to take up and act on any grievances arising from unemployment.

3. Every organization that affiliates with the National Unemployment Council shall be required to pay the regular fee for a charter plus such local affiliation fee as may be established by the by-laws of the Council in their city, county and State. Such affiliation constitutes an expression of agreement with and readiness to be governed by the program, Constitution, and aims of the N.U.C. in all matters related to the struggles against unemployment. In all other matters the affiliated organization retains complete autonomy.

4. In accordance with the needs of the workers and the principles of the N.U.C., all affiliated organizations and members are required to promote by every possible means the unity of the workers.

5. Wherever unaffiliated organizations exist side by side with organizations that accept our program in full, our affiliated organizations shall take the initiative in forming a "Federation" which shall be composed of delegates from all the organizations, elected on a basis of proportional representation. Such Federations have the task of effecting the maximum possible unity in action and policy despite organizational independence of the unaffiliated organizations.

6. Organizations that join us only in a united front are to retain their autonomy and organizational independence and are required only to be governed by the conditions on which the given united front is established.

7. In preparing united front conferences and in the course of united front actions, we address ourselves to the recognized officers and leading bodies of other organizations. At the same time we reserve the right and follow the practice of reaching the rank and file of such organizations with information on our proposals and plans and such differences as develop between the leaders and the U.C.

ARTICLE XI.

Finances, Dues, Charters

1. Every member of the N.U.C. shall receive a membership book on payment of five (5) cents initiation to the local treasurer.

2. Membership dues in the N.U.C. shall be not less than two (2) cents per month. Locals may by majority decision increase the local dues. No part of such additional local dues need be shared with any of the higher bodies.

3. Any one three months or more in arrears in dues payment shall not be considered in good standing.

4. Failure to become a member and remain in good standing shall not disqualify any honest worker from support by the organization when in need of help. Such worker must, however, be required to report to the Grievance Committee and attend the meeting at which decision is to be made on the action to be taken with regard to his grievance. This provision shall not apply in an emergency which requires action before a formal meeting can be held.

5. All workers shall be welcome at meetings of Unemployment Locals and may have a voice in discussions. Only members in good standing shall have the right to a vote.

6.   There shall be a strict accounting of all funds — the books being audited by an auditing committee of the rank and file every three months. Funds for official publications and literature shall be kept separate from general funds. Locals, city and county councils shall set up finance committees to work out ways and means of raising and assuring responsible handling of funds needed for the work.

ARTICLE XII.

Education
1.   Educational Committees shall be set up in the locals and higher bodies for the purpose of training promising militant workers, establishing forums, study circles, and of instituting a series of discussions in the locals through the reading of the National Unemployment Council pamphlets. Research departments should be set up where possible. Tours for National, State, and county speakers and organizers will be organized in conjunction with local Councils.

ARTICLE XIII.

Discipline
1.   Any member whose conduct is or may be harmful to the National Unemployment Council or any of its sub-divisions, or any other workers' organization, shall be disciplined.
2.   Stools, spies, scabs, habitual drunkards, constant disrupters, shall not be admitted to membership or tolerated within the organization. Any known as such shall be exposed and treated with the contempt which is due them.
3.   Charges shall be preferred to the Executive Committee which shall report its findings to an open meeting to which the member involved shall be invited. Charges should be made in written form. Appeals may be made to the next higher body up to the National Executive Board whose decision shall be final.

ARTICLE XIV.

Women's, Youth and Children's Divisions
1.   For the purpose of dealing more effectively with the special problems of these groups, locals and Councils may and should wherever necessary and possible, organize the following auxiliary organizations: (a) Women's, (b) Youth, (c) Children's, groups, clubs or auxiliaries of the Unemployment Council.
2.   Such auxiliaries may be chartered and shall operate in all respects in accordance with the program and Constitution of the N.U.C. and the by-laws of the State, County, city and local sub-divisions of which they are a part. They shall, however, develop in addition special programs, activities and procedures to conform to the special needs and problems of such groups.

Information on Supplies and Literature

The following supplies and literature are issued by the National Unemployment Council of the U.S. and can be obtained through city, county, state councils or directly from the National Office at 80 East 11th Street, New York City.

Every division of our movement and every local should as soon as possible after organization and at all times thereafter, be in a position to circulate our literature and supplies among the workers in the area in which these operate.

CHARTER

A Charter will be issued to any local, with a membership of 25 or more. This includes also such organizations as local unions, lodges and clubs which wish to be affiliated through the nearest Unemployment Council. Every council (delegate body) whether sectional, city, county or state, should also secure a charter as such. The fee for a charter is fifty cents.

MEMBERSHIP CARDS AND INITIATION FEE

Membership cards together with initiation stamps are supplied at the following rates:

To individual members	5¢ each	
To Locals	2¢	($2.50 per 100)
To City Councils	2¢	($2.00 per 100)
To County Councils	1¢	($1.50 per 100)
To State Councils	1¢	($1.00 per 100)

These rates are not to be altered by any subdivision excepting that a local may increase the rate to the individual member if this is decided by a two-thirds majority of the membership of the given local.

DUES STAMPS

The minimum dues of the National Unemployment Council is 2¢ per month. Dues stamps are supplied at the following rates:

To Locals	$1.00 per hundred
To City Councils	0.80 per hundred
To County Councils	0.60 per hundred
To State Committees	0.40 per hundred

MEMBERSHIP AND CAMPAIGN BUTTONS

Buttons with the emblem of the National Unemployment Council (an arm grasping at throat of death's head representing hunger with the slogans, "Fight Against Hunger — For the Workers Bill", and the name of our organization on the border) will be supplied at the following rates:

Campaign Buttons (Retail at 5¢ each)

In quantities of 3,000 or more	$10.00 per thousand
In quantities of 1,000 up to 3,000	$12.00 per thousand
In quantities of less than 1,000	$ 2.00 per hundred

Membership Buttons (Retail at 10¢ each)

In quantities of 100 or less	5¢ each
In quantities of 200 or more	$4.00 per hundred

PENNY CONTRIBUTION TICKETS

As a means of raising funds for our work through regular collections in the neighborhoods, at shops, union and lodge meetings and affairs, we issue rolls of Penny Tickets. These are similar to theatre tickets. They come in rolls of 1,000 tickets. We sell these at $2.00 per 1,000. The various subdivisions may sell them on the basis of the same percentage as is provided for dues. Each roll when sold at the rate of 1¢ per ticket nets $10.00.

COPIES OF THE WORKERS' BILL (H.R. 7598)

An exact reprint of the Workers' Bill as presented in Congress is available for general distribution. We supply these at the rate of $2.00 per thousand copies or 30¢ per hundred.

CAMPAIGN POST CARD

As one means of bringing pressure to bear upon all members of Congress for immediate enactment of our Bill (H.R. 7598) we issue a Post Card which carries a reproduction of the first page of the Bill and a message calling upon the Congressmen to support it. This card is to be sold or distributed to organizations and individuals who are to mail them in to the Congressmen and Senators from the given District and State.

We supply these cards at the rate of $2.00 per thousand or 25¢ per 100.

They may be resold at retail at the rate of two for one cent.

PETITION LISTS

Organizations that wish to conduct a signature campaign to force their city, county and state legislative bodies to memorialize Congress for enactment of our Bill, may secure petition lists for this purpose. Such lists also provide a good medium for getting names and addresses of those who are willing to support our fight against hunger. Those who sign should be called to neighborhood meetings and organized into locals.

We supply the lists at $2.50 per thousand; 35¢ per 100.

Appendix J

Unemployed Committee of Atlanta Leaflet, 1932

The following leaflet was used by the state of Georgia as the basis of the charge against Angelo Herndon in 1932 that he was guilty of inciting to insurrection.

THE LEAFLET
WORKERS OF ATLANTA!
EMPLOYED and UNEMPLOYED — Negro and
White — ATTENTION!
MEN and WOMEN OF ATLANTA :

Thousands of us, together with our families, are at this time facing starvation and misery and are about to be thrown out of our houses because the miserable charity hand-out that some of us were getting has been stopped! Hundreds of thousands of dollars have been collected from workers in this city for relief for the unemployed, and most of it has been squandered in high salaries for the heads of these relief agencies.

Mr. T. K. Glenn, president of the Community Chest, is reported to be getting a salary of $10,000 a year. Mr. Frank Neely, executive director of the Community Chest, told the County Commission Saturday that he gets $6,500 a year, while at the same time no worker, no matter how big his family, gets more than two dollars and a half to live on. If we count the salaries paid the secretaries and the investigators working in the thirty-eight relief stations in this city, it should not surprise us that the money for relief was used up and there is no more left to keep us from starvation. If we allow ourselves to starve while these fakers grow fat off our misery, it will be our own fault.

The bosses want us to starve peacefully and by this method save the money they have accumulated off our sweat and blood. We must force them to continue our relief and give more help. We must not allow them to stall us any longer with fake promises. The city and county authorities from the money they have already collected from us in taxes, and by taking the incomes of the bankers and other rich capitalists, can take care of every unemployed family in Atlanta. We must make them do it.

At a meeting of the County Commissioners last Saturday, it was proposed by Walter S. McNeal, Jr., to have the police round up all unemployed workers and their families and ship them back to the farms and make them work for just board and no wages, while just a few months ago these hypocrites were talking about forced labor in Soviet Russia, a country where there is no starvation and where the workers rule! Are we going to let them force us into slavery?

At this meeting Mr. Hendrix said that there were no starving families in Atlanta, that if there is he has not seen any. Let's all of us, white and Negroes, together, with our women folk and children, go to his office in the county court house on Pryor and Hunter Streets Thursday morning at 10 o'clock and show this faker that there is plenty of suffering in the city of Atlanta and demand that he give us immediate relief! Organize and fight for unemployment insurance at the expense of the government and the bosses! Demand immediate payment of the bonus to the ex- servicemen. Don't forget Thursday morning at the county court house.

Issued by the
Unemployed Committee of Atlanta,
P.O. Box 339

Reprinted from Angelo Herndon, *Let Me Live* (1937; reprint ed., New York: Arno Press, 1969).

Appendix K

A New Declaration of Independence by the Continental Congress of Workers and Farmers, May 1933

More than one hundred and fifty years ago our forefathers proclaimed in the Declaration of Independence that the supreme function of government is to make secure for men their inalienable right to life, liberty, and the pursuit of happiness.

Moreover, the fathers declared that

Whenever any form of government becomes destructive of these ends, it is the right of the people to alter or abolish it, and to institute a new government, laying its foundations on such principles, and organizing its powers in such form as to them shall seem most likely to effect their safety and happiness.

Such are the two basic principles of human liberty and genuine Americanism laid down by the founders of this Republic.

It has now come to pass that there has grown up in this nation a system of business, industry and finance which has enthroned economic kings and financial barons over our lives vastly more powerful, more irresponsible, and more dangerous to human rights than the political kings whom the fathers overthrew in our American revolution of 1776. These economic rulers now have such absolute control over the economic life of the people as to threaten the very foundation of this Republic.

Under this system of production for private profit these rulers have created conditions that are intolerable.

They have drawn billions in profit, rent, and interest; and they have slashed our wages and the prices of our farm products.

They have used the marvels of the machine age, not to lift the burden of toil from our shoulders, but to speed us up beyond human endurance, and to throw us jobless upon the streets.

They have taken the products of our labor, and not paid us enough to buy back the goods we have produced.

They have wasted our natural, technical, and human resources, and led us into ever more tragic periods of industrial chaos.

They have lived in mansions, and evicted us from our homes.

They have led us to trust in their banks, and then have stolen our savings.

They have invaded our civil liberties, and thrown our leaders into jail.

They have intrenched themselves in power by controlling the schools, the press, and the government.

They have spent billions on bombs and battleships while we have gone cold and hungry.

They have forced us to bleed and die in defense of their loans and markets abroad, and to kill our fellow workers in other countries.

They have done these things as part and parcel of a profit system which places the few in control of gigantic monopolies and puts profit above human life.

Since the first Declaration of Independence the American people have discovered and created the means for unheard-of wealth. Wide rivers have been tamed to provide electric power, huge mountains have been tunneled to give ore for the creation of new and marvelous machines, and the prairies have been made to yield rich crops. *Man's power to produce wealth has been increased a hundredfold, until now a life of security and abundance is possible for all.*

BUT TODAY THE NATION STARVES IN THE MIDST OF PLENTY. THE GIGANTIC MACHINES STAND IDLE, THE CROPS LIE IN WAREHOUSES OR ROT IN FIELDS.

The system is collapsing before our very eyes. It is destroying itself with a destruction that threatens the historic gains of human rights and the achievements of human civilization. It is for us, workers and farmers of America, to build now a new economic system of justice and freedom. Only through our organized power can mankind be freed from the crushing and needless bonds of poverty and insecurity.

We, the representatives of workers, and farmers' organizations, in Continental Congress assembled, call upon all those who toil to organize to achieve one supreme aim, a new economic system based upon the principles of cooperation, public ownership and democratic management, in which the planlessness, the waste, and the exploitation of our present order shall be eliminated and in which the natural resources and the basic industries of the country shall be planned and operated for the common good.

Farmers and workers of America! The wealth and knowledge of one hundred and fifty years of achievement are at our command if we will organize for power. We shall not starve in the midst of plenty! We are the majority. Workers and farmers everywhere, unite! Agitate, educate, organize! We have a world to win!

Broadside from the Continental Congress of Farmers and Workers, National Committee of Correspondence and Action, Chicago, Ill. (copy in Tamiment Institute Library of New York University).

From Philip S. Foner, ed. *We, the Other People* (Urbana: University of Illinois Press, 1976).

Appendix L

Declaration of Workers' and Farmers' Rights and Purposes, 1933

Adopted by the National Unemployed Leagues, July 4, 1933.

When, in a nation possessing unlimited resources, along with the greatest industrial and transportation equipment the world has ever known, there develops a condition wherein millions of citizens are forced into dire destitution and starvation through being denied to have access to the tools of production, then it becomes their duty to organize to change these conditions.

A new tyranny has developed through the control of our great industrial system by a few who manipulate the affairs of the nation selfishly and ruthlessly. The suffering and misery of millions of victims is of no consequence or weight in the operation of their affairs. Their only objective is more gold, more power. The motive behind all their actions is greed, while their technic is cunning.

Coldly indifferent to the consequences to future generations, helpless children are denied the elementary things necessary to their proper physical and mental development.

The home, the corner-stone of the American nation, is being destroyed by the economic anarchy throughout the land.

The youth of the nation are being turned into vagrants by the denial of the right to work and the destruction of the protecting influence of the home. Young boys and girls are forced into conditions which cause their moral and physical decay.

Millions of men and women after years of toil, broken in spirit and health, are thrown ruthlessly aside without proper provisions for their declining years.

Driven by heartless masters to the performance of greater tasks, countless thousands of workers are ruined in health and hurried to an early grave.

Throughout the land thousands of farmers are being dispossessed of their farms, evicted from their homes and brutally set into the highway; while millions more are struggling hopelessly under overwhelming burden of debt, awaiting the same fate.

Helpless against the aggression of concentrated wealth, large numbers of business men are being ruined and forced into the army of starvation.

Denied employment, the workers are given as a relief from the consequences of the anarchistic system under which they live an inadequate and degrading charity.

Private ownership and control have built a wall between the machines of production and the workers that keep the machines idle and the workers starving.

We hold that all children are entitled to conditions of health and happiness that will permit their proper development of race, color, creed or nationality.

That the interests of all workers are identical and that they should not be divided by religion, racial, political or national prejudices:

That all useful members of society are entitled to adequate sustenance without the stigma of charity:

That it is the first duty of government to provide for the health and happiness of the people of the nation:

That all persons have the duty and the right to work.

In order that these evils may be remedied and these ends accomplished, we determine and declare that the profit system with its meaningless depressions, its needless miseries, its suicidal wars and its gross injustices must come to an end, and we furthermore declare that it is the solemn duty of every worker and farmer to bend every effort through organization and through determined action in unity with all workers and farmers to fight to destroy this system and to set up a workers' and farmers' republic in America.

When our forefathers crushed the tyranny of kings, America was born. When the men of 1860 destroyed chattel slavery, America's development as a great industrial state was made possible. And when the men and women of today shall finally crush the tyranny of bankers and bosses, America shall at last be free.

Signed: Committee on the Declaration of Independence
Voice of the Unemployed, Aug. 1, 1933

From Philip Foner, ed., *We, the Other People* (Urbana: University of Illinois Press, 1976).

Appendix M

Preamble to the Constitution, Relief Workers' League of Greater New York, 1934

Recognizing the necessity for uniting the people of this nation for immediate and effective action against unemployment which confronts us on a mass scale; and

Understanding that the Government of the United States alone, of all nations still pursues the path of denying adequate relief and social insurance to the working people of America; and

Realizing the necessity for rallying the workers of the country against evictions and foreclosures, and for defense of their living and working standards;

We, the delegates from various relief job projects, representing thousands of skilled and unskilled workers, office, clerical, manual, technical, and professional workers, declare that our Aims and Purposes shall be:

1. To immediately improve wages and labor conditions;
2. To unite with the unemployed in common action for relief;
3. To actively support, and work for the enactment of the (National) Workers' Unemployment Insurance Bill which guarantees to every worker adequate relief from unemployment at the expense of the government and employers.

Recognizing the existing abuse and evils in the CWA administration, we declare that we shall not tolerate any discrimination against workers on the job, and that we shall defend the rights of the Negro, the single worker, and the foreign-born worker.

WE STAND FOR:

1. Workers employed on relief projects shall receive no less than Five (5) dollars per day and no less than Eighty (80) dollars per month.
2. All skilled work to be paid at the prevailing rate of wages of the trade unions.
3. Work relief wages shall be supplemented by the state where the income of the family is below the minimum relief allowance.
4. The electric and gas company shall suspend payment of deposits and abolish dollar minimum bill for all unemployed.
5. Free transportation to and from work where the fare is above ten cents.
6. No delinquency of payment of relief wages. All wages to be paid weekly on a definite pay day and up to date. No deduction for time lost because of bad weather or holidays.
7. Wages to be increased in proportion to inflation and to the rising cost of living.

8. Any worker injured or sick as a result of working on relief projects shall be paid full wages for the entire period of disability.

9. Free medical attention shall be furnished by the Civil Works Administrations.

10. No worker shall be denied relief because of refusing to accept work that calls for unusual physical exertion, requires absence from home, or residence in labor camps, or replacement of workers in labor conflicts.

11. C.W.A. to establish warm shelter for the purpose of rest and lunch periods, on all labor projects.

12. No termination of projects. C.W.A. to take immediate steps for continuation of work relief without any delay to the men on the jobs.

Rules And Regulations

1. Eligibility for membership.

All relief workers, regardless of age, color, creed, sex, or political affiliation, shall be entitled to join this organization if he or she abides by the principles and rules of the organization.

No one shall be allowed to join or be a member of this organization if he or she is a foreman, unless approved by the workers on the job and by the Executive Committee of the organization.

No one connected with the police department, private or public detective agencies shall be eligible for Membership.

2. Initiation and Dues.

The initiation fee for membership in this organization shall be ten cents. All members pay ten cents dues monthly to be collected at job meetings and turned in to the financial secretary. Dues can also be paid directly to the financial secretary.

3. Meetings.

Locals shall hold regular meetings at fixed intervals (about every two weeks) to be decided by membership of the locals.

4. Executive.

The executive committee shall constitute one or more job delegates from all job committees, in addition to the officers of the organization. All delegates or officers of the organization are subject to recall at any time by the rank and file.

Until job committees are established the general membership meeting has power to withdraw any member of the present executive committee or change any decision of the executive committee.

The highest authority of the organization is the General membership meeting which is empowered to change, approve, or amend any decision.

The executive committee shall consist of the following officers: Organizer, chairman, vice-chairman, recording secretary, financial secretary.

5. City Body.

The highest City Body shall be the Central Job Delegates Council, which shall consist of delegates elected by the men on their project, or by the membership of a local on the basis of one delegate for every 25 members. As the organization grows, the number of men necessary to elect a delegate will be raised.

The Central Job Delegates Council shall elect an executive committee of 25, including the officers of the Relief Workers' League, which shall be: President, Vice-president, Recording Secretary, Financial Secretary, and organizer. The Executive is empowered only to carry out the decisions of the Central Job Delegates Council, carry out the routine organization work, and shall report back to the Central Job Delegates Council, at each meeting of that body.

The Central Job Delegates Council shall meet once a month. The Executive Committee of the Relief Workers' League shall meet twice a month.

Any officer or member of the executive must obey the decisions of the membership and the majority of the executive committee. The permanent committees shall consist of: Ways and means, press, and organization and membership committee. Any executive member or committee member failing to attend three consecutive meetings will automatically be dropped from the executive.

Form of Organization

The Relief Workers' League shall be organized on the basis of job grievance committees numbering from five to nine members to be elected by the workers of the particular job or project. The job grievance committee shall elect a job organizer and deputy finance secretary. (One or more delegates depending on size of job shall be the representative at the executive committee of the Relief Workers' League.) Very small projects to be attached to the nearest big project.

Appendix N

Workers' Unemployment Old Age and Social Insurance Bill (H.R. 2827), 1935

Representative Ernest Lundeen (Farmer-Labor, Minn.) first placed this bill (as H.R. 7598) before the 73rd Congress, 2nd Session, on February 2, 1934. On May 15, 1935, the House Committee on Labor, with only one dissenting vote, reported favorably on the following version of the bill (H.R. 2827), which Representative Lundeen had introduced in the 74th Congress, 1st Session, January 3, 1935.

In the House of Representatives

January 3, 1935

Mr. LUNDEEN introduced the following bill; which was referred to the Committee on Labor and ordered to be printed.

A BILL

To provide for the establishment of unemployment, old age, and social insurance, and for other purposes.

Be it enacted by the Senate and House of Representatives of the United States of America in Congress assembled, That this Act shall be known by the title "The Workers' Unemployment, Old Age, & Social Insurance Act."

Sec. 2. The Secretary of Labor is hereby authorized and directed to provide for the immediate establishment of a system of unemployment insurance for the purpose of providing compensation for all workers and farmers above eighteen years of age, unemployed through no fault of their own. Such compensation shall be equal to average local wages, but shall in no case be less than $10 per week, plus $3 for each dependent. Workers willing and able to do full-time work but unable to secure full-time employment shall be entitled to receive the difference between their earnings and the average local wages for full-time employment. The minimum compensation guaranteed by this Act shall be increased in conformity with rises in the cost of living. Such unemployment insurance shall be administered and controlled, and the minimum compensation shall be adjusted by workers and farmers under rules and regulations which shall be prescribed by the Secretary of Labor in conformity with the purposes and provisions of this Act through unemployment insurance commissions directly elected by members of workers' and farmers' organizations.

Sec. 3. The Secretary of Labor is hereby further authorized and directed to provide for the immediate establishment of other forms of social insurance for the purpose of providing compensation for all workers and farmers who are unable to work because of sickness, old age, maternity, industrial injury, or any other disability. Such compensation shall be the same as provided by section 2 of this Act for unemployment insurance and shall be administered in like manner. Compensation for disability because of maternity shall be paid to women during the period of eight weeks previous and eight weeks following childbirth.

Sec. 4. All moneys necessary to pay compensation guaranteed by this Act and the cost of establishing and maintaining the administration of this Act shall be paid by the Government of the United States. All such moneys are hereby appropriated out of all funds in the Treasury of the United States not otherwise appropriated. Further taxation necessary to provide funds for the purposes of this Act shall be levied on inheritances, gifts, and individual and corporation incomes of $5,000 a year and over. The benefits of this Act shall be extended to workers, whether they be industrial, agricultural, domestic, office, or professional workers, and to farmers, without discrimination because of age, sex, race, color, religious or political opinion or affiliation. No worker or farmer shall be disqualified from receiving the compensation guaranteed by this Act because of past participation in strikes, or refusal to work in place of strikers, or at less than average local or trade-union wages, or under unsafe or unsanitary conditions, or where hours are longer than the prevailing union standards of a particular trade or locality, or at an unreasonable distance from home.

Appendix O

Constitution of the Workers Alliance

ARTICLE I

Name

The name of this Organization shall be WORKERS ALLIANCE OF AMERICA.

ARTICLE II

Membership

The Workers Alliance of America is a direct-membership organization. Any organization of unemployed and relief workers whose principles and constitution do not conflict with the principles and constitution of this organization shall be eligible for affiliation. This organization shall be a nation-wide alliance of organized state groups and local affiliates within unorganized states. Any state in which there [are] no affiliates or where the affiliates have not agreed on a combined state unit shall be considered unorganized. The NEB shall be authorized to call a representative conference to establish a state organization of the Alliance, in any state of the Union wherein at least 10 units are organized, providing said units extend into 3 or more counties.

ARTICLE III

Purpose

The purpose shall be to organize the forces of all unemployed, relief, and part-time workers of America and to make effective the principles established by the National Convention and the National Executive Board.

ARTICLE IV

Charters

Section 1. Charters to state organizations or locals in unorganized states shall be granted upon the vote of the NEB.

Section 2. Charters may be suspended by majority vote of NEB.

Section 3. Charters may be revoked by a 2/3 vote, after charges have been preferred in writing to the NEB. The NEB shall then give notice to the organization against whom charges have been preferred no later than 10 days after charges are entered, in writing at least 30 days prior to a hearing on these charges.

Section 4. Charter revocation may be made only upon the ground of failure to live up to the national constitution, the principles and policies of the Workers Alliance of America.

Section 5. An appeal from the decision of the NEB may be taken to the Convention of the Alliance by any organization of the Alliance, providing that notice of such appeal be filed with the NEB not later than 2 months after NEB decision.

Section 6. Where state groups have been organized and recognized by the NEB, the organization shall not be dissolved, except as herein provided, so long as three or more of the affiliates desire the continuance of the said State organization.

ARTICLE V

Dues
The price of dues stamps shall be 1¢ each to state organizations, and 2¢ to local or county affiliates in unorganized states. In addition, there may be a convention assessment not to exceed 10¢ per member for the financing of the National Convention. Each state shall determine county and local dues payment.

National Convention stamps shall be issued for this purpose.

ARTICLE VI

Representation to National Convention
Voting representation at the National Convention shall be upon the basis of average number of dues stamps purchased monthly by the state or other affiliated groups, except that organized state units shall be entitled to one additional delegate. The monthly average of dues stamps shall be computed from the date of the last convention call until the date of the next convention call. The National Executive Board shall decide on the number of delegates.

ARTICLE VII

National Convention
The National Convention shall be the supreme governing body. It shall be called by the NEB within 14 months following this convention upon a minimum of 60 days notice to affiliates. The time and date for the convention shall be fixed by the NEB.

ARTICLE VIII

National Executive Board
Section 1. The National Executive Board shall consist of the President, four Vice-Presidents, and twenty-two additional members elected by the

annual convention. They shall serve in the interim between national conventions.

Section 2. No more than three members of the NEB shall be from any one state. The NEB shall transact all business between regular national conventions. The NEB shall meet at least every four months, preferably in a different locality. A majority of the NEB shall constitute a quorum. The NEB, however, shall have power to delegate its authority to an action committee composed of its own members. For purposes of proper conduct of the business of the national office, an office committee may be selected, consisting of the President, Secretary-Treasurer, Organization Secretary, Editor and Business Manager of the Newspaper.

Section 3. The President shall have power to call special meetings of the NEB in case of emergency, upon three weeks notice to all members.

Section 4. Upon request of eight or more members of the NEB the President shall have sent out a call for a special NEB meeting. Upon the favorable response of ten members the President shall set a day and place and notify all members and state organizations, giving at least three weeks notice.

Section 5. The NEB shall employ a Secretary-Treasurer who shall be bonded in sufficient amount and be a member in good standing in the national organization. The Secretary-Treasurer shall handle all funds of the national organization and shall make a full financial report once each month to all NEB and advisory Committee members. The duties and salary of the Secretary-Treasurer shall be set by the NEB except where specifically defined in this Constitution. The National Secretary-Treasurer shall also gather statistics on relief and the works program; shall present grievances to various departments of the government; shall report matters pertinent to the organization that come before Congress or other governmental bodies; and shall arrange for hearings and demonstrations. In all those matters he shall be subject to the jurisdiction of the NEB. In addition the NEB shall employ an Organization Secretary who shall together with the Secretary-Treasurer, handle the affairs of the national organization, under the direction of the President and the NEB. The NEB shall be empowered to select organizers and all other necessary help to carry on the work of the national organization.

Section 6. The NEB shall be empowered to accept the affiliation of any group of unemployed and relief workers that accept this constitution and declaration of principles, and whose constitution and declaration of principles do not conflict with that of the WAA.

Section 7. The NEB shall be empowered to act in all matters not covered by this constitution.

Section 8. The NEB is instructed to work for the affiliation of all unemployed and relief work organizations; and to work for the closest possible relationship with the organized labor movement. No action limiting the independence of the WAA shall be taken however, without ratification at a national convention.

Section 9. Upon the occasion of a dispute within an affiliate or state organization that prevents the active functioning of the organization, and upon the request of 1/3 of the branches or units of the organization the NEB is empowered to appoint a committee of inquiry. Upon 2/3 vote of the NEB, the charter may be suspended and a re-organization ordered. In such cases the suspended organization shall be required to turn over all books, assets and other property to the NEB, which shall be returned to the organization when reorganized.

ARTICLE IX

Sub-committees
The NEB shall select a number of sub-committees that shall be responsible to it. These shall include an Organization Committee, a Legislative Committee, an Auditing Committee, a Finance Committee, a Newspaper Committee and such other committees as it deems necessary.

The duties and functions of such committees shall be defined by the NEB.

ARTICLE X

National Advisory Committee
There shall be a National Advisory Committee elected by the NEB, composed of not less than 15 and no more than 25 persons prominent in the organization of labor or sympathetic to the aims and purposes of the Workers Alliance of America. The duty of the Advisory Committee shall be to advise the NEB on policy and program, to help in securing funds to extend and promote the work of the Workers Alliance. The National Advisory Committee shall be called into session at least every six months. It shall elect its own officers. Its decision shall not be binding upon the NEB, nor shall it issue any public statements except with permission of the NEB.

ARTICLE XI

Vacancies on the NEB
Section 1.　In the event of the vacancy of the President for any reason, the first vice-president shall assume his office and occupy it until the next national convention. In this event, each vice-president shall assume the next highest place in the list. In the event of the vacancies of all of the vice-presidents, the NEB shall elect vice-presidents from its own numbers.

Section 2.　Vacancies on the NEB shall be filled from a list of alternates elected at the national convention, to take office in order of numbers of votes received. Balloting for alternates shall be carried on separately from that of NEB members.

ARTICLE XII

Appeal from NEB
Appeal from the decisions of the NEB shall be through referendum of the

general membership or through action of the national convention. A referendum may be initiated upon the official request of states or affiliates from at least 20% of the membership located in at least eight (8) states. Membership for the purposes of referendum shall be computed as the average monthly dues payments from the time of the last convention call to the date of the call for the referendum. At least thirty (30) days notice shall be given after the date of the call for referendum.

ARTICLE XIII

Recall
Recall proceedings on any NEB member, including President and Vice-President, may be initiated by a 2/3 vote of the NEB, or by petition of 25% of the membership located in at least eight (8) states. Membership for purposes of recall shall be computed from the issuance of the last convention call to the date of request for the recall. A date shall be set by the NEB for the recall vote and a majority membership shall govern.

ARTICLE XIV

Location of National Headquarters
The National Headquarters of the Workers Alliance of America shall be in Washington, D.C. The NEB may, however, establish regional offices in order to maintain the closest possible contact with its groups in various parts of the country.

AMENDMENTS

This constitution may be amended by a majority vote of the National Convention or by National Referendum.

Notes

Chapter 9

1. The Workingmen's Party of the United States sent what they called an Address to President Hays. The text of this address was published July 26, 1877, in the *New York World* and July 30, 1877, in the *St. Louis Globe Democrat.*

Chapter 15

1. As part of a nationwide campaign for a working day of only eight hours, 3,000 workers attended a meeting May 4, 1886, in Chicago's Haymarket Square. As the meeting was about to end, 160 policemen appeared and ordered those present to disperse. Someone who has never been identified threw a bomb among the police (seven of the sixty-six who were wounded later died). Police opened fire on the meeting, wounding 200 and killing several. Later, eight Anarchists, only one of whom was at the meeting, were arrested, tried, found guilty of the bombing, and sentenced to death. Albert Parsons was among those who were hanged.

Chapter 16

1. Several philanthropists financed Tannenbaum's education, and he later became a professor at Columbia University and an authority on labor and Latin America.

2. Many years later, Benjamin described that first Hunger March: "It [went] from Hull House to City Hall in Chicago. It was organized by Baron [an Anarchist — F.F.] and my two sisters, and they were in the forefront of it, carrying a great big black banner which went almost all across the street with just one word on it — a black banner with one word in white letters, 'HUNGER!'"

Chapter 17

1. For convenience, this book omits the sequence of names used by Communists for their party. Communist Party or CP is used throughout, no matter what variant of that title was in use at the time.

Chapter 19

1. Some of the film footage taken at the March 6 demonstration can be seen today at the Museum of Modern Art in New York.

Chapter 20

1. The title "Unemployed Council(s)" is used throughout this book instead of "Unemployment Council(s)." Officers of the organization tried without much success to have the second appellation accepted because they wanted the council(s) to be regarded as open to employed as well as unemployed workers.

2. In 1982 Anne Burlak Timpson, still prominent in labor circles, was one of eighteen women who received the Wonder Woman Award given by the Wonder Woman Foundation.

Chapter 22

1. At least two of those who took part in the People's Lobby conference, Elmer Cope and Carl Brannin, would soon be identified with an organization called the Unemployed League. The league was quite separate from the Unemployed Council, which had brought together the Hunger March.

Chapter 24

1. In subsequent years Cacchione began taking an active part in the whole political scene in Brooklyn. In 1941, to the consternation of old-line politicians, and aided by the system of proportional representation then in force, he, an avowed Communist, was elected to the New York City Council.

Chapter 25

1. Herndon's attorney, Benjamin J. Davis, was an African-American lawyer in Atlanta, the son of a leading Republican politician. Davis became a passionate partisan of the jobless, and he, like his client, joined the Communist Party. A few years later Davis became a member of the City Council of New York, elected as a Communist (as was Peter V. Cacchione, who had also entered left-wing politics by way of the unemployed movement).

Chapter 27

1. Borders had a good working relationship with Joseph L. Moss, head of the Cook County Department of Public Aid, who was very wary of the Unemployed Council. Moss, in fact, collaborated with the police in sending informers into the UC, according to Beth Shulman, who in 1987 made a study of the Chicago Workers Committee for the Chicago Institute of Labor and Industrial Relations. Shulman reported that Moss even passed along rumors that the UC had begun to arm its members.

Chapter 28

1. The IWW had organized what it called Unemployed Leagues in 1914.

2. Budenz, who was a founder of the CPLA, moved into the American Workers Party when the CPLA dissolved. Later he joined the Communist Party and became editor of the *Daily Worker.* Later still, after a reconversion to Roman Catholicism, he acted as a professional witness, testifying against Communists

before the House Committee on Un-American Activities (HUAC).

Chapter 34

1. The title of the organization in the beginning was Works Progress Administration. It was later changed to Work Projects Administration. Under both titles it was known as WPA.

2. Woodrum, after his victorious assault on the WPA, retired from Congress and took a post as a lobbyist for the Plant Food Council at a salary three times greater than his congressional pay.

3. J. Parnell Thomas (Republican, New Jersey), a member of the House Committee on Un American Activities, was particularly active in attacking as Communists the workers on the WPA arts projects. His hostility continued into the 1950s, when he was instrumental in sending ten Hollywood screenwriters and directors to prison. Thomas himself was convicted of padding his congressional payroll and was sent to the Danbury Federal Correctional Institution, where two of his prison mates were screenwriters, Ring Lardner, Jr., and Lester Cole, whom he had helped send there.

Chapter 36

1. Breitman's friends republished the pamphlet on the occasion of his death fifty years after the Workers Alliance had made a laughingstock of New Jersey's do-nothing legislature.

2. The United Cannery and Agricultural Processors and Agricultural Workers of America (CIO).

3. *How to Win Work at a Living Wage or a Decent Standard of Relief with the Workers Alliance of America.*

4. In *Eleanor and Franklin*, Joseph P. Lash reported the incident this way: "[Roosevelt] was not quite sure how the Communist problem should be handled in the organizations in which they were active. If there was a chance to save the organization he thought liberals should make the fight and not simply withdraw. That was the advice he sent to Aubrey Williams in regard to the Workers Alliance, the organization of the unemployed. 'FDR would like to see David Lasser change name & purge communists, who put Russia first,' Eleanor advised Williams" (p. 602). The quotation is a marginal note made by Eleanor Roosevelt on a letter from Aubrey Williams to her, November 11, 1939.

5. Benjamin served for a while as head of the International Workers Order, and then was District Organizer of the CP in St. Louis. After that, in 1944, he and the CP parted company. In 1982, explaining this severance of a lifetime relationship, Benjamin said in an article in *In These Times*, "The American CP abandoned socialism by failing to safeguard principles and fundamental aims in the mistaken belief that this was the only way to secure a place and play a role in the mass movements of the time." Benjamin died May 12, 1983.

6. Lasser was out of work as unemployment was drawing to a close just before the war. Letters in the Roosevelt Library at Hyde Park record efforts he made to get a government job. He did have a post in the Works Progress Administration

for a while; then the Senate added an amendment to the WPA appropriation bill specifying that no money could be spent on paying a salary to David Lasser. He then became a labor consultant to Secretary of Commerce Averell Harriman. When Harriman was made ambassador to the USSR, he asked Lasser to be a labor consultant to the Marshall Plan, but Lasser had scarcely started this work when he was declared a security risk on the basis of allegations by an informer, who has never been identified (this was the McCarthy period). Lasser was again unemployed. The man who had tried to purge the Workers Alliance of radicals was himself purged as a radical. He finally got work as a researcher and negotiator for the International Brotherhood of Electrical Workers, a post he held until his retirement in 1968. In 1980, President Carter informed David Lasser that he had been found not to be a security risk.

Epilogue

1. Just as this book went to press, evidence appeared that work was going forward in studies of the organized unemployed. *Labor History*, Vol. 3, no. 3 (1989), carried "A New War in Dixie: Communists and the Unemployed in Birmingham, Alabama, 1930–1933," by Robin D.J. Kelley. My own account of events in the South would have been more illuminating had I had this paper at hand as I researched. Additional materials that I did not know about have come to light and will make it possible for others to expand my too-meager treatment of such phenomena as the Unemployed Leagues and the activities, early in this century, of Ben Reitman and J. Eads How.

Sources

Chapter 1

American Citizen (New York). January 16, 1808.

American Citizen (Philadelphia). January 16, 1808.

Asbury, Herbert. *The Gangs of New York.* Garden City, N.Y.: Garden City Publishing Company, 1928.

Bobbe, Dorothie. *DeWitt Clinton.* New York: Minton, Balch & Company, 1933.

Brandt, Lilian. *An Impressionistic View of the Winter of 1930–1931 in New York City.* New York: Welfare Council of New York City, 1932.

Channing, Edward. *The History of the United States.* 6 vols. New York: Macmillan Company, 1905–1925.

City of New York. *Minutes of the Common Council of the City of New York, 1784–1831.* 21 vols. 1917.

Commons, John R., et al. *History of Labor in the United States.* 4 vols. New York: Macmillan Company, 1918–1935.

Daitchman, George. "Labor and the 'Welfare State' in Early New York," *Labor History* 4, no. 3 (Fall 1963).

Foner, Philip S. *History of the Labor Movement in the United States.* Vol. 1, *From Colonial Times to the Founding of the American Federation of Labor.* New York: International Publishers, 1947.

General Advertiser (Philadelphia). January 2, 1808.

Goold, William. *Portland in the Past.* Portland, Maine: Printed for the author by B. Thurston & Company, 1886.

Lamb, Martha Joanna Reade. *History of the City of New York: Its Origin, Rise and Progress.* 3 vols. New York: A. S. Barnes, 1877–1880.

Lambert, John. *Travels Through Canada and the United States of North America in the Years 1806, 1807, 1808.* London: Printed for C. Cradock and W. Joy by Edinburgh, Doig, and Stirling, 1813.

McMaster, John Bach. *History of the People of the United States from the Revolution to the Civil War.* 8 vols. New York: D. Appleton, c1883–c1913.

Mercantile Advertiser (New York). 1808.

Mohl, Raymond A. *Poverty in New York, 1783–1825.* New York: Oxford University Press, 1971.

Morris, Richard B. *Government and Labor in Early America.* New York: Columbia University Press, 1946.

Mushkat, Jerome. *Tammany, The Evolution of a Political Machine*. New York: Syracuse University Press, 1971.

Myers, Gustavus. *The History of Tammany Hall*. New York: Boni and Liveright, 1917.

New York Evening Post. December 21, 26, 1807; January 8, 9, March 12, 1808.

New York Gazette. 1808.

New York Herald. 1808.

Public Advertiser (New York). 1808.

Renwick, James. *A Discourse on the Character and Public Services of DeWitt Clinton.* New York: G. & C. & H. Carvill, 1829.

Roads, Samuel, Jr. *The History and Traditions of Marblehead.* Marblehead, Mass.: N. A. Lindsey & Company, 1897.

Scharf, J. Thomas, and Wescott Thompson. *History of Philadelphia.* 7 vols. Philadelphia: L. H. Everts & Company, 1884.

Sears, Louis Martin. *Jefferson and the Embargo.* New York: Octogan Books, 1966.

Shankle, George Earlie. *American Nicknames.* New York: The H. W. Wilson Company, 1937.

Spectator (New York). 1808.

Stokes, I. N. Phelps. *Iconography of Manhattan Island, 1498–1909.* New York: Robert H. Dodd, 1915–1928.

Werner, Morris. *Tammany Hall.* New York: Doubleday & Company, 1928.

Wilson, James Grant. *The Memorial History of the City of New-York from Its First Settlement to the Year 1892.* New York: New-York History Company, 1893.

Chapter 2

Arky, Louis H. "The Mechanic's Union of Trade Associations and the Foundation of the Philadelphia Working Men's Movement." *Pennsylvania Magazine of History and Biography* 76 (April 1952).

Basset, T. D. Seymour. "The Secular Utopian Socialists." In *Socialism and American Life*, Donald Drew Egbert and Stow Parsons, eds. Princeton, N.J.: Princeton University Press, 1952.

Bestor, Arthur Eugene, Jr. *Backwoods Utopias: The Sectarian and Owenite Phases of Communitarian Socialism in America, 1663–1829*. Philadelphia: University of Pennsylvania Press, 1950.

Byrdsall, F. *The History of the Loco-Foco, or Equal Rights Party, Its Movements, Conventions and Proceedings.* 1842. Reprint. New York: Burt Franklin, 1967.

Carey, Mathew. *Mathew Carey, Autobiography.* Brooklyn: E. L. Schwaab, 1942.

Carlton, Frank T. "The Workingmen's Party of New York." *Political Science Quarterly* 22, no. 3 (September 1907).

City of New York. *Minutes of the Common Council of the City of New York, 1784–1831.* 21 vols. 1917.

Columbian (New York). February 19, 1819.

Commercial Advertiser (New York). January 11, 1829.

Commons, John R., et al. *History of Labor in the United States.* 4 vols. New York: Macmillan Company, 1918–1935.

Evans, George Henry. "History of the Origin and Progress of the Working Men's Party in New York." *The Radical* 2 (1842).

Faulkner, Harold Underwood. *American Economic History.* 7th ed. New York: Harper & Brothers, 1954.

Flint, James. *Flint's Letters from America, 1818–1820.* 1882. Reprint. Cleveland: A. H. Clark, 1904.

Foner, Philip S. *History of the Labor Movement in the United States.* Vol. 1, *From Colonial Times to the Founding of the American Federation of Labor.* New York: International Publishers, 1947.

Free Inquirer (Harmony, Indiana). December 19, 1829; November 27, 1830.

Harris, David. *Socialist Origins in the United States: American Forerunners of Marx, 1817–1832.* Assen, The Netherlands: Van Gorcum & Company, 1966.

Hobsbawm, E. J. *Primitive Rebels: Studies in Archaic Forms of Social Movement in the 19th and 20th Centuries.* New York: W. W. Norton & Company, 1965.

Hugins, Walter. *Jacksonian Democracy and the Working Class: A Study of the New York Working Men's Movement, 1829–1837.* Stanford, Calif.: Stanford University Press, 1960.

Johnson, Oakley C., ed. *Robert Owen in the United States.* New York: Humanities Press, 1970.

Klebaner, Benjamin J. "Public Poor Relief in America, 1790–1860." *Pennsylvania Magazine of History and Biography,* October 1954.

Lamb, Martha Joanna Reade. *History of the City of New York: Its Origin, Rise and Progress.* 3 vols. New York: A. S. Barnes, 1877–1880.

Lightner, Otto G. *The History of Business Depressions.* New York: Northeastern Press, 1922.

McMaster, John Bach. *History of the People of the United States from the Revolution to the Civil War.* 8 vols. New York: D. Appleton, c1883–c1913.

Mechanic's Free Press (Philadelphia). September 25, 1830.

Mitchell, Broadus, and Louise Pearson Mitchell. *American Economic History.* Boston: Houghton Mifflin Company, 1947.

Mohl, Raymond A. *Poverty in New York: 1783–1825.* New York: Oxford University Press, 1971.

Montgomery, David. "The Working Classes of the Pre-Industrial American City, 1780–1830." *Labor History* 9 (1968).

Myers, Gustavus. *The History of Tammany Hall.* New York: Boni and Liveright, 1917.

New York Evening Post. December 21, 26, 1807; January 8, 9, March 12, 1808.

Niles Weekly Register (Baltimore). 1819, 1829.

Owen, Robert. *A View of Society, and Other Writings.* New York: E. P. Dutton & Co., 1966.

Parrington, Vernon L., Jr. *American Dreams: A Study of American Utopias.* New York: Russell and Russell, 1964.

Pessen, Edward. "The Working Men's Party Revisited." *Labor History* 4 (Fall 1963).

———. "Thomas Skidmore, Agrarian Reformer in the Early American Labor Movement." *New York History* 25 (July 1954).

Rezneck, Samuel. "The Depression of 1819–1822: A Social History." *American Historical Review* 39 (October 1933).

Rothbard, Murray N. *The Panic of 1819: Reactions and Policies.* New York: Columbia University Press, 1962.

Skidmore, Thomas. *The Rights of Man to Property!* New York: A. Ming Jr., 1829.

———, ed. *Moral Physiology Exposed and Refuted.* New York: Skidmore & Jacobus, 1831.

Stokes, I. N. Phelps. *Iconography of Manhattan Island, 1498–1909.* New York: Robert H. Dodd, 1915–1928.

Swisher, Carl Brent. *American Constitutional Development.* Boston: Houghton Mifflin Company, 1954.

Warden, D. B. *Statistical, Political, Historical Account of the United States of North America.* 3 vols. Edinburgh: A. Constable & Company, 1819.

Wright, Frances. *Views of Society and Manners in America.* Edited by Paul R. Baker. Cambridge, Mass.: Harvard University Press, 1963.

Chapters 3 and 4

Abbott, Edith. "Harriet Martineau and the Employment of Women in 1836." *Journal of Political Economy* 14 (1906).

Alexander, De Alva Standwood. *A Political History of the State of New York.* 3 vols. 1909. Reprint. Port Washington, N.Y.: I. J. Friedman, 1969.

American Monthly Magazine. April 1837.

Asbury, Herbert. *The Gangs of New York.* Garden City, N.Y.: Garden City Publishing Company, 1928.

Association for the Improvement of the Condition of the Poor (New York). *Annual Reports.* 1854, 1855.

Bimba, Anthony. *History of the American Working Class.* New York: International Publishers, c1927.

Brownson, Orestes Augustus. *Babylon is Falling.* Boston: J. R. Batts, 1937.

———. "The Laboring Classes." *Boston Quarterly Review*, July 1840.

Byrdsall, F. *The History of the Loco-Foco, or Equal Rights Party, Its Movements, Conventions and Proceedings.* 1842. Reprint. New York: Burt Franklin, 1967.

Carey, H. C. *Principles of Political Economy.* 3 vols. Philadelphia: Carey, Lea & Blanchard, 1837–1840.

Channing, William Ellery. *Lectures on the Elevation of the Labouring Portion of the Community*. Boston: W. D. Ticknor, 1840.

Cheyney, Edward Potts. *The Anti-Rent Agitation in the State of New York, 1839–1846*. Philadelphia: Porter & Coates, 1887.

City of New York. *Minutes of the Common Council of the City of New York, 1784–1831*. 21 vols. 1917.

Cole, Margaret. *Robert Owen of New Lanark, 1773–1858*. New York: Oxford University Press, 1953.

Commercial Advertiser (New York). 1837.

Commons, John R., et al. *History of Labor in the United States*. 4 vols. New York: Macmillan Company, 1918–1935.

Courier and Enquirer (New York). 1837.

Darling, Arthur B. "The Workingmen's Party in Massachusetts, 1833–1834." *American Historical Review* 29 (October 1923):81–86.

Dayton, Abram Child. *Last Days of Knickerbocker Life in New York*. New York: G. W. Harlan, 1882.

Dickens, Charles. *American Notes and Pictures from Italy*. 1844. Reprint. New York: Oxford University Press, 1957.

Foner, Philip S. *History of the Labor Movement in the United States*. Vol. 1, *From Colonial Times to the Founding of the American Federation of Labor*. New York: International Publishers, 1947.

Free Enquirer (New Harmony, Indiana). 1834.

Greeley, Horace. *Recollections of a Busy Life*. New York: J. B. Ford & Company, 1868.

———. *The Tribune Almanac*. New York: The Tribune Office, 1838.

Gutman, Herbert G. *Work, Culture, and Society in Industrializing America*. New York: Alfred A. Knopf, 1976.

Headley, J. T. *The Great Riots of New York, 1712 to 1873*. New York: E. B. Treat, 1873.

Heffner, William Clinton. *History of Poor Relief Legislation in Pennsylvania, 1682–1913*. Cleona, Penn.: Holzapfel Publishing Company, 1913.

Hugins, Walter. *Jacksonian Democracy and the Working Class: A Study of the New York Working Men's Movement, 1829–1837*. Stanford, Calif.: Stanford University Press, 1960.

Jenkins, John Stillwell. *History of Political Parties in the State of New York*. Auburn, N.Y.: Alden & Markham, 1846.

Johnson, Oakley C., ed. *Robert Owen in the United States*. New York: Humanities Press, 1970.

Journal of Commerce (New York). March 6, 1837.

The Knickerbocker (New York). May, March 1837.

Lamb, Martha Joanna Reade. *History of the City of New York: Its Origin, Rise and Progress*. 3 vols. New York: A. S. Barnes, 1877–1880.

McMaster, John Bach. *History of the People of the United States from the Revolution to the Civil War.* 8 vols. New York: D. Appleton, c1883–c1913.

Martineau, Harriet. *Society in America.* 1837. Reprint. Seymour Martin Lipset, ed. Gloucester, Mass.: P. Smith, 1968.

Mathews, Cornelius. *Arcturus,* January 1841.

Mott, Frank Luther. *A History of American Magazines.* 5 vols. Cambridge, Mass.: Harvard University Press, 1938–1968.

———. *American Journalism: A History of Newspapers in the United States through 260 Years, 1690 to 1950.* Rev. ed. New York: Macmillan Company, 1950.

National Laborer (Philadelphia). 1837.

Nevins, Allan, ed. *Diary of Philip Hone, 1828–1851.* 12 vols. 1927. Reprint. New York: Dodd, Mead & Company, 1936.

New Era. March 2, October 7, 1837.

New Haven Register. 1837.

New Yorker (Newspaper). April 22, May 27, 1837; January 20, 1838.

New York Evening Post. 1837.

New York Mirror. 1837.

New York Star. 1837.

New York Times. 1837.

Niles Weekly Register (Baltimore). January 10, February 25, August 12, 1837; February 13, 1840.

North American Review (Boston). 1837.

Norwalk Chronicle (Connecticut). 1837.

Pennsylvania Inquirer (Philadelphia). January 7, 1937.

Pessen, Edward. *Most Uncommon Jacksonians: Radical Leaders of the Early Labor Movement.* Albany: State University of New York Press, 1967.

Plain Dealer (New York). 1937.

Publius (Ogden, James De Peyster). *Remarks on the Currency of the United States.* New York: Wiley & Putnam, 1840.

Radical Reformer. 1836.

Rezneck, Samuel. *Business Depressions and Financial Panics: Essays in American Business and Economic History.* Westport, Conn.: Greenwood Publishing Corp., 1968.

Roosevelt, Clinton. *The Science of Government Founded on Rational Law.* New York: Dean & Trevett, 1841.

Rudé, George F. *The Crowd in History: A Study of Popular Disturbances in France and England 1730–1848.* New York: John Wiley & Sons, 1964.

Scharf, J. Thomas, and Wescott Thompson. *History of Philadelphia.* 7 vols. Philadelphia: L. H. Everts & Company, 1884.

Simpson, Stephen. *The Workingman's Manual.* Philadelphia: T. L. Bonsal, 1831.

Sketches of Popular Tumults: Illustrations of the Evils of Social Ignorance. London, 1833.

Spooner, Lysander. *Poverty: Its Illegal Cause and Legal Cure.* Boston: B. Marsh, 1846.

United States Gazette (Philadelphia). 1835.

United States Magazine and Democratic Review (Washington, D.C.). 1837.

Weekly Visitor, or Ladies Museum (New York). 1837.

Werner, Morris. *Tammany Hall.* New York: Doubleday & Company, 1928.

Williams, Mr. "Political Symptoms and Popular Rights." *North American Quarterly Review* (c1835).

Woolen, Evans. "Labor Troubles between 1834 and 1837." *Yale Review* 1 (May 1892).

Workingmen of Charlestown, Massachusetts. "An Address to their Brethren throughout the Commonwealth and the Union." *Boston Quarterly Review,* January 1841.

Chapter 5

Anonymous. *The Wealth and Biography of the Wealthy Citizens of the City of New York.* New York, 1855.

Association for the Improvement of the Condition of the Poor (New York). *Annual Reports.* 1854, 1855.

Bankers Magazine 15 (1855).

Cale, Edgar B. *The Organization of Labor in Philadelphia, 1850–1870.* Philadelphia: Edgar B. Cale, 1940.

The Citizen. February 3, December 23, 28, 1854; January 13, 15, 1855.

City of New York. *Minutes of the Common Council of the City of New York, 1784–1831.* 21 vols. 1854.

Faust, Albert Bernhart. *The German Element in the United States.* 2 vols. Boston: Houghton Mifflin Company, 1909.

Graham's American Monthly Magazine of Literature and Art (Philadelphia). 1854; January 1855.

Greeley, Horace. *The Crystal Palace and its Lessons: A Lecture.* New York: DeWitt and Davenport, 1852.

Leslie's Weekly. 1854, 1855.

Linn, William A. *Horace Greeley.* 1903. Reprint. New York: D. Appleton, 1912.

McGuffey, William Holmes. *McGuffey's Newly Revised Eclectic First Reader.* Cincinnati: W. B. Smith & Company, 1853.

McMaster, John Bach. *The Acquisition of Political, Social and Industrial Rights of Man in America.* New York: F. Ungar Publishing Company, 1961.

Mushkat, Jerome. *Tammany, The Evolution of a Political Machine.* New York: Syracuse University Press, 1971.

Myers, Gustavus. *The History of Tammany Hall.* 2nd ed., revised and enlarged. New York: Boni and Liveright, 1917.

National Labor Tribune (Pittsburgh). 1854, 1855.

Nevins, Allan, and Milton Halsey Thomas, eds. *The Diary of George Templeton Strong.* Seattle: University of Washington Press, 1988.

New York Herald. December 19, 22, 25, 26, 27, 30, 1854; January 6, 8, 9, 13, 14, 16, February 25, 1855.

New York Times. December 1854; January 1855.

New York Tribune. December 22, 23, 25, 30, 1854; January 6, 8, 1855.

Parrington, Vernon L., Jr. *American Dreams: A Study of American Utopias.* New York: Russell and Russell, 1964.

Putnam Monthly Magazine. 1854, 1855.

Sanger, William B. *History of Prostitution.* 1856. Revised. New York: Eugenics Publishing Company, 1937.

Schlueter, Hermann. *Die Internationale in Amerika.* Chicago: Deutsche Sprachgruppe der Sozialist Partei der Ver Staaten, 1918.

Weitling, Wilhelm Christian. *Garantieen der Harmonie und Freiheit.* Hamburg: Verlag des Verfassers, 1849.

Werner, Morris. *Tammany Hall.* New York: Doubleday & Company, 1928.

Chapter 6

Annual Report of the Board of Commissioners of the Central Park, 1858–1870.

Asbury, Herbert. *The Gangs of New York.* Garden City, N.Y.: Garden City Publishing Company, 1928.

Association for the Improvement of the Condition of the Poor (New York). *Annual Reports.* 1854, 1855.

Atlantic Monthly. November 1857.

Barlow, Elizabeth. *Frederick Law Olmsted in New York.* New York: Praeger, 1972.

Bimba, Anthony. *The Molly Maguires.* New York: International Publishers, c1932.

A Brief and Popular Account of the Panics and Revulsions in the U.S. from 1690 to 1857. New York: Members of the New York Press, 1857.

Brooklyn Times. October 21, 1857; July 12, 1858.

Carey, Henry Charles. *Principles of Social Science.* 1858–1859. Reprint. New York: A. M. Kelley, 1963.

Commons, John R., et al. *History of Labor in the United States.* 4 vols. New York: Macmillan Company, 1918–1935.

Ely, Richard T. *French and German Socialism In Modern Times.* New York: Harper & Brothers, 1883.

Evening Post (New York). 1857, 1858.

Fabos, Julius G., Gordon T. Milde, and V. Michael Weinmeyer. *Frederick Law Olmstead, Sr., Founder of Landscape Architecture in America.* Amherst: University of Massachusetts Press, 1968.

Feder, Leah Hannah. *Unemployment Relief in Periods of Depression: A Study of Measures Adopted in Certain American Cities, 1857 through 1922.* New York: Russell Sage Foundation, 1936.

Fein, Albert. *Frederick Law Olmstead and the American Environmental Tradition.* New York: George Braziller, 1972.

Foner, Philip S. *History of the Labor Movement in the United States.* Vol. 1, *From Colonial Times to the Founding of the American Federation of Labor.* New York: International Publishers, 1947.

Graham's American Monthly Magazine of Literature and Art (Philadelphia). 1857.

Greeley, Horace. *Why I Am A Whig: Reply To An Inquiring Friend.* New York: Tribune Office, 1852.

Harper's New Monthly Magazine. November 1857.

Harper's Weekly (New York). 1857, 1858.

Haswell, Charles H. *Reminiscences of an Octogenarian of the City of New York.* New York: Harper & Brothers, 1896.

A History of the Forgeries, Perjuries, and Other Crimes of our "Model" Mayor (New York). 1856.

Hoxie, Joseph. *Pauperism — Its Evils, Causes and Remedy.* New York: C. W. Baker, 1859.

Klebaner, Benjamin Joseph. *Public Poor Relief in America.* New York: Arno Press, 1976.

Frank Leslie's Illustrated Weekly (New York). 1857–1858.

Lossing, Benson John. *History of New York City to 1884.* Vol. 2. New York: G. E. Perine, 1884.

Marx, Karl, and Friedrich Engels. *Karl Marx and Frederick (sic) Engels: Selected Correspondence, 1846–1895.* 1934. Reprint. Translated by Dona Torr. New York: International Publishers, 1942.

McLaughlin, Charles C., ed. *Selected Letters of Frederick Law Olmstead.* Cambridge: Harvard University Press, 1960.

Nevins, Allan, and Milton Halsey Thomas, eds. *The Diary of George Templeton Strong.* Seattle: University of Washington Press, 1988.

New York Daily Times. November 7, 9, 11, 12, 24, 25, 1857.

New York Herald. 1857, 1858.

New York Post. 1857, 1858.

New York Tribune. 1857, 1858.

Obermann, Karl. *Joseph Weydemeyer: Pioneer of American Socialism.* New York: International Publishers, 1947.

Philadelphia Ledger. October 26, 1857.

Putnam's Monthly. 1857, 1858.

Reed, Henry Hope, and Sophia Duckworth. *Central Park: A History and a Guide.* New York: C. N. Potter, 1967.

Sanger, William B. *History of Prostitution.* 1856. Revised. New York: Eugenics Publishing Company, 1937.

Scharf, J. Thomas, and Wescott Thompson. *History of Philadelphia.* 7 vols. Philadelphia: L. H. Everts & Company, 1884.

Sylvis, James C. *The Life, Speeches, Labors and Essays of William H. Sylvis, Late President of the Iron Moulders International Union.* Philadelphia: Claxton Reusen & Hoffelfinger, 1872.

Wilson, James G., ed. *The Memorial History of the City of New York From Its First Settlements to the Year 1892.* 4 vols. New York: New York History Company, 1892–1893.

Chapter 7

Adamic, Louis. *Dynamite, The Story of Class Violence in America.* New York: Viking Press, 1931.

Association for the Improvement of the Condition of the Poor (New York). *Annual Reports.* 1873, 1874.

Boyer, Richard O., and Herbert M. Morais. *Labor's Untold Story.* 3rd ed., rev. New York: United Electrical, Radio & Machine Workers of America, 1976.

Broun, Heywood, and Margaret Leech. *Anthony Comstock, Roundsman of the Lord.* New York: A. & C. Boni, 1927.

Chicago Times. November 11, 17, 1873.

Chicago Tribune. November 13–18, 1873.

Dacus, Joseph A. *Annals of the Great Strikes in the United States: A Reliable History and Graphic Description of the Causes and Thrilling Events of the Labor Strikes and Riots of 1877.* 1877. Reprint. New York: Burt Franklin, 1969.

David, Henry. *The History of the Haymarket Affair; a Study in the American Social-Revolutionary and Labor Movements.* New York: Farrar & Rinehart, 1936.

Engels, Friedrich. *Socialism: Utopian and Scientific.* Edited by W. D. Henderson. Baltimore: Penguin Books, 1967.

Feder, Leah Hannah. *Unemployment Relief in Periods of Depression: A Study of Measures Adopted in Certain American Cities, 1857 through 1922.* New York: Russell Sage Foundation, 1936.

Foner, Philip S. *History of the Labor Movement in the United States.* Vol. 1, *From Colonial Times to the Founding of the American Federation of Labor.* New York: International Publishers, 1947.

———, ed. *The Formation of the Workingmen's Party of the United States: Proceedings of the Union Congress Held at Philadelphia, July 19–22, 1876.* New York: American Institute for Marxist Studies, 1976.

Garlin, Sender. *John Swinton: American Radical (1829–1901)*. New York: American Institute for Marxist Studies, 1976.

Gompers, Samuel. *Seventy Years of Life and Labor: An Autobiography*. New York: E. P. Dutton, 1925.

Gutman, Herbert G. "The Tompkins Square 'Riot' in New York City." *Labor History* 2 (Winter 1955).

———. "The Failure of the Movement by the Unemployed for Public Works in 1873." *Political Science Quarterly* 80 (June 1965)

———. *Power and Culture: Essays on the American Working Class*. Edited by Ira Berlin. New York: Pantheon Books, 1987.

Headley, J. T. *The Great Riots of New York, 1712–1873*. New York: E. B. Treat, 1873.

Johnson, Oakley. *Marxism in United States History Before the Russian Revolution (1876–1917)*. New York: Humanities Press, 1974.

Lambert, H. G. *Lambert's New York City Guide and Business Registry*. New York: H. G. Lambert & Company, 1873.

Frank Leslie's Illustrated Weekly (New York). January, February 1874.

Lynch, Dennis Tilden. *"Boss" Tweed: The Story of a Grim Generation*. New York: Boni & Liveright, 1927.

Marx, Karl, and Friedrich Engels. *Letters to Americans, 1848–1895: A Selection*. Edited by Alexander Trachtenberg. New York: International Publishers, 1953.

McCabe, James Dabney (Edwin Winston Martin, pseud.). *The History of the Great Riots*. Philadelphia: National Publishing Company, 1877.

McGuire, Peter J. *Diary*. Photocopied. Tamiment Library, New York University.

McNeill, George E., ed. *The Labor Movement: The Problem of Today*. New York: M. W. Hazen Company, 1888.

Myers, Gustavus. *The History of Tammany Hall*. 2nd ed., revised and enlarged. New York: Boni and Liveright, 1917.

Nevins, Allan, and Milton Halsey Thomas, eds. *The Diary of George Templeton Strong*. Seattle: University of Washington Press, 1988.

New Leader (New York). January 15, 1927.

New York. *New York State Assembly Journal*. January 14, 1874.

New York Post. January 13, 1874.

New York Sun. October 23, November 4, 1873; January 6, 14, 19, 1874.

New York Times. November 16, 1873; January 12–16, 1874; January 9, 16, 1927.

New York World. January 11, 12, 14, 19, 29, 1874.

Oberholtzer, E. P. *Jay Cooke: Financier of the Civil War*. 2 vols. Philadelphia: G. W. Jacobs & Company, 1907.

Philadelphia Bulletin. November 7, 1873.

Symes, Lillian, and Travers Clement. *Rebel America: The Story of Social Revolt in the United States.* New York: Harper & Brothers, 1934.

The Toiler. May 27, July 25, August 1, September 5, 1874.

Woodhull and Claflin's Weekly (New York). November 10, 1873.

Young, Alfred J. (curator of the New York Police Academy Museum). Letter to author, December 14, 1977.

Chapter 8

The Alarm (Chicago). October 4, 1884.

Ashbaugh, Carolyn. *Lucy Parsons: American Revolutionary.* Chicago: Charles H. Kerr, 1976.

Beard, Charles A., and Mary R. Beard. *The Rise of American Civilization.* Vol. 2. *The Industrial Era.* New York: Macmillan Company, 1927.

Boyer, Richard O., and Herbert M. Morais. *Labor's Untold Story.* 3rd ed., rev. New York: United Electrical, Radio & Machine Workers of America, 1976.

Calmer, Alan. *Labor Agitator: The Story of Albert R. Parsons.* New York: International Publishers, 1937.

Chicago Times. 1873–1874.

Chicago Tribune. 1873–1874.

Colcord, Joanna C. *Cash Relief.* New York: Russell Sage Foundation, 1936.

Commons, John R., et al. *History of Labor in the United States.* 4 vols. New York: Macmillan Company, 1918–1935.

Faulkner, Harold Underwood. *American Economic History.* 7th ed. New York: Harper & Brothers, 1954.

Feder, Leah Hannah. *Unemployment Relief in Periods of Depression: A Study of Measures Adopted in Certain American Cities,. 1857 through 1922.* New York: Russell Sage Foundation, 1936.

Foner, Philip S. *History of the Labor Movement in the United States.* Vol. 1, *From Colonial Times to the Founding of the American Federation of Labor.* New York: International Publishers, 1947.

———. *The Great Labor Uprising of 1877.* New York: Monad Press, 1977.

Frank Leslie's Illustrated Weekly (New York). January, February 1874.

Lewis, Lloyd, and Henry Justin Smith. *Chicago: The History of Its Reputation.* New York: Harcourt, Brace & Company, 1929.

McNeill, George E., ed. *The Labor Movement: The Problem of Today.* New York: The M. W. Hazen Company, 1888.

Mitchell, Broadus, and Louise Pearson Mitchell. *American Economic History.* Boston: Houghton Mifflin Company, 1947.

Parsons, Lucy E. *Life of Albert R. Parsons.* 2nd ed. rev. Chicago: Mrs. Lucy E. Parsons, 1903.

Symes, Lillian, and Travers Clement. *Rebel America: The Story of Social Revolt in the United States.* New York: Harper & Brothers, 1934.

Chapter 9

Aveling, Edward B. *The Chicago Anarchists*. London: W. R. Reeves, 1877.

Aveling, Edward B., and Eleanor Marx Aveling. *The Working-Class Movement in America*. 2nd ed. London: S. Sonnenschein & Company, 1891.

Bancroft, Hubert Howe. *History of the Pacific States: California*. San Francisco: History Company, 1884–1890.

———. *The Works of Hubert Howe Bancroft*. Vol. 37, *Popular Tribunals*. San Francisco: A. L. Bancroft & Company, 1887.

Browne, Carl. Letter to Ira B. Cross, September 2, 1908. Bancroft Library, University of California, Berkeley.

Bruce, Robert V. *1877, Year of Violence*. Indianapolis: Bobbs-Merrill Company, 1959.

Bryce, James. *The American Commonwealth*. 2 vols. New York: Macmillan Company, 1889.

Byington, Lewis Francis, and Oscar Lewis. *The History of San Francisco*. Chicago: S. J. Clarke Publishing Company, 1931.

Carlson, Oliver, and Ernest Sutherland Bates. *Hearst, Lord of San Simeon*. New York: Viking Press, 1936.

Commons, John R., et al. *History of Labor in the United States*. 4 vols. New York: Macmillan Company, 1918–1935.

Cross, Ira B. *History of the Labor Movement in California*. Berkeley: University of California Press, 1935.

Dacus, Joseph A. *Annals of the Great Strikes in the United States: A Reliable History and Graphic Description of the Causes and Thrilling Events of the Labor Strikes and Riots of 1877*. 1877. Reprint. New York: Burt Franklin, 1969.

Daily Alta Californian. January 4, 1878.

Foner, Philip S. *The Great Labor Uprising of 1877*. New York: Monad Press, 1977.

Garlin, Sender. "William Dean Howells and the Haymarket Era." Occasional Paper No. 33. New York: American Institute for Marxist Studies, 1979.

George, Henry. "The Kearney Agitation in California." *Popular Science Monthly* 17 (August 1880).

Hillquit, Morris. *The History of Socialism in the United States*. 1873. Reprint. 5th ed. New York: Russell & Russell, 1965.

Hunt, Rockwell D. *California's Stately Hall of Fame*. Stockton, Calif.: College of the Pacific, 1950.

Johnson, Oakley. *Marxism in United States History Before the Russian Revolution (1876–1917)*. New York: Humanities Press, 1974.

Kauer, Ralph. "Workingmen's Party of California." *Pacific Historical Review* 13 (September 1944).

Lawrence, John. "The Working Class and the Labor Movement." Ph.D. dissertation, University of California, Berkeley, 1979.

Nevins, Allan. *American Press Opinions*. Boston: D. C. Heath & Company, 1928.

Oser, Jacob. *Henry George*. New York: Twayne Publishers, 1974.

Roney, Frank. *Frank Roney, Irish Rebel and California Labor Leader, an Autobiography*. Edited by Ira B. Cross. Berkeley: University of California Press, 1931.

San Francisco Bulletin. 1877–1880.

San Francisco Call. 1877–1880.

San Francisco Chronicle. 1877–1880.

San Francisco Examiner. November 27, 1877; January 5, March 12, 1878; March 6, 1880; February 9, 10, 13, 18, 23, 28, 1881.

Saxton, Alexander. *The Indispensable Enemy: Labor and the Anti-Chinese Movement in California*. Berkeley: University of California Press, 1971.

Stedman, J. C. and R. A. Leonard. *The Workingmen's Party of California*. San Francisco: Bacon & Company, 1878.

Symes, Lillian and Travers Clement. *Rebel America: The Story of Social Revolt in the United States*. New York: Harper & Brothers, 1934.

Young, John P. *Journalism in California*. San Francisco: Chronicle Publishing Company, 1915.

———. *San Francisco: A History of the Pacific Coast Metropolis*. San Francisco: S. J. Clarke Publishing Company, 1912.

Chapters 10 and 11

The Alarm (Chicago). October 25, November 22, 29, 1884.

Ashbaugh, Carolyn. *Lucy Parsons: American Revolutionary*. Chicago: Charles H. Kerr, 1976.

Aveling, Edward B. *An American Journey*. New York: John W. Lovell Company, 1887.

———. *The Chicago Anarchists: A Statement of Facts*. London: W. Reeves, 1877.

Aveling, Edward B., and Eleanor Marx Aveling. *The Working-Class Movement in America*. 2nd ed. London: S. Sonnenschein & Company, 1891.

Bancroft, Hubert Howe. *The Works of Hubert Howe Bancroft*. Vol. 37, *Popular Tribunals*. San Francisco: A. L. Bancroft & Company, 1887.

Beard, Charles A., and Mary R. Beard. *The Rise of American Civilization*. Vol. 2, *The Industrial Era*. New York: Macmillan Company, 1927.

Bellamy, Edward. "How to Employ the Unemployed! Should the State or Municipality Provide Work for Its Unemployed?" *New Nation* 4, no. 4 (January 27, 1894).

Bloor, Ella Reeve. *We Are Many: An Autobiography by Ella Reeve Bloor.* New York: International Publishers, 1940.

Boyer, Richard O., and Herbert M. Morais. *Labor's Untold Story*. 3d ed., rev. New York: United Electrical, Radio & Machine Workers of America, 1976.

Buchanan, Joseph R. *The Story of a Labor Agitator.* New York: Outlook Company, 1903.

Byington, Lewis Francis, and Oscar Lewis. *The History of San Francisco.* Chicago: S. J. Clarke Publishing Company, 1931.

Calmer, Alan. *Labor Agitator: The Story of Albert R. Parsons.* New York: International Publishers, 1937.

Chicago Times. 1873–1874.

Chicago Tribune. 1873–1874.

Colcord, Joanna C. *Cash Relief.* New York: Russell Sage Foundation, 1936.

Commons, John R., et al. *History of Labor in the United States.* 4 vols. New York: Macmillan Company, 1918–1935.

David, Henry. *The History of the Haymarket Affair; a Study in the American Social-Revolutionary and Labor Movements.* New York: Farrar & Rinehart, 1936.

Drinnon, Richard. *Rebel in Paradise: A Biography of Emma Goldman.* New York: Bantam Books, 1973.

Engels, Friedrich. *The Labor Movement in America.* New York: L. Weiss, 1887.

Evening World Herald (Omaha). April 14, 16–24, 1894.

Faulkner, Harold Underwood. *American Economic History.* 7th ed. New York: Harper & Brothers, 1954.

Feder, Leah Hannah. *Unemployment Relief in Periods of Depression: A Study of Measures Adopted in Certain American Cities, 1857 through 1922.* New York: Russell Sage Foundation, 1936.

Field, Homer H., and Hon. Joseph R. Reed. *History of Pottawattamie County, Iowa, from the Earliest Historic Times to 1907.* 2 vols. Chicago: S. J. Clarke Publishing Company, 1907.

Fink, Leon. "Workingmen's Democracy: The Knights of Labor in Local Politics, 1886–1896." Ph.D. dissertation, University of Rochester, New York, 1977.

Foner, Philip S. *The Great Labor Uprising of 1877.* New York: Monad Press, 1977.

———. *History of the Labor Movement in the United States.* Vol. 2, *From the Founding of the A.F. of L. to the Emergence of American Imperialism.* 2nd ed. New York: International Publishers, 1975.

———, ed. *Autobiographies of the Haymarket Martyrs.* New York: Humanities Press, 1969.

Fusfeld, Daniel R. *The Rise and Repression of Radical Labor, USA, 1877–1918.* Chicago: Charles H. Kerr Publishing Company, 1980.

George, Henry. *Progress and Poverty: An Inquiry into the Cause of Industrial Depressions and of Increase of Want with Increase of Wealth — The Remedy.* New York: Henry George, 1879.

Goldman, Emma. *Living My Life.* New York: Alfred A. Knopf, 1931.

Hall, A. Cleveland. "An Observer in Coxey's Camp." *The Independent* 46 (May 17, 1894).

Harlan, Edgar R. *A Narrative History of the People of Iowa.* Chicago: American Historical Society, 1931.

Hooper, Osman C. "The Coxey Movement in Ohio." *Ohio State Archaeological and Historical Society Publications* 9 (1901).

John Swinton's Paper (New York). 1883, 1887.

Jones, Mary. *The Autobiography of Mother Jones*. 3rd ed. Edited by Mary Field Parton. Chicago: Illinois Labor History Society, 1976.

The Knight of Labor (Lynn, Mass.). July 18, 1885.

Lewis, Lloyd, and Henry Justin Smith. *Chicago: The History of its Reputation*. New York: Harcourt, Brace & Company, 1929.

"The Life of a Forgotten Giant: P. J. McGuire, Father of Labor Day." McGuire Papers, Tamiment Library, New York University.

Lloyd, Henry Demarest. "The Lords of Industry." *North American Review* 37 (June 1884).

Marx, Karl, and Friedrich Engels. *Letters to Americans, 1848–1895: A Selection*. Edited by Alexander Trachtenberg. New York: International Publishers, 1953.

McNeill, George E., ed. *The Labor Movement: The Problem of Today*. New York: M. W. Hazen Company, 1888.

Merriam, Eve. *The Voice of Liberty: The Story of Emma Lazarus*. New York: Farrar and Strauss, 1959.

Morris, George. "True History of Labor Day." *World Magazine*, September 1, 1983.

New York Herald. December 30, 1883.

New York Times. July 14, 1880; 1882; 1883.

Parsons, Lucy E. *Life of Albert R. Parsons*. 2nd ed. rev. Chicago; Mrs. Lucy E. Parsons, 1903.

Pennsylvania. *Report of the Committee Appointed to Investigate the Railroad Riots in July 1877*. Legal Document No. 29. Harrisburg, Pennsylvania, 1878.

Powderly, Terence V. "The Army of the Discontented." *North American Review* April 1885.

———. *Thirty Years of Labor, 1859–1889*. Columbus, Ohio: Excelsior Publishing House, 1890.

Steklov, Iurii Mikhailovich (G. M. Stekloff, pseud.). *History of the First International*. Translated by Eden & Cedar Paul. London: M. Lawrence, 1928.

Symes, Lillian, and Travers Clement. *Rebel America: The Story of Social Revolt in the United States*. New York: Harper & Brothers, 1934.

Tebbel, John. *An American Dynasty*. Garden City, N.Y.: Doubleday & Company, 1947

U.S. Bureau of Labor Statistics. *First Annual Report, 1886*.

Van Gelder, Lawrence. "Labor Day and the Man Who Began It All." *New York Times*, August 29, 1979.

Will, Thomas E. "The Unemployed: A Symposium." *Arena* 10 (October 1894).

Chapter 12

American Federation of Labor. *Proceedings of the American Federation of Labor 1881–1905.* Vol. 3, *1893–1896.* Bloomington, Ill.: Pantagraph Printing and Stationery Company, 1905–1906.

Bellamy, Edward. *Looking Backward, 2000–1887.* 1888. Reprint. Edited by John L. Thomas. Cambridge: Harvard University Press, 1967.

Briggs, John E. "Jack London, Impulsive Youth." *The Palimpsest* 52 (June 1971).

Buchanan, Joseph R. *The Story of a Labor Agitator.* New York: The Outlook Company, 1903.

Cedar Rapids Gazette (Iowa). July 21, 1957.

Chicago Tribune. May 15, 1894.

Closson, Carlos C., Jr. "The Unemployed in American Cities." *Quarterly Journal of Economics* 8 (January 1894).

Council Bluffs Directory (Iowa). 1893–1894.

The Council Bluffs Globe (Iowa). April 12, 13, 16, 17, 19, 21, 1894.

Council Bluffs Non-Pareil (Iowa). April 13–May 9, 1894.

Daily Gate City (Keokuk, Iowa). May 16, June 3, 1894.

Des Moines Leader (Iowa). April 15, 21, May 22, 1894.

Foner, Philip S. *History of the Labor Movement in the United States.* Vol. 2, *From the Founding of the A.F. of L. to the Emergence of American Imperialism.* 2nd ed. New York: International Publishers, 1975.

———, ed. *Jack London, American Rebel.* New York: Citadel Press, 1947.

Frank, Henry. "The Crusade of the Unemployed." *Arena* 10 (July 1894).

The Gladbrook Tama Northern (Gladbrook, Iowa). August 12, 1955.

Haywood, William D. *Bill Haywood's Book: The Autobiography of William D. Haywood.* New York: International Publishers, 1929.

Hicks, John D. *The Populist Revolt: A History of the Farmers' Alliance and the People's Party.* Lincoln: University of Nebraska Press, 1961.

Hooper, Osman C. "The Coxey Movement in Ohio." *Ohio State Archaeological and Historical Society Publications* 9 (1901).

Iowa Centennial. June 11, 1956.

Iowa State Register (Des Moines). April 25, 27, 29, May 3, 7, 1894.

Josephson, Matthew. *The Robber Barons.* New York: Alfred A. Knopf, 1967.

Journal of the Knights of Labor. September 14, October 12, 1873; January 8, 1894.

Kelley (*sic*), Charles T. "Are Radicals Insane?" *Current History Magazine,* May 1924.

The Labor Leader (Boston). September 23, 1893.

Langford, Norma Jean. "Kelly's Army." *The Iowan,* Summer 1970.

Lindsey, Almont. *The Pullman Strike, The Story of a Unique Experiment and of a Great Labor Upheaval.* Chicago: University of Chicago Press, 1942.

Lloyd, Henry Demarest. *Wealth Against Commonwealth.* New York: Harper & Brothers, 1894.

London, Charmian K. *The Book of Jack London.* 2 vols. New York: Century Company, 1921.

London, Jack. "A Jack London Diary. Tramping With Kelly Through Iowa." *The Palimpsest* 52 (June 1971). First published in *The Palimpsest* 7 (May 1926).

———. "The March of Kelly's Army. The Story of an Extraordinary Migration." *Cosmopolitan* 43 (October 1907).

———. "Hoboes That Pass in the Night." *Cosmopolitan* 44 (December 1907).

———. *The Road.* 1907. Reprint. Santa Barbara: Peregrine Publishers, 1907.

London, Joan. *Jack London and His Times.* New York: Doubleday, Doran & Company, 1939.

Madison, Charles A. *Critics and Crusaders: A Century of American Protest.* New York: Henry Holt & Company, 1947.

Marx, Karl, and Friedrich Engels. *Letters to Americans, 1848–1895: A Selection.* Edited by Alexander Trachtenberg. New York: International Publishers, 1953.

McCallum, Douglas. *The Dogs and the Fleas by One of the Dogs.* Chicago: Douglas McCallum, 1893.

McCook, J. J. "A Tramp Census and its Revelations." *Forum* 15 (August 1893).

McMurry, Donald L. *Coxey's Army: A Study of the Industrial Army Movement of 1894.* Boston: Little, Brown & Company, 1929.

Murphy, Joseph P. "The Army that Ate Pie for Breakfast." *Omaha World Herald,* April 15, 1971.

New York Times. April 29, May 2, 1894.

Omaha Bee (Nebraska). April 16, 17, 18, 20, 21, 22, 23, 24, 25, 26, 27, May 2, 7, 1894.

Omaha World Herald (Nebraska). April 25, 26, 27, 1892; May 2, 3, 5, 1894.

Ottumwa Courier (Iowa). April 21–May 29, 1894; September 14, 1946; July 1, 1976.

The Palimpsest (State Historical Society of Iowa). Special Issue on Jack London and Kelly's Army. Vol. 52 (June 1971).

Peterson, William J. "From Des Moines to Keokuk." *Palimpsest* 52 (June 1971).

Reeve, Carl. *The Life and Times of Daniel De Leon.* New York: Humanities Press, 1972.

Rezneck, Samuel. *Business Depressions and Financial Panics: Essays in American Business and Economic History.* Westport, Conn.: Greenwood Publishing Corp., 1968.

San Francisco Chronicle. April 8, 1894.

Saniel, Lucien. *Territorial Expansion.* New York: Labor News Company, c1898.

Saxton, Alexander. "San Francisco Labor and the Populist Progressive Insurgencies." *Pacific Historical Review* 24 (November 1965).

Schwantes, Carlos A. *Coxey's Army: An American Odyssey*. Lincoln: University of Nebraska Press, 1985.

Sioux City Journal (Iowa). April 13, 1913.

Stetson, H. L. "The Industrial Army." *The Independent* 46 (May 31, 1893).

Stuart Locomotive (Stuart, Iowa). April 20, 27, May 4, 1894.

Tygiel, Jules Everett. "Workingmen in San Francisco: 1880–1901." Ph.D. dissertation, University of California, Los Angeles, 1977.

Vincent, Henry. *The Story of the Commonweal*. Chicago: W. B. Conkey Company, 1894.

Vinson, Edrie Lee. "General Jacob Sechler Coxey and His Relationship to the Industrial Army of the Pacific Northwest." Master's thesis, Carroll College, Helena, Montana, 1973.

Washington Press (Washington, Iowa). May 16, 1894.

Woodcock, George. *Anarchism: A History of Libertarian Ideas and Movements*. Cleveland: World Publishing Company, 1962.

Wykoff, Walter A. *The Workers*. New York: Charles Scribner's Sons, 1899.

Zinn, Howard. *A People's History of the United States*. New York: Harper & Row, 1980.

Chapter 13

Cedar Rapids Gazette (Iowa). July 21, 1957.

Chicago Tribune. May 15, 1894.

Council Bluffs Globe (Iowa). April 17, 1894.

Council Bluffs Non-Pareil (Iowa). April 13–May 9, 1894; July 26, 1936.

Daily Gate City (Keokuk, Iowa). May 16, June 3, 1894.

Des Moines Leader (Iowa). April 15, May 22, 1894.

Des Moines Register (Iowa). November 13, 1927; May 1, 1938; May 26, 1968.

Frank, Henry. "The Crusade of the Unemployed." *Arena* 10 (July 1894).

Gaboury, William J. *Dissension in the Rockies: A History of Idaho Populism*. New York: Garland Publishing Company, 1988.

Hooker, Reverend George E. "The Unemployed in Boston." *The Independent*, April 18, 1894.

Iowa Centennial. June 11, 1956.

Iowa State Register. April 24, May 10, 11, 1894.

McMurry, Donald L. *Coxey's Army: A Study of the Industrial Army Movement of 1894*. Boston: Little, Brown & Company, 1929.

New York Graphic. June 20, 1946.

New York Times. April 23, 27, 29, May 1–5, 1894.

Omaha Bee (Nebraska). April 29, 1894.

Ottumwa Courier (Iowa). April 21–May 29, 1894; September 14, 1946; July 1, 1976.

Reeve, Carl. *The Life and Times of Daniel De Leon.* New York: Humanities Press, 1972.

Reichert, William O. "The Melancholy Political Thought of Morrison I. Swift." *New England Quarterly,* December 1976.

San Francisco Chronicle. April 8, 1894.

Schwantes, Carlos A. *Coxey's Army: An American Odyssey.* Lincoln: University of Nebraska Press, 1985.

Sioux City Journal (Iowa). April 13, 1913.

Splitter, Henry Winfred. "Concerning Vinette's Los Angeles Regiment of Coxey's Army." *Pacific Historical Review* 27 (February 1948).

Stimson, Grace Hillman. *Rise of the Labor Movement in Los Angeles.* Berkeley: University of California Press, 1955.

Stuart Locomotive (Stuart, Iowa). April 20, 27, May 4, 1894.

Swift, Morrison I. *A League of Justice or Is It Right to Rob Robbers?* Boston: Commonwealth Society, 1893.

——. *Capitalists Are the Cause of Unemployment.* Boston: Libbie Show Print, 1894.

——. *What a Tramp Learns in California.* San Francisco: Society of American Socialists, 1896.

Vincent, Henry. *The Story of the Commonweal.* Chicago: W. B. Conkey Company, 1894.

Vinson, Edrie Lee. "General Jacob Sechler Coxey and His Relationship to the Industrial Armies of the Pacific Northwest." Master's thesis, Carroll College, Helena, Montana, 1973.

Chapter 14

Andrews, Elisha Benjamin. *The United States in Our Own Times.* New York: Charles Scribner's Sons, 1903.

Austin, Shirley Plumer. "Coxey's Commonweal Army." *The Chautauquan,* June 1894.

Cedar Rapids Gazette (Iowa). July 21, 1957.

Chicago Tribune. March 25, May 2, 15, 1894.

Closson, Carlos C., Jr. "The Unemployed in American Cities." *Quarterly Journal of Economics* 8 (January 1894).

Council Bluffs Globe (Iowa). April 17, 20, 1894.

Council Bluffs Non-Pareil (Iowa). April 13–May 9, 1894; July 26, 1936.

Coxey, Jacob S. "Cause and Cure." January 1898. Jacob S. Coxey Papers. Massillon Museum, Massillon, Ohio.

——. "Coxey, His Own Story of the Commonweal." "Why the March to Washington in 1894." "Why the March to Washington in 1914." Jacob S. Coxey Papers. Massillon Museum, Massillon, Ohio.

Daily Gate City (Keokuk, Iowa). May 16, June 3, 1894.

Des Moines Leader (Iowa). April 15, May 22, 1894.

Des Moines Register (Iowa). November 13, 1927; May 1, 1938; May 26, 1968.

Des Moines Tribune (Iowa). May 3, 1975.

Foner, Philip S. *History of the Labor Movement in the United States.* Vol. 2, *From the Founding of the A.F. of L. to the Emergence of American Imperialism.* 2nd ed. New York: International Publishers, 1975.

Fusfeld, Daniel R. *The Rise and Repression of Radical Labor, USA, 1877–1918.* Chicago: Charles H. Kerr Publishing Company, 1980.

Garrett, Garet. "The Driver." *Saturday Evening Post,* December 24, 1921.

Heald, Edward Thornton. *The McKinley Era.* Vol. 2, *1875–1901.* Canton, Ohio: Stark County Historical Society, 1950.

Hooper, Osman C. "The Coxey Movement in Ohio." *Ohio State Archaeological and Historical Society Publications* 9 (1901).

Hicks, John D. *The Populist Revolt: A History of the Farmers' Alliance and the People's Party.* Lincoln: University of Nebraska Press, 1961.

Industrial Army Petitions. National Archives, Washington, D.C.

Iowa Centennial. June 11, 1956.

Iowa State Register. April 24, May 2, 8, 9, 1894.

Journal of the Knights of Labor. August 24, 1893.

The J. S. Coxey Good Roads Association of the United States. *Bulletin No. 6* (January 26, 1895). Jacob S. Coxey Papers. Massillon Museum, Massillon, Ohio.

Lewis, Lloyd, and Henry Justin Smith. *Chicago: The History of Its Reputation.* New York: Blue Ribbon Books, 1933.

McCallum, Douglas. *The Dogs and the Fleas by One of the Dogs.* Chicago: Douglas McCallum, 1893.

McMurry, Donald L. *Coxey's Army: A Study of the Industrial Army Movement of 1894.* Boston: Little, Brown & Company, 1929.

Myers, Chesterfield W. *Coxey's Warning: A Vindication of Coxeyism.* Chesterfield W. Myers, 1894.

Omaha World Herald (Nebraska). May 5, 1894.

Ottumwa Courier (Iowa). April 21–May 29, 1894; September 14, 1946; July 1, 1976.

Pugh, Edwin V. "General Jacob S. Coxey, Politician." Master's thesis, University of Pittsburgh, 1937.

Reeve, Carl. *The Life and Times of Daniel De Leon.* New York: Humanities Press, 1972.

San Francisco Chronicle. April 8, 1894.

Schwantes, Carlos A. *Coxey's Army: An American Odyssey.* Lincoln: University of Nebraska Press, 1985.

Sioux City Journal (Iowa). April 13, 1913.

Stead, William Thomas. "Coxeyism: A Character Sketch." *American Review of Reviews* 10 (July 1894).

———. *If Christ Came to Chicago: A Plea for the Union of All Who Love in the Service of All Who Suffer.* Chicago: Laird & Lee, 1894.

Stuart Locomotive (Stuart, Iowa). April 20, 27, May 4, 1894.

U.S. Congress. Senate. Miscellaneous Documents. 53rd Congress, 2nd Session, Docs. 151, 163, 171, 251.

Veblen, Thorstein B. "The Army of the Commonweal." *Journal of Political Economy* 2 (June 1894).

Vincent, Henry. *The Story of the Commonweal.* Chicago: W. B. Conkey Company, 1894.

Vinson, Edrie Lee. "General Jacob Sechler Coxey and His Relationship to the Industrial Armies of the Pacific Northwest." Master's thesis, Carroll College, Helena, Montana, 1973.

Chapter 15

Benjamin, Herbert. Interview with author, n.d.

Borough, Reuben. "The Chicago I Remember, 1907." *Illinois State Historical Society Journal* 59, no. 2 (Summer 1966).

Boston Herald. March 26, 1914.

Brandt, Lilian. *An Impressionistic View of the Winter of 1930–1931 in New York City.* New York: Welfare Council of New York City, 1932.

Brissenden, Paul F. *The I.W.W.* New York: Russell and Russell, 1957.

Bruns, Roger A. *The Damnedest Radical: The Life and World of Ben Reitman, Chicago's Celebrated Social Reformer, Hobo King, and Whorehouse Physician.* Urbana: University of Illinois Press, 1987.

Chaplin, Ralph. "Solidarity Forever." *Songs of Workers to Fan the Flames of Discontent.* 34th ed. Chicago: Industrial Workers of the World, 1974.

"The Church and the Unemployed." The *Masses*, April 1914.

Conlin, Joseph. *Bread and Roses Too: Studies of the Wobblies.* Westport, Conn.: Greenwood Press, 1969.

Coxey, Jacob S. Letter to Martin H. Glynn, Governor of New York, March 10, 1914. Jacob S. Coxey Papers. Massillon Museum, Massillon, Ohio.

Debs, Eugene V. *Voices of Revolt.* New York: International Publishers, 1928.

De Caux, Len. *Labor Radical from the Wobblies to CIO: A Personal History.* Boston: Beacon Press, 1970.

De Cleyre, Voltairine. "The Case in Philadelphia: An Appeal." *Mother Earth,* March, July, October, 1908.

Devine, Edward T. *Misery and Its Causes.* New York: Macmillan Company, 1909.

Dubofsky, Melvyn. *We Shall Be All: A History of the Industrial Workers of the World.* New York: Quadrangle/New York Times Book Company, 1969.

Feder, Leah Hannah. *Unemployment Relief in Periods of Depression: A Study of Measures Adopted in Certain American Cities, 1857 through 1922.* New York: Russell Sage Foundation, 1936.

Foner, Philip S. *The History of the Labor Movement in the United States.* Vol. 4, *The Industrial Workers of the World, 1905-1917.* New York: International Publishers, 1965.

Goldman, Emma. *Living My Life.* Salt Lake City: Gibbs Smith, 1982.

Gompers, Samuel. *Seventy Years of Life and Labor: An Autobiography.* New York: E. P. Dutton, 1925.

Haywood, William D. *Bill Haywood's Book: The Autobiography of William D. Haywood.* New York: International Publishers, 1929.

Industrial Union Bulletin. February 29, March 14, May 16, 23, July 25, September 19, December 12, 1908.

Industrial Workers of the World. *Proceedings of the First Convention of the Industrial Workers of the World.* 1905. Reprint. New York: New York Labor News Company, 1969.

Johnson, Oakley. *Marxism in United States History Before the Russian Revolution (1876-1917).* New York: Humanities Press, 1974.

Kipnis, Ira. *The American Socialist Movement, 1897-1912.* New York: Columbia University Press, 1952.

Kornbluh, Joyce L., ed. *Rebel Voices: An I.W.W. Anthology.* Ann Arbor: University of Michigan Press, 1964.

Kraditor, Aileen S. *The Radical Persuasion, 1890-1917.* Baton Rouge: University of Louisiana Press, 1981.

Mitchell, W. C. *Business Cycles and Their Causes.* Berkeley: University of California Press, 1971.

Mother Earth (New York). March, July, October 1908.

New York Times. April 9, 1905; January 4, 15, March 11, May 2, 21, 24, June 2, 5, 18, August 29, September 2, 8, October 10, December 2, 5, 15, 29, 1907; January 5, 9, 15, 21, 24, 27, 28, February 1, 7, 20, 21, 29, March 14, 29, 30, 31, April 4, 5, 7, 8, 12, 15, 19, 21, May 8, 9, 20, June 30, July 30, August 1, 12, 14, 26, September 8, October 4, 18, 25, November 3, December 18, 1908.

Piven, Frances Fox, and Richard A. Cloward. *Regulating the Poor: The Functions of Public Welfare.* New York: Vintage Books, 1971.

Preston, William, Jr. *Aliens and Dissenters: Federal Suppression of Radicals, 1903-1933.* Cambridge: Harvard University Press, 1963.

Ringenbach, Paul T. *Tramps and Reformers, 1873-1916: The Discovery of Unemployment in New York.* Westport, Conn.: Greenwood Press, 1973.

Solenberger, Alice W. *One Thousand Homeless Men.* New York: Russell Sage Foundation, 1911.

Swift, Morrison I. *There Must Be Revolution.* Boston: Liberty Press, 1932.

Thompson, Fred, and Patrick Murfin. *The I.W.W.: Its First Seventy Years, 1905–1975*. Chicago: Industrial Workers of the World, 1976.

"The Unemployed in the Churches of New York." *Survey* 31 (March 28, 1914).

Chapter 16

Alsberg, Henry G. "Was It Something Like This?" *The Masses*, April 1914.

Anderson, Nels. *The Hobo, The Sociology of Homeless Men*. Chicago: University of Chicago Press, 1923.

Ashbaugh, Carolyn. *Lucy Parsons: American Revolutionary*. Chicago: Charles H. Kerr, 1976.

Benjamin, Herbert. Interview with author, n.d.

———. Memoir. Herbert Benjamin Papers. Ernst Benjamin collection, Washington, D.C.

Bruns, Roger A. *The Damnedest Radical: The Life and World of Ben Reitman, Chicago's Celebrated Social Reformer, Hobo King, and Whorehouse Physician*. Urbana: University of Illinois Press, 1987.

Chaplin, Ralph. "Solidarity Forever." *Songs of Workers to Fan the Flames of Discontent*. 34th ed. Chicago: International Workers of the World, 1974.

———. *Wobbly: The Rough-and-Tumble Story of an American Radical*. Chicago: University of Chicago Press, 1948.

"The Church and the Unemployed." *The Masses*, April 1914.

Debs, Eugene V. *Voices of Revolt*. New York: International Publishers, 1928.

Dubovsky, Melvin. *We Shall Be All: A History of the Industrial Workers of the World*. New York: Quadrangle/New York Times Book Company, 1969.

Eastman, Max. "The Tannenbaum Crime." *The Masses*, May 1914.

Feder, Leah Hannah. *Unemployment Relief in Periods of Depression: A Study of Measures Adopted in Certain American Cities, 1857 through 1922*. New York: Russell Sage Foundation, 1936.

Flynn, Elizabeth Gurley. *Rebel Girl: An Autobiography, My First Life*. New York: International Publishers, 1973.

Foner, Philip S. *The History of the Labor Movement in the United States*. Vol. 4, *The Industrial Workers of the World, 1905–1917*. New York: International Publishers, 1965.

Gambs, John S. "The Decline of the I.W.W." Ph.D. dissertation, Columbia University, New York, 1932.

Garrison, Dee. *Mary Heaton Vorse, the Life of an American Insurgent*. Philadelphia: Temple University Press, 1989.

Goldman, Emma. *Living My Life*. Salt Lake City: Gibbs Smith, 1982.

Hall, Covington. "Us the Hoboes." *International Socialist Review*, April 1914.

"Helen Keller's New Book." *International Socialist Review*, December 1913.

Hill, Joe. "How to Make Work for the Unemployed." *International Socialist Review*, December 1914.

International Socialist Review. December 1913; February, May, June 1914.

Kauffman, Reginald Wright. "The March of the Hungry Men." *International Socialist Review*, May 1914.

Kedward, H. Roderick. *The Anarchists; The Men Who Shocked an Era.* New York: American Heritage Press, 1971.

Kipling, Rudyard. "The Workingman's Answer to the Capitalist Class." *International Socialist Review*, February 1914.

Kornbluh, Joyce L., ed. *Rebel Voices: An I.W.W. Anthology.* Ann Arbor: University of Michigan Press, 1964.

Labor Knight ("Published wherever Carl Browne goes and whenever he chooses."). Copies in the Bancroft Library, University of California, Berkeley.

Literary Digest. May 19, 1928.

London, Jack. "The Army of Revolution." *International Socialist Review*, May 1914.

London, Meyer. "The Unemployed." *The Masses*, April 1915.

Los Angeles Times. December 26, 27, 1913.

Madison, Charles A. *Critics and Crusaders: A Century of American Protest.* New York: Henry Holt & Company, 1947.

Marcy, Mary E. "How the Capitalists Solve the Problem of the Unemployed." *International Socialist Review*, May 1914.

Mitchell, W. C. *Business Cycles and Their Causes.* Berkeley: University of California Press, 1971.

Mother Earth (New York). February 1914.

New York Times. 1914. Passim.

Parsons, Lucy E. *Life of Albert E. Parsons.* 2nd ed., rev. Chicago, 1903.

Ringenbach, Paul T. *Tramps and Reformers, 1873–1916.* Westport, Conn.: Greenwood Press, 1973.

Ritterskamp, Godfred. "Unemployment and the Six-hour Day." *International Socialist Review*, January 1914.

San Francisco Chronicle. February 18, 19, 20, 21, 22, 23, 1914.

Sinclair, Upton. "To Frank Tannenbaum in Prison." *International Socialist Review*, June 1914.

Solidarity. 1914.

Steffens, Lincoln. *The Autobiography of Lincoln Steffens.* New York: Harcourt Brace & Company, 1931.

Tannenbaum, Frank. "Tannenbaum's Speech." *The Masses*, May 1914.

Thompson, Fred and Patrick Murfin. *The I.W.W.: Its First Seventy Years, 1905–1975.* Chicago: Industrial Workers of the World, 1976.

Tresca, Carlo. *The Unemployed and the I.W.W.* Chicago: Industrial Workers of the World, n.d.

"The Unemployed and the Churches of New York." *Survey* 31, no. 26 (March 28, 1914).

Vorse, Mary Heaton. *A Footnote to Folly: Reminiscences of Mary Heaton Vorse.* New York: Farrar and Rinehart, 1935.

Weinstein, James. *The Decline of Socialism in America, 1912–1925.* New York: Monthly Review Press, 1967.

Young, Arthur. "Carl Browne, The Labor Knight." *The Masses,* April 1914.

Chapter 17

Amter, Israel, and Sadie Van Veen. Memoirs. Tamiment Library, New York University.

Browder, Earl. *Unemployment: Why It Occurs and How to Fight It.* Chicago: Workers Party of America, 1924.

Chambers, Clarke A. *Seedtime of Reform: American Social Service and Social Action, 1918–1933.* Minneapolis: University of Minnesota Press, 1963.

Commons, John R. "Unemployment Compensation and Prevention." *Survey* 47 (October 1, 1921).

Draper, Theodore. *American Communism and Soviet Russia: The Formative Period.* New York: Viking Press, 1960.

Dunn, Robert W. *The Palmer Raids.* New York: International Publishers, 1948.

Faulkner, Harold Underwood. *American Economic History.* 7th ed. New York: Harper & Brothers, 1954.

Feder, Leah Hannah. *Unemployment Relief in Periods of Depression: A Study of Measures Adopted in Certain American Cities, 1857 through 1922.* New York: Russell Sage Foundation, 1936.

Foster, William Z. *Pages From A Worker's Life.* New York: International Publishers, 1939.

Gompers, Samuel. *Seventy Years of Life and Labor; An Autobiography.* New York: E. P. Dutton & Company, 1925.

Grin, Carolyn. "The Unemployment Conference of 1921: An Experiment in National Cooperative Planning." *Mid-America: An Historical Review* 55, no. 2 (April 1973).

Howard, Donald C. *The WPA and Federal Relief Policy.* New York: Russell Sage Foundation, 1943.

Josephson, Harold. "The Dynamics of Repression: New York During the Red Scare." *Mid-America: An Historical Review* 59, no. 3 (October 1977).

Kelley (sic), Charles T. "Are Radicals Insane?" *Current History* 20 (May 1924).

King, Willford Isbell. *Employment Hours and Earning in Prosperity and Depression United States, 1920–1922.* New York: National Bureau of Economic Research, 1923.

Lenin, V. I. *"Left-Wing" Communism: An Infantile Disorder.* New York: International Publishers, 1934.

Malyshev, Sergei. *Unemployed Councils in St. Petersburg in 1906.* San Francisco: Proletarian Publishers, 1976.

Nelson, Daniel. *Unemployment Insurance: The American Experience*. Madison: University of Wisconsin Press, 1969.

New York. Legislature. Joint Committee Investigating Seditious Activities and Revolutionary Radicalism. Albany, New York, 1920.

New York Times. May 14, 15, November 25, 1920; January 5, 6, 10, March 7, April 20, 30, May 6, 8, 11, August 23, 30, 31, September 9, 14, 15, 16, 17, 18, 19, 20, 21, 24, 26, October 10, November 13, 21, 25, 27, December 4, 22, 1921; February 5, 7, 8, 10, 12, 14, 20, March 4, 1922; February 7, 11, 14, March 19, April 26, June 9, 1928.

President's Conference on Unemployment: Emergency Measures Recommended for Recovery of Employment. Government Printing Office, Washington, D.C., 1921.

Preston, William, Jr. *Aliens and Dissenters: Federal Suppression of Radicals, 1903-1933*. Cambridge, Mass.: Harvard University Press, 1963.

Renshaw, Patrick. *The Wobblies: The Story of Syndicalism in the United States*. Garden City, N.Y.: Doubleday & Company, 1967.

Seymour, Helen. "The Organized Unemployed." Master's thesis, University of Chicago, 1937.

Symes, Lillian, and Travers Clement. *Rebel America: The Story of Social Revolt in the United States*. New York: Harper & Brothers, 1934.

U.S. Congress. *Congressional Record*. 67th Congress, 2nd Session, 1922. Vol. 62, pt. 9.

Wolfe, Alan. *The Seamy Side of Democracy: Repression in America*. New York: David McKay, 1973.

Chapter 18

Bart, Philip, ed. *Highlights of a Fighting History: Sixty Years of the Communist Party USA*. New York: International Publishers, 1979.

Bernstein, Irving. *The Lean Years: A History of the American Worker, 1920-1933*. Boston: Houghton Mifflin Company, 1960.

Brandt, Lilian. *An Impressionistic View of the Winter of 1930-1931 in New York City*. New York: Welfare Council of New York City, 1932.

Bremner, William H. *Depression Winters: New York Social Workers and the New Deal*. Philadelphia: Temple University Press, 1984.

Browder, Earl Russell. *Out of A Job*. New York: Workers Library Publishers, 1929.

———. "The October Plenum of the Central Committee, CPUSA." *The Communist* 8, no. 10 (November 1929).

Brown, Josephine Chaplin. *Public Relief, 1929-1939*. New York: Henry Holt & Co., 1949.

Business Week. October 7, 1931.

Cantwell, Robert. *Land of Plenty*. New York: Farrar and Rinehart, 1934.

Chambers, Clarke A. *Seedtime of Reform: American Social Service and Social Action, 1918–1933*. Minneapolis: University of Minnesota Press, 1963.

Colcord, Joanna C., et al. *Emergency Work Relief as Carried Out in Twenty-six American Communities, 1930–1931*. New York: Russell Sage Foundation, 1932.

Corey, Lewis. *The Decline of American Capitalism.* New York: Covici Friede, 1934.

Daily Worker (New York). October, November, December 9, 1929; January 23, 24, 27, March 5, 6, 7, 8, December 9, 1930.

De Caux, Len. *Labor Radical: From Wobblies to CIO, A Personal History.* Boston: Beacon Press, 1970.

Douglas, Paul H., and Aaron Director. *The Problem of Unemployment.* New York: Macmillan Company, 1931.

Ellis, Edward Robb. *A Nation in Torment: The Great American Depression, 1929–1939.* New York: Capricorn Books, 1971.

"Ex-General Coxey: Champion of the Jobless." *The Literary Digest*, May 19, 1928.

Fine, Nathan S. "Unemployment, a World-Wide Problem." *Current History*, September 1930.

Fox-Schwartz, Bonnie. "Unemployment Relief in Philadelphia, 1930–1932: A Study of the Depression's Impact on Volunteerism." *Philadelphia Public Ledger*, June 20, 1932.

Garraty, John A. *Unemployment in History: Economic Thought and Public Policy.* New York: Harper & Row, 1978.

Glazer, Nathan. *The Social Basis of American Communism.* New York: Harcourt Brace & World, 1961.

Gold, Michael. *Mike Gold: A Literary Anthology.* Edited by Michael Folsom. New York: International Publishers, 1972.

Hallgren, Mauritz. *Seeds of Revolt: A Study of American Life and the Temper of the American People During the Depression.* New York: Alfred A. Knopf, 1933.

Harper, Elsie D. *Out of a Job: Proposals for Unemployment Insurance.* New York: Woman's Press, 1931.

Hayes, E. P. *Activities of the President's Emergency Committee for Employment (October 7, 1930–August 19, 1931).* Printed for private circulation. Concord, N.H.: Rumford Press, 1936.

Hoover, Herbert. *New Day; Campaign Speeches of Herbert Hoover, 1928.* Stanford, Calif.: Stanford University Press, 1928.

Horan, James D. *The Desperate Years: From Stock Market Crash to World War II.* New York: Bonanza Books, 1962.

Kalar, Joseph. "Unemployed Anthology: Notes from Minnesota." *New Masses* 6 (September 30, 1930).

Kessler-Harris, Alice. "Stratifying by Sex: Understanding the History of Working Women." In *Labor Market Segmentation*, Richard C. Edwards, Michael

Reich, and David M. Gordon, eds. Lexington, Mass.: D. C. Heath & Company, 1975.

Komisar, Lucy. *Down and Out in the USA*. New York: Franklin Watts, 1973.

Lebergott, Stanley. *Manpower in Economic Growth*. New York: McGraw Hill, 1964.

Leonard, Jonathan Norton. *Three Years Down*. New York: Carrich and Evans, 1939.

MacDonald, G. B. "In Search of a Job." *Christian Century* 47 (April 23, 1930).

Maurer, David J. "Relief Problems and Politics in Ohio." In *The New Deal*, John Braeman et al., eds. Columbus: Ohio State University Press, 1975.

Maurer, Harry. *Not Working: An Oral History of the Unemployed*. New York: Holt, Rinehart, and Winston, 1979.

Minehan, Thomas. *Boy and Girl Tramps of America*. New York: Farrar and Rinehart, 1934.

Mitchell, Broadus. *Depression Decade: From New Era Through New Deal, 1921–1941*. New York: Rinehart & Company, 1947.

Myers, William Starr, and Walter H. Newton. *The Hoover Administration: A Documented Narrative*. New York: Charles Scribner's Sons, 1936.

Naison, Mark. *The Communist Party in Harlem: 1928–1936*. Urbana: University of Illinois Press, 1983.

Nathan, Robert R. *Estimate of Unemployment in the United States*. Geneva: International Labor Office, 1936.

New Republic. April 29, 1931.

New York Times. January 0, February 7, 11, 14, March 18, 19, 24, April 26, August 11, 1928; October 30, 1929; September 20, 1931.

"Our Immediate Tasks." *Party Organizer* 2, nos. 3 & 4, (March–April 1928).

Piven, Frances Fox, and Richard A. Cloward. *Regulating the Poor: The Functions of Public Welfare*. New York: Vintage Books, 1971.

———. *Poor People's Movements: Why They Succeed, How They Fail*. New York: Pantheon Books, 1977.

Prago, Albert. "The Organization of the Unemployed and the Role of the Radicals, 1929–1935." Ph.D. dissertation, Institute of Policy Studies, Washington, D.C., 1976.

President's Conference on Unemployment. "Recent Economic Changes." In *Out of a Job: Proposals For Unemployment Insurance*, Elsie D. Harper, ed. New York: Woman's Press, 1931.

"A Program on Unemployment." *The Communist* 7, no. 6 (June 1928).

Quinten, B. T. "Oklahoma Tribes; The Great Depression and the Indian Bureau." In *Hitting Home: The Great Depression in Town and Country*, Bernard Sternsher, ed. Chicago: Quadrangle Books, 1970.

Recreation Department of the Clearing House for Unemployed Homeless Men. *Breadline Frolics, a Minstrel*. Chicago, 1932.

Rubin, Charles. *The Log of Rubin the Sailor.* New York: International Publishers, 1973.

Schlesinger, Arthur M., Jr. *The Coming of the New Deal.* Boston: Houghton Mifflin Company, 1958.

———. *The Age of Roosevelt.* Vol. 1, *The Crisis of the Old Order: 1919–1932.* Boston: Houghton Mifflin Company, 1957.

Searls, Virginia C. "Cuyahoga County Relief Administration Clients as Members of the Unemployment Council." Master's thesis, Western Reserve University, Cleveland, Ohio, 1935.

Seymour, Helen. "The Organized Unemployed." Master's thesis, University of Chicago, 1937.

Shannon, David. *The Great Depression.* New York: Prentice Hall, 1960.

———. *The Socialist Party of America: A History.* New York: Macmillan Company, 1955.

Socialist Labor Party. *Unemployment . . . Why?* New York, 1957.

Swift, Morrison I. *There Must Be Revolution.* Boston: Liberty Press, 1934.

Thompson, Fred, and Patrick Murfin. *The I.W.W.: Its First Seventy Years, 1905–1975.* Chicago: Industrial Workers of the World, 1976.

Unemployed (New York). No. 5 (1932).

Vorse, Mary Heaton. *A Footnote to Folly: Reminiscences of Mary Heaton Vorse.* New York: Farrar and Rinehart, 1935.

Warren, Harris Gaylord. *Herbert Hoover and the Great Depression.* New York: Oxford University Press. 1959.

Wecter, Dixon. *The Age of the Great Depression.* New York: Macmillan Company, 1948.

Wolfe, Alan. *The Seamy Side of Democracy: Repression in America.* New York: David McKay, 1973.

Chapter 19

Amter, Israel, and Sadie Van Veen. Memoirs. Tamiment Library, New York University.

Bell, Daniel. *Marxian Socialism in the United States.* Princeton, N.J.: Princeton University Press, 1967.

Benjamin, Herbert. Memoirs. Herbert Benjamin Papers. Ernst Benjamin collection, Washington, D.C.

Bernstein, Irving. *The Lean Years: A History of the American Worker, 1920–1933.* Boston: Houghton Mifflin Company, 1960.

Boyer, Richard O., and Herbert M. Morais. *Labor's Untold Story.* 3rd ed., rev. New York: United Electrical, Radio & Machine Workers of America, 1976.

Brandt, Lilian. *Glimpses of New York in Previous Depressions: A Confidential Interim Report Made as a Feature of the Study of Social Welfare During the Business Depression.* New York: Welfare Council Research Bureau, 1933.

Brecher, Jeremy. *Strike!* San Francisco: Straight Arrow Books, 1972.

Browder, Earl. *Out of A Job.* New York: Workers Library Publishers, 1929.

Brown, Josephine Chaplin. *Public Relief, 1929–1939.* New York: Henry Holt & Co., 1949.

Catholic Worker (New York). Vol. 1, no. 1 (1933).

"Comintern Instructions to the Forthcoming Party Congress." *Communist International,* March 1929.

The Communist. May 1930, September 1930.

Daily News (New York). March 7, 1930.

Daily Worker (New York). December 9, 1929; January 23, 24, 27, March 5, 6, 7, 8, December 9, 1930.

Daily World (New York). March 6, 8, 1969.

DeCaux, Len. *Labor Radical: From Wobblies to CIO, A Personal History.* Boston: Beacon Press, 1970.

Dos Passos, John. "Back To Red Hysteria." *New Republic,* July 2, 1930.

Drake, St. Clair, and Horace R. Cayton. *Black Metropolis: A Study of Negro Life in a Northern City.* 1945. Reprint. New York: Harper & Row, 1966.

Draper, Theodore. *The Roots of American Communism.* New York: Viking Press, 1957.

Ellis, Edward Robb. *A Nation in Torment: The Great American Depression, 1929–1939.* New York: Capricorn Books, 1971.

Engdahl, J. Louis. *Sedition! To Protest and Organize Against War, Hunger, and Unemployment.* New York: International Labor Defense, 1930.

Foner, Philip O. *Women and the American Labor Movement from World War I to the Present.* New York: Free Press, 1979.

Foster, William Z. *From Bryan to Stalin.* New York: International Publishers, 1937.

———. *Pages From A Worker's Life.* New York: International Publishers, 1939.

Garraty, John A. *Unemployment in History: Economic Thought and Public Policy.* New York: Harper & Row, 1978.

Glazer, Nathan. *The Social Basis of American Communism.* New York: Harcourt Brace & World, 1961.

Grant, Joanne, ed. *Black Protest: History, Documents, and Analyses, 1619 to the Present.* Greenwich, Conn.: Fawcett Publications, 1968.

Hallgren, Mauritz. *Seeds of Revolt: A Study of American Life and the Temper of the American People During the Depression.* New York: Alfred A. Knopf, 1933.

Hathaway, C. A. "An Examination of Our Failure to Organize the Unemployed." *The Communist,* September 1930.

Herald Tribune (New York). March 7, 1930.

Herndon, Angelo. *Let Me Live.* 1937. Reprint. New York: Arno Press, 1969.

Horan, James D. *The Desperate Years.* New York: Bonanza Books, 1962.

"How Many Apples a Day Keep the Wolf Away?" *Literary Digest*, December 6, 1930.

Howe, Irving, and Lewis Coser. *The American Communist Party: A Critical History (1919–1957)*. Boston: Beacon Press, 1957.

Keylin, Arleen, ed. *The Depression Years as Reported by The New York Times*. New York: New York Times Company, 1969.

Labor Research Association. *Labor Fact Book I*. New York: International Publishers, 1931.

Labour Monthly (London). February 1927.

Lasswell, Harold, and Dorothy Blumenstock. *World Revolutionary Propaganda*. New York: Alfred A. Knopf, 1939.

Leab, Daniel J. "United We Eat: The Creation and Organization of the Unemployed Councils in 1930." *Labor History* 8 (1967).

Leonard, Jonathan Norton. *Three Years Down*. New York: Carrick and Evans, 1939.

Liberator. March 8, 15, 1930.

Mikhailov, B. Y., et al., eds. *Recent History of the Labor Movement in the United States: 1918–1939*. Moscow, 1977.

Naison, Mark. *The Communist Party in Harlem: 1928–1936*. Urbana: University of Illinois Press, 1983.

Nelson, Steve. *The Volunteers*. New York: Masses and Mainstream, 1953.

Nelson, Steve, James R. Barrett, and Rob Ruck. *Steve Nelson, American Radical*. Pittsburgh: University of Pittsburgh Press, 1981.

New Republic. March 26, 1931.

New York Herald Tribune. March 7, 1930.

New York Times. February 25, March 5, 6, 7, 8, 15, 17, 26, May 2, 1930; June 1931.

New York World. March 7, 1930.

"No One Has Starved." *Fortune*, September 1932.

North, Joseph. *Robert Minor, Artist and Crusader: An Informal Biography*. New York: International Publishers, 1956.

Olgin, M. J. "From March Sixth to May First." *The Communist*, May 1930.

Party Organizer (New York). 1930. Passim.

Pen and Hammer. *Don't Take It Lying Down*. New York: National Committee, Unemployed Councils, July 1932.

Piven, Frances Fox, and Richard A. Cloward. *Poor People's Movements: Why They Succeed, How They Fail*. New York: Pantheon Books, 1977.

————. *Regulating the Poor: The Functions of Public Welfare*. New York: Vintage Books, 1971.

Prago, Albert. "The Organization of the Unemployed and the Role of the Radicals, 1929–1935." Ph.D. dissertation, Institute of Policy Studies, Washington, D.C., 1976.

Preston, William, Jr. *Aliens and Dissenters: Federal Suppression of Radicals, 1903–1933*. Cambridge, Mass.: Harvard University Press, 1963.

Richmond, Alexander. *A Long View From the Left: Memoirs of an American Revolutionary*. Boston: Houghton Mifflin Company, 1973.

Rosenzweig, Roy. "Organizing the Unemployed." *Radical America*, July–August 1976.

Schneiderman, William. *Dissent on Trial: The Story of a Political Life*. Minneapolis: MEP Publications, 1983.

Seymour, Helen. "The Organized Unemployed." Master's thesis, University of Chicago, 1937.

Simon, Rita James. *As We Saw The Thirties*. Urbana: University of Illinois Press, 1967.

Sternsher, Bernard. *Hitting Home: The Great Depression in Town and Country*. Chicago: Quadrangle Books, 1970.

Unemployed Council Papers. Tamiment Library, New York University.

U.S. Congress. Senate. Subcommittee of the Committee on the Judiciary. *Guide to Communist Tactics Among the Unemployed*. Washington, D.C.: U.S. Government Printing Office, 1961.

Vorse, Mary Heaton. *A Footnote to Folly: Reminiscences of Mary Heaton Vorse*. New York: Farrar and Rinehart, 1935.

Walker, C. R. "Relief and Revolution." *Forum* 88 (August–September 1932).

Winter, Carl. "Unemployed Struggles of the Thirties." *Political Affairs*, September–October 1969.

Zipser, Arthur. "March 6, 1930 — A Day To Remember." *Daily World*, February 28, 1980.

———. *Working Class Giant: The Life of William Z. Foster*. New York: International Publishers, 1981.

Chapter 20

Adams, Grace. *Workers on Relief*. New Haven, Conn.: Yale University Press, 1939.

Allen, A. "Unemployed Work — Our Weak Point." *The Communist*, August 1932.

Allen, James. Interview with author, 1985.

American Civil Liberties Union. *What Rights For the Unemployed?* New York: ACLU, 1935.

Amsterdam News (New York). October 8, 1930.

Amter, Israel. *Why the Workers' Unemployment Insurance Bill?* New York: Workers Library Publishers, 1933.

———. "The Revolutionary Upsurge and the Struggles of the Unemployed." *The Communist*, February 1933.

"Beloved Alliance Organizer Devoted Life to Workers." *Social Welfare*, March 10, 1938.

Benjamin, Herbert. Interview with Theodore Draper. Theodore Draper Papers, Robert E. Woodruff Library, Emory University, Atlanta, Georgia.

——. Memoirs. Herbert Benjamin Papers. Ernst Benjamin collection, Washington, D.C.

——. "Notes on the Work of the Block Committees." *Party Organizer*, May–June 1932.

——. *United Action For the Right to Live.* New York: National Committee, Unemployed Councils, 1933.

——. "The Unemployed Movement." *The Communist,* June 1931.

Bloor, Ella Reeve. *We Are Many; an Autobiography by Ella Reeve Bloor.* New York: International Publishers, 1940.

Boyer, Richard O. and Herbert M. Morais. *Labor's Untold Story.* 3rd ed., rev. New York: United Electrical, Radio & Machine Workers of America, 1976.

Brandt, Joe. "How Our Block Committees Work." *Party Organizer* 5 (May–June 1932).

Browder, Earl. "One Year of Struggle of the Unemployed in the USA." *International Press Correspondence (Inprecorr),* March 19, 1931.

——. "Report of the Political Committee to the Twelfth Central Committee Plenum." *The Communist,* January 1931.

Brown, Josephine Chaplin. *Public Relief, 1929–1939.* New York: Henry Holt & Co., 1949.

Burlak, Ann. See Timpson.

Carpenter, David. "The Communist Party: Leader in the Struggle of the Unemployed." *Political Affairs* 39 (September 1949).

Catholic Worker (New York). Vol. 1, no. 1 (1933).

Chambers, Clarke A. *Seedtime of Reform: American Social Service and Social Action, 1918–1933.* Minneapolis: University of Minnesota Press, 1963.

Cochran, Bert. *Labor and Communism: The Conflict that Shaped American Unions.* Princeton, N.J.: Princeton University Press, 1977.

Communist International 8, no. 10 (June 1, 1931).

Cross, Frank Clay. "Revolution in Colorado." *The Nation* 138, no. 3579 (February 7, 1934).

Daily Worker (New York). December 8, 1930; January 31, 1931; October 24, 1934; March 3, 5, 1938.

Davidow, Mike. Letter to author, May 17, 1983.

Davis, Benjamin J. *Communist Councilman from Harlem: Autobiographical Notes Written in a Federal Penitentiary.* New York: International Publishers, 1969.

Drake, St. Clair, and Horace R. Cayton. *Black Metropolis: A Study of Negro Life in a Northern City.* 1945. Reprint. New York: Harper & Row, 1966.

Foner, Philip S. *Women and the American Labor Movement from World War I to the Present.* New York: Free Press, 1979.

Foster, William Z. *From Bryan to Stalin.* New York: International Publishers, 1937.

Garraty, John A. *Unemployment in History: Economic Thought and Public Policy.* New York: Harper & Row, 1978.

Gates, John. *The Story of an American Communist.* New York: Thomas Nelson & Sons, 1958.

Gebert, B. K. "After the Chicago Massacre." *International Press Correspondence (Inprecorr)*, August 27, 1931.

Glick, Brian. "The Thirties: Organizing the Unemployed." *Liberation* 12, no. 6–7 (September 1967).

Grant, Joanne, ed. *Black Protest: History, Documents, and Analyses, 1619 to the Present.* Greenwich, Conn.: Fawcett Publications, 1968.

Hathaway, Clarence. "Our Failure to Organize the Unemployed." *The Communist*, September 1930.

Haywood, Harry. *Black Bolshevik: Autobiography of an Afro-American Communist.* Chicago: Liberator Press, 1978.

High, Stanley. "Who Organized the Unemployed?" *Saturday Evening Post*, July 9, 1938.

Hofstadter, Richard and Michael Wallace, eds. *American Violence: A Documentary.* New York: Alfred A. Knopf, 1970.

Hudson, Hosea. *Black Worker in the Deep South.* New York: International Publishers, 1972.

Hunger Fighter (Chicago). April 6, 12, 1932; April 1935.

Johnson, Oakley C. "Helen Lynch, Organizer of the Unemployed." *World Magazine*, March 9, 1974.

Keeran, Roger. *The Communist Party and the Auto Workers Unions.* Bloomington: Indiana University Press, 1980.

Labor Research Association. *Labor Fact Book I.* New York: International Publishers, 1931.

Labor Unity 7, no. 4 (April 1932); no. 12 (December 1932).

Lasswell, Harold and Dorothy Blumenstock. *World Revolutionary Propaganda.* New York: Alfred A. Knopf, 1939.

Lasswell, James. *Shovels and Guns.* New York: International Publishers, 1935.

Leab, Daniel J. "United We Eat: The Creation and Organization of the Unemployed Councils in 1930." *Labor History* 8 (1967).

Lightfoot, Claude M. *Chicago Slums to World Politics: Autobiography of Claude M. Lightfoot.* Edited by Timothy V. Johnson. New York: New Outlook Publishers, 1985.

Malyshev, Sergei. *Unemployed Councils in St. Petersburg in 1906.* San Francisco: Proletarian Publishers, 1976.

Martin, Charles H. *The Angelo Herndon Case and Southern Justice.* Baton Rouge: Louisiana State University Press, 1976.

Naison, Mark. *The Communist Party in Harlem: 1928–1936*. Urbana: University of Illinois Press, 1983.

National Committee, Unemployed Councils. *Make the Democrats Keep Their Promises*. New York: Workers Library Publishers, 1933.

National Unemployment Council of the USA. *Constitution and Regulations*. New York: Workers Library Publishers, 1934.

————. *Newsletter*. New York, March 31, 1936.

Nelson, Steve, James R. Barrett, and Rob Ruck. *Steve Nelson, American Radical*. Pittsburgh: University of Pittsburgh Press, 1981.

New Republic. March 26, 1931.

North, Joseph, ed. *New Masses: An Anthology of the Rebel Thirties*. New York: International Publishers, 1969.

Olgin, M. J. "From March Sixth to May First." *The Communist*, May 1930.

Ottley, Roi, and William J. Weatherby, eds. "The Depression in Harlem." In *Hitting Home: The Great Depression in Town and Country*, Bernard Sternsher, ed. Chicago: Quadrangle Books, 1970.

Painter, Nell Irwin. *The Narrative of Hosea Hudson: His Life as a Negro Communist*. Cambridge, Mass.: Harvard University Press, 1979.

Party Organizer. August 1931; November 1931; May–June 1932; January, May–June, August–September 1933.

Pen and Hammer. *Don't Take It Lying Down*. New York: National Committee, Unemployed Councils, July 1932.

Piatnitsky, O. "Unemployment in the Present World Economic Crisis and the Tasks of the Communist Parties and the Revolutionary Trade Union Movement." *International Press Correspondence (Inprecorr)*, August 17, 1931.

Piven, Frances Fox, and Richard A. Cloward. *Poor People's Movements: Why They Succeed, How They Fail*. New York: Pantheon Books, 1977.

————. *Regulating the Poor: The Functions of Public Welfare*. New York: Vintage Books, 1971.

Prago, Albert. "The Organization of the Unemployed and the Role of the Radicals, 1929–1935." Ph.D. dissertation, Institute of Policy Studies, Washington, D.C., 1976.

Preis, Art. *Labor's Giant Step: Twenty Years of the CIO*. New York: Pioneer Publishers, 1964.

"Resolution on Work Among the Unemployed." *The Communist*, October 1931.

Richmond, Alexander. *A Long View From the Left: Memoirs of an American Revolutionary*. Boston: Houghton Mifflin Company, 1973.

Schlesinger, Arthur M., Jr. *The Age of Roosevelt*. Vol. 1, *The Crisis of the Old Order: 1919–1932*. Boston: Houghton Mifflin Company, 1957.

————. *The Coming of the New Deal*. Boston: Houghton Mifflin Company, 1958.

Schneiderman, William. *Dissent on Trial: The Story of a Political Life*. Minneapolis: MEP Publications, 1983.

Schulman, Elizabeth. "The Workers Are Finding a Voice: The Chicago Workers Committee and the Relief Struggles of 1932." Advance draft of a research proposal, December 1, 1986. In author's collection.

Searls, Virginia C. "Cuyahoga County Relief Administration Clients as Members of the Unemployment Council." Master's thesis, Western Reserve University, Cleveland, Ohio, 1935.

Seymour, Helen. "The Organized Unemployed." Master's thesis, University of Chicago, 1937.

Severn, Clara. "We Begin to March." *Monthly Review*, December 1934.

Southern Worker. 1932–1933.

Terkel, Studs. *Hard Times*. New York: Pantheon Books, 1970.

Thomas, Norman. "The Thirties as a Socialist Recalls Them." In *As We Saw The Thirties*, Rita J. Simon, ed. Urbana: University of Illinois Press, 1967.

Timpson, Ann Burlak. Interview with author, 1989.

Unemployed Council Papers. Tamiment Library, New York University.

U.S. Congress. Senate. Subcommittee of the Committee on the Judiciary. *Guide to Communist Tactics Among the Unemployed*. Washington, D.C.: U.S. Government Printing Office, 1961.

Van Veen, Sadie. Memoirs of Israel Amter and Sadie Van Veen. Tamiment Library, New York University.

———. *Our Children Cry For Bread*. New York: National Committee, Unemployed Councils, 1933.

Varga, E. "The Problems of the Increase in Chronic Unemployment." *Communist International* 10 (September 1, 1933).

Walker, C. R. "Relief and Revolution." *Forum*, September 1932.

Winter, Carl. "Unemployed Struggles in the Thirties." *Political Affairs*, September–October 1969.

———. Letter to author, July 1989.

Wilson, Edmund. "Communists and Cops." *New Republic* 65 (February 11, 1931).

Wolters, Raymond. *Negroes and the Great Depression: The Problem of Economic Recovery*. Westport, Conn.: Greenwood Publishing Corp., 1970.

Yoneda, Karl G. *Ganbatte: Sixty-Year Struggle of a Kibei Worker*. Los Angeles: Asian American Studies Center, UCLA, 1983.

Chapter 21

Bernstein, Irving. *The Lean Years: A History of the American Worker, 1920–1933*. Boston: Houghton Mifflin Company, 1960.

Brannin, Carl. "Northwest Unemployed Organizer." *Labor Age* 21 (June 1932).

Brown, Josephine Chaplin. *Public Relief, 1929–1939*. New York: Henry Holt & Co., 1949.

Colcord, Joanna C. "People Without Money." *New Outlook*, December 1932.

Davenport, Walter. "They Help Themselves." *Colliers*, December 31, 1932.

Heckert, Fritz. "The Prague Conference on the Unemployment Question." *International Press Correspondence (Inprecorr)*, September 10, 1931.

Hillman, Arthur. *The Unemployed Citizen's Leagues of Seattle*. Seattle: University of Washington Press, 1934.

Kerr, Clark. "Productive Enterprises of the Unemployed, 1931–1938." Ph.D. dissertation, University of California, Berkeley, 1939.

Kerr, Clark, and P. S. Taylor. "The Self-Help Cooperatives in California." In *Essays in Social Economics*, E. T. Grether, ed. Berkeley: University of California Press, 1935.

Leab, Daniel J. "Barter and Self-Help Groups, 1932–1933." *Mid-Continent American Studies Journal*, Spring 1966.

Nelson, Steve, James R. Barrett, and Rob Ruck. *Steve Nelson, American Radical*. Pittsburgh: University of Pittsburgh Press, 1981.

New Frontier. March 1933.

Oppenheimer, Irene B. "The Organization of the Unemployed." Master's thesis, Columbia University, New York, 1940.

Party Organizer (New York). October 1934.

Springer, Gertrude. "Shock Troops to the Rescue." *Survey*, January 1933.

Unemployed Citizen (Seattle). December 16, 1932.

U.C.L. Chronicle (Tacoma, Wash.). August 24, 1932.

U.C.L. Educational Bulletin. Lessons 1–9, n.d.

The Voice of the Unemployed. National Non-Profit Co-operative Newspaper (New Llano, La.). June 1, July 1, 15, August 1, September 1, 1933.

Weishaar, W., and W. W. Parrish. *Men Without Money*. New York: G. P. Putnam's Sons, 1933.

Wells, Hulet M. "They Organize in Seattle." *Survey*, March 15, 1932.

Chapter 22

Benjamin, Herbert. Interview with Theodore Draper. Theodore Draper Papers, Robert E. Woodruff Library, Emory University, Atlanta, Georgia.

———. Memoirs. Herbert Benjamin Papers. Ernst Benjamin collection, Washington, D.C.

———. Interview with author, n.d.

Better America Foundation Newsletter (Los Angeles). November 2, 1931.

Browder, Earl. Interview by J. Starobin, Oral History Collection, Columbia University, New York, 1964.

———. *The Reminiscences of J. Earl Browder*. Library of Congress Microfiche ILX84 1369.

Daily Mirror (New York). December 8, 1931.

Davis, Benjamin J. *Communist Councilman from Harlem: Autobiographical Notes Written in a Federal Penitentiary*. New York: International Publishers, 1969.

De Caux, Len. *Labor Radical: From Wobblies to CIO, A Personal History*. Boston: Beacon Press, 1970.

Dos Passos, John. "Red Day on Capitol Hill." *New Republic*, December 23, 1931.

Dyson, Lowell K. *Red Harvest: The Communist Party and American Farmers*. Lincoln: University of Nebraska Press, 1982.

Evening Graphic (New York). December 2, 1931.

Foster, William Z. *Pages From a Worker's Life*. New York: International Publishers, 1939.

———. "The Worker's Power — The National Hunger March Showed It!" *Labor Unity* 7, no. 1 (January 1932).

Glassford, Pelham D. Papers. University of California, Los Angeles.

Keeran, Roger. *The Communist Party and the Auto Workers Unions*. Bloomington: Indiana University Press, 1980.

Kornbluh, Joyce L., ed. *Rebel Voices: An I.W.W. Anthology*. Ann Arbor: University of Michigan Press, 1964.

Mostovets, Nikolai. *Henry Winston: Profile of a US Communist*. Moscow: Progress Publishers, 1983.

Naison, Mark. *The Communist Party in Harlem: 1928–1936*. Urbana: University of Illinois Press, 1983.

National Committee of Unemployment Councils. *The Demands of the National Hunger March*. New York: 1931.

New York Evening Post. December 6, 7, 8, 1931.

New York Times. December 6, 7, 8, 1931.

Party Organizer. December 1931.

People's Lobby Bulletin. December 1931, January 1932.

Piven, Frances Fox, and Richard A. Cloward. *Regulating the Poor: The Functions of Public Welfare*. New York: Vintage Books, 1971.

Political Affairs. September–October 1969.

Prago, Albert. "The Organization of the Unemployed and the Role of the Radicals, 1929–1935." Ph.D. dissertation, Institute of Policy Studies, Washington, D.C., 1976.

Schlesinger, Arthur M., Jr. *The Coming of the New Deal*. Boston: Houghton Mifflin Company, 1958.

Thomas, Norman. "The Thirties as a Socialist Recalls Them." In *As We Saw The Thirties*, Rita J. Simon, ed. Urbana: University of Illinois Press, 1967.

Unemployed Council Papers. Tamiment Library, New York University.

Van Veen, Sadie. Memoirs of Israel Amter and Sadie Van Veen. Tamiment Library, New York University.

Washington Post. December 6, 1931.

Winter, Carl. "Unemployed Struggles in the Thirties." *Political Affairs*, September–October 1969.

Chapter 23

Baskin, Alex. "The Ford Hunger March." *Labor History*, Summer 1972.

Bird, Caroline. *The Invisible Scar.* New York: David McKay Company, 1966.

Bonosky, Phillip. *Brother Bill McKie: Building the Union at Ford.* New York: International Publishers, 1953.

Boyer, Richard O., and Herbert M. Morais. *Labor's Untold Story.* 3rd ed., rev. New York: United Electrical, Radio & Machine Workers of America, 1976.

Detroit Free Press. March 8, 1932.

Detroit News. March 8, 1932.

Detroit Times. March 8, 1932.

Ford Worker 7, no. 3 (March 1932). Issued by the Ford Section of the Communist Party of the USA, Detroit, Michigan.

Foster, William Z. *Pages From a Worker's Life.* New York: International Publishers, 1939.

Hofstadter, Richard, and Michael Wallace, eds. *American Violence: A Documentary.* New York: Alfred A. Knopf, 1970.

Johnson, Oakley. "After the Dearborn Massacre." *New Republic*, March 30, 1932.

Keeran, Roger. *The Communist Party and the Auto Workers Unions.* Bloomington: Indiana University Press, 1980.

Montgomery, David. *Workers' Control in America.* New York: Cambridge University Press, 1979.

New Force (Detroit). March–April 1932. Published by the John Reed Club of Detroit.

New Masses. May 1932.

New York Times. March 8, 1932.

Piven, Frances Fox, and Richard A. Cloward. *Regulating the Poor: The Functions of Public Welfare.* New York: Vintage Books, 1971.

Prago, Albert. "The Organization of the Unemployed and the Role of the Radicals, 1929–1935." Ph.D. dissertation, Institute of Policy Studies, Washington, D.C., 1976.

Schlesinger, Arthur M., Jr. *The Age of Roosevelt.* Vol. 1, *The Crisis of the Old Order: 1919–1932.* Boston: Houghton Mifflin Company, 1957.

Sugar, Maurice. *The Ford Hunger March.* Berkeley, Calif.: Meiklejohn Civil Liberties Institute, 1980.

———. Papers. Archives of Labor History and Urban Affairs, Reuther Library, Wayne State University, Detroit, Michigan.

Sward, Keith. *The Legend of Henry Ford.* New York: Rinehart & Company, 1948.

Zipser, Arthur. *Working Class Giant: The Life of William Z. Foster.* New York: International Publishers, 1981.

Chapter 24

Bart, Philip, ed., *Highlights of a Fighting History: Sixty Years of the Communist Party USA.* New York: International Publishers, 1979.

Bernstein, Irving. *The Lean Years: A History of the American Worker, 1920–1933.* Boston: Houghton Mifflin Company, 1960.

Bonosky, Phillip. *Brother Bill McKie: Building the Union at Ford.* New York: International Publishers, 1953.

Cowley, Malcolm. "The Flight of the Bonus Army." *New Republic,* August 17, 1932.

Daily Worker (New York). June, July 1932.

Daily World (New York). February 3, 1982.

Daniels, Roger. *The Bonus March: An Episode of the Great Depression.* Westport, Conn.: Greenwood Publishing Corp., 1971.

Dos Passos, John. "Washington and Chicago. 1. The Veterans Come Home to Roost." *New Republic,* June 29, 1932.

Douglas, Jack. *Veterans on the March.* New York: Workers Library Publishers, 1934.

Ellis, Edward Robb. *A Nation in Torment: The Great American Depression, 1929–1939.* New York: Capricorn Books, 1971.

Gerson, Simon W. *Pete: The Story of Peter V. Cacchione, New York's First Communist Councilman.* New York: International Publishers, 1976.

Glassford, Pelham D. Papers. University of California, Los Angeles.

Hofstadter, Richard, and Michael Wallace, eds. *American Violence: A Documentary.* New York: Alfred A. Knopf, 1970.

Hoover, Herbert. *Memoirs.* Vol. 2, *The Great Depression, 1929–1941.* New York: Macmillan Company, 1952.

Lisio, Donald J. *The President and Protest: Hoover, Conspiracy and the Bonus Riot.* Columbia: University of Missouri Press, 1974.

Myers, William Starr, and Walter H. Newton. *The Hoover Administration: A Documented Narrative.* New York: Charles Scribner's Sons, 1936.

New York Times. July 28, 29, 1932.

Prago, Albert. "The Organization of the Unemployed and the Role of the Radicals, 1929–1935." Ph.D. dissertation, Institute of Policy Studies, Washington, D.C., 1976.

Terkel, Studs. *Hard Times.* New York: Pantheon Books, 1970.

The Unemployed (New York). 1932.

The Washington Post. July 29, 1932.

Chapter 25

Benjamin, Herbert. Memoirs. Herbert Benjamin Papers. Ernst Benjamin collection, Washington, D.C.

Bernstein, Irving. *The Lean Years: A History of the American Worker, 1920–1933.* Boston: Houghton Mifflin Company, 1960.

Brecher, Jeremy. *Strike!* San Francisco: Straight Arrow Books, 1972.

Bremner, William H. *Depression Winters: New York Social Workers and the New Deal.* Philadelphia: Temple University Press, 1984.

Chambers, Clarke A. *Seedtime of Reform: American Social Service and Social Action, 1918–1933.* Minneapolis: University of Minnesota Press, 1963.

Garraty, John A. *Unemployment in History: Economics, Thought, and Public Policy.* New York: Harper & Row, 1978.

Hallgren, Mauritz. "How Many Hungry?" *The Nation,* February 10, 1932.

Herndon, Angelo. *Let Me Live.* 1937. Reprint. New York: Arno Press, 1969.

Hunger Fighter (New Haven, Conn.). 1932.

Industrial Worker (Chicago). 1932.

Lasswell, Harold, and Dorothy Blumenstock. *World Revolutionary Propaganda: A Chicago Study.* New York: Alfred A. Knopf, 1939.

"Local Struggles and the Building of the Unemployed Councils in Preparation for the Hunger March." *Party Organizer,* January 1932.

"No One Has Starved." *Fortune,* September 1932.

Painter, Nell Irwin. *The Narrative of Hosea Hudson: His Life as a Negro Communist in the South.* Cambridge: Harvard University Press, 1979.

Piven, Frances Fox, and Richard A. Cloward. *Poor People's Movements: Why They Succeed, How They Fail.* New York: Pantheon Books, 1977.

Record, Wilson. *The Negro and the Communist Party.* Chapel Hill: University of North Carolina Press, 1951.

Thompson, Fred, and Patrick Murfin. *The I.W.W.: Its First Seventy Years, 1905–1975.* Chicago: Industrial Workers of the World, 1976.

Winter, Carl. Interview with author, November 1989.

Chapter 26

American Civil Liberties Union. *What Rights for the Unemployed?* New York: ACLU, 1935.

Amter, Israel. *The March Against Hunger.* New York: National Committee, Unemployed Councils, 1933.

———. "National Hunger and the Next Steps." *Party Organizer,* January 1933.

Benjamin, Herbert. Interview with Theodore Draper. Theodore Draper Papers, Robert E. Woodruff Library, Emory University, Atlanta, Georgia.

———. Memoirs. Herbert Benjamin Papers. Ernst Benjamin collection, Washington, D.C.

———. "Hunger Marchers and the Police." *New Republic,* January 11, 1933.

Bernstein, Irving. *The Lean Years: A History of the American Worker, 1920–1933.* Boston: Houghton Mifflin Company, 1960.

Boyer, Richard O., and Herbert M. Morais. *Labor's Untold Story.* 3rd ed., rev. New York: United Electrical, Radio & Machine Workers of America, 1976.

Cantwell, Robert. "The Hunger Marchers' Victory." *Common Sense,* January 19, 1933.

Cowley, Malcolm. "Red Day in Washington." *New Republic,* December 21, 1932.

Dahlberg, Edward. "Hunger on the March." *Nation,* December 28, 1932.

Davis, Benjamin J. *Communist Councilman from Harlem: Autobiographical Notes Written in a Federal Penitentiary.* New York: International Publishers, 1969.

Day, Dorothy. *The Long Loneliness: The Autobiography of Dorothy Day.* New York: Harper & Brothers, 1952.

Dos Passos, John. "Red Day on Capitol Hill." *New Republic,* December 23, 1931.

Father Cox's Blue Shirt News (Pittsburgh). June 25, 1932.

Grant, Joanne, ed. *Black Protest: History, Documents, and Analyses, 1619 to the Present.* Greenwich, Conn.: Fawcett Publishers, 1968.

Hallgren, Mauritz. *Seeds of Revolt: A Study of American Life and the Temper of the American People During the Depression.* New York: Alfred A. Knopf, 1933.

Herndon, Angelo. *Let Me Live.* 1937. Reprint. New York: Arno Press, 1969.

———. "You Cannot Kill the Working Class." In *Black Protest: History, Documents, and Analyses, 1619 to the Present,* Joanne Grant, ed. Greenwich, Conn.: Fawcett Publishers, 1968.

Hoover, Herbert. *The New Day; Campaign Speeches of Herbert Hoover, 1928.* Stanford: Stanford University Press, 1928.

Hunger Fighter (New Haven, Conn.). December 14, 1932.

Industrial Worker (Chicago). February 9, 1932.

Kornbluh, Joyce L., ed. *Rebel Voices: An I.W.W. Anthology.* Ann Arbor: University of Michigan Press, 1964.

Kravif, Hy. "The Press and the Unemployed." *Social Work Today* 3, no. 2 (November 1935).

Labor Research Association. *Labor Fact Book II.* New York: International Publishers, 1934.

———. *Labor Fact Book III.* New York: International Publishers, 1936.

Lasswell, Harold, and Dorothy Blumenstock. *World Revolutionary Propaganda: A Chicago Study.* New York: Alfred A. Knopf, 1939.

Martin, Charles H. *The Angelo Herndon Case and Southern Justice.* Baton Rouge: Louisiana State University Press, 1976.

New Frontier. December 12, 1932.

New Leader (New York). 1932.

New York Daily News. December 4, 1932.

New York Herald Tribune. January 8, 17, 1932.

New York Times. November 8, December 1932; January 1933.

New York World Telegram. November 3, 1932.

"No One Has Starved." *Fortune,* September 1932.

Party Organizer. January 1933.

People's Lobby Bulletin. January 1932.

Piven, Frances Fox, and Richard A. Cloward. *Poor People's Movements: Why They Succeed, How They Fail.* New York: Pantheon Books, 1977.

———. *Regulating the Poor: The Functions of Public Welfare.* New York: Vintage Books, 1971.

Prago, Albert. "The Organization of the Unemployed and the Role of the Radicals, 1929–1935." Ph.D. dissertation, Institute of Policy Studies, Washington, D.C., 1976.

Reynolds, W. "Involving the A.F. of L. in the Hunger March." *Party Organizer,* January 1932.

Robinson, Edgar Eugene, and Vaughn Davis Bornet. *Herbert Hoover, President of the United States.* Stanford, Calif.: Hoover Institution Press, 1975.

Romasco, Albert U. *The Poverty of Abundance: Hoover, the Nation, the Depression.* New York: Oxford University Press, 1965.

Time. November 28, 1932.

Timpson, Ann Burlak. Letter to author, April 1983.

Unemployed Citizen (Seattle). December 16, 1932.

Unemployed Council. Papers. Tamiment Library, New York University.

Walker, C. R. "Relief and Revolution." *Forum,* September 1932.

Weyl, Nathaniel. "Organizing Hunger." *New Republic,* December 14, 1932.

Wickens, James F. "Depression and the New Deal in Colorado." In *The New Deal,* John Braeman, Robert H. Bremner, and David Brody, eds. Columbus: Ohio State University Press, 1975.

Chapter 27

Anderson, Nels. *The Right To Work.* New York: Modern Age Books, 1938.

Bell, Daniel. *Marxian Socialism in the United States.* Princeton, N.J.: Princeton University Press, 1967.

Benjamin, Herbert. Memoirs. Herbert Benjamin Papers. Ernst Benjamin collection, Washington, D.C.

Borders, Karl. "The Unemployed Strike Out for Themselves." *Survey,* April 15, 1932.

———. "When the Unemployed Organize." *The Unemployed,* no. 5 (1932).

Brecher, Jeremy. *Strike!* San Francisco: Straight Arrow Books, 1972.

Budenz, Louis Francis. "Organizing the Jobless." *Labor Age,* December–January 1933.

Colcord, Joanna C. "People Without Money." *New Outlook,* December 1932.

The Communist. June 1931.

Cope, Elmer F. Papers. Ohio Historical Society, Columbus, Ohio.

Davis, S. M. "Muste and Brookwood." *Militant,* May 27, 1933.

Drake, St. Clair, and Horace R. Cayton. *Black Metropolis: A Study of Negro Life in a Northern City.* 1945. Reprint. New York: Harper & Row, 1966.

Gambs, John S. "United We Eat." *Survey Graphic* 23, no. 8 (August 1934).

Glick, Brian. "The Thirties: Organizing the Unemployed." *Liberation* 12, no. 6–7 (September 1967).

Greenstein, Harry. "The Maryland Emergency Relief Program — Past and Future." Paper presented to the Maryland Conference of Social Work, February 25, 1935.

Keeran, Roger. *The Communist Party and the Auto Workers Unions.* Bloomington: Indiana University Press, 1980.

Lasser, David. *The Conquest of Space.* New York: Penguin Press, 1931.

———. "Toward Building a National Unemployed Organization." *New Leader* 17, no. 52 (December 29, 1934).

Lasswell, Harold, and Dorothy Blumenstock. *World Revolutionary Propaganda: A Chicago Study.* New York: Alfred A. Knopf, 1939.

Naison, Mark. *The Communist Party in Harlem: 1928–1936.* Urbana: University of Illinois Press, 1983.

The New Frontier (Chicago). December 12, 26, 1932; January 8, February 8, 22, March 4, 22, April 19, 1933.

New York Herald Tribune. January 29, 1934.

Ohio Unemployed League Songs. Columbus: Ohio Unemployed League, 1933.

Piven, Frances Fox, and Richard A. Cloward. *Regulating the Poor: The Functions of Public Welfare.* New York: Vintage Books, 1971.

Prago, Albert. "The Organization of the Unemployed and the Role of the Radicals, 1929–1935." Ph.D. dissertation, Institute of Policy Studies, Washington, D.C., 1976.

Preis, Art. *Labor's Giant Step: Twenty Years of the CIO.* New York: Pioneer Publishers, 1964.

Robinson, Jo Ann. *Abraham Went Out: A Biography of A. J. Muste.* Philadelphia: Temple University Press, 1983.

Rosenzweig, Roy. "Socialism in Our Time: The Socialist Party and the Unemployed, 1929–1936." *Labor History* 20, no. 4 (Fall 1979).

Schultz, Edward. "The Musteites Kid the Jobless." *Labor Unity,* December 1932.

Seymour, Helen. "The Organized Unemployed." Master's thesis, University of Chicago, 1937.

Shannon, David. *The Great Depression.* New York: Prentice Hall, 1960.

Simon, Rita James, ed. *As We Saw The Thirties: Essays on Social and Political Movements of a Decade.* Urbana: University of Illinois Press, 1967.

Stockham, J. R. "An Analysis of the Organizational Structure, Aims, and Tactics of the Workers' Alliance of America in Franklin County and Cuyahoga County, Ohio, and in Hennepin County, Minnesota." Master's thesis, Ohio State University, 1938.

Unemployed Citizen. December 16, 1932; February 17, 1933.

Unemployed Citizen's League. National Archives, Washington D.C.

Unemployed News (Unemployed Citizen's League of Philadelphia and Unemployed Union of Camden County). April 22, 1933.

Unemployed Union. September 3, 1934 — June 24, 1935.

Vanguard (Seattle). 1933, 1934.

Chapter 28

Bailey, Bill. Interviewed by Carrie Jenkins. August 27, 1989.

Benjamin, Herbert. Papers. Ernst Benjamin collection, Washington, D.C.

Borders, Karl. "The Unemployed Strike Out for Themselves." *Survey,* April 15, 1932.

Brown, Josephine Chaplin. *Public Relief, 1929–1939.* New York: Henry Holt & Co., 1949.

Budenz, Louis Francis. "Organizing the Jobless." *Labor Age,* December–January 1933.

———. "We Can Organize the Jobless." *Labor Age,* February–March 1933.

Cope, Elmer F. Papers. Ohio Historical Society, Columbus, Ohio.

Dobbs, Farrell. *Teamster Politics.* New York: Pathfinder Press, 1975.

Feeley, Diane. *In Unity There is Strength: The Struggle of the Unemployed Throughout the 1930s.* Pittsburgh, 1983.

Glick, Brian. "The Thirties: Organizing the Unemployed." *Liberation* 12, no. 6–7 (September 1967).

Hillman, Arthur. *The Unemployed Citizens' Leagues of Seattle.* Seattle: University of Washington Press, 1934.

Howard, Donald S. *The WPA and Federal Relief Policy.* New York: Russell Sage Foundation, 1943.

Howe, Harry A. "Unemployed Begin To Act." *Labor Age,* August 1932.

Johnson, Arnold. "Give Us Relief Or We'll Take It." *Modern Monthly,* February 1954. First published in *Modern Monthly,* 1934.

Keeran, Roger. *The Communist Party and the Auto Workers Unions.* Bloomington: Indiana University Press, 1980.

McKinney, Earnest Rice. "The Reminiscences of Earnest Rice McKinney." Interview by Ed Edwin, 1961. Columbia University Oral History Collection, New York.

Mitchell, Broadus. *Depression Decade: From New Era Through New Deal, 1921–1941.* New York: Rinehart and Company, 1947.

Nelson, Bruce. *Workers on the Waterfront: Seamen, Longshoremen, and Unionism in the 1930s.* Urbana: University of Illinois Press, 1988.

Prago, Albert. "The Organization of the Unemployed and the Role of the Radicals, 1929–1935." Ph.D. dissertation, Institute of Policy Studies, Washington, D.C., 1976.

Preis, Art. *Labor's Giant Step: Twenty Years of the CIO.* New York: Pioneer Publishers, 1964.

Quin, Mike. *The Big Strike.* Olema, Calif.: Olema Publishing Company, 1949.

Richmond, Alexander. *A Long View from the Left: Memoirs of an American Revolutionary.* Boston: Houghton Mifflin Company, 1973.

Robinson, Jo Ann. *Abraham Went Out: A Biography of A. J. Muste.* Philadelphia: Temple University Press, 1983.

Rosenzweig, Roy. "Organizing the Unemployed." *Radical America,* July–August 1976.

———. "Radicals and the Jobless: The Musteites and the Unemployed Leagues, 1932–1934." *Labor History* 16 (Winter 1975).

Schulman, Elizabeth. "The Workers Are Finding a Voice: The Chicago Workers Committee and the Relief Struggles of 1932." Advance draft of a research proposal, December 1, 1986. In author's collection.

Seymour, Helen. "The Organized Unemployed." Master's thesis, University of Chicago, 1937.

Stockham, J. R. "An Analysis of the Organizational Structure, Aims, and Tactics of the Workers' Alliance of America in Franklin County and Cuyahoga County, Ohio, and in Hennepin County, Minnesota." Master's thesis, Ohio State University, 1938.

Unemployed Citizen. December 16, 1932 — February 17, 1933.

Unemployed News (Philadelphia). April 22, 1933. Paper of the Unemployed Citizen's League of Philadelphia and the Unemployed Union of Camden County.

The Voice of the Workers 2, no. 19 (1934); 4, no. 17 (1936). Organ of the Lehigh County Unemployed League.

Chapter 29

Bartlett, Lenore K. "The Attack on the Townsend Plan." *Social Work Today* 3, no. 8 (May 1936).

Bennett, David H. *Demagogues in the Depression: American Radicals and the Union Party, 1932–1936.* New Brunswick, N.J.: Rutgers University Press, 1969.

———. "The Year of the Old Folks' Revolt." *American Heritage* 16, no. 1 (December 1964).

Crowell, Chester T. "The Townsend Plan: A Challenge to Congress." *American Mercury* 34, no. 136 (April 1935).

Epstein, Abraham. "Facing Old Age." *American Scholar* 3, no. 2 (Spring 1934).

Harris, Herbert. "Dr. Townsend's Marching Soldiers." *Current History* 43, no. 2 (February 1936).

Holtzman, Abraham. *The Townsend Movement: A Political Study.* New York: Bookman Associates, 1936.

Johnson, Julie E., ed. *Old Age Pension.* New York: H. W. Wilson Co., 1935.

Nueberger, Richard L. "The Townsend Plan Exposed." *The Nation,* October 30, 1935.

Nueberger, Richard L., and Kelley Loe. *An Army of the Aged.* Caldwell, Idaho: Caxton Printers, 1936.

Piven, Frances Fox, and Richard A. Cloward. *Regulating the Poor: The Functions of Public Welfare.* New York: Vintage Books, 1971.

Stack, Celeste. "Whither Townsendism?" *New Masses* 20, no. 5 (July 28, 1936).

U.S. Congress. *Congressional Record,* 74th Congress, 1st Session, H.R. 7154, April 1, 1935. (John S. McGroarty of California introduced a bill backed by the Townsend movement.)

Chapter 30

Blake, Fay, and H. Newman. "Upton Sinclair's EPIC Campaign." *California History,* Fall 1984.

Harris, Leon. *Upton Sinclair: American Rebel.* New York: Thomas Y. Crowell, 1975.

Mcfadden, Bernarr. "Upton Sinclair Wants to Sell Us Government Ownership." *Liberty* 2, no. 42 (October 20, 1934).

McWilliams, Carey. "Poverty, Pensions, and Panaceas: California in the Thirties." *Working Papers,* Fall 1974.

Mitchell, Greg. "Upton Sinclair's EPIC Campaign." *The Nation,* August 4–11, 1984.

———. "Summer of '34." *Working Papers,* November–December 1982.

Sinclair, Upton. *I, Governor of California, and How I Ended Poverty: A True Story of the Future.* New York: Farrar and Rinehart, 1933.

———. "What I Am Really Going To Do." *Liberty* 2 (October 20, 1934).

———. "End Poverty in Civilization." *The Nation,* September 26, 1934.

———. "What the EPIC Plan Means." *Literary Digest,* October 13, 1934.

———. "The Future of EPIC." *The Nation,* November 28, 1934.

Unseem, Michael. *Protests in America.* Indianapolis: Bobbs-Merrill Company, 1975.

Chapter 31

Bennett, David H. *Demagogues in the Depression: American Radicals and the Union Party, 1932–1936.* New Brunswick, N.J.: Rutgers University Press, 1969.

Brinkley, Alan. *Voices of Protest: Huey Long, Father Coughlin, and the Great Depression.* New York: Alfred A. Knopf, 1982.

Carter, Hodding, and Gerald L.K. Smith. "How Come Huey Long? — Bogeyman — or Superman?" *New Republic,* February 13, 1985.

Davis, Forrest. "Father Coughlin." *Atlantic Monthly* 156, no. 6 (December 1935).

Deutsch, Hermann B. "Huey Long — The Last Phase." *Saturday Evening Post* 208, no. 15 (October 12, 1935).

Graham, Hugh D., ed. *Huey Long.* Englewood Cliffs, N.J.: Prentice-Hall, 1970.

Long, Huey P. *Every Man a King: The Autobiography of Huey P. Long.* New Orleans: National Book Company, 1933.

Magil, A. B. *The Truth About Father Coughlin.* New York: Workers Library Publishers, 1935.

———. "Father Coughlin's Army." *New Masses* 14, no. 1 (January 1, 1935).

Piven, Frances Fox, and Richard A. Cloward. *Regulating the Poor: The Functions of Public Welfare.* New York: Vintage Books, 1971.

Shenton, James P. "The Coughlin Movement and the New Deal." *Political Science Quarterly* 73, no. 3 (September 1958).

Simon, Rita James. *As We Saw the Thirties: Essays on Social and Political Movements of a Decade.* Urbana: University of Illinois Press, 1967.

Spivak, John L. *Shrine of the Silver Dollar.* New York: Modern Age Books, 1940.

Swing, Raymond Gram. *Forerunners of American Fascism.* New York: Julian Messner, 1935.

Ward, Louis B. *Father Charles E. Coughlin: An Authorized Biography.* Detroit: Tower Publications, 1933.

Williams, T. Harry. *Huey Long.* New York: Alfred A. Knopf, 1969.

Chapter 32

Albany Evening News (New York). October 31, 1934.

American Civil Liberties Union. *What Rights For the Unemployed?* New York: ACLU, 1935.

Anderson, Nels. *The Right to Work.* New York: Modern Age Books, 1938.

Bass, Thomas A. "A Reborn CCC Shapes Young Lives With An Old Idea." *Smithsonian,* April 1983.

Brown, Josephine Chaplin. *Public Relief, 1929-1939.* New York: Henry Holt & Co., 1949.

Folsom, Franklin. Eyewitness notes about events on May 26, 1934, and the opening day of the Civil Works Administration, December 1933.

Hopkins, Harry L. *Spending to Save: The Complete Story of Relief.* 1936. Reprint. Seattle: University of Washington Press, 1972.

Howard, Donald S. *The WPA and Federal Relief Policy.* New York: Russell Sage Foundation, 1943.

Hunger Fighter (New York). June 2, 1934.

International News Service. November 1, 1934.

Knickerbocker News (Albany). October 31, 1934.

Lasswell, James. *Shovels and Guns: The CCC in Action.* New York: International Publishers, 1935.

Naison, Mark. *The Communist Party in Harlem: 1928–1936.* Urbana: University of Illinois Press, 1983.

New York Evening Journal. December 29, 1933.

New York Herald Tribune. December 12, 20, 1933; January 19, 23, 24, 1934.

New York News. May 27, 28, 1934.

New York Times. December 16, 1933; January 19, 1934.

Piven, Frances Fox, and Richard A. Cloward. *Regulating the Poor: The Functions of Public Welfare.* New York: Vintage Books, 1971.

Prago, Albert. "The Organization of the Unemployed and the Role of the Radicals, 1929–1935." Ph.D. dissertation, Institute of Policy Studies, Washington, D.C., 1976.

Preis, Art. *Labor's Giant Step: Twenty Years of the CIO.* New York: Pioneer Publishers, 1964.

Schlesinger, Arthur M., Jr. *The Age of Roosevelt.* Vol. 2, *The Coming of the New Deal.* Boston: Houghton Mifflin Company, 1957.

Sparks, Leonard. *How to Win Jobs.* New York: Communist Party, n.d.

These Are Our Lives: As told by the people and written by members of the Federal Writer's Project of the Works Progress Administration in North Carolina, Tennessee, and Georgia. Chapel Hill: University of North Carolina Press, 1939.

Times-Union (Albany, N.Y.). October 31, 1934.

Wickens, James F. "Depression and the New Deal in Colorado." In *The New Deal,* John Braeman, Robert H. Bremner, and David Brody, eds. Columbus: Ohio State University Press, 1975.

Wolters, Raymond. *Negroes and the Great Depression: The Problem of Economic Recovery.* Westport, Conn.: Greenwood Publishing Corporation, 1970.

Chapter 33

Amter, Israel. *Why the Workers' Unemployment Insurance Bill? How It Can Be Won.* New York: Workers Library Publishers, 1933.

———. "More Leadership in the Struggle for Unemployment Insurance." *Party Organizer,* May–June 1933.

———. "Work Among the Unemployed." *Party Organizer,* August–September 1933.

———. "Resolution on the Application of the Open Letter by Section One Conference, Detroit District." *Party Organizer,* August–September 1933.

Bart, Philip, et al., eds. *Highlights of a Fighting History: 60 Years of the Communist Party USA.* New York: International Publishers, 1979.

Benjamin, Herbert. *Shall It Be Hunger Doles or Unemployment Insurance?* New York: Workers Library Publishers, 1934.

———. "We Forgot Our Motivation." *In These Times*, December 8–14, 1983.

———. "Mass Struggle Will Force the Government to Provide Jobless Insurance." *Daily Worker*, November 26, 1931.

Bernstein, Irving. *The Lean Years: A History of the American Worker, 1920–1933*. Boston: Houghton Mifflin Company, 1960.

Braeman, John, Robert H. Bremner, and David Brody. *The New Deal: The National Level*. Columbus: Ohio State University Press, 1975.

Bremner, William H. *Depression Winters: New York Social Workers and the New Deal*. Philadelphia: Temple University Press, 1984.

Brogan, Denis W. *The Era of Franklin D. Roosevelt: A Chronicle of the New Deal and Global War*. New Haven, Conn.: Yale University Press, 1950.

Browder, Earl. "The American Communist Party." In *As We Saw the Thirties*, Rita J. Simon, ed. Urbana: University of Illinois Press, 1967.

———. *Unemployment Insurance: The Burning Issue of the Day*. New York: Workers Library Publishers, April 1935.

Burnham, Grace. *Social Insurance*. New York: International Pamphlets, 1932.

———. *Work or Wages*. New York: International Pamphlets, 1930.

Douglas, Jack. *Veterans on the March*. New York: Workers Library Publishers, 1934.

Draper, Theodore. Papers. Robert E. Woodruff Library, Emory University, Atlanta, Georgia.

Feeley, Diane. *In Unity There is Strength: The Struggle of the Unemployed Throughout the 1930s*. Pittsburgh, 1983.

Fisher, Jacob. *The Response of Social Work to the Depression*. Boston: G. K. Hall & Company, 1980.

Foster, William Z. "Marxism and the American Working Class." *Political Affairs* 32, no. 10 (November 1953).

Garraty, John A. *Unemployment in History: Economics, Thought, and Public Policy*. New York: Harper & Row, 1978.

Gates, John. *The Story of an American Communist*. New York: Thomas Nelson & Sons, 1958.

Gusev, S. I. "The Tasks of the CP of the USA in the Struggle for Social Insurance." *Communist International*, no. 8 (May 1, 1933).

Gusev, S. I., and Earl Browder. "Tasks of the American Communist Party in Organizing the Struggle for Social Insurance." *The Communist*, September 1933.

Harper, Elsie D. *Out of a Job: Proposals for Unemployment Insurance*. New York: Woman's Press, 1931.

Johnson, Oakley C. *The Day is Coming: Life and Work of Charles E. Ruthenberg*. New York: International Publishers, 1957.

Meyers, William Starr, and Walter H. Newton. *The Hoover Administration: A Documented Narrative*. New York: Charles Scribner's Sons, 1936.

Mikhailov, B. Y., et al., eds. *Recent History of the Labor Movement in the United States: 1918–1939*. Moscow, 1977.

Muste, A. J. "Unemployment Insurance: The Alternative to Charity." *The Unemployed*, January 1931.

Nelson, Daniel. *Unemployment Insurance: The American Experience, 1915–1932*. Madison: University of Wisconsin Press, 1969.

Nelson, Steve, James R. Barrett, and Rob Ruck. *Steve Nelson, American Radical*. Pittsburgh: University of Pittsburgh Press, 1981.

New Leader (New York). September 22, 1934.

New York Times. January 25, 27, December 5, 15, 1933; January 27, 1934; June 17, September 10, October 25, 1935.

People's Lobby Bulletin. May 1932.

Perkins, Frances. "Unemployment Insurance." *Survey Graphic* 67, no. 3 (November 1, 1931).

Piven, Frances Fox, and Richard A. Cloward. *Regulating the Poor: The Functions of Public Welfare*. New York: Vintage Books, 1971.

Rosenzweig, Roy. "Organizing the Unemployed." *Radical America*, July–August 1976.

Schlesinger, Arthur M., Jr. *The Age of Roosevelt*. Vol. 2, *The Coming of the New Deal*. Boston: Houghton Mifflin Company, 1957.

U.S. Congress. House. 74th Congress, 1st Session, Report no. 418, Committee on Labor. *We Are For H.R. 2827*. Reprint issued by the National Joint Action Committee for Genuine Social Insurance, New York, May 1935.

U.S. Congress. Senate. Committee on the Judiciary. *Guide to Communist Tactics Among the Unemployed*. Washington, D.C.: U.S. Government Printing Office, 1961.

Weinstock, Louis. "Depression Struggles." *Daily World*, September 6, 1969.

———. "The History of the Unemployment Insurance Bill of 1932: an excerpt from an oral history." In *The Right to Earn a Living in the United States*. Meiklejohn Civil Liberties Institute Symposium Journal. Berkeley, California, 1982.

Why Unemployment Insurance? New York: New York A. F. of L. Trade Union Committee for Unemployment Insurance and Relief, n.d.

Yellowitz, Irwin. "The Origins of Unemployment Reform." *Labor History*, Fall 1968.

Chapter 34

Aaron, Daniel. "Guidebooks and Meal Tickets." *Times Literary Supplement*, July 28, 1978.

"Art For Everybody." *Look*, May 9, 1939.

Banks, Ann, ed. *First Person America*. New York: Alfred A. Knopf, 1980.

Biddle, Livingston. *Our Government and the Arts: A Perspective from the Inside*. New York: ACA Books, 1988.

Fox, Daniel. "The Achievement of the Federal Writers Project." *American Quarterly* 13, no. 1 (Spring 1961).

Howard, Donald S. *The WPA and Federal Relief Policy*. New York: Russell Sage Foundation, 1943.

Johns, Orrick. *Time of Our Lives: The Story of My Father and Myself*. New York: Stackpole Sons, 1937.

McDonald, William F. *Federal Relief Administration and the Arts*. Columbus: Ohio State University Press, 1969.

Mangione, Jerre. *An Ethnic at Large: A Memoir of the Thirties and Forties*. Philadelphia: University of Pennsylvania Press, 1983.

———. *The Dream and the Deal: The Federal Writers Project, 1935–1943*. Philadelphia: University of Pennsylvania Press, 1983.

New York City Projects Council. *Your Job*. New York: Uptown Cooperative Press, 1936.

Oakland Tribune (Oakland, Calif.). August 13, 1939; May 9, 1940.

O'Connor, Frances V., ed. *Art For the Millions: Essays from the 1930s by Artists and Administrators of the WPA Federal Arts Project*. Boston: New York Graphic Society, 1973.

———. *The New Deal Art Projects: An Anthology of Memoirs*. Washington, D.C.: Smithsonian Institution Press, 1972.

Ogden, August Raymond. *The Dies Committee: A Study of the Special House Committee for the Investigation of Un-American Activities, 1938–1944*. Washington, D.C.: Catholic University of America Press, 1945.

Penkower, Marty Noam. *The Federal Writers' Project: A Study in Government Patronage of the Arts*. Urbana: University of Illinois Press, 1977.

San Francisco Examiner. July 13, 1939; March 12, May 16, 1940.

Sargent, James E. "Clifton A. Woodrum of Virginia: A Southern Progressive in Congress, 1923–1945." *Virginia Magazine of History and Biography* 89, no. 3 (July 1981).

———. "Woodrum's Economy Bloc: The Attack on Roosevelt's WPA, 1937–1939." *Virginia Magazine of History and Biography* 93, no. 2 (April 1985).

University of Chicago Roundtable. *Relief and the WPA*. Chicago, 1939.

U.S. Department of Health, Education, and Welfare. *Public Attitudes Toward Social Security, 1935–1965*. Washington, D.C., U.S. Government Printing Office, Research Report 33, 1970.

Whitcomb, Robert. "Delegate to Washington." *Commonweal*, April 6, 1934.

Whiting, Cecile. *Antifascism in American Art*. New Haven, Conn.: Yale University Press, 1989.

Chapter 35

Benjamin, Herbert. Interview. Oral History Collection, Butler Library, Columbia University, November 18, 1976.

Blackstock, Nelson. "Max Geldman: A Leader of 1930s Unemployed Movement." *The Militant,* January 13, 1989.

A Call to Militant Members of the Workers Alliance. c1937.

Dobbs, Farrell. *Teamster Politics.* New York: Pathfinder Press, 1975.

Northwest Organizer (Minneapolis, Minn.). December 31, 1936.

Sargent, James E. "Clifton A. Woodrum of Virginia: A Southern Progressive in Congress, 1923–1945." *Virginia Magazine of History and Biography* 89, no. 3 (July 1981).

———. "Woodrum's Economy Bloc: The Attack on Roosevelt's WPA, 1937–1939." *Virginia Magazine of History and Biography* 93, no. 2 (April 1985).

Stockham, J. R. "An Analysis of the Organizational Structure, Aims, and Tactics of the Workers' Alliance of America in Franklin County and Cuyahoga County, Ohio, and in Hennepin County, Minnesota." Master's thesis, Ohio State Unversity, 1938.

Schmitz, Anthony. "Another Time, Another Place: Minneapolis, '34." *In These Times,* September 5–11, 1984.

Chapter 36

Anderson, Nels. "Pressure Groups." *Survey Graphic,* March 1936.

Bell, Tom. "The Pecan Strike." *Current,* May 22, 1986.

Benjamin, Herbert. "Discussion on Unemployed Convention." Undated typescript. Herbert Benjamin Papers. Ernst Benjamin collection, Washington, D.C.

———. "Unemployment Unity Convention." Typescript of a report to the Communist Party, 1936. Herbert Benjamin Papers. Ernst Benjamin collection, Washington, D.C.

———. Letter to James E. Sargent, August 31, 1981. Herbert Benjamin Papers. Ernst Benjamin collection, Washington, D.C.

———. "Six Months After the Unification of the Unemployed." Typescript, 1936. Herbert Benjamin Papers. Ernst Benjamin collection, Washington, D.C.

———. "Unity in the Unemployment Field." *The Communist,* April 1936.

———. "We Forgot Our Motivation." *In These Times,* December 8–14, 1983.

Bonosky, Phillip. "A Letter to Mrs. Roosevelt." *Mainstream,* January 1963.

Breitman, George. *The Trenton Siege: By the Army of Unoccupation.* New York: Fourth International Tendency, 1986.

———. Letter to Unit #78, White Collar and Professional Division, Workers Alliance of New Jersey. November 4, 1936. Herbert Benjamin Papers. Ernst Benjamin collection, Washington, D.C.

Cope, Elmer. Letters to A. J. Muste. November 11, 1932; November 20, 1932; February 29, 1933. Elmer F. Cope Papers. Ohio Historical Society, Columbus, Ohio.

———. Letter to V. C. Bauhof. November 20, 1932. Elmer F. Cope Papers. Ohio Historical Society, Columbus, Ohio.

Creel, George. Letter to Stephen Early. June 28, 1939. Roosevelt Library, Hyde Park, New York.

Daily Worker (New York). May 11, 1936.

Dennis, Peggy. *The Autobiography of an American Communist: A Personal View of a Political Life, 1925–1975.* Westport, Conn.: Lawrence Hill, 1977.

Folsom, Franklin. Notes made during the unity convention of the Workers Alliance in Washington, D.C., 1936.

Fraser, Steve, and Gary Gerstle, eds. *The Rise and Fall of the New Deal Order, 1930–1980.* Princeton, N.J.: Princeton University Press, 1989.

Gummell, W. T. Letter to Paul Rasmussen. January 9, 1936. Herbert Benjamin Papers. Ernst Benjamin collection, Washington, D.C.

Heinmann, Hal R. Letter to unidentified person. January 19, 1937. Herbert Benjamin Papers. Ernst Benjamin collection, Washington, D.C.

Howard, Donald S. *The WPA and Federal Relief Policy.* New York: Russell Sage Foundation, 1943.

Hudson, Hosea. *Black Worker in the Deep South.* New York: International Publishers, 1972.

Ingram, Frank. "On the Resignation of David Lasser from the Presidency of the Workers Alliance of America on June 18, 1940." Mimeograph. Herbert Benjamin Papers. Ernst Benjamin collection, Washington, D.C.

Kever, Jeannie. "La Pasionera Still Speaks Out for Justice." *San Antonio Light,* n.d.

Labor Research Association. *Labor Fact Book IV.* New York: International Publishers, 1938.

———. *Labor Fact Book V.* New York: International Publishers, 1941.

Lash, Joseph P. *Eleanor and Franklin.* New York: W. W. Norton, 1971.

Lasser, David. Letters to President Roosevelt, Eleanor Roosevelt, and members of Roosevelt's staff. Roosevelt Library, Hyde Park, New York.

———. *The $60 at 60 Pension Plan.* Washington, D.C.: Workers Alliance of America, 1939.

———. "To the Members of the Workers Alliance." Letter, n.d. Herbert Benjamin Papers. Ernst Benjamin collection, Washington, D.C.

———. Letter to author, August 3, 1989.

———. "An Answer to the NAC Statement of June 21." Mimeograph, with pages missing, 1936. Herbert Benjamin Papers. Ernst Benjamin collection, Washington, D.C.

. "To the Members of the National Executive Board of the Workers Alliance of America." Mimeograph, June 18, 1940. Herbert Benjamin Papers. Ernst Benjamin collection, Washington, D.C.

. "Why I Quit the Workers Alliance." *New York Post,* August 7, 8, 9, 10, 12, 13, 1940.

Mason, Olga. "Establishing the Unity of the Unemployed Workers." *Party Organizer,* May–June 1933.

McKinney, Earnest Rice. "The Reminiscences of Earnest Rice McKinney." Interview by Ed Edwin, 1961. Columbia University Oral History Collection, New York.

Minnesota Workers Alliance. *Proceedings and Reports: Third Annual Convention,* December 9, 10, 11, 1938.

Muste, A. J. Letters to Elmer Cope, February 18, March 15, April 29, 1983. Elmer F. Cope Papers. Ohio Historical Society, Columbus, Ohio.

Naison, Mark. *The Communist Party in Harlem: 1928–1936.* Urbana: University of Illinois Press, 1983.

New York Times. August 2, 1936; April 8, July 26, August 23, 25, 1937.

Ogden, August Raymond. *The Dies Committee: A Study of the Special House Committee for the Investigation of Un-American Activities, 1938–1944.* Washington, D.C.: Catholic University of America Press, 1945.

Oppenheimer, Irene B. "The Organization of the Unemployed." Master's thesis, Columbia University, New York, 1940.

Painter, Nell Irwin. *The Narrative of Hosea Hudson: His Life as a Negro Communist.* Cambridge: Harvard University Press, 1979.

People's Press 1, no. 52 (October 24, 1936).

Perkins, George. Letter to Elmer Cope, November 29, 1932. Elmer F. Cope Papers. Ohio Historical Society, Columbus, Ohio.

Piven, Frances Fox, and Richard A. Cloward. *Poor People's Movements: Why They Succeed, How They Fail.* New York: Pantheon Books, 1977.

. *Regulating the Poor: The Functions of Public Welfare.* New York: Vintage Books, 1971.

Prago, Albert. "The Organization of the Unemployed and the Role of the Radicals, 1929–1935." Ph.D. dissertation, Institute of Policy Studies, Washington, D.C., 1976.

Professional Worker (Berkeley, Calif.). March 22, April 26, May 3, August 1937.

"Resolution on Political Action in the 1936 Election." Typescript draft apparently prepared for the second national convention of the Workers Alliance of America. 1936. Herbert Benjamin Papers. Ernst Benjamin collection, Washington, D.C.

Rips, Geoffrey. "Emma Tenayuca: Alive and Active in San Antonio." *San Antonio Women's Magazine* 2, no. 1 (1985).

. "Living History: Emma Tenayuca Tells Her Story." *Texas Observer* 75, no. 21 (October 28, 1983).

Rogg, Nathan. "The Unemployed Unite." *Social Work Today* 3, no. 9 (June 1936).

Rosenzweig, Roy. "Organizing the Unemployed." *Radical America*, July–August 1976.

San Francisco Call-Bulletin. June 6, 1940.

San Francisco Chronicle. May 18, 1940; December 13, 1942.

San Francisco Examiner. July 28, 1941.

Sargent, James E. "Proposal to the National Endowment for the Humanities." Letter, September 14, 1981. Herbert Benjamin Papers. Ernst Benjamin collection, Washington, D.C.

Seymour, Helen. "The Organized Unemployed." Master's thesis, University of Chicago, 1937.

Socialist Builder (Chicago). Nos. 1 and 2 (February 1937). (Paper of the National Unemployment Committee of the Socialist Party.)

Stockham, J. R. "An Analysis of the Organizational Structure, Aims, and Tactics of the Workers' Alliance of America in Franklin County and Cuyahoga County, Ohio, and in Hennepin County, Minnesota." Master's thesis, Ohio State Unversity, 1938.

Tenayuca, Emma. Interview with author, January 1990.

Terkel, Studs. *Hard Times.* New York: Pantheon Books, 1970.

Turner, Allan. "A Night that Changed San Antonio." *Houston Chronicle*, December 14, 1986.

Unemployed Leagues. "Minutes of a Conference at Reading, Pennsylvania." February 17, 1933. Author's collection.

U.S. Congress. *Congressional Record.* Hearings of the Special Committee on Un-American Propaganda Activities. 75th Congress, 3rd Session. August 12–20, 23, 1938. Vol. 1

U.S. Department of Health, Education, and Welfare. *Public Attitudes Toward Social Security, 1935–1965.* Research Report 33. Washington D.C., U.S. Government Printing Office, 1970.

Washington Post. April 8, 1936.

Washington Star. April 7, 10, 1936.

Washington Times. April 9, 11, 1936.

West, Don, ed. *Songs for Kentucky Workers.* Lexington, KY: Kentucky Workers Alliance, n.d.

Workers Alliance 1, no. 12 (April 1936).

Workers Alliance of America. *How to Win With the Workers Alliance.* Washington, D.C., 1937.

———. *How to Win Work at a Living Wage or a Decent Standard of Relief with the Workers Alliance of America.* Washington D.C., 1937.

———. *Official Call to the Second National Convention.* Washington, D.C., 1936.

———. *Proceedings of the Second National Convention, April 7–10, 1936.* New York: Uptown Cooperative Press, 1936.

————. *Report of the National Executive Board to the Second National Convention.* 1936.

Workers Alliance of America, Administrative Committee. "Statement on the Resignation of David Lasser." Mimeograph, n.d. Herbert Benjamin Papers. Ernst Benjamin collection, Washington, D.C.

Workers Alliance of America National Bulletin (Washington, D.C.). June 22, 1940.

Index